D1611738

Introduction to Econometrics

Introduction
to
ECONOMETRICS

Henri Theil

University of Chicago

Prentice-Hall, Inc., Englewood Cliffs, New Jersey 07632

Library of Congress Cataloging in Publication Data

THEIL, HENRI.
    Introduction to econometrics.

    Includes bibliographical references and index.
    1. Econometrics. I. Title.
HB139.T47   330'.01   77-14972
ISBN 0-13-481028-7

PRENTICE-HALL INTERNATIONAL, INC., *London*
PRENTICE-HALL OF AUSTRALIA PTY. LIMITED, *Sydney*
PRENTICE-HALL OF CANADA, LTD., *Toronto*
PRENTICE-HALL OF INDIA PRIVATE LIMITED, *New Delhi*
PRENTICE-HALL OF JAPAN, INC., *Tokyo*
PRENTICE-HALL OF SOUTHEAST ASIA PTE. LTD., *Singapore*
WHITEHALL BOOKS LIMITED, *Wellington, New Zealand*

Contents

v

part one
THE SIMPLE REGRESSION MODEL

chapter 12

The Testing of Hypotheses   *171*

chapter 13

The Functional Form of a Relation   *186*

chapter 14

Consumer Demand Equations   *200*

part three

EXTENSIONS OF THE REGRESSION MODEL

chapter 18

Aggregation   *288*

chapter 19

Generalized Least Squares and Related Procedures   *299*

chapter 20

Introduction to Simultaneous-Equation Problems: Static Equation Systems   *319*

part four
PREDICTION AND CONTROL

Appendix   *396*

Problems   *424*

References   *427*

Statistical Tables   *433*

Index   *443*

Preface

The main objective of this book is to enable the reader to understand applied econometric studies. The prerequisites for reading the book consist of elementary calculus through partial differentiation, apart from high school algebra and one or two courses in economics; further details are provided on page xvii. A second objective is to provide more advanced material in the sections marked by an asterisk. These sections can either be used for supplementary reading or for the second course in a two-course sequence.

Acknowledgments

I have used several preliminary versions of this book in the introductory econometrics course for MBA and college students in Chicago. Their reactions were a major determinant of the present form of the book. I am also indebted to Professors Walter D. Fisher (Northwestern University), Robert McNown (University of Colorado), and Houston Stokes (University of Illinois), who made detailed comments on an earlier draft; to Kenneth Laitinen, who provided comments on successive drafts while assisting in the teaching of the course; to Professors Jacques Drèze (University of Louvain) and Teun Kloek (Erasmus University, Rotterdam) and my colleagues William Wecker and Victor Zarnowitz, who commented on parts of the book; and to Prentice-Hall's Frank Enenbach, who is *almost* on our faculty and persuaded me to give the book to his firm. I want to express my great appreciation for the hard work and cheerfulness of my secretary, Mrs. Janice Ricks, and her predecessor, Mrs. Kathleen Masulis, who typed and retyped and checked and rechecked galleys and page proofs.

The Institute of Mathematical Statistics kindly permitted me to include the table of the Von Neumann ratio; so did the Biometrika Trustees for the t, χ^2, F, and Durbin-Watson tables. These Trustees and Longman Group Ltd. informed me that some columns of the t table are from *Statistical Tables for Biological, Agricultural and Medical Research* by Fisher and Yates (sixth edition, 1974). I am grateful to the Literary Executor of the late Sir Ronald A. Fisher, F.R.S., to Dr. Frank Yates, F.R.S., and to Longman Group Ltd., London, for permission to reprint these columns.

HENRI THEIL

Chicago, Illinois

The Design and Use
of This Book

Each chapter consists of one or more opening paragraphs and several sections (e.g., Section 3.2 is the second section of Chapter 3). Most sections contain an opening paragraph and several (unnumbered) subsections. Formulas are indicated by two numbers, the first for the chapter and the second for the order of occurrence; for example, eq. (5.3) is the third equation in Chapter 5. Tables and figures are numbered consecutively throughout the book. To facilitate finding a table or figure, its page number is usually mentioned.

The Appendix consists of eight sections, labeled A to H. Formulas in the Appendix are indicated by the letter of the section followed by the number of the order of occurrence.

Prerequisites

Elementary calculus is a prerequisite for reading this book, but analytical integration is not used. The reader can work his way through the material on continuous distributions in Sections 4.1 and 4.2 by simply remembering that the probabilities of discrete distributions (Chapter 3) are replaced by the density function and summation by integration.

Apart from the elementary calculus prerequisite, the book presumes no further mathematical or statistical preparation. Statistics is developed from scratch. The use of the summation operator $\sum$ is explained in Section 2.2. On the other hand, if the reader has a sufficient command of matrix algebra, he will appreciate the concise style of the Appendix. No attempt is made to explain matrix algebra in this book, but an instructor who uses the book for a two-course sequence will not find it difficult to provide the necessary material for Sections A and B of the Appendix in his second course.

The Four Parts of the Book

Since the book is introductory, it should emphasize the standard linear model. Accordingly, the main objective of Part One is this model for one explanatory variable, that of Part Two is the extension for more variables and the associated statistical inference techniques, whereas the discussion of such topics as generalized and two-stage least squares is postponed until Chapters 19 to 21 at the end of Part Three. In a book of this kind it is impossible to describe even a medium-sized simultaneous-equation model adequately; the familiar Klein Model I must do the work. To provide a compensation, I decided to discuss predictions and prediction errors in some detail, as well as certain elements of control theory, in Chapters 22 and 23, which constitute Part Four.

Given the presumption that the reader knows little or no mathematical statistics, it would be a disadvantage to have all statistics in one or several chapters at the beginning. Few persons would be able to digest all this material. Therefore, statistics is introduced successively in the first three parts of the book. Chapters 3 and 4 in Part One describe discrete and continuous distributions and the first elements of point estimation theory; this statistical basis is sufficient through Chapter 9. The second statistical installment is Chapters 10 to 12 in Part Two, dealing with multivariate normality, χ^2, t, confidence intervals, and hypothesis testing. The third is Chapters 15 and 16 at the beginning of Part Three on large-sample distribution theory, Bayesian inference, and related matters. This division of the statistical material into successive stages has obvious additional advantages when the reader is a student who takes an introductory mathematical statistics course concurrently.

An important question is at which stage the reader should be advised to be suspicious. Should he be told each time immediately after a new approach is introduced how it can go wrong because the data may violate the underlying assumptions? Or should these warnings be postponed until the stage at which he has developed some feeling for the relationship among the various approaches? I prefer the latter alternative, since the former runs the risk of generating confusion rather than understanding. For example, it would be very troublesome to explain the consequences of an erroneous specification of the relations estimated when properties of least squares are discussed in Chapters 5 and 8. Accordingly, doubts are spread in Chapter 17, which deals with specification and observational errors, and in Chapter 18 (on the consequences of aggregation) and in Section 23.2 (on economy-wide econometric models).

Using the Book in the Classroom

The econometrician analyzes statistical data. Thus, when an instructor teaches an introductory econometrics course, he should expect that his students will want to see some "real" data at an early stage. But if these students know little or no statistics, there is the risk that they will spend weeks wading through algebraic symbols before they see anything "real." How can this problem be resolved?

I find it useful to divide my class sessions (about 75 minutes each) into two or three parts, so that several topics can be discussed in each session and one of these can be data analysis. An additional advantage of this division-into-parts is that it reduces the accumulation of mathematical results, so that it avoids a situation in which students are asked to apply results which they have not fully digested.

For example, in the first session the instructor may want to start with the first few pages of Section 1.1, which describe (among others) a consumption-income relation, and then move to Section 2.1, where such a relation is considered for fictitious data. He assigns Section 2.2 for the second session and moves on to Section 2.3 until the discussion of the least-squares principle, eq. (2.25). He then proceeds to the opening paragraph of Chapter 7, which contains real data (Table 12), and discusses the questions raised in that paragraph. The last topic discussed in the first session is Section 3.1 on univariate discrete distributions. In the next two sessions the instructor completes Chapters 2 and 3. As soon as Chapter 2 is completed, he goes through Section 7.1, where least squares is applied to the data of Table 12. This means that at an early stage of the course students have seen how data are used to obtain an income elasticity and a price elasticity. Further details on this course are provided in the Teacher's Manual.

The application of econometric methods to actual economic data is a prominent feature of this book. There are two ways in which applications can be presented: Either numerous examples are discussed briefly, or few examples are discussed in more detail. I prefer the latter alternative, because numerous brief discussions easily lead to a superficial attitude, which is unfortunately too common in applied econometric studies. Accordingly, the above-mentioned data of Table 12 figure prominently in the confidence intervals and statistical tests of Chapters 11 and 12, and Klein's Model I plays an important role in several sections of Chapters 21 and 23. Obviously, discussing few examples has a disadvantage also, but this can be eliminated to a large degree by means of a display of scatter diagrams referring to different areas of application. Several such diagrams are mentioned in the opening paragraph of the References at the end of this book.

Chapters 14 and 22 should be viewed as contrasts. Chapter 22 is mainly empirical and serves to provide the student with an idea of the degree of accuracy which he can expect from economic predictions and of the decline of this accuracy when the prediction refers to a more distant future. Chapter 14 provides a link between economic theory and econometric analysis. The economic theory used in this chapter is that of utility maximization subject to a budget constraint, which yields Slutsky symmetry. Usually, this symmetry is viewed as no more than an interesting academic result, but it has practical implications. Ignoring income effects (which are usually small), the instructor can describe Slutsky symmetry for his students as follows: A one-dollar increase in the price of your product has an effect on the demand for your competitor's product which is equal to the effect on the demand for your product of a one-dollar increase in the price of your competitor's product. When Slutsky symmetry is described in this way, students will be better motivated to derive it theoretically, test it statistically, and impose it on the estimates.

Starred Sections

From Chapter 10 onward, certain sections (sometimes all sections) of most chapters are marked by an asterisk. Such sections can be omitted in a first reading; later sections without asterisks are independent of earlier sections with asterisks except for an occasional sentence in parentheses or brackets. The instructor can delete the starred sections in an elementary course, although the allocation of stars is obviously arbitrary to some degree.

Deleting starred sections in an introductory course is particularly attractive when this course is part of a two-course sequence: The instructor can then ask students to review the earlier sections, discussed in the first course, before he proceeds to the later sections of the same chapter in the second course. However, even if the sections without asterisks are discussed in one single course, without a second-course follow-up, the students will have a fairly detailed knowledge of the standard linear model, including confidence intervals and t tests, some knowledge of simultaneous-equation models and of specification, heteroscedasticity, and autocorrelation problems, as well as an appreciation of the analysis of numerical economic data in conjunction with the corresponding economic theory.

List of Tables

List of Figures

chapter 1

What Econometrics Is About

Econometrics is concerned with the application of statistical methods and statistical data to problems in economics, business, and related areas. The econometrician uses such data to solve problems in a systematic way.

For example, consider the distribution of total personal income in some country and some year over the individual income recipients. We can count the number of persons earning between zero and $1000, between $1000 and $2000, between $2000 and $3000, and so on. When we have completed this count, an income distribution emerges. Does this distribution obey a simple mathematical law? When we repeat the count for a later year, has the distribution changed? Does the later year reveal more or less income inequality? What is a satisfactory way of measuring income inequality?

These are questions which econometrics tries to answer. The example considers only one variable: income. Much of econometrics is concerned with relationships among several variables. In this chapter we shall describe a typology and indicate the use of such relationships.

1.1 Typology of Economic Relations

Behavioral Relations

Let C be per capita consumption (total consumer expenditure divided by the population) in some country and some year. Let Y be per capita income in the same year, and consider the relation

$$(1.1) \qquad C = \beta_0 + \beta Y$$

This is an equation which describes per capita consumption linearly in terms of per capita income. It answers the following question: If the incomes of the individual consumers increase, so that per capita income also increases, how does this affect per capita consumption? The answer provided by (1.1) is that each additional dollar of per capita income generates β additional dollars of per capita consumption. This is an explicit answer only when we know β. The acquisition of such knowledge by means of data on per capita income and consumption is among the tasks of econometrics. Another task of econometrics is to verify whether the relation is indeed linear, as postulated by (1.1).

Equation (1.1) is an example of a *behavioral relation*. It describes how consumers behave, on the average, with respect to their total expenditures on goods and services, given their incomes. The words "on the average" are used to stress that (1.1) is a per capita relationship.

Technical Relations

There are behavioral relations for consumers, such as (1.1), and also for firms and other economic agents, but not all economic relations are behavioral relations. A counterexample is

$$(1.2) \qquad\qquad P = cK^{\alpha}L^{\beta}$$

where P is the maximum output of a factory during a year (measured in physical units) that can be attained when the capital stock in that year equals K and the total number of man-hours employed equals L.

Equation (1.2) is called a *technical relation*. Specifically, it is a production function of the Cobb-Douglas form. If it is valid, we can compute the maximum output for any combination of the variables K and L, provided the constants c, α, and β are known. It is the task of econometrics to use appropriate data such that this knowledge becomes available and to verify whether (1.2) is an appropriate form for the production function.

Note that (1.2) is not linear in the variables K and L. However, when we take logarithms, (1.2) becomes

$$(1.3) \qquad\qquad \log P = \log c + \alpha \log K + \beta \log L$$

which is linear in the variables $\log K$ and $\log L$. Thus, a simple logarithmic transformation changes the nonlinear relation (1.2) into the linear relation (1.3). This is important, because in Chapters 2 and 5 we shall show that the linearity assumption plays an important role in econometrics. In Section 13.1 we shall provide a more systematic discussion.

Definitional, Equilibrium, and Institutional Relations

There are three other groups of relations besides behavioral and technical relations. One is the *identity* or *definitional relation*, an equation that holds identically in its variables simply because these variables are defined so that the equation must hold. Examples are

(1.4)   price $\times$ quantity $=$ dollar value (for any good)

(1.5)   net worth $=$ total assets $-$ total liabilities

(1.6)   net investment $=$ change in capital stock

A fourth type of economic relation is the *equilibrium* or *adjustment equation*. For example, consider the market of some good and assume that it is cleared in each year. This implies

(1.7)   supply $=$ demand

which is an equilibrium equation that holds for each year.

A fifth type is the *institutional equation*, such as

(1.8)   sales tax revenue $= .05 \times$ dollar sales

which applies when a government imposes a 5 percent sales tax on a certain group of goods. More generally, institutional equations describe relationships among variables that result from institutionally imposed (usually government-imposed) arrangements. Another example is the amount of income tax to be paid by an individual as a function of his net income and the number of his dependents.

There is an important difference between eqs. (1.4) to (1.8) on the one hand and the behavioral and technical relations (1.1) and (1.2) on the other in that the former contain no unknown coefficients. We have unknown coefficients in the latter equations [β_0 and β in (1.1) and c, α, and β in (1.2)], the determination of which is an econometric problem. Also, there is no uncertainty as to the form of the relationships (1.4) to (1.8), whereas econometric analysis may show that it is preferable to modify the form of the behavioral and technical relations (1.1) and (1.2).

Therefore, definitional, equilibrium, and institutional relationships are less interesting from an econometric point of view, but we shall find in Chapter 20 that they do play a role in the analysis of systems of equations.

Static and Dynamic Relations

The five groups of relations discussed above constitute a typology based on the economic nature of the relationship. Another distinction is the timing of the variables which occur in the equation. In (1.1) both variables (C and Y) refer to the same period—the same year in this case. Such a relation is called *static*. However, suppose that per capita consumption depends not only on current per capita income but also on last year's per capita income. If the relation is linear, it can be written as

(1.9) $C_t = \beta_0 + \beta_1 Y_t + \beta_2 Y_{t-1}$

where C_t and Y_t are per capita consumption and income, respectively, in year t, and Y_{t-1} is per capita income in year $t-1$.

Equation (1.9) is an example of a *dynamic* behavioral equation; such an equation contains variables that are dated differently. Another example is

$$(1.10) \qquad C_t = \beta_0 + \beta_1 Y_t + \lambda C_{t-1}$$

which contains per capita consumption of year $t-1$ on the right. If $\lambda > 0$, (1.10) implies that a larger consumption last year stimulates consumption this year. The specification (1.10) is of the type proposed by Koyck (1954) and is further considered in Section 21.1.

Technical relations can also be dynamic. For example, suppose that capital goods bought in different years have different productivities and extend (1.2) to

$$(1.11) \qquad P_t = cK_t^{\alpha} K_{t-1}^{\alpha'} K_{t-2}^{\alpha''} \ldots L_t^{\beta}$$

where P_t is the maximum output of a factory that can be attained in year t when its labor force in that year consists of L_t man-hours and when it uses a capital stock consisting of K_t units bought in year t, K_{t-1} units bought in year $t-1$, and so on.

See Problems 4 and 5 at the end of this chapter for static and dynamic definitional and institutional relations.

Micro- and Macrorelations

A third distinction between economic relations is by the number of economic agents involved. Equations (1.2) and (1.11) describe the technology of one factory; they are called technical *microrelations*. On the other hand, (1.1), (1.9), and (1.10) refer to the "average" behavior of all consumers in a country; such equations are called behavioral *macrorelations*. If C and Y in (1.1) are not per capita variables but the consumption and income, respectively, of one household, this equation becomes a behavioral microrelation. Similarly, if P, K, and L in (1.2) stand for the total output, capital stock, and labor force of all manufacturing firms in some country, this equation becomes a technical macrorelation. (Total output is then measured in dollars at constant prices, not in physical units.) These examples show that the micro/macro distinction applies equally to behavioral and technical relations, as does the static/dynamic distinction.

The micro/macro distinction is also important with respect to the conceptual origin of behavioral relations. In most cases they originate with economic theory, such as utility maximization in the consumer's case and cost minimization or profit maximization in the case of the firm. Note that these theories are microeconomic in nature, so that they yield microrelations, not macrorelations. The problem of how to obtain macrorelations from microrelations is the subject of *aggregation theory*, which is considered in Chapter 18.

1.2   The Use of Numerically Specified Economic Relations

Suppose that we have succeeded in the econometric objective of finding numerical values for the coefficients c, α, and β of the production function (1.2) or for β_0, β_1, and β_2 of the consumption function (1.9). What have we accomplished?

First, we have learned something about the operation of the economy, or at least of a segment of the economy. For example, suppose that β_1 and β_2 in (1.9) turn out to be equal, so that current per capita income (Y_t) and last year's per capita income (Y_{t-1}) have equal weight with respect to current per capita consumption (C_t). We may view β_2 as measuring the income effect on consumption with a one-year lag and β_1 as measuring the effect with a zero lag. Hence, $\beta_1 = \beta_2$ implies that income affects consumption with an *average lag* of one-half year. On the other hand, if $\beta_1 > \beta_2 > 0$, current income has a greater weight than last year's income, and the average lag is less than one-half year.

Second, if we are confident that our numerically specified relation also applies to the future, we can use it for *prediction*. In the early months of year t we obtain data on year $t-1$, including Y_{t-1} of the consumption function (1.9). If β_1 in (1.9) happens to be zero, we can use this equation to predict C_t. If β_1 does not vanish (which is more likely), we need a prediction of Y_t to predict C_t. This required prediction of Y_t may be available from other sources. The subject of prediction is pursued more systematically in Section 11.4 and Chapters 22 and 23.

Third, when we have an appropriate set of behavioral, technical, and other relations, we can try to use these for the purpose of *control;* that is, we use them to design a system of actions so that our variables behave in a well-defined desirable manner. This subject is considered in Section 23.3.

Problems

All problems refer to Section 1.1.

1   Would you consider a negative numerical value of β plausible for the consumption function (1.1)? Explain your answer.

2   Prove that if $\alpha + \beta = 1$ in the production function (1.2), a proportionate change in the quantities of the production factors (K and L) raises output (P) in the same proportion. Also prove that if $\alpha + \beta$ is larger (smaller) than 1 and if K and L are raised proportionately, the relative increase in P is larger (smaller) than that in K and L. (*Note*: The first case, $\alpha + \beta = 1$, is known as "constant returns to scale.")

3   (*Continuation*) Formulate the condition on the coefficients of the dynamic

production function (1.11) under which this function has constant returns to scale.

4   Verify that (1.4) and (1.5) are static definitional relations and that (1.6) is dynamic.

5   The U.S. federal income tax allows the possibility of income averaging over the past three years. Explain how this can be interpreted as a dynamic institutional relation.

6   Modify (1.5) and (1.6) so that they become definitional macrorelations.

part one

THE
SIMPLE
REGRESSION
MODEL

chapter 2

Fitting
a Straight Line

We return to the consumption function $C = \beta_0 + \beta Y$ of (1.1) and imagine that we have data on per capita income (Y) and consumption (C) for a number of years. The problem of determining β_0 and β would be trivial if the data were in perfect agreement with the linear relationship implied by $C = \beta_0 + \beta Y$, but such perfection is a very rare phenomenon. To become an econometrician, one must learn to live with this lack of perfection.

2.1 Data and Theoretical Relations

We imagine that data are available for seven consecutive years, indicated by 1, 2, ..., 7 and shown in column (1) of Table 1. Columns (2) and (3) contain

TABLE 1

Data on two variables

Year (1)	Per capita income (x) (2)	Per capita consumption (y) (3)	(4)
1	100	89	Small
2	105	93	Small
3	110	97	Large
4	108	98	Deleted
5	106	96	Small
6	109	100	Large
7	111	99	Large

per capita income and consumption in each year. We label these variables as x and y in order to stress that this is a fictitious example which serves to illustrate a more general problem. Column (4) of the table is explained later in this section.

The Scatter of Observation Points

A convenient way of analyzing the relation between two variables is by means of a diagram (Figure 1) with x measured horizontally and y vertically. The seven observations of Table 1 are represented by seven points [Figure 1(a)] which clearly indicate that they are not located on a straight line, thus contradicting the theory that per capita consumption can be described as a linear function of per capita income. The seven points constitute a scatter which suggests that there is no simple relation between the two variables.

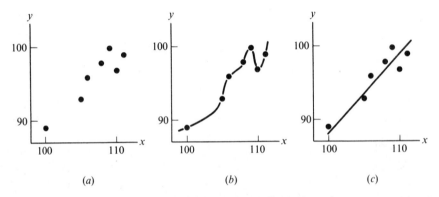

FIGURE 1   Analysis of a scatter of observation points

It is, of course, possible to draw a curve that contains all seven points. This is illustrated in Figure 1(b). However, it is quite doubtful whether this curve represents a satisfactory picture of the relationship between per capita consumption and income. One reason for doubt is that the curve moves downward in one income interval, indicating that a higher per capita income reduces rather than raises per capita consumption. Another reason is that if an eighth observation becomes available, it is very unlikely that this observation will be exactly on the curve of Figure 1(b). This means that the curve would have to be refitted each time a new observation becomes available and that we can never be sure that the curve we are using will agree with the next observation.

It seems much more plausible to accept the fact that there are deviations and to use a simple theoretical relation between x and y to fit the observations; the word *theoretical* is used to stress that the relation is not in exact agreement with the observations. In this chapter we use a linear relation, represented by the straight line of Figure 1(c), which appears to fit the seven observations reasonably well.

A Method of Fitting a Straight Line

Figure 2 illustrates a method of fitting straight lines which is close to Wald's (1940) approach. This is a very simple method, which is one reason we discuss it here. Another reason is that in Section 5.4 we shall find it convenient to compare this method with that of least squares. The least-squares approach is described in Section 2.3.

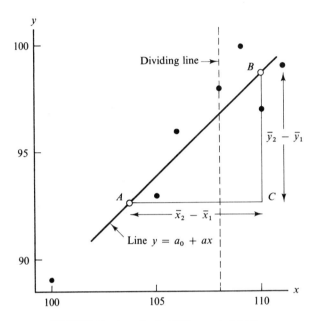

FIGURE 2   A method of fitting a straight line

We divide the observations of Table 1 into two groups of equal size according to the values of the variable x. This division is indicated by the broken vertical dividing line in Figure 2. Since we have an odd number of observations (7), we disregard the middle observation and thus obtain two groups consisting of three observations each. They are indicated by "small" in column (4) of Table 1 for the three observations to the left of the dividing line (these are the three observations with the smallest x value) and by "large" for the three observations to the right of the dividing line.

Next we compute the arithmetic average x value, written $\bar{x}_1$, of the three observations to the left of the broken line. An inspection of Table 1 yields

$$(2.1) \qquad \bar{x}_1 = \frac{100 + 105 + 106}{3} = 103\tfrac{2}{3}$$

We also compute $\bar{y}_1$, the average y value of the same three observations:

$$(2.2) \qquad \bar{y}_1 = \frac{89 + 93 + 96}{3} = 92\tfrac{2}{3}$$

The point $(\bar{x}_1, \bar{y}_1)$ is indicated by the small circle at A in Figure 2. Its two coordinates are the arithmetic means of the corresponding coordinates of the three observations to the left of the dividing line. This point is called the *center of gravity* of these three observations.

We proceed in the same way for the three points to the right of the dividing line. This leads to B, the center of gravity of these three points, with the following coordinates:

$$(2.3) \qquad \bar{x}_2 = \frac{110 + 109 + 111}{3} = 110$$

$$(2.4) \qquad \bar{y}_2 = \frac{97 + 100 + 99}{3} = 98\tfrac{2}{3}$$

We have thus obtained two centers of gravity, A and B, and we use these to define a linear equation in x and y,

$$(2.5) \qquad y = a_0 + ax$$

This equation corresponds to the straight line through A and B in Figure 2. Its slope (a) equals the ratio of BC to AC:

$$(2.6) \qquad a = \frac{\bar{y}_2 - \bar{y}_1}{\bar{x}_2 - \bar{x}_1} = \frac{98\tfrac{2}{3} - 92\tfrac{2}{3}}{110 - 103\tfrac{2}{3}} = \frac{6}{6\tfrac{1}{3}} \approx .947$$

The intercept or constant term (a_0) is obtained by substituting (2.6) in $\bar{y}_1 = a_0 + a\bar{x}_1$ or in $\bar{y}_2 = a_0 + a\bar{x}_2$. Using the latter approach, as well as (2.3) and (2.4), we obtain

$$(2.7) \qquad a_0 = \bar{y}_2 - a\bar{x}_2 = 98\tfrac{2}{3} - \frac{6}{6\tfrac{1}{3}} \times 110 \approx -5.54$$

which completes the numerical specification of the coefficients of (2.5).

2.2   On Sums, Arithmetic Means, and Mean Squares and Products

The coordinates of the two centers of gravity discussed in Section 2.1 are obtained as ratios, with numerators equal to certain sums of observations on variables [see the middle members of eqs. (2.1) to (2.4)]. We shall meet such sums frequently in this book. It is therefore convenient to introduce here the summation operator $\sum$.

The Summation Operator

Let x_i be income earned in year i, so that $x_1 + x_2 + x_3$ equals total income earned in years 1, 2, and 3. We write this as

$$\sum_{i=1}^{3} x_i = x_1 + x_2 + x_3$$

where $i = 1$ below $\sum$ indicates that the summation is over i (the subscript of x_i after $\sum$) and that the summation starts at $i = 1$, and where 3 above $\sum$ indicates that the summation terminates at $i = 3$. Therefore,

$$\sum_{i=2}^{6} x_i = x_2 + x_3 + x_4 + x_5 + x_6$$

and

$$\sum_{i=5}^{10} x_i - \sum_{i=9}^{12} x_i = x_5 + x_6 + x_7 + x_8 + x_9 + x_{10} - (x_9 + x_{10} + x_{11} + x_{12})$$

$$= x_5 + x_6 + x_7 + x_8 - (x_{11} + x_{12}) = \sum_{i=5}^{8} x_i - \sum_{i=11}^{12} x_i$$

which the reader is invited to verify.

Summation Rules

If k is a constant (such as $k = 3$), then

$$(2.8) \qquad \sum_{i=1}^{n} (kx_i) = k \sum_{i=1}^{n} x_i$$

To prove this result, we write the left-hand side as

$$kx_1 + kx_2 + \cdots + kx_n = k(x_1 + x_2 + \cdots + x_n) = k \sum_{i=1}^{n} x_i$$

which completes the proof.

When x and y are two variables whose observations are in pairs, (x_1, y_1), (x_2, y_2), $\ldots$, as in Table 1, then

$$(2.9) \qquad \sum_{i=1}^{n} (x_i + y_i) = \sum_{i=1}^{n} x_i + \sum_{i=1}^{n} y_i$$

Proof:

$$\sum_{i=1}^{n} (x_i + y_i) = (x_1 + y_1) + (x_2 + y_2) + \cdots + (x_n + y_n)$$

$$= (x_1 + x_2 + \cdots + x_n) + (y_1 + y_2 + \cdots + y_n)$$

$$= \sum_{i=1}^{n} x_i + \sum_{i=1}^{n} y_i$$

Next, let x, y, and z be three variables whose observations are in triples, (x_1, y_1, z_1), (x_2, y_2, z_2), $\ldots$, and let k_1, k_2, and k_3 be constants. Then

$$(2.10) \qquad \sum_{i=1}^{n} (k_1 x_i + k_2 y_i + k_3 z_i) = k_1 \sum_{i=1}^{n} x_i + k_2 \sum_{i=1}^{n} y_i + k_3 \sum_{i=1}^{n} z_i$$

which the reader is invited to verify using (2.8) and (2.9).

The Arithmetic Mean

Let x_1, x_2, $\ldots$, x_n be the values taken by the variable x. The arithmetic mean of these values is defined as

$$(2.11) \qquad \bar{x} = \frac{1}{n} \sum_{i=1}^{n} x_i$$

which satisfies

(2.12)
$$\sum_{i=1}^{n} (x_i - \bar{x}) = 0$$

or, in words, if we measure all values taken by a variable as a deviation from their arithmetic mean $(x_1 - \bar{x}, \ldots, x_n - \bar{x})$, then the sum of these values thus measured is zero.

To prove (2.12) we apply (2.10) in the first step below and (2.11) in the second:

$$\sum_{i=1}^{n} (x_i - \bar{x}) = \sum_{i=1}^{n} x_i - (\bar{x} + \bar{x} + \cdots + \bar{x})$$
$$= n\bar{x} - n\bar{x} = 0$$

Mean Squares and Mean Products

Let $(x_1, y_1), \ldots, (x_n, y_n)$ be the values taken by the variables x and y, and let $\bar{x}$ and $\bar{y} = (y_1 + \cdots + y_n)/n$ be the two arithmetic means. We have

(2.13)
$$\sum_{i=1}^{n} (x_i - \bar{x})(y_i - \bar{y}) = \sum_{i=1}^{n} (x_i - \bar{x})y_i$$

To prove this we write the left-hand side as

$$\sum_{i=1}^{n} [(x_i - \bar{x})y_i - \bar{y}(x_i - \bar{x})] = \sum_{i=1}^{n} (x_i - \bar{x})y_i - \bar{y} \sum_{i=1}^{n} (x_i - \bar{x})$$
$$= \sum_{i=1}^{n} (x_i - \bar{x})y_i$$

where the first equal sign is based on (2.10), with $\bar{y}$ treated as a constant, and the second on (2.12).

We divide both sides of (2.13) by n:

(2.14)
$$\frac{1}{n} \sum_{i=1}^{n} (x_i - \bar{x})(y_i - \bar{y}) = \frac{1}{n} \sum_{i=1}^{n} (x_i - \bar{x})y_i$$

The left-hand side is the arithmetic mean of all products (for short, the *mean product*) of the two variables, both being measured as deviations from their own means ($\bar{x}$ and $\bar{y}$). We conclude from (2.14) that to compute such a mean product, it is sufficient to measure only one of the two variables as a deviation from the mean. Note that this formulation-in-words is symmetric in the two variables, whereas the right-hand side of (2.14) is not symmetric. But the left-hand side is symmetric (interchanging the roles of x and y leaves the expression unchanged), so that we must have

(2.15)
$$\frac{1}{n} \sum_{i=1}^{n} (x_i - \bar{x})(y_i - \bar{y}) = \frac{1}{n} \sum_{i=1}^{n} x_i(y_i - \bar{y})$$

Next use (2.10) and (2.11) to write the right-hand side of (2.15) as

$$\frac{1}{n} \sum_{i=1}^{n} x_i y_i - \frac{\bar{y}}{n} \sum_{i=1}^{n} x_i = \frac{1}{n} \sum_{i=1}^{n} x_i y_i - \bar{x}\bar{y}$$

Therefore,

$$(2.16) \qquad \frac{1}{n} \sum_{i=1}^{n} (x_i - \bar{x})(y_i - \bar{y}) = \frac{1}{n} \sum_{i=1}^{n} x_i y_i - \bar{x}\bar{y}$$

The first term on the right is the mean product, with neither variable measured as the deviation from the mean. The equation shows that to obtain the mean product when both variables are measured as deviations from their means, we have to subtract the product of these means.

If $y_i = x_i$ for each i, (2.13) and (2.16) become

$$(2.17) \qquad \sum_{i=1}^{n} (x_i - \bar{x})^2 = \sum_{i=1}^{n} (x_i - \bar{x})x_i$$

$$(2.18) \qquad \frac{1}{n} \sum_{i=1}^{n} (x_i - \bar{x})^2 = \frac{1}{n} \sum_{i=1}^{n} x_i^2 - \bar{x}^2$$

The left-hand side of (2.18) is the *mean square* of the x_i's measured as deviations from their mean.

Double Summation

Sometimes we have symbols with two subscripts and we want to sum over both. Table 2 provides an example, with H rows (H values of the first subscript) and K columns (K values of the second subscript). The first row contains all p's whose first subscript is 1. Consequently, the first row sum (the sum of all p's in the first row) is $p_{11} + p_{12} + \cdots + p_{1K}$, which is abbreviated as $\sum_k p_{1k}$ in the table. Similarly, the first column sum is $p_{11} + p_{21} + \cdots + p_{H1}$, which is abbreviated as $\sum_h p_{h1}$.

TABLE 2

Summation across rows and columns

	First column	Second column		Kth column	Row sums
First row	p_{11}	p_{12}	$\cdots$	p_{1K}	$\sum_k p_{1k}$
Second row	p_{21}	p_{22}	$\cdots$	p_{2K}	$\sum_k p_{2k}$
	.	.		.	.
	.	.		.	.
Hth row	p_{H1}	p_{H2}	$\cdots$	p_{HK}	$\sum_k p_{Hk}$
Column sums	$\sum_h p_{h1}$	$\sum_h p_{h2}$	$\cdots$	$\sum_h p_{hK}$	S

The symbol S in the lower-right corner of Table 2 stands for the sum of all p's of the table. When we sum first across rows and then add the row sums, we obtain

$$S = \sum_{k=1}^{K} p_{1k} + \sum_{k=1}^{K} p_{2k} + \cdots + \sum_{k=1}^{K} p_{Hk} = \sum_{h=1}^{H} \left(\sum_{k=1}^{K} p_{hk} \right)$$

By summing first across columns and then adding the column sums, we find

$$S = \sum_{h=1}^{H} p_{h1} + \sum_{h=1}^{H} p_{h2} + \cdots + \sum_{h=1}^{H} p_{hK} = \sum_{k=1}^{K} \left(\sum_{h=1}^{H} p_{hk} \right)$$

It should be evident that it is irrelevant in which order we sum over the subscripts. We write the result as

(2.19)
$$S = \sum_{h=1}^{H} \sum_{k=1}^{K} p_{hk}$$

which is a double summation over h and k. In the right-hand side we add HK (H times K) terms.

Separation of Double Sums

In Chapter 3 we shall meet double sums of the form

(2.20)
$$\sum_{h=1}^{H} \sum_{k=1}^{K} p_{hk} x_h$$

Since x_h does not involve the subscript k, the summation over k can be confined to p_{hk}. This becomes clearer when we write (2.20) in full detail:

$$
\begin{array}{ll}
p_{11}x_1 + p_{12}x_1 + \cdots + p_{1K}x_1 & \text{(for } h = 1) \\
+p_{21}x_2 + p_{22}x_2 + \cdots + p_{2K}x_2 & \text{(for } h = 2) \\
\cdots\cdots\cdots\cdots\cdots\cdots\cdots \\
+p_{H1}x_H + p_{H2}x_H + \cdots + p_{HK}x_H & \text{(for } h = H)
\end{array}
$$

The sum of the terms in the first line is $x_1 \sum_k p_{1k}$ [see (2.8)]. Therefore,

(2.21)
$$\sum_{h=1}^{H} \sum_{k=1}^{K} p_{hk} x_h = \sum_{h=1}^{H} \left(x_h \sum_{k=1}^{K} p_{hk} \right)$$

which shows that to compute the double sum on the left, we can perform two single summations, each over one subscript only. First, we sum p_{hk} over k and multiply the result by x_h, which yields the expression in parentheses. Second, we sum this expression over h.

Sometimes it is possible to separate a double sum completely, as in

$$\sum_{h=1}^{H} \sum_{k=1}^{K} x_h y_k$$

which is equal to

$$
\begin{array}{ll}
x_1 y_1 + x_1 y_2 + \cdots + x_1 y_K & \text{(for } h = 1) \\
+x_2 y_1 + x_2 y_2 + \cdots + x_2 y_K & \text{(for } h = 2) \\
\cdots\cdots\cdots\cdots\cdots\cdots\cdots \\
+x_H y_1 + x_H y_2 + \cdots + x_H y_K & \text{(for } h = H)
\end{array}
$$

When we sum line by line, we obtain

$$x_1 \sum_{k=1}^{K} y_k + x_2 \sum_{k=1}^{K} y_k + \cdots + x_H \sum_{k=1}^{K} y_k = (x_1 + x_2 + \cdots + x_H) \sum_{k=1}^{K} y_k$$

Therefore,

(2.22)
$$\sum_{h=1}^{H}\sum_{k=1}^{K} x_h y_k = \left(\sum_{h=1}^{H} x_h\right)\left(\sum_{k=1}^{K} y_k\right)$$

The right-hand side is the product of two sums, which is thus equal to a double sum consisting of HK terms of the form $x_h y_k$. Note that it is immaterial in which order we sum on the right (first over h and then over k or vice versa). This is in contrast to the right-hand side of (2.21), where we must first sum p_{hk} over k.

When $H = K$ and $x_1 = y_1, \ldots, x_H = y_H$ in (2.22), we obtain

(2.23)
$$\sum_{h=1}^{H}\sum_{k=1}^{H} x_h x_k = \left(\sum_{h=1}^{H} x_h\right)^2$$

which equates the square of the sum of H terms to the sum of H^2 terms. The latter terms contain H squares ($x_1^2, \ldots, x_H^2$).

2.3 Fitting a Straight Line by Least Squares

The most well-known method of fitting a line is by least squares. To simplify the exposition we start with the case in which the line is constrained to go through the origin.

Least Squares Through the Origin

The algebraic representation of the straight line through the origin is

(2.24)
$$y = bx$$

which amounts to a proportionality of x and y with b as proportionality constant. Our objective is to specify b numerically on the basis of observations.

Figure 3 contains a straight line through the origin and five observation points, none of which is located on the line. The vertical deviations of the points from this line are indicated by broken lines. Note that these deviations are sometimes positive (when the point is above the line $y = bx$) and sometimes negative (when the point is below the line).

The situation is considered in more detail for one of the observation points, labeled the ith point. Its horizontal coordinate is x_i (as shown below the horizontal axis), and its vertical coordinate is y_i, which would be equal to bx_i if (2.24) were true for the ith point. However, this point is actually above rather than on the line $y = bx$ of Figure 3, so that this point has a positive deviation $y_i - bx_i$ with respect to this line. The *principle of least squares*, abbreviated as LS, states that the line to be selected is the one which minimizes the sum of the squares of these deviations over all observations. Algebraically, with n observations, this amounts to minimizing

(2.25)
$$G(b) = \sum_{i=1}^{n} (y_i - bx_i)^2$$

with respect to b.

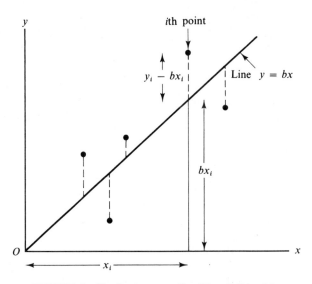

FIGURE 3   The least-squares line through the origin

The LS Slope Through the Origin

To implement the criterion (2.25), we apply a method known as *completing the square*. Using (2.10), we write the right-hand side of (2.25) as

$$\sum_{i=1}^{n} (b^2 x_i^2 - 2b x_i y_i + y_i^2) = b^2 \sum_{i=1}^{n} x_i^2 - 2b \sum_{i=1}^{n} x_i y_i + \sum_{i=1}^{n} y_i^2$$

Hence, we can write (2.25) in the form

$$G(b) = \left[b^2 \sum_{i=1}^{n} x_i^2 - 2b \sum_{i=1}^{n} x_i y_i + \frac{\left(\sum_{i=1}^{n} x_i y_i \right)^2}{\sum_{i=1}^{n} x_i^2} \right] + \sum_{i=1}^{n} y_i^2 - \frac{\left(\sum_{i=1}^{n} x_i y_i \right)^2}{\sum_{i=1}^{n} x_i^2}$$

The expression in brackets is the square of

$$b \sqrt{\sum_{i=1}^{n} x_i^2} - \frac{\sum_{i=1}^{n} x_i y_i}{\sqrt{\sum_{i=1}^{n} x_i^2}}$$

so that we obtain

$$(2.26) \qquad G(b) = \left(b \sqrt{\sum_{i=1}^{n} x_i^2} - \frac{\sum_{i=1}^{n} x_i y_i}{\sqrt{\sum_{i=1}^{n} x_i^2}} \right)^2 + \sum_{i=1}^{n} y_i^2 - \frac{\left(\sum_{i=1}^{n} x_i y_i \right)^2}{\sum_{i=1}^{n} x_i^2}$$

The last two terms on the right do not involve b, so that minimizing $G(b)$ with respect to b is equivalent to minimizing the squared difference immediately to the right of the equal sign. The minimum value of this square is zero, which is attained when b satisfies

$$b\sqrt{\sum_{i=1}^{n} x_i^2} = \frac{\sum_{i=1}^{n} x_i y_i}{\sqrt{\sum_{i=1}^{n} x_i^2}}$$

We divide both sides by the square root of $\sum_i x_i^2$:

(2.27)
$$b = \frac{\sum_{i=1}^{n} x_i y_i}{\sum_{i=1}^{n} x_i^2}$$

This is the LS solution of the slope coefficient b in the proportionality (2.24).

Unconstrained Least Squares

When the linear relation between y and x is not constrained to go through the origin, it takes the form

(2.28)
$$y = b_0 + bx$$

so that there are now two coefficients (the intercept or constant term b_0 and the slope b) which must be adjusted. Figure 4 provides a picture of this line; the vertical deviation of the ith point from the line is now $y_i - b_0 - bx_i$. Thus, LS requires that

(2.29)
$$G(b_0, b) = \sum_{i=1}^{n} (y_i - b_0 - bx_i)^2$$

be minimized with respect to both b_0 and b.

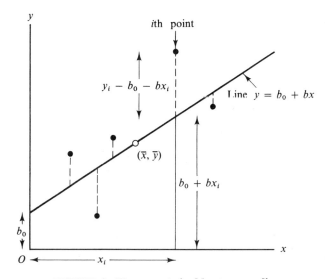

FIGURE 4   The unconstrained least-squares line

With $\bar{x}$ and $\bar{y}$ defined as the arithmetic means of the x_i's and y_i's, respectively, we have

$$y_i - b_0 - bx_i = [y_i - \bar{y} - b(x_i - \bar{x})] + (\bar{y} - b\bar{x} - b_0)$$

so that (2.29) can be written as the sum over $i = 1, \ldots, n$ of

$$[y_i - \bar{y} - b(x_i - \bar{x})]^2 + (\bar{y} - b\bar{x} - b_0)^2$$
$$+ 2(\bar{y} - b\bar{x} - b_0)[y_i - \bar{y} - b(x_i - \bar{x})]$$

Hence, applying (2.10), we obtain

$$G(b_0, b) = \sum_{i=1}^{n} [y_i - \bar{y} - b(x_i - \bar{x})]^2 + n(\bar{y} - b\bar{x} - b_0)^2$$
$$+ 2(\bar{y} - b\bar{x} - b_0) \sum_{i=1}^{n} (y_i - \bar{y}) - 2b(\bar{y} - b\bar{x} - b_0) \sum_{i=1}^{n} (x_i - \bar{x})$$

It follows from (2.12) that the two sums in the second line vanish. Therefore,

$$(2.30) \qquad G(b_0, b) = \sum_{i=1}^{n} [y_i - \bar{y} - b(x_i - \bar{x})]^2 + n(\bar{y} - b\bar{x} - b_0)^2$$

The Intercept and the Slope of the Unconstrained LS Line

The result (2.30) shows that the sum of the squared deviations (2.29) can be written as the sum of two terms. Since b_0 does not occur in the first term, minimizing $G(\ )$ with respect to b_0 is equivalent to minimizing the second term with respect to b_0. The minimum value of this term is zero, which is attained when we specify b_0 as

$$(2.31) \qquad b_0 = \bar{y} - b\bar{x}$$

This result expresses the intercept b_0 in terms of the slope b and the arithmetic means of the two variables.

Since the second term of (2.30) vanishes under (2.31), the sum of the squared deviations now becomes equal to the first term:

$$\sum_{i=1}^{n} [y_i - \bar{y} - b(x_i - \bar{x})]^2$$

Note that this expression is equivalent to the right-hand side of (2.25) when we measure y_i and x_i in (2.25) as deviations from their respective means. We can then apply the developments described in the subsection below (2.25), which leads to the following modification of (2.27):

$$(2.32) \qquad b = \frac{\sum_{i=1}^{n} (x_i - \bar{x})(y_i - \bar{y})}{\sum_{i=1}^{n} (x_i - \bar{x})^2}$$

This result enables us to obtain the slope b from the observations, after which (2.31) yields the intercept b_0. Since (2.31) can be written in the form $\bar{y} = b_0 + b\bar{x}$, we conclude that $(\bar{x}, \bar{y})$, the center of gravity of the observations, is located on the LS line. This point is shown in Figure 4. Note that it is the center of gravity of all n observations, whereas A and B in Figure 2 are the centers of gravity of the points to the left and to the right, respectively, of the dividing line.

Applications to the Data of Table 1

For the seven-year data of Table 1 on page 9, we have

(2.33) $$\bar{x} = 107, \qquad \bar{y} = 96$$

(2.34) $$\sum_{i=1}^{7} (x_i - \bar{x})(y_i - \bar{y}) = 80$$

(2.35) $$\sum_{i=1}^{7} (x_i - \bar{x})^2 = 84$$

so that (2.32) and (2.31) yield

(2.36) $$b = \tfrac{80}{84} \approx .952, \qquad b_0 = 96 - \tfrac{80}{84} \times 107 \approx -5.90$$

Note that this slope and intercept differ from the values of a and a_0 in (2.6) and (2.7), which we obtained from the same data but by means of a different method.

To obtain the coefficient (2.27), the slope of the LS line through the origin, we multiply (2.16) and (2.18) by n:

(2.37) $$\sum_{i=1}^{n} (x_i - \bar{x})(y_i - \bar{y}) = \sum_{i=1}^{n} x_i y_i - n\bar{x}\bar{y}$$

(2.38) $$\sum_{i=1}^{n} (x_i - \bar{x})^2 = \sum_{i=1}^{n} x_i^2 - n\bar{x}^2$$

Substitution of (2.33) to (2.35) and $n = 7$ in these two equations gives $\sum_i x_i y_i = 71{,}984$ and $\sum_i x_i^2 = 80{,}227$, so that (2.27) yields

(2.39) $$b = \frac{71{,}984}{80{,}227} \approx .897$$

This result differs from the b given in (2.36). Both results are derived by LS from the same data, but (2.39) is based on a line through the origin, whereas the line corresponding to (2.36) does not go through the origin ($b_0 \neq 0$).

Least-Squares Adjusted Values and Residuals

We return to (2.28) and write

(2.40) $$\hat{y}_i = b_0 + b x_i \qquad\qquad i = 1, \ldots, n$$

where b_0 and b are given in (2.31) and (2.32). Equation (2.40) defines the *LS adjusted value* of y_i; this value ($\hat{y}_i$) would be equal to y_i for each i if the LS fit were perfect, i.e., if all n points were located on the LS line. Usually the fit is not perfect, so that the deviations from the LS line,

(2.41) $$e_i = y_i - \hat{y}_i = y_i - b_0 - b x_i \qquad\qquad i = 1, \ldots, n$$

are nonzero for at least some values of the subscript i. The e_i defined in (2.41) is known as the *LS residual* for the ith observation. A comparison of (2.41) with (2.29) shows that the LS procedure minimizes the sum of squares of these residuals.

The first equal sign in (2.41) implies that the observed y_i is equal to the sum of the LS adjusted value $\hat{y}_i$ and the residual e_i. This decomposition is shown in Table 3 for the data of Table 1. The last row of Table 3 contains the arithmetic mean of the entries in each column. Note that the arithmetic mean of the residuals is zero; this is necessarily so. To prove this we sum the first and third members of (2.41) over i:

$$(2.42) \qquad \sum_{i=1}^{n} e_i = \sum_{i=1}^{n} y_i - nb_0 - b \sum_{i=1}^{n} x_i$$

By dividing by n we obtain the arithmetic mean of the residuals on the left, which is thus equal to $\bar{y} - b_0 - b\bar{x}$ and hence, in view of (2.31), to zero. Note that the arithmetic mean of the residuals is, in general, not zero when they are obtained from the LS line through the origin (see Problem 7).

TABLE 3

Least-squares adjusted values and residuals for the data of Table 1

Year	x_i	$\hat{y}_i = b_0 + bx_i$	e_i	y_i
1	100	89.33	−.33	89
2	105	94.10	−1.10	93
3	110	98.86	−1.86	97
4	108	96.95	1.05	98
5	106	95.05	.95	96
6	109	97.90	2.10	100
7	111	99.81	−.81	99
Arithmetic mean	107	96.00	.00	96

The LS Residual Sum of Squares

Since the LS adjustment minimizes the sum of squares of the residuals, it is worthwhile to verify what the value of this minimum is. For this purpose we substitute $b_0 = \bar{y} - b\bar{x}$ in (2.41), which gives

$$e_i = y_i - (\bar{y} - b\bar{x}) - bx_i = y_i - \bar{y} - b(x_i - \bar{x})$$

We square the first and third members,

$$e_i^2 = (y_i - \bar{y})^2 + b^2(x_i - \bar{x})^2 - 2b(x_i - \bar{x})(y_i - \bar{y})$$

and sum over i:

$$(2.43) \qquad \sum_{i=1}^{n} e_i^2 = \sum_{i=1}^{n} (y_i - \bar{y})^2 + b^2 \sum_{i=1}^{n} (x_i - \bar{x})^2 - 2b \sum_{i=1}^{n} (x_i - \bar{x})(y_i - \bar{y})$$

We have $b \sum_i (x_i - \bar{x})^2 = \sum_i (x_i - \bar{x})(y_i - \bar{y})$ in view of (2.32), and therefore $-2b^2 \sum_i (x_i - \bar{x})^2 = -2b \sum_i (x_i - \bar{x})(y_i - \bar{y})$. We use this to combine the last two terms in (2.43),

$$(2.44) \qquad \sum_{i=1}^{n} e_i^2 = \sum_{i=1}^{n} (y_i - \bar{y})^2 - b^2 \sum_{i=1}^{n} (x_i - \bar{x})^2$$

or, in more explicit form,

$$(2.45) \qquad \sum_{i=1}^{n} (y_i - b_0 - bx_i)^2 = \sum_{i=1}^{n} (y_i - \bar{y})^2 - b^2 \sum_{i=1}^{n} (x_i - \bar{x})^2$$

We have $\sum_i (y_i - \bar{y})^2 = 88$ for the data of Table 1. Using (2.35) and (2.36) also, we thus obtain the following value of the LS residual sum of squares:

$$(2.46) \qquad 88 - (\tfrac{80}{84})^2 84 \approx 11.81$$

The reader should verify that for LS adjustment through the origin, (2.45) is to be changed into

$$(2.47) \qquad \sum_{i=1}^{n} (y_i - bx_i)^2 = \sum_{i=1}^{n} y_i^2 - b^2 \sum_{i=1}^{n} x_i^2$$

where b is now as defined in (2.27). We have $\sum_i y_i^2 = 64{,}600$ for the data of Table 1. Using the figures shown in (2.39) also, we obtain

$$(2.48) \qquad 64{,}600 - \left(\frac{71{,}984}{80{,}227}\right)^2 80{,}227 \approx 12.07$$

which is larger than the value shown in (2.46). This is not surprising, because (2.48) is the minimum of the sum of the squared deviations obtained by adjusting only one coefficient (the slope). It stands to reason that when we adjust two coefficients (the slope and the intercept) the minimum will certainly not be larger and will usually be smaller.

Alternative Derivation of the LS Coefficients

The solution (2.27) of the LS slope through the origin was obtained by completing the square as shown in (2.26). When we extended the procedure to include a constant term b_0, we wrote the expression to be minimized as the sum of two terms [see (2.30)]; we used one term for minimization with respect to b_0 and found that the subsequent minimization with respect to the slope could be reduced to that of LS through the origin. This means that we complete the square in that case also. But when the number of coefficients adjusted is larger than two, as will be the case in Chapter 7, completing the square is no longer convenient. It is then more attractive to equate derivatives to zero. The developments below describe how this procedure works in the case of fitting straight lines.

Consider again the function (2.25), written as

$$G(b) = b^2 \sum_{i=1}^{n} x_i^2 - 2b \sum_{i=1}^{n} x_i y_i + \sum_{i=1}^{n} y_i^2$$

Minimizing this function can be performed by differentiating it with respect to b:

$$(2.49) \qquad \frac{dG}{db} = 2b \sum_{i=1}^{n} x_i^2 - 2 \sum_{i=1}^{n} x_i y_i$$

A necessary condition for a minimum of $G(b)$ is $dG/db = 0$, which directly yields the b of (2.27).

To handle (2.29) similarly, we write it in the form (2.30). The first right-hand term in (2.30) can be written as

$$\sum_{i=1}^{n} [(y_i - \bar{y})^2 - 2b(x_i - \bar{x})(y_i - \bar{y}) + b^2(x_i - \bar{x})^2]$$

$$= \sum_{i=1}^{n} (y_i - \bar{y})^2 - 2b \sum_{i=1}^{n} (x_i - \bar{x})(y_i - \bar{y}) + b^2 \sum_{i=1}^{n} (x_i - \bar{x})^2$$

We can thus write (2.30) in the form

$$(2.50) \qquad G(b_0, b) = \sum_{i=1}^{n} (y_i - \bar{y})^2 - 2b \sum_{i=1}^{n} (x_i - \bar{x})(y_i - \bar{y})$$
$$+ b^2 \sum_{i=1}^{n} (x_i - \bar{x})^2 + n(\bar{y} - b\bar{x} - b_0)^2$$

A necessary condition for a minimum of $G(b_0, b)$ is that its partial derivative with respect to b_0 vanishes:

$$(2.51) \qquad \frac{\partial G}{\partial b_0} = -2n(\bar{y} - b\bar{x} - b_0) = 0$$

This implies $\bar{y} - b\bar{x} - b_0 = 0$, in agreement with (2.31). Next consider the partial derivative of (2.50) with respect to b:

$$(2.52) \qquad \frac{\partial G}{\partial b} = -2 \sum_{i=1}^{n} (x_i - \bar{x})(y_i - \bar{y}) + 2b \sum_{i=1}^{n} (x_i - \bar{x})^2 - 2n\bar{x}(\bar{y} - b\bar{x} - b_0)$$

The second necessary condition is $\partial G/\partial b = 0$. On combining this with (2.51) and (2.52), we obtain

$$-2 \sum_{i=1}^{n} (x_i - \bar{x})(y_i - \bar{y}) + 2b \sum_{i=1}^{n} (x_i - \bar{x})^2 = 0$$

which yields the b of (2.32).

2.4 Some Questions

In Sections 2.1 and 2.3 we described two methods of fitting a straight line which yield different solutions when applied to the same data. Which method should be preferred? The LS procedure uses a well-defined criterion (that of minimizing the sum of squares of the deviations), which may be considered as an advantage over the method of Section 2.1. However, it is not difficult to invent a different criterion, such as minimizing the sum of the absolute values of the deviations. What is the special merit of least squares? More generally, why should deviations be small, or "as small as possible" in some mathematical sense? Is there a general economic law which states that deviations have such properties?

Also, we measured the deviations in Figures 3 and 4 vertically (in a direction parallel to the y axis). Why don't we measure them horizontally? Why not in a direction which is perpendicular to the fitted straight line? Why not in any other direction?

These are among the questions to which we shall address ourselves in this book. The answers will be based on a combination of economic and statistical considerations. Econometrics uses both economic and statistical tools. In the next two chapters we shall consider the elements of statistical distribution and estimation theory, after which we shall return to the fitting of straight lines in Chapter 5.

Problems

Problems 1–3 refer to Section 2.1, 4–6 to Section 2.2, and 7–11 to Section 2.3.

1 Suppose that the curve in Figure 1(b) is obtained by fitting a polynomial through the seven points. Of which degree should this polynomial be?

2 Verify that $\bar{y}_2$ in (2.4), which is the y coordinate of the center of gravity of the three points with the largest x values in Table 1, is *not* equal to the arithmetic mean of the three largest y values in that table.

3 Verify that $\bar{y}_1 - a\bar{x}_1$ equals a_0 shown in (2.7), using (2.1), (2.2), and (2.6).

4 Prove (2.10).

5 Prove (2.15) directly, without using symmetry considerations.

6 Prove that the sum of the p's in the second and third rows of Table 2 is equal to

$$\sum_{h=2}^{3} \sum_{k=1}^{K} p_{hk}$$

How many p's are added in this expression?

7 Consider the two-observation case ($n = 2$) with the following values of the two variables:

$$x_1 = 1, \quad y_1 = 1$$
$$x_2 = 2, \quad y_2 = 1\tfrac{1}{2}$$

Verify that (2.27) yields $b = .8$ and that the two LS deviations $y_1 - bx_1$ and $y_2 - bx_2$ have an arithmetic mean equal to .05.

8 (*Continuation*) Without making any computations, can you assert what the values of the two deviations are when the LS line is not constrained to pass through the origin?

9 (*Continuation*) Consider the three-observation case ($n = 3$) with the following values of the two variables:

$$x_1 = 0, \quad y_1 = 0$$
$$x_2 = 1, \quad y_2 = 1$$
$$x_3 = 3, \quad y_3 = 2$$

Verify that (2.27) yields $b = .7$ and that the arithmetic mean of the LS deviations is $\frac{1}{15}$. Next verify that (2.31) and (2.32) yield $b = \frac{9}{14}$ and $b_0 = \frac{1}{7}$.

10 Use (2.27) to verify (2.47).

11 Consider the three-decimal approximation .897 for b [see (2.39)]. Verify that when this approximation is used in (2.48), rather than the ratio 71,984/80,227, the result is 48.63, which is more than four times as large as the correct result 12.07. (*Note*: This substantial discrepancy illustrates the danger of rounding in the intermediate steps of the computation. When a computer is used, it is frequently appropriate to apply double precision.)

chapter 3

Discrete Distribution Theory

We mentioned in Section 2.4 the need for statistical distribution theory. This leads to the subject of random variables. The expression "X is a random variable" means that there is a particular probability of occurrence associated with each possible value of X; equivalent expressions are "X is subject to a probability distribution" and "X is stochastic." The word *variate* is also used frequently as a synonym for random variable.

The objective of this chapter is to develop the theory of discrete distributions; the random variable X can then take only selected values. The extension to continuous distribution theory is described in Chapter 4.

3.1 Univariate Discrete Distributions

Let X take one of the values $x_1, x_2, \ldots, x_H$ with probabilities $p_1, p_2, \ldots, p_H$. This is expressed by

$$(3.1) \qquad\qquad \mathrm{P}[X = x_h] = p_h \qquad\qquad h = 1, \ldots, H$$

or, in words, the probability is p_h that X takes the value x_h.

Constraints on Probabilities

Probabilities are necessarily nonnegative:

$$(3.2) \qquad\qquad\qquad p_h \geq 0 \qquad\qquad\qquad h = 1, \ldots, H$$

Also, they add up to 1,

(3.3)
$$\sum_{h=1}^{H} p_h = 1$$

because it is certain that X takes one of the values $x_1, \ldots, x_H$.

For example, let X be the number showing when a balanced die is rolled. The possible values are then 1, 2, 3, 4, 5, and 6, and the probability of each of these values is $\frac{1}{6}$:

(3.4)
$$P[X = h] = p_h = \tfrac{1}{6} \qquad\qquad h = 1, \ldots, 6$$

The distribution (3.4) is shown in Figure 5. The six possible values are measured horizontally, and the associated probabilities are displayed by vertical line segments, all with length $\frac{1}{6}$. Note that (3.4) satisfies the conditions (3.2) and (3.3).

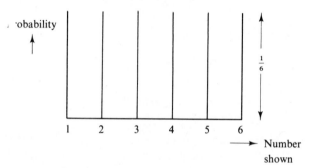

FIGURE 5   **Example of a probability distribution**

The Expectation of a Random Variable

The expectation of the random variable X, written $\mathcal{E}X$, is defined as the weighted mean of the values which it can take $(x_1, \ldots, x_H)$ with weights equal to the corresponding probabilities:

(3.5)
$$\mathcal{E}X = \sum_{h=1}^{H} p_h x_h$$

For the distribution (3.4), we have, using (2.8) with $k = \frac{1}{6}$,

(3.6)
$$\mathcal{E}X = \tfrac{1}{6}(1 + 2 + 3 + 4 + 5 + 6) = 3\tfrac{1}{2}$$

The expectation of X is frequently referred to as the *mean* of the distribution of X, or simply as the mean of X. The reader is advised to make a careful distinction between the mean of a random variable and the arithmetic mean $\bar{x}$ of a set of numbers $x_1, \ldots, x_n$ defined in (2.11).

The Variance of a Random Variable

The mean of X is a measure of the central tendency of its distribution. Frequently we also want a measure of the degree of dispersion around the mean. One such measure is the *variance* of X, written var X. It is obtained by writing all values which X can take as a deviation from the mean $\mathcal{E}X$, squaring each deviation, and then weighting the squared deviations with weights equal to the corresponding probabilities:

$$(3.7) \qquad \text{var } X = \sum_{h=1}^{H} p_h(x_h - \mathcal{E}X)^2$$

Note that variances are always nonnegative, because squares are nonnegative, and the squares in (3.7) are multiplied by probabilities which are also nonnegative [see (3.2)].

The right-hand side of (3.7) can be written as

$$\sum_{h=1}^{H} p_h(x_h - \mathcal{E}X)^2 = \sum_{h=1}^{H} p_h[x_h^2 + (\mathcal{E}X)^2 - 2x_h\mathcal{E}X]$$
$$= \sum_{h=1}^{H} p_h x_h^2 + (\mathcal{E}X)^2 \sum_{h=1}^{H} p_h - 2\mathcal{E}X \sum_{h=1}^{H} p_h x_h$$
$$= \sum_{h=1}^{H} p_h x_h^2 + (\mathcal{E}X)^2 - 2(\mathcal{E}X)^2$$
$$= \sum_{h=1}^{H} p_h x_h^2 - (\mathcal{E}X)^2$$

where the second equal sign is based on (2.10) and the third on (3.3) and (3.5). On combining this result with (3.7), we thus obtain

$$(3.8) \qquad \text{var } X = \sum_{h=1}^{H} p_h x_h^2 - (\mathcal{E}X)^2$$

If X is a random variable with values $x_1, \ldots, x_H$ and probabilities $p_1, \ldots, p_H$, then X^2 is also random; X^2 takes the values $x_1^2, \ldots, x_H^2$ with the same probabilities. Hence, $\sum_h p_h x_h^2$ in (3.8) is the weighted mean of the values which X^2 can take with weights equal to the corresponding probabilities. Thus, going back to the expectation definition (3.5), we conclude that $\sum_h p_h x_h^2$ is the expectation of X^2, and we can write (3.8) as

$$(3.9) \qquad \text{var } X = \mathcal{E}(X^2) - (\mathcal{E}X)^2$$

or, in words, the variance of a random variable is equal to the expectation of its square minus the square of its expectation.

Four Remarks on Expectations and Variances

(1) Note that $\mathcal{E}X$ and var X are not random. They are constants which summarize certain properties of the distribution of the random variable X. It is X which is random, not $\mathcal{E}X$ and var X. In the case of (3.4), the number shown by the die is a random variable, and its expectation is $3\frac{1}{2}$ [see (3.6)].

(2) The variance can be interpreted as an expectation. In (3.7) we take a weighted mean of $(x_1 - \mathcal{E}X)^2, \ldots, (x_H - \mathcal{E}X)^2$ with weights equal to the probabilities $p_1, \ldots, p_H$, so that (3.7) is the expectation of $(X - \mathcal{E}X)^2$,

$$(3.10) \qquad \text{var } X = \mathcal{E}[(X - \mathcal{E}X)^2]$$

or, in words, the variance of X is equal to the expectation of the square of this random variable with the understanding that this variable is to be measured as a deviation from its own expectation.

(3) More generally, consider any function $g(X)$ of X, such as X^3 or $\alpha + \beta X$, where α and β are constants. Since $g(X) = g(x_h)$ if $X = x_h$, $g(X)$ is a random variable which takes the values $g(x_1), \ldots, g(x_H)$ with probabilities $p_1, \ldots, p_H$. Accordingly, the expectation of a function $g(X)$ of the random variable X with distribution (3.1) is defined as

$$(3.11) \qquad \mathcal{E}[g(X)] = \sum_{h=1}^{H} p_h g(x_h)$$

(4) The expression $(x_h - \mathcal{E}X)^2$ in (3.7) is positive except when $x_h = \mathcal{E}X$. For two different values, $x_h \neq x_k$, it is evidently impossible to have both $x_h = \mathcal{E}X$ and $x_k = \mathcal{E}X$. Hence, if p_h and p_k are both nonzero, either $p_h(x_h - \mathcal{E}X)^2$ or $p_k(x_k - \mathcal{E}X)^2$ or both must be positive. Thus, (3.7) implies that the variance of X is positive as soon as X takes two different values with nonzero probabilities. Equivalently, a zero variance of X implies that it takes just one value, with unit probability. In that case X is said to be *nonrandom* or *nonstochastic*.

The Standard Deviation of a Random Variable

An alternative measure of dispersion is the standard deviation of X, written σ_X, which is defined as the (positive) square root of the variance:

$$(3.12) \qquad \sigma_X = \sqrt{\operatorname{var} X}$$

A slight advantage of the standard deviation over the variance is that it is measured in the same units as the random variable itself. For example, if X is measured in centimeters, the variance (3.7) is expressed in square centimeters and the standard deviation (3.12) in centimeters.

For the distribution (3.4) the first right-hand term of (3.8) equals

$$\tfrac{1}{6}(1^2 + 2^2 + 3^2 + 4^2 + 5^2 + 6^2) = \tfrac{91}{6}$$

By substituting (3.6) for $\mathcal{E}X$ in the second right-hand term of (3.8), we obtain

$$\operatorname{var} X = \tfrac{91}{6} - (3\tfrac{1}{2})^2 = \tfrac{35}{12}$$

Application of (3.12) yields $\sigma_X = \sqrt{\tfrac{35}{12}} \approx 1.71$. Hence, when a balanced die is rolled, the number showing is a random variable with mean $3\tfrac{1}{2}$ and a standard deviation slightly in excess of 1.7.

An Infinite Number of Values

In (3.1) we assume that X can take H values, where H is a finite number. This is satisfied by (3.4) with $H = 6$. However, suppose that X can take all positive integer values $(1, 2, 3, \ldots, 10, 11, \ldots, 100, 101, \ldots, 1000, 1001, \ldots)$. We then write (3.5) and (3.11) as

(3.13) $$\mathcal{E}X = \sum_h p_h x_h, \qquad \mathcal{E}[g(X)] = \sum_h p_h g(x_h)$$

where it is to be understood that the summations are over all values of the subscript h for which $p_h > 0$. Since we are summing an infinite number of terms, it is possible that the sum is not finite, in which case the expectations of X and/or $g(X)$ do not exist. This must be checked for each case; examples are given in Problems 3 and 4. Whenever we discuss general properties of expectations and variances in this book, it will be assumed that they exist.

3.2 Multivariate Discrete Distributions

We mentioned on page 1 that much of econometrics is concerned with relationships among several variables. It is therefore appropriate to extend the distribution theory of one random variable to that of several random variables.

The Bivariate Discrete Distribution

Suppose that we have a pair of random variables (X, Y), where X takes the values $x_1, x_2, \ldots$ and Y takes the values $y_1, y_2, \ldots$ in such a way that

(3.14) $$P[X = x_h, Y = y_k] = p_{hk} \qquad \begin{matrix} h = 1, 2, \ldots \\ k = 1, 2, \ldots \end{matrix}$$

The left-hand side is the probability of the simultaneous occurrence of two *events*, one event being $X = x_h$ and the other $Y = y_k$.

Equation (3.14) defines the bivariate distribution of the random pair (X, Y). Its probabilities satisfy

(3.15) $$p_{hk} \geq 0 \qquad h = 1, 2, \ldots ; k = 1, 2, \ldots$$

(3.16) $$\sum_h \sum_k p_{hk} = 1$$

where the summation in (3.16) is over the entire range of both h and k. Note that (3.15) and (3.16) are immediate extensions of (3.2) and (3.3).

It is instructive to compare the probabilities p_{hk} of our bivariate distribution with the p's of Table 2 on page 15. This table is reproduced, with some modifications, as Table 4. The column headings now correspond to the events $Y = y_1$, $Y = y_2, \ldots$, and the rows similarly refer to $X = x_1$, $X = x_2, \ldots$. To qualify as probabilities, the p's must satisfy two conditions: They must be nonnegative [see (3.15)], and they must add up to 1 [see (3.16)]. This explains why S in the lower-right corner of Table 2, defined in (2.19), becomes 1 in Table 4.

TABLE 4

The bivariate probability distribution

	$Y = y_1$	$Y = y_2$	$\cdots$	$Y = y_K$	Marginal distribution of X
$X = x_1$	p_{11}	p_{12}	$\cdots$	p_{1K}	$p_1.$
$X = x_2$	p_{21}	p_{22}	$\cdots$	p_{2K}	$p_2.$
.	.	.		.	.
.	.	.		.	.
.	.	.		.	.
$X = x_H$	p_{H1}	p_{H2}	$\cdots$	p_{HK}	$p_H.$
Marginal distribution of Y	$p_{.1}$	$p_{.2}$	$\cdots$	$p_{.K}$	1

The Marginal Distributions of a Bivariate Distribution

By summing (3.14) over the entire range of k we obtain

$$\sum_k \text{P}[X = x_h, Y = y_k] = \sum_k p_{hk}$$

The expression on the left is simply $\text{P}[X = x_h]$, the probability that X equals x_h irrespective of the value taken by Y. Therefore,

$$(3.17) \qquad \text{P}[X = x_h] = p_{h.}, \qquad \text{where } p_{h.} = \sum_k p_{hk}$$

which defines the *marginal distribution* of X. This distribution states that when no attention is paid to Y, X takes the values $x_1, x_2, \ldots$ with probabilities $p_1., p_2., \ldots$. The probabilities of the marginal distribution of X are the row sums shown in the last column of Table 4, which should be compared with the row sums of Table 2 on page 15.

Similarly, by summing (3.14) over h, we obtain the marginal distribution of Y:

$$(3.18) \qquad \text{P}[Y = y_k] = p_{.k}, \qquad \text{where } p_{.k} = \sum_h p_{hk}$$

The probabilities of the marginal distribution of Y are the column sums shown in the last row of Table 4.

It should be noted that the probabilities of the two marginal distributions satisfy the constraints (3.2) and (3.3), which apply to ordinary univariate distributions. They are nonnegative, because $p_{h.}$ and $p_{.k}$ in (3.17) and (3.18) are defined as sums of p_{hk}'s which are nonnegative [see (3.15)]. Both $p_1., p_2., \ldots$ and $p_{.1}, p_{.2}, \ldots$ add up to 1, because the sum of all p_{hk}'s equals 1 [see (3.16)].

Table 5 gives two numerical examples of a bivariate distribution, with X taking two values (1 and 2) and Y three values (1, 2, and 3). Note that the two distributions differ but that the marginal distributions are pairwise identical.

TABLE 5

Two examples of a bivariate distribution

	$Y = 1$	$Y = 2$	$Y = 3$	*Marginal*
		First distribution		
$X = 1$	$p_{11} = .2$	$p_{12} = .05$	$p_{13} = 0$	$p_1. = .25$
$X = 2$	$p_{21} = .2$	$p_{22} = .35$	$p_{23} = .2$	$p_2. = .75$
Marginal	$p_{.1} = .4$	$p_{.2} = .4$	$p_{.3} = .2$	1
		Second distribution		
$X = 1$	$p_{11} = .1$	$p_{12} = .1$	$p_{13} = .05$	$p_1. = .25$
$X = 2$	$p_{21} = .3$	$p_{22} = .3$	$p_{23} = .15$	$p_2. = .75$
Marginal	$p_{.1} = .4$	$p_{.2} = .4$	$p_{.3} = .2$	1

The Means and Variances of a Bivariate Distribution

Let $g(X, Y)$ be a function of the random pair (X, Y). We extend the definition (3.11) as follows:

$$(3.19) \qquad \mathcal{E}[g(X, Y)] = \sum_h \sum_k p_{hk} g(x_h, y_k)$$

If $g(X, Y) = X$, (3.19) yields the expectation of X in the bivariate distribution of (X, Y),

$$(3.20) \qquad \mathcal{E}X = \sum_h \sum_k p_{hk} x_h = \sum_h p_{h.} x_h$$

where the last step is based on (2.21) and (3.17). It follows from (3.10) that the variance of X is obtained by specifying $g(X, Y)$ as $(X - \mathcal{E}X)^2$:

$$(3.21) \qquad \operatorname{var} X = \sum_h \sum_k p_{hk}(x_h - \mathcal{E}X)^2 = \sum_h p_{h.}(x_h - \mathcal{E}X)^2$$

We conclude from (3.20) and (3.21) that the mean and the variance of X in the bivariate distribution of (X, Y) are essentially univariate concepts; they are the mean and the variance of the marginal distribution of X. Similarly,

$$(3.22) \qquad \mathcal{E}Y = \sum_k p_{.k} y_k, \qquad \operatorname{var} Y = \sum_k p_{.k}(y_k - \mathcal{E}Y)^2$$

which is obtained by substituting $g(X, Y) = Y$ and $g(X, Y) = (Y - \mathcal{E}Y)^2$ in (3.19).

For the two distributions of Table 5 we find

$$(3.23) \qquad \begin{array}{lll} \mathcal{E}X = 1\frac{3}{4}, & \operatorname{var} X = \frac{3}{16}, & \sigma_X \approx .433 \\ \mathcal{E}Y = 1\frac{4}{5}, & \operatorname{var} Y = \frac{14}{25}, & \sigma_Y \approx .748 \end{array}$$

where the standard deviations (σ_X and σ_Y) are computed as the square roots of the corresponding variances, in agreement with (3.12). Note that both bivariate distributions of Table 5 have the same pair of means ($\mathcal{E}X$ and $\mathcal{E}Y$) and the same pair of variances (var X and var Y) because they have the same pair of marginal distributions.

The Covariance

The covariance of the random pair (X, Y), written cov (X, Y), is defined as the expectation of the product of X and Y with the understanding that X and Y are measured as deviations from their own expectations. Thus, we can apply (3.19) with $g(X, Y)$ interpreted as $(X - \mathcal{E}X)(Y - \mathcal{E}Y)$:

$$(3.24) \qquad \text{cov } (X, Y) = \mathcal{E}[(X - \mathcal{E}X)(Y - \mathcal{E}Y)]$$
$$= \sum_h \sum_k p_{hk}(x_h - \mathcal{E}X)(y_k - \mathcal{E}Y)$$

Recall that the means and variances given in (3.20) to (3.22) are essentially univariate. In contrast to this, the covariance (3.24) is a truly bivariate concept. We shall find in Section 3.4 that the covariance plays a role in the analysis of linear combinations of random variables. Also, we shall see in Section 6.2 how the covariance provides a measure of the degree to which two random variables are linearly related.

The expression in the second line of (3.24) can be written as

$$\sum_h \sum_k p_{hk} x_h y_k - \mathcal{E}Y \sum_h \sum_k p_{hk} x_h - \mathcal{E}X \sum_h \sum_k p_{hk} y_k + \mathcal{E}X\mathcal{E}Y \sum_h \sum_k p_{hk}$$

It follows from (3.16), (3.20), and $\sum_h \sum_k p_{hk} y_k = \mathcal{E}Y$ that this can be simplified to

$$(3.25) \qquad \text{cov } (X, Y) = \sum_h \sum_k p_{hk} x_h y_k - \mathcal{E}X\mathcal{E}Y$$
$$= \mathcal{E}(XY) - \mathcal{E}X\mathcal{E}Y$$

Hence, the covariance of two random variables is equal to the expectation of their product minus the product of their expectations.

We have $\sum_h \sum_k p_{hk} x_h y_k = 3.15$ for the second distribution of Table 5 and $\mathcal{E}X\mathcal{E}Y = 3.15$ [see (3.23)], so that (3.25) yields a zero covariance for this distribution. For the first distribution we obtain

$$(3.26) \qquad \text{cov } (X, Y) = 3.3 - 3.15 = .15$$

which is a positive value.

Distributions in Three and More Dimensions

Extensions to a number of random variables larger than two are conceptually straightforward. It is essentially a matter of adding a subscript to the probability for each additional variable:

$$(3.27) \qquad P[X = x_h, Y = y_k, Z = z_l] = p_{hkl}$$

The interested reader will find further details in Problems 6 to 8.

3.3   Conditional Distributions and Stochastic Independence

Consider the first distribution of Table 5 and imagine that we know that $Y = 1$. What can we say about the distribution of X given this knowledge?

Such questions are of considerable importance in econometrics. When translated into the language of consumption and income, they can be phrased in the form, "What is the probability distribution of consumption given that income takes a particular numerical value?"

Conditional Discrete Distributions

If $Y = 1$ holds in the first distribution of Table 5, only the first column of the distribution is relevant. This column consists of $p_{11} = .2$, $p_{21} = .2$, and $p_{.1} = .4$. Hence, if we know that $Y = 1$ (which happens 40 percent of the time because $p_{.1} = .4$), then $X = 1$ and $X = 2$ are equally likely (because $p_{11} = p_{21}$). This is formalized by the statements

$$(3.28) \qquad P[X = 1 \mid Y = 1] = \frac{p_{11}}{p_{.1}} = \frac{.2}{.4} = .5$$

$$(3.29) \qquad P[X = 2 \mid Y = 1] = \frac{p_{21}}{p_{.1}} = \frac{.2}{.4} = .5$$

The first member in (3.28) should be read as the conditional probability of $X = 1$ given $Y = 1$. It is defined as the ratio of the joint probability of the two events ($X = 1$ *and* $Y = 1$) to the probability of the condition ($Y = 1$). In (3.29) we have the conditional probability of $X = 2$ given $Y = 1$. Note that the division by the probability of the condition, $P[Y = 1] = p_{.1} = .4$, ensures that the conditional probabilities add up to 1, as they should: $.5 + .5 = 1$.

Table 6 contains three conditional distributions of X, all based on the first distribution of Table 5, given $Y = 1$, $Y = 2$, and $Y = 3$. When the condition is $Y = 2$, we divide p_{12} and p_{22} by $p_{.2}$; when it is $Y = y_3$, we divide p_{13} and p_{23} by $p_{.3}$. Note that $X = 2$ holds with unit probability in the last distribution, so that X ceases to be random conditionally on $Y = 3$.

TABLE 6

Three conditional distributions

	Given Y = 1	Given Y = 2	Given Y = 3
$X = 1$	$.2/.4 = .5$	$.05/.4 = .125$	$0/.2 = 0$
$X = 2$	$.2/.4 = .5$	$.35/.4 = .875$	$.2/.2 = 1$

The extension of (3.28) and (3.29) to the more general bivariate distribution of Table 4 is

$$(3.30) \qquad P[X = x_h \mid Y = y_k] = \frac{P[X = x_h, Y = y_k]}{P[Y = y_k]} = \frac{p_{hk}}{p_{.k}}$$

Hence, if $Y = y_k$, X takes the values $x_1, x_2, \ldots$ with the probabilities $p_{1k}/p_{.k}$, $p_{2k}/p_{.k}, \ldots$. Note that this conditional probability is defined only if $p_{.k} \neq 0$, i.e., if the probability of the condition ($Y = y_k$) does not vanish.

We also have the conditional probability of $Y = y_k$ given $X = x_h$, which is obtained by simply interchanging the roles of $X = x_h$ and $Y = y_k$ in (3.30):

$$(3.31) \qquad P[Y = y_k \,|\, X = x_h] = \frac{P[X = x_h,\, Y = y_k]}{P[X = x_h]} = \frac{p_{hk}}{p_{h.}}$$

Thus, if $X = x_h$, Y takes the values y_1, y_2, ... with the probabilities $p_{h1}/p_{h.}$, $p_{h2}/p_{h.}$, ... (provided $p_{h.} \neq 0$). Table 7 contains two conditional distributions of Y, both based on the first distribution of Table 5, given $X = 1$ and $X = 2$. Note that the sum of the conditional probabilities in each column of Table 6 equals 1 and that those of Table 7 add up to 1 in each row. (This holds for the second row only approximately because of rounding errors.)

TABLE 7

Two other conditional distributions

	$Y = 1$	$Y = 2$	$Y = 3$
Given $X = 1$	$.2/.25 = .8$	$.05/.25 = .2$	$0/.25 = 0$
Given $X = 2$	$.2/.75 \approx .267$	$.35/.75 \approx .467$	$.2/.75 \approx .267$

Conditional Means and Variances

The conditional mean and variance of X given $Y = y_k$ are defined in accordance with (3.5) and (3.7), but they are obviously based on probabilities of the form (3.30):

$$(3.32) \qquad \mathcal{E}(X \,|\, Y = y_k) = \sum_h \frac{p_{hk}}{p_{.k}} x_h$$

$$(3.33) \qquad \operatorname{var}(X \,|\, Y = y_k) = \sum_h \frac{p_{hk}}{p_{.k}} [x_h - \mathcal{E}(X \,|\, Y = y_k)]^2$$

The conditional mean and variance of Y given $X = x_h$ are similarly based on (3.31):

$$(3.34) \qquad \mathcal{E}(Y \,|\, X = x_h) = \sum_k \frac{p_{hk}}{p_{h.}} y_k$$

$$(3.35) \qquad \operatorname{var}(Y \,|\, X = x_h) = \sum_k \frac{p_{hk}}{p_{h.}} [y_k - \mathcal{E}(Y \,|\, X = x_h)]^2$$

For example, the means and variances of the three conditional distributions of Table 6 are

$$(3.36) \qquad \begin{array}{ll} \mathcal{E}(X \,|\, Y = 1) = 1.5, & \operatorname{var}(X \,|\, Y = 1) = .25 \\ \mathcal{E}(X \,|\, Y = 2) = 1.875, & \operatorname{var}(X \,|\, Y = 2) = .109375 \\ \mathcal{E}(X \,|\, Y = 3) = 2, & \operatorname{var}(X \,|\, Y = 3) = 0 \end{array}$$

Note that these numerical results all differ from the unconditional mean and variance ($\mathcal{E}X$ and var X) shown in (3.23). Also note that in (3.36) the conditional expectation of X increases when Y takes a larger value and that the conditional variance of X decreases.

Stochastic Independence

The random variables X and Y are said to be stochastically independent when

$$(3.37) \qquad p_{hk} = p_{h.}p_{.k} \qquad \text{for all pairs } (h, k)$$

This implies that $p_{hk}/p_{.k} = p_{h.}$ in (3.30), so that the conditional distribution of X given $Y = y_k$ (for any k with $p_{.k} \neq 0$) is identical to the marginal distribution (3.17) of X. Another implication of (3.37) is $p_{hk}/p_{h.} = p_{.k}$, so that the conditional distribution (3.31) of Y given $X = x_h$ (for any h for which $p_{h.} \neq 0$) is identical to the marginal distribution (3.18) of Y.

We conclude that *under stochastic independence any knowledge about X (such as $X = x_h$) is worthless for the formulation of probability statements on Y and vice versa.* Also, since the conditional distributions are identical to the corresponding marginal distribution, the conditional means and variances must be identical to the corresponding unconditional mean and variance. This may be verified by comparing (3.32) to (3.35) with (3.20) to (3.22).

REMARKS:

(1) The reader should verify that the second distribution of Table 5 satisfies condition (3.37) of stochastic independence.

(2) Stochastic independence implies that the conditional means and variances are equal to the corresponding unconditional mean and variance, but checking that the conditional means and variances are equal to their unconditional counterparts is not sufficient to conclude that there is stochastic independence. To verify whether X and Y are stochastically independent, we have to check whether (3.37) is true.

Products of Functions of Independent Random Variables

Let $g_1(X)$ and $g_2(Y)$ be functions of X and Y, respectively, and let X and Y be stochastically independent. We consider the expectation of the product of $g_1(X)$ and $g_2(Y)$ using (3.19):

$$\begin{aligned}
\mathcal{E}[g_1(X)g_2(Y)] &= \sum_h \sum_k p_{hk} g_1(x_h) g_2(y_k) \\
&= \sum_h \sum_k p_{h.}p_{.k} g_1(x_h) g_2(y_k) \\
&= [\sum_h p_{h.} g_1(x_h)][\sum_k p_{.k} g_2(y_k)]
\end{aligned}$$

The second equal sign is based on the independence condition (3.37), and the third on the separation proposition (2.22) for the double sum. [Interpret x_h of (2.22) as $p_{h.}g_1(x_h)$ and y_k as $p_{.k}g_2(y_k)$.] Since the expressions in brackets in the last line are simply the expectations of $g_1(X)$ and $g_2(Y)$, we thus have

$$(3.38) \qquad \mathcal{E}[g_1(X)g_2(Y)] = \mathcal{E}[g_1(X)]\mathcal{E}[g_2(Y)]$$

or, in words, if X and Y are stochastically independent, the product of any function of X and any function of Y has an expectation equal to the product of the expectations of the two functions.

Take $g_1(X) = X$ and $g_2(Y) = Y$, so that $\mathcal{E}(XY) = \mathcal{E}X\mathcal{E}Y$ is implied by (3.38) under stochastic independence. On comparing this with (3.25) we conclude that *independent random variables have a zero covariance*. Note that this result agrees with the zero covariance of the second distribution of Table 5 [see the discussion preceding (3.26) and remark (1) at the end of the previous subsection]. Also note that the converse is not true: If X and Y have a zero covariance, they need not be stochastically independent. This matter is further pursued in Section 6.2.

Extensions to Three and More Dimensions

To extend the definition of stochastic independence to more than two random variables, we write (3.37) in the form

$$P[X = x_h, \ Y = y_k] = P[X = x_h]P[Y = y_k]$$

for all pairs (h, k). The extension to the trivariate distribution (3.27) is

$$(3.39) \qquad P[X = x_h, \ Y = y_k, Z = z_l] = P[X = x_h]P[Y = y_k]P[Z = z_l]$$

for all triples (h, k, l), where $P[X = x_h]$, $P[Y = y_k]$, and $P[Z = z_l]$ are probabilities of the marginal distributions of X, Y, and Z, respectively. If (3.39) holds for each (h, k, l), the three random variables are said to be *independently distributed*. The extension to four and more variables is obvious. If X, Y, and Z are independently distributed, we have

$$(3.40) \qquad \mathcal{E}[g_1(X)g_2(Y)g_3(Z)] = \mathcal{E}[g_1(X)]\mathcal{E}[g_2(Y)]\mathcal{E}[g_3(Z)]$$

which is an extension of (3.38). Also, if X, Y, and Z are independently distributed, the covariances of X and Y, of X and Z, and of Y and Z are all zero. The interested reader should consult Problems 14 and 15.

3.4   The Algebra of Expectations

Linear combinations of random variables play an important role in this book. It is convenient to derive here the mean and the variance of such a combination.

The Expectation of a Linear Combination of Random Variables

Consider the linear combination $Z = \alpha_0 + \alpha_1 X + \alpha_2 Y$ of two random variables X and Y, where the α's are constants. It follows from (3.14) that Z equals $\alpha_0 + \alpha_1 x_h + \alpha_2 y_k$ with probability p_{hk}. Hence, (3.19) yields

$$\mathcal{E}Z = \sum_h \sum_k p_{hk}(\alpha_0 + \alpha_1 x_h + \alpha_2 y_k)$$
$$= \alpha_0 \sum_h \sum_k p_{hk} + \alpha_1 \sum_h \sum_k p_{hk} x_h + \alpha_2 \sum_h \sum_k p_{hk} y_k$$

Using (3.16), (3.20), and $\sum_h \sum_k p_{hk} y_k = \mathcal{E}Y$, we thus obtain

$$(3.41) \qquad \mathcal{E}(\alpha_0 + \alpha_1 X + \alpha_2 Y) = \alpha_0 + \alpha_1 \mathcal{E}X + \alpha_2 \mathcal{E}Y$$

which states that the expectation of a linear combination of two random variables is equal to *the same linear combination* (with the same α's) of the expectations of these variables. Note that this holds even when X and Y are not stochastically independent. Also note that (3.41) for $\alpha_1 = \alpha_2 = 0$ implies $\mathcal{E}\alpha_0 = \alpha_0$; that is, the expectation of a constant is equal to this constant.

The result (3.41) holds for any linear combination of n random variables $X_1, \ldots, X_n$ (see Problem 17 for $n = 3$). If these variables have expectations $\mathcal{E}X_1, \ldots, \mathcal{E}X_n$, then

$$(3.42) \qquad \mathcal{E}\left(\alpha_0 + \sum_{i=1}^{n} \alpha_i X_i\right) = \alpha_0 + \sum_{i=1}^{n} \alpha_i \mathcal{E}X_i$$

where $\alpha_0, \alpha_1, \ldots, \alpha_n$ are arbitrary constants.

The Variance of a Linear Combination

We return to the expectation of the function $g(X, Y)$ defined in (3.19). The variance of this function is defined as

$$(3.43) \qquad \operatorname{var} g(X, Y) = \sum_h \sum_k p_{hk}\{g(x_h, y_k) - \mathcal{E}[g(X, Y)]\}^2$$

which is a direct extension of the variance of X given in (3.21). When $g(\quad)$ is specified as $Z = \alpha_0 + \alpha_1 X + \alpha_2 Y$, we can use (3.41) to write (3.43) as

$$\operatorname{var} Z = \sum_h \sum_k p_{hk}[\alpha_0 + \alpha_1 x_h + \alpha_2 y_k - (\alpha_0 + \alpha_1 \mathcal{E}X + \alpha_2 \mathcal{E}Y)]^2$$
$$= \sum_h \sum_k p_{hk}[\alpha_1(x_h - \mathcal{E}X) + \alpha_2(y_k - \mathcal{E}Y)]^2$$

The expression in the second line can be evaluated as follows:

$$\sum_h \sum_k p_{hk}[\alpha_1^2(x_h - \mathcal{E}X)^2 + \alpha_2^2(y_k - \mathcal{E}Y)^2 + 2\alpha_1\alpha_2(x_h - \mathcal{E}X)(y_k - \mathcal{E}Y)]$$
$$= \alpha_1^2 \sum_h \sum_k p_{hk}(x_h - \mathcal{E}X)^2 + \alpha_2^2 \sum_h \sum_k p_{hk}(y_k - \mathcal{E}Y)^2$$
$$+ 2\alpha_1\alpha_2 \sum_h \sum_k p_{hk}(x_h - \mathcal{E}X)(y_k - \mathcal{E}Y)$$

The first term after the equal sign is equal to $\alpha_1^2 \operatorname{var} X$ in view of (3.21), and the second term equals $\alpha_2^2 \operatorname{var} Y$. Using (3.24) also, we thus obtain

$$(3.44) \quad \operatorname{var}(\alpha_0 + \alpha_1 X + \alpha_2 Y) = \alpha_1^2 \operatorname{var} X + \alpha_2^2 \operatorname{var} Y + 2\alpha_1\alpha_2 \operatorname{cov}(X, Y)$$

which shows that the variance of a linear combination of X and Y involves the variances of both and also their covariance. Note that α_0 does not occur on the right; adding a constant to a random variable does not affect its variance.

Assume now that X and Y are stochastically independent, so that their covariance vanishes [see the paragraph below (3.38)]. Then (3.44) is simplified to

$$(3.45) \qquad \operatorname{var}(\alpha_0 + \alpha_1 X + \alpha_2 Y) = \alpha_1^2 \operatorname{var} X + \alpha_2^2 \operatorname{var} Y$$

This result holds more generally. If $X_1, \ldots, X_n$ are independently distributed, then

$$(3.46) \qquad \operatorname{var}\left(\alpha_0 + \sum_{i=1}^{n} \alpha_i X_i\right) = \sum_{i=1}^{n} \alpha_i^2 \operatorname{var} X_i$$

so that the variance of a linear combination of random variables is a linear combination of the variances of these variables. Note that the coefficient of var X_i on the right in (3.46) is the square of the coefficient of X_i on the left. Again note that the additive constant α_0 does not occur on the right.

Also note that (3.45) and (3.46) are based on the independence assumption, whereas (3.41) and (3.42) do not require this assumption. When there is no independence, the variance of a linear combination of random variables involves the covariances of these variables [see (3.44) for the two-variable case]. These matters are further pursued in the last subsection of Section 6.2.

Standardized Random Variables

Let X be a random variable with expectation $\mathcal{E}X$ and standard deviation σ_X. We subtract $\mathcal{E}X$ from X to obtain $X - \mathcal{E}X$, which has zero expectation, $\mathcal{E}(X - \mathcal{E}X) = 0$; this follows from (3.41) with $\alpha_0 = -\mathcal{E}X$, $\alpha_1 = 1$, and $\alpha_2 = 0$. Next we divide by σ_X. The resulting ratio also has zero expectation:

$$(3.47) \qquad \mathcal{E}\left(\frac{X - \mathcal{E}X}{\sigma_X}\right) = 0$$

This follows from (3.41) with the α's specified as

$$(3.48) \qquad \alpha_0 = -\frac{\mathcal{E}X}{\sigma_X}, \qquad \alpha_1 = \frac{1}{\sigma_X}, \qquad \alpha_2 = 0$$

The variance of $(X - \mathcal{E}X)/\sigma_X$ is 1,

$$(3.49) \qquad \mathrm{var}\left(\frac{X - \mathcal{E}X}{\sigma_X}\right) = 1$$

which follows from (3.44) with the α's specified in (3.48).

We conclude from (3.47) and (3.49) that when X is measured from its expectation and then divided by its standard deviation, the resulting expression $(X - \mathcal{E}X)/\sigma_X$ has zero expectation and unit variance. Random variables with this expectation and this variance are called *standardized* random variables.

Problems

Problems 1–4 refer to Section 3.1, 5–8 to Section 3.2, 9–15 to Section 3.3, and 16–18 to Section 3.4.

1 Let X take the values a and $a + 2$ with probability $\frac{1}{2}$ each. Prove that $\mathcal{E}X = a + 1$ and var $X = 1$.

2 Let X take the values a, $a + 1$, and $a + 2$ with probability $\frac{1}{3}$ each. Prove that $\mathcal{E}X = a + 1$ and var $X = \frac{2}{3}$.

3 A person tosses a coin; the probabilities of heads and tails are $\frac{1}{2}$ each. If heads show up, he receives $1 and the game is terminated. If tails show up, he tosses the coin again and receives \$2 when heads show up at that time, after which the game is terminated. If tails show up again, he tosses the coin and receives \$3 when heads show up, and so on. Thus, his gain is a random variable which takes the value \$1 with probability $\frac{1}{2}$, \$2 with probability $\frac{1}{4}$, \$3 with probability $\frac{1}{8}$, \$4 with probability $\frac{1}{16}$, etc. (Hence the gain is a random variable which takes an infinite number of values.) Prove that the expected gain (the expectation of the gain) is \$2.

4   (*Continuation*) We modify the rules of the game so that the gain is \$1 with probability $\frac{1}{2}$, \$2 with probability $\frac{1}{4}$, \$4 with probability $\frac{1}{8}$, \$8 with probability $\frac{1}{16}$, etc.; hence, the amount is doubled in each next step. Prove that the gain is a random variable whose expectation is infinitely large.

5   Verify the numerical results (3.23) as well as the two covariances of Table 5 [see (3.26) and the lines preceding that equation].

6   Formulate the constraints on the probabilities p_{hkl} of (3.27). Then sum (3.27) over the entire range of k and l to obtain

$$P[X = x_h] = p_{h..}, \quad \text{where } p_{h..} = \sum_k \sum_l p_{hkl}$$

and similarly,

$$P[Y = y_k] = p_{.k.}, \quad \text{where } p_{.k.} = \sum_h \sum_l p_{hkl}$$

$$P[Z = z_l] = p_{..l}, \quad \text{where } p_{..l} = \sum_h \sum_k p_{hkl}$$

The probabilities $p_{h..}$, $p_{.k.}$, and $p_{..l}$ are those of the marginal distributions of X, Y, and Z, respectively. Verify that they are nonnegative and add up to 1 when summed over the appropriate range of the subscript.

7   (*Continuation*) Extend (3.19) to

$$\mathcal{E}[g(X, Y, Z)] = \sum_h \sum_k \sum_l p_{hkl} g(x_h, y_k, z_l)$$

and indicate how $g(X, Y, Z)$ must be specified to yield

$$\mathcal{E}X = \sum_h p_{h..} x_h, \quad \text{var } X = \sum_h p_{h..} (x_h - \mathcal{E}X)^2$$

Define the means and variances of Y and Z also.

8   (*Continuation*) Specify $g(X, Y, Z) = (X - \mathcal{E}X)(Y - \mathcal{E}Y)$ to obtain

$$\text{cov } (X, Y) = \sum_h \sum_k p_{hk.} (x_h - \mathcal{E}X)(y_k - \mathcal{E}Y)$$

Also derive the covariances of X and Z and of Y and Z. (*Note*: This result shows that the covariance is essentially a bivariate concept, even in a trivariate distribution, in the same way that the mean and the variance are univariate concepts.)

9   Prove

$$\text{var } (X \mid Y = y_k) = \sum_h \frac{p_{hk}}{p_{.k}} x_h^2 - [\mathcal{E}(X \mid Y = y_k)]^2$$

Formulate and prove a similar result for var $(Y \mid X = x_h)$.

10   (*Continuation*) Verify the conditional means and variances shown in (3.36).

Also verify the following conditional means and variances for Table 7:

$$\mathcal{E}(Y\,|\,X=1)=1.2, \qquad \text{var}\,(Y\,|\,X=1)=.16$$
$$\mathcal{E}(Y\,|\,X=2)=2, \qquad \text{var}\,(Y\,|\,X=2)\approx.533$$

Compare these results with the corresponding unconditional mean and variance shown in (3.23), and draw your conclusions.

11 Prove that the weighted mean, with weights equal to the probabilities of the corresponding conditions, of the conditional means is equal to the unconditional mean:

$$\sum_k p_{.k}\mathcal{E}(X\,|\,Y=y_k)=\mathcal{E}X$$
$$\sum_h p_{h.}\mathcal{E}(Y\,|\,X=x_h)=\mathcal{E}Y$$

(*Note*: The conditional variances do not follow this simple rule.)

12 Prove that if X and Y are stochastically independent, knowledge of the probabilities of their marginal distributions is sufficient to compute the complete array of all bivariate probabilities.

13 Verify that X and Y are stochastically independent in the second distribution of Table 5. For this distribution, compute the probabilities of the conditional distributions (similarly to Tables 6 and 7), and verify that they are equal to the probabilities of the corresponding marginal distributions shown in Table 5.

14 (*Continuation of Problem 6*) Write the independence condition (3.39) as

$$p_{hkl}=p_{h..}p_{.k.}p_{..l} \qquad \text{for all triples } (h,k,l)$$

and prove (3.40) under this condition.

15 (*Continuation*) Prove that the covariances of Problem 8 all vanish when X, Y, and Z are independently distributed.

16 Prove the following:

$$\text{cov}\,(\alpha_0+\alpha_1 X+\alpha_2 Y,\ \beta_0+\beta_1 X+\beta_2 Y)=\alpha_1\beta_1\,\text{var}\,X$$
$$+\alpha_2\beta_2\,\text{var}\,Y+(\alpha_1\beta_2+\alpha_2\beta_1)\,\text{cov}\,(X,Y)$$

where the α's and β's are constants. (*Hint*: First express both $\alpha_0+\alpha_1 X+\alpha_2 Y$ and $\beta_0+\beta_1 X+\beta_2 Y$ as deviations from their expectations.)

17 (*Continuation of Problem 6*) Prove, without using the independence condition of Problem 14, that

$$\mathcal{E}(\alpha_0+\alpha_1 X+\alpha_2 Y+\alpha_3 Z)=\alpha_0+\alpha_1\mathcal{E}X+\alpha_2\mathcal{E}Y+\alpha_3\mathcal{E}Z$$

where the α's are constants.

18 (*Continuation*) Prove the following:

$$\text{var}\,(\alpha_0+\alpha_1 X+\alpha_2 Y+\alpha_3 Z)=\alpha_1^2\,\text{var}\,X+\alpha_2^2\,\text{var}\,Y+\alpha_3^2\,\text{var}\,Z$$
$$+2\alpha_1\alpha_2\,\text{cov}\,(X,Y)+2\alpha_1\alpha_3\,\text{cov}\,(X,Z)$$
$$+2\alpha_2\alpha_3\,\text{cov}\,(Y,Z)$$

chapter 4

Continuous

Distribution Theory

and

Statistical Inference

The developments of discrete distribution theory in Chapter 3 are necessary for the understanding of econometrics but not sufficient. The reason is that most economic variables do not take selected values but all values, or all values in a certain range or interval. For example, per capita consumption can take all values from zero onward. Accordingly, the first objective of this chapter is to extend the analysis of Chapter 3 to continuous distributions. The second objective is to develop the first principles of statistical inference.

4.1 Univariate Continuous Distributions

We assume that the random variable X can take all values in the interval (a, b), where $a < b$. We may have $a = -\infty$ and $b = \infty$ as special cases. Consider then the probability statement

$$(4.1) \qquad \qquad P[x < X \le x + dx] = f(x)\,dx \qquad \qquad a \le x < b$$

or, in words, the probability that X takes a value in a small interval to the right of x is proportional to $f(x)$, the value of the *probability density function* at x. The proportionality coefficient is dx, the width of the interval $(x, x + dx)$. Examples are given in Figures 6 and 7 later in this section.

Constraints on the Probability Density Function

Since the left-hand side of (4.1) is a probability for any $dx > 0$, the probability density function (for short, the density function) must take nonnegative values. Also, its integral over (a, b) must be 1, because it is certain that X takes one of the values between a and b. Therefore,

(4.2) $$f(x) \geq 0 \qquad\qquad a \leq x < b$$

(4.3) $$\int_a^b f(x)\, dx = 1$$

which should be compared with (3.2) and (3.3). This comparison suggests that the probabilities of Chapter 3 are replaced by the density function, and sums by integrals. We shall find that this is indeed systematically the case.

For example, let X be uniformly distributed over the interval from a to b:

(4.4) $$f(x) = \frac{1}{b - a} \qquad\qquad a \leq x < b$$

Hence, the density function is a constant in the interval (a, b); it is illustrated by the straight line parallel to the horizontal axis in Figure 6. When we identify

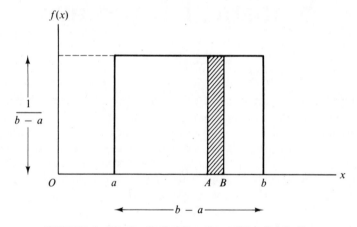

FIGURE 6   The density function of a uniform distribution

OA and AB with x and dx, respectively, the shaded area in the figure is equal to the probability (4.1). Condition (4.3) requires that the total area between the density line and the horizontal axis be 1. This is satisfied by (4.4), because the area is that of a rectangle with length $b - a$ and height $1/(b - a)$. In most cases the density function behaves as a curve (Figure 7 on p. 46 is an example); condition (4.3) then requires that the area below the density curve equal 1. Condition (4.2) is obviously also satisfied by (4.4).

Expectation, Variance, and Standard Deviation

The expectation (or mean) of the random variable X with density function $f(\ )$ is defined in accordance with (3.5) but with probabilities replaced by the density function and summation by integration:

$$(4.5) \qquad \mathcal{E}X = \int_a^b xf(x)\, dx$$

The expectation of a function $g(X)$ of X is similarly defined as

$$(4.6) \qquad \mathcal{E}[g(X)] = \int_a^b g(x)f(x)\, dx$$

which should be compared with (3.11).

By specifying $g(X) = (X - \mathcal{E}X)^2$, with $\mathcal{E}X$ defined in (4.5), we obtain the variance of X:

$$(4.7) \qquad \text{var } X = \int_a^b (x - \mathcal{E}X)^2 f(x)\, dx$$

Also, by proceeding as in the developments leading to (3.8) but with sums replaced by integrals, we obtain

$$(4.8) \qquad \text{var } X = \mathcal{E}(X^2) - (\mathcal{E}X)^2$$

where $\mathcal{E}(X^2)$ is defined, in agreement with (4.6), as the integral of $x^2 f(x)\, dx$ over x from a to b. Note that (4.8) agrees with (3.9) for discrete distributions. The reader may want to verify that the uniform distribution (4.4) has an expectation equal to $\frac{1}{2}(a + b)$, which is the midpoint of the interval (a, b), and a variance equal to $\frac{1}{12}(b - a)^2$, which is one-twelfth of the squared width of the interval. The standard deviation of X is defined, similarly to (3.12), as

$$(4.9) \qquad \sigma_X = \sqrt{\text{var } X}$$

where var X is now as defined in (4.7).

When $a = b$ in (4.1), the distribution of X degenerates so that X takes only one value and hence becomes nonstochastic; its variance is then zero. When the range (a, b) of X is infinitely large (either $a = -\infty$ or $b = \infty$ or both), its mean and variance may not exist. This must be checked for each case.

The Normal Distribution

A random variable with density function

$$(4.10) \qquad f(x) = \frac{1}{\sqrt{2\pi}} e^{(-1/2)x^2} \qquad -\infty < x < \infty$$

is said to be normally distributed with zero mean and unit variance; here $e \approx 2.71828$ is the base of the natural logarithms. A generalization is

$$(4.11) \qquad f(x) = \frac{1}{\sigma\sqrt{2\pi}} \exp\left\{ -\frac{1}{2} \frac{(x - \mu)^2}{\sigma^2} \right\} \qquad -\infty < x < \infty$$

where $\exp\{z\}$ stands for e^z. The density function (4.11) is that of the normal distribution with mean μ and variance σ^2.

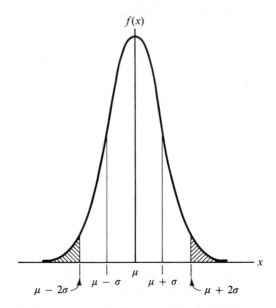

FIGURE 7   The density function of a normal distribution

Figure 7 provides a picture of the density function (4.11). Its form is symmetric, with a maximum at the mean μ. The area below the curve and between the vertical lines at $\mu - \sigma$ and $\mu + \sigma$ is .683 (in three decimal places). This means that if X is normally distributed, the probability is .683 that X will take a value less than one standard deviation (σ) from the mean. The area below the curve and between the vertical lines at $\mu - 2\sigma$ and $\mu + 2\sigma$ is .954. Since the total area below a density curve is always 1, the area below the curve to the left of $\mu - 2\sigma$ plus that to the right of $\mu + 2\sigma$ is thus $1 - .954 = .046$. Given the symmetry of the normal density curve, the probability of finding a value of X exceeding $\mu + 2\sigma$ is therefore .023 and that of finding a value less than $\mu - 2\sigma$ is also .023. The last two figures correspond to the shaded areas in Figure 7.

4.2   Multivariate Continuous Distribution Theory

The Bivariate Continuous Distribution

Consider the random pair (X, Y), where X can take any value in the interval (a_1, b_1) and Y any value in (a_2, b_2) in such a way that

(4.12) $P[x < X \le x + dx, y < Y \le y + dy] = f(x, y)\, dx\, dy$

where $a_1 \le x < b_1$ and $a_2 \le y < b_2$. The left-hand side of (4.12) is the probability of the joint occurrence of two events,

$$x < X \le x + dx \quad \text{and} \quad y < Y \le y + dy$$

and $f(x, y)$ in the right-hand side of (4.12) is the density function of the joint distribution of X and Y. This function satisfies

(4.13) $f(x, y) \ge 0$ $a_1 \le x < b_1, a_2 \le y < b_2$

(4.14) $\int_{a_1}^{b_1} \int_{a_2}^{b_2} f(x, y) \, dx \, dy = 1$

which is the bivariate extension of (4.2) and (4.3) and also the continuous version of (3.15) and (3.16).

We can visualize the bivariate density function in a three-dimensional space with x and y measured horizontally and f vertically. The double integral in (4.14) is then the content of the three-dimensional area below the density surface. This is the extension of the two-dimensional area below the density curve in Figure 7. An example (that of the bivariate normal distribution) is discussed in Section 10.1.

Marginal Continuous Distributions

By integrating (4.12) over y from a_2 to b_2, we obtain

$$P[x < X \le x + dx] = \left[\int_{a_2}^{b_2} f(x, y) \, dy \right] dx$$

This can be written as

(4.15) $P[x < X \le x + dx] = f_1(x) \, dx$ $a_1 \le x < b_1$

where

(4.16) $f_1(x) = \int_{a_2}^{b_2} f(x, y) \, dy$ $a_1 \le x < b_1$

is the density function of the marginal distribution of X. This result is the continuous version of (3.17). Similarly, integration of (4.12) over x from a_1 to b_1 yields

(4.17) $P[y < Y \le y + dy] = f_2(y) \, dy$ $a_2 \le y < b_2$

where $f_2(\quad)$ is the density function of the marginal distribution of Y:

(4.18) $f_2(y) = \int_{a_1}^{b_1} f(x, y) \, dx$ $a_2 \le y < b_2$

Note that (4.15) takes the same form as (4.1) except that $f(x)$ in (4.1) now becomes the density function (4.16) of the marginal distribution of X. This density function takes nonnegative values, because the integrand in (4.16) is nonnegative [see (4.13)]. Also, it follows from (4.14) that the integral of $f_1(x)$ equals 1. The marginal density function (4.18) has the same properties.

Expectations, Variances, and the Covariance

The bivariate extension of (4.6) is

$$(4.19) \qquad \mathcal{E}[g(X, Y)] = \int_{a_1}^{b_1} \int_{a_2}^{b_2} g(x, y) f(x, y) \, dx \, dy$$

which is also the continuous version of (3.19). When we specify X for $g(X, Y)$ in (4.19) to obtain $\mathcal{E}X$, the right-hand side of (4.19) becomes

$$\int_{a_1}^{b_1} \int_{a_2}^{b_2} x f(x, y) \, dx \, dy = \int_{a_1}^{b_1} x \left[\int_{a_2}^{b_2} f(x, y) \, dy \right] dx = \int_{a_1}^{b_1} x f_1(x) \, dx$$

By comparing the third member with (4.5), we find that $\mathcal{E}X$ in the bivariate continuous distribution of (X, Y) is equal to the mean of the marginal distribution of X. The following results, which are continuous versions of (3.20) to (3.22), may be similarly verified:

$$(4.20) \qquad \begin{aligned} \mathcal{E}X &= \int_{a_1}^{b_1} x f_1(x) \, dx, \qquad \text{var } X = \int_{a_1}^{b_1} (x - \mathcal{E}X)^2 f_1(x) \, dx \\ \mathcal{E}Y &= \int_{a_2}^{b_2} y f_2(y) \, dy, \qquad \text{var } Y = \int_{a_2}^{b_2} (y - \mathcal{E}Y)^2 f_2(y) \, dy \end{aligned}$$

To obtain the covariance we substitute $(X - \mathcal{E}X)(Y - \mathcal{E}Y)$ for the function $g(X, Y)$ in (4.19):

$$\begin{aligned} (4.21) \qquad \text{cov } (X, Y) &= \mathcal{E}[(X - \mathcal{E}X)(Y - \mathcal{E}Y)] \\ &= \int_{a_1}^{b_1} \int_{a_2}^{b_2} (x - \mathcal{E}X)(y - \mathcal{E}Y) f(x, y) \, dx \, dy \\ &= \mathcal{E}(XY) - \mathcal{E}X \mathcal{E}Y \end{aligned}$$

This is the continuous version of (3.24) and (3.25). The reader interested in intermediate steps for the last equal sign in (4.21) should consult Problem 3.

Conditional Continuous Distributions

In Section 3.3 we obtained the probabilities of conditional discrete distributions by dividing the joint probabilities p_{hk} by the probability of the condition. We now modify the second member of (3.30) to

$$\frac{P[x < X \le x + dx, y < Y \le y + dy]}{P[y < Y \le y + dy]} = \frac{f(x, y) \, dx \, dy}{f_2(y) \, dy} = \frac{f(x, y)}{f_2(y)} \, dx$$

where the first equal sign is based on (4.12) and (4.17). We write this result more succinctly as

$$(4.22) \qquad P[x < X \le x + dx \,|\, Y = y] = \frac{f(x, y)}{f_2(y)} \, dx$$

and refer to the ratio $f(x, y)/f_2(y)$ as the conditional density function of X given $Y = y$. This function exists when $f_2(y) \ne 0$. Similarly,

$$(4.23) \qquad P[y < Y \le y + dy \,|\, X = x] = \frac{f(x, y)}{f_1(x)} \, dy$$

where $f(x, y)/f_1(x)$ is the conditional density function of Y given $X = x$. The condition here is $f_1(x) \neq 0$.

The conditional means are the following continuous versions of (3.32) and (3.34):

$$(4.24) \qquad \mathcal{E}(X \mid Y = y) = \frac{1}{f_2(y)} \int_{a_1}^{b_1} xf(x, y)\, dx$$

$$(4.25) \qquad \mathcal{E}(Y \mid X = x) = \frac{1}{f_1(x)} \int_{a_2}^{b_2} yf(x, y)\, dy$$

Note that we can put $f_2(y)$ before the integration sign in (4.24) because it does not involve the integration variable x and that the same holds for $f_1(x)$ in (4.25) with respect to y. The conditional variances are similarly conditional versions of (3.33) and (3.35):

$$(4.26) \qquad \mathrm{var}\,(X \mid Y = y) = \frac{1}{f_2(y)} \int_{a_1}^{b_1} [x - \mathcal{E}(X \mid Y = y)]^2 f(x, y)\, dx$$

$$(4.27) \qquad \mathrm{var}\,(Y \mid X = x) = \frac{1}{f_1(x)} \int_{a_2}^{b_2} [y - \mathcal{E}(Y \mid X = x)]^2 f(x, y)\, dy$$

It is important to recognize that, in general, the conditional mean and variance (4.24) and (4.26) are functions of y and that the conditional mean and variance (4.25) and (4.27) are functions of x. The reader should compare this with (3.36) and Problem 10 on page 41 for the discrete case.

Independent Continuous Random Variables

Two random variables X and Y with joint density function $f(x, y)$ are said to be stochastically independent when this function satisfies

$$(4.28) \qquad f(x, y) \equiv f_1(x)f_2(y) \qquad a_1 \leq x < b_1, a_2 \leq y < b_2$$

where $\equiv$ stands for "identically equal to" (for any values of x and y). Under (4.28) we have

$$\frac{f(x, y)}{f_2(y)} \equiv f_1(x), \qquad \frac{f(x, y)}{f_1(x)} \equiv f_2(y)$$

so that the conditional density function of X given $Y = y$ with $f_2(y) \neq 0$ is identical to the marginal density function (4.16) of X, and, similarly, the conditional density function of Y given $X = x$ with $f_1(x) \neq 0$ is identical to the marginal density function (4.18) of Y. As in the analogous discrete case (3.37), the independence condition (4.28) implies that knowledge of X is worthless for the formulation of probability statements on Y and vice versa.

We mentioned at the end of the previous subsection that, in general, the conditional mean and variance of X given $Y = y$ are functions of y and that the conditional mean and variance of Y given $X = x$ are functions of x. But if X and Y are stochastically independent, the former mean and variance are not functions of y, and the latter are not functions of x. This follows from the fact that, under (4.28), the conditional density functions are all identical to the corresponding marginal density function. It may also be verified directly by substituting (4.28) in (4.24) to (4.27).

If $g_1(X)$ and $g_2(Y)$ are functions of X and Y, respectively, and if the joint density function of (X, Y) satisfies the independence condition (4.28), then

$$(4.29) \qquad \mathcal{E}[g_1(X)g_2(Y)] = \mathcal{E}[g_1(X)]\mathcal{E}[g_2(Y)]$$

This is the continuous version of (3.38); its derivation is similar, with sums replaced by integrals. By substituting $g_1(X) = X$ and $g_2(Y) = Y$ and using (4.21), we find that the independence condition (4.28) implies that X and Y have a zero covariance.

Stochastic Independence of More Than Two Random Variables

Let $X_1, X_2, \ldots, X_n$ be n random variables which satisfy

$$P[x_1 < X_1 \leq x_1 + dx_1, x_2 < X_2 \leq x_2 + dx_2, \ldots, x_n < X_n \leq x_n + dx_n]$$
$$= f(x_1, x_2, \ldots, x_n) \, dx_1 \, dx_2 \ldots dx_n$$

so that $f(x_1, x_2, \ldots, x_n)$ is the joint density function of the n random variables. These variables are said to be independently distributed when

$$(4.30) \qquad f(x_1, x_2, \ldots, x_n) \equiv f_1(x_1)f_2(x_2) \ldots f_n(x_n)$$

where $f_i(x_i)$ is the marginal density function of X_i. This is the extension of (4.28) for n random variables and also the continuous version of (3.39) for general n.

As an example, let $X_1, X_2, \ldots, X_n$ be independently and normally distributed with zero mean and unit variance. The density function of this distribution is given in (4.10), so that the right-hand side of (4.30) becomes

$$(4.31) \qquad \frac{1}{\sqrt{2\pi}} e^{(-1/2)x_1^2} \frac{1}{\sqrt{2\pi}} e^{(-1/2)x_2^2} \cdots \frac{1}{\sqrt{2\pi}} e^{(-1/2)x_n^2}$$
$$= \frac{1}{(\sqrt{2\pi})^n} e^{(-1/2)x_1^2} e^{(-1/2)x_2^2} \cdots e^{(-1/2)x_n^2}$$

We have, for any values $a_1, a_2, \ldots, a_n$,

$$(4.32) \qquad e^{a_1} e^{a_2} \ldots e^{a_n} = e^{a_1 + a_2 + \cdots + a_n} = \exp\left\{\sum_{i=1}^{n} a_i\right\}$$

where $\exp\{z\}$, as in (4.11), stands for e^z. By substituting the third member of (4.32) in the right-hand side of (4.31), with a_i interpreted as $-\frac{1}{2}x_i^2$, we obtain

$$(4.33) \qquad f(x_1, x_2, \ldots, x_n) = \frac{1}{(\sqrt{2\pi})^n} \exp\left\{-\frac{1}{2}\sum_{i=1}^{n} x_i^2\right\}$$

which is the joint density function of n independently and normally distributed random variables with zero mean and unit variance.

Next, let $X_1, X_2, \ldots, X_n$ be independently and normally distributed with mean μ and variance σ^2. Hence, the density function of each X_i is as shown in (4.11), so that the right-hand side of (4.30) is now

$$\frac{1}{\sigma\sqrt{2\pi}} \exp\left\{-\frac{1}{2}\frac{(x_1 - \mu)^2}{\sigma^2}\right\} \frac{1}{\sigma\sqrt{2\pi}} \exp\left\{-\frac{1}{2}\frac{(x_2 - \mu)^2}{\sigma^2}\right\} \times \cdots$$

$$\times \frac{1}{\sigma\sqrt{2\pi}} \exp\left\{-\frac{1}{2}\frac{(x_n - \mu)^2}{\sigma^2}\right\}$$

The reader should verify, using (4.32), that this yields

$$(4.34) \qquad f(x_1, x_2, \ldots, x_n) = \frac{1}{(\sigma\sqrt{2\pi})^n} \exp\left\{-\frac{1}{2\sigma^2} \sum_{i=1}^{n} (x_i - \mu)^2\right\}$$

which is the joint density function of n independent normal variates with mean μ and variance σ^2.

Linear Combinations of Continuous Random Variables

Equation (3.42) also holds when $X_1, \ldots, X_n$ have a continuous distribution:

$$(4.35) \qquad \mathcal{E}\left(\alpha_0 + \sum_{i=1}^{n} \alpha_i X_i\right) = \alpha_0 + \sum_{i=1}^{n} \alpha_i \mathcal{E} X_i$$

We prove this here for $n = 2$, with a random pair (X, Y). The left-hand side is then the expectation of $\alpha_0 + \alpha_1 X + \alpha_2 Y$. It follows from (4.19) that this expectation is equal to

$$\int_{a_1}^{b_1} \int_{a_2}^{b_2} (\alpha_0 + \alpha_1 x + \alpha_2 y) f(x, y)\, dx\, dy = \alpha_0 \int_{a_1}^{b_1} \int_{a_2}^{b_2} f(x, y)\, dx\, dy$$

$$+ \alpha_1 \int_{a_1}^{b_1} \int_{a_2}^{b_2} x f(x, y)\, dx\, dy$$

$$+ \alpha_2 \int_{a_1}^{b_1} \int_{a_2}^{b_2} y f(x, y)\, dx\, dy$$

The first term on the right equals α_0 [see (4.14)]. The second is a multiple α_1 of the double integral considered below (4.19) and is thus equal to $\alpha_1 \mathcal{E} X$. The third term is similarly equal to $\alpha_2 \mathcal{E} Y$, so that

$$(4.36) \qquad \mathcal{E}(\alpha_0 + \alpha_1 X + \alpha_2 Y) = \alpha_0 + \alpha_1 \mathcal{E} X + \alpha_2 \mathcal{E} Y$$

which proves (4.35) for $n = 2$.

To obtain the variance of $\alpha_0 + \alpha_1 X + \alpha_2 Y$, we first subtract the expectation (4.36), which gives $\alpha_1(X - \mathcal{E} X) + \alpha_2(Y - \mathcal{E} Y)$. The variance is then equal to the expectation of the square of this difference. When we work this out (the reader interested in details should consult Problem 6), we obtain

$$(4.37) \quad \mathrm{var}(\alpha_0 + \alpha_1 X + \alpha_2 Y) = \alpha_1^2 \, \mathrm{var}\, X + \alpha_2^2 \, \mathrm{var}\, Y + 2\alpha_1\alpha_2 \, \mathrm{cov}\,(X, Y)$$

which is the extension of (3.44) for the continuous case. If X and Y are stochastically independent, their covariance is zero [see the discussion below (4.29)], so that (4.37) can be simplified accordingly. More generally, if $X_1, X_2, \ldots, X_n$ are continuously distributed and satisfy the independence condition (4.30), then

$$(4.38) \qquad \operatorname{var}\left(\alpha_0 + \sum_{i=1}^{n} \alpha_i X_i\right) = \sum_{i=1}^{n} \alpha_i^2 \operatorname{var} X_i$$

This is the extension of (3.46) for the continuous case.

The results (3.47) and (3.49) for standardized random variables apply to continuous distributions also. In particular, a normal variate with zero mean and unit variance is called a *standardized normal variate*. Hence, (4.10) is the density function of a standardized normal variate, and (4.33) is the joint density function of n independent standardized normal variates.

4.3   Statistical Inference

Random Samples and Unknown Parameters

Let $X_1, X_2, \ldots, X_n$ be independently and identically distributed; that is, we assume that they are n independent random variables and that they all have the same distribution. This is also expressed by saying that $(X_1, \ldots, X_n)$ is a *random sample* of size n drawn from this distribution.

If the distribution from which the sample is drawn is continuous with density function $f(x)$, the joint density function of the sample is of the following form [see (4.30)]:

$$(4.39) \qquad f(x_1)f(x_2) \ldots f(x_n)$$

The right-hand side of (4.34) provides an example, the X_i's being independently and identically distributed according to the normal law with mean μ and variance σ^2. We start here with the simple case $\sigma^2 = 1$, so that (4.34) becomes

$$(4.40) \qquad \frac{1}{(\sqrt{2\pi})^n} \exp\left\{-\frac{1}{2} \sum_{i=1}^{n} (x_i - \mu)^2\right\}$$

Imagine that we do not know the mean μ and that we consider μ as an unknown parameter (an unknown constant). We want to acquire knowledge about this parameter by means of a random sample. That is, we suppose that a random sample $(X_1, \ldots, X_n)$ has been drawn, so that we have n numerical values. How can we use these values to draw conclusions on the unknown mean μ of their normal distribution?

An example is illustrative. Table 8 contains 50 sample values, which we may interpret as profit margins on Pintos in percentage form, one Pinto dealer being drawn at random from each of the 50 American states. (The figures are actually obtained from random sampling numbers.) Given our knowledge that these numbers have been obtained by 50 independent random drawings from a normal distribution with mean μ and unit variance, how can we use them to draw numerical conclusions on μ, the mean profit margin?

TABLE 8

The outcome of a random sample of profit margins

Number	Profit margin	Number	Profit margin	Number	Profit margin
1	10.11	18	10.21	35	8.97
2	9.11	19	8.67	36	10.35
3	10.99	20	11.70	37	9.18
4	10.50	21	9.08	38	11.76
5	9.05	22	11.73	39	9.32
6	10.81	23	10.66	40	9.12
7	9.72	24	8.31	41	9.86
8	8.36	25	12.13	42	10.77
9	8.56	26	7.80	43	8.39
10	10.01	27	11.57	44	9.33
11	10.24	28	8.15	45	10.58
12	10.46	29	7.76	46	8.94
13	10.02	30	9.85	47	10.51
14	7.91	31	9.55	48	9.76
15	12.08	32	9.97	49	8.40
16	9.20	33	11.01	50	10.29
17	10.27	34	11.19		

Techniques of Statistical Inference

There are several ways in which this question can be answered. Four answers are outlined below. The explanations are given in terms of the distribution (4.40) and the example of Table 8 and therefore refer to the case of a continuous distribution. Each of the four approaches also applies to unknown parameters of discrete distributions, but the exposition is simplified when we continue our discussion based on continuous distributions.

(1) We may use a certain function of the sample values to approximate μ. Given that μ in (4.40) is the mean of the normal distribution from which the sample is drawn, an obvious choice is the arithmetic mean of the 50 sample values of Table 8, which is 9.845. In other words, we use one single numerical value, computed from the sample, to approximate the unknown μ. This leads to the theory of *point estimation*, which is described in Section 4.4.

(2) A disadvantage of using one single numerical value is that it will usually differ from μ. To overcome this objection we may decide to formulate an interval (A, B), the limits of which (A and B) are computed from the sample values, in such a way that there will be sufficiently great confidence that μ lies in this interval. This leads to the theory of *interval estimation*, which is considered briefly at the end of Section 4.4 and more extensively in Chapter 11.

(3) We may also be interested in testing a particular hypothesis about μ, such as $\mu = 10.5$. Given our knowledge that the figures of Table 8 have been obtained from a normal distribution with mean μ and unit variance, do these data support the hypothesis $\mu = 10.5$, or are they evidence that this hypothesis

should be rejected? Answering such questions belongs to the theory of *hypothesis testing*, which is considered in Chapter 12.

(4) The three approaches outlined above have in common their treatment of μ as an unknown constant. The view of *Bayesian inference* is different. Bayesians would argue that the econometrician has certain prior judgments on μ even before he has seen the outcome of the random sample. To incorporate these judgments, Bayesians treat μ as a random variable and formulate the prior judgments on μ by means of a so-called prior density function. The random sample then serves to change the prior judgments into posterior convictions. The method of Bayesian inference is considered in Chapter 16.

4.4   Point Estimation

Estimators and Estimates

Let $(X_1, \ldots, X_n)$ be a random sample with joint density function (4.40). In approach (1) in the preceding section we suggested using the arithmetic mean 9.845 of the sample values of Table 8 to approximate μ. Let us first consider the arithmetic mean of $X_1, \ldots, X_n$:

$$(4.41) \qquad\qquad \bar{X} = \frac{1}{n} \sum_{i=1}^{n} X_i$$

Note that $\bar{X}$ is *not* identical to the arithmetic mean 9.845 mentioned above. The X_i's in (4.41) are random variables; hence, $\bar{X}$ is also random. The numbers of Table 8 are values taken by the X_i's once the sample has been drawn; these numbers are not random, nor is their arithmetic mean 9.845.

This distinction is essential. We are interested in the numerical value of μ in (4.40) and use formula (4.41) to pursue this goal. When (4.41) is applied to the numbers of Table 8, we obtain an *estimate* of μ equal to 9.845, whereas $\bar{X}$ defined in (4.41)—the function of the random sample $(X_1, \ldots, X_n)$ before the sample is specified numerically—is called an *estimator* of μ. An estimator is a random variable; an estimate is a value taken by the estimator for a particular sample.

Estimates may vary from sample to sample. For example, if we draw a second Pinto dealer from each American state, the 50 profit margins will differ from those shown in Table 8, and the arithmetic mean of the 50 new numbers may be, say, 10.003 rather than 9.845. But if such samples are randomly selected, we can evaluate the variability of their arithmetic means (9.845, 10.003, etc.) by means of the distribution of the estimator (4.41). This distribution is known as the *sampling distribution* of the estimator. To evaluate an estimation procedure, we must analyze the sampling distribution.

Unbiased Estimators and Unbiased Estimates

The first property to be examined here is the expectation of the sampling distribution. Thus, we take the expectation of (4.41),

$$(4.42) \qquad \mathcal{E}\bar{X} = \mathcal{E}\left(\frac{1}{n}\sum_{i=1}^{n} X_i\right) = \frac{1}{n}\sum_{i=1}^{n} \mathcal{E}X_i = \frac{n\mu}{n} = \mu$$

where the second equal sign is based on (4.35) with $\alpha_0 = 0$ and $\alpha_i = 1/n$ for $i = 1, \ldots, n$ and the third on the fact that each X_i has the same expectation μ.

We conclude from (4.42) that the estimator $\bar{X}$ of the parameter μ has an expectation equal to this parameter. The estimator is then said to be *unbiased*; the expectation of the sampling distribution coincides with the parameter which the estimator serves to approximate. Equivalently, the difference $\bar{X} - \mu$ between the estimator and the parameter, which is known as the *sampling error* of the estimator, then has zero expectation:

$$(4.43) \qquad \mathcal{E}(\bar{X} - \mu) = \mathcal{E}\bar{X} - \mu = \mu - \mu = 0$$

When the estimator is unbiased, the numerical estimate (9.845 in the case of Table 8) is frequently also called unbiased. An unbiased estimate is simply the numerical realization of an unbiased estimator for a particular sample.

REMARKS:

(1) The successive steps in (4.42) do not involve the assumption that the X_i's are normally distributed. These steps show that whenever we draw a random sample from some distribution with mean μ, the estimator (4.41) is unbiased with respect to μ. On the other hand, if the sample is indeed from a normal distribution, then it can be shown that the sampling distribution of $\bar{X}$ is also normal. This is pursued in Section 10.1.

(2) The assumption that $(X_1, \ldots, X_n)$ is a random sample implies that $X_1, \ldots, X_n$ are independently distributed (see the first paragraph of Section 4.3). This independence is not used in the successive steps of (4.42). The second step is based on the general proposition that the expectation of a linear combination of random variables is equal to the same linear combination of the expectations, which holds even when the random variables are not independent. The third step in (4.42) is based on the proposition that all X_i's have the same expectation μ, which does not involve the independence assumption either.

On Various Kinds of Means

We emphasize that the discussion of the two previous subsections includes as many as four kinds of means.

First, there is the unknown parameter μ which we want to estimate. This μ is the mean or expected value of the distribution from which the random sample is drawn. Frequently, we refer to μ as the unknown mean of the *population* from which the sample is drawn or, more briefly, as the population mean.

Second, $\bar{X}$ defined in (4.41) is also a mean, viz., the arithmetic mean of the random sample (the sample mean). This mean is a random variable, whereas the population mean μ is an unknown constant.

Third, the number 9.845 is a mean, too; it is the arithmetic mean of the sample values that have actually been drawn (see Table 8). It differs from (4.41) in that it is not random and from μ in that it is a *known* number.

Fourth, there is $\mathcal{E}\bar{X}$, the expectation of the sample mean. Since $\mathcal{E}\bar{X}$ is an expectation, it is a mean, viz., of the sampling distribution of $\bar{X}$. We proved in (4.42) that $\mathcal{E}\bar{X}$ equals μ, which means—by definition—that the sample mean $\bar{X}$ is an unbiased estimator of the population mean μ.

Biased Estimators and Bias Corrections

To show an example of a biased estimator we assume that $(X_1, \ldots, X_n)$ is a random sample from a normal distribution with mean μ and variance σ^2, both μ and σ^2 being unknown, so that the joint density function is now as specified in (4.34). Let us use the mean square of the X_i's, measured as deviations from their arithmetic mean $\bar{X}$, as an estimator of σ^2:

$$(4.44) \qquad \frac{1}{n} \sum_{i=1}^{n} (X_i - \bar{X})^2$$

We shall prove in the next subsection that the expectation of this estimator is

$$(4.45) \qquad \mathcal{E}\left[\frac{1}{n} \sum_{i=1}^{n} (X_i - \bar{X})^2\right] = \frac{n-1}{n}\sigma^2$$

Since $(n-1)/n < 1$, this shows that the estimator is *biased downward*; its expectation is smaller than the parameter σ^2 which it serves to estimate. Note that (4.45) also holds for random drawings from nonnormal distributions with finite variance σ^2.

Although bias should not be the only consideration, it is worth noting that in this case the bias can be easily corrected. Consider the alternative estimator

$$(4.46) \qquad s^2 = \frac{1}{n-1} \sum_{i=1}^{n} (X_i - \bar{X})^2$$

which is obtained by multiplying the original estimator (4.44) by the constant $n/(n-1)$. It follows from (4.35) that the expectation of s^2 is equal to $n/(n-1)$ multiplied by the expectation of (4.44). Thus, using (4.45), we obtain

$$(4.47) \qquad \mathcal{E}(s^2) = \frac{n}{n-1} \frac{n-1}{n}\sigma^2 = \sigma^2$$

which proves that s^2 is an unbiased estimator of σ^2 (also for nonnormal distributions).

The Sampling Variance of an Estimator

Unbiasedness of an estimator implies only that the sampling error has zero expectation. It does not exclude the possibility that the sampling error takes large values (positive or negative) with a considerable probability. To analyze this aspect we consider the variance of the sampling distribution, known as the *sampling variance* of the estimator. We apply this to $\bar{X}$ using (4.38), which shows that if $X_1, \ldots, X_n$ are independently distributed, the variance of $\sum_i \alpha_i X_i$ is equal to a weighted sum of the variances of the X_i's with weights equal to the squares of the α_i's. In (4.41) each α_i equals $1/n$. If we use (4.34), each X_i has variance σ^2. Therefore,

$$(4.48) \qquad \operatorname{var} \bar{X} = \frac{\sigma^2}{n^2} + \frac{\sigma^2}{n^2} + \cdots + \frac{\sigma^2}{n^2} \qquad (n \text{ terms})$$

$$= n\left(\frac{\sigma^2}{n^2}\right) = \frac{\sigma^2}{n}$$

Hence, the sampling variance of $\bar{X}$ decreases when the sample size n increases. This agrees with intuition; when we draw a larger sample, we should expect that the sample mean $\bar{X}$ will tend to be closer to the population mean μ.

The result (4.48) can be used to prove (4.45). Consider

$$\sum_{i=1}^{n} (X_i - \bar{X})^2 = \sum_{i=1}^{n} [(X_i - \mu) - (\bar{X} - \mu)]^2$$

$$= \sum_{i=1}^{n} [(X_i - \mu)^2 + (\bar{X} - \mu)^2 - 2(X_i - \mu)(\bar{X} - \mu)]$$

$$= \sum_{i=1}^{n} (X_i - \mu)^2 + n(\bar{X} - \mu)^2 - 2(\bar{X} - \mu)\sum_{i=1}^{n} (X_i - \mu)$$

Since $\sum_i (X_i - \mu) = n(\bar{X} - \mu)$, this yields, after multiplication by $1/n$,

$$\frac{1}{n}\sum_{i=1}^{n} (X_i - \bar{X})^2 = \frac{1}{n}\sum_{i=1}^{n} (X_i - \mu)^2 + (\bar{X} - \mu)^2 - 2(\bar{X} - \mu)^2$$

$$= \frac{1}{n}\sum_{i=1}^{n} (X_i - \mu)^2 - (\bar{X} - \mu)^2$$

Then take the expectation:

$$(4.49) \qquad \mathcal{E}\left[\frac{1}{n}\sum_{i=1}^{n} (X_i - \bar{X})^2\right] = \mathcal{E}\left[\frac{1}{n}\sum_{i=1}^{n} (X_i - \mu)^2\right] - \mathcal{E}[(\bar{X} - \mu)^2]$$

It follows from (4.35) that the first term on the right is a weighted sum of the expectations of $(X_1 - \mu)^2, \ldots, (X_n - \mu)^2$ with all weights equal to $1/n$. Since these expectations are all equal to σ^2, this term also equals σ^2. The term which is subtracted is the variance of $\bar{X}$, which is given in (4.48). Hence, (4.49) becomes

$$\mathcal{E}\left[\frac{1}{n}\sum_{i=1}^{n} (X_i - \bar{X})^2\right] = \sigma^2 - \frac{\sigma^2}{n} = \frac{n-1}{n}\sigma^2$$

which proves (4.45). Note that this proof does not require the X_i's to be normally distributed.

The Standard Error of an Estimate

If $\sigma^2 = 1$, as is the case in (4.40), the variance (4.48) equals $1/n$. When this is applied to Table 8 ($n = 50$), we find that the standard deviation of $\bar{X}$ is $\sqrt{\frac{1}{50}} \approx .141$. The estimate 9.845 is thus a value taken by the estimator $\bar{X}$ which has mean μ [see (4.42)] and standard deviation .141. Let us use the fact (not proved here) that the sampling distribution of $\bar{X}$ is normal if the sample is drawn from a normal distribution. Also recall from the discussion of Figure 7 on page 46 that there is a .954 probability that a normally distributed random variable takes a value less than two standard deviations from the mean. In this case the implication is that, apart from a probability $1 - .954 = .046$, the difference between 9.845 and the mean μ will not exceed $2 \times .141$, and hence μ will not be smaller than $9.845 - 2(.141) \approx 9.6$ and not be larger than $9.845 + 2(.141) \approx 10.1$. Thus, we obtain an interval (9.6, 10.1) for μ; our high degree of confidence that μ lies in this interval is measured by the fact that the probability is only .046 that we are wrong.

The above procedure is straightforward because the assumption $\sigma^2 = 1$ implies that the variance (4.48) is known. If σ^2 is unknown, we can estimate (4.48) by s^2/n, where s^2 is defined in (4.46). Given that s^2 is an unbiased estimator of σ^2, s^2/n is an unbiased estimator of the sampling variance (4.48) of the estimator $\bar{X}$ of μ:

$$(4.50) \qquad \mathcal{E}\left(\frac{s^2}{n}\right) = \frac{1}{n}\mathcal{E}(s^2) = \frac{\sigma^2}{n}$$

For the data of Table 8 we have $s^2 = 1.3461$, yielding $s^2/n \approx .02692$ for $n = 50$. Its square root is .164, which is known as the standard error of the estimate 9.845 of μ. *The standard error of an estimate of μ is an estimate of the standard deviation of the sampling distribution of the estimator of μ.* In the previous paragraph we used the standard deviation .141 (based on the assumption $\sigma^2 = 1$). If we replace it by the standard error .164 and proceed in the same way, we conclude that μ will not be smaller than $9.845 - 2(.164) \approx 9.5$ and not be larger than $9.845 + 2(.164) \approx 10.2$, apart from a probability .046. This is the *twice-the-standard-error rule* (or *two-sigma rule*). This rule is not an exact procedure, because we approximate σ^2 by s^2. Also note the use of the normal distribution. In our case $\bar{X}$ is normally distributed if the sample is from a normal distribution (which has not been proved here). The two-sigma rule is frequently applied when the estimator is not normally distributed, which amounts to another approximation. The discussion of this subject is continued in Section 11.2.

Problems

Problems 1 and 2 refer to Section 4.1, 3–7 to Section 4.2, and 8 and 9 to Section 4.4.

1 Let X have a normal distribution with density function (4.11). Use the probability statements made in the last paragraph of Section 4.1 to obtain numerical values of the following probabilities:

$$P[X > \mu], \qquad P[\mu + \sigma < X \le \mu + 2\sigma], \qquad P[X > \mu - \sigma]$$

2 For the uniform distribution (4.4), prove by direct integration:

$$\mathcal{E}X = \tfrac{1}{2}(a + b), \qquad \mathcal{E}(X^2) = \tfrac{1}{3}(a^2 + ab + b^2)$$

Also prove that var $X = \frac{1}{12}(b - a)^2$. (*Hint:* Use $\int x^{k-1}\,dx = x^k/k$ for any $k > 0$.)

3 The expression in the second line of (4.21) equals

$$\int_{a_1}^{b_1}\int_{a_2}^{b_2} (xy - y\mathcal{E}X - x\mathcal{E}Y + \mathcal{E}X\mathcal{E}Y)f(x, y)\,dx\,dy$$

This integral can be written as the sum of four terms:

$$\int_{a_1}^{b_1}\int_{a_2}^{b_2} xyf(x, y)\,dx\,dy - \mathcal{E}X \int_{a_1}^{b_1}\int_{a_2}^{b_2} yf(x, y)\,dx\,dy$$
$$- \mathcal{E}Y \int_{a_1}^{b_1}\int_{a_2}^{b_2} xf(x, y)\,dx\,dy + \mathcal{E}X\mathcal{E}Y \int_{a_1}^{b_1}\int_{a_2}^{b_2} f(x, y)\,dx\,dy$$

Evaluate each of these four terms to obtain the expression in the last line of (4.21).

4 Prove that if (4.30) is true and if the relevant expectations exist (are finite),

$$\mathcal{E}[g_1(X_1)g_2(X_2)\ldots g_n(X_n)] = \mathcal{E}[g_1(X_1)]\mathcal{E}[g_2(X_2)]\ldots\mathcal{E}[g_n(X_n)]$$

where $g_i(X_i)$ is an arbitrary function of X_i $(i = 1, \ldots, n)$.

5 Let $X_1, X_2, \ldots, X_n$ be normally and independently distributed, X_i having mean μ_i and standard deviation σ_i $(i = 1, \ldots, n)$. Prove that the joint density function of the X_i's takes the form

$$\frac{1}{\sigma_1\sigma_2\ldots\sigma_n(\sqrt{2\pi})^n} \exp\left\{-\frac{1}{2}\sum_{i=1}^{n}\frac{(x_i - \mu_i)^2}{\sigma_i^2}\right\}$$

Indicate how (4.34) is a special case of this density function.

6 Prove that the left-hand side of (4.37) equals

$$\int_{a_1}^{b_1}\int_{a_2}^{b_2} [\alpha_1(x - \mathcal{E}X) + \alpha_2(y - \mathcal{E}Y)]^2 f(x, y)\,dx\,dy$$

and that this integral can be written as

$$\alpha_1^2 \int_{a_1}^{b_1}\int_{a_2}^{b_2} (x - \mathcal{E}X)^2 f(x, y)\,dx\,dy + \alpha_2^2 \int_{a_1}^{b_1}\int_{a_2}^{b_2} (y - \mathcal{E}Y)^2 f(x, y)\,dx\,dy$$
$$+ 2\alpha_1\alpha_2 \int_{a_1}^{b_1}\int_{a_2}^{b_2} (x - \mathcal{E}X)(y - \mathcal{E}Y)f(x, y)\,dx\,dy$$

Verify that this is equivalent to the right-hand side of (4.37).

7 Extend Problem 16 on page 42 to the case in which (X, Y) has a continuous distribution.

8   Prove that the square of the standard error described in the last paragraph of Section 4.4 is an unbiased estimate of the sampling variance of the estimator $\bar{X}$. Be careful when you use the words estimate and estimator.

9   Does the unbiasedness of s^2 [see (4.47)] imply that s is an unbiased estimator of σ? If yes, prove this; if no, describe the direction of the bias. [*Hint*: Use (4.8) with X interpreted as s.]

chapter 5

Two-Variable Regression

In this chapter we return to the subject considered in Chapter 2: fitting straight lines. The discussion will now be extended by means of the theory of statistical estimation developed in Section 4.4. This requires the formulation of a statistical model, which takes place in Section 5.1.

5.1 The Standard Linear Model

A Consumption-Income Relation

In Chapter 2 we applied our fitting procedures to a linear relation between per capita income and consumption (Table 1 on page 9). The discussion of the present section is simplified when we use a cross-sectional microrelation between income (x) and total consumption expenditure (y) of individual family households.

Specifically, consider all families in some country whose incomes in a certain year are equal to x_1. We should expect that the amounts which these families spend differ because income is not the only factor which determines consumption. This is illustrated in the three-dimensional Figure 8, which has two horizontal axes for income (x) and consumption (y). The straight line parallel to the y axis at $x = x_1$ refers to the families with income equal to x_1. If it were true that income determines consumption uniquely, there would be one particular y value corresponding to $x = x_1$. But factors other than income affect different consumers differently, which is indicated in Figure 8 by the density

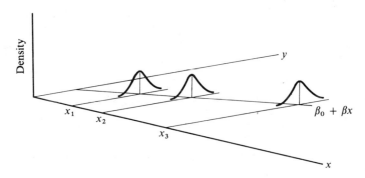

FIGURE 8   A consumption-income relation

curve drawn above the straight line at $x = x_1$. Thus, we assume that given $x = x_1$ consumption is a random variable; this is part of the statistical model to be developed. The vertical axis in the figure refers to the density of the distribution of consumption.

Next consider all families with income $x_2 > x_1$. Again, we should expect that their expenditures differ. But we should also expect that, due to the higher income of this group, their consumption expenditures will be larger on the average.

The Conditional Mean and Variance of Consumption

Consider n income values $x_1, \ldots, x_n$. Our next assumption is that we independently draw at random one household from the group of all households corresponding to each of these incomes. Furthermore, the idea of a larger average consumption corresponding to a larger income will now be made more specific. We assume that the conditional expectation of the household's consumption (y_i) given its income (x_i) is a linear function of x_i:

$$(5.1) \qquad \mathcal{E}(y_i \,|\, x_i) = \beta_0 + \beta x_i \qquad\qquad i = 1, \ldots, n$$

Finally, we assume that the conditional variance of y_i given x_i is a constant:

$$(5.2) \qquad \operatorname{var}(y_i \,|\, x_i) = \sigma^2 \qquad\qquad i = 1, \ldots, n$$

The linear function (5.1) is illustrated in Figure 8 by means of a straight line in the horizontal plane. The three density curves in the figure illustrate assumption (5.2); they all have the same standard deviation (σ).

It is instructive to compare (5.1) and (5.2) with (3.36), where we have conditional means of X which increase with the value taken by Y and conditional variances of X which decrease with the value taken by Y. In (5.1) the conditional mean of consumption, given income, is assumed to vary with income, but in a very particular way: It is a linear function of income. Assumption (5.2) is even more restrictive: The conditional variance of consumption, given income, is not supposed to vary at all with income.

The Standard Linear Model for Two Variables

The preceding paragraphs describe the features of the standard linear model for two variables. This model can be summarized as follows:

(1) One of the two variables is the *dependent variable*, and the other is the *explanatory variable*. In our example the former variable is consumption, and the latter is income.

(2) We operate conditionally on n values $x_1, \ldots, x_n$ taken by the explanatory variable. These values are treated as constants. The associated values $y_1, \ldots, y_n$ taken by the dependent variable are random and satisfy the condition of stochastic independence.

(3) The conditional mean and variance of y_i given x_i satisfy (5.1) and (5.2), where β_0, β, and σ^2 are unknown parameters. Our objective will be to estimate these parameters.

The three density curves of Figure 8 are those of normal distributions. The assumption of normality is not made here. If it is made, several important results can be obtained in addition to those derived later in this chapter; these will be pursued in Chapters 10 to 12.

The Disturbance Formulation

We define $\epsilon_i = y_i - (\beta_0 + \beta x_i)$, which is equivalent to

$$(5.3) \qquad\qquad y_i = \beta_0 + \beta x_i + \epsilon_i \qquad\qquad i = 1, \ldots, n$$

Returning to the consumption-income relation, we may view ϵ_i as the combined effect on consumption (y_i) of all factors other than income (x_i). Since β_0, β, and x_i in (5.3) are constants and y_i is random, ϵ_i must be random also.

The ϵ_i's are called the *disturbances* of the consumption-income equation. The equation would be "undisturbed" if consumption were an exact linear function of income, but this is not realistic owing to the numerous factors (other than income) which affect consumption. These factors are frequently called the *neglected variables* in the equation. In (5.3) only income (x_i) is introduced explicitly as an explanatory variable; all other variables affecting consumption are thus neglected, their combined effect being represented by a random disturbance ϵ_i.

We take the conditional expectation of both sides of (5.3), given x_i:

$$\mathcal{E}(y_i | x_i) = \beta_0 + \beta x_i + \mathcal{E}(\epsilon_i | x_i)$$

This result in conjunction with (5.1) implies

$$(5.4) \qquad\qquad \mathcal{E}(\epsilon_i | x_i) = 0 \qquad\qquad i = 1, \ldots, n$$

Next subtract (5.1) from (5.3) and square both sides:

$$[y_i - \mathcal{E}(y_i | x_i)]^2 = \epsilon_i^2$$

If we take the conditional expectation (given x_i) of both sides of this equation, we obtain σ^2 on the left [see (5.2)]. On the right we obtain

$$\mathcal{E}(\epsilon_i^2 \mid x_i) = \text{var}\,(\epsilon_i \mid x_i) + [\mathcal{E}(\epsilon_i \mid x_i)]^2 = \text{var}\,(\epsilon_i \mid x_i)$$

where the first equal sign is based on (4.8) with X interpreted as ϵ_i (given x_i) and the second on (5.4). Therefore,

$$(5.5) \qquad\qquad \text{var}\,(\epsilon_i \mid x_i) = \sigma^2 \qquad\qquad i = 1, \ldots, n$$

A major advantage of the disturbance formulation is that it allows us to drop the inconvenient conditional notation. We simply write (5.4) and (5.5) in the form

$$(5.6) \qquad\qquad \mathcal{E}\epsilon_i = 0 \qquad\qquad i = 1, \ldots, n$$

$$(5.7) \qquad\qquad \text{var}\,\epsilon_i = \sigma^2 \qquad\qquad i = 1, \ldots, n$$

where it is to be understood that $x_1, \ldots, x_n$ are constants. If we add to this the assumption

$$(5.8) \qquad\qquad \epsilon_1, \ldots, \epsilon_n \text{ are independently distributed}$$

then $y_1, \ldots, y_n$ are also independently distributed in agreement with statement (2) in the preceding subsection.

The independence condition (5.8) implies that $\epsilon_1, \ldots, \epsilon_n$ have pairwise zero covariances. We can combine this property with (5.7) in the form

$$(5.9) \qquad\qquad \mathcal{E}(\epsilon_i \epsilon_j) = \begin{cases} \sigma^2 & \text{if } i = j \\ 0 & \text{if } i \neq j \end{cases}$$

In the first line of (5.9) we have $\mathcal{E}(\epsilon_i^2)$, which equals var ϵ_i because (5.6) states that $\mathcal{E}\epsilon_i = 0$ [see (4.8)]. In the second line we have the covariance of two different disturbances [see (4.21) and (5.6)].

A Dichotomy of Variables and Coefficients

It is instructive to consider the above algebraic concepts according to two criteria: whether they are constants or random variables, and whether they are observable or unobservable. This is pursued in Table 9. The values $x_1, \ldots, x_n$ taken by the explanatory variable are treated as constants, and they are known; hence, they are both constant and observable. The parameters β_0, β, and σ^2 are also constants, but they are unknown (not observable). The values $y_1, \ldots, y_n$ taken by the dependent variable are not constants but random. They are

TABLE 9

A dichotomy of variables and coefficients

	Observable	Not observable
Constant	$x_1, \ldots, x_n$	β_0, β, σ^2
Random	$y_1, \ldots, y_n$	$\epsilon_1, \ldots, \epsilon_n$

observable in the sense that their numerical realizations can be observed. In the case of the consumption-income relation, y_i stands for the consumption of a randomly selected family with income x_i; once the family has been selected, we can observe its consumption. The disturbances are random variables whose realizations cannot be observed; they are unobservable random variables. To find such a realization we would need β_0 and β in (5.3), but neither β_0 nor β is observable.

Some Comments on the Standard Linear Model

The objective of this chapter is statistical inference in the standard linear model, particularly by least squares. This will be continued in Chapter 8 for the case in which there is more than one explanatory variable and in Chapters 10 to 12 under the condition that the disturbances are normally distributed. However, the assumptions of the standard linear model are restrictive in certain respects. Several restrictions are indicated below, along with references to sections and chapters in which generalizations are discussed.

First, there is the linearity assumption of the conditional expectation in (5.1). This linearity is restrictive, although not so much as it may seem; this will be explained in Section 13.1. Second, there is the constancy of the variance in (5.7) and the independence in (5.8). These two assumptions are further considered in Sections 19.1 and 19.2.

The constancy of the values taken by the explanatory variable is another matter. There are situations in which, due to the general interdependence of economic phenomena, it is difficult to argue that the dependent variable takes random and the explanatory variable takes nonrandom values. Such situations are considered in Chapters 20 and 21. Also, the values taken by the explanatory variable may be measured imperfectly; economic data are frequently not perfect. If the measurement errors are random, the observed values of the explanatory variables are not constant but random. This problem is considered in Section 17.4.

5.2   Least Squares Through the Origin

In this section we assume that $\beta_0 = 0$, so that the conditional expectation (5.1) is proportional to x_i and (5.3) is simplified to

$$(5.10) \qquad\qquad y_i = \beta x_i + \epsilon_i \qquad\qquad i = 1, \ldots, n$$

Our first objective will be to estimate β, for which we shall use the LS solution (2.27):

$$(5.11) \qquad\qquad b = \frac{\sum_{i=1}^{n} x_i y_i}{\sum_{i=1}^{n} x_i^2}$$

This b is an estimator of β in (5.10). The change in interpretation should be noted. In Chapter 2 we fitted a straight line through the origin [see (2.24)] and used the LS principle to determine the slope of this line. *Here there is no question of "determining" the slope.* The slope of the model (5.10) is β, which is an unknown parameter, and the LS coefficient (5.11) is an *estimator* of this parameter.

The Unbiasedness of the LS Slope Estimator

We use (5.10) in

$$\sum_{i=1}^{n} x_i y_i = \sum_{i=1}^{n} x_i(\beta x_i + \epsilon_i) = \beta \sum_{i=1}^{n} x_i^2 + \sum_{i=1}^{n} x_i \epsilon_i$$

which we substitute in (5.11):

$$(5.12) \qquad b = \beta + \frac{\sum_{i=1}^{n} x_i \epsilon_i}{\sum_{i=1}^{n} x_i^2} \quad \text{or} \quad b - \beta = \frac{\sum_{i=1}^{n} x_i \epsilon_i}{\sum_{i=1}^{n} x_i^2}$$

Hence, the sampling error $b - \beta$ is a linear combination of $\epsilon_1, \ldots, \epsilon_n$ with weights equal to $x_1/A, \ldots, x_n/A$, where

$$(5.13) \qquad A = \sum_{i=1}^{n} x_i^2$$

These weights are completely determined by $x_1, \ldots, x_n$ and are hence constants. Thus, the expectation of $b - \beta$ is the same linear combination of the expectations of the ϵ_i's. Using (5.6), we thus find $\mathcal{E}(b - \beta) = 0$ or

$$(5.14) \qquad \mathcal{E}b = \beta$$

which proves that the LS coefficient (5.11) is an unbiased estimator of the slope β in (5.10). Note that this result is independent of (5.9); the only assumptions used are (5.6) and the constancy of the values $x_1, \ldots, x_n$ taken by the explanatory variable.

The Sampling Variance of the LS Slope Estimator

We square the second equation in (5.12),

$$(5.15) \qquad (b - \beta)^2 = \frac{\left(\sum_{i=1}^{n} x_i \epsilon_i\right)^2}{\left(\sum_{i=1}^{n} x_i^2\right)^2} = \frac{\sum_{i=1}^{n} \sum_{j=1}^{n} x_i x_j \epsilon_i \epsilon_j}{\left(\sum_{i=1}^{n} x_i^2\right)^2}$$

where the second step is based on (2.23). The variance of b is equal to the expectation of $(b - \mathcal{E}b)^2 = (b - \beta)^2$ [see (5.14)], so that it is obtained by taking the expectation of (5.15). Using the third member of that equation, we find that var b is equal to the expectation of a linear combination of n^2 products of disturbances, $\epsilon_i \epsilon_j$, with weights of the form $x_i x_j / A^2$, where A is defined in (5.13). These weights are determined by $x_1, \ldots, x_n$ and are hence all constants. Therefore,

$$(5.16) \qquad \operatorname{var} b = \frac{1}{A^2} \sum_{i=1}^{n} \sum_{j=1}^{n} x_i x_j \mathcal{E}(\epsilon_i \epsilon_j)$$

Table 10 contains all terms which are summed in the right-hand side of (5.16). Note that the entries along the main diagonal in the table, from upper left

TABLE 10

**Components of the sampling variance of
the least-squares slope estimator**

	$j = 1$	$j = 2$	$j = n$
$i = 1$	$(x_1^2/A^2)\mathcal{E}(\epsilon_1^2)$	$(x_1 x_2/A^2)\mathcal{E}(\epsilon_1 \epsilon_2)$ $\cdots$	$(x_1 x_n/A^2)\mathcal{E}(\epsilon_1 \epsilon_n)$
$i = 2$	$(x_2 x_1/A^2)\mathcal{E}(\epsilon_2 \epsilon_1)$	$(x_2^2/A^2)\mathcal{E}(\epsilon_2^2)$ $\cdots$	$(x_2 x_n/A^2)\mathcal{E}(\epsilon_2 \epsilon_n)$
	.	.	.
	.	.	.
	.	.	.
$i = n$	$(x_n x_1/A^2)\mathcal{E}(\epsilon_n \epsilon_1)$	$(x_n x_2/A^2)\mathcal{E}(\epsilon_n \epsilon_2)$ $\cdots$	$(x_n^2/A^2)\mathcal{E}(\epsilon_n^2)$

$(i = j = 1)$ to lower right $(i = j = n)$, contain expectations of squares of disturbances, whereas those not in the diagonal contain expectations of products of two different disturbances. The latter expectations are all zero according to (5.9), so that it is sufficient to add the entries along the main diagonal:

$$\operatorname{var} b = \frac{1}{A^2} \sum_{i=1}^{n} x_i^2 \mathcal{E}(\epsilon_i^2)$$

But (5.9) for $i = j$ implies $\mathcal{E}(\epsilon_i^2) = \sigma^2$, so that

$$\operatorname{var} b = \frac{\sigma^2}{A^2} \sum_{i=1}^{n} x_i^2$$

which may be further simplified to

$$(5.17) \qquad \operatorname{var} b = \frac{\sigma^2}{\sum\limits_{i=1}^{n} x_i^2}$$

in view of (5.13).

Comments on the Variance of the LS Slope Estimator

The derivations of the previous subsection clearly show that the variance-covariance condition (5.9) on the disturbances is essential for the simple result (5.17). The interpretation of this result can be conveniently given in three steps.

First, the smaller the variance σ^2 of the disturbances, the more accurate is the LS estimator as measured by its sampling variance. This is intuitively plausible. When σ^2 becomes smaller, the density curves of Figure 8 become "tighter" around their means. In the extreme case $\sigma^2 = 0$ these curves degenerate so that all families have consumption expenditures at these means; β can then be trivially determined from this "undisturbed" consumption-income relation.

Second, to assess the effect of the number of observations (n), it is convenient to write (5.17) as

$$(5.18) \qquad \text{var } b = \frac{\sigma^2/n}{(1/n) \sum_{i=1}^{n} x_i^2}$$

Hence, given $(1/n) \sum_i x_i^2$ (to be discussed in the next paragraph) and σ^2, the sampling variance of the LS coefficient declines when we have more observations. This is also plausible; it is directly comparable to the effect of n on the sampling variance of $\bar{X}$ in (4.48).

Third, the sampling variance of b depends on the behavior of the explanatory variable. It declines when $(1/n) \sum_i x_i^2$, which is the mean square of the values of this variable, takes a larger value (given σ^2 and n). Figure 9 illustrates the effect of this mean square. The solid line in Figure 9(a) is the LS line through the origin and five observation points. The solid LS line in Figure 9(b) has the same slope, but the five observations from which it is computed are much closer to the origin. Hence the x_i's and also their mean square are smaller in Figure 9(b) than in Figure 9(a), so that (5.18) implies that the variance of the LS slope estimator is larger in the former figure than in the latter. This is illustrated in each figure by the pair of broken lines between which all five points are located. The angle between the broken lines is much larger in Figure 9(b) than in Figure 9(a), suggesting that there is more uncertainty as to the true slope β in Figure 9(b), which agrees with the theoretical result based on (5.18).

Note that the broken lines have no particular theoretical interpretation. It is not correct that the true line (with slope β) must be between the broken lines. These lines are used here as a simple intuitive device to clarify the effect of the mean square of the x_i's on the accuracy of the LS slope estimator as measured by the sampling variance (5.18).

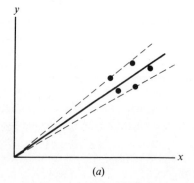
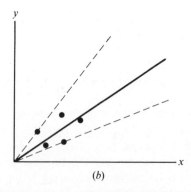

(a)   (b)

FIGURE 9   The effect of the mean square of the explanatory variable on the accuracy of the LS slope estimator

The LS Estimator of the Disturbance Variance

The slope β is not the only unknown parameter; the variance σ^2 of the disturbances $\epsilon_1, \ldots, \epsilon_n$ is equally unknown. Since the ϵ_i's are the deviations from the true line $y = \beta x$, it is natural to consider the deviations of the observation points from the LS line, $y_i - bx_i$ for $i = 1, \ldots, n$. Recall that we analyzed these deviations geometrically in Figure 3 on page 18.

We use (5.10) in

$$y_i - bx_i = \beta x_i + \epsilon_i - bx_i = \epsilon_i - (b - \beta)x_i$$

We square the first and third members,

$$(y_i - bx_i)^2 = \epsilon_i^2 + (b - \beta)^2 x_i^2 - 2(b - \beta)x_i \epsilon_i$$

and sum over i:

$$\sum_{i=1}^{n} (y_i - bx_i)^2 = \sum_{i=1}^{n} \epsilon_i^2 + (b - \beta)^2 \sum_{i=1}^{n} x_i^2 - 2(b - \beta) \sum_{i=1}^{n} x_i \epsilon_i$$

But $\sum_i x_i \epsilon_i = (b - \beta) \sum_i x_i^2$ in view of the second equation in (5.12). Therefore,

(5.19)
$$\sum_{i=1}^{n} (y_i - bx_i)^2 = \sum_{i=1}^{n} \epsilon_i^2 - (b - \beta)^2 \sum_{i=1}^{n} x_i^2$$

We take the expectation of the right-hand side, which yields $n\sigma^2$ for the first term in view of (5.9). Since $x_1, \ldots, x_n$ are constants, the second term becomes minus the variance of b multiplied by $\sum_i x_i^2$. Thus, using (5.17), we obtain

$$\mathcal{E}\left[\sum_{i=1}^{n} (y_i - bx_i)^2\right] = n\sigma^2 - \frac{\sigma^2}{\sum_{i=1}^{n} x_i^2} \sum_{i=1}^{n} x_i^2$$

which can be simplified to

(5.20)
$$\mathcal{E}\left[\sum_{i=1}^{n} (y_i - bx_i)^2\right] = (n - 1)\sigma^2$$

Thus, when we define

(5.21)
$$s^2 = \frac{1}{n-1} \sum_{i=1}^{n} (y_i - bx_i)^2$$

we have

(5.22)
$$\mathcal{E}(s^2) = \sigma^2$$

Hence, s^2 is an unbiased estimator of σ^2. This estimator is equal to the sum of the squares of the deviations, which is minimized by LS [see (2.25)], divided by the number of observations less 1.

Recapitulation of the Mathematical Procedure

The mathematical derivations of this section will be repeated, with some modifications, in Sections 5.3 and 8.2. It is therefore convenient to summarize the procedure here.

To obtain the sampling error of b, we started with the definition (5.11) and substituted the right-hand side of (5.10) for y_i. This yields the result, shown in (5.12), that the sampling error of b is a linear combination of the ϵ_i's with constant weights, which proves that b is unbiased. Next, to obtain the sampling variance of b, we square the sampling error [see (5.15)] and take the expectation. This sampling variance is derived from condition (5.9) and involves the parameter σ^2 as shown in (5.17).

To estimate σ^2, we take the sum of squares of the deviations from the LS line as our starting point; this sum of squares is the expression which is minimized by LS. Again, we use (5.10) to eliminate y_i, yielding (5.19), which expresses the sum of squares of the deviations in terms of the random ϵ_i's, the nonrandom x_i's, and $(b - \beta)^2$. Then we take the expectation, using the variance of b for $\mathcal{E}[(b - \beta)^2]$. This yields (5.20), which shows that the expected sum of squares of the deviations from the LS line is a multiple $n - 1$ of σ^2. Thus, by dividing the sum of squares of these deviations by $n - 1$ (which is a constant), we obtain the unbiased estimator (5.21) of σ^2.

5.3   Unconstrained Least Squares

In this section we abandon the assumption $\beta_0 = 0$ and return to the more general form (5.3). Hence, both β and β_0 must now be estimated, for which purpose we use the LS coefficients given in (2.31) and (2.32):

$$(5.23) \qquad b_0 = \bar{y} - b\bar{x}$$

$$(5.24) \qquad b = \frac{\sum_{i=1}^{n} (x_i - \bar{x})(y_i - \bar{y})}{\sum_{i=1}^{n} (x_i - \bar{x})^2}$$

In this section we shall use eqs. (2.12), (2.13), and (2.17) of Section 2.2. It is convenient to reproduce them here:

$$(5.25) \qquad \sum_{i=1}^{n} (x_i - \bar{x}) = 0$$

$$(5.26) \qquad \sum_{i=1}^{n} (x_i - \bar{x})(y_i - \bar{y}) = \sum_{i=1}^{n} (x_i - \bar{x})y_i$$

$$(5.27) \qquad \sum_{i=1}^{n} (x_i - \bar{x})^2 = \sum_{i=1}^{n} (x_i - \bar{x})x_i$$

The Unbiasedness and Sampling Variance of the LS Slope Estimator

It follows from (5.26) that (5.24) can be written as

$$(5.28) \qquad b = \frac{\sum_{i=1}^{n} (x_i - \bar{x})y_i}{\sum_{i=1}^{n} (x_i - \bar{x})^2}$$

We use (5.3) to write the right-hand numerator as

$$\sum_{i=1}^{n} (x_i - \bar{x})y_i = \sum_{i=1}^{n} (x_i - \bar{x})(\beta_0 + \beta x_i + \epsilon_i)$$

$$= \beta_0 \sum_{i=1}^{n} (x_i - \bar{x}) + \beta \sum_{i=1}^{n} (x_i - \bar{x})x_i + \sum_{i=1}^{n} (x_i - \bar{x})\epsilon_i$$

$$= \beta \sum_{i=1}^{n} (x_i - \bar{x})^2 + \sum_{i=1}^{n} (x_i - \bar{x})\epsilon_i$$

where the last step is based on (5.25) and (5.27). Thus, after dividing by $\sum_i (x_i - \bar{x})^2$, we find that (5.28) yields

$$(5.29) \qquad b = \beta + \frac{\sum_{i=1}^{n} (x_i - \bar{x})\epsilon_i}{\sum_{i=1}^{n} (x_i - \bar{x})^2} \quad \text{or} \quad b - \beta = \frac{\sum_{i=1}^{n} (x_i - \bar{x})\epsilon_i}{\sum_{i=1}^{n} (x_i - \bar{x})^2}$$

Note that (5.29) is equivalent to (5.12) except that the x_i's are now all measured as deviations from their arithmetic mean. The reader should verify that, subject to this modification, all further results of Section 5.2 through eq. (5.18) are valid for the present model. Therefore,

$$(5.30) \qquad \mathcal{E}b = \beta$$

$$(5.31) \qquad \text{var } b = \frac{\sigma^2}{\sum_{i=1}^{n} (x_i - \bar{x})^2} = \frac{\sigma^2/n}{(1/n)\sum_{i=1}^{n} (x_i - \bar{x})^2}$$

so that the LS slope estimator (5.24) is unbiased and has a sampling variance which is proportional to the disturbance variance σ^2, inversely proportional to the number of observations, and also inversely proportional to the mean square of the x_i's measured as deviations from $\bar{x}$.

The Unbiasedness of the LS Estimator of the Constant Term

We sum both sides of (5.3) over i,

$$\sum_{i=1}^{n} y_i = n\beta_0 + \beta \sum_{i=1}^{n} x_i + \sum_{i=1}^{n} \epsilon_i$$

and divide by n:

$$(5.32) \qquad \bar{y} = \beta_0 + \beta\bar{x} + \bar{\epsilon}, \qquad \text{where } \bar{\epsilon} = \frac{1}{n} \sum_{i=1}^{n} \epsilon_i$$

Next we substitute $\beta_0 + \beta\bar{x} + \bar{\epsilon}$ for $\bar{y}$ in $b_0 = \bar{y} - b\bar{x}$ [see (5.23)] to obtain $b_0 = \beta_0 + \beta\bar{x} + \bar{\epsilon} - b\bar{x} = \beta_0 + \bar{\epsilon} - (b - \beta)\bar{x}$, and hence

$$(5.33) \qquad b_0 - \beta_0 = \bar{\epsilon} - (b - \beta)\bar{x}$$

The left-hand side is the sampling error of the LS constant-term estimator b_0. The equation shows that this sampling error is equal to the difference between the arithmetic mean $\bar{\epsilon}$ of the n disturbances and the sampling error of b multiplied by $\bar{x}$. The random variable $\bar{\epsilon}$ has zero expectation (because it is a linear combination of $\epsilon_1, \ldots, \epsilon_n$, each of which has zero expectation), and $(b - \beta)\bar{x}$ also has zero expectation (because b is an unbiased estimator of β and $\bar{x}$ is a constant). Therefore, the right-hand side of (5.33) has zero expectation, so that $\mathcal{E}(b_0 - \beta_0) = 0$, and hence

$$(5.34) \qquad\qquad \mathcal{E}b_0 = \beta_0$$

This proves that the LS constant-term estimator is unbiased.

The Sampling Variance of the LS Constant-Term Estimator

Since b_0 is unbiased, its variance is obtained by squaring the sampling error (5.33),

$$(b_0 - \beta_0)^2 = \bar{\epsilon}^2 + \bar{x}^2(b - \beta)^2 - 2\bar{x}(b - \beta)\bar{\epsilon}$$

and then taking the expectation:

$$(5.35) \qquad \operatorname{var} b_0 = \mathcal{E}(\bar{\epsilon}^2) + \bar{x}^2 \operatorname{var} b - 2\bar{x}\mathcal{E}[(b - \beta)\bar{\epsilon}]$$

The following results are proved at the end of this section:

$$(5.36) \qquad\qquad \mathcal{E}(\bar{\epsilon}^2) = \frac{\sigma^2}{n}$$

$$(5.37) \qquad\qquad \mathcal{E}[(b - \beta)\bar{\epsilon}] = 0$$

On combining these two results with (5.35) and (5.31), we obtain

$$(5.38) \qquad \operatorname{var} b_0 = \mathcal{E}(\bar{\epsilon}^2) + \bar{x}^2 \operatorname{var} b = \sigma^2 \left[\frac{1}{n} + \frac{\bar{x}^2}{\sum_{i=1}^{n}(x_i - \bar{x})^2} \right]$$

which shows that the sampling variance of the LS constant-term estimator consists of two parts, one of which is the expectation of $\bar{\epsilon}^2$ and the other of which involves the variance of the LS slope estimator b. We have $\bar{x} = 0$ when $(\bar{x}, \bar{y})$, the center of gravity of the n observation points, lies on the y axis [see Figure 10(a)]. In that case (5.38) yields $\operatorname{var} b_0 = \mathcal{E}(\bar{\epsilon}^2) = \sigma^2/n$, and the variance of the

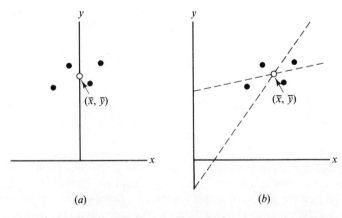

(a)   (b)

FIGURE 10   The impact of the center of gravity of the observation points on the variance of the LS constant-term estimator

slope estimator plays no role in the variance of b_0. When $\bar{x}$ is large (positive or negative), as it is in Figure 10(b), the variance of b can play a substantial role in that of b_0, so that there is then considerable uncertainty as to the value of the true intercept β_0 due to the uncertainty of the slope β. This is indicated in Figure 10(b) by the two broken lines through the center of gravity $(\bar{x}, \bar{y})$; one of these lines implies a positive value of the intercept and the other a negative value. Note that, as in Figure 9, the broken lines are illustrative only and have no special theoretical meaning with respect to the "true" line $y = \beta_0 + \beta x$.

The LS Estimator of the Disturbance Variance

We return to the LS residual $e_i = y_i - b_0 - bx_i$ defined in (2.41). By substituting (5.3) for y_i, we obtain

$$e_i = \beta_0 + \beta x_i + \epsilon_i - b_0 - bx_i$$
$$= \epsilon_i - (b_0 - \beta_0) - (b - \beta)x_i$$
$$= \epsilon_i - \bar{\epsilon} - (b - \beta)(x_i - \bar{x})$$

where the last step is based on (5.33). We square this result,

$$e_i^2 = (\epsilon_i - \bar{\epsilon})^2 + (b - \beta)^2(x_i - \bar{x})^2 - 2(b - \beta)(x_i - \bar{x})(\epsilon_i - \bar{\epsilon})$$

and sum over i:

$$(5.39) \qquad \sum_{i=1}^{n} e_i^2 = \sum_{i=1}^{n} (\epsilon_i - \bar{\epsilon})^2 + (b - \beta)^2 \sum_{i=1}^{n} (x_i - \bar{x})^2$$
$$- 2(b - \beta) \sum_{i=1}^{n} (x_i - \bar{x})(\epsilon_i - \bar{\epsilon})$$

To evaluate the last term on the right we consider

$$\sum_{i=1}^{n} (x_i - \bar{x})(\epsilon_i - \bar{\epsilon}) = \sum_{i=1}^{n} (x_i - \bar{x})\epsilon_i - \bar{\epsilon} \sum_{i=1}^{n} (x_i - \bar{x})$$
$$= \sum_{i=1}^{n} (x_i - \bar{x})\epsilon_i$$
$$= (b - \beta) \sum_{i=1}^{n} (x_i - \bar{x})^2$$

where the second equal sign is based on (5.25) and the third on (5.29). By substituting this result in (5.39), we obtain

$$(5.40) \qquad \sum_{i=1}^{n} e_i^2 = \sum_{i=1}^{n} (\epsilon_i - \bar{\epsilon})^2 - (b - \beta)^2 \sum_{i=1}^{n} (x_i - \bar{x})^2$$

We proceed to take the expectation of (5.40). At the end of this section we prove the following result for the first term on the right:

$$(5.41) \qquad \mathcal{E}\left[\sum_{i=1}^{n} (\epsilon_i - \bar{\epsilon})^2 \right] = (n - 1)\sigma^2$$

The second right-hand term in (5.40) has an expectation equal to $-\text{var } b$ multiplied by $\sum_i (x_i - \bar{x})^2$, which equals $-\sigma^2$ in view of (5.31). Hence, the expectation of (5.40) is

$$(5.42) \qquad \mathcal{E}\left(\sum_{i=1}^{n} e_i^2 \right) = (n - 1)\sigma^2 - \sigma^2 = (n - 2)\sigma^2$$

Therefore, when we define

(5.43) $$s^2 = \frac{1}{n-2} \sum_{i=1}^{n} e_i^2 = \frac{1}{n-2} \sum_{i=1}^{n} (y_i - b_0 - bx_i)^2$$

we have

(5.44) $$\mathcal{E}(s^2) = \sigma^2$$

An unbiased estimator of the disturbance variance is thus obtained by dividing the sum of the squares of the residuals by $n-2$.

Degrees of Freedom

Why do we have $n-2$ in (5.43), whereas we had $n-1$ in (5.21)? An intuitive answer to this question is provided by the minimization principle of least squares described in Section 2.3. When we force the LS line to go through the origin, we minimize the function (2.25),

$$G(b) = \sum_{i=1}^{n} (y_i - bx_i)^2$$

by varying one coefficient (b). When we do not force the LS line to go through the origin, we minimize the function (2.29),

$$G(b_0, b) = \sum_{i=1}^{n} (y_i - b_0 - bx_i)^2$$

by varying two coefficients (b_0 and b). It stands to reason that when we minimize a residual sum of squares by adjusting two coefficients rather than one, the minimum value will tend to be smaller; indeed, we found this to be true for the example considered in Section 2.3 [see the discussion below (2.48)]. Thus, it is not surprising that the expected sum of squares (5.42), based on the adjustment of two coefficients, is smaller than the expectation (5.20), which is based on the adjustment of only one coefficient.

To obtain an unbiased estimator of σ^2, we divide the left-hand side of (5.19) by $n-1$ and that of (5.40) by $n-2$. The number of observations (n) minus the number of coefficients adjusted is called the number of *degrees of freedom*. The unbiased estimators (5.21) and (5.43) of the disturbance variance are both equal to the sum of squares of the deviations divided by the number of degrees of freedom.

The Regression Terminology

The LS equation

(5.45) $$y_i = b_0 + bx_i + e_i$$

is frequently called a *regression equation*. This terminology goes back to applications of LS to a problem in biology in the nineteenth century, with y_i interpreted as the height of a male and x_i as that of his father. It was found that sons of tall fathers also tend to be tall but on average not so tall as their fathers; similarly, short fathers have short sons but on average not so short. Hence, there is a "regression" toward the mean height in successive generations. The regression terminology is used on a large scale, but the specialized original meaning of the word is part of history.

Equation (5.45) gives the regression of the dependent variable (y) on the explanatory variable (x). The latter variable is frequently called the *regressor* and the former the *regressand*. We "run" a regression of a regressand on a regressor. In (5.45) we have one regressor; this is the case of *simple regression* or two-variable (x and y) regression. The special case discussed in Section 5.2 is that of a simple regression through the origin. When we run a regression of one regressand on several regressors (several explanatory variables), we have a *multiple regression*, to be discussed in Chapter 8. The straight line which is the geometric picture of the equation $y = b_0 + bx$ is known as the *regression line* and the coefficients of this equation (the b's) as the *regression coefficients*. The standard linear model described in Section 5.1 is sometimes called the *linear regression model*.

A Numerical Example

We proceed to apply the above results to the $n = 7$ observations in Table 1 on page 9. In (2.36) we obtained

(5.46)
$$b = \frac{\sum_{i=1}^{7} (x_i - \bar{x})(y_i - \bar{y})}{\sum_{i=1}^{7} (x_i - \bar{x})^2} = \frac{80}{84} \approx .952$$

(5.47)
$$b_0 = 96 - \tfrac{80}{84} \times 107 \approx -5.90$$

To estimate σ^2, we consider the LS residual sum of squares derived in (2.45) and (2.46) for the data of Table 1, which appeared to be 11.81. It follows from (5.43) that this is to be divided by $n - 2 = 7 - 2$ to yield the unbiased estimate of σ^2:

(5.48)
$$s^2 = \frac{11.81}{5} \approx 2.362$$

We have $\sigma^2/\sum_i (x_i - \bar{x})^2 = \sigma^2/84$ for the variance of b in view of (5.31). Using (5.48), we obtain $\sqrt{2.362/84} \approx .17$ for the standard error of the slope estimate. Next, using $n = 7$ and $\bar{x} = 107$ [see (2.33)], we compute the standard error of the constant-term estimate from (5.38) by taking the square root of

(5.49)
$$2.362\left(\frac{1}{7} + \frac{107^2}{84}\right) \approx 2.362(.14 + 136.30) \approx 322.3$$

which yields a standard error of 18.0. We write the result as

(5.50)
$$y = -5.9 + .95x + \text{residual}$$
$$(18.0) \quad (.17)$$

This is the regression of y on x in numerical form, with standard errors added in parentheses below the corresponding estimates. Note that these estimates have one decimal place less than in (5.46) and (5.47). This change is made because the order of magnitude of the standard errors indicates that the extra decimal place of the estimates has little meaning.

Comparison with LS Through the Origin

In (2.39) we obtained the following slope coefficient of the LS line through the origin from the same data:

$$(5.51) \qquad b = \frac{\sum_{i=1}^{7} x_i y_i}{\sum_{i=1}^{7} x_i^2} = \frac{71,984}{80,227} \approx .897$$

Also, we obtained 12.07 for the sum of the squared deviations from the corresponding LS line [see (2.47) and (2.48)]. Hence, (5.21) implies the following unbiased estimate of σ^2:

$$(5.52) \qquad s^2 = \frac{12.07}{6} \approx 2.011$$

This estimate is smaller than that obtained in (5.48), which is due to the larger number of degrees of freedom ($6 > 5$) in the present case. However, note that it is not generally true that the unbiased σ^2 estimate obtained from LS through the origin is below the estimate obtained from unconstrained LS.

We use (5.17) for the sampling variance of the LS slope estimator through the origin. An unbiased estimate of this variance is obtained from (5.52): $s^2/\sum_i x_i^2 = 2.011/80,227 \approx .00002507$. The square root of this estimate is .005 (in three decimal places), which is the standard error of the slope estimate (5.51). We write the result as

$$(5.53) \qquad y = .897x + \text{residual}$$
$$(.005)$$

which should be compared with (5.50).

Application of the two-sigma rule (see the end of Section 4.4) to the slope in (5.53) yields $.897 - 2(.005) = .887$ as a lower bound for β and $.897 + 2(.005) = .907$ as an upper bound. The corresponding interval based on (5.50) is from $.95 - 2(.17) \approx .6$ to $.95 + 2(.17) \approx 1.3$. The width of the interval $(.6, 1.3)$ exceeds that of $(.887, .907)$ considerably. The implication is that *if we are willing to assume that the true income-consumption relation is a proportionality relation*, we can estimate the slope of this relation with far greater precision than without this assumption.

Figure 11 clarifies why there is such a large difference in the precision of the slope estimators with and without constant term. This figure contains the seven observation points of Table 1 and is identical to Figure 1 on page 10 except that it shows the origin of the coordinate system. If the regression line is not required

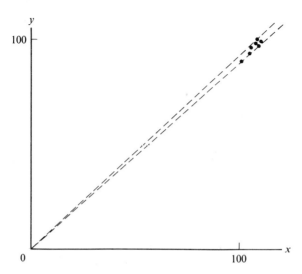

FIGURE 11   The effect of the constant-term constraint on the
precision of the slope estimator

to go through the origin, the only information we have on the slope of the
consumption-income relation is the location of the seven observation points.
But if we assume that this relation is a proportionality, the line must go through
the origin, which is equivalent to very "potent" information. This is indicated
by the two broken lines between which all seven points are located; the angle
between these lines is quite small. As in the case of Figures 9 and 10, the broken
lines are illustrative only.

Derivations

In Section 4.4 we considered independently distributed random variables
$X_1, \ldots, X_n$ with mean μ and variance σ^2. The disturbances $\epsilon_1, \ldots, \epsilon_n$ are
independently distributed with zero mean and variance σ^2, so that the results
obtained for the X_i's in Section 4.4 apply to the ϵ_i's with μ specified as zero.
We conclude from (4.45) that $\sum_i (X_i - \bar{X})^2$ has expectation $(n - 1)\sigma^2$; hence,
the same is true for $\sum_i (\epsilon_i - \bar{\epsilon})^2$, which proves (5.41). Next consider (4.48),
var $\bar{X} = \sigma^2/n$. Since var X equals $\mathcal{E}[(\bar{X} - \mu)^2]$, which becomes $\mathcal{E}(\bar{\epsilon}^2)$ when
applied to the ϵ_i's, this proves (5.36).

To prove (5.37), we use (5.29) and (5.32) in

$$(b - \beta)\bar{\epsilon} = \frac{\sum\limits_{i=1}^{n} (x_i - \bar{x})\epsilon_i}{\sum\limits_{i=1}^{n} (x_i - \bar{x})^2} \left(\frac{1}{n} \sum\limits_{j=1}^{n} \epsilon_j \right) = \frac{\sum\limits_{i=1}^{n} \sum\limits_{j=1}^{n} (x_i - \bar{x})\epsilon_i\epsilon_j}{n \sum\limits_{i=1}^{n} (x_i - \bar{x})^2}$$

The third member is a weighted sum of the n^2 disturbance products $\epsilon_i\epsilon_j$ with
weights equal to $x_i - \bar{x}$ divided by the denominator of this member. Since

these weights are constants, we have

(5.54)
$$\mathcal{E}[(b - \beta)\bar{\epsilon}] = \frac{\sum_{i=1}^{n} \sum_{j=1}^{n} (x_i - \bar{x})\mathcal{E}(\epsilon_i \epsilon_j)}{n \sum_{i=1}^{n} (x_i - \bar{x})^2}$$

To evaluate the numerator on the right we use (5.9),

$$\sum_{i=1}^{n} \sum_{j=1}^{n} (x_i - \bar{x})\mathcal{E}(\epsilon_i \epsilon_j) = \sum_{i=1}^{n} (x_i - \bar{x})\mathcal{E}(\epsilon_i^2) = \sigma^2 \sum_{i=1}^{n} (x_i - \bar{x}) = 0$$

where the last step is based on (5.25). On combining this result with (5.54), we obtain (5.37).

5.4   An Optimal Property of Least-Squares Estimation

It was stated in Section 2.4 that LS has the advantage of a well-defined criterion—that of minimizing the sum of squares of the deviations. This advantage is no longer relevant when we use LS as a method for estimating unknown parameters. However, LS has another and more fundamental advantage under the standard linear model. Within a certain class of estimators, to be explained below, LS estimators have minimum sampling variance.

Linear Estimators

We return to the standard linear model and define a linear estimator of an unknown parameter as any linear function $C_1 y_1 + \cdots + C_n y_n$ of the random values taken by the dependent variable, where $C_1, \ldots, C_n$ are constants. Note that the LS slope estimator $b = \sum_i x_i y_i / \sum_i x_i^2$ given in (5.11) is linear, because it takes the form $\sum_i C_i y_i$ when C_i is specified as

$$\frac{x_i}{x_1^2 + \cdots + x_n^2} \qquad i = 1, \ldots, n$$

As in Section 5.2, we start with the case $\beta_0 = 0$ and specify β as the parameter to be estimated, so that $b^* = \sum_i C_i y_i$, with unspecified constants $C_1, \ldots, C_n$, is the general form of a linear estimator of β. To provide a link between b^* and the LS estimator $b = \sum_i x_i y_i / \sum_i x_i^2$, we write b^* as

$$b^* = \left(C_1 - \frac{x_1}{\sum_{i=1}^{n} x_i^2} \right) y_1 + \cdots + \left(C_n - \frac{x_n}{\sum_{i=1}^{n} x_i^2} \right) y_n + \frac{x_1 y_1 + \cdots + x_n y_n}{\sum_{i=1}^{n} x_i^2}$$

Since the last term on the right is simply b, we can write this in the simpler form

(5.55)
$$b^* = b + \sum_{i=1}^{n} c_i y_i, \qquad \text{where } c_i = C_i - \frac{x_i}{\sum_{j=1}^{n} x_j^2}$$

Both the C_i's and the x_i's are constants; hence, the c_i's are constants too.

Unbiased Linear Estimators

An unbiased linear estimator is a linear estimator which is unbiased. To verify under which condition b^* is unbiased, we substitute $\beta x_i + \epsilon_i$ for y_i in (5.55),

$$(5.56) \qquad b^* = b + \sum_{i=1}^{n} c_i(\beta x_i + \epsilon_i) = b + \beta \sum_{i=1}^{n} c_i x_i + \sum_{i=1}^{n} c_i \epsilon_i$$

and take the expectation of the first and third members,

$$(5.57) \qquad \mathcal{E}b^* = \beta + \beta \sum_{i=1}^{n} c_i x_i$$

where use is made of the unbiasedness of the LS estimator ($\mathcal{E}b = \beta$), of $\mathcal{E}\epsilon_i = 0$, and of the constancy of the c_i's and x_i's. We conclude from (5.57) that the estimator is unbiased, $\mathcal{E}b^* = \beta$, if and only if

$$(5.58) \qquad \sum_{i=1}^{n} c_i x_i = 0$$

in which case (5.56) can be simplified to

$$(5.59) \qquad b^* = b + \sum_{i=1}^{n} c_i \epsilon_i$$

We conclude that b^* in (5.55) is the general form of a linear estimator of β and that condition (5.58) ensures that it is unbiased.

The LS Slope Estimator Through the Origin Is Best Linear Unbiased

We subtract β from both sides of (5.59),

$$b^* - \beta = (b - \beta) + \sum_{i=1}^{n} c_i \epsilon_i$$

and square both sides,

$$(b^* - \beta)^2 = (b - \beta)^2 + \left(\sum_{i=1}^{n} c_i \epsilon_i\right)^2 + 2(b - \beta) \sum_{i=1}^{n} c_i \epsilon_i$$

after which we take the expectation. Since b^* and b are both unbiased if (5.58) is true, the expectations of the two terms immediately to the left and right of the equal sign become the variances of b^* and b, so that we obtain

$$\operatorname{var} b^* = \operatorname{var} b + \mathcal{E}\left[\left(\sum_{i=1}^{n} c_i \epsilon_i\right)^2\right] + 2\mathcal{E}\left[(b - \beta) \sum_{i=1}^{n} c_i \epsilon_i\right]$$

It is shown in the next paragraph that the last term vanishes,

$$(5.60) \qquad \mathcal{E}\left[(b - \beta) \sum_{i=1}^{n} c_i \epsilon_i\right] = 0$$

which yields

$$(5.61) \qquad \operatorname{var} b^* = \operatorname{var} b + \mathcal{E}\left[\left(\sum_{i=1}^{n} c_i \epsilon_i\right)^2\right] \geq \operatorname{var} b$$

where the inequality sign is based on the fact that the second term in the middle member is the expectation of a square and is therefore nonnegative. We conclude from (5.61) that the variance of b^* is never smaller than the variance (5.17) of the LS estimator. In other words, the latter estimator is *best linear unbiased* in the sense that among all estimators of β that are also linear and unbiased the LS estimator has the smallest possible sampling variance. (This result does not exclude the possibility that a nonlinear unbiased estimator of β exists with a smaller sampling variance than that of the LS estimator. However, this possibility will not be pursued here.)

To prove (5.60) we use (5.12), which shows that the left-hand side of (5.60) is the expectation of

$$\frac{\sum_{i=1}^{n} x_i \epsilon_i}{\sum_{i=1}^{n} x_i^2} \sum_{j=1}^{n} c_j \epsilon_j = \frac{\sum_{i=1}^{n} \sum_{j=1}^{n} c_j x_i \epsilon_i \epsilon_j}{\sum_{i=1}^{n} x_i^2}$$

Since $c_1, \ldots, c_n, x_1, \ldots, x_n$ are all constants, the left-hand side of (5.60) is thus equal to

$$\frac{\sum_{i=1}^{n} \sum_{j=1}^{n} c_j x_i \mathcal{E}(\epsilon_i \epsilon_j)}{\sum_{i=1}^{n} x_i^2} = \frac{\sum_{i=1}^{n} c_i x_i \mathcal{E}(\epsilon_i^2)}{\sum_{i=1}^{n} x_i^2} = \frac{\sigma^2 \sum_{i=1}^{n} c_i x_i}{\sum_{i=1}^{n} x_i^2} = 0$$

where the first equal sign is based on (5.9) for $i \neq j$, the second on (5.9) for $i = j$, and the third on the unbiasedness condition (5.58). This completes the proof of (5.60).

Extension to Unconstrained LS Estimation

We proceed to the LS estimators b_0 and b defined in (5.23) and (5.24) for the case in which β_0 is not constrained to be zero. Both are linear estimators. For b this follows directly from (5.28). Given that b is linear in $y_1, \ldots, y_n$,

$$b_0 = \bar{y} - b\bar{x} = \frac{1}{n} \sum_{i=1}^{n} y_i - b\bar{x}$$

is obviously also linear in $y_1, \ldots, y_n$. We know from (5.30) and (5.34) that b and b_0 are both unbiased. It can be shown under the conditions of the standard linear model that both are best linear unbiased. If β_0 is unknown, no linear unbiased estimators of β and β_0 exist whose sampling variances are smaller than var b and var b_0, respectively, given in (5.31) and (5.38). The proof is similar to that of the previous subsection but will not be given here.

The following example is instructive. In Section 2.1 we considered the slope coefficient (2.6),

(5.62)
$$a = \frac{\bar{y}_2 - \bar{y}_1}{\bar{x}_2 - \bar{x}_1}$$

It is shown in the next subsection that a is a linear unbiased estimator of the slope β in (5.3) and that for the data of Table 1 on page 9 the sampling variance of a equals a multiple .0166 of σ^2. The variance of the LS estimator is

$$\text{var } b = \frac{\sigma^2}{\sum_{i=1}^{7} (x_i - \bar{x})^2} = \frac{\sigma^2}{84}$$

which is a multiple .0119 of σ^2 and hence about 30 percent smaller than the variance of a.

We conclude that the estimator (5.62), though unbiased, has the disadvantage of a larger sampling variance relative to the LS estimator. This is important, but we should not forget that the discussion of Figure 11 has shown that a different specification ($\beta_0 = 0$ or $\beta_0 \neq 0$) may lead to much larger differences between the sampling variances of estimators of the same parameter (β). Such a situation is not uncommon in econometrics.

Derivations

The pairs $(\bar{x}_1, \bar{y}_1)$ and $(\bar{x}_2, \bar{y}_2)$ in (5.62) are the centers of gravity of two sets of observation points in Figure 2 on page 11. Table 1 shows that $\bar{y}_1 = \frac{1}{3}(y_1 + y_2 + y_5)$ and $\bar{y}_2 = \frac{1}{3}(y_3 + y_6 + y_7)$. Using (5.3), we thus have

$$\bar{y}_1 = \beta_0 + \tfrac{1}{3}\beta(x_1 + x_2 + x_5) + \tfrac{1}{3}(\epsilon_1 + \epsilon_2 + \epsilon_5)$$
$$\bar{y}_2 = \beta_0 + \tfrac{1}{3}\beta(x_3 + x_6 + x_7) + \tfrac{1}{3}(\epsilon_3 + \epsilon_6 + \epsilon_7)$$

By subtracting and using $\bar{x}_1 = \frac{1}{3}(x_1 + x_2 + x_5)$ and $\bar{x}_2 = \frac{1}{3}(x_3 + x_6 + x_7)$, we find

$$\bar{y}_2 - \bar{y}_1 = \beta(\bar{x}_2 - \bar{x}_1) + \tfrac{1}{3}(\epsilon_3 + \epsilon_6 + \epsilon_7 - \epsilon_1 - \epsilon_2 - \epsilon_5)$$

so that (5.62) yields

(5.63) $$a = \beta + \frac{\epsilon_3 + \epsilon_6 + \epsilon_7 - \epsilon_1 - \epsilon_2 - \epsilon_5}{3(\bar{x}_2 - \bar{x}_1)}$$

Since $\bar{x}_1$ and $\bar{x}_2$ are constants and the ϵ_i's have zero expectation, a is an unbiased estimator of the true slope β. It is also a linear estimator; this follows from (5.62). To obtain the variance of a we consider $(a - \beta)^2$, which is equal to the square of the right-hand ratio in (5.63), and then take the expectation,

$$\mathcal{E}\left[\frac{(\epsilon_3 + \epsilon_6 + \epsilon_7 - \epsilon_1 - \epsilon_2 - \epsilon_5)^2}{9(\bar{x}_2 - \bar{x}_1)^2}\right] = \frac{\mathcal{E}[(\epsilon_3 + \epsilon_6 + \epsilon_7 - \epsilon_1 - \epsilon_2 - \epsilon_5)^2]}{9(\bar{x}_2 - \bar{x}_1)^2}$$

where the equal sign is based on the constancy of $\bar{x}_1$ and $\bar{x}_2$. The expectation in the right-hand numerator is the sum of the expectations of six squared disturbances (the squares of $\epsilon_3, \epsilon_6, \ldots, \epsilon_5$) plus the sum of the expectations of certain products of disturbances. It follows from (5.9) that the latter expectations are all zero and that the former are equal to σ^2 each. Hence, the variance of a is equal to $6\sigma^2$ divided by $9(\bar{x}_2 - \bar{x}_1)^2$, which yields $.0166\sigma^2$ for the specifications (2.1) and (2.3) of $\bar{x}_1$ and $\bar{x}_2$.

Problems

Problems 1 and 2 refer to Section 5.1, 3 and 4 to Section 5.2, 5–8 to Section 5.3, and 9 and 10 to Section 5.4.

1 Suppose that (5.1) is replaced by

$$\mathcal{E}(y_i \,|\, x_i) = \beta_0 + \beta \log x_i \qquad\qquad i = 1, \ldots, n$$

Does this modification fall under the standard linear model?

2 When applied to a consumption-income relation, Figure 8 implies that the expenditures of families with an income of \$10,000 have the same standard deviation as the expenditures of families with an income of \$50,000. Do you consider this a plausible assumption? (*Note:* Generalizations are considered in Section 19.1.)

3 In the paragraph preceding (5.18), it is stated that β can be trivially determined when $\sigma^2 = 0$. Why is "determined" used here, rather than "estimated"?

4 Verify the following proposition: The unbiasedness of the σ^2 estimator (5.21) does require condition (5.9) but that of the slope estimator (5.11) does not.

5 Prove that when (5.12) is replaced by (5.29), eqs. (5.13) to (5.18) and Table 10 remain valid, provided that $x_1, \ldots, x_n$ are replaced by $x_1 - \bar{x}, \ldots, x_n - \bar{x}$.

6 Compare the expression in brackets in (5.38) with the expressions in parentheses in (5.49). Verify that for the data of Table 1 the uncertainty as to the slope b dominates the variance of b_0, and use Figures 10(b) and 11 to argue that this is as could be expected.

7 Compute the two-sigma interval for β_0 in (5.50), and verify that $\beta_0 = 0$ is included in this interval.

8 Prove that the squares of the standard errors shown in (5.50) are unbiased estimates of the sampling variances of the corresponding LS estimators. Make a careful distinction between estimates and estimators.

9 Use (5.9) to prove that if $c_1, \ldots, c_n$ are constants,

$$\mathcal{E}\left[\left(\sum_{i=1}^{n} c_i \epsilon_i \right)^2 \right] = \sigma^2 \sum_{i=1}^{n} c_i^2$$

Compare this with (5.61) to conclude that the variance of b^* always exceeds that of b except when all c_i's vanish, that is, except when b^* is identical to the LS estimator. (*Note:* This result proves that among all linear unbiased estimators of β *only* LS yields the smallest possible sampling variance.)

10 Is s^2 defined in (5.21) a linear estimator? Is $s = \sqrt{s^2}$ a linear estimator?

chapter 6

Two-Variable Correlation

This chapter, which completes Part One of the book, starts with the following question: If we fit a straight line, how good is the fit? The answer is formulated in Section 6.1 by means of the correlation coefficient of the two variables involved. In Sections 6.2 and 6.3 we shall define the correlation coefficient of two random variables and that of the estimators of two unknown parameters.

6.1 The Correlation Coefficient of Observation Pairs

Definition of a Correlation Coefficient

Consider two variables, x and y, whose observations are in pairs, (x_1, y_1), $\ldots$, (x_n, y_n), as in Table 1 on page 9. The correlation coefficient of these observation pairs (also called the correlation coefficient of the variables x and y) is defined as

$$(6.1) \qquad r = \frac{\sum\limits_{i=1}^{n}(x_i - \bar{x})(y_i - \bar{y})}{\sqrt{\sum\limits_{i=1}^{n}(x_i - \bar{x})^2 \sum\limits_{i=1}^{n}(y_i - \bar{y})^2}}$$

where $\bar{x}$ and $\bar{y}$ are the arithmetic means of the x_i's and the y_i's, respectively. Note that the right-hand side of (6.1) is symmetric in the two variables; it does not change when we interchange the roles of x and y.

83

For example, for Table 1 we have $n = 7$ and

(6.2)
$$\sum_{i=1}^{7} (x_i - \bar{x})^2 = 84, \qquad \sum_{i=1}^{7} (y_i - \bar{y})^2 = 88$$

(6.3)
$$\sum_{i=1}^{7} (x_i - \bar{x})(y_i - \bar{y}) = 80$$

so that (6.1) yields

(6.4)
$$r = \frac{80}{\sqrt{84 \times 88}} \approx .930$$

Hence, the correlation coefficient of per capita income and per capita consumption as revealed by Table 1 is .930 in three decimal places.

It is instructive to compare (6.1) with the LS slope coefficient (2.32),

(6.5)
$$b = \frac{\sum_{i=1}^{n} (x_i - \bar{x})(y_i - \bar{y})}{\sum_{i=1}^{n} (x_i - \bar{x})^2}$$

which is not symmetric in the two variables. However, since the numerators in (6.1) and (6.5) are the same, and since the two denominators are positive, r and b must have the same sign.

Constraints on the Correlation Coefficient

Consider eq. (2.44), reproduced here:

(6.6)
$$\sum_{i=1}^{n} e_i^2 = \sum_{i=1}^{n} (y_i - \bar{y})^2 - b^2 \sum_{i=1}^{n} (x_i - \bar{x})^2$$

We divide both sides by $\sum_i (y_i - \bar{y})^2$,

$$\frac{\sum_{i=1}^{n} e_i^2}{\sum_{i=1}^{n} (y_i - \bar{y})^2} = 1 - \frac{b^2 \sum_{i=1}^{n} (x_i - \bar{x})^2}{\sum_{i=1}^{n} (y_i - \bar{y})^2}$$

$$= 1 - \frac{\left[\sum_{i=1}^{n} (x_i - \bar{x})(y_i - \bar{y})\right]^2}{\sum_{i=1}^{n} (x_i - \bar{x})^2 \sum_{i=1}^{n} (y_i - \bar{y})^2}$$

where the second step is based on (6.5). A comparison with (6.1) shows that we have proved

(6.7)
$$1 - r^2 = \frac{\sum_{i=1}^{n} e_i^2}{\sum_{i=1}^{n} (y_i - \bar{y})^2}$$

The right-hand side is the ratio of two sums of squares and hence cannot be negative, so that $1 - r^2 \geq 0$ or $r^2 \leq 1$. This is equivalent to

(6.8)
$$-1 \leq r \leq 1$$

or, in words, the correlation coefficient of the observation pairs $(x_1, y_1), \ldots,$ (x_n, y_n) cannot be below -1 or above 1.

Discussion of Numerical Values of the Correlation Coefficient

We have $r^2 = 1$ in (6.7) if and only if $\sum_i e_i^2 = 0$, that is, when $e_1 = \cdots = e_n = 0$ and hence when the LS fit is perfect. Thus, $r^2 < 1$, and hence $-1 < r < 1$ as soon as the LS fit is imperfect. To verify whether $r = 1$ or $r = -1$ holds under a perfect fit, we recall from the discussion below (6.5) that r and the LS slope b always have the same sign. Therefore, $r = 1$ holds when all n observation points are on a straight line with increasing slope ($b > 0$), and $r = -1$ holds when all points are on a straight line with decreasing slope.

These two cases are illustrated by the two scatter diagrams at the top of Figure 12. The two diagrams below these exhibit substantial but imperfect correlations, and the next two are cases of low correlation. The last diagram on the left indicates that there is no association between the two variables at all, $r = 0$. However, note that $r = 0$ does not imply that there is no such association. The correlation coefficient measures only the degree to which the variables are *linearly* related. In the diagram in the lower-right corner y is a quadratic function of x. This relation is exact; nevertheless, x and y are uncorrelated ($r = 0$).

6.2   The Correlation Coefficient of Two Random Variables

The mean and the variance of a distribution may be viewed as the probabilistic versions of the arithmetic mean and the mean square, respectively, of n numbers. In this section we shall consider the probabilistic version of the correlation coefficient r.

The Correlation Coefficient of a Random Pair

We write (6.1) in the form

$$(6.9) \qquad r = \frac{(1/n) \sum\limits_{i=1}^{n} (x_i - \bar{x})(y_i - \bar{y})}{\sqrt{(1/n) \sum\limits_{i=1}^{n} (x_i - \bar{x})^2 (1/n) \sum\limits_{i=1}^{n} (y_i - \bar{y})^2}}$$

so that r becomes the mean product of the observation pairs divided by the square root of the product of the two mean squares, both variables being measured as deviations from their arithmetic means.

Our objective is to define the correlation coefficient ρ of a random pair (X, Y) with finite and nonzero variances. The clue is the interpretation of the covariance as the probabilistic version of the mean product in the numerator

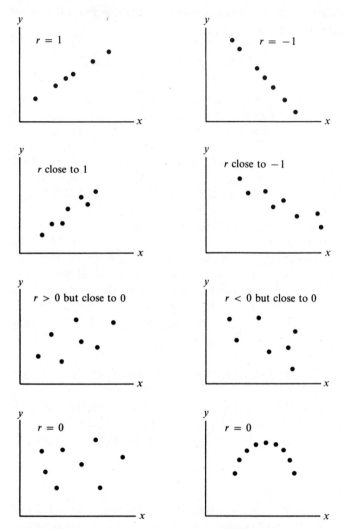

FIGURE 12 The correlation coefficients of eight scatter diagrams

of (6.9). This gives

(6.10)
$$\rho = \frac{\text{cov}(X, Y)}{\sqrt{\text{var } X \text{ var } Y}} = \frac{\text{cov}(X, Y)}{\sigma_X \sigma_Y}$$

where σ_X and σ_Y are the standard deviations of X and Y, respectively.

Constraints on the Correlation Coefficient

The correlation coefficient ρ is constrained by

(6.11)
$$-1 \le \rho \le 1$$

which is similar to (6.8). To prove (6.11) we consider (3.44) with $\alpha_0 = 0$:

(6.12) $\text{var} (\alpha_1 X + \alpha_2 Y) = \alpha_1^2 \text{ var } X + \alpha_2^2 \text{ var } Y + 2\alpha_1\alpha_2 \text{ cov } (X, Y)$

This holds for any values of the constants α_1 and α_2. We specify $\alpha_1 = 1/\sigma_X$ and $\alpha_2 = 1/\sigma_Y$, so that the left-hand side of (6.12) becomes the variance of $X/\sigma_X + Y/\sigma_Y$. Since the first two terms on the right become

$$\alpha_1^2 \text{ var } X = \frac{\text{var } X}{\sigma_X^2} = 1, \qquad \alpha_2^2 \text{ var } Y = \frac{\text{var } Y}{\sigma_Y^2} = 1$$

we thus have

(6.13) $\text{var} \left(\dfrac{X}{\sigma_X} + \dfrac{Y}{\sigma_Y} \right) = 2 + 2 \dfrac{\text{cov } (X, Y)}{\sigma_X \sigma_Y} = 2(1 + \rho)$

Next we specify $\alpha_1 = 1/\sigma_X$ and $\alpha_2 = -1/\sigma_Y$ in (6.12), which gives

(6.14) $\text{var} \left(\dfrac{X}{\sigma_X} - \dfrac{Y}{\sigma_Y} \right) = 2 - 2 \dfrac{\text{cov } (X, Y)}{\sigma_X \sigma_Y} = 2(1 - \rho)$

The first member of (6.13) is a variance and hence nonnegative, so that the third member implies $1 + \rho \geq 0$ and hence $\rho \geq -1$. Similarly, the nonnegativity of the variance in (6.14) implies $\rho \leq 1$, which completes the proof of (6.11).

Perfectly Correlated Random Variables

We conclude from (6.13) that $\rho = -1$ (the smallest possible value) holds if and only if the variance in the first member vanishes. Thus, $\rho = -1$ implies that the expression

(6.15) $\dfrac{X}{\sigma_X} + \dfrac{Y}{\sigma_Y}$

becomes nonstochastic [see remark (4) on page 30]. The first distribution of Table 11 provides an example. The random pair (X, Y) takes the values $(1, 3)$ and $(3, 1)$ with probability .3 each and $(2, 2)$ with probability .4. The other six bivariate probabilities are all zero, which is indicated by blank entries. The reader should verify that this distribution has the following variances and covariance:

(6.16) $\text{var } X = \text{var } Y = .6, \qquad \text{cov } (X, Y) = -.6$

Hence, (6.10) yields $\rho = -.6/\sqrt{(.6)(.6)} = -1$. This distribution is illustrated in Figure 13(a), where the values of X and Y are measured along the two axes. The points $(1, 3)$, $(2, 2)$, and $(3, 1)$ are indicated by A_1, A_2, and A_3, respectively; these are the only points at which (X, Y) has nonzero probability. Note that these three points are on a downward-sloping straight line and that their coordinates satisfy $X + Y = 4$. Thus, the first distribution of Table 11 is such that $X + Y$ equals a constant. Since the standard deviations of X and Y are both equal to $\sqrt{.6}$ [see (6.16)], the random variable (6.15) takes the form

$$\frac{X}{\sigma_X} + \frac{Y}{\sigma_Y} = \frac{X + Y}{\sqrt{.6}}$$

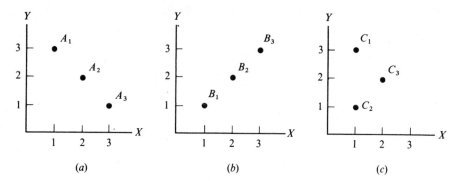

FIGURE 13   Perfectly correlated and uncorrelated random variables

TABLE 11

Perfectly correlated and uncorrelated random variables

	$Y = 1$	$Y = 2$	$Y = 3$	Marginal
First distribution ($\rho = -1$)				
$X = 1$			$p_{13} = .3$	$p_{1.} = .3$
$X = 2$		$p_{22} = .4$		$p_{2.} = .4$
$X = 3$	$p_{31} = .3$			$p_{3.} = .3$
Marginal	$p_{.1} = .3$	$p_{.2} = .4$	$p_{.3} = .3$	1
Second distribution ($\rho = 1$)				
$X = 1$	$p_{11} = .3$			$p_{1.} = .3$
$X = 2$		$p_{22} = .4$		$p_{2.} = .4$
$X = 3$			$p_{33} = .3$	$p_{3.} = .3$
Marginal	$p_{.1} = .3$	$p_{.2} = .4$	$p_{.3} = .3$	1
Third distribution ($\rho = 0$)				
$X = 1$	$p_{11} = .3$		$p_{13} = .3$	$p_{1.} = .6$
$X = 2$		$p_{22} = .4$		$p_{2.} = .4$
Marginal	$p_{.1} = .3$	$p_{.2} = .4$	$p_{.3} = .3$	1

which is also a constant (equal to $4/\sqrt{.6}$) and hence nonstochastic, in agreement with the statement made below (6.15).

The second distribution of Table 11, illustrated in Figure 13(b), is an example of the other extreme. Here the two variances and the covariance are all equal to .6, so that $\rho = 1$ [see (6.10)], and the three points with nonzero probability (B_1, B_2, and B_3) are on an upward straight line.

These results hold generally. Two discrete random variables X and Y are *perfectly correlated* ($\rho = \pm 1$) if and only if the values which they take with nonzero probability are on a straight line; these values are then linearly related. We have $\rho = -1$ when the linear relation is decreasing [Figure 13(a)] and $\rho = 1$ when it is increasing [Figure 13(b)].

Uncorrelated and Stochastically Independent Random Variables

When $\rho \neq 0$, the random variables X and Y are said to be *correlated*; when $\rho = 0$, they are called *uncorrelated*. It follows from (6.10) that if X and Y have a zero covariance, they are uncorrelated. We know from the paragraph below (3.38) that if X and Y are stochastically independent, they have a zero co-variance. Thus, two random variables are necessarily uncorrelated when they are stochastically independent.

The converse is not true. If X and Y are uncorrelated, they need not be stochastically independent. The third distribution of Table 11, which is illustrated in Figure 13(c), provides an example. The reader should verify that its covariance vanishes, implying $\rho = 0$, but that the distribution does not satisfy the independence condition (3.37). Figures 13(a) to 13(c) illustrate that the correlation coefficient ρ of X and Y measures the degree to which these random variables are *linearly* related. In this respect ρ is similar to r as described at the end of Section 6.1.

REMARKS:

(1) Recall eq. (3.44), reproduced here:

(6.17) $\operatorname{var}(\alpha_0 + \alpha_1 X + \alpha_2 Y) = \alpha_1^2 \operatorname{var} X + \alpha_2^2 \operatorname{var} Y + 2\alpha_1\alpha_2 \operatorname{cov}(X, Y)$

If X and Y are stochastically independent, the covariance term on the right vanishes. But independence is stronger than necessary for this result; it is sufficient that X and Y are uncorrelated. More generally, if $X_1, \ldots, X_n$ are pairwise all uncorrelated (which is a weaker condition than "are independently distributed"), then

(6.18) $$\operatorname{var}\left(\alpha_0 + \sum_{i=1}^{n} \alpha_i X_i\right) = \sum_{i=1}^{n} \alpha_i^2 \operatorname{var} X_i$$

(2) If (X, Y) has a continuous distribution, the correlation coefficient ρ is also defined according to (6.10) but with the variances and covariance defined as integrals rather than sums. This ρ, too, is subject to the constraint (6.11). Remark (1) also applies to continuous distributions in that (6.18) holds when $X_1, \ldots, X_n$ are all pairwise uncorrelated.

(3) We assumed in (5.8) that the disturbances $\epsilon_1, \ldots, \epsilon_n$ of the standard linear model are independently distributed. For the analysis of Chapter 5, it is actually sufficient to assume that they are all pairwise uncorrelated (see Problem 6).

6.3   The Sampling Covariance and Correlation Coefficient of the Estimators of Two Parameters

Since estimators of parameters are random variables, the correlation coefficient of two estimators is a special case of the correlation coefficient of two random variables. As an example, we consider the LS estimators b and b_0 of

β and β_0 in $y_i = \beta_0 + \beta x_i + \epsilon_i$ [see (5.3)]. Both estimators are unbiased, so that their covariance (usually called the sampling covariance on the analogy of the sampling variance) is obtained by multiplying their sampling errors and taking the expectation. For this purpose we use (5.33) and (5.37), reproduced here:

(6.19)
$$b_0 - \beta_0 = \bar{\epsilon} - (b - \beta)\bar{x}$$
(6.20)
$$\mathcal{E}[(b - \beta)\bar{\epsilon}] = 0$$

The product of the sampling errors of b and b_0 is, in view of (6.19), equal to

$$(b - \beta)(b_0 - \beta_0) = (b - \beta)\bar{\epsilon} - (b - \beta)^2 \bar{x}$$

It follows from (6.20) that the first term on the right has zero expectation. Therefore,

(6.21)
$$\operatorname{cov}(b, b_0) = -\bar{x} \operatorname{var} b$$

which shows that (given var $b > 0$) the covariance of the LS slope and constant-term estimators has a sign opposite to that of the arithmetic mean $\bar{x}$ of the explanatory variable.

The sampling correlation coefficient of b and b_0 is obtained by dividing the covariance (6.21) by the square root of the product of the two variances. For the data of Table 1 on page 9 this yields a correlation coefficient of $-.9995$ in four decimal places (see Problem 7 for its derivation), so that b and b_0 are very highly negatively correlated in this case. This means that if a particular sample yields a slope estimate b exceeding β, chances are that its constant-term estimate b_0 is below β_0 and vice versa. Such interactions of estimates of two parameters are particularly important for the econometric analysis of linear combinations of parameters (see Section 8.2).

Problems

Problems 1 and 2 refer to Section 6.1, 3–6 to Section 6.2, and 7 to Section 6.3.

1 Prove that the observations $(x, y) = (1, 9), (2, 4), (3, 1), (4, 0), (5, 1), (6, 4)$, and $(7, 9)$ are all located on the curve $y = (x - 4)^2$, and verify that the correlation coefficient (6.1) of these seven observation pairs is zero.

2 Let (x_i, y_i) for $i = 1, \ldots, n$ be the observation pairs of two variables x and y. Prove that the correlation coefficient (6.1) of x and y equals the correlation coefficient of $x + A_1$ and $y + A_2$, where A_1 and A_2 are arbitrary constants. Next prove that if c_1 and c_2 are both positive or both negative constants, the correlation coefficient of $c_1 x + A_1$ and $c_2 y + A_2$ equals r defined in (6.1) and that this coefficient equals $-r$ if c_1 and c_2 are constants of opposite sign. [Note: These results prove that the correlation coefficient of $x + $ constant and $y + $ constant equals the correlation r of (x, y), that

the correlation coefficient of any linear function of x and any linear function of y equals the same r if the two functions are both increasing or both decreasing, and that this correlation coefficient equals $-r$ if one of these functions is increasing and the other is decreasing.]

3   (*Continuation*) Extend this result for the correlation coefficient ρ of a random pair (X, Y). In particular, prove that the correlation coefficient of (a) $1 + X$ and $2 - 3Y$ is $-\rho$, (b) $1 - X$ and $2 - 3Y$ is ρ, and (c) $1 - X$ and $2 + 3Y$ is $-\rho$.

4   Compute the means, variances, and covariances of the three distributions of Table 11. Also verify that the third distribution does not satisfy (3.37).

5   Verify that the correlation coefficient of the first distribution of Table 5 on page 33 is equal to $3/\sqrt{42} \approx .463$. What is the correlation coefficient of the second distribution of that table?

6   Verify that if the ϵ_i's are uncorrelated random variables with zero mean and variance σ^2, they satisfy conditions (5.6) and (5.9) and that these are the only conditions on the ϵ_i's used in Chapter 5 except for the proof of (5.36) and (5.41) at the end of Section 5.3 (where the ϵ_i's are assumed to be independent). Prove that (5.36) and (5.41) are also true if the ϵ_i's are uncorrelated with zero mean and variance σ^2.

7   Verify that for the data of Table 1 on page 9 the covariance (6.21) equals $-107\sigma^2/84$ and the sampling correlation coefficient of b and b_0 equals $-107/\sqrt{11,461} \approx -.9995$. [*Hint*: Use the numbers given in the discussion preceding (5.49), and use (5.38) for the variance of b_0.]

part two

THE
MULTIPLE
REGRESSION
MODEL

chapter 7

Fitting
a Plane

The problems in which we shall be interested in this and several later chapters can be illustrated with the following example, which was also used by Theil and Nagar (1961) and Theil (1971, p. 102). We observe that the volume of textile consumption per capita in the Netherlands was subject to a substantial increasing trend from 1923 to 1931, after which its behavior became more irregular during the later years of the 1930s. The relevant time series is shown in column (1) of Table 12. Several questions may be asked. Given that consumer demand theory indicates real income and relative prices as the variables that determine the consumption of goods and services, to what extent do statistical data show that these variables account for the variation of textile consumption over time? Can we use these data to determine or estimate the degree to which textile consumption is sensitive to a change in income and the textile price? Once we have found such a relationship, can we use it to predict textile consumption in some future year? Can we test the hypothesis that, for example, textile consumption is completely insensitive to changes in income?

In this chapter we shall extend the LS adjustment procedure of Section 2.3 to the case of several variables, and we shall apply the result to Table 12. The specific questions raised in the previous paragraph are answered in Chapters 8 to 12.

TABLE 12

**Time series dealing with the consumption of
textile in the Netherlands, 1923–1939**

Year	Volume of textile consumption per capita* (1)	Real income per capita* (2)	Relative price of textile* (3)	$\log_{10}$ (1) (4)	$\log_{10}$ (2) (5)	$\log_{10}$ (3) (6)
1923	99.2	96.7	101.0	1.99651	1.98543	2.00432
1924	99.0	98.1	100.1	1.99564	1.99167	2.00043
1925	100.0	100.0	100.0	2.00000	2.00000	2.00000
1926	111.6	104.9	90.6	2.04766	2.02078	1.95713
1927	122.2	104.9	86.5	2.08707	2.02078	1.93702
1928	117.6	109.5	89.7	2.07041	2.03941	1.95279
1929	121.1	110.8	90.6	2.08314	2.04454	1.95713
1930	136.0	112.3	82.8	2.13354	2.05038	1.91803
1931	154.2	109.3	70.1	2.18808	2.03862	1.84572
1932	153.6	105.3	65.4	2.18639	2.02243	1.81558
1933	158.5	101.7	61.3	2.20003	2.00732	1.78746
1934	140.6	95.4	62.5	2.14799	1.97955	1.79588
1935	136.2	96.4	63.6	2.13418	1.98408	1.80346
1936	168.0	97.6	52.6	2.22531	1.98945	1.72099
1937	154.3	102.4	59.7	2.18837	2.01030	1.77597
1938	149.0	101.6	59.5	2.17319	2.00689	1.77452
1939	165.5	103.8	61.3	2.21880	2.01620	1.78746

*Index base 1925 = 100.

7.1   Fitting a Plane by Least Squares

The Case of Three Variables

We return to the straight line $y = b_0 + bx$ of (2.28) and extend this to

(7.1) $$y = b_0 + b_1 x_1 + b_2 x_2$$

which describes y in terms of two x variables rather than one. The geometric picture of (7.1) is that of a plane in a three-dimensional space, with the three variables (y, x_1, and x_2) measured along the three axes.

In Table 1 on page 9 our observations are in pairs, (x_i, y_i) for $1, \ldots, n$ ($n = 7$ in Table 1). In (7.1) we have three variables; thus, we assume that the data are in triples, (y_i, x_{1i}, x_{2i}) for $i = 1, \ldots, n$, or, more explicitly,

(7.2)
$$(y_1, x_{11}, x_{21})$$
$$(y_2, x_{12}, x_{22})$$
$$\vdots$$
$$(y_n, x_{1n}, x_{2n})$$

In Figure 4 on page 19 we found that the observation pairs are not on a straight line. We applied the LS principle by minimizing

$$G(b_0, b) = \sum_{i=1}^{n} (y_i - b_0 - bx_i)^2$$

with respect to b_0 and b. Similarly, we shall usually find that the n observations (7.2) contradict (7.1) by not being on a plane. The LS principle then requires that the plane be determined by minimizing

(7.3) $$G(b_0, b_1, b_2) = \sum_{i=1}^{n} (y_i - b_0 - b_1 x_{1i} - b_2 x_{2i})^2$$

with respect to b_0, b_1, and b_2.

The LS Constant Term

The partial derivative of (7.3) with respect to b_0 equals

$$\frac{\partial G}{\partial b_0} = -2 \sum_{i=1}^{n} (y_i - b_0 - b_1 x_{1i} - b_2 x_{2i})$$

A necessary condition for a minimum G is that this derivative equals zero:

(7.4) $$-2 \sum_{i=1}^{n} y_i + 2nb_0 + 2b_1 \sum_{i=1}^{n} x_{1i} + 2b_2 \sum_{i=1}^{n} x_{2i} = 0$$

When we introduce the arithmetic means of the three variables,

(7.5) $$\bar{y} = \frac{1}{n} \sum_{i=1}^{n} y_i, \qquad \bar{x}_1 = \frac{1}{n} \sum_{i=1}^{n} x_{1i}, \qquad \bar{x}_2 = \frac{1}{n} \sum_{i=1}^{n} x_{2i}$$

we can write (7.4), after dividing by $2n$, as

(7.6) $$b_0 = \bar{y} - b_1 \bar{x}_1 - b_2 \bar{x}_2$$

which is a direct extension of (2.31).

The Normal Equations for the LS Slope Coefficients

Substitution of (7.6) in (7.3) gives

(7.7) $$\sum_{i=1}^{n} [y_i - (\bar{y} - b_1 \bar{x}_1 - b_2 \bar{x}_2) - b_1 x_{1i} - b_2 x_{2i}]^2$$

$$= \sum_{i=1}^{n} [y_i - \bar{y} - b_1(x_{1i} - \bar{x}_1) - b_2(x_{2i} - \bar{x}_2)]^2$$

We proceed to differentiate the right-hand side with respect to b_1 and equate the derivative to zero:

$$-2 \sum_{i=1}^{n} (x_{1i} - \bar{x}_1)[y_i - \bar{y} - b_1(x_{1i} - \bar{x}_1) - b_2(x_{2i} - \bar{x}_2)] = 0$$

This is equivalent to

(7.8) $$b_1 \sum_{i=1}^{n} (x_{1i} - \bar{x}_1)^2 + b_2 \sum_{i=1}^{n} (x_{1i} - \bar{x}_1)(x_{2i} - \bar{x}_2)$$

$$= \sum_{i=1}^{n} (x_{1i} - \bar{x}_1)(y_i - \bar{y})$$

Next we evaluate the partial derivative of the right-hand side of (7.7) with respect to b_2 and equate it to zero,

$$-2 \sum_{i=1}^{n} (x_{2i} - \bar{x}_2)[y_i - \bar{y} - b_1(x_{1i} - \bar{x}_1) - b_2(x_{2i} - \bar{x}_2)] = 0$$

which is equivalent to

$$(7.9) \qquad b_1 \sum_{i=1}^{n} (x_{1i} - \bar{x}_1)(x_{2i} - \bar{x}_2) + b_2 \sum_{i=1}^{n} (x_{2i} - \bar{x}_2)^2$$
$$= \sum_{i=1}^{n} (x_{2i} - \bar{x}_2)(y_i - \bar{y})$$

Equations (7.8) and (7.9) form a system of two linear equations, known as the *normal equations*, in the slope coefficients b_1 and b_2, from which these coefficients can be solved under certain conditions. These conditions will be discussed in Section 8.3.

The Variables of Table 12

The LS procedure described above will now be applied to the data on the volume of textile consumption per capita in column (1) of Table 12. Recall from the opening paragraph of this chapter that, according to consumer demand theory, the demand for each good is determined by real income and relative prices. Thus, we use real income per capita as one of our variables. Total real income is defined as total money income of private consumers divided by the cost-of-living index. To obtain real income per capita we divide this ratio by the population size:

$$(7.10) \qquad \frac{\text{total money income of private consumers}}{\text{population size} \times \text{cost-of-living index}}$$

We use only one relative price, viz., that of textile, which is approximated by the retail price index of clothing. The relative price of textile is then defined as

$$(7.11) \qquad \frac{\text{retail price index of clothing}}{\text{cost-of-living index}}$$

The volume of textile consumption is computed by dividing the total money value of textile consumption bought by private consumers by the retail price index of clothing. To obtain the volume per capita we divide, as in (7.10), by the population size:

$$(7.12) \qquad \frac{\text{total money value of textile consumption by private consumers}}{\text{population size} \times \text{retail price index of clothing}}$$

The numerical values of the variables (7.10), (7.11), and (7.12), expressed in index form with base 100 in 1925, are shown in columns (2), (3), and (1), respectively, of Table 12.

Application of LS to Table 12

Recall from the discussion below eq. (1.3) in Section 1.1 that a simple logarithmic transformation is in certain cases sufficient to ensure that the equation takes a linear form. In the application to be discussed we use this property by computing the LS plane in logarithmic form (with logarithms to the base 10); further details on this matter are provided in Section 8.1. Thus, the variable y in (7.1) is interpreted as the logarithm of the volume of textile consumption per capita,

(7.13) $y = \log_{10}$ (volume of textile consumption per capita)

and x_1 and x_2 are similarly defined as

(7.14) $x_1 = \log_{10}$ (real income per capita)

(7.15) $x_2 = \log_{10}$ (relative price of textile)

The values taken by the variables (7.13) to (7.15) are shown in the last three columns of Table 12. The figures in the successive rows of these three columns can be identified with the n observations (7.2) for $n = 17$ (because we have 17 annual observations in Table 12).

We use columns (5) and (6) of Table 12 to obtain

(7.16) $\sum_{i=1}^{17} (x_{1i} - \bar{x}_1)^2 = .00793,$ $\sum_{i=1}^{17} (x_{2i} - \bar{x}_2)^2 = .14794$

(7.17) $\sum_{i=1}^{17} (x_{1i} - \bar{x}_1)(x_{2i} - \bar{x}_2) = .00761$

Using column (4) also, we find

(7.18) $\sum_{i=1}^{17} (x_{1i} - \bar{x}_1)(y_i - \bar{y}) = .00276$

(7.19) $\sum_{i=1}^{17} (x_{2i} - \bar{x}_2)(y_i - \bar{y}) = -.11392$

By substituting these numerical values in (7.8) and (7.9), we obtain

(7.20) $\begin{aligned} .00793b_1 + .00761b_2 &= .00276 \\ .00761b_1 + .14794b_2 &= -.11392 \end{aligned}$

These are the two normal equations which are linear in the slopes b_1 and b_2, with the following solution:

(7.21) $b_1 = 1.1430,$ $b_2 = -.8289$

Next we use the last three columns of Table 12 to obtain the arithmetic averages of the three variables:

(7.22) $\bar{y} = 2.12214,$ $\bar{x}_1 = 2.01223,$ $\bar{x}_2 = 1.87258$

When the values shown in (7.21) and (7.22) are substituted in (7.6), we obtain

(7.23) $b_0 = 1.3742$

This completes the computation of the LS coefficients. Using (7.21) and (7.23), we write the equation of the LS plane as

(7.24) $$y = 1.3742 + 1.1430x_1 - .8289x_2$$

or, in more explicit form, as

(7.25) $\log_{10}$ (textile consumption per capita)
$$= 1.3742 + 1.1430 \log_{10} \text{ (real income per capita)}$$
$$-.8289 \log_{10} \text{ (relative textile price)}$$

We conclude from the positive coefficient (1.1430) of the logarithm of real income per capita that an increase in real income raises the volume of textile consumption and from the negative coefficient ($-.8289$) of the relative textile price that an increase in this price reduces the volume of textile consumption. These signs of the two slope coefficients agree with what could have been expected a priori. We shall return to this result in Sections 8.1 and 8.2.

7.2   Extensions

When we have more than two x variables, say K, we extend (7.1) to

(7.26) $$y = b_0 + b_1 x_1 + \cdots + b_K x_K$$

and the observations (7.2) to

$$(y_1, x_{11}, \ldots, x_{K1})$$
$$(y_2, x_{12}, \ldots, x_{K2})$$

(7.27)
$$\vdots$$

$$(y_n, x_{1n}, \ldots, x_{Kn})$$

The expression to be minimized is now

(7.28) $$G(b_0, b_1, \ldots, b_K) = \sum_{i=1}^{n} (y_i - b_0 - b_1 x_{1i} - \cdots - b_K x_{Ki})^2$$

LS Through the Origin

We start with the case of a zero intercept ($b_0 = 0$) for $K = 3$, so that (7.28) is simplified to

(7.29) $$G(b_1, b_2, b_3) = \sum_{i=1}^{n} (y_i - b_1 x_{1i} - b_2 x_{2i} - b_3 x_{3i})^2$$

The partial derivatives of this function are

$$\frac{\partial G}{\partial b_1} = -2 \sum_{i=1}^{n} x_{1i}(y_i - b_1 x_{1i} - b_2 x_{2i} - b_3 x_{3i})$$

$$\frac{\partial G}{\partial b_2} = -2 \sum_{i=1}^{n} x_{2i}(y_i - b_1 x_{1i} - b_2 x_{2i} - b_3 x_{3i})$$

$$\frac{\partial G}{\partial b_3} = -2 \sum_{i=1}^{n} x_{3i}(y_i - b_1 x_{1i} - b_2 x_{2i} - b_3 x_{3i})$$

When we equate these derivatives to zero, we obtain three normal equations which are linear in the three slope coefficients b_1, b_2, and b_3:

(7.30)
$$b_1 \sum_{i=1}^{n} x_{1i}^2 + b_2 \sum_{i=1}^{n} x_{1i}x_{2i} + b_3 \sum_{i=1}^{n} x_{1i}x_{3i} = \sum_{i=1}^{n} x_{1i}y_i$$
$$b_1 \sum_{i=1}^{n} x_{1i}x_{2i} + b_2 \sum_{i=1}^{n} x_{2i}^2 + b_3 \sum_{i=1}^{n} x_{2i}x_{3i} = \sum_{i=1}^{n} x_{2i}y_i$$
$$b_1 \sum_{i=1}^{n} x_{1i}x_{3i} + b_2 \sum_{i=1}^{n} x_{2i}x_{3i} + b_3 \sum_{i=1}^{n} x_{3i}^2 = \sum_{i=1}^{n} x_{3i}y_i$$

Note that, in contrast to the earlier normal equations (7.8) and (7.9), the x's and y's in (7.30) are not measured as deviations from their arithmetic means.

The extension of (7.30) for larger values of K is straightforward. For example, if $K = 4$, we add a term $-b_4 x_{4i}$ within the parentheses on the right in (7.29) and differentiate with respect to all four b's. When the four derivatives are put equal to zero, we obtain four normal equations, each of which is linear in the four slope coefficients.

Unconstrained LS

Next we shall consider the case in which the constant term must also be adjusted. Thus, for $K = 3$, we extend (7.29) to

(7.31)
$$G(b_0, b_1, b_2, b_3) = \sum_{i=1}^{n} (y_i - b_0 - b_1 x_{1i} - b_2 x_{2i} - b_3 x_{3i})^2$$

The partial derivative with respect to b_0 is

$$\frac{\partial G}{\partial b_0} = -2 \sum_{i=1}^{n} (y_i - b_0 - b_1 x_{1i} - b_2 x_{2i} - b_3 x_{3i})$$

When we equate this to zero, we obtain

(7.32)
$$b_0 = \bar{y} - b_1 \bar{x}_1 - b_2 \bar{x}_2 - b_3 \bar{x}_3$$

where $\bar{y}$, $\bar{x}_1$, and $\bar{x}_2$ are defined in (7.5) and $\bar{x}_3$ is similarly the arithmetic mean of $x_{31}, \ldots, x_{3n}$. Note that (7.32) is the extension of (7.6).

We proceed to substitute (7.32) in (7.31). This yields

(7.33)
$$\sum_{i=1}^{n} [y_i - \bar{y} - b_1(x_{1i} - \bar{x}_1) - b_2(x_{2i} - \bar{x}_2) - b_3(x_{3i} - \bar{x}_3)]^2$$

which is now to be minimized with respect to b_1, b_2, and b_3. But note that (7.33) is identical to the right-hand side of (7.29) except that the four variables are now measured as deviations from their arithmetic means. Thus, subject to this modification, we obtain the same normal equations as those shown in (7.30). We simplify the notation by introducing

(7.34)
$$X_{1i} = x_{1i} - \bar{x}_1, \qquad X_{2i} = x_{2i} - \bar{x}_2, \qquad X_{3i} = x_{3i} - \bar{x}_3$$

so that the normal equations become

$$b_1 \sum_{i=1}^{n} X_{1i}^2 \quad + b_2 \sum_{i=1}^{n} X_{1i}X_{2i} + b_3 \sum_{i=1}^{n} X_{1i}X_{3i} = \sum_{i=1}^{n} X_{1i}(y_i - \bar{y})$$

$$(7.35) \quad b_1 \sum_{i=1}^{n} X_{1i}X_{2i} + b_2 \sum_{i=1}^{n} X_{2i}^2 \quad + b_3 \sum_{i=1}^{n} X_{2i}X_{3i} = \sum_{i=1}^{n} X_{2i}(y_i - \bar{y})$$

$$b_1 \sum_{i=1}^{n} X_{1i}X_{3i} + b_2 \sum_{i=1}^{n} X_{2i}X_{3i} + b_3 \sum_{i=1}^{n} X_{3i}^2 \quad = \sum_{i=1}^{n} X_{3i}(y_i - \bar{y})$$

This result extends the normal equations (7.8) and (7.9) for $K = 3$. The general extension based on (7.28) should now be clear. First, we differentiate (7.28) with respect to b_0. When this derivative is equated to zero, we obtain

$$(7.36) \qquad b_0 = \bar{y} - b_1 \bar{x}_1 - \cdots - b_K \bar{x}_K$$

Next we substitute (7.36) in (7.28), which gives

$$(7.37) \qquad \sum_{i=1}^{n} (y_i - \bar{y} - b_1 X_{1i} - \cdots - b_K X_{Ki})^2$$

where the X's are, as in (7.34), x's measured as deviations from their arithmetic means. Finally, we differentiate (7.37) with respect to $b_1, \ldots, b_K$ and equate each of these derivatives to zero. This yields K normal equations, all linear in $b_1, \ldots, b_K$, the first of which is

$$(7.38) \quad b_1 \sum_{i=1}^{n} X_{1i}^2 + b_2 \sum_{i=1}^{n} X_{1i}X_{2i} + \cdots + b_K \sum_{i=1}^{n} X_{1i}X_{Ki} = \sum_{i=1}^{n} X_{1i}(y_i - \bar{y})$$

A Special Case

It follows from (6.1) that the correlation coefficient of the observation pairs on the first two x variables is

$$\frac{\sum_{i=1}^{n} (x_{1i} - \bar{x}_1)(x_{2i} - \bar{x}_2)}{\sqrt{\sum_{i=1}^{n} (x_{1i} - \bar{x}_1)^2 \sum_{i=1}^{n} (x_{2i} - \bar{x}_2)^2}}$$

Hence, these variables are uncorrelated when $\sum_i (x_{1i} - \bar{x}_1)(x_{2i} - \bar{x}_2) = 0$, which is equivalent to $\sum_i X_{1i}X_{2i} = 0$ in view of (7.34). Suppose that the first x variable is uncorrelated with all others:

$$\sum_{i=1}^{n} X_{1i}X_{2i} = \cdots = \sum_{i=1}^{n} X_{1i}X_{Ki} = 0$$

It follows that (7.38) now becomes $b_1 \sum_i X_{1i}^2 = \sum_i X_{1i}(y_i - \bar{y})$, which has the following solution for b_1:

$$(7.39) \qquad b_1 = \frac{\sum_{i=1}^{n} X_{1i}(y_i - \bar{y})}{\sum_{i=1}^{n} X_{1i}^2} = \frac{\sum_{i=1}^{n} (x_{1i} - \bar{x}_1)(y_i - \bar{y})}{\sum_{i=1}^{n} (x_{1i} - \bar{x}_1)^2}$$

This b_1 is evidently identical to the LS slope coefficient which we obtain by fitting a straight line for y and x_1 only, ignoring all other x variables. Next suppose that the x variables are *all* pairwise uncorrelated, $\sum_i X_{hi}X_{ki} = 0$ for all pairs (h, k) with $h \neq k$. Then the slopes $b_1, \ldots, b_K$ obtained from the normal equations are all equal to the LS slope coefficients of the straight lines fitted for y and the corresponding x variable. This is immediately clear from (7.35) for $K = 3$, where the first equation contains only b_1, the second only b_2, and the third only b_3.

However, uncorrelated x variables are the exception rather than the rule in econometrics. This may be illustrated by means of the normal equations (7.20), where $\sum_i X_{1i}X_{2i} = .00761 \neq 0$. In such cases, the b's obtained from the normal equations will *not* be identical to the corresponding b's obtained from fitting straight lines (see Problem 5).

7.3   Analysis of Residuals

There are certain diagrams which enable the analyst to obtain a better understanding of the relation obtained from LS. These diagrams are based on the LS residuals and adjusted values, which will be considered first.

LS Adjusted Values and Residuals

With $b_1, \ldots, b_K$ obtained from the normal equations and b_0 from (7.36), we define the LS adjusted value of y_i as

$$(7.40) \qquad \hat{y}_i = b_0 + b_1 x_{1i} + \cdots + b_K x_{Ki} \qquad\qquad i = 1, \ldots, n$$

This is a generalization of (2.40). The corresponding residual is

$$(7.41) \qquad e_i = y_i - \hat{y}_i = y_i - (b_0 + b_1 x_{1i} + \cdots + b_K x_{Ki})$$

The residuals $e_1, \ldots, e_n$ have a zero arithmetic mean. This may be verified by summing the first and third members of (7.41) over i:

$$\sum_{i=1}^n e_i = \sum_{i=1}^n y_i - nb_0 - b_1 \sum_{i=1}^n x_{1i} - \cdots - b_K \sum_{i=1}^n x_{Ki}$$

The right-hand side equals $n(\bar{y} - b_0 - b_1\bar{x}_1 - \cdots - b_K\bar{x}_K)$, which is zero in view of (7.36). Therefore, the sum of the e_i's and hence their arithmetic mean are both zero.

By summing the first two members of (7.41) over i and dividing the result by n, we obtain

$$\frac{1}{n}\sum_{i=1}^n e_i = \frac{1}{n}\sum_{i=1}^n y_i - \frac{1}{n}\sum_{i=1}^n \hat{y}_i$$

Since the left-hand side vanishes and the first term on the right equals $\bar{y}$, this proves

$$(7.42) \qquad \frac{1}{n}\sum_{i=1}^n \hat{y}_i = \bar{y}$$

so that the LS adjusted values have an arithmetic mean equal to that of the observed y_i's.

The above results on arithmetic means are valid only when the adjusted equation contains a constant term (b_0). When the LS plane is fitted through the origin, eq. (7.42) need not be true, and the residuals need not have a zero arithmetic mean. An example is given in Problem 6.

Zero-Correlation Properties of the Residuals

Substitution of (7.36) in (7.41) yields

$$(7.43) \qquad \begin{aligned} e_i &= y_i - \bar{y} - b_1(x_{1i} - \bar{x}_1) - \cdots - b_K(x_{Ki} - \bar{x}_K) \\ &= y_i - \bar{y} - b_1 X_{1i} - \cdots - b_K X_{Ki} \end{aligned}$$

where the second step is based on (7.34). Next multiply (7.43) by X_{1i},

$$X_{1i}e_i = X_{1i}(y_i - \bar{y}) - b_1 X_{1i}^2 - \cdots - b_K X_{1i}X_{Ki}$$

and sum over i:

$$\sum_{i=1}^{n} X_{1i}e_i = \sum_{i=1}^{n} X_{1i}(y_i - \bar{y}) - b_1 \sum_{i=1}^{n} X_{1i}^2 - \cdots - b_K \sum_{i=1}^{n} X_{1i}X_{Ki}$$

The right-hand side is zero in view of the normal equation (7.38). Therefore, $\sum_i X_{1i}e_i = \sum_i (x_{1i} - \bar{x}_1)e_i = 0$. The reader should verify that this holds for each of the x variables:

$$(7.44) \qquad \sum_{i=1}^{n} (x_{hi} - \bar{x}_h)e_i = 0 \qquad\qquad h = 1, \ldots, K$$

We conclude that the LS residuals have a zero product sum with the values taken by each x variable. Note that the latter values are measured as deviations from their arithmetic mean ($\bar{x}_h$) and that we have just proved that the arithmetic mean of the e_i's is zero. Therefore, when we apply the correlation coefficient (6.1) to the n observation pairs (x_{hi}, e_i), we shall find a zero value: Each x variable is uncorrelated with the LS residuals.

We write (7.36) in the form $\bar{y} = b_0 + b_1\bar{x}_1 + \cdots + b_K\bar{x}_K$ and subtract this from (7.40):

$$(7.45) \qquad \hat{y}_i - \bar{y} = b_1(x_{1i} - \bar{x}_1) + \cdots + b_K(x_{Ki} - \bar{x}_K)$$

We multiply both sides of this equation by e_i and sum over i:

$$\begin{aligned} \sum_{i=1}^{n} (\hat{y}_i - \bar{y})e_i &= \sum_{i=1}^{n} [b_1(x_{1i} - \bar{x}_1) + \cdots + b_K(x_{Ki} - \bar{x}_K)]e_i \\ &= b_1 \sum_{i=1}^{n} (x_{1i} - \bar{x}_1)e_i + \cdots + b_K \sum_{i=1}^{n} (x_{Ki} - \bar{x}_K)e_i \end{aligned}$$

It follows from (7.44) that each of the K terms in the second line vanishes. Therefore,

$$(7.46) \qquad \sum_{i=1}^{n} (\hat{y}_i - \bar{y})e_i = 0$$

which states that the LS residuals have a zero product sum with the LS adjusted values, the latter being measured as deviations from their arithmetic mean [see (7.42)]. Thus, the correlation coefficient (6.1) applied to the n observation pairs $(\hat{y}_i, e_i)$ is zero.

A Decomposition

The first equal sign in (7.41) implies $e_i = y_i - \bar{y} - (\hat{y}_i - \bar{y})$. We write this in the form

(7.47) $$y_i - \bar{y} = (\hat{y}_i - \bar{y}) + e_i \qquad\qquad i = 1,\ldots,n$$

which expresses $y_i - \bar{y}$ as the sum of the corresponding LS adjusted value and the LS residual. In addition, this LS adjusted value is expressed in (7.45) as the sum of the contributions of all x variables.

Table 13 contains the components of (7.47) and (7.45) for the textile example, the data of which are given in Table 12 on page 96. The first column gives

TABLE 13

Decomposition of textile consumption

Year	$y_i - \bar{y}$	$\hat{y}_i - \bar{y}$	$b_1(x_{1i} - \bar{x}_1)$	$b_2(x_{2i} - \bar{x}_2)$	e_i
1923	−.1256	−.1398	−.0306	−.1092	.0142
1924	−.1265	−.1295	−.0235	−.1060	.0030
1925	−.1221	−.1196	−.0140	−.1056	−.0026
1926	−.0745	−.0603	.0098	−.0701	−.0142
1927	−.0351	−.0436	.0098	−.0534	.0086
1928	−.0517	−.0354	.0311	−.0665	−.0163
1929	−.0390	−.0331	.0369	−.0701	−.0059
1930	.0114	.0059	.0436	−.0377	.0055
1931	.0659	.0524	.0302	.0223	.0135
1932	.0642	.0589	.0117	.0472	.0053
1933	.0779	.0650	−.0056	.0706	.0129
1934	.0259	.0262	−.0373	.0636	−.0004
1935	.0120	.0251	−.0322	.0573	−.0131
1936	.1032	.0996	−.0260	.1256	.0036
1937	.0662	.0779	−.0022	.0801	−.0116
1938	.0510	.0752	−.0061	.0813	−.0241
1939	.0967	.0751	.0045	.0706	.0216
Arithmetic mean	.0000	.0000	.0000	.0000	.0000

the logarithm of the volume of textile consumption per capita in each year, measured as a deviation from the arithmetic mean of these logarithms over all 17 years. The figure at the top in this column $(-.1256)$ is computed by subtracting $\bar{y} = 2.12214$ [see (7.22)] from the corresponding figure (1.99651) in column (4) of Table 12. The third column of Table 13 contains the contribution of real income per capita and the fourth that of the relative textile price, with b_1 and b_2 as shown in (7.21). By adding these two columns, we obtain, in view of (7.45), the $n = 17$ values of $\hat{y}_i - \bar{y}$, which are given in the second column. The last column contains the residuals. As (7.47) shows, these can be obtained by subtracting the second column from the first. (There are discrepancies of at most one unit in the fourth decimal place due to the fact that each figure is rounded individually.)

The Decomposition in Graphical Form

Figure 14 displays the decomposition of Table 13 in graphical form. There are two lines on top, both measuring the volume of textile consumption per capita in logarithmic form. The solid line represents observed behavior (y_i), and the broken line gives the LS adjusted value ($\hat{y}_i$). Below these two lines are the two components of the LS adjusted value, one for real income per capita ($b_1 x_{1i} = 1.1430 x_{1i}$) and one for the relative textile price ($b_2 x_{2i} = -.8289 x_{2i}$). The line at the bottom shows the LS residuals (the vertical distances between the two lines on top). Note that all variables in the figure (y_i, $\hat{y}_i$, $1.1430 x_{1i}$, and $-.8289 x_{2i}$) are measured as deviations from their respective arithmetic means.

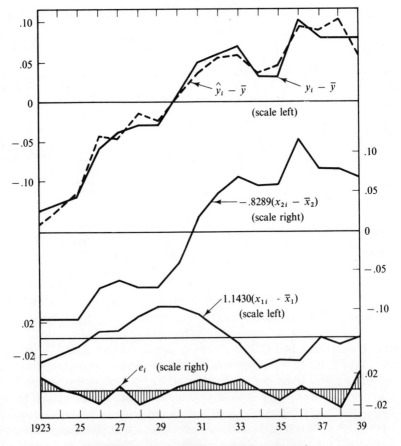

FIGURE 14 Decomposition of textile consumption

Figure 14 is useful in several respects. It shows how closely the logarithm of the volume of textile consumption per capita is approximated by the LS adjustment. In particular, it is worthwhile to check the turning points and to verify whether the two top lines are similar in this respect. In this example the agreement is satisfactory. Also, the figure shows whether a particular change in textile consumption in a certain year is the result of the behavior of one of the x variables, or of the combined influence of several x variables, or of residual effects. It also shows the variables that are more important. In the case of Figure 14 the relative textile price ($-.8289x_{2i}$) seems to dominate real income ($1.1430x_{1i}$). Finally, the figure allows a graphical inspection of residuals. For example, there may be "outliers," in which case the analyst should ponder their causes.

In Figure 14 we describe the logarithm of the volume of textile consumption per capita and its components as functions of time. The LS procedure is frequently applied to cross-sectional rather than time series data (compare the consumption-income relation of Section 5.1), in which case such a figure makes no sense.

Partial Scatter Diagrams

In Figure 1(c) on page 10 we fitted a straight line through certain data for a two-variable relation. The justification was that these data are in reasonable agreement with a linear function. We can extend this to (7.1) by fitting a plane in the three-dimensional space and verifying whether the n observation points are reasonably close to the plane, but such a construction is expensive. When we have three x variables, we would have to work in a four-dimensional space, which is even worse.

A substitute is a series of two-dimensional planes, one for each x variable, with that variable measured horizontally and y corrected for the effect of all other x variables measured vertically. For example, take the first x variable (x_1). The value of y_i corrected for the effect of $x_{2i}, \ldots, x_{Ki}$ and measured as a deviation from the arithmetic mean is

$$y_i - \bar{y} - b_2(x_{2i} - \bar{x}_2) - \cdots - b_K(x_{Ki} - \bar{x}_K) = b_1(x_{1i} - \bar{x}_1) + e_i$$

where the equal sign is based on (7.43). This is applied in Figure 15(a) to the textile example, where $x_{1i} - \bar{x}_1$ is measured along the horizontal axis and

(7.48) $\qquad y_i - \bar{y} + .8289(x_{2i} - \bar{x}_2) = 1.1430(x_{1i} - \bar{x}_1) + e_i$

along the vertical axis. The left-hand side of (7.48) is the ith observation on the logarithm of the volume of textile consumption per capita, corrected for the effect of the relative textile price. This is abbreviated as "textile consumption corrected for price effect" above the vertical axis. The right-hand variable in (7.48), $x_{1i} - \bar{x}_1$, is similarly abbreviated as "income variable" to the right of the horizontal axis.

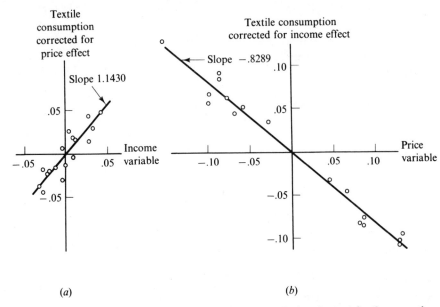

(a)   (b)

FIGURE 15   Partial scatter diagrams for the textile example (see the text for the corrections along the vertical axes)

Figure 15(b) displays the relation between textile consumption and the relative textile price in the same way. Here the vertical variable is

$$y_i - \bar{y} - 1.1430(x_{1i} - \bar{x}_1) = -.8289(x_{2i} - \bar{x}_2) + e_i$$

which is the logarithm of the volume of textile consumption per capita corrected for the effect of real income per capita.

The two scatters of Figure 15 (known as partial scatter diagrams) indicate that the linear form of the LS equation (7.24) is a satisfactory approximation. Notice the much smaller range of variation of the logarithm of real income per capita in Figure 15(a) compared with that of the logarithm of the relative textile price in Figure 15(b). This difference is in agreement with that between the two sums of squares shown in (7.16).

Problems

Problems 1 and 2 refer to Section 7.1, 3–5 to Section 7.2, and 6–9 to Section 7.3.

1   Use (7.6) to prove that the LS fit of (7.1) through the points (7.2) is such that the LS plane goes through the center of gravity $(\bar{x}_1, \bar{x}_2, \bar{y})$ of these points.

2   Substitute the solution (7.21) in the left-hand sides of eqs. (7.20), and compare the result with the right-hand sides.

3 Prove that the normal equations (7.30) can be written in double-sum form,

$$\sum_{k=1}^{3} b_k \sum_{i=1}^{n} x_{hi}x_{ki} = \sum_{i=1}^{n} x_{hi}y_i$$

where $h = 1, 2,$ and 3. Provide a similar formulation for the normal equations (7.35).

4 Equation (7.38) is the first normal equation for K explanatory variables. Derive the second normal equation.

5 Suppose that rather than solving b_1 and b_2 from the normal equations (7.20) we derive them by fitting a straight line for y and the corresponding x variable. Verify that this yields

$$b_1 = \frac{.00276}{.00793} \approx .35, \qquad b_2 = \frac{-.11362}{.14794} \approx -.77$$

Compare this with (7.21), and state your conclusions.

6 Consider the following three triples of observations:

$$\begin{aligned} x_{11} &= 1, & x_{21} &= 0, & y_1 &= 3 \\ x_{12} &= 0, & x_{22} &= 1, & y_2 &= 1\tfrac{1}{2} \\ x_{13} &= 1, & x_{23} &= 1, & y_3 &= 6 \end{aligned}$$

We apply LS through the origin. Prove that the normal equations are

$$b_1 \sum_{i=1}^{n} x_{1i}^2 + b_2 \sum_{i=1}^{n} x_{1i}x_{2i} = \sum_{i=1}^{n} x_{1i}y_i$$
$$b_1 \sum_{i=1}^{n} x_{1i}x_{2i} + b_2 \sum_{i=1}^{n} x_{2i}^2 = \sum_{i=1}^{n} x_{2i}y_i$$

where $n = 3$ in this case. Verify that this yields $b_1 = 3\tfrac{1}{2}$ and $b_2 = 2$ and that the three residuals $y_i - b_1 x_{1i} - b_2 x_{2i}$ are $-\tfrac{1}{2}, -\tfrac{1}{2},$ and $\tfrac{1}{2}$ for $i = 1, 2,$ and 3, respectively. Conclude that these residuals do not have a zero arithmetic mean (compare Problem 7 on page 25).

7 (*Continuation*) Without making any computations, can you assert what the values of the three residuals are when the LS plane is not constrained to pass through the origin?

8 Let the number of x variables be K. Prove that if the LS plane is constrained to pass through the origin, the first normal equation is

$$b_1 \sum_{i=1}^{n} x_{1i}^2 + \cdots + b_K \sum_{i=1}^{n} x_{1i}x_{Ki} = \sum_{i=1}^{n} x_{1i}y_i$$

and that this is equivalent to

$$\sum_{i=1}^{n} x_{1i}(y_i - b_1 x_{1i} - \cdots - b_K x_{Ki}) = 0$$

Since the expression in parentheses is the ith residual obtained from LS through the origin, this proves that the first x variable has a zero product sum with these residuals. [Note that, in contrast to (7.44), x_{1i} is not measured as a deviation from $\bar{x}_1$.] Extend this result to the other x variables.

9 The arithmetic means in the last row of Table 13 are all zero. Prove that this is necessarily so.

chapter 8

Multiple

Regression

In this chapter we shall extend the two-variable regression analysis of Chapter 5 to more variables by means of the LS procedure of Chapter 7. Our first concern is an extension of the standard linear model.

8.1 Extension of the Standard Linear Model

A Statistical Model for Textile Consumption

In Section 5.1 we considered a cross-sectional microrelation between consumption and income. We assumed that for n income values $x_1, \ldots, x_n$ one household is drawn independently at random from the group of all households corresponding to each of these incomes. For the analysis of textile in Section 7.1, which is based on time series data, we proceed differently. We assume that for each year $i = 1923, \ldots, 1939$ the observed value of the volume of textile consumption per capita [column (1) of Table 12 on page 96] is the realization of a random variable. The distribution of such a random variable describes in probabilistic form the set of values which textile consumption could have taken in year i, whereas actually only one value is observed. Our assumption is not concerned with this particular numerical value; it deals with the random process which generates such a value. Our view of the world is that what history shows is just one of the numerous developments that could have taken place, with different probabilities.

As in Section 5.1, we shall be mainly interested in certain conditional expectations and variances. We write y_i, x_{1i}, and x_{2i} for the logarithms of, respectively, the volume of textile consumption per capita, real income per capita, and the relative textile price, all in year i [compare (7.13) to (7.15)]. We assume that the conditional expectation of y_i given x_{1i} and x_{2i} is a linear function of the conditioning factors,

$$(8.1) \qquad \mathcal{E}(y_i \,|\, x_{1i}, x_{2i}) = \beta_0 + \beta_1 x_{1i} + \beta_2 x_{2i}$$
$$i = 1923, \ldots, 1939$$

where β_0, β_1, and β_2, are unknown parameters. Also, we assume that the conditional variance of y_i given x_{1i} and x_{2i} is a constant,

$$(8.2) \qquad \text{var}\,(y_i \,|\, x_{1i}, x_{2i}) = \sigma^2 \qquad i = 1923, \ldots, 1939$$

where σ^2 is an unknown positive parameter which measures the extent to which textile consumption is affected by variables other than income and the textile price (the neglected variables). In addition, we shall make an independence assumption, to be stated in the next subsection. The reader should compare this paragraph with page 62 for the two-variable case.

A General Formulation

In this chapter we shall extend the standard linear model to the case of one dependent variable and an arbitrary number of explanatory variables. In the example of the previous subsection, the dependent variable is the logarithm of the volume of textile consumption per capita, and the explanatory variables are the logarithms of real income per capita and of the relative textile price. As in Section 5.1, we operate conditionally on the n values taken by each explanatory variable; these values are treated as constants. The associated values $y_1, \ldots, y_n$ of the dependent variable are treated as random.

The disturbance formulation of Chapter 5 is also useful here. For the case of textile it takes the form

$$(8.3) \qquad y_i = \beta_0 + \beta_1 x_{1i} + \beta_2 x_{2i} + \epsilon_i$$

where ϵ_i is the disturbance of year i, which describes the combined effect on y_i of all factors other than real income per capita and the relative textile price. We assume that

$$(8.4) \qquad \mathcal{E}\epsilon_i = 0 \qquad i = 1923, \ldots, 1939$$

which is equivalent to (8.1) combined with the treatment of all x values as constants. We also assume that var $\epsilon_i = \sigma^2$ for each i, which is equivalent to (8.2), and that the ϵ_i's are independently distributed. These assumptions imply

$$(8.5) \qquad \mathcal{E}(\epsilon_i \epsilon_j) = \begin{cases} \sigma^2 & \text{if } i = j \\ 0 & \text{if } i \neq j \end{cases}$$

The specifications (8.3) to (8.5) should be compared with (5.3), (5.6), and (5.9). The dichotomy of Table 9 on page 64 also applies to the present case, except that the observable constants now include the values taken by all explanatory variables, and the unobservable constants (the unknown parameters) include more than one slope parameter.

Income and Price Elasticities

The final result of Section 7.1 is given in the equivalent forms (7.24) and (7.25), which are reproduced here:

(8.6) $$y = 1.3742 + 1.1430x_1 - .8289x_2$$

(8.7) $\log_{10}$ (textile consumption per capita)
$$= 1.3742 + 1.1430 \log_{10} \text{ (real income per capita)}$$
$$- .8289 \log_{10} \text{ (relative textile price)}$$

With T defined as the volume of textile consumption per capita, Y as real income per capita, and p as the relative textile price, we take the antilog of (8.7):

(8.8) $$T = 10^{1.3742} Y^{1.1430} p^{-.8289}$$
$$= 23.7 Y^{1.1430} p^{-.8289}$$

This equation is a numerical specification of the relation

(8.9) $$T = c Y^{\alpha} p^{\beta}$$

where c, α, and β are constants.

The derivatives of (8.9) are not constants but vary with Y and p. For example, the partial derivative with respect to Y is

$$\frac{\partial T}{\partial Y} = \alpha c Y^{\alpha-1} p^{\beta}$$

We multiply this by Y/T,

(8.10) $$\frac{\partial T}{\partial Y} \frac{Y}{T} = \frac{\alpha c Y^{\alpha} p^{\beta}}{T} = \alpha$$

where the last step is based on (8.9). Thus, for the relation (8.9) the derivative $\partial T/\partial Y$ multiplied by Y/T equals the constant α.

To interpret (8.10) we imagine that Y increases by a small amount ΔY in (8.9), p remaining constant, and write ΔT for the change in T caused by ΔY. Then the first member of (8.10) equals the limit for $\Delta Y \to 0$ of

(8.11) $$\frac{\Delta T}{\Delta Y} \frac{Y}{T} = \frac{\Delta T/T}{\Delta Y/Y}$$

Suppose that Y increases by 1 percent, $\Delta Y/Y = .01$; then the right-hand side of (8.11) is the percentage change in T caused by the 1 percent increase in Y. Given that both sides of (8.11) are equal to the first member of (8.10) for sufficiently small ΔY, the constant α in (8.10) is thus the *income elasticity* of the demand for textile: When real income increases by a small proportion, the relative textile price remaining unchanged, then the proportionate change in the volume of textile consumption is a multiple α of the proportionate change in real income.

The income elasticity is specified as 1.1430 in (8.8), which means that a 1 percent real income increase raises the volume of textile consumption by 1.1430 percent. Similarly, the *price elasticity* of the demand for textile is β in (8.9), which is specified as $-.8289$ in (8.8); hence, a 1 percent increase in the relative price reduces the volume of textile consumption by .8289 percent.

Four Remarks

(1) The statement, based on (8.9), that a 1 percent increase in Y changes T by α percent is an approximation which is adequate for small changes and will be used in this chapter. In Section 13.2 we shall provide further details on the nature of this approximation.

(2) The specification (8.9) postulates that the income and price elasticities (α and β) are constant over time. This is convenient, and the evidence shown in Figure 15 on page 108 is encouraging. However, such elasticities may actually vary and depend on the levels of real income and the relative textile price. We shall have more to say about this specification in Section 17.1.

(3) Equations (8.7) and (8.8) contain only the relative price of textile, not of other goods and services. This specification should be viewed as a convenient approximation. A more detailed introduction to consumer demand theory is given in Section 14.1.

(4) In the discussion preceding (8.5) we assumed that the ϵ_i's are independently distributed. As in the case of Chapter 5, the analysis of this chapter requires only that the ϵ_i's are all pairwise uncorrelated [see remark (3) on page 89].

8.2 Least Squares in Multiple Regression

We write (8.6) in the form

(8.12) $y = 1.37 + 1.14x_1 - .83x_2 + \text{residual}$

                                   (.31)   (.16)   (.04)

which is a multiple regression, to be compared with the simple regression (5.50). The point estimates in (8.12) have fewer decimal places than in (8.6); this change is made because of the size of the standard errors. These standard errors, shown in (8.12) in parentheses below the corresponding estimates, will be derived in this section.

Review of Earlier Results

As in Section 5.3, we shall need eqs. (2.12), (2.13), and (2.17) of Section 2.2, which are reproduced here:

(8.13) $$\sum_{i=1}^{n} (x_i - \bar{x}) = 0$$

(8.14)
$$\sum_{i=1}^{n} (x_i - \bar{x})(y_i - \bar{y}) = \sum_{i=1}^{n} (x_i - \bar{x})y_i$$

(8.15)
$$\sum_{i=1}^{n} (x_i - \bar{x})^2 = \sum_{i=1}^{n} (x_i - \bar{x})x_i$$

The normal equations (7.8) and (7.9) are our starting point:

$$b_1 \sum_{i=1}^{n} (x_{1i} - \bar{x}_1)^2 + b_2 \sum_{i=1}^{n} (x_{1i} - \bar{x}_1)(x_{2i} - \bar{x}_2) = \sum_{i=1}^{n} (x_{1i} - \bar{x}_1)(y_i - \bar{y})$$

$$b_1 \sum_{i=1}^{n} (x_{1i} - \bar{x}_1)(x_{2i} - \bar{x}_2) + b_2 \sum_{i=1}^{n} (x_{2i} - \bar{x}_2)^2 = \sum_{i=1}^{n} (x_{2i} - \bar{x}_2)(y_i - \bar{y})$$

It follows from (8.14), with x_i interpreted as x_{1i} and hence $\bar{x}$ as $\bar{x}_1$, that the right-hand side of the first normal equation is equal to

$$\sum_{i=1}^{n} (x_{1i} - \bar{x}_1)y_i$$

When we proceed similarly for the second normal equation, we obtain

(8.16)
$$b_1 \sum_{i=1}^{n} (x_{1i} - \bar{x}_1)^2 + b_2 \sum_{i=1}^{n} (x_{1i} - \bar{x}_1)(x_{2i} - \bar{x}_2) = \sum_{i=1}^{n} (x_{1i} - \bar{x}_1)y_i$$

$$b_1 \sum_{i=1}^{n} (x_{1i} - \bar{x}_1)(x_{2i} - \bar{x}_2) + b_2 \sum_{i=1}^{n} (x_{2i} - \bar{x}_2)^2 = \sum_{i=1}^{n} (x_{2i} - \bar{x}_2)y_i$$

The Solution of the Normal Equations

Our first objective is to obtain explicit solutions of the LS slope coefficients b_1 and b_2, for which purpose we introduce a more convenient notation. We use the definition (6.1) for the correlation coefficient of the two explanatory variables:

(8.17)
$$r = \frac{\sum_{i=1}^{n} (x_{1i} - \bar{x}_1)(x_{2i} - \bar{x}_2)}{\sqrt{\sum_{i=1}^{n} (x_{1i} - \bar{x}_1)^2 \sum_{i=1}^{n} (x_{2i} - \bar{x}_2)^2}}$$

Thus, when we also define

(8.18)
$$S_1 = \sqrt{\sum_{i=1}^{n} (x_{1i} - \bar{x}_1)^2}, \qquad S_2 = \sqrt{\sum_{i=1}^{n} (x_{2i} - \bar{x}_2)^2}$$

we have

(8.19)
$$rS_1 S_2 = \sum_{i=1}^{n} (x_{1i} - \bar{x}_1)(x_{2i} - \bar{x}_2)$$

and the normal equations (8.16) can be written as

(8.20)
$$S_1^2 b_1 + r S_1 S_2 b_2 = \sum_{i=1}^{n} (x_{1i} - \bar{x}_1)y_i$$

(8.21)
$$r S_1 S_2 b_1 + S_2^2 b_2 = \sum_{i=1}^{n} (x_{2i} - \bar{x}_2)y_i$$

Next we multiply (8.21) by rS_1/S_2,

$$r^2 S_1^2 b_1 + rS_1 S_2 b_2 = \frac{rS_1}{S_2} \sum_{i=1}^{n} (x_{2i} - \bar{x}_2) y_i$$

and subtract this from (8.20):

$$(1 - r^2)S_1^2 b_1 = \sum_{i=1}^{n} (x_{1i} - \bar{x}_1) y_i - \frac{rS_1}{S_2} \sum_{i=1}^{n} (x_{2i} - \bar{x}_2) y_i$$

$$= \sum_{i=1}^{n} \left[x_{1i} - \bar{x}_1 - \frac{rS_1}{S_2}(x_{2i} - \bar{x}_2) \right] y_i$$

Thus, when we define

(8.22) $$A_{1i} = \frac{x_{1i} - \bar{x}_1 - (rS_1/S_2)(x_{2i} - \bar{x}_2)}{(1 - r^2)S_1^2}$$

we have the following solution of b_1:

(8.23) $$b_1 = \sum_{i=1}^{n} A_{1i} y_i$$

It follows from symmetry considerations that the solution of b_2 is obtained by interchanging the subscripts 1 and 2. Since r defined in (8.17) is symmetric in x_1 and x_2, this yields

(8.24) $$b_2 = \sum_{i=1}^{n} A_{2i} y_i$$

where

(8.25) $$A_{2i} = \frac{x_{2i} - \bar{x}_2 - (rS_2/S_1)(x_{1i} - \bar{x}_1)}{(1 - r^2)S_2^2}$$

The Unbiasedness of the LS Slope Estimators

When we substitute (8.3) in (8.23), we obtain

(8.26) $$b_1 = \sum_{i=1}^{n} A_{1i}(\beta_0 + \beta_1 x_{1i} + \beta_2 x_{2i} + \epsilon_i)$$

$$= \beta_0 \sum_{i=1}^{n} A_{1i} + \beta_1 \sum_{i=1}^{n} A_{1i} x_{1i} + \beta_2 \sum_{i=1}^{n} A_{1i} x_{2i} + \sum_{i=1}^{n} A_{1i} \epsilon_i$$

In the next subsection we shall prove

(8.27) $$\sum_{i=1}^{n} A_{1i} = 0$$

(8.28) $$\sum_{i=1}^{n} A_{1i} x_{1i} = 1$$

(8.29) $$\sum_{i=1}^{n} A_{1i} x_{2i} = 0$$

Substitution of these results in (8.26) yields $b_1 = \beta_1 + \sum_i A_{1i} \epsilon_i$, which is equivalent to

(8.30) $$b_1 - \beta_1 = \sum_{i=1}^{n} A_{1i} \epsilon_i$$

A comparison of (8.30) and (8.23) shows that the sampling error $b_1 - \beta_1$ is the same function of the ϵ_i's as the estimator b_1 is of the y_i's. Also, since r, S_1, and S_2 defined in (8.17) and (8.18) are determined by the x_{1i}'s and x_{2i}'s, A_{1i} defined in (8.22) is also determined by these x's. Therefore, the A_{1i}'s are constants, so that (8.4) and (8.30) imply that b_1 is an unbiased estimator of β_1. Similarly, b_2 is an unbiased estimator of β_2, as will be shown in the next subsection.

Derivations

We use (8.22) in

$$\sum_{i=1}^{n} A_{1i} = \frac{1}{(1 - r^2)S_1^2} \sum_{i=1}^{n} (x_{1i} - \bar{x}_1) - \frac{rS_1}{(1 - r^2)S_1^2 S_2} \sum_{i=1}^{n} (x_{2i} - \bar{x}_2)$$

Both sums on the right vanish in view of (8.13), with x_i interpreted as x_{1i} and x_{2i}, respectively. This proves (8.27).

To verify (8.28), we consider

$$\sum_{i=1}^{n} A_{1i}x_{1i} = \frac{1}{(1 - r^2)S_1^2} \sum_{i=1}^{n} (x_{1i} - \bar{x}_1)x_{1i} - \frac{rS_1}{(1 - r^2)S_1^2 S_2} \sum_{i=1}^{n} (x_{2i} - \bar{x}_2)x_{1i}$$

It follows from (8.15), with x_i interpreted as x_{1i}, that the first sum on the right equals $\sum_i (x_{1i} - \bar{x}_1)^2$. Similarly, (8.14) with x_i interpreted as x_{2i} and y_i as x_{1i} shows that the second sum equals

$$\sum_{i=1}^{n} (x_{2i} - \bar{x}_2)(x_{1i} - \bar{x}_1)$$

so that $\sum_i A_{1i}x_{1i}$ is equal to

$$\frac{1}{(1 - r^2)S_1^2} \sum_{i=1}^{n} (x_{1i} - \bar{x}_1)^2 - \frac{rS_1}{(1 - r^2)S_1^2 S_2} \sum_{i=1}^{n} (x_{1i} - \bar{x}_1)(x_{2i} - \bar{x}_2)$$

$$= \frac{1}{(1 - r^2)S_1^2} S_1^2 - \frac{r}{(1 - r^2)S_1 S_2} rS_1 S_2 = \frac{1}{1 - r^2}(1 - r^2) = 1$$

where the first equal sign is based on (8.18) and (8.19). This completes the proof of (8.28).

Finally, to verify (8.29), we consider

$$\sum_{i=1}^{n} A_{1i}x_{2i} = \frac{1}{(1 - r^2)S_1^2} \sum_{i=1}^{n} (x_{1i} - \bar{x}_1)x_{2i} - \frac{rS_1}{(1 - r^2)S_1^2 S_2} \sum_{i=1}^{n} (x_{2i} - \bar{x}_2)x_{2i}$$

which we similarly write as

$$\frac{1}{(1 - r^2)S_1^2} \sum_{i=1}^{n} (x_{1i} - \bar{x}_1)(x_{2i} - \bar{x}_2) - \frac{rS_1}{(1 - r^2)S_1^2 S_2} \sum_{i=1}^{n} (x_{2i} - \bar{x}_2)^2$$

$$= \frac{1}{(1 - r^2)S_1^2} rS_1 S_2 - \frac{r}{(1 - r^2)S_1 S_2} S_2^2 = \frac{1}{1 - r^2}\left(\frac{rS_2}{S_1} - \frac{rS_2}{S_1}\right) = 0$$

This completes the proof of (8.29).

For the sampling error of b_2 we have, with A_{2i} defined in (8.25),

(8.31)
$$b_2 - \beta_2 = \sum_{i=1}^{n} A_{2i}\epsilon_i$$

This is similar to (8.30) and establishes the unbiasedness of b_2. The derivation of (8.31) is a matter of interchanging the subscripts 1 and 2 in (8.30), but it is of course also possible to derive (8.31) directly (see Problem 5).

The Sampling Variances of the LS Slope Estimators

Since b_1 has expectation β_1, we obtain the variance of b_1 by squaring both sides of (8.30),

$$(b_1 - \beta_1)^2 = \left(\sum_{i=1}^{n} A_{1i}\epsilon_i\right)^2 = \sum_{i=1}^{n}\sum_{j=1}^{n} A_{1i}A_{1j}\epsilon_i\epsilon_j$$

and then taking the expectation. Using the constancy of the A's as well as (8.5), we thus obtain

$$\text{var } b_1 = \sum_{i=1}^{n}\sum_{j=1}^{n} A_{1i}A_{1j}\mathcal{E}(\epsilon_i\epsilon_j) = \sum_{i=1}^{n} A_{1i}^2\mathcal{E}(\epsilon_i^2) = \sigma^2 \sum_{i=1}^{n} A_{1i}^2$$

In the next subsection we shall prove

(8.32)
$$\sum_{i=1}^{n} A_{1i}^2 = \frac{1}{(1-r^2)\sum_{i=1}^{n}(x_{1i} - \bar{x}_1)^2}$$

so that the result is

(8.33)
$$\text{var } b_1 = \frac{\sigma^2}{(1-r^2)\sum_{i=1}^{n}(x_{1i} - \bar{x}_1)^2}$$

By interchanging the subscripts 1 and 2, we obtain

(8.34)
$$\text{var } b_2 = \frac{\sigma^2}{(1-r^2)\sum_{i=1}^{n}(x_{2i} - \bar{x}_2)^2}$$

The results (8.33) and (8.34) are the extension of the sampling variance (5.31) for the slope estimators in multiple regressions on two explanatory variables. The factor $1 - r^2$ which occurs in this extension is further discussed in Section 8.3.

More Derivations

The square of A_{1i} defined in (8.22) equals

(8.35)
$$\frac{(x_{1i} - \bar{x}_1)^2 + (r^2 S_1^2/S_2^2)(x_{2i} - \bar{x}_2)^2 - (2rS_1/S_2)(x_{1i} - \bar{x}_1)(x_{2i} - \bar{x}_2)}{(1-r^2)^2 S_1^4}$$

Since the denominator $(1 - r^2)^2 S_1^4$ does not involve the subscript i, we obtain the sum of the squares of the A_{1i}'s by summing the numerator over i and then dividing the sum by this denominator. Using (8.18) and (8.19), we find that the sum of the numerator equals

$$\sum_{i=1}^{n} (x_{1i} - \bar{x}_1)^2 + \frac{r^2 S_1^2}{S_2^2} \sum_{i=1}^{n} (x_{2i} - \bar{x}_2)^2 - \frac{2rS_1}{S_2} \sum_{i=1}^{n} (x_{1i} - \bar{x}_1)(x_{2i} - \bar{x}_2)$$

$$= S_1^2 + \frac{r^2 S_1^2}{S_2^2} S_2^2 - \frac{2rS_1}{S_2} r S_1 S_2 = (1 - r^2) S_1^2$$

When we divide the third member by the denominator of (8.35), we obtain $1/(1 - r^2) S_1^2$. This is equal to the right-hand side of (8.32), so that the proof of (8.32) is thus completed.

The LS Estimator of the Disturbance Variance

The LS residual corresponding to the disturbance ϵ_i of (8.3) is defined as

$$(8.36) \qquad\qquad e_i = y_i - b_0 - b_1 x_{1i} - b_2 x_{2i}$$

where b_0, b_1, and b_2 are the LS estimators of β_0, β_1, and β_2. In Sections 5.2 and 5.3 we proved, for simple regressions with and without constant term, that an unbiased estimator of the disturbance variance σ^2 is obtained by dividing the residual sum of squares by the number of degrees of freedom: the number of observations (n) minus the number of coefficients adjusted. In the present case three b's are adjusted, so that there are $n - 3$ degrees of freedom. Accordingly, the LS estimator of σ^2 is defined as

$$(8.37) \qquad\qquad s^2 = \frac{1}{n - 3} \sum_{i=1}^{n} e_i^2$$

which is indeed an unbiased estimator:

$$(8.38) \qquad\qquad \mathcal{E}(s^2) = \sigma^2$$

This unbiasedness is not proved here, but in Appendix B we provide a proof (involving matrix algebra) for unbiased σ^2 estimation with an arbitrary number of explanatory variables.

Application to the Demand for Textile

We have 17 annual observations in Table 12 on page 96, which yield $17 - 3 = 14$ degrees of freedom. The 17 residuals shown in the last column of Table 13 on page 105 have a sum of squares equal to .002567 (in six decimal places). It follows from (8.37) that this is to be divided by 14 to yield an unbiased estimate of σ^2:

$$(8.39) \qquad\qquad s^2 = \frac{.002567}{14} \approx .0001833$$

For the correlation coefficient r defined in (8.17), when applied to the logarithms of real income per capita and the relative textile price, we use (7.16) and (7.17), which gives

$$(8.40) \qquad r = \frac{.00761}{\sqrt{(.00793)(.14794)}} \approx .222$$

Next, by substituting s^2 for σ^2 in (8.33) and (8.34), we obtain the following estimates of the sampling variances of b_1 and b_2:

$$(8.41) \qquad \frac{s^2}{(1 - r^2) \sum\limits_{i=1}^{17} (x_{1i} - \bar{x}_1)^2} \approx .024324$$

$$(8.42) \qquad \frac{s^2}{(1 - r^2) \sum\limits_{i=1}^{17} (x_{2i} - \bar{x}_2)^2} \approx .001304$$

The standard errors .16 and .04 in (8.12) are the square roots of the estimated variances (8.41) and (8.42), respectively. Note in particular that the standard error .04 of the estimate $-.83$ of the price elasticity is much smaller than the standard error .16 of the estimate 1.14 of the income elasticity. A comparison of the left-hand sides of (8.41) and (8.42) shows that this is exclusively due to the difference between $\sum_i (x_{1i} - \bar{x}_1)^2 = .00793$ and $\sum_i (x_{2i} - \bar{x}_2)^2 = .14794$. The latter value, when divided by 17, is the mean square of the logarithms of the relative textile price (measured as deviations from their arithmetic mean), which is thus considerably larger than the mean square of the logarithms of real income per capita. Such mean squares are a measure of variability of the values of an explanatory variable. The results (8.41) and (8.42) illustrate that an accurate estimation of a slope coefficient requires that the values of the corresponding explanatory variable be sufficiently dispersed. The difference in dispersion of the two explanatory variables in this case is also illustrated by the two partial scatter diagrams in Figure 15 on page 108.

The Sampling Covariance of the LS Slope Estimators

In Section 6.3 we considered the sampling covariance of the LS slope and constant-term estimators for a simple regression. We shall extend this now to the covariance of the slope estimators b_1 and b_2. Since these are unbiased estimators of β_1 and β_2, respectively, their covariance is obtained by multiplying (8.30) and (8.31),

$$(b_1 - \beta_1)(b_2 - \beta_2) = \left(\sum_{i=1}^{n} A_{1i}\epsilon_i\right)\left(\sum_{j=1}^{n} A_{2j}\epsilon_j\right) = \sum_{i=1}^{n} \sum_{j=1}^{n} A_{1i}A_{2j}\epsilon_i\epsilon_j$$

and taking the expectation. Using the constancy of the A's and (8.5), we thus obtain

$$\text{cov}\,(b_1, b_2) = \sum_{i=1}^{n} \sum_{j=1}^{n} A_{1i}A_{2j}\mathcal{E}(\epsilon_i\epsilon_j) = \sum_{i=1}^{n} A_{1i}A_{2i}\mathcal{E}(\epsilon_i^2) = \sigma^2 \sum_{i=1}^{n} A_{1i}A_{2i}$$

and hence, using

$$(8.43) \qquad \sum_{i=1}^{n} A_{1i}A_{2i} = -\frac{r}{(1 - r^2)S_1 S_2}$$

as well as the definitions of S_1 and S_2 given in (8.18),

$$(8.44) \qquad \text{cov}\,(b_1, b_2) = -\frac{r\sigma^2}{(1 - r^2)\sqrt{\sum_{i=1}^{n}(x_{1i} - \bar{x}_1)^2 \sum_{i=1}^{n}(x_{2i} - \bar{x}_2)^2}}$$

The derivation of (8.43) is similar to that of (8.32); intermediate steps are given in Problem 7.

Estimating a Linear Combination of Slope Parameters

The sampling covariance of b_1 and b_2 plays a role in the analysis of linear combinations of β_1 and β_2. For example, let there be a 1 percent increase in real income per capita and a 2 percent decrease in the relative textile price. Since β_1 and β_2 in (8.3) are the income and price elasticity, respectively, of the demand for textile, the effect on the volume of textile consumption per capita is an increase of $\beta_1 - 2\beta_2$ percent. The LS estimate of $\beta_1 - 2\beta_2$ is

$$(8.45) \qquad b_1 - 2b_2 = 1.1430 - 2(-.8289) \approx 2.80$$

where the first equal sign is based on the LS coefficients given in (8.6). Hence, the LS estimated effect of the income and price changes mentioned above is an increase of 2.80 percent in the volume of textile consumption per capita.

More generally, let the linear combination be $w_1\beta_1 + w_2\beta_2$, where w_1 and w_2 are constants. The estimator of this combination is $w_1b_1 + w_2b_2$, which is unbiased and has the following variance in view of (4.37):

$$(8.46) \quad \text{var}\,(w_1b_1 + w_2b_2) = w_1^2 \,\text{var}\, b_1 + w_2^2 \,\text{var}\, b_2 + 2w_1w_2 \,\text{cov}\,(b_1, b_2)$$

In the case discussed in the previous paragraph we have $w_1 = 1$ and $w_2 = -2$, so that

$$(8.47) \qquad \text{var}\,(b_1 - 2b_2) = \text{var}\, b_1 + 4 \,\text{var}\, b_2 - 4 \,\text{cov}\,(b_1, b_2)$$

The variances and covariance on the right are given in (8.33), (8.34), and (8.44). All three involve the unknown parameter σ^2, which we replace by s^2, leading to the estimates (8.41) and (8.42) of var b_1 and var b_2. For the covariance (8.44) we proceed similarly, using (8.40) for r and (7.16) for the sums of squares of the x_{1i}'s and x_{2i}'s. This yields an estimate of $-.001251$ of the covariance of b_1 and b_2. Substitution of these results in (8.47) gives the following estimate of the variance of $b_1 - 2b_2$:

$$(8.48) \qquad .024324 + 4(.001304) - 4(-.001251) \approx .0345$$

The square root of .0345 is .19 in two decimal places. Hence, the LS estimate of 2.80 percent obtained from (8.45) has a standard error of .19 percent. Applying the two-sigma rule, we obtain a lower bound of $2.80 - 2(.19) \approx 2.4$ percent for the increase in the volume of textile consumption per capita and an upper bound of $2.80 + 2(.19) \approx 3.2$ percent.

The LS Estimator of the Constant Term

By summing (8.3) over i and dividing the result by n, we obtain

$$(8.49) \qquad \bar{y} = \beta_0 + \beta_1 \bar{x}_1 + \beta_2 \bar{x}_2 + \frac{1}{n} \sum_{i=1}^{n} \epsilon_i$$

We write $b_0 = \bar{y} - b_1 \bar{x}_1 - b_2 \bar{x}_2$ [see (7.6)] in the form $\bar{y} = b_0 + b_1 \bar{x}_1 + b_2 \bar{x}_2$ and subtract this from (8.49) to obtain

$$(8.50) \qquad b_0 - \beta_0 = \frac{1}{n} \sum_{i=1}^{n} \epsilon_i - \bar{x}_1 (b_1 - \beta_1) - \bar{x}_2 (b_2 - \beta_2)$$

$$= \frac{1}{n} \sum_{i=1}^{n} \epsilon_i - \bar{x}_1 \sum_{i=1}^{n} A_{1i} \epsilon_i - \bar{x}_2 \sum_{i=1}^{n} A_{2i} \epsilon_i$$

where the second step is based on (8.30) and (8.31). Since the expression in the second line of (8.50) is a weighted sum of the ϵ_i's with constant weights, the unbiasedness of b_0 follows directly from (8.4).

The sampling variance of b_0 is obtained by squaring (8.50) and taking the expectation. This yields

$$(8.51) \qquad \text{var } b_0 = \frac{\sigma^2}{n} + \bar{x}_1^2 \text{ var } b_1 + \bar{x}_2^2 \text{ var } b_2 + 2\bar{x}_1 \bar{x}_2 \text{ cov } (b_1, b_2)$$

which is an extension of (5.38). The reader who is interested in the derivation of (8.51) should consult Problem 11.

All four terms in the right-hand side of (8.51) involve the unknown parameter σ^2. If we replace σ^2 by s^2 given in (8.39) and use $n = 17$ as well as (7.22) for $\bar{x}_1$ and $\bar{x}_2$, the following estimate of var b_0 results:

$$(8.52) \qquad \frac{.0001833}{17} + (2.01223)^2(.024324) + (1.87258)^2(.001304)$$

$$+ 2(2.01223)(1.87258)(-.001251) \approx .0936$$

The square root of .0936 is .31 (in two decimal places), which is the standard error of the constant-term estimate shown in (8.12).

8.3 Multicollinearity

The variance results (8.33) and (8.34) may be written as

$$(8.53) \qquad \text{var } b_h = \frac{\sigma^2}{(1 - r^2) \sum_{i=1}^{n} (x_{hi} - \bar{x}_h)^2} \qquad h = 1, 2$$

which should be compared with $\sigma^2 / \sum_i (x_i - \bar{x})^2$, the sampling variance of the LS slope estimator which we obtained in (5.31) for simple regressions. The major difference is evidently the factor $1 - r^2$ in the denominator of (8.53).

This factor equals 1 and can thus be ignored in (8.53) when the two explanatory variables are uncorrelated ($r = 0$). We considered the case of uncorrelated explanatory variables in the last subsection of Section 7.2 but noted at the end of that subsection that this is an exceptional case in econometrics. Here, we shall find it convenient to start with the other extreme, $r^2 = 1$, in which case the denominator of (8.53) vanishes.

An Algebraic Approach

If $r^2 = 1$ in (8.53), then either $r = 1$ or $r = -1$ for the two x variables in (8.17). Recall from Section 6.1 that $r^2 = 1$ implies that these variables are linearly related,

$$(8.54) \qquad\qquad x_{2i} = a_0 + a x_{1i} \qquad\qquad i = 1, \ldots, n$$

where $a > 0$ if $r = 1$ and $a < 0$ if $r = -1$. Let us write (8.3) in the form

$$y_i = \beta_0 + \beta_1 x_{1i} + \beta_2' x_{2i} + (\beta_2 - \beta_2') x_{2i} + \epsilon_i$$

where β_2' is an arbitrary constant. For x_{2i} in the third term we substitute the right-hand side of (8.54):

$$y_i = \beta_0 + \beta_1 x_{1i} + \beta_2'(a_0 + a x_{1i}) + (\beta_2 - \beta_2') x_{2i} + \epsilon_i$$

This can be written as

$$(8.55) \qquad y_i = \beta_0 + \beta_2' a_0 + (\beta_1 + \beta_2' a) x_{1i} + (\beta_2 - \beta_2') x_{2i} + \epsilon_i$$

which is a linear relation with slope coefficients $\beta_1 + \beta_2' a$ and $\beta_2 - \beta_2'$ and constant term $\beta_0 + \beta_2' a_0$. If $\beta_2' = 0$, these three coefficients become β_1, β_2, and β_0, respectively, so that (8.55) is then identical to (8.3). But since β_2' is arbitrary, (8.55) yields infinitely many specifications of the relation between y and the explanatory variables x_1 and x_2.

The cause of this problem is the linear relation (8.54). If the two explanatory variables are linearly related, there is no way in which we can separate the effects of these variables on y in (8.3). This follows from the fact that the slope coefficients in (8.55) vary arbitrarily when β_2' is given different values. In fact, the LS normal equations yield no unique solutions under (8.54). Note that (8.54) amounts to a second linear relation, viz., between x_1 and x_2, in addition to the linear relation (8.3) in which we are interested. Accordingly, the problem considered here is known as *multicollinearity*.

A Geometric Approach

Figure 16 illustrates the multicollinearity problem in a three-dimensional space, with x_1 and x_2 measured along two horizontal axes and y along the vertical axis. Assume first that the ϵ_i's are all zero in (8.3), so that y is an exact linear function of x_1 and x_2. The observation points (x_{1i}, x_{2i}, y_i) for $i = 1, \ldots, n$ are then all located in a plane in the (x_1, x_2, y) space. This is the plane

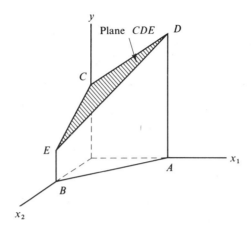

FIGURE 16   Illustration of multicollinearity

through C, D, and E in the figure. But if $r = \pm 1$, the observations on x_1 and x_2 are on a straight line, indicated by AB in the (x_1, x_2) plane, so that the points (x_{1i}, x_{2i}, y_i) are not only in the plane CDE but also vertically above AB. That is, all n points must be on the line DE in the plane CDE, the lines AD and BE both being vertical (parallel to the y axis). It is obvious, however, that there are infinitely many planes through the straight line DE. This is equivalent to saying that if $r = \pm 1$, the n observation points (x_{1i}, x_{2i}, y_i) do not enable us to obtain a unique regression plane in the (x_1, x_2, y) space.

Above we assumed that y is an exact linear function of x_1 and x_2. If it is not, as is the case under (8.3) when the disturbance variance σ^2 is nonzero, the points (x_{1i}, x_{2i}, y_i) are randomly scattered above and below the plane CDE. If $r = \pm 1$, these points are all in the vertical plane through AB, so that they are randomly scattered above and below the line DE. As in the case of the previous paragraph, such observation points do not enable us to obtain a unique plane in the (x_1, x_2, y) space.

Extreme and Near-Extreme Multicollinearity

The case $r^2 = 1$ ($r = 1$ or $r = -1$) is that of extreme multicollinearity. When r is not equal but close to 1 or -1, we have near-extreme multicollinearity. In applied econometrics this occurs much more frequently than extreme multi-collinearity. In particular, when the observations take the form of time series data, we may easily have near-extreme multicollinearity because different explana-tory variables may be subject to similar trends and almost simultaneous ups and downs.

If r is not equal to but close to 1 or -1, then $1 - r^2$ is positive but small, so that the sampling variance (8.53) is large, which implies that the LS slope estimators b_1 and b_2 are inaccurate. This result is not difficult to understand.

Estimating β_1 and β_2 of (8.3) is an attempt to assess the separate effects of x_1 and x_2 on y. But if r is close to 1 or -1, x_1 and x_2 are almost exactly linear functions of each other. It stands to reason that it is very difficult to separate the effects of x_1 and x_2 when their behavior as revealed by the n observations is so similar. This difficulty is reflected by the large value of the variances of the LS slope coefficients of the two variables.

The geometry of Figure 16 is also illustrative for near-extreme multicollinearity. If r is close but not equal to 1 or -1, the observation pairs (x_{1i}, x_{2i}) are rather close to the line AB in the (x_1, x_2) plane (see the two diagrams immediately below the top in Figure 12 on page 86). Accordingly, the points representing the observation triples (x_{1i}, x_{2i}, y_i) are then not all above or below DE, as they are under extreme multicollinearity. These points are characterized by certain horizontal deviations from the line DE; typically, most of these points are located inside a "cigar" around DE. Such horizontal deviations imply that the normal equations can be solved to yield unique solutions of b_1 and b_2 and hence a unique regression plane. However, the fact that these deviations tend to be small implies that the present situation is close to extreme multicollinearity, so that the variance (8.53) takes a large value.

8.4 Extensions

The above analysis can be generalized for three and more explanatory variables, but the derivations are tedious. It is much more attractive to use matrix algebra, as is done in Appendix B. The main results are summarized below.

The General Case

(1) When (8.3) is extended to include more explanatory variables, the slope coefficients b_1, b_2, ... obtained from the normal equations and $b_0 = \bar{y} - b_1\bar{x}_1 - b_2\bar{x}_2 - \ldots$ are unbiased estimators of the corresponding β's. This result is based on the zero expectations of the ϵ_i's and the constancy of the x_i's; it does not require condition (8.5).

(2) The generalization for more explanatory variables involves the sampling variances of all LS coefficients and the sampling covariances of all pairs of LS coefficients. These variances and covariances do require condition (8.5). In Section 9.3, where the discussion of multicollinearity continues, we shall provide a simple extension of the variance result (8.53).

(3) As in (8.44) and (8.53), the sampling variances and covariances involve the unknown σ^2. An unbiased estimator of σ^2, similar to (8.37), is obtained by dividing the sum of squares of the LS residuals by the number of degrees of freedom: the number of observations (n) minus the number of coefficients adjusted. For example, there are $n - 4$ degrees of freedom when there are three slope coefficients and a constant term. The unbiasedness of this σ^2 estimator requires condition (8.5).

(4) When (8.3) is modified so that it contains more explanatory variables

but no constant term ($\beta_0 = 0$), unbiased estimators of the β's are obtained from the normal equations in which the x's are not measured as deviations from their arithmetic means. Such normal equations are shown in (7.30) for three slope coefficients. The number of degrees of freedom in this case is $n - 3$ (because no constant term is adjusted).

The Gauss-Markov Theorem

In Section 5.4 we proved for simple regressions that under the standard linear model with $\beta_0 = 0$ the LS slope estimator through the origin is best linear unbiased in the sense that it has minimum sampling variance in the class of all unbiased linear estimators of β. We stated thereafter that the unconstrained LS estimators of β and β_0 have the same property when $\beta_0 = 0$ is not imposed. This result can be extended for multiple regression: The LS estimators b_0, b_1, and b_2 of β_0, β_1, and β_2 in (8.3) are all best linear unbiased.

The Gauss-Markov theorem, which is proved in Appendix B, provides a further extension. Consider *any linear combination* of the β's of (8.3), such as $\beta_1 - 2\beta_2$. The corresponding LS estimator $b_1 - 2b_2$ is linear in the y_i's [see (8.23) and (8.24)], and it is unbiased; its sampling variance is obtained from (8.47). The Gauss-Markov theorem states that there is no other unbiased linear estimator of $\beta_1 - 2\beta_2$ which has a smaller sampling variance. Thus, 2.80 in (8.45) is a best linear unbiased estimate of $\beta_1 - 2\beta_2$; .0345 in (8.48) is an unbiased estimate of the sampling variance of the LS estimator $b_1 - 2b_2$; and this sampling variance is the smallest variance of any unbiased linear estimator of $\beta_1 - 2\beta_2$.

The linear combination $\beta_1 - 2\beta_2$ is just one example. We may extend (8.3) so that it contains any number of β's, say β_0, β_1, β_2, β_3, and β_4, and consider any linear combination of these, say $w_1\beta_1 + w_3\beta_3 + w_4\beta_4$, where the w's are constants. The Gauss-Markov theorem states that the LS expression $w_1b_1 + w_3b_3 + w_4b_4$ is a best linear unbiased estimator of this combination.

Problems

Problems 1 and 2 refer to Section 8.1, 3–12 to Section 8.2, 13 and 14 to Section 8.3, and 15 and 16 to Section 8.4.

1 Verify from (8.9) that $\partial T/\partial p = \beta c Y^\alpha p^{\beta-1}$. Use this to prove that β is the elasticity of the demand for textile with respect to the relative textile price, and explain in words what that means.

2 Prove that the income elasticity in the first member of (8.10) can be written in the form of a logarithmic derivative:

$$\frac{\partial T}{\partial Y} \frac{Y}{T} = \frac{\partial \log T}{\partial \log Y}$$

(*Note*: This result also holds when the elasticity is not a constant.)

3 Verify the solution (8.24) of the normal equations (8.20) and (8.21) directly, without using symmetry considerations.

4 It is stated below (8.30) that the sampling error $b_1 - \beta_1$ is the same function of the ϵ_i's as the estimator b_1 is of the y_i's. Verify that the LS slope estimators in Sections 5.2 and 5.3 have the same property.

5 Verify (8.31) directly. (*Hint*: Prove first that $\sum_i A_{2i} = \sum_i A_{2i}x_{1i} = 0$ and $\sum_i A_{2i}x_{2i} = 1$.)

6 Verify that the unbiasedness of the LS estimators b_0, b_1, and b_2 requires the constancy of the x_{1i}'s and x_{2i}'s and the validity of (8.4) but not the validity of (8.5). [*Note*: The unbiasedness property (8.38) does require (8.5).]

7 Prove (8.43). [*Hint*: First multiply A_{1i} and A_{2i} as shown in (8.22) and (8.25), and verify that the product $A_{1i}A_{2i}$ equals a ratio whose denominator is the square of $(1 - r^2)S_1S_2$. Then sum the numerator over i, and use (8.18) and (8.19) to verify that this sum is equal to $-r(1 - r^2)S_1S_2$.]

8 Use (8.33), (8.34), and (8.44) to prove that the sampling correlation coefficient of the LS slope coefficients equals $-r$, that is, minus the correlation coefficient of the observation pairs (x_{1i}, x_{2i}) of the two explanatory variables. (*Note*: This result holds only for regressions on two explanatory variables with constant term.)

9 In the discussion preceding (8.46) it is stated that $w_1b_1 + w_2b_2$ is an unbiased estimator of $w_1\beta_1 + w_2\beta_2$. Prove that this estimator is indeed unbiased when w_1 and w_2 are constants.

10 Use (8.3) to prove that the percentage change in the volume of textile consumption per capita which results from (a) a 1 percent increase in real income per capita and (b) a 2 percent increase in the relative textile price equals $\beta_1 + 2\beta_2$. Verify that an unbiased estimate of this change is a decrease of .515 percent in the volume of textile consumption per capita and that the standard error of this estimate is .16 percent. [*Hint*: Make appropriate changes in (8.45) and (8.48).]

11 Write $\bar{\epsilon} = (\epsilon_1 + \cdots + \epsilon_n)/n$ and use (8.50) to prove that the sampling variance of b_0 equals

$$\mathcal{E}(\bar{\epsilon}^2) + \bar{x}_1^2 \text{ var } b_1 + \bar{x}_2^2 \text{ var } b_2 + 2\bar{x}_1\bar{x}_2 \text{ cov } (b_1, b_2)$$
$$- 2\bar{x}_1\mathcal{E}[(b_1 - \beta_1)\bar{\epsilon}] - 2\bar{x}_2\mathcal{E}[(b_2 - \beta_2)\bar{\epsilon}]$$

Verify that this yields (8.51) if

$$\mathcal{E}(\bar{\epsilon}^2) = \frac{\sigma^2}{n}, \qquad \mathcal{E}[(b_1 - \beta_1)\bar{\epsilon}] = \mathcal{E}[(b_2 - \beta_2)\bar{\epsilon}] = 0$$

which is to be proved. [*Hint*: See the last subsection of Section 5.3 and use (8.30) for $b_1 - \beta_1$.]

12 Verify that the numerical results in the second members of (8.41), (8.42), and (8.52) are unbiased estimates of the sampling variances of b_1, b_2, and b_0, respectively. Also verify that the estimate $-.001251$ of the sampling covariance of b_1 and b_2 [see the discussion preceding (8.48)] is unbiased and that .0345 in (8.48) is an unbiased estimate of the sampling variance of $b_1 - 2b_2$.

13 Verify that (8.20) becomes $S_1^2 b_1 + S_1 S_2 b_2 = \sum_i (x_{1i} - \bar{x}_1) y_i$ when $r = 1$. Multiply this by S_2 / S_1:

$$S_1 S_2 b_1 + S_2^2 b_2 = \frac{S_2}{S_1} \sum_{i=1}^{n} (x_{1i} - \bar{x}_1) y_i$$

Prove that this is identical to (8.21) if $r = 1$, so that $r = 1$ implies that the two normal equations are effectively only one equation and, therefore, do not enable us to obtain both b_1 and b_2. [*Hint*: If $r = 1$, the observation pairs (x_{1i}, x_{2i}) are on a straight line whose slope is equal to the ratio of the two S's.] Then extend this result to the case $r = -1$.

14 Let s^2, $\sum_i (x_{1i} - \bar{x}_1)^2$, and $\sum_i (x_{2i} - \bar{x}_2)^2$ remain as they are in (8.41) and (8.42), but consider the following alternative values of r: $r = 0$, $r = .222$ [see (8.40)], and $r = .99$. Compute the standard errors of the slope coefficients under these three different specifications, and draw your conclusions.

15 Read the last sentence in the next-to-last paragraph of Section 8.4, and provide a similar interpretation for the numbers .515 and .16 in Problem 10.

16 Prove that the best linear unbiasedness of b and b_0 (stated in Section 5.4) is a special case of the Gauss-Markov theorem.

chapter 9

Multiple
Correlation

In Section 9.1 we shall address ourselves to one of the questions raised in the opening paragraph of Chapter 7. Given that demand theory indicates real income and relative prices as the factors determining the consumption of goods and services, to what extent do these variables account for the observed variation of textile consumption over time? In Section 9.2 we shall consider a related question, viz., whether it is possible to measure the contribution of each explanatory variable (real income and the relative textile price in this case) to the explanation of textile consumption. In Section 9.3 we shall return to the multicollinearity discussion of Section 8.3 and extend it to the case of three and more explanatory variables.

It should be understood that *all* regressions in this chapter contain a constant term. The case without constant terms is more complicated; see Theil (1971, pp. 175–178).

9.1 The Coefficient of Multiple Correlation

Review of Earlier Results

In this section we shall use the LS adjusted values and residuals which were introduced in Section 7.3. They are defined in (7.40) and (7.41), reproduced below:

(9.1) $$\hat{y}_i = b_0 + b_1 x_{1i} + \cdots + b_K x_{Ki}$$
(9.2) $$e_i = y_i - \hat{y}_i = y_i - (b_0 + b_1 x_{1i} + \cdots + b_K x_{Ki})$$

We shall use eqs. (7.42) and (7.45) to (7.47). It is convenient to reproduce these also:

(9.3)
$$\frac{1}{n} \sum_{i=1}^{n} \hat{y}_i = \bar{y}$$

(9.4)
$$\hat{y}_i - \bar{y} = b_1(x_{1i} - \bar{x}_1) + \cdots + b_K(x_{Ki} - \bar{x}_K)$$

(9.5)
$$\sum_{i=1}^{n} (\hat{y}_i - \bar{y})e_i = 0$$

(9.6)
$$y_i - \bar{y} = (\hat{y}_i - \bar{y}) + e_i$$

Definition of the Multiple Correlation Coefficient

The multiple correlation coefficient R associated with the regression of a dependent variable y on K explanatory variables $x_1, \ldots, x_K$ is defined as the ordinary correlation coefficient of the LS adjusted values and the observed values of the dependent variable. It follows from (9.3) that this correlation coefficient can be written as

(9.7)
$$R = \frac{\sum_{i=1}^{n} (\hat{y}_i - \bar{y})(y_i - \bar{y})}{\sqrt{\sum_{i=1}^{n} (\hat{y}_i - \bar{y})^2 \sum_{i=1}^{n} (y_i - \bar{y})^2}}$$

We use (9.6) to write the numerator of (9.7) as

$$\sum_{i=1}^{n} (\hat{y}_i - \bar{y})(y_i - \bar{y}) = \sum_{i=1}^{n} (\hat{y}_i - \bar{y})[(\hat{y}_i - \bar{y}) + e_i]$$
$$= \sum_{i=1}^{n} (\hat{y}_i - \bar{y})^2 + \sum_{i=1}^{n} (\hat{y}_i - \bar{y})e_i$$

It follows from (9.5) that this can be simplified to

(9.8)
$$\sum_{i=1}^{n} (\hat{y}_i - \bar{y})(y_i - \bar{y}) = \sum_{i=1}^{n} (\hat{y}_i - \bar{y})^2$$

which we substitute in (9.7):

(9.9)
$$R = \frac{\sum_{i=1}^{n} (\hat{y}_i - \bar{y})^2}{\sqrt{\sum_{i=1}^{n} (\hat{y}_i - \bar{y})^2 \sum_{i=1}^{n} (y_i - \bar{y})^2}} = \frac{\sqrt{\sum_{i=1}^{n} (\hat{y}_i - \bar{y})^2}}{\sqrt{\sum_{i=1}^{n} (y_i - \bar{y})^2}}$$

The square root in the numerator of the third member is nonnegative, so that $R \geq 0$. But since R is defined as the ordinary correlation coefficient of the pairs $(\hat{y}_1, y_1), \ldots, (\hat{y}_n, y_n)$, we also have $R \leq 1$. Therefore,

(9.10)
$$0 \leq R \leq 1$$

which shows that the range of the multiple correlation coefficient is one-half that of the ordinary correlation coefficient.

The Multiple Correlation Coefficient of a Simple Regression

When we have a simple rather than a multiple regression ($K = 1$), we can simplify the numerator in the third number of (9.9) by means of (9.4),

$$(9.11) \qquad \sqrt{\sum_{i=1}^{n} (\hat{y}_i - \bar{y})^2} = \sqrt{b_1^2 \sum_{i=1}^{n} (x_{1i} - \bar{x}_1)^2}$$

$$= |b_1| \sqrt{\sum_{i=1}^{n} (x_{1i} - \bar{x}_1)^2}$$

where $|b_1|$ is the absolute value of b_1 (equal to b_1 if $b_1 \geq 0$ and to $-b_1$ if $b_1 < 0$). This b_1 for a simple regression is

$$b_1 = \frac{\sum_{i=1}^{n} (x_{1i} - \bar{x}_1)(y_i - \bar{y})}{\sum_{i=1}^{n} (x_{1i} - \bar{x}_1)^2}$$

$$= \frac{\sum_{i=1}^{n} (x_{1i} - \bar{x}_1)(y_i - \bar{y})}{\sqrt{\sum_{i=1}^{n} (x_{1i} - \bar{x}_1)^2 \sum_{i=1}^{n} (y_i - \bar{y})^2}} \frac{\sqrt{\sum_{i=1}^{n} (y_i - \bar{y})^2}}{\sqrt{\sum_{i=1}^{n} (x_{1i} - \bar{x}_1)^2}}$$

The first ratio in the second line is the correlation coefficient of y and x_1, to be written r_{01}, where the subscript 0 refers to y and 1 to x_1. Since the square roots in the second ratio are both positive, we thus have

$$|b_1| = |r_{01}| \frac{\sqrt{\sum_{i=1}^{n} (y_i - \bar{y})^2}}{\sqrt{\sum_{i=1}^{n} (x_{1i} - \bar{x}_1)^2}}$$

which we substitute in (9.11):

$$(9.12) \qquad \sqrt{\sum_{i=1}^{n} (\hat{y}_i - \bar{y})^2} = |r_{01}| \sqrt{\sum_{i=1}^{n} (y_i - \bar{y})^2}$$

On comparing this with (9.9), we obtain $R = |r_{01}|$; that is, when the regression is simple rather than multiple, the multiple correlation coefficient equals the absolute value of the ordinary correlation coefficient of the two variables.

The Coefficient of Determination and Its Complement

We return to the more general case of multiple regression and square both sides of (9.6) and then sum over i:

$$\sum_{i=1}^{n} (y_i - \bar{y})^2 = \sum_{i=1}^{n} (\hat{y}_i - \bar{y})^2 + \sum_{i=1}^{n} e_i^2 + 2 \sum_{i=1}^{n} (\hat{y}_i - \bar{y}) e_i$$

It follows from (9.5) that this can be simplified, after division by n, to

$$(9.13) \qquad \frac{1}{n} \sum_{i=1}^{n} (y_i - \bar{y})^2 = \frac{1}{n} \sum_{i=1}^{n} (\hat{y}_i - \bar{y})^2 + \frac{1}{n} \sum_{i=1}^{n} e_i^2$$

The left-hand side is the mean square of the observed values of the dependent variable, measured as deviations from $\bar{y}$. This mean square is a measure of the observed variation of this variable, so that (9.13) amounts to a decomposition of this variation in terms of an LS adjusted component and a residual component.

Next square the first and third members of (9.9),

$$(9.14) \qquad R^2 = \frac{\sum_{i=1}^{n} (\hat{y}_i - \bar{y})^2}{\sum_{i=1}^{n} (y_i - \bar{y})^2} = \frac{(1/n) \sum_{i=1}^{n} (\hat{y}_i - \bar{y})^2}{(1/n) \sum_{i=1}^{n} (y_i - \bar{y})^2}$$

and divide (9.13) by its left-hand side, which gives 1 on the left and R^2 for the first term on the right [see (9.14)], so that the second term must be $1 - R^2$. Therefore,

$$(9.15) \qquad 1 - R^2 = \frac{\sum_{i=1}^{n} e_i^2}{\sum_{i=1}^{n} (y_i - \bar{y})^2} = \frac{(1/n) \sum_{i=1}^{n} e_i^2}{(1/n) \sum_{i=1}^{n} (y_i - \bar{y})^2}$$

Equations (9.14) and (9.15) provide a decomposition of the observed variation of the dependent variable in terms of proportions. A proportion R^2 of this variation is accounted for by the LS adjusted values $\hat{y}_1, \ldots, \hat{y}_n$ and hence, in view of (9.4), by the explanatory variables. The complement $1 - R^2$ is the residual proportion and is therefore not accounted for by the explanatory variables. The squared multiple correlation coefficient (R^2) is frequently called the *coefficient of determination* of the regression.

Application to the Demand for Textile

The multiple correlation coefficient for textile consumption, obtained by applying either (9.7) or (9.9) to the first two columns of Table 13 on page 105, is

$$(9.16) \qquad R = .9871$$

implying

$$(9.17) \qquad R^2 = .9744, \qquad 1 - R^2 = .0256$$

Hence, almost $97\frac{1}{2}$ percent of the variation in the logarithm of the volume of textile consumption per capita is accounted for by the two explanatory variables (the logarithms of real income per capita and the relative textile price), and only a little over $2\frac{1}{2}$ percent is residual.

It is not necessary to compute the LS adjusted values $\hat{y}_1, \ldots, \hat{y}_n$ to obtain R. Using (9.8) and (9.4), we have

$$\sum_{i=1}^{n} (\hat{y}_i - \bar{y})^2 = \sum_{i=1}^{n} (\hat{y}_i - \bar{y})(y_i - \bar{y})$$

$$= \sum_{i=1}^{n} [b_1(x_{1i} - \bar{x}_1) + \cdots + b_K(x_{Ki} - \bar{x}_K)](y_i - \bar{y})$$

$$= b_1 \sum_{i=1}^{n} (x_{1i} - \bar{x}_1)(y_i - \bar{y}) + \cdots + b_K \sum_{i=1}^{n} (x_{Ki} - \bar{x}_K)(y_i - \bar{y})$$

so that (9.14) can be written as

$$(9.18) \quad R^2 = \frac{b_1 \sum_{i=1}^{n} (x_{1i} - \bar{x}_1)(y_i - \bar{y}) + \cdots + b_K \sum_{i=1}^{n} (x_{Ki} - \bar{x}_K)(y_i - \bar{y})}{\sum_{i=1}^{n} (y_i - \bar{y})^2}$$

Hence, the computation of R^2 can be based on the LS slope coefficients, which are obtained from the normal equations, and the sums of certain squares and products of variables.

9.2 The Incremental Contributions of Explanatory Variables

Given that R^2 defined in (9.14) measures the degree to which the variation in the dependent variable is accounted for by the explanatory variables and that $1 - R^2$ measures the residual component [see (9.15)], the next question is whether it is possible to measure the contribution of each explanatory variable separately. It seems that (9.18) provides a simple solution. Its right-hand numerator is the sum of K terms, one for each explanatory variable. Accordingly, we consider the idea of interpreting the ratio

$$(9.19) \quad \frac{b_h \sum_{i=1}^{n} (x_{hi} - \bar{x}_h)(y_i - \bar{y})}{\sum_{i=1}^{n} (y_i - \bar{y})^2}$$

as the contribution of the hth explanatory variable to the variation in the dependent variable $(h = 1, \ldots, K)$. The sum of these K contributions equals R^2 [see (9.18)], which is good, but there is the difficulty (see Problem 4) that the ratio (9.19) may be negative, which is very bad. This destroys the usefulness of (9.19) as a measure of the contribution of the hth explanatory variable to the variation in the dependent variable.

The Incremental Contribution of an Explanatory Variable

An alternative approach is in terms of "marginal" or "incremental" contributions. That is, we consider the increase in R^2 which results from the inclusion of the hth explanatory variable in the regression, given that the other $K - 1$ variables are included. To evaluate this increase we consider first the situation in which the hth variable is not included. Thus, we run a regression of y on $x_1, \ldots, x_{h-1}, x_{h+1}, \ldots, x_K$, which yields the following LS slope coefficients:

$$(9.20) \quad b_1^*, \ldots, b_{h-1}^*, b_{h+1}^*, \ldots, b_K^*$$

We write R_h for the associated multiple correlation coefficient, where the subscript (h) refers to the excluded variable (x_h). It follows from (9.18) that R_h can be obtained from

$$(9.21) \quad R_h^2 \sum_{i=1}^{n} (y_i - \bar{y})^2 = \sum_{k \neq h} b_k^* \sum_{i=1}^{n} (x_{ki} - \bar{x}_k)(y_i - \bar{y})$$

where $\sum_{k \neq h}$ stands for summation over $k = 1, \ldots, K$ excluding $k = h$.

Thus, when x_h is included (along with $x_1, \ldots, x_{h-1}, x_{h+1}, \ldots, x_K$), the squared multiple correlation coefficient is R^2, and when x_h is excluded, it is R_h^2. The *incremental contribution* of x_h to the explanation of the variation of the dependent variable is accordingly defined as $R^2 - R_h^2$. In contrast to the ratio (9.19), such a contribution cannot be negative:

$$(9.22) \qquad R^2 - R_h^2 \geq 0 \qquad\qquad h = 1, \ldots, K$$

To prove this inequality, we note that LS (by definition) minimizes the residual sum of squares. Hence, in view of (9.15), LS minimizes $1 - R^2$, or maximizes R^2. Similarly, the coefficients (9.20) are determined by maximizing R_h^2 obtained from (9.21), but the latter maximization is subject to the constraint that x_h has a zero coefficient (because x_h is excluded). Constrained maximization cannot yield a higher squared multiple correlation coefficient. Therefore, $R_h^2 \leq R^2$, which proves (9.22).

The Sum of the Incremental Contributions

Suppose that we compute the incremental contribution $R^2 - R_h^2$ for each of the K explanatory variables. Is the sum of these incremental contributions equal to total contribution R^2 of all these variables?

To answer this question we consider first the case in which the K explanatory variables are all uncorrelated,

$$(9.23) \qquad \sum_{i=1}^{n} (x_{hi} - \bar{x}_h)(x_{ki} - \bar{x}_k) = 0$$

for all pairs (h, k) with $h \neq k$. We know from the last subsection of Section 7.2 that the LS slope coefficients can then be obtained from simple regressions,

$$(9.24) \qquad b_k = \frac{\sum_{i=1}^{n} (x_{ki} - \bar{x}_k)(y_i - \bar{y})}{\sum_{i=1}^{n} (x_{ki} - \bar{x}_k)^2}$$

for $k = 1, \ldots, K$. If all x variables are uncorrelated, this is certainly true for the $K - 1$ which remain after x_h is deleted; hence, the LS slope coefficients (9.20) become $b_k^* = b_k$ as shown in (9.24) for $k \neq h$. Therefore, we can write (9.21) with the asterisk deleted from b_k^*,

$$R_h^2 \sum_{i=1}^{n} (y_i - \bar{y})^2 = \sum_{k \neq h} b_k \sum_{i=1}^{n} (x_{ki} - \bar{x}_k)(y_i - \bar{y})$$

We subtract this equation from (9.18), written in the form

$$R^2 \sum_{i=1}^{n} (y_i - \bar{y})^2 = \sum_{k=1}^{K} b_k \sum_{i=1}^{n} (x_{ki} - \bar{x}_k)(y_i - \bar{y})$$

with the following result:

$$(9.25) \qquad (R^2 - R_h^2) \sum_{i=1}^{n} (y_i - \bar{y})^2 = b_h \sum_{i=1}^{n} (x_{hi} - \bar{x}_h)(y_i - \bar{y})$$

Note that (9.25) holds for $h = 1, \ldots, K$ when (9.23) is true for all pairs $h \neq k$. Thus, we can sum (9.25) over h,

$$\sum_{h=1}^{K} (R^2 - R_h^2) \sum_{i=1}^{n} (y_i - \bar{y})^2 = \sum_{h=1}^{K} b_h \sum_{i=1}^{n} (x_{hi} - \bar{x}_h)(y_i - \bar{y})$$
$$= R^2 \sum_{i=1}^{n} (y_i - \bar{y})^2$$

where the second step is based on (9.18). By dividing the left-hand side and the expression in the second line by $\sum_i (y_i - \bar{y})^2$, we obtain

$$(9.26) \qquad \sum_{h=1}^{K} (R^2 - R_h^2) = R^2$$

which proves that if all explanatory variables are uncorrelated, the sum of their incremental contributions is equal to their total contribution R^2.

The Multicollinearity Effect

If (9.23) is not true for one or several pairs (h, k) with $h \neq k$, so that the observation pairs (x_{hi}, x_{ki}) have a nonzero correlation coefficient, the result (9.26) will in general not be true either. Recall from Section 8.3 that a nonzero correlation coefficient ($r \neq 0$) of x_1 and x_2 indicates the existence of some degree of multicollinearity. Accordingly, we refer to the excess of the total contribution R^2 of the explanatory variables over the sum of their incremental contributions,

$$(9.27) \qquad R^2 - \sum_{h=1}^{K} (R^2 - R_h^2)$$

as the *multicollinearity effect* in the decomposition of R^2. The value of this effect may be positive, zero, or negative. The subject of multicollinearity for three or more explanatory variables is considered in Section 9.3.

The Corrected Multiple Correlation Coefficient

Recall from remark (3) on page 124 that the LS residual sum of squares has to be divided by the number of degrees of freedom, not by the number of observations, to provide an unbiased estimator of σ^2 under the standard linear model. In the case of textile consumption, with three coefficients adjusted, this amounts to using the estimator (8.37),

$$(9.28) \qquad \frac{1}{n-3} \sum_{i=1}^{n} e_i^2$$

It is also customary to divide $\sum_i (y_i - \bar{y})^2$ by $n - 1$ rather than by n to obtain the mean square of the dependent variable around $\bar{y}$:

$$(9.29) \qquad \frac{1}{n-1} \sum_{i=1}^{n} (y_i - \bar{y})^2$$

This is done on the analogy of the unbiased estimator of the variance [see (4.46)] and (4.47)], but it should be emphasized that there is no question of unbiased estimation in the present case, because the standard linear model implies that $y_1, \ldots, y_n$ have different expectations [see (8.1)] and hence different distributions.

When we apply the modifications (9.28) and (9.29) to the third member of (9.15), we obtain the *corrected* multiple correlation coefficient $\bar{R}$, which is defined by

$$(9.30) \qquad 1 - \bar{R}^2 = \frac{[1/(n-3)] \sum_{i=1}^{n} e_i^2}{[1/(n-1)] \sum_{i=1}^{n} (y_i - \bar{y})^2} = \frac{n-1}{n-3}(1 - R^2)$$

or, equivalently,

$$(9.31) \qquad \bar{R}^2 = R^2 - \frac{2}{n-3}(1 - R^2)$$

Hence, $\bar{R}^2 < R^2$ (unless $R^2 = 1$, in which case $\bar{R}^2 = 1$ also). The correction thus amounts to reducing the value of the squared multiple correlation coefficient. We may have a negative $\bar{R}^2$, in which case its square root $(\bar{R})$ is usually not computed. A generalization of (9.31) for an arbitrary number of coefficients adjusted is given in Problem 5.

The modifications (9.30) and (9.31) are motivated by considerations of bias, but note that $\bar{R}^2$ is not an unbiased estimator of a parameter, because no such parameter has been defined. The multiple correlation coefficient is used here as a descriptive measure of the goodness of fit of a multiple regression. Nevertheless, it is good practice to use $\bar{R}^2$ rather than R^2, because R^2 tends to give an overly optimistic picture of the fit of the regression, particularly when the number of explanatory variables is not very small compared with the number of observations.

Application to the Demand for Textile

Table 14 provides a summary for the textile example. The first two lines contain the incremental contributions of the logarithms of real income per

TABLE 14

**Multiple correlation and incremental contributions
for textile consumption**

Incremental contribution of income	$R^2 - R_1^2 =$	.098
Incremental contribution of textile price	$R^2 - R_2^2 =$	.963
Multicollinearity effect	$R^2 - \sum_h (R^2 - R_h^2) =$	−.087
		+
Total contribution of explanatory variables	$R^2 =$	.974
Correction	$R^2 - \bar{R}^2 =$	.004
		−
Proportion accounted for by explanatory variables	$\bar{R}^2 =$	.971

capita (x_1) and the relative textile price (x_2). Here R^2 is as shown in (9.17), while R_1 and R_2 are in this case the ordinary correlations of the logarithm of the volume of textile consumption per capita and x_2 and x_1, respectively. The sum of the two incremental contributions is 1.061, which indicates that this total may exceed 1. The multicollinearity effect is obtained by subtracting 1.061 from R^2. The correction (9.30) amounts to

$$(9.32) \qquad 1 - \bar{R}^2 = \tfrac{16}{14}(.0256) = .0292, \qquad \bar{R}^2 = .9708$$

Hence, when the correction is made, about 97 percent of the mean square of the logarithm of the volume of textile consumption per capita is accounted for by the two explanatory variables, and about 3 percent is residual. Note that the size of the correction, $R^2 - \bar{R}^2$, is very modest in this case. The correction is larger when R^2 is smaller and when the number of explanatory variables is larger (see Problems 5 and 6).

The $\bar{R}^2$ shown in (9.32) is on the high side. By and large, $\bar{R}$'s tend to be rather close to 1 when the data used are characterized by a considerable degree of aggregation. In our example we have aggregation both over a large number of individuals and over an important class of commodities, because the dependent variable covers all consumers in the Netherlands and all goods of the large textile group. When we run a cross-section regression explaining textile expenditures by individual households, we should expect an $\bar{R}^2$ which is much smaller (of the order of .5 or even less). When we run a regression explaining the expenditures on girls' dresses by individual households, $\bar{R}^2$ will usually be still smaller. The time period is also important. A cross-section survey covering a month will generally produce smaller $\bar{R}$'s than a survey that lasts a year. These statements reflect the fact that, in many cases, aggregation over individuals or over commodities or over time tends to reduce the importance of neglected variables. We shall have more to say about $\bar{R}^2$ in Section 17.1.

9.3   More on Multicollinearity

The Sampling Variance of an LS Slope Estimator

In (8.33) and (8.34) we obtained a simple result for the sampling variance of the LS slope estimators in regressions on two explanatory variables with a constant term. We write it in the form (8.53),

$$(9.33) \qquad \operatorname{var} b_h = \frac{\sigma^2}{(1 - r^2) \sum_{i=1}^{n} (x_{hi} - \bar{x}_h)^2} \qquad h = 1, 2$$

where r is the correlation coefficient of the observation pairs (x_{1i}, x_{2i}).

This result can be extended for regressions on any number (K) of explanatory variables with a constant term; for a proof (which involves matrix algebra), see Theil (1971, pp. 165–166). The generalized result for any of the K slope estimators is

$$(9.34) \qquad \text{var } b_h = \frac{\sigma^2}{(1 - P_h^2) \sum_{i=1}^{n} (x_{hi} - \bar{x}_h)^2} \qquad h = 1, \ldots, K$$

where P_h is the multiple correlation coefficient associated with the LS regression of x_h on the $K - 1$ other explanatory variables $(x_1, \ldots, x_{h-1}, x_{h+1}, \ldots, x_K)$. Note that this regression is *not* the same as that of y on the latter x's, considered in the discussion preceding (9.20). The regression corresponding to P_h describes x_h, not y, as a linear function of all other x's. This regression need not have any economic meaning; it should be viewed as an auxiliary regression which serves to define the multiple correlation coefficient P_h in the variance formula (9.34).

For $K = 2$, (9.34) reduces to (9.33), as it obviously should. This follows from the result, obtained below (9.12), that P_h equals the absolute value of the correlation coefficient of the pairs (x_{1i}, x_{2i}) when the auxiliary regression just mentioned is the simple regression of x_1 on x_2 or of x_2 on x_1.

Multicollinearity Among Three or More Explanatory Variables

When $P_h = 1$ holds in (9.34), x_h is an exact linear function of the $K - 1$ other explanatory variables for all n observations. This is the case of extreme multicollinearity for a regression of y on K variables; it implies that the normal equations have no unique solution for the LS slope coefficients $b_1, \ldots, b_K$. Accordingly, the variance (9.34) explodes. When P_h is not equal but close to 1, x_h is almost an exact linear function of the $K - 1$ other explanatory variables. This is the case of near-extreme multicollinearity, which (9.34) signals by a large variance of b_h.

Note that the linear relation among the x's which causes the multicollinearity need not involve all x's. For example, we may have $K = 5$ and $x_{1i} = 3x_{3i} - x_{5i}$ for $i = 1, \ldots, n$. If this holds exactly, then $P_1 = 1$; if it holds almost exactly, then P_1 is almost 1. It should be clear that when there are more explanatory variables, the danger of near-extreme multicollinearity increases. We know from (9.22) that adding an explanatory variable tends to raise the multiple correlation coefficient. Similarly, when x_h is expressed linearly in terms of $K - 1$ other x's to yield P_h and when K and hence also $K - 1$ increase, this will typically raise P_h also.

Although (9.34) is an attractive formula in that it provides valuable insight into the behavior of the sampling variance of an LS slope estimator under conditions of near-extreme multicollinearity, we should not view (9.34) as a recommendation to compute multiple correlation coefficients $P_1, \ldots, P_K$ for the derivation of standard errors. Efficient computer programs are based on inverses of matrices (see Appendix B).

Problems

Problems 1–3 refer to Section 9.1, 4–7 to Section 9.2, and 8 to Section 9.3.

1   Verify that (6.7) is a special case of (9.15).

2   Verify how the result $R = |r_{01}|$ for $K = 1$, stated below (9.12), can be obtained from (9.18).

3   (*Continuation*) Suppose that the K explanatory variables are all pairwise uncorrelated,

$$\sum_{i=1}^{n} (x_{hi} - \bar{x}_h)(x_{ki} - \bar{x}_k) = 0$$

for each pair (h, k) with $h \neq k$. Use (9.18) to prove that R^2 is in that case equal to the sum of the squares of the K correlation coefficients of the observation pairs $(x_{1i}, y_i), \ldots, (x_{Ki}, y_i)$ for $i = 1, \ldots, n$.

4   Consider a regression of y on x_1 and x_2 with a constant term. The three variables have unit sums of squares (all values measured as deviations from the corresponding arithmetic means). The product sums are

$$\sum_{i=1}^{n} (x_{1i} - \bar{x}_1)(y_i - \bar{y}) = .2$$

$$\sum_{i=1}^{n} (x_{2i} - \bar{x}_2)(y_i - \bar{y}) = .8$$

$$\sum_{i=1}^{n} (x_{1i} - \bar{x}_1)(x_{2i} - \bar{x}_2) = .5$$

Verify that the LS slope coefficient b_1 is negative, and use this to prove that the ratio (9.19) for $h = 1$ is also negative.

5   Extend (9.31) for any number of explanatory variables (and a constant term) to

$$\bar{R}^2 = R^2 - \frac{\text{number of explanatory variables}}{\text{number of degrees of freedom}}(1 - R^2)$$

Use this result to prove that the correction, $R^2 - \bar{R}^2$, increases when there are more explanatory variables and when the uncorrected R^2 takes a smaller value. [*Note:* In Theil (1971, pp. 178–182), K stands for the number of coefficients adjusted (the number of explanatory variables plus 1 for the constant term).]

6   (*Continuation*) For $n = 17$, compute $\bar{R}^2$ for two, three, and four explanatory variables—with constant term—and for $R^2 = .9, .7, .5, .3,$ and .1 ($3 \times 5 = 15$ combinations). Draw your conclusions.

7   Consider a regression of y on x_1 and x_2 (with a constant term). We have

$$\sum_{i=1}^{n} (x_{1i} - \bar{x}_1)(y_i - \bar{y}) = \sum_{i=1}^{n} (x_{2i} - \bar{x}_2)(y_i - \bar{y}) = 0$$

Prove that $\bar{R}^2 < 0$. Also prove that $b_1 = b_2 = 0$.

8   Remark (3) on page 124 states that σ^2 is estimated unbiasedly by the ratio of the residual sum of squares to the number of degrees of freedom. Use this result to prove that an unbiased estimator of var b_h given in (9.34) is the ratio of the expression

$$\frac{(1 - R^2)(1/n) \sum_{i=1}^{n} (y_i - \bar{y})^2}{(1 - P_h^2)(1/n) \sum_{i=1}^{n} (x_{hi} - \bar{x}_h)^2}$$

to the number of degrees of freedom. Discuss this result, and show (a) that if more variation of y is accounted for by $x_1, \ldots, x_K$, this lowers the standard error of b_h and (b) that if more variation of x_h is accounted for by $x_1, \ldots, x_{h-1}, x_{h+1}, \ldots, x_K$, this raises the standard error of b_h.

chapter 10

Multivariate Normality and Maximum Likelihood

The multivariate normal distribution plays a central role in multivariate statistical theory. A property which characterizes this particular distribution is the fact that any linear combination of multinormal variates is itself normally distributed. This property plays an important role in the analysis of this and later chapters.

The development of multivariate normal theory is therefore the first objective of this chapter. The second is the estimation method of maximum likelihood, which is an alternative to the least-squares method. It will appear in Section 12.3 that the maximum-likelihood procedure yields, as a by-product, a general method of testing statistical hypotheses.

10.1 The Multivariate Normal Distribution

The density function of the univariate normal distribution is given in (4.11) and reproduced here:

$$(10.1) \qquad f(x) = \frac{1}{\sigma\sqrt{2\pi}} \exp\left\{-\frac{1}{2}\frac{(x-\mu)^2}{\sigma^2}\right\} \qquad -\infty < x < \infty$$

Here μ is the mean of the distribution, σ is the standard deviation, and hence σ^2 is the variance. We can thus write (10.1) "in words" as

$$(10.2) \qquad f(x) = \frac{1}{\sqrt{2\pi \times \text{variance}}} \exp\left\{-\frac{1}{2}\frac{(x-\text{mean})^2}{\text{variance}}\right\}$$

The Bivariate Normal Distribution

Consider a random pair (X, Y) with correlation coefficient ρ. We write μ_1 for the mean of X, μ_2 for the mean of Y, and σ_1 and σ_2 for the standard deviations of X and Y, respectively. The distribution of (X, Y) is said to be bivariate normal when its joint density function takes the form

(10.3) $$f(x, y) = \frac{1}{2\pi\sigma_1\sigma_2\sqrt{1 - \rho^2}} \exp\{g(x, y)\}$$

where

(10.4) $$g(x, y) = -\frac{1}{2(1 - \rho^2)}$$
$$\times \left[\frac{(x - \mu_1)^2}{\sigma_1^2} + \frac{(y - \mu_2)^2}{\sigma_2^2} - \frac{2\rho(x - \mu_1)(y - \mu_2)}{\sigma_1\sigma_2} \right]$$

The range of the bivariate normal distribution is $-\infty < x < \infty$ and $-\infty < y < \infty$, which is an extension of the range $-\infty < x < \infty$ of the univariate normal distribution (10.1). If we measure x and y along two horizontal axes and the density function (10.3) along the vertical axis, the resulting picture of this function is that of a mountain with a peak at $x = \mu_1, y = \mu_2$. This picture is the extension of the normal curve shown in Figure 7 on page 46.

Equations (10.3) and (10.4) show that the bivariate normal distribution is determined by five parameters: the two means (μ_1 and μ_2), the two standard deviations (σ_1 and σ_2), and the correlation coefficient (ρ). It is to be understood that $\rho^2 < 1$ in (10.3) and (10.4); the limiting cases $\rho = \pm 1$ are not considered here.

Uncorrelated Normal Variates Are Stochastically Independent

If X and Y are uncorrelated ($\rho = 0$), we can simplify (10.4) to

$$g(x, y) = -\frac{1}{2}\frac{(x - \mu_1)^2}{\sigma_1^2} - \frac{1}{2}\frac{(y - \mu_2)^2}{\sigma_2^2}$$

and hence (10.3) to

(10.5) $$f(x, y) = \frac{1}{2\pi\sigma_1\sigma_2} \exp\left\{ -\frac{1}{2}\frac{(x - \mu_1)^2}{\sigma_1^2} - \frac{1}{2}\frac{(y - \mu_2)^2}{\sigma_2^2} \right\}$$
$$= \frac{1}{\sqrt{2\pi\sigma_1^2}} \exp\left\{ -\frac{1}{2}\frac{(x - \mu_1)^2}{\sigma_1^2} \right\} \frac{1}{\sqrt{2\pi\sigma_2^2}} \exp\left\{ -\frac{1}{2}\frac{(y - \mu_2)^2}{\sigma_2^2} \right\}$$

where the second step is based on $e^{a+b} = e^a e^b$ with a and b appropriately specified [see (4.32)].

It follows from (10.2) that the expression in the second line of (10.5) is equal to the univariate normal density function with mean μ_1 and standard deviation σ_1, multiplied by the univariate normal density function with mean μ_2 and standard deviation σ_2. Thus, going back to the independence definition (4.28), we conclude that *under bivariate normality the two random variables are sto-chastically independent when they are uncorrelated* ($\rho = 0$).

We emphasize that this result is specific for the bivariate normal distribution. We know from Section 6.2 that random variables may be uncorrelated without being independent, but the result obtained in the previous paragraph shows that this cannot occur when their distribution is bivariate normal.

The Conditional Distributions Are Univariate Normal

Recall from (4.23) that the conditional density function of Y given $X = x$ is obtained by dividing the joint density $f(x, y)$ by the density $f_1(x)$ of the marginal distribution of X. This ratio is evaluated in the next subsection with the following result:

$$(10.6) \quad \frac{f(x, y)}{f_1(x)} = \frac{1}{\sqrt{2\pi\sigma_2^2(1 - \rho^2)}} \exp\left\{ -\frac{1}{2} \frac{[y - \mu_2 - \rho\sigma_2(x - \mu_1)/\sigma_1]^2}{\sigma_2^2(1 - \rho^2)} \right\}$$

A comparison with (10.2) shows that this conditional distribution is univariate normal with the following mean and variance:

$$(10.7) \quad \mathcal{E}(Y \mid X = x) = \mu_2 + \frac{\rho\sigma_2}{\sigma_1}(x - \mu_1), \qquad \text{var}(Y \mid X = x) = \sigma_2^2(1 - \rho^2)$$

The conditional distribution of X given $Y = y$ is obtained similarly. It follows from symmetry considerations that this distribution is univariate normal with the following mean and variance:

$$(10.8) \quad \mathcal{E}(X \mid Y = y) = \mu_1 + \frac{\rho\sigma_1}{\sigma_2}(y - \mu_2), \qquad \text{var}(X \mid Y = y) = \sigma_1^2(1 - \rho^2)$$

We conclude from (10.7) and (10.8) that under bivariate normality the conditional mean of either random variable given the other is a linear function of the latter and that the conditional variance is a constant. Note that this is similar to the standard linear model for two variables, which postulates that the conditional mean of y_i given x_i is a linear function of x_i and that the conditional variance of y_i is a constant [see (5.1) and (5.2)]. But note also that (10.7) and (10.8) are completely symmetric in the two random variables, whereas the standard linear model is asymmetric in the sense that it makes no probability statements on the values $x_1, \ldots, x_n$ of the explanatory variable.

Derivations for the Conditional Distributions

Since the marginal distribution of X is normal with mean μ_1 and standard deviation σ_1, $f_1(x)$ is obtained from (10.1) by substituting μ_1 and σ_1 for μ and σ, respectively. Using (10.3) also, we find that the left-hand ratio in (10.6) equals

$$(10.9) \quad \frac{\sigma_1\sqrt{2\pi}}{2\pi\sigma_1\sigma_2\sqrt{1 - \rho^2}} \exp\left\{ g(x, y) - \left[-\frac{1}{2} \frac{(x - \mu_1)^2}{\sigma_1^2} \right] \right\}$$

$$= \frac{1}{\sqrt{2\pi\sigma_2^2(1 - \rho^2)}} \exp\left\{ g(x, y) + \frac{1}{2} \frac{(x - \mu_1)^2}{\sigma_1^2} \right\}$$

It follows from (10.4) that the expression in curled brackets equals

$$-\frac{1}{2(1-\rho^2)}\left[\frac{(x-\mu_1)^2}{\sigma_1^2}+\frac{(y-\mu_2)^2}{\sigma_2^2}-\frac{2\rho(x-\mu_1)(y-\mu_2)}{\sigma_1\sigma_2}\right]$$
$$+\frac{1}{2}\frac{(x-\mu_1)^2}{\sigma_1^2}$$

which we write as a multiple $-1/2(1-\rho^2)$ of

$$\frac{(x-\mu_1)^2}{\sigma_1^2}+\frac{(y-\mu_2)^2}{\sigma_2^2}-\frac{2\rho(x-\mu_1)(y-\mu_2)}{\sigma_1\sigma_2}-(1-\rho^2)\frac{(x-\mu_1)^2}{\sigma_1^2}$$
$$=\frac{(y-\mu_2)^2}{\sigma_2^2}-\frac{2\rho(x-\mu_1)(y-\mu_2)}{\sigma_1\sigma_2}+\frac{\rho^2(x-\mu_1)^2}{\sigma_1^2}$$
$$=\left[\frac{y-\mu_2}{\sigma_2}-\frac{\rho(x-\mu_1)}{\sigma_1}\right]^2$$

Multiplication by $-1/2(1-\rho^2)$ gives

$$-\frac{1}{2(1-\rho^2)}\left[\frac{y-\mu_2}{\sigma_2}-\frac{\rho(x-\mu_1)}{\sigma_1}\right]^2$$
$$=-\frac{1}{2}\frac{[y-\mu_2-(\rho\sigma_2/\sigma_1)(x-\mu_1)]^2}{\sigma_2^2(1-\rho^2)}$$

Substitution of the right-hand side in the curled brackets of (10.9) completes the proof of (10.6).

Linear Combinations of Normal Variates Are Normally Distributed

Let (X, Y) have any distribution (not necessarily normal) with means μ_1 and μ_2, standard deviations σ_1 and σ_2, and correlation coefficient ρ. Define $Z = \alpha X + \beta Y$, where α and β are constants. We know that the mean of Z is

(10.10) $$\mathcal{E}Z = \alpha\mu_1 + \beta\mu_2$$

and that its variance is

(10.11) $$\begin{aligned}\text{var } Z &= \alpha^2 \text{ var } X + \beta^2 \text{ var } Y + 2\alpha\beta \text{ cov } (X, Y)\\ &= \alpha^2\sigma_1^2 + \beta^2\sigma_2^2 + 2\alpha\beta\rho\sigma_1\sigma_2\end{aligned}$$

It can be shown that if (X, Y) has a bivariate normal distribution, *any* linear combination (with constant coefficients) of X and Y has a univariate normal distribution. Thus, for Z defined above, the probability that $z < Z \le z + dz$ equals

(10.12) $$\frac{1}{\sqrt{2\pi(\alpha^2\sigma_1^2 + \beta^2\sigma_2^2 + 2\alpha\beta\rho\sigma_1\sigma_2)}}$$
$$\times \exp\left\{-\frac{1}{2}\frac{(z - \alpha\mu_1 - \beta\mu_2)^2}{\alpha^2\sigma_1^2 + \beta^2\sigma_2^2 + 2\alpha\beta\rho\sigma_1\sigma_2}\right\} dz$$

It follows from (10.2) that this is the density function, multiplied by dz, of the normal distribution with mean (10.10) and variance (10.11).

In particular, if X and Y have zero mean and unit variance, so that (10.3) becomes

(10.13) $$f(x, y) = \frac{1}{2\pi\sqrt{1 - \rho^2}} \exp\left\{-\frac{x^2 + y^2 - 2\rho xy}{2(1 - \rho^2)}\right\}$$

and if $Z = X + Y$ [$\alpha = \beta = 1$ in (10.10) and (10.11)], then (10.12) is simplified to

(10.14) $$\frac{1}{2\sqrt{\pi(1 + \rho)}} \exp\left\{-\frac{z^2}{4(1 + \rho)}\right\}$$

A comparison with (10.2) shows that (10.14) is the density function of the normal distribution with zero mean and variance $2(1 + \rho)$. This variance agrees with (10.11) for $\alpha = \beta = \sigma_1 = \sigma_2 = 1$. To simplify the mathematics, we shall derive (10.14) in the next subsection rather than the more general result (10.12).

Derivations for the Normality of a Linear Combination

To clarify the procedure, we shall start with a discrete rather than the normal distribution. Let X and Y be random variables which take positive integer values, so that $Z = X + Y$ also takes positive integer values. We are interested in the probability that Z equals 5. The event $Z = 5$ takes place when (X, Y) equals $(1, 4)$, $(2, 3)$, $(3, 2)$, or $(4, 1)$. Hence $P[Z = 5]$ is obtained by adding the probabilities that (X, Y) takes any of these four values:

$$P[Z = 5] = \sum_{x=1}^{4} P[X = x, Y = 5 - x]$$

More generally,

(10.15) $$P[Z = z] = \sum_{x=1}^{z-1} P[X = x, Y = z - x]$$

where z is any integer value larger than 1.

When we proceed to continuous distributions, probabilities become density functions, and summation becomes integration. Since the normal distribution has a range from $-\infty$ to ∞, the continuous version of (10.15) is thus

(10.16) $$f(z) = \int_{-\infty}^{\infty} f(x, z - x)\, dx$$

where the integrand is specified in (10.13):

(10.17) $$f(x, z - x) = \frac{1}{2\pi\sqrt{1 - \rho^2}} \exp\left\{-\frac{x^2 + (z - x)^2 - 2\rho x(z - x)}{2(1 - \rho^2)}\right\}$$

Thus, we have to prove that the integral of (10.17) over x equals (10.14). We shall do so by completing the square.

We write the numerator of the ratio in curled brackets in (10.17) as

$$
\begin{aligned}
x^2 &+ (z^2 + x^2 - 2zx) - 2\rho(zx - x^2) \\
&= 2(1 + \rho)(x^2 - zx) + z^2 \\
&= 2(1 + \rho)(x^2 - zx + \tfrac{1}{4}z^2) + (1 - \tfrac{1}{2} - \tfrac{1}{2}\rho)z^2 \\
&= 2(1 + \rho)(x - \tfrac{1}{2}z)^2 + \tfrac{1}{2}(1 - \rho)z^2
\end{aligned}
$$

This shows that the expression in curled brackets in (10.17) equals

$$-\frac{2(1+p)(x-\tfrac{1}{2}z)^2}{2(1-p^2)} - \frac{\tfrac{1}{2}(1-p)z^2}{2(1-p^2)} = -\frac{(x-\tfrac{1}{2}z)^2}{1-p} - \frac{z^2}{4(1+p)}$$

Since $2\pi\sqrt{1-p^2}$ equals the product of $\sqrt{\pi(1-p)}$ and $2\sqrt{\pi(1+p)}$, we can thus write the right-hand side of (10.17) as the product of

(10.18)
$$\frac{1}{\sqrt{\pi(1-p)}} \exp\left\{-\frac{(x-\tfrac{1}{2}z)^2}{1-p}\right\}$$

and

(10.19)
$$\frac{1}{2\sqrt{\pi(1+p)}} \exp\left\{-\frac{z^2}{4(1+p)}\right\}$$

Thus, we must multiply (10.18) and (10.19) and then integrate over x [see (10.16)]. But note that (10.19) does not involve x, so that the integration can be confined to (10.18). Also note that (10.18) is the density function of the normal distribution with mean $\tfrac{1}{2}z$ and variance $\tfrac{1}{2}(1-p)$ [see (10.2)], so that its integral over x from $-\infty$ to ∞ must be 1. Therefore, the integral over x of the product of (10.18) and (10.19) is simply equal to (10.19). The proof is completed by noticing that (10.19) is identical to (10.14).

The Multivariate Normal Distribution

The bivariate density function (10.3) takes the form of a constant (equal to the reciprocal of $2\pi\sigma_1\sigma_2\sqrt{1-p^2}$) multiplied by the exponent of $g(x, y)$ defined in (10.4). The multivariate normal density function of an n-tuple $(X_1, \ldots, X_n)$ is similarly equal to a constant multiplied by the exponent of

(10.20)
$$g(x_1, \ldots, x_n) = -\tfrac{1}{2} \sum_{i=1}^{n} \sum_{j=1}^{n} a_{ij}(x_i - \mu_i)(x_j - \mu_j)$$

where $\mu_1, \ldots, \mu_n$ are the means of $X_1, \ldots, X_n$ and the a_{ij}'s are determined by the variances and covariances of the X_i's. For example, (10.20) becomes (10.4) for $n = 2$ when we specify the a_{ij}'s as

(10.21)
$$a_{11} = \frac{1}{\sigma_1^2(1-p^2)}, \qquad a_{22} = \frac{1}{\sigma_2^2(1-p^2)}$$

(10.22)
$$a_{12} = a_{21} = -\frac{1}{\sigma_1\sigma_2(1-p^2)}$$

which the reader should verify. Since p equals the covariance divided by the square root of the product of the two variances, the results (10.21) and (10.22) confirm that the a_{ij}'s of (10.20) are determined by the variances and covariances.

Further details on the multivariate normal distribution are provided in Appendix C, including proofs of some of the propositions which follow in the next subsection. These propositions are all direct extensions of properties of the bivariate normal distribution discussed above.

Properties of the Multivariate Normal Distribution

(1) If $(X_1, \ldots, X_n)$ is multivariate normal with means $\mu_1, \ldots, \mu_n$ and standard deviations $\sigma_1, \ldots, \sigma_n$, the marginal distribution of X_i is univariate normal with mean μ_i and standard deviation σ_i ($i = 1, \ldots, n$).

(2) Under the same condition, the conditional distribution of each X_i, given the $n - 1$ other X's, is univariate normal. The conditional mean is a linear function of the values taken by the latter X's, and the conditional variance is a constant.

(3) Under the same condition, any linear combination (with constant coefficients) of $X_1, \ldots, X_n$ has a univariate normal distribution, and any pair of such combinations has a bivariate normal distribution.

(4) If $X_1, \ldots, X_n$ are all uncorrelated, all a_{ij}'s with different subscripts vanish, so that (10.20) is simplified to

$$g(x_1, \ldots, x_n) = -\tfrac{1}{2} \sum_{i=1}^n a_{ii}(x_i - \mu_i)^2$$

The exponent of $g(x_1, \ldots, x_n)$ is then equal to

$$\exp\{-\tfrac{1}{2}a_{11}(x_1 - \mu_1)^2 - \cdots - \tfrac{1}{2}a_{nn}(x_n - \mu_n)^2\}$$

which we write, using $\exp\{A_1 + \cdots + A_n\} = e^{A_1} \cdots e^{A_n}$, as

(10.23) $$\exp\{-\tfrac{1}{2}a_{11}(x_1 - \mu_1)^2\} \exp\{-\tfrac{1}{2}a_{22}(x_2 - \mu_2)^2\} \cdots$$
$$\times \exp\{-\tfrac{1}{2}a_{nn}(x_n - \mu_n)^2\}$$

Each of these exponents is that of the univariate normal density function (10.2) with mean μ_i and variance $1/a_{ii}$ ($i = 1, \ldots, n$). Therefore, in view of the independence definition (4.30), if $X_1, \ldots, X_n$ have a multivariate normal distribution and if they are uncorrelated, they are independently distributed. [See Problem 5 for the normalizing constants associated with the exponents in (10.23).]

The Arithmetic Mean of a Random Sample from a Normal Distribution

Let $(X_1, \ldots, X_n)$ be a random sample from a normal distribution with mean μ and variance σ^2. The density function of the sample is given in (4.34), which we write as

(10.24) $$f(x_1, \ldots, x_n) = \frac{1}{(\sigma\sqrt{2\pi})^n} \exp\left\{-\frac{1}{2}\sum_{i=1}^n \frac{(x_i - \mu)^2}{\sigma^2}\right\}$$

This is a special case of the multivariate normal distribution, with all means equal to μ ($\mathscr{E}X_i = \mu$ for $i = 1, \ldots, n$), all variances equal to σ^2, and all covariances equal to zero.

The arithmetic mean of the X_i's is

(10.25) $$\bar{X} = \frac{1}{n} \sum_{i=1}^n X_i$$

which is a linear combination of the X_i's. Therefore, in view of proposition (3) above, $\bar{X}$ is normally distributed.

*10.2 The Method of Maximum Likelihood

Let $(X_1, \ldots, X_n)$ be a random sample from some distribution which is characterized by an unknown parameter θ. This θ may be the mean of this distribution, or its variance, or any other parameter; we use θ as a general symbol for an unknown parameter. We write $f(x \mid \theta)$ for the density function of the distribution; the insertion of θ within the parentheses indicates that the form of the density curve depends on the value of θ. The density function (4.39) of the sample thus becomes

(10.26) $$f(x_1 \mid \theta) f(x_2 \mid \theta) \cdots f(x_n \mid \theta)$$

The Likelihood Function and the Maximum-Likelihood Estimate

We shall be interested in the value which the density function (10.26) takes when it is evaluated at the sample values $X_1, \ldots, X_n$:

(10.27) $$f(X_1 \mid \theta) f(X_2 \mid \theta) \cdots f(X_n \mid \theta)$$

Note that this expression, in contrast to (10.26), is random because the X's are random. An example of (10.27) is

(10.28) $$\frac{1}{(2\pi)^{n/2}} \exp\left\{ -\frac{1}{2} \sum_{i=1}^{n} (X_i - \theta)^2 \right\}$$

which is the joint density function of a random sample from a normal distribution with mean θ and unit variance, evaluated at the random sample values $X_1, \ldots, X_n$.

We may view (10.27) as the probability density of obtaining the sample, given that θ is the parameter value. Alternatively, we may view (10.27) as a function of θ, given the sample. To emphasize the latter viewpoint, we write (10.27) as

(10.29) $$L(X_1, \ldots, X_n; \theta)$$

which is known as the *likelihood function*. Suppose now that the sample has been drawn, so that $X_1, \ldots, X_n$ take numerical values. The value of the likelihood function (10.29) then still depends on θ. The method of *maximum likelihood* proposes to use as an estimate of θ the value $\hat{\theta}$ which maximizes the likelihood function,

(10.30) $$L(X_1, \ldots, X_n; \hat{\theta}) \geq L(X_1, \ldots, X_n; \tilde{\theta})$$

where $\tilde{\theta}$ is any other estimate of θ. The underlying intuitive idea is that we should prefer a parameter value which implies a large probability density of the sample drawn, rather than a value which declares that the sample is less probable. This approach yields a class of estimates, called maximum-likelihood estimates.

Example

Suppose that a random sample of size n is drawn from a normal distribution with mean θ and unit variance, so that the likelihood function takes the form (10.28):

$$(10.31) \qquad L(X_1, \ldots, X_n; \theta) = \frac{1}{(2\pi)^{n/2}} \exp\left\{-\frac{1}{2} \sum_{i=1}^{n} (X_i - \theta)^2\right\}$$

The method of maximum likelihood maximizes this function by varying θ. To implement this maximization, we note that $\log L$ is an increasing function of L, so that we can just as well maximize the (natural) logarithm of L:

$$(10.32) \qquad \log_e L(X_1, \ldots, X_n; \theta) = -\frac{n}{2} \log_e 2\pi - \frac{1}{2} \sum_{i=1}^{n} (X_i - \theta)^2$$

Maximizing this function is equivalent to minimizing

$$\sum_{i=1}^{n} (X_i - \theta)^2 = \sum_{i=1}^{n} [X_i - \bar{X} - (\theta - \bar{X})]^2$$
$$= \sum_{i=1}^{n} (X_i - \bar{X})^2 + n(\theta - \bar{X})^2 - 2(\theta - \bar{X}) \sum_{i=1}^{n} (X_i - \bar{X})$$
$$= \sum_{i=1}^{n} (X_i - \bar{X})^2 + n(\theta - \bar{X})^2$$

The θ value which minimizes the expression in the last line is $\hat{\theta} = \bar{X}$, so that the sample mean $\bar{X}$ is the maximum-likelihood estimate of the mean θ of the normal distribution with unit variance.

When $X_1, \ldots, X_n$ are random (before the sample is actually drawn), so is $\bar{X}$, and $\hat{\theta} = \bar{X}$ is then the maximum-likelihood *estimator* of θ of this normal distribution. Note that, more generally, the solution $\hat{\theta}$ of the maximum problem (10.30) is a function of the sample $(X_1, \ldots, X_n)$.

Maximum-Likelihood Estimation of Several Parameters

When a distribution is characterized by several unknown parameters (several θ's), we maximize the likelihood function with respect to each parameter. As an example, consider a random sample of size n from a normal distribution with unknown mean μ and unknown variance σ^2. The likelihood function is now

$$(10.33) \quad L(X_1, \ldots, X_n; \mu, \sigma^2) = \frac{1}{(2\pi\sigma^2)^{n/2}} \exp\left\{-\frac{1}{2\sigma^2} \sum_{i=1}^{n} (X_i - \mu)^2\right\}$$

which has the following logarithm:

$$(10.34) \qquad \log_e L(X_1, \ldots, X_n; \mu, \sigma^2)$$
$$= -\frac{n}{2} \log_e 2\pi - \frac{n}{2} \log_e \sigma^2 - \frac{1}{2\sigma^2} \sum_{i=1}^{n} (X_i - \mu)^2$$

To maximize (10.34) with respect to μ and σ^2, we consider its derivatives:

(10.35)
$$\frac{\partial \log_e L}{\partial \mu} = \frac{1}{\sigma^2} \sum_{i=1}^{n} (X_i - \mu)$$

(10.36)
$$\frac{\partial \log_e L}{\partial \sigma^2} = -\frac{n/2}{\sigma^2} + \frac{\sum_{i=1}^{n} (X_i - \mu)^2}{2\sigma^4}$$

The right-hand side of (10.35) equals $n(\bar{X} - \mu)/\sigma^2$. Thus, by equating this derivative to zero, we find that $\bar{X}$ is the maximum-likelihood estimator of μ (as in the case of the previous subsection). When we substitute this solution in the derivative (10.36),

$$-\frac{n/2}{\sigma^2} + \frac{\sum_{i=1}^{n} (X_i - \bar{X})^2}{2\sigma^4} = \frac{n}{2\sigma^4}\left[-\sigma^2 + \frac{1}{n} \sum_{i=1}^{n} (X_i - \bar{X})^2 \right]$$

and equate that derivative to zero also, we find that

(10.37)
$$\hat{\sigma}^2 = \frac{1}{n} \sum_{i=1}^{n} (X_i - \bar{X})^2$$

is the maximum-likelihood estimator of σ^2. We know from (4.45) that this is a biased estimator; hence, maximum-likelihood estimators are not necessarily unbiased.

*10.3 Maximum-Likelihood Estimation in the Standard Linear Model

The Standard Linear Model Under Normality

In this section we shall apply the maximum-likelihood method to estimate the parameters of the standard linear model. The disturbances are assumed to be normally distributed. Hence, given that the model postulates that they are uncorrelated with zero mean and the same variance, they are now independently distributed according to the same normal law. We shall consider in Sections 15.2 and 16.4 how this normality assumption can be justified.

In particular, consider eq. (8.3) of Section 8.1, reproduced here:

(10.38)
$$y_i = \beta_0 + \beta_1 x_{1i} + \beta_2 x_{2i} + \epsilon_i \qquad i = 1, \ldots, n$$

If $\epsilon_1, \ldots, \epsilon_n$ are independent normal variates with zero mean and variance σ^2, their joint density function is

$$\frac{1}{(2\pi\sigma^2)^{n/2}} \exp\left\{-\frac{1}{2\sigma^2} \sum_{i=1}^{n} \epsilon_i^2\right\}$$

We use (10.38) to substitute $y_i - \beta_0 - \beta_1 x_{1i} - \beta_2 x_{2i}$ for ϵ_i, which yields the following likelihood function:

(10.39) $L(y_1, \ldots, y_n; \beta_0, \beta_1, \beta_2, \sigma^2)$
$$= \frac{1}{(2\pi\sigma^2)^{n/2}} \exp\left\{-\frac{1}{2\sigma^2} \sum_{i=1}^{n} (y_i - \beta_0 - \beta_1 x_{1i} - \beta_2 x_{2i})^2\right\}$$

In the left-hand side of (10.39), $y_1, \ldots, y_n$, are the random sample values similar to $X_1, \ldots, X_n$ in the left-hand side of (10.33). The x_{1i}'s and x_{2i}'s are not introduced as arguments of $L(\ )$ in (10.39); they are known constants under the standard linear model.

The Maximum-Likelihood Coefficient Estimators

The logarithm of (10.39) is

(10.40) $\log_e L(y_1, \ldots, y_n; \beta_0, \beta_1, \beta_2, \sigma^2)$

$$= -\frac{n}{2} \log_e 2\pi - \frac{n}{2} \log_e \sigma^2 - \frac{1}{2\sigma^2} \sum_{i=1}^{n} (y_i - \beta_0 - \beta_1 x_{1i} - \beta_2 x_{2i})^2$$

Maximum-likelihood estimates are obtained by selecting those parameter values for which (10.39) or, equivalently, its logarithm (10.40) takes the largest value. Note, then, that the third right-hand term in (10.40) is the only one containing the β's and that this term is equal to a negative constant $(-1/2\sigma^2)$ multiplied by

(10.41) $$\sum_{i=1}^{n} (y_i - \beta_0 - \beta_1 x_{1i} - \beta_2 x_{2i})^2$$

Hence, the maximum-likelihood estimates of the β's are those values which minimize (10.41). But this criterion is precisely that of least squares. Therefore, under the assumption of normally distributed disturbances, *maximum-likelihood estimation of the β's is equivalent to LS estimation*, so that the maximum-likelihood estimators of β_0, β_1, and β_2 are identical to the corresponding LS estimators b_0, b_1, and b_2.

We know from (8.30), (8.31), and (8.50) that the sampling errors of these estimators are linear combinations of the disturbances. Therefore, if the disturbances are normally distributed, the coefficient estimators b_0, b_1, and b_2 are normally distributed with means equal to the corresponding β's.

The Maximum-Likelihood Estimator of the Disturbance Variance

Substitution of the maximum-likelihood solution in (10.41) gives

$$\sum_{i=1}^{n} (y_i - b_0 - b_1 x_{1i} - b_2 x_{2i})^2 = \sum_{i=1}^{n} e_i^2$$

which we substitute in (10.40):

(10.42) $\log_e L(y_1, \ldots, y_n; b_0, b_1, b_2, \sigma^2)$

$$= -\frac{n}{2} \log_e 2\pi - \frac{n}{2} \log_e \sigma^2 - \frac{1}{2\sigma^2} \sum_{i=1}^{n} e_i^2$$

To estimate σ^2 by maximum likelihood, we maximize (10.42) by varying σ^2. Thus, we differentiate (10.42) with respect to σ^2,

(10.43) $-\frac{n/2}{\sigma^2} + \frac{1}{2\sigma^4} \sum_{i=1}^{n} e_i^2$

which we equate to zero, yielding

(10.44)
$$\frac{1}{n} \sum_{i=1}^{n} e_i^2$$

as the maximum-likelihood estimator of σ^2. We know from (8.37) and (8.38) that the estimator (10.44) is not unbiased. This result is similar to that obtained below (10.37).

Problems

Problems 1–5 refer to Section 10.1, 6 and 7 to Section 10.2, and 8–10 to Section 10.3.

1 Let (X, Y) have a bivariate normal distribution with means μ_1 and μ_2, standard deviations σ_1 and σ_2, and correlation coefficient p. Prove directly (not using symmetry considerations) that the conditional distribution of X given $Y = y$ is normal with the mean and variance shown in (10.8).

2 Let (X, Y) have a bivariate normal distribution. Is $3X - Y$ normally distributed? Is $3X^2 - Y$ normally distributed? Explain your answer.

3 Let the density function of (X, Y) be as shown in (10.13). Prove that X and Y are both standardized normal variates. Are they independent standardized normal variates?

4 Verify that, for $n = 2$, (10.20) is equivalent to (10.4) when the a_{ij}'s are specified as shown in (10.21) and (10.22).

5 Prove that

$$\sqrt{\frac{a_{ii}}{2\pi}} \exp \left\{ -\frac{1}{2} a_{ii}(x_i - \mu_i)^2 \right\}$$

is the density function of the normal distribution with mean μ_i and variance $1/a_{ii}$. Use this result to verify that each exponent in (10.23) must be multiplied by $\sqrt{a_{ii}/2\pi}$ in order to yield the density function of the corresponding variate X_i. (*Note*: If $X_1, \ldots, X_n$ are not uncorrelated, so that there are nonzero a_{ij}'s with $i \neq j$, the variance of X_i is not $1/a_{ii}$.)

6 Write $\mathcal{E}(\hat{\sigma}^2) - \sigma^2$ for the bias of the estimator (10.37) of σ^2. Prove that this bias converges to zero when n increases indefinitely.

7 Verify that, for any given value of σ^2, the function (10.34) is maximized by equating μ to $\bar{X}$. [*Hint*: See the developments below (10.32).] Substitute $\bar{X}$ for μ in (10.34):

$$\log_e L(X_1, \ldots, X_n; \bar{X}, \sigma^2)$$
$$= -\frac{n}{2} \log_e 2\pi - \frac{n}{2} \log_e \sigma^2 - \frac{1}{2\sigma^2} \sum_{i=1}^{n} (X_i - \bar{X})^2$$

Differentiate this function with respect to σ^2 to obtain the maximum-likelihood solution (10.37). Also compute the second derivative with respect to

σ^2. Verify that this is negative at the solution (10.37), thus confirming that we have a maximum.

8 Extend (10.38) to an equation containing an arbitrary number of explanatory variables, and assume that $\epsilon_1, \ldots, \epsilon_n$ are independent normal variates with zero mean and variance σ^2. Prove that (a) the maximum-likelihood estimators of the constant term and all slope coefficients are identical to the corresponding LS estimators and (b) the maximum-likelihood estimator of σ^2 equals the residual sum of squares divided by n.

9 (*Continuation*) Extend this result to equations without constant term ($\beta_0 = 0$).

10 Prove that the second-order derivative of (10.42) with respect to σ^2 is equal to $n/2\sigma^4 - (1/\sigma^6) \sum_i e_i^2$. Evaluate this derivative at the solution (10.44), and complete the proof that this solution corresponds to a maximum of the likelihood function.

chapter 11

Confidence
and
Prediction Intervals

This chapter and the next develop statistical inference methods other than the point estimation procedure described in Section 4.4. To implement these methods, we need two distributions associated with the normal, which are described in Section 11.1. Proofs of the statements made in that section can be found in any introductory statistical text.

11.1 Two Distributions Associated with the Normal

The Chi-Square Distribution

Let $Z_1, \ldots, Z_n$ be independent standardized normal variates (zero mean and unit variance). The sum of their squares,

$$(11.1) \qquad Z_1^2 + \cdots + Z_n^2$$

can be shown to have the chi-square (χ^2) distribution with n degrees of freedom. (The relationship with the degrees of freedom introduced in Section 5.3 is explained in Section 11.3.) The density function of a χ^2 variate with n degrees of freedom, indicated by $\chi^2(n)$, is illustrated in Figure 17 for $n = 1$, 2, and 6. The range of the distribution is from 0 to ∞ for any value of n. The distribution is skew with a tail in the direction of ∞, but it becomes more symmetric when n increases. The mean of the distribution is equal to the number of degrees of freedom, and the variance equals twice this number:

$$(11.2) \qquad \mathcal{E}[\chi^2(n)] = n, \qquad \operatorname{var} \chi^2(n) = 2n$$

A table of the χ^2 distribution is given at the end of this book.

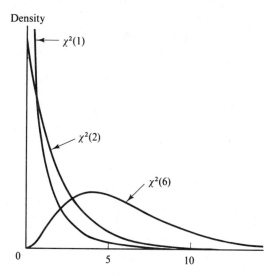

FIGURE 17   Density functions of the χ^2 distributions with one, two, and six degrees of freedom

The Student Distribution

Let $Z_1, \ldots, Z_n, Z_{n+1}$ be independent standardized normal variates, and consider the following expression:

$$(11.3) \qquad \frac{Z_{n+1}}{\sqrt{(1/n)\sum_{i=1}^{n} Z_i^2}} = \frac{Z_{n+1}}{\sqrt{Z_1^2 + \cdots + Z_n^2}}\sqrt{n}$$

We know from (11.1) that the denominator on the right is the square root of a χ^2 variate with n degrees of freedom. Since $Z_1, \ldots, Z_n$ are distributed independently of Z_{n+1} (by assumption), the ratio immediately to the right of the equal sign in (11.3) is thus the ratio of a standardized normal variate (Z_{n+1}) to the square root of an independent χ^2 variate. When such a ratio is multiplied by the square root of the number of degrees of freedom of the χ^2 variate, as is the case on the right in (11.3), the resulting expression is distributed as Student's t with n degrees of freedom, indicated by $t(n)$. Thus, both sides of (11.3) are distributed as $t(n)$. The mean and the variance of the Student distribution are

$$(11.4) \qquad \mathcal{E}[t(n)] = 0, \qquad \operatorname{var} t(n) = \frac{n}{n-2}$$

Note that the variance exists only for $n \geq 3$ [see the paragraph below (4.9)].

Figure 18 illustrates the density function of the Student distribution for $n = 4$ degrees of freedom, along with the density function of the standardized normal distribution. Both are symmetric around the zero mean, but the Student distribution has thicker tails. When the number of degrees of freedom increases

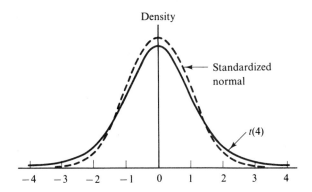

FIGURE 18 Density functions of the standardized normal distribution and of the t distribution with four degrees of freedom

indefinitely, the Student distribution becomes indistinguishable from the standardized normal distribution. A table of the Student distribution is given at the end of this book.

The Sampling Distribution of the Estimators of the Mean and the Variance

Let $(X_1, \ldots, X_n)$ be a random sample from a normal distribution with unknown mean μ and unknown variance σ^2. Hence, the density function of the sample is given in (4.34), which we write as

$$(11.5) \qquad f(x_1, \ldots, x_n) = \frac{1}{(\sigma\sqrt{2\pi})^n} \exp\left\{-\frac{1}{2}\sum_{i=1}^{n}\frac{(x_i - \mu)^2}{\sigma^2}\right\}$$

To estimate μ we use $\bar{X} = (1/n)\sum_i X_i$. Since $\bar{X}$ is a linear combination of multinormal variates, the distribution of $\bar{X}$ is normal. Also recall from (4.42) and (4.48) that this distribution has mean μ and variance σ^2/n. Since a univariate normal distribution is determined by its mean and variance [see (10.2)], the sampling distribution of $\bar{X}$ is thus completely specified.

To estimate σ^2 we use s^2 defined in (4.46),

$$(11.6) \qquad s^2 = \frac{1}{n-1}\sum_{i=1}^{n}(X_i - \bar{X})^2$$

which we multiply by $(n-1)/\sigma^2$:

$$(11.7) \qquad \frac{(n-1)s^2}{\sigma^2} = \frac{1}{\sigma^2}\sum_{i=1}^{n}(X_i - \bar{X})^2$$

It is shown in Appendix C that if $(X_1, \ldots, X_n)$ is a random sample from a normal distribution with mean μ and variance σ^2, (I) the right-hand side of (11.7) is distributed as $\chi^2(n-1)$ and (II) $\bar{X}$ and this right-hand side are stochastically independent.

REMARKS:

(1) Since the left-hand side of (11.7) equals s^2 multiplied by the constant $(n - 1)/\sigma^2$, the independence property (II) implies that $\bar{X}$ and s^2 are also stochastically independent. Hence, the joint density function of $\bar{X}$ and s^2 is the product of the density function of $\bar{X}$ and that of s^2. The density function of $\bar{X}$ is that of the normal distribution with mean μ and variance σ^2/n. The density function of s^2 follows from the fact that $(n - 1)s^2/\sigma^2$ is distributed as $\chi^2(n - 1)$. Thus, the joint density function of $(\bar{X}, s^2)$ is specified completely.

(2) In the right-hand side of (11.7) we have the sum of n squares. In (11.1) we also have the sum of n squares, with distribution $\chi^2(n)$. Why is the distribution $\chi^2(n - 1)$ in the case of (11.7)? To clarify this we note that if X_i is normal with mean μ and variance σ^2, $(X_i - \mu)/\sigma$ is standardized normal, so that the independence of the X_i's implies that the random variable

$$\sum_{i=1}^{n} \left(\frac{X_i - \mu}{\sigma} \right)^2 = \frac{1}{\sigma^2} \sum_{i=1}^{n} (X_i - \mu)^2$$

is distributed as $\chi^2(n)$. In (11.7) we have $\bar{X}$ rather than μ on the right, and $(X_i - \bar{X})/\sigma$ does not have unit variance. However, the right-hand side of (11.7) can be written as the sum of the squares of $n - 1$ independent standardized normal variates; the use of $\bar{X}$ instead of μ "absorbs" one degree of freedom, leading to $\chi^2(n - 1)$ rather than $\chi^2(n)$. The interested reader should consult Problem 3, where this matter is pursued for $n = 1$ and $n = 2$.

11.2 Confidence Intervals

In Section 4.4 we developed the theory of point estimation, which yields one numerical value as an approximation of the unknown parameter, given the sample drawn. The analyst may want more than such a single value. He may want an interval (A, B) so that there will be great confidence that the parameter lies in this interval.

A Confidence Interval Based on the Normal Distribution

Let $(X_1, \ldots, X_n)$ be a random sample from a normal distribution with unknown mean μ and unit variance, so that the arithmetic mean $\bar{X}$ is normally distributed with mean μ and variance $1/n$. We know from the table of the normal distribution that there is a .95 probability that a normal variate lies in the interval (mean $\pm 1.960 \times$ standard deviation). Therefore,

$$(11.8) \qquad P\left[\mu - \frac{1.960}{\sqrt{n}} \leq \bar{X} \leq \mu + \frac{1.960}{\sqrt{n}} \right] = .95$$

By subtracting $\mu + \bar{X}$ from each member, we find that the double inequality within brackets is equivalent to

$$-\bar{X} - \frac{1.960}{\sqrt{n}} \leq -\mu \leq -\bar{X} + \frac{1.960}{\sqrt{n}}$$

which, in turn, is equivalent to

$$\bar{X} - \frac{1.960}{\sqrt{n}} \le \mu \le \bar{X} + \frac{1.960}{\sqrt{n}}$$

so that we can write (11.8) in the form

(11.9) $$P\left[\bar{X} - \frac{1.960}{\sqrt{n}} \le \mu \le \bar{X} + \frac{1.960}{\sqrt{n}}\right] = .95$$

The result (11.9) is interpreted as a *confidence interval* $(\bar{X} \pm 1.96/\sqrt{n})$ for the parameter μ with *confidence coefficient* .95. Thus, we have obtained an interval (A, B), in agreement with the objective stated in the opening paragraph of this section, but we should be very careful as to its interpretation. What is random within brackets in (11.9) is $\bar{X}$, not μ. Hence, the interval (A, B) is random in the sense that its end points,

$$A = \bar{X} - \frac{1.960}{\sqrt{n}} \quad \text{and} \quad B = \bar{X} + \frac{1.960}{\sqrt{n}}$$

are random variables. It is therefore better to read (11.9) as "The probability is .95 that the interval $(\bar{X} \pm 1.96/\sqrt{n})$ contains μ" rather than "The probability is .95 that μ lies in the interval $(\bar{X} \pm 1.96/\sqrt{n})$."

Example

Consider the sample shown in Table 8 on page 53 and assume that the $n = 50$ profit margins are obtained by random drawings from a normal distribution with mean μ and unit variance. Since the arithmetic mean of the 50 sample values is 9.845, the double inequality on the left in (11.9) takes the following form for this sample:

(11.10) $$9.845 - \frac{1.960}{\sqrt{50}} \le \mu \le 9.845 + \frac{1.960}{\sqrt{50}}$$

Using $1.96/\sqrt{50} \approx .277$, we obtain $9.57 \le \mu \le 10.12$. It is impossible to say whether, for a particular sample, such an interval does or does not contain μ. However, (11.9) shows that if we construct confidence intervals with a .95 confidence coefficient a large number of times, it will turn out in about 95 percent of all cases that the interval actually contains the parameter and, hence, in about 5 percent of all cases that the parameter is outside the interval.

The selection of the confidence coefficient (.95 in the above example) is a matter to be decided by the analyst. If he raises this coefficient, the procedure becomes more reliable: There will be fewer cases in which the parameter is outside the interval. But at the same time he reduces the precision of his numerical statement, because a higher confidence coefficient raises the width of the confidence interval. For example, if we select a .99 confidence coefficient, we use the fact that there is a .99 probability that a normal variate lies in the interval (mean $\pm 2.576 \times$ standard deviation). This shows that 1.960 in (11.9) must be replaced by 2.576, which raises the width of the confidence interval by more than 30 percent.

A Confidence Interval Based on the Student Distribution

The result (11.9) is so simple because the normal distribution of $X_1, \ldots, X_n$ has unit variance by assumption. If this variance is an unknown parameter σ^2, the variance of $\bar{X}$ equals σ^2/n, and the ratio $1.960/\sqrt{n}$ in (11.9) becomes $1.960\sigma/\sqrt{n}$, which cannot be computed from the sample because σ is unknown. To solve this problem we consider

$$(11.11) \qquad \frac{(\bar{X} - \mu)/(\sigma/\sqrt{n})}{\sqrt{(n-1)s^2/\sigma^2}} \sqrt{n-1} = \frac{(\bar{X} - \mu)\sqrt{n}}{s}$$

Since $\bar{X}$ is normally distributed with mean μ and variance σ^2/n (and hence standard deviation $\sigma/\sqrt{n}$), the ratio of $\bar{X} - \mu$ to $\sigma/\sqrt{n}$ in the left-hand numerator of (11.11) is a standardized normal variate. We know from property (I) stated below (11.7) that $(n-1)s^2/\sigma^2$ is distributed as $\chi^2(n-1)$ and from property (II) that it is independent of $\bar{X}$. Therefore, the left-hand side of (11.11) is the ratio of a standardized normal variate to the square root of an independent χ^2 variate, multiplied by the square root of the number of degrees of freedom of this χ^2 variate. Thus, going back to the lines preceding (11.4), we conclude that the left-hand side of (11.11) and hence the right-hand side also are distributed as $t(n-1)$. This enables us to obtain a confidence interval for μ based on the Student distribution.

Second Example

Consider again Table 8 on page 53, for which $n = 50$, so that $t(n-1)$ becomes $t(49)$. The table of the Student distribution with 49 degrees of freedom shows that this t variate exceeds 2.010 with probability .025. Given that the distribution is symmetric around zero, the inequality $t(49) < -2.010$ has the same probability. Therefore,

$$(11.12) \qquad P[-2.010 \leq t(49) \leq 2.010] = .95$$

Since (11.11) for $n = 50$ is distributed as $t(49)$, the double inequality on the left in (11.12) yields

$$-2.010 \leq \frac{(\bar{X} - \mu)\sqrt{50}}{s} \leq 2.010$$

This is equivalent to

$$-2.010\frac{s}{\sqrt{50}} \leq \bar{X} - \mu \leq 2.010\frac{s}{\sqrt{50}}$$

and also to

$$(11.13) \qquad \bar{X} - 2.010\frac{s}{\sqrt{50}} \leq \mu \leq \bar{X} + 2.010\frac{s}{\sqrt{50}}$$

When we substitute the observed values 9.845 for $\bar{X}$ and $\sqrt{1.3461}$ for s, we obtain $9.52 \leq \mu \leq 10.17$ as a confidence interval corresponding to the .95 confidence coefficient [see (11.12)]. Note that the width of this interval exceeds that of the interval obtained below (11.10) under the assumption $\sigma^2 = 1$.

Comparison with the Two-Sigma Rule

At this stage the reader is advised to go back to the last subsection of Section 4.4 on standard errors and the two-sigma rule. This rule proposes an interval obtained from the estimate by adding and subtracting twice the standard error, and it states that this interval contains the parameter apart from a probability .046. In (11.13) the multiple of the standard error is 2.010 rather than 2, and the probability that the interval does not contain the parameter is .05 rather than .046. These differences are rather small, but they can be much larger when the sample is smaller.

In contrast to the two-sigma rule, confidence intervals based on the Student distribution provide an exact procedure for μ if the distribution from which the sample is drawn is normal with mean μ and variance σ^2. In the next section we shall extend the approach to confidence intervals for the β's and σ^2 of the standard linear model.

11.3   Confidence Intervals in the Standard Linear Model

Review of Earlier Results

We consider again eq. (8.3) in Section 8.1,

$$(11.14) \qquad y_i = \beta_0 + \beta_1 x_{1i} + \beta_2 x_{2i} + \epsilon_i \qquad\qquad i = 1, \ldots, n$$

as well as the sampling variance (8.33) of the LS estimator b_1 of β_1:

$$(11.15) \qquad \operatorname{var} b_1 = \frac{\sigma^2}{(1 - r^2) \sum_{i=1}^{n} (x_{1i} - \bar{x}_1)^2}$$

This variance is unknown because σ^2 is unknown. But since s^2 defined in (8.37) is an unbiased estimator of σ^2,

$$(11.16) \qquad s^2 = \frac{1}{n-3} \sum_{i=1}^{n} e_i^2, \qquad \mathcal{E}(s^2) = \sigma^2$$

the expression

$$(11.17) \qquad s_{b_1}^2 = \frac{s^2}{(1 - r^2) \sum_{i=1}^{n} (x_{1i} - \bar{x}_1)^2}$$

is an unbiased estimator of the variance (11.15). The corresponding estimate is the square of the standard error of b_1 [see (8.41)]. Our first objective is to use this standard error to obtain a confidence interval for β_1.

The Chi-Square Distribution of the Residual Sum of Squares

We assume that $\epsilon_1, \ldots, \epsilon_n$ are independent normal variates with zero mean and variance σ^2. We know from (8.30), (8.31), and (8.50) that the sampling errors of the b's are linear combinations of the ϵ_i's; hence, b_0, b_1 and b_2 are normally distributed with means equal to the corresponding β's.

We multiply the first equation in (11.16) by $(n - 3)/\sigma^2$:

$$(11.18) \qquad \frac{(n-3)s^2}{\sigma^2} = \frac{1}{\sigma^2} \sum_{i=1}^{n} e_i^2$$

Here $n - 3$ is the number of degrees of freedom in the demand equation for textile. More generally, let us write n' for the number of degrees of freedom: the number of observations (n) minus the number of coefficients adjusted [see remark (3) on page 124]. We extend (11.16) to $s^2 = (1/n') \sum_i e_i^2$ and hence (11.18) to

$$(11.19) \qquad \frac{n's^2}{\sigma^2} = \frac{1}{\sigma^2} \sum_{i=1}^{n} e_i^2$$

It is shown in Appendix C that, under the assumption on the ϵ_i's stated in the previous paragraph, (I) the right-hand side of (11.19) is distributed as $\chi^2(n')$ and (II) this right-hand side and hence s^2 on the left also are stochastically independent of the LS coefficient estimators (the b's). The reader should compare these propositions with those stated below (11.7).

The n' defined below (11.18) is the number of degrees of freedom of the regression. Proposition (I) implies that the LS residual sum of squares of this regression, when divided by σ^2, has a χ^2 distribution with the same number of degrees of freedom. This should clarify the relationship between the degrees of freedom of a regression and a χ^2 variate.

A Confidence Interval for a Coefficient

Given that b_1 is normally distributed with mean β_1 and variance (11.15), the ratio $(b_1 - \beta_1)/\sqrt{\text{var } b_1}$ is a standardized normal variate. It follows from propositions (I) and (II) above that this ratio is independent of $n's^2/\sigma^2$ and that $n's^2/\sigma^2$ is distributed as $\chi^2(n')$. Thus, we can conclude from the discussion preceding (11.4) that

$$(11.20) \qquad \frac{(b_1 - \beta_1)/\sqrt{\text{var } b_1}}{\sqrt{n's^2/\sigma^2}} \sqrt{n'} = \frac{b_1 - \beta_1}{\sqrt{(s^2/\sigma^2)\,\text{var } b_1}} = \frac{b_1 - \beta_1}{s_{b_1}}$$

is distributed as $t(n')$. The last step in (11.20) is based on (11.15) and (11.17).

This result enables us to obtain a confidence interval for β_1 based on the Student distribution. We have 17 annual observations in the regression for textile, so $n' = 17 - 3 = 14$. The table of the Student distribution shows

$$(11.21) \qquad P[-2.145 \le t(14) \le 2.145] = .95$$

The LS estimate b_1 of the income elasticity of the demand for textile is 1.1430 [see (7.21)], and s_{b_1} equals $\sqrt{.024324} \approx .1560$ [see (8.41)], which yields the ratio of $1.1430 - \beta_1$ to $.1560$ for the third member of (11.20). Thus, the double inequality on the left in (11.21) becomes

$$-2.145 \leq \frac{1.1430 - \beta_1}{.1560} \leq 2.145$$

which is equivalent to $-.335 \leq 1.143 - \beta_1 \leq .335$ and also (in two decimal places) to $.81 \leq \beta_1 \leq 1.48$. This is a confidence interval for the income elasticity of the demand for textile at the .95 confidence coefficient [see (11.21)]. The reader should verify, using the relevant results of Chapter 8 (see Problem 9), that the three β's of the demand equation for textile have the following confidence intervals, each in two decimal places at the .95 confidence coefficient:

(11.22)
$$.72 \leq \beta_0 \leq 2.03 \qquad \text{(constant term)}$$
$$.81 \leq \beta_1 \leq 1.48 \qquad \text{(income elasticity)}$$
$$-.91 \leq \beta_2 \leq -.75 \qquad \text{(price elasticity)}$$

A Confidence Interval for the Disturbance Variance

Recall from proposition (I) below (11.19) that $n's^2/\sigma^2$ is distributed as $\chi^2(n')$. The table of the χ^2 distribution with $n' = 14$ degrees of freedom shows that this χ^2 variate is less than 5.63 with probability .025 and is larger than 26.12 with the same probability, so that

(11.23)
$$P[5.63 \leq \chi^2(14) \leq 26.12] = .95$$

Hence, $5.63 \leq 14s^2/\sigma^2 \leq 26.12$ or, equivalently, $14s^2/26.12 \leq \sigma^2 \leq 14s^2/5.63$ holds with probability .95. When we substitute .002567 for $14s^2$ [see (8.39)], we obtain (.00010, .00046) as a confidence interval for σ^2 at the .95 confidence coefficient.

A Linear Combination of Coefficients

In (8.45) we estimated $\beta_1 - 2\beta_2$, where β_1 and β_2 are the income and price elasticities of the demand for textile. Our objective is now to obtain a confidence interval for such a linear combination of β's.

Let $w_1\beta_1 + w_2\beta_2$ be this linear combination, where w_1 and w_2 are constants. Its LS estimator is $w_1b_1 + w_2b_2$, which is unbiased. The sampling variance of this estimator is given in (8.46),

(11.24) $\quad \text{var}(w_1b_1 + w_2b_2) = w_1^2 \text{ var } b_1 + w_2^2 \text{ var } b_2 + 2w_1w_2 \text{ cov } (b_1, b_2)$

where var b_1 is given in (11.15), var b_2 takes the same form except that the subscripts 1 and 2 must be interchanged, and cov (b_1, b_2) is given in (8.44) and reproduced here:

$$\text{cov}(b_1, b_2) = -\frac{r\sigma^2}{(1 - r^2)\sqrt{\sum_{i=1}^{n}(x_{1i} - \bar{x}_1)^2 \sum_{i=1}^{n}(x_{2i} - \bar{x}_2)^2}}$$

When we substitute these results in (11.24) and use the notation (8.18),

$$S_1 = \sqrt{\sum_{i=1}^{n}(x_{1i} - \bar{x}_1)^2}, \qquad S_2 = \sqrt{\sum_{i=1}^{n}(x_{2i} - \bar{x}_2)^2}$$

we obtain

$$\text{var}(w_1 b_1 + w_2 b_2) = w_1^2 \frac{\sigma^2}{(1 - r^2)S_1^2} + w_2^2 \frac{\sigma^2}{(1 - r^2)S_2^2}$$
$$- 2w_1 w_2 \frac{r\sigma^2}{(1 - r^2)S_1 S_2}$$

which can be simplified to

$$(11.25) \qquad \text{var}(w_1 b_1 + w_2 b_2) = \frac{\sigma^2}{1 - r^2} \left(\frac{w_1^2}{S_1^2} + \frac{w_2^2}{S_2^2} - \frac{2r w_1 w_2}{S_1 S_2} \right)$$

A Confidence Interval for a Linear Combination

Since $w_1 b_1 + w_2 b_2$ equals $w_1 \beta_1 + w_2 \beta_2$ plus a linear combination of normally distributed disturbances, $w_1 b_1 + w_2 b_2 - (w_1 \beta_1 + w_2 \beta_2)$ is normal with zero mean and variance (11.25), so that

$$(11.26) \qquad \frac{w_1 b_1 + w_2 b_2 - (w_1 \beta_1 + w_2 \beta_2)}{(\sigma/\sqrt{1 - r^2})\sqrt{(w_1/S_1)^2 + (w_2/S_2)^2 - 2r w_1 w_2/S_1 S_2}}$$

is a standardized normal variate. Recall the propositions stated below (11.19), according to which $n's^2/\sigma^2$ is distributed as $\chi^2(n')$ and is stochastically independent of the two b's in (11.26). Thus, by dividing (11.26) by $\sqrt{n's^2/\sigma^2} = (s/\sigma)\sqrt{n'}$ and multiplying by $\sqrt{n'}$, we obtain

$$(11.27) \qquad \frac{w_1 b_1 + w_2 b_2 - (w_1 \beta_1 + w_2 \beta_2)}{(s/\sqrt{1 - r^2})\sqrt{(w_1/S_1)^2 + (w_2/S_2)^2 - 2r w_1 w_2/S_1 S_2}}$$

which is distributed as $t(n')$.

We apply (11.27) to the linear combination $\beta_1 - 2\beta_2$ mentioned at the beginning of the previous subsection, so that the numerator takes the following value [see (8.45)]:

$$b_1 - 2b_2 - (\beta_1 - 2\beta_2) \approx 2.801 - (\beta_1 - 2\beta_2)$$

A comparison with (11.25) shows that the denominator of (11.27) is simply the standard error of $w_1 b_1 + w_2 b_2$, which is $\sqrt{.03454} \approx .186$ in the present case [see (8.48)]. Thus, using $n' = 14$ and (11.21), we obtain the double inequality

$$(11.28) \qquad -2.145 \leq \frac{2.801 - (\beta_1 - 2\beta_2)}{.186} \leq 2.145$$

which yields (after multiplication by .186 and subtraction of 2.801) a confidence interval (2.40, 3.20) for $\beta_1 - 2\beta_2$ with confidence coefficient .95. This interval is almost identical to that obtained below (8.48) from the two-sigma rule.

Confidence Regions for Several Coefficients

Each of the three confidence intervals in (11.22) has a .95 confidence coefficient. Hence, each of these intervals is obtained by a statistical procedure which guarantees a .95 probability that the interval contains the corresponding parameter. But what is the probability that a confidence interval for β_1 and one for β_2 *both* contain their parameter?

Consider Table 15, where $\beta_1 \in I_1$ indicates that β_1 is in the confidence interval, $\beta_1 \notin I_1$ that β_1 is outside the interval, and similarly for β_2 and I_2. Hence, we have $2 \times 2 = 4$ possible outcomes, each of which has a probability (p_{11}, p_{12}, p_{21}, p_{22}). The table may be viewed as a bivariate discrete distribution, to be compared with those shown in Table 5 on page 33. The marginal probabilities $p_{1.}$ and $p_{.1}$ are the confidence coefficients (both .95) of the two confidence intervals separately, and $p_{2.}$ and $p_{.2}$ are their complements (both .05).

TABLE 15

Confidence intervals for two parameters

	$\beta_2 \in I_2$	$\beta_2 \notin I_2$	*Marginal*
$\beta_1 \in I_1$	p_{11}	p_{12}	$p_{1.} = .95$
$\beta_1 \notin I_1$	p_{21}	p_{22}	$p_{2.} = .05$
Marginal	$p_{.1} = .95$	$p_{.2} = .05$	1

We are interested in p_{11}, the probability that both confidence intervals contain their parameter. Since one of the four possible outcomes must occur, the four probabilities ($p_{11}, p_{12}, p_{21}, p_{22}$) must add up to 1. Therefore,

$$(11.29) \qquad p_{11} = 1 - p_{12} - p_{21} - p_{22}$$
$$= 1 - (p_{12} + p_{22}) - (p_{21} + p_{22}) + p_{22}$$
$$= 1 - p_{.2} - p_{2.} + p_{22}$$

We have $p_{.2} = p_{2.} = .05$ and $p_{22} \geq 0$, so that (11.29) implies that $p_{11} \geq .9$. Hence, given that (.81, 1.48) is the realization of I_1 for our sample in (11.22) and that $(-.91, -.75)$ is the realization of I_2, the shaded rectangular region shown in Figure 19 is a confidence region for the parameter pair (β_1, β_2) with a confidence coefficient at least equal to .9.

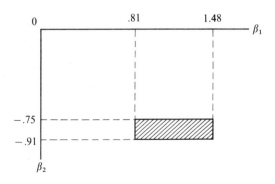

FIGURE 19 A confidence region for the income and price elasticities of the demand for textile

Note that the exact confidence coefficient is unknown, although we know a lower limit (.9) for this coefficient. It is also possible to construct an area in the form of an ellipse for which the confidence coefficient is known; see, for example, Theil (1971, pp. 132–134).

*11.4   Regression Predictions

The Nature of a Regression Prediction

Suppose we have computed a regression of a dependent variable on certain explanatory variables. Can we use such a regression to predict a future value of the dependent variable? The answer is affirmative, provided two conditions are satisfied. First, the relationship should be stable, which amounts to unchanged values of the β's and σ^2. Second, the prediction of the value of the dependent variable requires the corresponding values of the explanatory variables to be known. It is a conditional prediction, given the values of the explanatory variables.

As an example, consider the demand equation (11.14) for textile. The right-hand variables are the logarithms of real income per capita and the relative textile price. Let these variables take the values x_{1*} and x_{2*} in some year after the sample period (1923–1939). Our objective is to predict y_*, the logarithm of the volume of textile consumption per capita in that year, using

$$(11.30) \qquad y_* = \beta_0 + \beta_1 x_{1*} + \beta_2 x_{2*} + \epsilon_*$$

where ϵ_* is a random variable with zero mean and variance σ^2.

The difference between predicting and estimating should be noted. *Estimating* is using a random sample to approximate unknown parameters (unknown constants), such as the β's in (11.30). *Predicting* is using a random sample to approximate values taken by random variables, such as y_* and ϵ_* in (11.30).

Above we used expressions such as "to predict a future value" and "in some year after the sample period," which suggest that the data should have the form of time series. We emphasize that this need not be so and that the analysis which follows is equally applicable to cross-sectional data, for example, the case in which household expenditures are predicted from income and family size (two explanatory variables) for households which are not included in the sample.

Predictor and Predictand

Let $\epsilon_1, \ldots, \epsilon_n, \epsilon_*$ be independent random variables with zero mean and variance σ^2. Then the conditional distribution of ϵ_* given $\epsilon_1, \ldots, \epsilon_n$ is independent of the latter ϵ's and is hence identical to the marginal distribution of ϵ_*, so that there is no way in which we can use the sample to infer about ϵ_*. If we predict ϵ_* by its expectation (zero), predicting y_* from (11.30) becomes equivalent to estimating the expectation of y_*,

$$(11.31) \qquad \mathcal{E}y_* = \beta_0 + \beta_1 x_{1*} + \beta_2 x_{2*}$$

Substitution of the LS estimators for the β's on the right yields

(11.32) $$\hat{y}_* = b_0 + b_1 x_{1*} + b_2 x_{2*}$$

which is a point estimator of $\mathcal{E}y_*$ (a point estimator of an unknown constant) and also a *point predictor* of y_* (a point predictor of a random variable). The random variable to be predicted (y_*) is called the *predictand*. We shall be particularly interested in the error $\hat{y}_* - y_*$ of the predictor; this error is another random variable. When we compute (11.32) for a numerically specified sample, the b's become estimates (rather than estimators), and the associated $\hat{y}_*$ becomes a numerically specified point prediction.

Unbiased Predictors

By subtracting (11.31) from (11.32), we obtain the sampling error of the estimator $\hat{y}_*$ of $\mathcal{E}y_*$:

(11.33) $$\hat{y}_* - \mathcal{E}y_* = b_0 - \beta_0 + x_{1*}(b_1 - \beta_1) + x_{2*}(b_2 - \beta_2)$$

Similarly, by subtracting (11.30) from (11.32), we obtain

(11.34) $$\hat{y}_* - y_* = b_0 - \beta_0 + x_{1*}(b_1 - \beta_1) + x_{2*}(b_2 - \beta_2) - \epsilon_*$$

and hence, using (11.33),

(11.35) $$\hat{y}_* - y_* = (\hat{y}_* - \mathcal{E}y_*) - \epsilon_*$$

This result shows that the error $\hat{y}_* - y_*$ of the predictor $\hat{y}_*$ is equal to the difference between the sampling error of the estimator $\hat{y}_*$ of $\mathcal{E}y_*$ and the disturbance component ϵ_* of the predictand y_*.

We treat x_{1*} and x_{2*} as constants, because we operate conditionally on these two values. The unbiasedness of the b's in (11.33) then implies that $\hat{y}_* - \mathcal{E}y_*$ has zero expectation. Since ϵ_* also has zero expectation (by assumption), (11.35) yields

(11.36) $$\mathcal{E}(\hat{y}_* - y_*) = 0$$

or, in words, the error $\hat{y}_* - y_*$ of the predictor $\hat{y}_*$ has zero expectation. This is expressed by saying that $\hat{y}_*$ is an *unbiased predictor*. Note that this predictor does not have an expectation equal to the predictand y_*; this predictand is a random variable. The expectation of an unbiased predictor is equal to the expectation of the predictand, which is verified by writing (11.36) in the form $\mathcal{E}\hat{y}_* - \mathcal{E}y_* = 0$.

The Variance of the Prediction Error

Given that $\hat{y}_*$ has expectation $\mathcal{E}y_*$, we obtain the variance of $\hat{y}_*$ by squaring both sides of (11.33),

$$\begin{aligned}(\hat{y}_* - \mathcal{E}y_*)^2 = {}&(b_0 - \beta_0)^2 + x_{1*}^2(b_1 - \beta_1)^2 + x_{2*}^2(b_2 - \beta_2)^2\\&+ 2x_{1*}(b_0 - \beta_0)(b_1 - \beta_1) + 2x_{2*}(b_0 - \beta_0)(b_2 - \beta_2)\\&+ 2x_{1*}x_{2*}(b_1 - \beta_1)(b_2 - \beta_2)\end{aligned}$$

and then taking the expectation. This yields

(11.37) $\text{var } \hat{y}_* = \text{var } b_0 + x_{1*}^2 \text{ var } b_1 + x_{2*}^2 \text{ var } b_2 + 2x_{1*} \text{ cov } (b_0, b_1)$
$+ 2x_{2*} \text{ cov } (b_0, b_2) + 2x_{1*}x_{2*} \text{ cov } (b_1, b_2)$

Since the prediction error $\hat{y}_* - y_*$ has zero expectation in view of (11.36), we obtain the variance of this error by squaring (11.35) and taking the expectation:

$$\mathcal{E}[(\hat{y}_* - y_*)^2] = \mathcal{E}[(\hat{y}_* - \mathcal{E}y_*)^2] + \mathcal{E}(\epsilon_*^2) - 2\mathcal{E}[(\hat{y}_* - \mathcal{E}y_*)\epsilon_*]$$

The first term on the right is the variance (11.37); the second equals σ^2; and the third vanishes (as will be shown in the next paragraph). Therefore,

(11.38) $\mathcal{E}[(\hat{y}_* - y_*)^2] = \text{var } \hat{y}_* + \sigma^2$

which shows that the variance of the prediction error consists of two parts. One component (σ^2) reflects our inability to predict the random component ϵ_* of y_*. The other component, var $\hat{y}_*$ given in (11.37), results from the use of the LS coefficients, rather than the β's, in the prediction formula (11.32).

To verify $\mathcal{E}[(\hat{y}_* - \mathcal{E}y_*)\epsilon_*] = 0$ we use (11.33):

(11.39) $\mathcal{E}[(\hat{y}_* - \mathcal{E}y_*)\epsilon_*] = \mathcal{E}[(b_0 - \beta_0)\epsilon_*] + x_{1*}\mathcal{E}[(b_1 - \beta_1)\epsilon_*]$
$+ x_{2*}\mathcal{E}[(b_2 - \beta_2)\epsilon_*]$

It follows from (8.30), (8.31), and (8.50) that the three expressions in brackets on the right are all linear combinations of $\epsilon_1, \ldots, \epsilon_n$, multiplied by ϵ_*. Since all $n + 1$ disturbances are uncorrelated with zero mean by assumption, the product of any such combination and ϵ_* has zero expectation, which implies that both sides of (11.39) vanish.

A Prediction Interval Based on the Student Distribution

If $\epsilon_1, \ldots, \epsilon_n, \epsilon_*$ are normally distributed, we can extend the theory of confidence intervals to yield a prediction interval for y_*. To simplify the exposition, we shall consider the case of a simple regression through the origin, so that the right-hand sides of (11.31) and (11.32) can be written as βx_* and $b x_*$, respectively, and (11.37) as

$$\text{var } \hat{y}_* = x_*^2 \text{ var } b = \frac{\sigma^2 x_*^2}{\sum_{i=1}^{n} x_i^2}$$

where the second step is based on (5.17). Hence, (11.38) becomes

(11.40) $\mathcal{E}[(\hat{y}_* - y_*)^2] = \sigma^2\left(1 + \frac{x_*^2}{S^2}\right),$ where $S^2 = \sum_{i=1}^{n} x_i^2$

Since $\hat{y}_* - y_* = b x_* - y_*$ is a linear combination of normal variates ($\epsilon_1, \ldots, \epsilon_n, \epsilon_*$), it is also normally distributed. Hence, in view of (11.36) and (11.40), the ratio

(11.41) $\dfrac{b x_* - y_*}{\sigma\sqrt{1 + x_*^2/S^2}}$

is a standardized normal variate. Next consider the propositions below (11.19), where $n' = n - 1$ in the present case. They imply that $(n - 1)s^2/\sigma^2$, with s^2 defined in (5.21), is distributed as $\chi^2(n - 1)$ and is stochastically independent of the ratio (11.41). [This independence follows from (1) the independence of b and s^2 and (2) the fact that the random component ϵ_* of y_* in (11.41) is also independent of the sample from which s^2 is obtained.] Therefore the expression

$$(11.42) \qquad \frac{(bx_* - y_*)/\sigma\sqrt{1 + x_*^2/S^2}}{\sqrt{(n-1)s^2/\sigma^2}}\sqrt{n-1} = \frac{bx_* - y_*}{s\sqrt{1 + x_*^2/S^2}}$$

is distributed as $t(n - 1)$.

We use the table of the Student distribution to obtain t_α from

$$(11.43) \qquad P[-t_\alpha \leq t(n - 1) \leq t_\alpha] = 1 - 2\alpha$$

For example, for $n = 50$ and $\alpha = .025$ (implying $1 - 2\alpha = .95$) we obtain $t_{.025} = 2.010$ from (11.12). Next we substitute the right-hand side of (11.42) for $t(n - 1)$ in (11.43):

$$P\left[-t_\alpha \leq \frac{bx_* - y_*}{s\sqrt{1 + x_*^2/S^2}} \leq t_\alpha\right] = 1 - 2\alpha$$

By multiplying the expressions in brackets by $s\sqrt{1 + x_*^2/S^2}$ and subtracting bx_*, we obtain

$$(11.44) \qquad P[bx_* - t_\alpha s\sqrt{1 + x_*^2/S^2} \leq y_* \leq bx_* + t_\alpha s\sqrt{1 + x_*^2/S^2}] = 1 - 2\alpha$$

which yields a prediction interval for y_*.

A Geometric Illustration

To clarify this result, we write the double inequality in brackets in (11.44) in the form $A \leq y_* \leq B$, where

$$(11.45) \qquad A = bx_* - t_\alpha s\sqrt{1 + \frac{x_*^2}{S^2}}, \qquad B = bx_* + t_\alpha s\sqrt{1 + \frac{x_*^2}{S^2}}$$

which are the end points of the prediction interval for y_*. These end points, viewed as functions of x_*, are the two branches of the hyperbola which is shown in Figure 20. The straight line through the origin is the regression line $y = bx$, which is determined by the sample (indicated by $n = 10$ black dots). This regression line yields the point prediction $\hat{y}_* = bx_*$ for any value of x_*. The width of the interval, $B - A$, is a multiple $2t_\alpha s$ of the square root of $1 + x_*^2/S^2$. This width takes the smallest value $(2t_\alpha s)$ at $x_* = 0$ and increases when x_* takes larger (positive or negative) values. Hence, the prediction becomes less accurate when it is made at a larger absolute value of x_*. This is intuitively obvious, since the regression is required to go through the origin and thus yields less uncertainty as to y when x is close to zero than when x is far from zero. If this requirement is not imposed, the most accurate prediction is made at the arithmetic mean $\bar{x}$ of the values taken by the explanatory variable. The interested reader should consult Problems 14 to 16 on this matter.

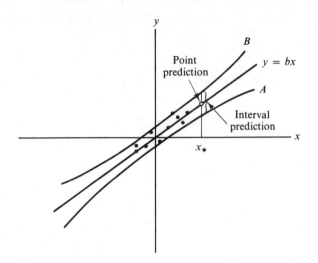

FIGURE 20   Regression prediction

We conclude from (11.44) and (11.45) that $A \leq y_* \leq B$ holds with probability $1 - 2\alpha$. Note that A, B, and y_* are *all* random. This is in contrast to a confidence interval $A \leq \theta \leq B$ for a parameter θ with confidence coefficient $1 - 2\alpha$. In the latter case, A and B are random, but θ is a constant.

Problems

Problems 1–3 refer to Section 11.1, 4 and 5 to Section 11.2, 6–13 to Section 11.3, and 14–16 to Section 11.4.

1 Verify that proposition (I) below (11.7), combined with the mean of the χ^2 distribution given in (11.2), implies the unbiasedness of the σ^2 estimator (11.6). [*Note*: The χ^2 distribution refers specifically to random sampling from a normal distribution, but the estimator (11.6) is unbiased even when the random sample is from a nonnormal distribution with mean μ and variance σ^2.]

2 (*Continuation*) Prove that if the random sample is from a normal distribution with mean μ and variance σ^2, the estimator s^2 of σ^2 has a sampling variance equal to $2\sigma^4/(n - 1)$.

3 For $n = 1$, prove that the right-hand side of (11.7) is zero, and verify that this agrees with the χ^2 distribution with zero degrees of freedom. [*Hint*: Use (11.2).] For $n = 2$, verify that the right-hand side of (11.7) equals

$$\frac{1}{\sigma^2}\left(X_1 - \frac{X_1 + X_2}{2}\right)^2 + \frac{1}{\sigma^2}\left(X_2 - \frac{X_1 + X_2}{2}\right)^2 = \left(\frac{X_1 - X_2}{\sigma\sqrt{2}}\right)^2$$

and prove that this is distributed as $\chi^2(1)$.

4 Extend (11.10) to obtain a confidence interval (9.48, 10.21) for μ at the .99 confidence coefficient, using the fact that there is a .99 probability that a normal variate lies in (mean $\pm$ 2.576 × standard deviation). Compare this confidence interval with that corresponding to the .95 confidence coefficient, and draw your conclusions.

5 Extend (11.13) to obtain a confidence interval for μ at the .99 confidence coefficient, using the fact that $|t(49)| \leq 2.68$ has probability .99.

6 Verify that the propositions below (11.19) contain those stated below (11.7) as a special case. [*Hint*: Specify $\beta_1 = \beta_2 = 0$ in (11.14).]

7 A χ^2 variate with 49 degrees of freedom has a .95 probability of lying between 31.1 and 69.7. Use this information as well as $s^2 = 1.3461$ to obtain a confidence interval (.95, 2.12) for σ^2 from Table 8 on page 53.

8 (*Continuation*) The confidence interval contains $\sigma^2 = 1$. Suppose that $\sigma^2 = 1$ had been outside the interval. What would you conclude, given the knowledge that Table 8 is obtained from a (reliable) computer program for random normal sample numbers with mean 10 and unit variance?

9 Verify the confidence intervals for β_0 and β_2 in (11.22). [*Hint*: Use (8.6), (8.42), and (8.52).]

10 (*Continuation*) Suppose that we write the confidence interval for β_2 in the following form:

$$P[-.91 \leq \beta_2 \leq -.75] = .95$$

What is wrong with this statement?

11 (*Continuation*) Construct confidence intervals for β_0, β_1, and β_2 with confidence coefficient .99, using $P[|t(14)| \leq 2.977] = .99$.

12 Verify that the ratio (11.27) contains the third member of (11.20) as a special case for $w_1 = 1$, $w_2 = 0$.

13 We have $P[\beta_1 \in I_1] = P[\beta_2 \in I_2] = .95$ in Table 15 and conclude

$$P[\beta_1 \in I_1 \text{ and } \beta_2 \in I_2] = (.95)^2 = .9025$$

What is wrong with this conclusion?

14 Consider a simple regression of y on x with constant term. Let $\hat{y}_*$ be the predictor of y_* at $x = x_*$. Verify that (11.37) in this case becomes

$$\text{var } \hat{y}_* = \text{var } b_0 + x_*^2 \text{ var } b + 2x_* \text{ cov } (b, b_0)$$
$$= \frac{\sigma^2}{n} + \frac{\sigma^2(x_* - \bar{x})^2}{\sum_{i=1}^{n} (x_i - \bar{x})^2}$$

[*Hint*: Use (5.31), (5.38), and (6.21).]

15 (*Continuation*) Verify that the prediction interval in brackets in (11.44) becomes

$$b_0 + bx_* - t_\alpha s \sqrt{1 + \frac{1}{n} + \frac{1}{k}(x_* - \bar{x})^2}$$
$$\leq y_* \leq b_0 + bx_* + t_\alpha s \sqrt{1 + \frac{1}{n} + \frac{1}{k}(x_* - \bar{x})^2}$$

where $k = \sum_i (x_i - \bar{x})^2$, s is given in (5.43), and t_α is obtained from

$$P[-t_\alpha \leq t(n-2) \leq t_\alpha] = 1 - 2\alpha$$

16 (*Continuation*) Verify that the end points of the new prediction interval, when viewed as functions of x_*, are the two branches of a hyperbola. Also prove that the minimum width of this interval is

$$2t_\alpha s \sqrt{1 + \frac{1}{n}}$$

and that this minimum is reached at $x_* = \bar{x}$.

chapter 12

The Testing

of

Hypotheses

The theories of point estimation and confidence intervals yield procedures to approximate an unknown parameter by means of the outcome of a random sample. The theory of hypothesis testing approaches the problem from a different angle; it asks whether the sample allows us to decide for or against the hypothesis that the parameter takes a particular value.

12.1 The First Fundamentals of Hypothesis Testing

Some Basic Concepts

Let $(X_1, \ldots, X_n)$ be a random sample from a normal distribution with unknown mean μ and unit variance. We want to use this sample to decide whether it is true that $\mu = \mu_0$, where μ_0 is a given number. We refer to $\mu = \mu_0$ as the *null hypothesis* and indicate it by H_0. This hypothesis is tested against an *alternative hypothesis*, indicated by H_1, which may state that $\mu \neq \mu_0$ (μ equals any number other than μ_0). Other possible specifications of H_1 are $\mu > \mu_0$ and $\mu < \mu_0$. For simplicity, we shall assume in this section that H_1 specifies $\mu \neq \mu_0$.

To test H_0 against the alternative H_1, we formulate a *test statistic*, which is some function of the random sample; we compute the value of this statistic for the sample that has been drawn and proceed to accept or reject H_0 on the basis of this numerical value. In the example of the previous paragraph, we may take $\bar{X} = (1/n) \sum_i X_i$ as the test statistic. We know that $\bar{X}$ is normally distributed with mean μ and variance $1/n$. If H_0 is true, the mean of this normal distribution is μ_0. If H_1 is true, this mean is $\mu \neq \mu_0$. An obvious procedure is to accept H_0 if the $\bar{X}$ of the sample drawn is sufficiently close to μ_0 and to reject H_0 in favor of H_1 if this $\bar{X}$ is far from μ_0.

Example

Let the data of Table 8 on page 53 be the outcome of a random sample ($n = 50$) from a normal distribution with mean μ and unit variance. The null hypothesis is $\mu = 11$, to be tested against the alternative hypothesis $\mu \neq 11$. Consider, then, (11.8), reproduced below:

$$(12.1) \qquad \mathrm{P}\left[\mu - \frac{1.960}{\sqrt{n}} \leq \bar{X} \leq \mu + \frac{1.960}{\sqrt{n}}\right] = .95$$

Hence, for $n = 50$, $\bar{X}$ lies in the interval ($\mu \pm 1.96/\sqrt{50}$) with .95 probability, whatever the value of μ may be. If H_0 is true, this value is 11, in which case $\bar{X}$ lies in ($11 \pm 1.96/\sqrt{50}$) with .95 probability. When the observed $\bar{X}$ is outside this interval, we reject H_0 in favor of H_1. This rejection thus takes place when the observed $\bar{X}$ is either larger than $11 + 1.96/\sqrt{50} \approx 11.28$ or smaller than $11 - 1.96/\sqrt{50} \approx 10.72$. The $\bar{X}$ of Table 8 is 9.845 and thus smaller than 10.72. Therefore, we reject the null hypothesis $\mu = 11$ against the alternative hypothesis $\mu \neq 11$.

Figure 21 shows the density function of the distribution of the test statistic $\bar{X}$ under H_0 (normal, mean 11, variance $\frac{1}{50}$). The set of values > 11.28 and < 10.72 is called the *critical region* of this test statistic for this null hypothesis. If the observed value of the statistic falls in this region, as is the case here ($9.845 < 10.72$), the null hypothesis is rejected. If the observed value of the statistic does not fall in this region, the null hypothesis is accepted. It follows from (12.1) for $n = 50$ that if the null hypothesis is true, $\bar{X}$ is outside the critical region with probability .95 and hence inside the critical region with probability .05. Given the symmetry of the normal distribution, the critical region of this example consists of two components with probability .025 each. The corresponding areas are shaded in Figure 21.

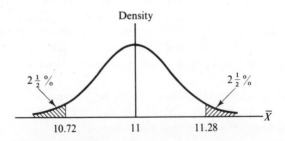

FIGURE 21   The critical region of a test statistic

Errors of the First and the Second Kind

The mathematics of hypothesis testing is quite close to that of confidence intervals, but the interpretation is different. In the case of confidence intervals, the interval may contain the parameter (which is good) or it may not contain the parameter (which is bad). In the case of hypothesis testing there are four possibilities, because either H_0 or H_1 is true and the test either accepts or rejects H_0:

(1) H_0 is true and the test statistic is not in the critical region, so that H_0 is accepted. This is a correct decision because H_0 is true.

(2) H_0 is not true (hence, H_1 is true) and the test statistic is in the critical region, so that H_0 is rejected in favor of H_1. This is also a correct decision.

(3) H_0 is true and the test statistic is in the critical region, so that H_0 is rejected. This is an error, known as an *error of the first kind*: The null hypothesis is rejected although it is true. In the example of the previous subsection such an error occurs when $\mu = 11$ (H_0 is true) and $\bar{X}$ exceeds 11.28 or is below 10.72; the probability of this error is .05 (see the shaded areas in Figure 21).

(4) H_0 is not true (hence, H_1 is true) and the test statistic is not in the critical region, so that H_0 is accepted. This is an *error of the second kind*: H_0 is accepted but not true.

The Probability of an Error

Ideally we would like to minimize the probability of both kinds of errors, but this is not a feasible approach. The standard procedure is to fix the probability of a first-kind error at a particular level: .05 in Figure 21. The analyst is then said to test his null hypothesis at the 5 percent *significance level*. The associated bounds of the critical region (10.72 and 11.28 in Figure 21) are called the 5 percent *significance limits* of the test statistic.

The probability of a second-kind error depends on the question of which specific hypothesis within the set of all hypotheses covered by H_1 is true. This is illustrated in Figure 22 for a random sample of size $n = 100$ from a normal distribution with mean μ and unit variance. The null hypothesis (H_0) states that $\mu = \mu_0$; the alternative hypothesis (H_1) states that $\mu \neq \mu_0$. The distribu-

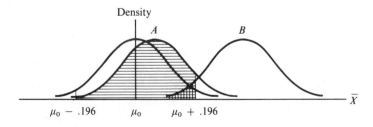

FIGURE 22   The probability of a second-kind error

tion of $\bar{X}$ is normal with mean μ and variance $1/n = .01$. If H_0 is true, this distribution has mean μ_0, so that there is a .95 probability that $\bar{X}$ falls in $(\mu_0 \pm .196)$, where $.196 = 1.96/\sqrt{n}$ for $n = 100$ [see (12.1)]. The corresponding density curve is shown on the far left in Figure 22. If the true value of μ differs only a little from μ_0, as is the case for the density curve labeled A, the probability that $\bar{X}$ falls in $(\mu_0 \pm .196)$ will not be far below .95; this probability is equal to the horizontally shaded area in Figure 22. Hence, the probability of a second-kind error is large when the null hypothesis, though untrue, is not far from the truth. On the other hand, if the true value of μ differs substantially from μ_0, the probability of a second-kind error is much smaller, as indeed we would like it to be. This is illustrated by the density curve B in Figure 22. Only a small portion of the area below this curve is above $(\mu_0 \pm .196)$, as is shown by the double-shaded area. Hence, if the hypothesis corresponding to curve B is true, the probability of a second-kind error is small.

12.2   Hypothesis Testing in the Standard Linear Model

We return to the demand equation (8.3) for textile,

$$(12.2) \qquad y_i = \beta_0 + \beta_1 x_{1i} + \beta_2 x_{2i} + \epsilon_i$$

Our first objective is to test hypotheses on the income and price elasticities (β_1 and β_2) under the assumption that the ϵ_i's are independent normal variates with zero mean and variance σ^2.

Testing a Hypothesis on a Coefficient

We test the null hypothesis (H_0) that the demand for textile has unitary income elasticity, $\beta_1 = 1$, against the alternative (H_1) that this elasticity is either larger or smaller than 1. We select the 5 percent significance level for this test, so that the probability is .05 that we will reject $\beta_1 = 1$ when in fact it is true.

Recall from (11.20) that $(b_1 - \beta_1)/s_{b_1}$ is distributed as $t(n')$, where $n' = 17 - 3 = 14$ for the textile example. If H_0 is true, $(b_1 - \beta_1)/s_{b_1}$ is equal to $(b_1 - 1)/s_{b_1}$, which takes the value

$$(12.3) \qquad \frac{1.1430 - 1}{\sqrt{.024324}} \approx .92$$

for the sample drawn [see (7.21) and (8.41)]. The result .92 is the value taken by the Student test statistic for our sample; if it is in the critical region, we reject H_0. Thus, we need the critical region of this Student test statistic at the 5 percent significance level. The solution is provided by (11.21), reproduced below,

$$(12.4) \qquad P[-2.145 \leq t(14) \leq 2.145] = .95$$

which shows that this region consists of all values larger than 2.145 in absolute value. The observed value, given in (12.3), is not in the critical region; hence, the hypothesis of unitary income elasticity is acceptable at the 5 percent significance level.

Next consider the null hypothesis $\beta_2 = -.75$, to be tested against the alternative $\beta_2 \neq -.75$ at the 5 percent significance level. As in the previous paragraph, we use the Student distribution $t(n') = t(14)$ of $(b_2 - \beta_2)/s_{b_2}$, which equals $(b_2 + .75)/s_{b_2}$ if H_0 is true. For the sample drawn [see (7.21) and (8.42)] this is

$$(12.5) \qquad \frac{-.8289 + .75}{\sqrt{.001304}} \approx -2.18$$

It follows from (12.4) that this is outside the 5 percent significance limits. Hence, the value of the Student test statistic is in the critical region, and the null hypothesis $\beta_2 = -.75$ is rejected in favor of $\beta_2 \neq -.75$.

The Effect of the Significance Level

Accepting or rejecting a null hypothesis is not independent of the significance level chosen. Consider the same H_0, $\beta_2 = -.75$, again to be tested against the alternative $\beta_2 \neq -.75$, but now at the 1 percent significance level. The value of the Student test statistic is -2.18 as in (12.5), but we must now use

$$(12.6) \qquad P[-2.977 \leq t(14) \leq 2.977] = .99$$

which shows that the 1 percent significance limits are ± 2.977. The observed value -2.18 is within these limits, so that $\beta_2 = -.75$ is accepted at the 1 percent significance level. This is in contrast to the rejection stated below (12.5). The difference results from the fact that a 1 percent significance level is more conservative from the viewpoint of rejecting H_0: The probability of rejecting H_0 when it is true is only .01, rather than .05. We express this result by saying that the price elasticity of the demand for textile is significantly different from $-.75$ at the 5 percent level but not significantly different from $-.75$ at the 1 percent level.

Testing a Hypothesis on the Disturbance Variance

Our next null hypothesis is $\sigma = .01$, to be tested against the alternative hypothesis $\sigma \neq .01$ at the 5 percent significance level. Recall from the discussion below (11.19) that $n's^2/\sigma^2$ is distributed as $\chi^2(n')$. For $n' = 14$ this equals $14s^2/(.01)^2$ under H_0, which takes the value $.002567/(.01)^2 = 25.67$ for the sample drawn [see (8.39)]. Next we use (11.23), reproduced here,

$$(12.7) \qquad P[5.63 \leq \chi^2(14) \leq 26.12] = .95$$

which shows that 5.63 and 26.12 are the 5 percent significance limits of this χ^2 test statistic. The observed value 25.67 is between these limits; hence, $\sigma = .01$ is an acceptable hypothesis at the 5 percent significance level.

t Ratios

Consider the null hypothesis that the demand for textile is completely insensitive to changes in real income, $\beta_1 = 0$, to be tested against $\beta_1 \neq 0$ at the 5 percent significance level. Again, recall from (11.20) that $(b_1 - \beta_1)/s_{b_1}$ is distributed as $t(n') = t(14)$. Under the present null hypothesis, this Student statistic takes the form b_1/s_{b_1}, which equals $1.1430/.1560 \approx 7.3$ for the sample drawn. This is larger than 2.145 and hence in the critical region [see (12.4)], so that the hypothesis of a zero income elasticity of the demand for textile must be rejected (in favor of a nonzero value) at the 5 percent significance level. Hence, this elasticity is significantly different from zero at the 5 percent level.

The ratio of the point estimate b_1 to its standard error s_{b_1} is thus the Student test statistic for the null hypothesis $\beta_1 = 0$. The absolute value of this ratio is known as a *t ratio*. Sometimes regressions are presented with *t* ratios, rather than standard errors, in parentheses below the point estimates:

$$(12.8) \qquad y = 1.37 + 1.14x_1 - .83x_2 + \text{residual}$$
$$(4.5) \quad (7.3) \quad (23.0)$$

Here 4.5 and 23.0 are *t* ratios for testing the hypotheses $\beta_0 = 0$ and $\beta_2 = 0$, respectively (see Problem 3 for the numerical values of these two ratios). Equation (12.8) should be compared with (8.12), reproduced here,

$$(12.9) \qquad y = 1.37 + 1.14x_1 - .83x_2 + \text{residual}$$
$$(.31) \quad (.16) \quad (.04)$$

where the numbers in parentheses are standard errors.

The presentation (12.8) is not recommended, because it forces the user of the regression to compute standard errors (by dividing point estimates by *t* ratios) if he is interested in null hypotheses other than zero values of the parameters. A direct presentation of standard errors, as is done in (12.9), is preferable, also because confidence intervals can then be obtained more easily.

Testing a Linear Combination of Coefficients

Next consider the null hypothesis

$$(12.10) \qquad w_1\beta_1 + w_2\beta_2 = w_0$$

where the w's are given numbers. Recall the statement made below (11.27), according to which the ratio

$$\frac{w_1b_1 + w_2b_2 - (w_1\beta_1 + w_2\beta_2)}{(s/\sqrt{1 - r^2})\sqrt{(w_1/S_1)^2 + (w_2/S_2)^2 - 2rw_1w_2/S_1S_2}}$$

is distributed as $t(n')$. Therefore, if (12.10) is true, the ratio

$$(12.11) \qquad \frac{w_1b_1 + w_2b_2 - w_0}{(s/\sqrt{1 - r^2})\sqrt{(w_1/S_1)^2 + (w_2/S_2)^2 - 2rw_1w_2/S_1S_2}}$$

is distributed as $t(n')$.

As an example, we shall consider the null hypothesis that the income and price elasticities of the demand for textile are equal apart from sign, $\beta_1 = -\beta_2$. This can be written as $\beta_1 + \beta_2 = 0$ and hence falls under (12.10) with $w_1 = w_2 = 1$ and $w_0 = 0$, so that (12.11) becomes

$$(12.12) \qquad \frac{b_1 + b_2}{(s/\sqrt{1 - r^2})\sqrt{(1/S_1)^2 + (1/S_2)^2 - 2r/S_1 S_2}}$$

which is distributed as $t(n') = t(14)$ under H_0. The value of the numerator for the sample drawn is $1.1430 + (-.8289) = .3141$ [see (7.21)] and that of the denominator is $.1521$, as will be shown in the next paragraph. Hence, (12.12) takes the value

$$(12.13) \qquad \frac{.3141}{.1521} \approx 2.07$$

which is less than the 5 percent significance limit of the Student distribution with 14 degrees of freedom shown in (12.4). Therefore, if the test is against the alternative hypothesis $\beta_1 + \beta_2 \neq 0$ at the 5 percent significance level, the null hypothesis is acceptable.

The square of the denominator in (12.12) equals

$$(12.14) \qquad \frac{s^2}{(1 - r^2)S_1^2} + \frac{s^2}{(1 - r^2)S_2^2} + 2\frac{-rs^2}{(1 - r^2)S_1 S_2}$$

The first two terms in (12.14) are the unbiased estimates of the sampling variances of b_1 and b_2 given in (8.41) and (8.42). The third term is twice the unbiased estimate of their sampling covariance [see (8.44)]. The latter estimate is $-.001251$ [see the discussion preceding (8.48)], so that (12.14) becomes $.024324 + .001304 + 2(-.001251) = .023126$, which has a square root equal to the denominator of (12.13).

One-Tailed and Two-Tailed Tests

In the applications discussed so far, we have assumed that if the null hypothesis states that $\theta = \theta_0$ for some parameter or parameter combination θ, the alternative hypothesis states that $\theta \neq \theta_0$, which means *either* $\theta < \theta_0$ or $\theta > \theta_0$. But suppose that the analyst admits *only* the alternative hypothesis $\theta < \theta_0$, or *only* $\theta > \theta_0$. For example, if θ measures the effect of a fertilizer on crop output, the analyst may know that this effect cannot be negative, which amounts to $\theta \geq 0$. Alternatively, the analyst may be convinced on a priori grounds that the price elasticity of the demand for textile is not larger in absolute value than the income elasticity, $-\beta_2 \leq \beta_1$, which is equivalent to $\beta_1 + \beta_2 \geq 0$. Then, if he wants to test the null hypothesis $\beta_1 + \beta_2 = 0$, he should do so against the alternative hypothesis $\beta_1 + \beta_2 > 0$. As before, we select the 5 percent significance level.

The clue is the appropriate choice of the critical region for the test statistic (12.12). It should be obvious that a large positive value of $b_1 + b_2$, but certainly

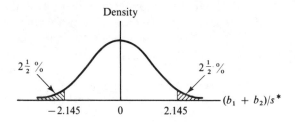

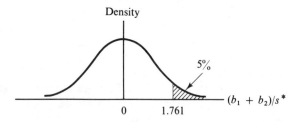

FIGURE 23 The critical regions of two-tailed and one-tailed tests

not a large negative value, is evidence supporting the alternative hypothesis $\beta_1 + \beta_2 > 0$. This is illustrated in Figure 23. The horizontal variable is the ratio (12.12), indicated by $(b_1 + b_2)/s^*$, where s^* is an abbreviation of the denominator of (12.12). The vertical variable is the density of (12.12) under H_0 (the Student density with 14 degrees of freedom). In the test against the alternative hypothesis $\beta_1 + \beta_2 \neq 0$, the critical region consists of two parts: the points on the horizontal axis to the left of -2.145 and those to the right of 2.145 [see (12.4)]. The areas below the density curve above both parts of this critical region are shaded in the upper part of Figure 23. The lower part of the figure refers to the alternative hypothesis $\beta_1 + \beta_2 > 0$. Since only positive values of $b_1 + b_2$ present evidence in favor of this hypothesis, we select a critical region to the right of the origin. This region consists of all points on the horizontal axis to the right of 1.761, because the probability that $t(14) > 1.761$ is equal to .05. The observed value of the test statistic given in (12.13) is in this region, so that we must reject $\beta_1 + \beta_2 = 0$ in favor of $\beta_1 + \beta_2 > 0$ at the 5 percent significance level.

Note that this conclusion differs from that drawn below (12.13) when we tested $\beta_1 + \beta_2 = 0$ against $\beta_1 + \beta_2 \neq 0$ at the *same* significance level. The difference is that the present test is a *one-tailed* test, whereas the previous one is a *two-tailed* test, as is evident from the shaded areas in Figure 23. The two-tailed test is designed to verify whether the sum of the income and price elasticities is significantly different from zero; the one-tailed test serves to verify whether this sum is significantly positive.

*12.3   Likelihood Ratio Tests

Consider the following null hypothesis for the demand equation (12.2) for textile:

(12.15) $$\beta_1 = \beta_2 = 0$$

This hypothesis declares that the demand for textile is completely insensitive to changes in real income and the relative textile price. To test a hypothesis which consists of two equations [$\beta_1 = 0$ and $\beta_2 = 0$ in (12.15)], it is convenient to use a so-called likelihood ratio test. Again, we assume that the ϵ_i's are independent normal variates with zero mean and variance σ^2.

Preliminary Discussion of Likelihood Ratio Tests and the F Distribution

Recall from Section 10.2 that maximum-likelihood estimates are obtained by maximizing the likelihood function. Thus, when these estimates are substituted in the likelihood function, we obtain the maximum value of this function, which we call the unconstrained maximum. This terminology is motivated by the consideration that the null hypothesis (12.15) may be viewed as a constraint on the coefficients of (12.2). If we impose this constraint when maximizing the likelihood function, the value of this function can obviously not exceed the unconstrained maximum. The procedure is thus to compute the constrained maximum, i.e., the largest value which the likelihood function can take under the null hypothesis. If we find that the constrained maximum is too much below the unconstrained maximum, we conclude that the sample yields evidence against the null hypothesis. In the next three subsections we shall evaluate these two maxima for the null hypothesis (12.15), after which a more general discussion follows.

In Section 11.1 we introduced two distributions associated with the normal: χ^2 and t. The test of (12.15) requires a third. Let X and Y be stochastically independent χ^2 variates with m and n degrees of freedom, respectively. We divide each by the number of degrees of freedom, X/m and Y/n, and consider their ratio:

(12.16) $$\frac{X/m}{Y/n} = F(m, n)$$

This ratio is distributed as F with m and n degrees of freedom. A table of the F distribution is given at the end of this book.

The Unconstrained Likelihood Maximum

The logarithm of the likelihood function associated with (12.2) takes the form (10.40), which is reproduced here:

(12.17) $\log_e L(y_1, \ldots, y_n; \beta_0, \beta_1, \beta_2, \sigma^2)$

$$= -\frac{n}{2} \log_e 2\pi - \frac{n}{2} \log_e \sigma^2 - \frac{1}{2\sigma^2} \sum_{i=1}^{n} (y_i - \beta_0 - \beta_1 x_{1i} - \beta_2 x_{2i})^2$$

In the developments below (10.40), we first maximized this function with respect
to the β's, which yields the LS estimators b_0, b_1, b_2 as the maximum-likelihood
estimators of the β's. Hence, given a fixed value of σ^2, the maximum of (12.17),
obtained by varying the β's, is

(12.18)
$$-\frac{n}{2}\log_e 2\pi - \frac{n}{2}\log_e \sigma^2 - \frac{1}{2\sigma^2}\sum_{i=1}^n e_i^2$$

which is equal to the right-hand side of (10.42). We then maximized this expression by varying σ^2, yielding $(1/n)\sum_i e_i^2$ as the maximum-likelihood estimator of
σ^2 [see (10.44)]. When we substitute this solution for σ^2 in the third term of
(12.18), we obtain

$$-\frac{1}{(2/n)\sum_{i=1}^n e_i^2}\sum_{i=1}^n e_i^2 = -\frac{n}{2}$$

so that (12.18) becomes

(12.19)
$$-\frac{n}{2}\log_e 2\pi - \frac{n}{2}\log_e \left(\frac{1}{n}\sum_{i=1}^n e_i^2\right) - \frac{n}{2}$$

which is the largest value that the logarithmic likelihood function (12.17) can
take.

The Constrained Likelihood Maximum

When we impose the null hypothesis (12.15), the function (12.17) becomes

(12.20) $\log_e L(y_1, \ldots, y_n; \beta_0, 0, 0, \sigma^2)$
$$= -\frac{n}{2}\log_e 2\pi - \frac{n}{2}\log_e \sigma^2 - \frac{1}{2\sigma^2}\sum_{i=1}^n (y_i - \beta_0)^2$$

This function involves two "free" parameters, viz., β_0 and σ^2 which (12.15)
leaves unspecified. Our objective is now to maximize (12.20) by varying β_0 and
σ^2, which yields the maximum of (12.17) that is compatible with the null
hypothesis (12.15).

We differentiate (12.20) with respect to β_0 and σ^2:

(12.21)
$$\frac{\partial \log_e L}{\partial \beta_0} = \frac{1}{\sigma^2}\sum_{i=1}^n (y_i - \beta_0)$$

(12.22)
$$\frac{\partial \log_e L}{\partial \sigma^2} = -\frac{n/2}{\sigma^2} + \frac{\sum_{i=1}^n (y_i - \beta_0)^2}{2\sigma^4}$$

The right-hand side of (12.21) equals $n(\bar{y} - \beta_0)/\sigma^2$, where $\bar{y}$ is the arithmetic
mean of $y_1, \ldots, y_n$. Thus, by equating (12.21) to zero, we obtain $\bar{y}$ as the
maximum-likelihood solution of β_0. When we substitute this solution in the
derivative (12.22),

$$-\frac{n/2}{\sigma^2} + \frac{\sum_{i=1}^n (y_i - \bar{y})^2}{2\sigma^4} = \frac{n}{2\sigma^4}\left[-\sigma^2 + \frac{1}{n}\sum_{i=1}^n (y_i - \bar{y})^2\right]$$

and equate that derivative to zero also, we find that

(12.23) $$\frac{1}{n}\sum_{i=1}^{n}(y_i - \bar{y})^2$$

is the maximum-likelihood solution of σ^2. Next we substitute the solutions $\bar{y}$ for β_0 and (12.23) for σ^2 in the third term of (12.20),

$$-\frac{1}{(2/n)\sum_{i=1}^{n}(y_i - \bar{y})^2}\sum_{i=1}^{n}(y_i - \bar{y})^2 = -\frac{n}{2}$$

so that (12.20) becomes

(12.24) $$-\frac{n}{2}\log_e 2\pi - \frac{n}{2}\log_e\left[\frac{1}{n}\sum_{i=1}^{n}(y_i - \bar{y})^2\right] - \frac{n}{2}$$

This is the maximum value of (12.20), obtained by varying β_0 and σ^2, and also the constrained maximum of (12.17) subject to (12.15).

The Likelihood Ratio

The likelihood ratio λ is defined as the ratio of the constrained maximum of the likelihood function to the unconstrained maximum. Therefore,

$$\log_e \lambda = \log_e \frac{\text{constrained maximum}}{\text{unconstrained maximum}}$$
$$= \log_e(\text{constrained maximum}) - \log_e(\text{unconstrained maximum})$$

Since (12.19) and (12.24) are the two relevant maxima of the logarithmic likelihood function (unconstrained and constrained), we thus obtain $\log_e \lambda$ by subtracting the former from the latter. This gives

$$\log_e \lambda = \frac{n}{2}\log_e\left(\frac{1}{n}\sum_{i=1}^{n}e_i^2\right) - \frac{n}{2}\log_e\left[\frac{1}{n}\sum_{i=1}^{n}(y_i - \bar{y})^2\right]$$

$$= \frac{n}{2}\log_e\frac{(1/n)\sum_{i=1}^{n}e_i^2}{(1/n)\sum_{i=1}^{n}(y_i - \bar{y})^2} = \frac{n}{2}\log_e(1 - R^2)$$

where the last step is based on (9.15). Thus, after taking antilogs, we obtain

(12.25) $$\lambda = (1 - R^2)^{n/2}$$

which expresses the likelihood ratio for testing the null hypothesis (12.15) in terms of the multiple correlation coefficient of the regression.

The Principle of a Likelihood Ratio Test

In the three previous subsections we developed the likelihood ratio for a particular case, but the general principle should be clear. We have several parameters, and the null hypothesis (H_0) specifies that some of these, but not all, take certain numerical values [such as the zero values of β_1 and β_2 in

(12.15)]. We compute the maximum of the likelihood function, given these numerical values (which is the constraint imposed by H_0), by varying the parameters which H_0 leaves unspecified: β_0 and σ^2 in the case of (12.15). The likelihood ratio λ is defined as the ratio of this constrained maximum to the unconstrained maximum of the likelihood function. By construction, λ is at most equal to 1. This is confirmed by (12.25) because $1 - R^2 \leq 1$ follows from $R \geq 0$.

The likelihood ratio test states that H_0 is to be rejected when λ is less than some critical number which is determined by the significance level that the analyst decides to use. The underlying idea is that H_0 must be considered as an unrealistic hypothesis when the largest probability density which is consistent with this hypothesis, given the sample drawn, is too far below the largest value of this density that can be attained when we do not impose H_0. This principle generates a class of tests; its implementation for the null hypothesis (12.15) is described in the next subsection.

Implementation of the Likelihood Ratio Test

We have $1 - R^2 = \lambda^{2/n}$ from (12.25), and hence $R^2 = 1 - \lambda^{2/n}$, so that

$$(12.26) \qquad \frac{R^2}{1 - R^2} = \frac{1 - \lambda^{2/n}}{\lambda^{2/n}} = \lambda^{-2/n} - 1$$

which shows that the likelihood ratio for (12.15) is directly related to the ratio of R^2 to $1 - R^2$. Next we use (9.14) and (9.15),

$$\frac{R^2}{1 - R^2} = \frac{\sum_{i=1}^{n} (\hat{y}_i - \bar{y})^2}{\sum_{i=1}^{n} e_i^2} = \frac{\sum_{i=1}^{n} [b_1(x_{1i} - \bar{x}_1) + b_2(x_{2i} - \bar{x}_2)]^2}{\sum_{i=1}^{n} e_i^2}$$

where the last step is based on (9.4) for $K = 2$. We write this result as

$$(12.27) \qquad \frac{R^2}{1 - R^2} = \frac{(1/\sigma^2) \sum_{i=1}^{n} [b_1(x_{1i} - \bar{x}_1) + b_2(x_{2i} - \bar{x}_2)]^2}{(1/\sigma^2) \sum_{i=1}^{n} e_i^2}$$

Recall from proposition (I) below (11.19) that the right-hand denominator is distributed as $\chi^2(n')$. It is shown in the next subsection that this denominator is stochastically independent of the numerator and that the latter is distributed as $\chi^2(2)$ if the null hypothesis (12.15) is true. Thus, going back to the discussion preceding and following (12.16), we find that in this case the likelihood ratio test can be implemented by means of the F distribution. We must divide the numerator and the denominator of (12.27) by their degrees of freedom (2 and n'), yielding

$$(12.28) \qquad \frac{R^2/2}{(1 - R^2)/n'} = \frac{n'R^2}{2(1 - R^2)}$$

which is distributed as $F(2, n')$ if (12.15) is true.

We apply this result to the demand for textile, using $n' = 14$ and $R^2 = .9744$ [see (9.17)], which yields a value of well over 200 for the test statistic (12.28). Since the 1 percent significance limit of $F(2, 14)$ is 6.51, this presents overwhelming evidence against the null hypothesis (12.15).

Derivations

The right-hand numerator of (12.27) involves only b_1 and b_2 (apart from σ^2 and the x_{1i}'s and x_{2i}'s, which are all constants); the independence of the numerator and the denominator then follows directly from proposition (II) below (11.19).

Next we write this numerator as

$$\frac{1}{\sigma^2}\left[b_1^2 \sum_{i=1}^{n}(x_{1i} - \bar{x}_1)^2 + b_2^2 \sum_{i=1}^{n}(x_{2i} - \bar{x}_2)^2 + 2b_1b_2 \sum_{i=1}^{n}(x_{1i} - \bar{x}_1)(x_{2i} - \bar{x}_2)\right]$$

which equals $(S_1^2 b_1^2 + S_2^2 b_2^2 + 2rS_1S_2b_1b_2)/\sigma^2$ in view of (8.18) and (8.19). We write this as

$$\frac{1}{\sigma^2}(S_1^2 b_1^2 + r^2 S_2^2 b_2^2 + 2rS_1S_2b_1b_2) + \frac{1}{\sigma^2}(1 - r^2)S_2^2 b_2^2$$

$$= \left(\frac{S_1b_1 + rS_2b_2}{\sigma}\right)^2 + \left(\frac{\sqrt{1 - r^2}\, S_2b_2}{\sigma}\right)^2$$

so that the right-hand numerator of (12.27) is equal to the sum of the squares of the ratios

(12.29) $$\frac{S_1b_1 + rS_2b_2}{\sigma} \quad \text{and} \quad \frac{\sqrt{1 - r^2}\, S_2b_2}{\sigma}$$

We shall prove in the next paragraph that, under the null hypothesis (12.15), these two ratios are independent standardized normal variates. Hence, the sum of their squares is distributed as $\chi^2(2)$, as stated below (12.27).

Both ratios in (12.29) are linear combinations of b_1 and b_2. Since b_1 and b_2 are normally distributed, these ratios are therefore also normally distributed. The expectations of the ratios are obtained by substituting β_1 and β_2 for b_1 and b_2 and are hence equal to zero under (12.15). The variance of the first ratio is

$$\frac{1}{\sigma^2}\,\text{var}\,(S_1b_1 + rS_2b_2) = \frac{1}{\sigma^2}[S_1^2\,\text{var}\,b_1 + r^2 S_2^2\,\text{var}\,b_2 + 2rS_1S_2\,\text{cov}\,(b_1, b_2)]$$

$$= \frac{\sigma^2}{\sigma^2(1 - r^2)}\left(\frac{S_1^2}{S_1^2} + \frac{r^2 S_2^2}{S_2^2} + 2rS_1S_2\frac{-r}{S_1S_2}\right)$$

$$= \frac{1}{1 - r^2}(1 + r^2 - 2r^2) = 1$$

where the second equal sign is based on (8.33), (8.34), and (8.44). The variance of the second ratio in (12.29) is also 1:

$$\frac{(1 - r^2)S_2^2}{\sigma^2}\,\text{var}\,b_2 = \frac{(1 - r^2)S_2^2}{\sigma^2}\,\frac{\sigma^2}{(1 - r^2)S_2^2} = 1$$

To verify that the two ratios are stochastically independent it is sufficient, given their normality, to prove that they are uncorrelated. This matter is pursued in Problem 10.

Extensions

Testing the null hypothesis (12.15) is frequently referred to as "testing the significance of the regression." If (12.15) is true, neither explanatory variable exerts any influence on the dependent variable; the values taken by the latter variable are equal to a constant (β_0) plus a random disturbance (ϵ_i). The procedure can be extended to include regressions on any number (K) of explanatory variables plus a constant term. We state, but do not prove, that the only changes are that $1 - R^2$ in the right-hand denominator of (12.28) is to be multiplied by K rather than 2 and that (12.28) thus modified is distributed as $F(K, n')$ if the null hypothesis $\beta_1 = \cdots = \beta_K = 0$ is true.

The likelihood ratio procedure is not confined to the testing of zero values of certain parameters. We refer to Theil (1971, pp. 141–145), where the hypothesis $\beta_1 = -\beta_2 = 1$ is tested for the demand for textile.

We conclude by noting that whereas the multiple correlation coefficient was introduced in Chapter 9 as a descriptive measure of the goodness of fit of a regression, the analysis of this section has shown that this coefficient plays an important role in the statistical testing of the significance of the regression. But it should also be noted that this testing requires the assumptions of the standard linear model with normally distributed disturbances. No such assumptions were used in Section 9.1.

Problems

Problems 1 and 2 refer to Section 12.1, 3–6 to Section 12.2, and 7–11 to Section 12.3.

1 In the discussion below (12.1) we reject the null hypothesis $\mu = 11$ at the 5 percent significance level. Verify that $\mu = 10.1$ is an acceptable hypothesis at the same significance level.

2 (*Continuation*) If we accept $\mu = 10.1$ in this way, does that mean that $\mu = 10.1$ is true?

3 Verify the t ratios of the constant term and the price elasticity of the demand for textile shown in (12.8). [*Hint*: Use (8.6), (8.42), and (8.52).]

4 Verify that the null hypothesis $\beta_2 = -1$ (a unitary price elasticity of the demand for textile) must be rejected in favor of $\beta_2 \neq -1$ at the 1 percent significance level. [*Hint*: Use (8.6), (8.42), and (12.6).]

5 (*Continuation*) Without further information on the Student distribution with 14 degrees of freedom, can you conclude that $\beta_2 = -1$ must also be

rejected against $\beta_2 > -1$ at the same significance level? (*Hint*: Compare Figure 23.)

6 Use $P[\chi^2(14) \leq 23.68] = .95$ to verify that the null hypothesis $\sigma = .01$ for textile must be rejected against the alternative hypothesis $\sigma > .01$ at the 5 percent significance level. [*Hint*: See the discussion preceding (12.7).]

7 Compare the definitions of the χ^2 and t distributions in Section 11.1 and of the F distribution in the first subsection of Section 12.3. Prove that if a random variable Z is distributed as $t(n)$, Z^2 is distributed as $F(1, n)$.

8 Verify that, for any given value of σ^2, the function (12.20) is maximized by equating β_0 to $\bar{y}$. [*Hint*: Prove that $\sum_i (y_i - \beta_0)^2$ is equal to the sum of $\sum_i (y_i - \bar{y})^2$ and $n(\beta_0 - \bar{y})^2$.] Substitute $\bar{y}$ for β_0 in (12.20):

$$\log_e L(y_1, \ldots, y_n; \bar{y}, 0, 0, \sigma^2)$$
$$= -\frac{n}{2} \log_e 2\pi - \frac{n}{2} \log_e \sigma^2 - \frac{1}{2\sigma^2} \sum_{i=1}^{n} (y_i - \bar{y})^2$$

Differentiate this function twice with respect to σ^2 to verify (a) the maximum-likelihood solution (12.23) of σ^2 and (b) the fact that the function is indeed maximized.

9 We reject the null hypothesis (12.15) in the paragraph below (12.28). Does this conclusion surprise you, given the results of earlier tests performed on the same data? Explain your answer.

10 Verify that the covariance of the two ratios in (12.29) equals

$$\frac{1}{\sigma^2} \operatorname{cov} (S_1 b_1 + r S_2 b_2, \sqrt{1 - r^2} \, S_2 b_2)$$

Use Problem 7 on page 59 to verify that this covariance is equal to

$$\frac{\sqrt{1 - r^2} \, S_1 S_2}{\sigma^2} \operatorname{cov} (b_1, b_2) + \frac{r\sqrt{1 - r^2} \, S_2^2}{\sigma^2} \operatorname{var} b_2$$

and prove that this is zero.

11 (*Continuation*) The statement below (12.29) implies that, under null hypothesis (12.15), the two ratios in (12.29) are (a) independent, (b) normally distributed, (c) with zero mean, and (d) with unit variance. Verify which of these four properties require the validity of (12.15) and which do not.

chapter 13

The Functional Form

of

a Relation

The standard linear model describes the expectation of the dependent variable as a linear function of the explanatory variables. The objective of this chapter is to investigate how *linear* should be interpreted and what kind of functions can be handled by this model.

13.1 The Meaning of Linearity

The textile example has shown that the linearity condition is not so restrictive as it may seem to be, because the explanatory variables defined in (7.14) and (7.15) are the logarithms of real income per capita and of the relative price of textile. Hence, we can afford linearity in the logarithms. As we know from Section 8.1, our approach is based on the assumption that the income elasticity β_1 and the price elasticity β_2 of the demand for textile are (unknown) constants. A constant-elasticity function is nonlinear, but when we take logarithms, a linear function in the logarithms of the original variables emerges. There are, as we shall shortly see, many cases in which a nonlinear function can be made linear.

A Linear Interpretation of a Nonlinear Function

Let y be a dependent variable whose expectation is a quadratic function of two variables, u and v,

(13.1) $$y_i = \beta_1 u_i + \beta_2 v_i + \beta_3 u_i^2 + \beta_4 v_i^2 + \beta_5 u_i v_i + \epsilon_i$$

where ϵ_i is a random disturbance with zero expectation. We define

$$x_{1i} = u_i, \qquad x_{2i} = v_i, \qquad x_{3i} = u_i^2, \qquad x_{4i} = v_i^2, \qquad x_{5i} = u_i v_i$$

so that (13.1) can be written as

(13.2) $$y_i = \beta_1 x_{1i} + \beta_2 x_{2i} + \beta_3 x_{3i} + \beta_4 x_{4i} + \beta_5 x_{5i} + \epsilon_i$$

In (13.1) we have a nonlinear function in the original explanatory variables u and v, whereas (13.2) is linear in $x_1, \ldots, x_5$. Note that the nature of the function has not changed; we have merely chosen different labels for our variables, x_3 for u^2, x_4 for v^2, and so on.

Similarly, consider the relation

(13.3) $$y_i = \beta_0 + \beta \log_e x_i + \epsilon_i$$

which is nonlinear in x but which can be handled by the standard linear model by means of the simple device of treating $\log_e x$ as the explanatory variable. In (13.3), the derivative of y with respect to x equals β/x, which converges to zero as x increases. This property can be realistic in a cross-sectional analysis with y interpreted as household expenditure on some group of goods and x as family income.

A third example is

(13.4) $$y_i = \beta_0 + \frac{\beta}{x_i} + \epsilon_i$$

which is nonlinear in x but linear in $1/x$. The derivative of y with respect to x is now $-\beta/x^2$, which also converges to zero as x increases. In this case the expectation of y converges to β_0 (a constant) as $x \to \infty$. This is in contrast to (13.3), where y increases or decreases beyond bounds; as $x \to \infty$, the expectation of y in (13.3) becomes ∞ (if $\beta > 0$) or $-\infty$ (if $\beta < 0$). These limiting considerations are important when the values $x_1, \ldots, x_n$ taken by the explanatory variable are characterized by a large spread.

Transforming a Nonlinear Function into a Linear Function

The three examples discussed above have in common that the equations become linear by an appropriate reinterpretation of the explanatory variables: by either taking the square of such a variable, or the product of two such variables, or the logarithm, or the reciprocal. A different case is

(13.5) $$y_i = \exp\left\{\beta_0 - \frac{\beta}{x_i} + \epsilon_i\right\} \qquad\qquad \beta > 0$$

which is nonlinear. But if we take the logarithm of both sides,

(13.6) $$\log_e y_i = \beta_0 - \frac{\beta}{x_i} + \epsilon_i$$

the right-hand side is linear in $1/x$ and the standard linear model can be applied to $\log_e y$ as the dependent variable and $1/x$ as the explanatory variable. This relationship is S-shaped (see Problem 1), which can be realistic for cross-sectional analysis with $y =$ household expenditure on a group of goods and $x =$ family income.

The difference between (13.5) and the examples discussed in the previous subsection should be noted. In each of the latter cases, the dependent variable is unchanged, but in (13.5) we replace y by $\log_e y$, as is shown in (13.6), so that the new dependent variable ($\log_e y$) has an expectation which is a linear function of $1/x$. This is possible only because (13.5) has its disturbance ϵ_i in the exponent. If we change (13.5) into

$$(13.7) \qquad y_i = \exp\left\{\beta_0 - \frac{\beta}{x_i}\right\} + \epsilon_i$$

taking logarithms on both sides yields

$$\log_e y_i = \log_e \left(\exp\left\{\beta_0 - \frac{\beta}{x_i}\right\} + \epsilon_i\right)$$

The logarithm on the right is a nonlinear function of ϵ_i, and the expectation of this logarithm is not a linear function of $1/x_i$.

Two Interpretations of Linearity

In the two previous subsections we have shown that the linearity condition is not so restrictive as it seemed in the first instance. It implies only that the expectation of the dependent variable [y in (13.1), (13.3), and (13.4), $\log_e y$ in (13.6)] is linear in certain *known functions* of the explanatory variables, such as squares, products, reciprocals, or logarithms. If an expression is linear in this way, it can be written as

$$(13.8) \qquad \beta_1 z_1(x_1, x_2, \ldots) + \beta_2 z_2(x_1, x_2, \ldots) + \cdots$$

where $z_h(x_1, x_2, \ldots)$ for $h = 1, 2, \ldots$ is a known function of the variables x_1, $x_2, \ldots$. But, obviously, the expression (13.8) is also linear in the parameters $\beta_1, \beta_2, \ldots$. Therefore, we may also say that the linearity condition of the standard linear model amounts to *linearity of the expectation of the dependent variable in the unknown parameters*. The reader should verify that this holds for (13.1), (13.3), (13.4), and (13.6) if $\mathcal{E}\epsilon_i = 0$. A counterexample is

$$(13.9) \qquad y_i = \beta_0 + \beta_1 e^{\beta_2 x_i} + \epsilon_i$$

where the β's are unknown parameters and ϵ_i is a random disturbance with zero mean. The expectation of y_i is now linear in $e^{\beta_2 x_i}$, but this is not a known function of x_i because β_2 is unknown. Also, the expectation of y_i is linear in β_0 and β_1 but nonlinear in β_2.

13.2   The Use of Logarithms

Logarithms played a role in the analysis of the demand for textile (see Table 12 on page 96) and also in several examples discussed in Section 13.1. In fact, logarithms are quite important in econometrics, the major reason being that they measure *relative effects*. Certain properties of logarithms are described in this section.

An Inequality for Natural Logarithms

The natural logarithm of x satisfies

(13.10)
$$\log_e x = x - 1 \quad \text{if } x = 1$$
$$< x - 1 \quad \text{if } x \neq 1$$

This inequality is illustrated in Figure 24, which contains the straight line $y = x - 1$ as well as the curve $y = \log_e x$. The curve is evidently below the straight line except at $x = 1$, in agreement with (13.10).

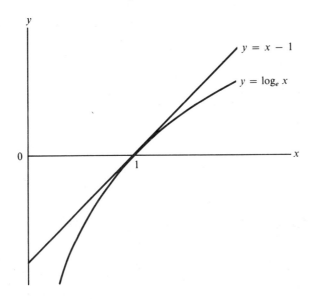

FIGURE 24 An inequality for natural logarithms

The proof of the first line of (13.10) is trivial. To verify the second line it is sufficient to prove that the derivative of $y = \log_e x$ is smaller than 1 (smaller than the slope 1 of the straight line $y = x - 1$) for $x > 1$ and larger than 1 for $x < 1$. This is indeed true, because the derivative of $y = \log_e x$ is $1/x$, which is < 1 for $x > 1$ and > 1 for $x < 1$.

The reader should verify, by applying a Taylor expansion of $y = \log_e x$ at $x = 1$, that

(13.11)
$$\log_e x \approx x - 1 - \tfrac{1}{2}(x - 1)^2$$

This result provides an approximation to $\log_e x$ that can be used when x is close to 1.

Percentage Changes and Log-changes

Let z be a variable which takes positive values only. We write z_t and z_{t-1} for its values in periods t and $t - 1$, so that z_t, z_{t-1}, and z_t/z_{t-1} are all positive. When we interpret x of (13.10) and (13.11) as z_t/z_{t-1}, we obtain

$$(13.12) \qquad \log_e \frac{z_t}{z_{t-1}} \leq \frac{z_t}{z_{t-1}} - 1 = \frac{z_t - z_{t-1}}{z_{t-1}}$$

$$(13.13) \qquad \log_e \frac{z_t}{z_{t-1}} \approx \frac{z_t - z_{t-1}}{z_{t-1}} - \frac{1}{2} \left(\frac{z_t - z_{t-1}}{z_{t-1}} \right)^2$$

The third member of (13.12) is the relative change (the percentage change divided by 100) in the variable from $t - 1$ to t. The first member is equal to $\log_e z_t - \log_e z_{t-1}$ and is thus the change in the natural logarithm. For brevity, we shall refer to this change as the *log-change* in the variable from $t - 1$ to t. It follows from (13.12) that the log-change is never larger and usually smaller than the relative change and from (13.13) that the difference between the two is small when the change is small. For the developments which follow, it will be convenient to write D for the log-change operator:

$$(13.14) \qquad Dz_t = \log_e z_t - \log_e z_{t-1} = \log_e \frac{z_t}{z_{t-1}}$$

An important advantage of the log-change over the relative change is its symmetry (apart from sign) with respect to the time subscripts. That is, if we consider the change in reverse direction, from t to $t - 1$, the log-change becomes

$$(13.15) \qquad \log_e \frac{z_{t-1}}{z_t} = -\log_e \frac{z_t}{z_{t-1}}$$

Note that the relative change does not have this property:

$$(13.16) \qquad \frac{z_{t-1} - z_t}{z_t} \neq -\frac{z_t - z_{t-1}}{z_{t-1}} \qquad \text{if } z_t \neq z_{t-1}$$

This inequality reflects the simple fact that a 25 percent increase followed by a 25 percent decrease does not restore the variable to its original level: $1.25(.75) = .9375 \neq 1$. To attain the original level, the 25 percent increase should be followed by a 20 percent decrease: $1.25(.8) = 1$. In the same way, a 25 percent increase from $t - 1$ to t is equivalent to a 20 percent decrease from t to $t - 1$, which amounts to $-.2 \neq -.25$ in (13.16). But the log-change corresponding to a 25 percent increase is .2231 and that corresponding to a 20 percent decrease is $-.2231$ (both in four decimal places); the agreement of these two numbers apart from sign is in accordance with (13.15).

Elasticities Further Considered

We noted in remark (1) on page 113 that the percentage-change interpretation of elasticities is an approximation which is adequate for small changes. Consider eq. (8.8), reproduced here:

(13.17)
$$T = 10^{1.3742}Y^{1.1430}p^{-.8289}$$
$$= 23.7Y^{1.1430}p^{-.8289}$$

Under the percentage-change interpretation, a 1 percent increase in p reduces T by .8289 percent. To verify this, let p increase by 1 percent, Y remaining unchanged, so that $p^{-.8289}$ in (13.17) becomes

$$(1.01p)^{-.8289} = 1.01^{-.8289}p^{-.8289} \approx .99179p^{-.8289}$$

This implies a proportionate decrease in T equal to $1 - .99179 = .00821$ or .821 percent. This is not equal but at least close to the decrease of .8289 percent mentioned above.

Next consider a 25 percent increase in p, so that the percentage-change rule yields a decline of $25(.8289) \approx 20.7$ percent for T. In (13.17) on the right, $p^{-.8289}$ now becomes

$$(1.25p)^{-.8289} = 1.25^{-.8289}p^{-.8289} \approx .831p^{-.8289}$$

so that the proportionate decrease in T is now $1 - .831 = .169$, or 16.9 percent. This shows that the 20.7 percent mentioned above is considerably in error. The error increases when the changes are larger (see also Problem 5).

Let us add a subscript t to the variables in (13.17) in order to indicate that we consider their values in year t. When we divide both sides by the same equation for $t - 1$, we obtain

$$\frac{T_t}{T_{t-1}} = \left(\frac{Y_t}{Y_{t-1}}\right)^{1.1430}\left(\frac{p_t}{p_{t-1}}\right)^{-.8289}$$

We proceed to take logarithms,

$$\log_e \frac{T_t}{T_{t-1}} = 1.1430 \log_e \frac{Y_t}{Y_{t-1}} - .8289 \log_e \frac{p_t}{p_{t-1}}$$

and use the log-change notation (13.14):

(13.18)
$$DT_t = 1.1430DY_t - .8289Dp_t$$

We conclude that the constant-elasticity relation (13.17) becomes linear (without constant term) when it is formulated in terms of log-changes and that the coefficients of this linear relation are the elasticities. Demand equations involving log-changes will be further considered in Section 14.2.

The Base of the Logarithms

The logarithms in Table 12 on page 96 are to the base 10. This has no effect on the income and price elasticities, because the same base is used for the logarithm of the variable on the left (the volume of textile consumption per capita) as for those on the right (real income per capita and the relative textile price). The situation is different for the constant term and the disturbance variance σ^2. When we equate the factors immediately to the right of the equal signs in (13.17) to each other, $10^{1.3742} = 23.7$, we see that the number 10 does play a crucial role in the antilog of the LS constant-term estimate $b_0 = 1.3742$. To verify the effect of the base of the logarithm on σ^2, we use

(13.19) $$\log_a x = (\log_a b)(\log_b x)$$

which holds for any positive values of a, b, and x. When we interpret x as the volume of textile consumption and a and b as e and 10, respectively, we find that the natural logarithm of this volume is obtained from the logarithm to the base 10 by multiplication by $\log_e 10 \approx 2.3026$. Since the disturbance ϵ_t is the random component of the logarithm of the volume of textile consumption, its standard deviation σ is to be multiplied by the same number when we use natural logarithms and the variance σ^2 by the square of this number. Accordingly, the estimate s^2 given in (8.39) takes the following values for natural logarithms:

(13.20) $$s^2 = (2.3026)^2(.0001833) \approx .000972$$

Log-changes and Growth Rates

The use of log-changes is also convenient for the analysis of average growth rates, exponential trends, and deviations from such trends. A brief exposition is given in this subsection and the next; for alternative methods of measuring trends, see Problems 8 and 9. We also refer the reader to Sections 22.1 and 22.2 on the use of log-changes in the analysis of predictions, which has certain features in common with the account that follows here.

We are interested in the change in some variable x from t to $t + T$, where T is a positive integer. The log-change is

$$\log_e x_{t+T} - \log_e x_t = \log_e \frac{x_{t+1}}{x_t} + \log_e \frac{x_{t+2}}{x_{t+1}} + \cdots + \log_e \frac{x_{t+T}}{x_{t+T-1}}$$

Hence, the total log-change from t to $t + T$ is simply the sum of the intervening one-period log-changes. By dividing the equation by T and using the log-change notation (13.14), we obtain

(13.21) $$\frac{1}{T} \log_e \frac{x_{t+T}}{x_t} = \frac{1}{T} \sum_{s=1}^{T} Dx_{t+s}$$

The right-hand side is the average of T successive log-changes, which measures the *average growth rate* of x from t to $t + T$. The left-hand side shows that the computation of this rate requires only a comparison of the values of x in the first and last periods.

Growth rates are frequently analyzed for variables which satisfy a multiplicative relation. Let x_t be gross national product in current dollars ("money-GNP") in period t, y_t the GNP deflator in t, and z_t gross national product in constant dollars ("real GNP"). Their multiplicative relation is

(13.22) $$z_t = \frac{x_t}{y_t}$$

with the following log-change:

$$Dz_t = \log_e \frac{z_t}{z_{t-1}} = \log_e \frac{x_t/y_t}{x_{t-1}/y_{t-1}} = \log_e \frac{x_t}{x_{t-1}} - \log_e \frac{y_t}{y_{t-1}}$$

This can be written as

(13.23) $$Dz_t = Dx_t - Dy_t$$

or, in words, the log-change in real GNP equals the log-change in money-GNP minus the log-change in the deflator. Next we replace t by $t + s$ in (13.23), sum over $s = 1, \ldots, T$, and divide by T:

(13.24) $$\frac{1}{T} \sum_{s=1}^{T} Dz_{t+s} = \frac{1}{T} \sum_{s=1}^{T} Dx_{t+s} - \frac{1}{T} \sum_{s=1}^{T} Dy_{t+s}$$

Hence, the average growth rate of real GNP equals the average growth rate of money-GNP minus the average growth rate of the deflator.

Exponential Trends and Deviations from the Trend

If x is an exponential function of time, $x_t = x_0 e^{\alpha t}$, each log-change equals α:

$$\begin{aligned} Dx_t &= \log_e x_0 e^{\alpha t} - \log_e x_0 e^{\alpha(t-1)} \\ &= \log_e x_0 + \alpha t - [\log_e x_0 + \alpha(t-1)] = \alpha \end{aligned}$$

The exponential form represents a very special case, but it happens more frequently that a variable has a strong exponential trend. Let us write m_x for the right-hand side of (13.21),

(13.25) $$m_x = \frac{1}{T} \sum_{s=1}^{T} Dx_{t+s}$$

so that $m_x = \alpha$ if $x_t = x_0 e^{\alpha t}$ holds for each t. If x has an exponential trend, we may ask how large the deviations from this trend tend to be. A simple measure is provided by

(13.26) $$\frac{1}{T} \sum_{s=1}^{T} (Dx_{t+s} - m_x)^2$$

which is the mean square of the log-changes around their mean m_x during the periods $t + 1, \ldots, t + T$.

We write (13.24) as $m_z = m_x - m_y$, where m_z and m_y are defined similarly to (13.25). We subtract this from (13.23), with t replaced by $t + s$:

$$Dz_{t+s} - m_z = (Dx_{t+s} - m_x) - (Dy_{t+s} - m_y)$$

We square both sides,

$$\begin{aligned} (Dz_{t+s} - m_z)^2 &= (Dx_{t+s} - m_x)^2 + (Dy_{t+s} - m_y)^2 \\ &\quad - 2(Dx_{t+s} - m_x)(Dy_{t+s} - m_y) \end{aligned}$$

which we sum over $s = 1, \ldots, T$ and then divide by T:

(13.27) $$\begin{aligned} \frac{1}{T} \sum_{s=1}^{T} (Dz_{t+s} - m_z)^2 &= \frac{1}{T} \sum_{s=1}^{T} (Dx_{t+s} - m_x)^2 + \frac{1}{T} \sum_{s=1}^{T} (Dy_{t+s} - m_y)^2 \\ &\quad - \frac{2}{T} \sum_{s=1}^{T} (Dx_{t+s} - m_x)(Dy_{t+s} - m_y) \end{aligned}$$

The first term on the right is the mean square (13.26), which we introduced as a measure of the size of the deviations from the exponential trend. Hence, (13.27) states that the mean square of these deviations for real GNP equals the sum of the mean squares for money-GNP and the deflator, minus twice the mean product of the deviations of the latter two variables. This mean product has the same sign as the correlation coefficient of these deviations [see (6.1)]. Therefore, if the average size of these deviations as measured by the first two right-hand terms in (13.27) is considered as fixed, the average size of the real-GNP deviations is larger when the deviations of money-GNP and the deflator are negatively correlated than when they are positively correlated.

13.3   Dummy Variables

The standard linear model assumes that the explanatory variables take numerical values, which excludes "qualitative" variables. However, there is a simple device to handle such variables.

War and Peace

Let y be the consumption of durables, which we assume to be a linear function of wage income (x_1) and nonwage income (x_2). Our sample includes peace years and war years. We assume that the constant term of the linear function is not the same in peace and war. When there is peace, we have

$$(13.28) \qquad y_i = \beta_0 + \beta_1 x_{1i} + \beta_2 x_{2i} + \epsilon_i$$

and when there is war,

$$(13.29) \qquad y_i = \beta_0' + \beta_1 x_{1i} + \beta_2 x_{2i} + \epsilon_i$$

It is, of course, possible to apply LS to peace years and war years separately, but such a procedure ignores the fact that the slope parameters β_1 and β_2 in (13.28) and (13.29) are the same. Let us introduce the variable x_3,

$$(13.30) \qquad x_{3i} = \begin{cases} 0 & \text{if the } i\text{th year is a peace year} \\ 1 & \text{if the } i\text{th year is a war year} \end{cases}$$

as well as the parameter

$$(13.31) \qquad \beta_3 = \beta_0' - \beta_0$$

The reader should verify that

$$(13.32) \qquad y_i = \beta_0 + \beta_1 x_{1i} + \beta_2 x_{2i} + \beta_3 x_{3i} + \epsilon_i$$

covers both (13.28) and (13.29) and hence applies to peace as well as war. The "zero-one" variable (13.30), which is commonly known as a *dummy variable*, thus enables us to handle the qualitative distinction between peace and war.

Seasonal Effects

A dummy variable can be used for each qualitative explanatory variable which takes two values, such as peace and war, white and nonwhite, Protestant and Catholic, and so on. More generally, if a qualitative variable takes r values, its effect on the dependent variable can be handled by means of $r - 1$ dummy variables.

The following is an example for $r = 4$. Let y_i be the volume of per capita consumption of soft drinks in period i, time being measured in quarters. Let x_{1i} be real per capita income, x_{2i} the relative price of soft drinks, and consider

$$(13.33) \qquad y_i = \beta_0 + \beta_1 x_{1i} + \beta_2 x_{2i} + \beta_3 x_{3i} + \beta_4 x_{4i} + \beta_5 x_{5i} + \epsilon_i$$

where $x_{3i} = 1$ if i falls in the first quarter of any year and 0 otherwise, $x_{4i} = 1$ if i falls in the second quarter of any year and 0 otherwise, and $x_{5i} = 1$ if i falls in the third quarter of any year and 0 otherwise. The reader should verify that β_3 in (13.33) measures the excess (positive or negative) of the consumption of soft drinks in the first quarter over that in the fourth and that β_4 and β_5 have similar interpretations.

Dummy Variables as Dependent Variables

There are situations in which the dependent variable is of a qualitative nature. Consider a cross-section study of family households, with some families buying a car and other families not buying a car. Suppose that the question of whether or not a family buys a car depends on its income, apart from random effects. This suggests that we should introduce a dummy variable $y_i = 1$ if the ith family buys a car and $y_i = 0$ if it does not and consider a model of the form $y_i = \beta_0 + \beta x_i + \epsilon_i$ or $y_i = \beta_0 + \beta \log x_i + \epsilon_i$, where x_i is family income and ϵ_i is a random disturbance.

It appears that this approach is not fruitful, since dummy variables used as dependent variables violate the assumptions of the standard linear model. A more fruitful approach is to formulate a model which describes the conditional probability of car purchase (or some transformation of this probability), given that income equals x_i. This leads to the subject of logit and probit analysis, which are beyond the scope of this book; for further details on this matter, see Theil (1971, pp. 628–636).

*13.4   Linearization

There are numerous functional forms which do not satisfy the linearity condition discussed at the end of Section 13.1. A linear approximation, frequently known as linearization, can be useful.

The CES Production Function

Consider the constant-elasticity-of-substitution (CES) production function,

$$(13.34) \qquad P_i = c[\alpha K_i^{-\rho} + (1 - \alpha)L_i^{-\rho}]^{-1/\rho}e^{\epsilon_i}$$

where P_i, K_i, and L_i are output, capital, and labor, respectively, in year i; ϵ_i is a random disturbance with zero mean; and c, α, and ρ are unknown parameters which satisfy $c > 0$, $0 < \alpha < 1$, $\rho > -1$. By taking logarithms, we obtain

$$(13.35) \qquad \log_e P_i = \log_e c - \frac{1}{\rho} \log_e [\alpha K_i^{-\rho} + (1 - \rho)L_i^{-\rho}] + \epsilon_i$$

which is nonlinear in the parameters. Following Kmenta (1967), we assume that ρ is not far from zero and apply a Taylor series approximation at $\rho = 0$. This is implemented in the next subsection, and the result is

$$(13.36) \quad \log_e \frac{P_i}{L_i} \approx \log_e c + \alpha \log_e \frac{K_i}{L_i} - \frac{1}{2}\rho\alpha(1 - \alpha)\left(\log_e \frac{K_i}{L_i}\right)^2 + \epsilon_i$$

where $\approx$ indicates that second and higher powers of ρ are ignored.

The dependent variable in (13.36) is $\log_e (P/L)$. Ignoring the approximation, we conclude that the expectation of this variable is a linear function of $\log_e (K/L)$ and $[\log_e (K/L)]^2$, both of which are known functions of K and L, and also a linear function of the parameters $\log_e c$, α, and $-\frac{1}{2}\rho\alpha(1 - \alpha)$. Once we have estimates of these parameters, we can compute the implied estimates of c and ρ. The problem of obtaining standard errors of these implied estimates is considered in Section 15.2.

Derivations

For notational convenience, we delete the disturbance ϵ_i and the subscript i from (13.35). Then subtract $\log_e L$ from both sides:

$$(13.37) \quad \log_e \frac{P}{L} = \log_e c - \log_e L - \frac{1}{\rho} \log_e [\alpha K^{-\rho} + (1 - \alpha)L^{-\rho}]$$

$$= \log_e c - \frac{1}{\rho}\{\rho \log_e L + \log_e [\alpha K^{-\rho} + (1 - \alpha)L^{-\rho}]\}$$

$$= \log_e c - \frac{1}{\rho}\{\log_e L^{\rho} + \log_e [\alpha K^{-\rho} + (1 - \alpha)L^{-\rho}]\}$$

The expression in curled brackets in the last line can be written as

$$\log_e \{L^{\rho}[\alpha K^{-\rho} + (1 - \alpha)L^{-\rho}]\} = \log_e \left[\alpha \left(\frac{K}{L}\right)^{-\rho} + 1 - \alpha\right]$$

Since $K/L = \exp\{\log_e (K/L)\}$, the right-hand side equals

$$(13.38) \qquad f(\rho) = \log_e (\alpha e^{-k\rho} + 1 - \alpha)$$

where

$$(13.39) \qquad k = \log_e \frac{K}{L}$$

Substitution of (13.38) for the expression in curled brackets in (13.37) gives

$$(13.40) \qquad \log_e \frac{P}{L} = \log_e c - \frac{f(\rho)}{\rho}$$

We write $f'(\rho)$ and $f''(\rho)$ for the first- and second-order derivatives of the function (13.38). The reader should verify that

$$(13.41) \qquad f'(\rho) = \frac{-\alpha k}{\alpha + (1 - \alpha)e^{k\rho}}, \qquad f''(\rho) = \frac{\alpha(1 - \alpha)k^2 e^{k\rho}}{[\alpha + (1 - \alpha)e^{k\rho}]^2}$$

and that $f(0) = 0$, $f'(0) = -\alpha k$, $f''(0) = \alpha(1 - \alpha)k^2$. Therefore, a Taylor expansion applied to $f(\rho)$ at $\rho = 0$ in (13.40) gives

$$\log_e \frac{P}{L} = \log_e c - \frac{-\alpha k \rho + \frac{1}{2}\alpha(1 - \alpha)k^2\rho^2 + \cdots}{\rho}$$
$$= \log_e c + \alpha k - \tfrac{1}{2}\alpha(1 - \alpha)k^2\rho + \cdots$$

Substitution of (13.39) for k completes the proof of (13.36).

The CES function (13.34) is equivalent to a Cobb-Douglas production function for $\rho = 0$. The interested reader should consult Problem 14.

Problems

Problems 1–3 refer to Section 13.1, 4–9 to Section 13.2, 10–12 to Section 13.3, and 13 and 14 to Section 13.4.

1 To analyze (13.5), ignore the disturbance and prove that y converges to 0 when x converges from positive values to 0. Also prove the following:

$$\frac{dy}{dx} = \frac{\beta}{x^2}e^{\beta_0 - \beta/x}, \qquad \frac{d^2y}{dx^2} = \frac{\beta}{x^3}\left(\frac{\beta}{x} - 2\right)e^{\beta_0 - \beta/x}$$

Use these results to verify the following behavior of y as a function of x. Starting at 0 for $x = 0$, y increases with increasing slope (dy/dx) until a point of inflection at $x = \frac{1}{2}\beta$, after which y increases with decreasing slope until a horizontal asymptote at $y = e^{\beta_0}$. Draw a picture, and verify that the relation is S-shaped.

2 (*Continuation*) Let (13.6) be applied to cross-section data with $y =$ household expenditure on a group of goods and $x =$ family income. Let the sample show values of y ranging from \$100 to \$1000 except for one household which spends no money on these goods; hence, for this household, the left-hand side of (13.6) equals $-\infty$, which cannot be handled in the LS computations. Suppose someone advises you to replace the zero expenditure by a fictitious one-dollar expenditure, so that the LS computations can be carried out. Is this sound advice? [*Hint*: Compare the one-dollar expenditure with the equally fictitious one-cent expenditure, and verify the sensitivity; to simplify the computations, use logarithms to the base 10

rather than natural logarithms. The result shows that (13.6) is an unattractive specification when the sample includes zero-expenditure households.]

3 Verify that if ϵ_t has zero mean, y_i in (13.1), (13.3), and (13.4) has an expectation which is linear in the parameters (the β's). Then state and prove a similar proposition for (13.6).

4 Verify the Taylor expansion (13.11), and prove that the third-order term is $\frac{1}{3}(x - 1)^3$.

5 Let Y increase by 1 percent in (13.17), p remaining unchanged; verify that T increases by 1.144 percent. Let Y increase by 25 percent, p remaining unchanged; verify that T increases by 29.1 percent. Compare these results with those obtained from the percentage-change approximation rule, and state your conclusions. [*Note*: A comparison with the results for the price elasticity, described below (13.17), illustrates the fact that the approximation is worse when the elasticity is farther from 1.]

6 Use a numerical specification of x_t, x_{t+1}, and x_{t+2} (all positive) to show that the following inequality can hold:

$$\frac{x_{t+2} - x_t}{x_t} \neq \frac{x_{t+1} - x_t}{x_t} + \frac{x_{t+2} - x_{t+1}}{x_{t+1}}$$

Compare this with (13.21), and state your conclusions.

7 (*Continuation*) For z_t defined in (13.22), prove that the following inequality can hold:

$$\frac{z_t - z_{t-1}}{z_{t-1}} \neq \frac{x_t - x_{t-1}}{x_{t-1}} - \frac{y_t - y_{t-1}}{y_{t-1}}$$

Compare this with (13.23), and state your conclusions.

8 For the change in a variable x from t to $t + T$, define the average relative change ξ, compounded over the T intervening periods, as $x_{t+T} = x_t(1 + \xi)^T$. Prove that this implies

$$\xi = \left(\frac{x_{t+T}}{x_t}\right)^{1/T} - 1$$

Define η and ζ similarly for the variables y and z, respectively. Prove that if (13.22) is true,

$$1 + \zeta = \frac{1 + \xi}{1 + \eta}$$

and that this implies $\zeta = (\xi - \eta)/(1 + \eta)$. Compare this with (13.24), written as $m_z = m_x - m_y$, and state your conclusions.

9 (*Continuation*) As another method for obtaining an average relative change, consider $x_{t+s} = x_t(1 + \xi')^s$ for $s = 1, \ldots, T$, and take logarithms of both sides, adding a residual on the right:

$$\log_e x_{t+s} = \log_e x_t + s \log_e (1 + \xi') + \text{residual}$$

Then determine $\log_e (1 + \xi')$ by LS. Prove that this yields

$$\log_e (1 + \xi') = \frac{1}{c} \sum_{s=1}^{T} s \log_e \frac{x_{t+s}}{x_t}, \qquad \text{where } c = \sum_{s=1}^{T} s^2$$

Define η' and ζ' similarly for the variables y and z, and prove that $\zeta' = (\xi' - \eta')/(1 + \eta')$ if the variables satisfy (13.22).

10 Verify that (13.32), with x_3 and β_3 defined in (13.30) and (13.31), covers both (13.28) and (13.29).

11 Prove that β_3 in (13.33) measures the (positive or negative) excess of the consumption of soft drinks in the first quarter over that in the fourth. Provide similar interpretations for β_4 and β_5. Which sign do you expect for β_5 in the Northern Hemisphere?

12 (*Continuation*) No separate dummy variable x_{6i} is introduced for the fourth quarter ($x_{6i} = 1$ if i falls in the fourth quarter of any year and 0 otherwise). What would happen if we did introduce this variable? (*Hint*: See Section 9.3.)

13 For $f(\rho)$ defined in (13.38), verify the derivatives in (13.41) as well as $f(0) = 0$, $f'(0) = -\alpha k$, and $f''(0) = \alpha(1 - \alpha)k^2$.

14 L'Hôpital's rule states that if $g(\rho)/h(\rho)$, the ratio of two functions of ρ, takes the form 0/0 at $\rho = 0$, we obtain the limit of this ratio for $\rho \to 0$ from the ratio of the derivatives of $g(\rho)$ and $h(\rho)$ at $\rho = 0$. Apply this rule to

$$g(\rho) = \log_e [\alpha K_i^{-\rho} + (1 - \alpha)L_i^{-\rho}], \qquad h(\rho) = \rho$$

and prove that this yields the following form of (13.35) for $\rho \to 0$:

$$\log_e P_i = \log_e c + \alpha \log_e K_i + (1 - \alpha) \log_e L_i + \epsilon_i$$

Verify that this equation is equivalent to the Cobb-Douglas production function (1.2) in the special case $\alpha + \beta = 1$.

chapter 14

Consumer
Demand
Equations

It occurs too often that econometricians run a regression without giving much thought to the economic theory behind the relation which they want to estimate. They will then run the risk of overlooking plausible theoretical constraints on the coefficients of this relation. Successful econometric studies pay appropriate attention to both economic theory and the data. In this chapter, which completes Part Two of the book, we shall illustrate the combined use of theory and data in the analysis of consumer demand—one of the oldest topics in applied econometrics. For example, it was observed more than 100 years ago (Engel's law, based on the study of family budget data) that the amount which a consumer spends on food increases when his income increases but that the *proportion* of income spent on food declines when income rises.

14.1 Introduction to Consumer Demand Theory

The Utility Function and the Budget Constraint

Let there be N goods available in the market place at prices $p_1, \ldots, p_N$. Consumer demand theory postulates that the consumer's tastes can be described by a utility function,

$$(14.1) \qquad u = u(q_1, \ldots, q_N)$$

which measures the consumer's satisfaction when he buys and consumes q_1 units of the first good, q_2 units of the second, and so on. We assume that $u(\ )$ is an increasing function of its N arguments.

The consumer's objective is to select the values of the q_i's which maximize the utility function subject to his financial limitations. These limitations are expressed by

(14.2) $$\sum_{i=1}^{N} p_i q_i = m$$

The product of p_i and q_i is the expenditure on the ith good; hence, the left-hand side of (14.2) is total expenditure on all goods. Thus, (14.2) is a budget constraint which states that total expenditure equals m. For brevity, we shall frequently refer to m as the consumer's income.

The consumer is supposed to take m and the p_i's as given, so that his objective is to maximize (14.1) subject to (14.2) for given $m, p_1, \ldots, p_N$. We assume that the utility function is such that this problem has a unique solution with positive q_i's for any values of income and prices in which we shall be interested. We write this solution as

(14.3) $$q_i = f_i(m, p_1, \ldots, p_N) \qquad\qquad i = 1, \ldots, N$$

which is a system of N demand equations, each describing the consumption of some good in terms of income and the prices of all N goods.

Real Income and Relative Prices

When income and all prices are multiplied by $k > 0$, (14.2) becomes $\sum_i (k p_i) q_i = km$, which implies exactly the same constraint on the q_i's as the original budget constraint (14.2). Also, since income and prices do not occur in (14.1), the utility function is not affected when income and prices are multiplied by k. Therefore, when this function is maximized subject to the budget constraint, with income and all prices multiplied by $k > 0$, the quantities remain unchanged. Hence, the demand equations (14.3) satisfy

(14.4) $$f_i(km, kp_1, \ldots, kp_N) = f_i(m, p_1, \ldots, p_N)$$

for $i = 1, \ldots, N$ and any $k > 0$.

When we interpret k as the reciprocal of a deflator P, the arguments in the left-hand side of (14.4) become m/P (real income) and $p_1/P, \ldots, p_N/P$ (relative prices). Hence, using this interpretation as well as (14.3), we obtain

(14.5) $$q_i = f_i\left(\frac{m}{P}, \frac{p_1}{P}, \ldots, \frac{p_N}{P}\right) \qquad\qquad i = 1, \ldots, N$$

which describes the demand for each good as a function of real income and all relative prices. The demand equation for textile discussed in Section 8.1 is a special case of (14.5), with only one relative price (the relative textile price).

Price Substitution and Slutsky Symmetry and Negativity

The deflator P is some function of the prices $p_1, \ldots, p_N$ and can thus be written as $P(p_1, \ldots, p_N)$, so that the relative prices become

$$\frac{p_1}{P(p_1, \ldots, p_N)}, \ldots, \frac{p_N}{P(p_1, \ldots, p_N)}$$

This shows that the last N arguments in (14.5) are all determined by $p_1, \ldots, p_N$; hence, these arguments can just as well be replaced by the undeflated prices $p_1, \ldots, p_N$. Thus, writing $\bar{m} = m/P$ for real income, we formulate the demand equations as

$$(14.6) \qquad q_i = q_i(\bar{m}, p_1, \ldots, p_N) \qquad i = 1, \ldots, N$$

which describes the demand for each good as a function of real income and the undeflated prices.

Note the difference between (14.3) and (14.6). The derivative $\partial f_i/\partial p_j$ of (14.3) describes the effect of a change in p_j on the demand for the ith good when money income (m) remains constant, whereas $\partial q_i/\partial p_j$ of (14.6) describes the effect when real income ($\bar{m}$) remains constant. The latter effect is the *substitution effect* of the change in p_j on the demand for the ith good. It was shown by Slutsky (1915) that if the utility function is appropriately differentiable, these effects are symmetric,

$$(14.7) \qquad \frac{\partial q_i}{\partial p_j} = \frac{\partial q_j}{\partial p_i} \qquad i, j = 1, \ldots, N$$

which is known as *Slutsky symmetry*. Also, the derivatives with respect to the corresponding price are all negative,

$$(14.8) \qquad \frac{\partial q_i}{\partial p_i} < 0 \qquad i = 1, \ldots, N$$

which is *Slutsky negativity*. Both properties are further considered later in this section.

In addition, we have

$$(14.9) \qquad \sum_{j=1}^{N} p_j \frac{\partial q_i}{\partial p_j} = 0 \qquad i = 1, \ldots, N$$

The left-hand side is the effect of proportionate changes in all prices on the demand for the ith good. We know from (14.4) that this effect is zero, as (14.9) states it to be, when m also changes proportionately. This condition is indeed satisfied, because taking the derivative $\partial q_i/\partial p_j$ of (14.6) implies that real income ($\bar{m}$) is kept constant, which is possible only if money income (m) changes proportionately to the prices.

Demand Equations with Constant Elasticities

As an example of a particular mathematical form of demand equations, we shall consider the following system ($i = 1, \ldots, N$):

$$(14.10) \qquad \log_e q_i = a_i + b_i \log_e \bar{m} + \sum_{j=1}^{N} c_{ij} \log_e p_j$$

Here $a_i, b_i, c_{i1}, \ldots, c_{iN}$ are constants, with b_i the income elasticity of the demand for the ith good and

(14.11)
$$c_{ij} = \frac{\partial q_i}{\partial p_j} \frac{p_j}{q_i} \qquad\qquad i, j = 1, \ldots, N$$

the elasticity of the demand for the ith good with respect to p_j (for a constant real income).

To verify the implications of Slutsky symmetry under (14.10), we multiply (14.7) by p_j/q_i. This gives c_{ij} on the left, while the right-hand side becomes

$$\frac{\partial q_j}{\partial p_i} \frac{p_j}{q_i} = \frac{\partial q_j}{\partial p_i} \frac{p_i}{q_j} \frac{p_j q_j}{p_i q_i} = c_{ji} \frac{p_j q_j}{p_i q_i}$$

so that Slutsky symmetry amounts to

(14.12)
$$\frac{c_{ij}}{c_{ji}} = \frac{p_j q_j}{p_i q_i} \qquad\qquad i, j = 1, \ldots, N$$

Since the c_{ij}'s are constant under (14.10), the left-hand side of (14.12) is also constant. Hence, Slutsky symmetry requires constant ratios of the expenditures on all N goods, irrespective of the values of income and all prices. This is unrealistic, which means that the constant-elasticity model (14.10) is not attractive when we are interested in Slutsky symmetry.

Indifference Curves

The Slutsky symmetry and negativity conditions (14.7) and (14.8) are derived in Appendix D; here we shall derive them along geometric lines for the case of two goods ($N = 2$). The quantities of these goods are measured along the two axes of Figure 25(a). The straight line AB is the budget line whose coordinates (q_1, q_2) satisfy

(14.13)
$$p_1 q_1 + p_2 q_2 = m$$

If the consumer spends all his money on the first good, (14.13) implies that he buys m/p_1 units of that good. Therefore, OA equals m/p_1 and, similarly, OB equals m/p_2, where B is the point at which the consumer spends all his money on the second good.

To find the point which the consumer actually selects, we must introduce his utility function $u = u(q_1, q_2)$. The three curves in Figure 25(a) are contour lines of this function at which utility is constant; these curves are known as *indifference curves*. Since utility is an increasing function of both q_1 and q_2, curve I corresponds to a higher utility level than that of curve II, and the latter corresponds to a higher utility level than that of curve III. Thus, the consumer will select the point on the budget line which is located on the highest indifference curve. This point is P at which curve II touches the budget line. Note that the slope of this indifference curve at P is equal to the slope of the budget line. Also note that the slope of this curve increases algebraically when we move from left to right; this means that when q_1 increases more and more, the decline

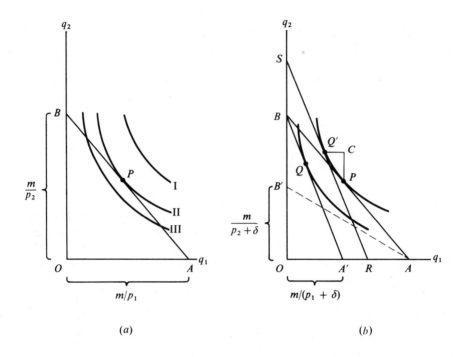

(a)   (b)

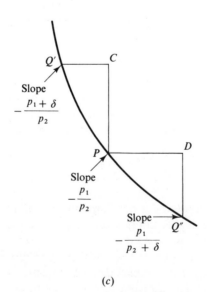

(c)

FIGURE 25   Slutsky symmetry and negativity for the case of two goods

204

in q_2 which is permitted to occur without loss of satisfaction (i.e., utility remaining unchanged) becomes smaller and smaller.

A Taylor Expansion

Each indifference curve may be viewed as describing q_2 as a function of q_1 at a constant utility level. We assume that the utility function $u(q_1, q_2)$ has continuous second-order derivatives, so that the same is true for each indifference curve. For the proof of Slutsky symmetry we shall find it convenient to use a second-order Taylor approximation of the indifference curve through P,

$$(14.14) \qquad q_2 - \bar{q}_2 = \alpha_0(q_1 - \bar{q}_1) + \tfrac{1}{2}\alpha(q_1 - \bar{q}_1)^2$$

where $\bar{q}_1$ and $\bar{q}_2$ are the coordinates of P, while α_0 and α are the first and second derivatives, respectively, at P. Hence, α_0 is the slope of the indifference curve at P, which is equal to the slope of the budget line (14.13). Since (14.13) can be written as

$$(14.15) \qquad q_2 = \frac{m}{p_2} - \frac{p_1}{p_2}q_1$$

and thus has slope $-p_1/p_2$, we must have $\alpha_0 = -p_1/p_2$. Therefore, (14.14) becomes

$$(14.16) \qquad q_2 - \bar{q}_2 = -\frac{p_1}{p_2}(q_1 - \bar{q}_1) + \tfrac{1}{2}\alpha(q_1 - \bar{q}_1)^2$$

which has the following derivative:

$$(14.17) \qquad \frac{dq_2}{dq_1} = -\frac{p_1}{p_2} + \alpha(q_1 - \bar{q}_1)$$

This is the algebraic version of the slope of the indifference curve through P, obtained from a quadratic approximation. This slope increases algebraically when $\alpha > 0$ (see the end of the previous subsection).

Slutsky Negativity in the Two-Good Case

Suppose now that p_1 increases by a small amount $\delta > 0$, so that the budget constraint (14.13) changes into

$$(14.18) \qquad (p_1 + \delta)q_1 + p_2q_2 = m$$

and the budget line AB changes into $A'B$, as shown in Figure 25(b). The new optimal point is Q at which an indifference curve touches the line $A'B$. This curve corresponds to a lower utility level because the price increase makes the consumer poorer than he was before. Suppose that we compensate the consumer for this price increase by raising his income by an amount δ':

$$(14.19) \qquad (p_1 + \delta)q_1 + p_2q_2 = m + \delta'$$

Since the prices are the same in (14.19) as in (14.18), the budget line corresponding to (14.19) must be parallel to $A'B$ for any value of δ'. This may be verified by solving (14.18) and (14.19) for q_2, similarly to (14.15), which yields the same slope coefficient $-(p_1 + \delta)/p_2$.

We proceed to select δ' so that the consumer can attain exactly the same utility level as that which he enjoyed at P. This yields the budget line RS (parallel to $A'B$), which touches the indifference curve through P at Q'. We conclude that Q' is the new optimal point after the price increase from p_1 to $p_1 + \delta$ when this increase is compensated by an income increase so that the original utility level is restored. This compensation is equivalent to a constant *real* income. Therefore, the move from P to Q' (along the indifference curve that goes through P) is exclusively the result of the substitution effect of the price increase from p_1 to $p_1 + \delta$. This move consists of a decrease in q_1 equal to $Q'C$ and an increase in q_2 equal to PC [see Figure 25(b)]. The decrease in q_1 caused by the increase in p_1 confirms (14.8).

Slutsky Symmetry in the Two-Good Case

For $N = 2$ the Slutsky symmetry property (14.7) amounts to only one symmetry relation:

$$(14.20) \qquad \frac{\partial q_2}{\partial p_1} = \frac{\partial q_1}{\partial p_2}$$

Given that the move from P to Q' involves a q_2 increase equal to PC, the derivative on the left in (14.20) is equal to the ratio of this increase to the increase δ in p_1 in the limit for $\delta \to 0$:

$$(14.21) \qquad \frac{\partial q_2}{\partial p_1} = \lim_{\delta \to 0} \frac{PC}{\delta}$$

To evaluate the ratio PC/δ we use the quadratic approximation (14.16) with derivative (14.17). When the consumer is at Q', this derivative equals the slope $-(p_1 + \delta)/p_2$ of the budget line RS, so that

$$-\frac{p_1 + \delta}{p_2} = -\frac{p_1}{p_2} + \alpha(q_1 - \bar{q}_1)$$

which yields $q_1 - \bar{q}_1 = -\delta/\alpha p_2$. We substitute this in (14.16):

$$(14.22) \qquad q_2 - \bar{q}_2 = \frac{\delta p_1}{\alpha p_2^2} + \frac{\delta^2}{2\alpha p_2^2}$$

But $q_2 - \bar{q}_2$ equals PC because we are considering the move from P to Q'. Therefore, after dividing both sides of (14.22) by δ, we have $PC/\delta = p_1/\alpha p_2^2 + \delta/2\alpha p_2^2$ and hence, using (14.21),

$$(14.23) \qquad \frac{\partial q_2}{\partial p_1} = \lim_{\delta \to 0} \frac{PC}{\delta} = \frac{p_1}{\alpha p_2^2}$$

Next, to derive $\partial q_1/\partial p_2$, we assume that p_2 increases to $p_2 + \delta$, p_1 remaining unchanged, so that the budget line changes from AB to the broken line AB'

in Figure 25(b). As in the paragraph below (14.19), we provide an income compensation so that the consumer can attain the indifference curve through P, but now at the prices $(p_1, p_2 + \delta)$. Thus, whereas the relevant point in the previous paragraph was Q' at which the indifference curve has a slope equal to $-(p_1 + \delta)/p_2$, the relevant point is now Q'' [see Figure 25(c), which uses a larger scale] at which the slope is $-p_1/(p_2 + \delta)$. The effect of the increase δ in the price p_2 on q_1 equals PD in Figure 25(c), so that

$$(14.24) \qquad \frac{\partial q_1}{\partial p_2} = \lim_{\delta \to 0} \frac{PD}{\delta}$$

To find PD, we equate the slope (14.17) to $-p_1/(p_2 + \delta)$,

$$-\frac{p_1}{p_2 + \delta} = -\frac{p_1}{p_2} + \alpha(q_1 - \bar{q}_1)$$

where $q_1 - \bar{q}_1$ equals PD in this case. This gives $PD = \delta p_1/\alpha p_2(p_2 + \delta)$ and hence $PD/\delta = p_1/\alpha p_2(p_2 + \delta)$ with limit $p_1/\alpha p_2^2$ as $\delta \to 0$. Hence, (14.24) implies $\partial q_1/\partial p_2 = p_1/\alpha p_2^2$. A comparison with (14.23) completes the proof of (14.20).

14.2   The Rotterdam Model

Consumer Demand Theory as an Allocation Theory

We concluded below (14.12) that the constant-elasticity model (14.10) is not attractive from the viewpoint of Slutsky symmetry. To make further progress, it is useful to note that consumer demand theory is in effect an allocation theory: It is concerned with the dollar amount to be allocated to each good, given the total amount available (m) and the prices of all goods $(p_1, \ldots, p_N)$. This is equivalent to saying that consumer demand theory is concerned with the N allocation proportions,

$$(14.25) \qquad w_i = \frac{p_i q_i}{m} \qquad\qquad i = 1, \ldots, N$$

which are known as the *budget shares* of the N goods. In this section we shall develop demand equations which are formulated in terms of changes in budget shares over time.

Note that the N budget shares add up to 1,

$$(14.26) \qquad \sum_{i=1}^{N} w_i = 1$$

which follows from (14.2) after dividing both sides by m. Also note that the proportion of income spent on food, mentioned in the opening paragraph of this chapter, is nothing but the combined budget share of all goods that fall under food.

The Change in a Budget Share and Its Three Components

Let $F(v_1, \ldots, v_n)$ be a differentiable function of n arguments. We consider the differential of this function,

$$(14.27) \qquad dF = \sum_{k=1}^{n} \frac{\partial F}{\partial v_k} dv_k$$

which gives us the change in the value of the function when all arguments are subject to infinitesimal changes. We apply this to (14.25), which describes w_i as a function of three arguments: p_i, q_i, and m. Since the partial derivatives of this function are q_i/m, p_i/m, and $-p_iq_i/m^2$, respectively, (14.27) yields

$$dw_i = \frac{q_i}{m} dp_i + \frac{p_i}{m} dq_i - \frac{p_iq_i}{m^2} dm$$

$$= \frac{p_iq_i}{m} \frac{dp_i}{p_i} + \frac{p_iq_i}{m} \frac{dq_i}{q_i} - \frac{p_iq_i}{m} \frac{dm}{m}$$

This can be written in a more elegant form,

$$(14.28) \qquad dw_i = w_i d(\log_e p_i) + w_i d(\log_e q_i) - w_i d(\log_e m)$$

which shows how the change in the ith budget share consists of three parts: one which is attributable to the change in the ith price, one for the change in the ith quantity, and one for the income change.

Recall that the consumer decides on the N quantities and takes income and prices as given. Accordingly, we select $w_i d(\log_e q_i)$, the quantity component of dw_i in (14.28), as the dependent variable of the demand equation for the ith good. This selection has several merits:

(1) Using the *quantity component*, rather than either of the two other components of dw_i, emphasizes that the quantity bought is the variable controlled by the consumer.

(2) Using a component of the *change* in a budget share will enable us to handle the partial derivatives in the Slutsky relations (14.7) and (14.8) and in (14.9). This statement is verified in the next subsection.

(3) Using components of changes in *budget shares* emphasizes that consumer demand theory is an allocation theory.

A Demand System in Infinitesimal Changes

We write (14.6) in logarithmic form:

$$\log_e q_i = \log_e q_i(\bar{m}, p_1, \ldots, p_N)$$
$$= \log_e q_i(e^{\log_e \bar{m}}, e^{\log_e p_1}, \ldots, e^{\log_e p_N})$$

The second line shows that (14.6) can be viewed as describing the logarithm of a quantity in terms of the logarithms of real income and all prices. We apply (14.27) to this logarithmic function:

$$d(\log_e q_i) = \frac{\partial \log q_i}{\partial \log \bar{m}} d(\log_e \bar{m}) + \sum_{j=1}^{N} \frac{\partial \log q_i}{\partial \log p_j} d(\log_e p_j)$$

This can be written in the equivalent form

$$(14.29) \qquad d(\log_e q_i) = \frac{\partial \log q_i}{\partial \log m} d(\log_e \bar{m}) + \sum_{j=1}^{N} \frac{\partial \log q_i}{\partial \log p_j} d(\log_e p_j)$$

because $\partial(\log q_i)/\partial(\log \bar{m}) = \partial(\log q_i)/\partial(\log m)$. This is so because the partial-derivative procedure implies that prices are kept constant in the evaluation of these two derivatives, so that the changes in money income (m) and real income ($\bar{m}$) are identical.

Next we multiply (14.29) by w_i:

$$w_i d(\log_e q_i) = w_i \frac{\partial \log q_i}{\partial \log m} d(\log_e \bar{m}) + w_i \sum_{j=1}^{N} \frac{\partial \log q_i}{\partial \log p_j} d(\log_e p_j)$$

$$= \frac{p_i q_i}{m} \frac{\partial q_i}{\partial m} \frac{m}{q_i} d(\log_e \bar{m}) + \frac{p_i q_i}{m} \sum_{j=1}^{N} \frac{\partial q_i}{\partial p_j} \frac{p_j}{q_i} d(\log_e p_j)$$

This can be simplified to

$$(14.30) \qquad w_i d(\log_e q_i) = p_i \frac{\partial q_i}{\partial m} d(\log_e \bar{m}) + \sum_{j=1}^{N} \frac{p_i p_j}{m} \frac{\partial q_i}{\partial p_j} d(\log_e p_j)$$

The left-hand side is the quantity component of the ith budget share change in (14.28). The coefficient of $d(\log_e p_j)$ on the right is

$$(14.31) \qquad \frac{p_i p_j}{m} \frac{\partial q_i}{\partial p_j} = \frac{p_j p_i}{m} \frac{\partial q_j}{\partial p_i}$$

where the equal sign is based on (14.7). Hence, Slutsky symmetry is equivalent to symmetry of the coefficients of the logarithmic price changes in the model (14.30). Also,

$$(14.32) \qquad \sum_{j=1}^{N} \frac{p_i p_j}{m} \frac{\partial q_i}{\partial p_j} = \frac{p_i}{m} \sum_{j=1}^{N} p_j \frac{\partial q_i}{\partial p_j} = 0$$

where the last step is based on (14.9).

Slutsky Coefficients

An approximation is necessary to implement the model (14.30) for data on finite (rather than infinitesimal) changes. We approximate $d(\log_e p_j)$ by Dp_{jt}, the log-change in the jth price from period $t - 1$ to period t [see (13.14)], and we replace the substitution term on the far right in (14.30) by

$$(14.33) \qquad \sum_{j=1}^{N} \pi_{ij} Dp_{jt}, \qquad \text{where } \pi_{ij} = \frac{p_i p_j}{m} \frac{\partial q_i}{\partial p_j}$$

This π_{ij} is called the (i, j)th *Slutsky coefficient*. It follows from (14.31) and (14.32) that the Slutsky coefficients satisfy

$$(14.34) \qquad\qquad \pi_{ij} = \pi_{ji} \qquad\qquad\qquad i, j = 1, \ldots, N$$

$$(14.35) \qquad\qquad \sum_{j=1}^{N} \pi_{ij} = 0 \qquad\qquad\qquad i = 1, \ldots, N$$

Also, the negativity condition (14.8) combined with the π_{ij} definition in (14.33) yields

$$(14.36) \qquad\qquad \pi_{ii} < 0 \qquad\qquad i = 1, \ldots, N$$

Marginal Shares

We write the coefficient of $d(\log_e \bar{m})$ in (14.30) as

$$(14.37) \qquad\qquad \mu_i = p_i \frac{\partial q_i}{\partial m} = \frac{\partial(p_i q_i)}{\partial m}$$

where the last equal sign is based on the fact that when we take the partial derivative of $p_i q_i$ with respect to m, p_i must be treated as a constant.

The coefficient μ_i is called the ith *marginal share*. It follows from the third member of (14.37) that this share answers the following question: If income goes up by one dollar, how much of this increase is allocated to the ith good? Note that a marginal share may be negative, viz., when the demand for a good declines as income increases ($\partial q_i / \partial m < 0$, the case of a so-called inferior good).

The marginal shares add up to 1,

$$(14.38) \qquad\qquad \sum_{i=1}^{N} \mu_i = 1$$

which is similar to (14.26) for budget shares. To prove (14.38), we differentiate (14.2) with respect to m, yielding $\sum_i p_i(\partial q_i/\partial m) = 1$. This is equivalent to (14.38) in view of (14.37).

A Demand Model in Finite Changes

Next consider the left-hand side of (14.30), where $d(\log_e q_i)$, to be approximated by Dq_{it}, is multiplied by w_i. In the finite-change version we have a budget share in t (w_{it}) and one in $t - 1$ ($w_{i,t-1}$). Our choice is their arithmetic average,

$$(14.39) \qquad\qquad \bar{w}_{it} = \tfrac{1}{2}(w_{i,t-1} + w_{it})$$

so that the finite-change demand equation has $\bar{w}_{it} Dq_{it}$ on the left. This equation takes the form

$$(14.40) \qquad\qquad \bar{w}_{it} Dq_{it} = \mu_i DQ_t + \sum_{j=1}^{N} \pi_{ij} Dp_{jt} + \epsilon_{it} \qquad\qquad i = 1, \ldots, N$$

where $\sum_j \pi_{ij} Dp_{jt}$ is the substitution term [see (14.33)] and ϵ_{it} is a random disturbance with zero mean, while

$$(14.41) \qquad\qquad DQ_t = \sum_{i=1}^{N} \bar{w}_{it} Dq_{it}$$

is the log-change in real income. The definition (14.41) is clarified in the next subsection.

The model (14.40), with the μ_i's and π_{ij}'s treated as unknown parameters, is the absolute price version of the so-called Rotterdam Model of systems of

consumer demand equations. There is also a relative price version in which the
Dp_{jt}'s are deflated by a price index, but this will not be considered here. For
further details, see Theil (1975–1976, Chapters 1 and 2).

The Measurement of Real Income

The sum of the left-hand side of (14.28) over $i = 1, \ldots, N$ is zero because
(14.26) holds identically for any values of income and prices. Thus, by summing
(14.28) over i, we obtain

$$0 = \sum_{i=1}^{N} w_i d(\log_e p_i) + \sum_{i=1}^{N} w_i d(\log_e q_i) - d(\log_e m)$$

This is equivalent to

$$(14.42) \qquad d(\log_e m) = \sum_{i=1}^{N} w_i d(\log_e p_i) + \sum_{i=1}^{N} w_i d(\log_e q_i)$$

which shows that the logarithmic change in the consumer's total expenditure
is the sum of a price component and a quantity component. These two components are known as the two Divisia indexes (a price index and a quantity
or volume index) of total expenditure.

Recall from the discussion preceding (14.6) that $\bar{m} = m/P$ is real income,
where P is a price index used to deflate money income. Let us define P as the
Divisia price index,

$$(14.43) \qquad d(\log_e P) = \sum_{i=1}^{N} w_i d(\log_e p_i)$$

so that (14.42), with the first term subtracted from both sides, becomes

$$d(\log_e m) - d(\log_e P) = \sum_{i=1}^{n} w_i d(\log_e q_i)$$

which is equivalent to

$$(14.44) \qquad d\left(\log_e \frac{m}{P}\right) = \sum_{i=1}^{N} w_i d(\log_e q_i)$$

The left-hand side is the logarithmic change in real income, the deflation being
performed by means of the Divisia price index. Thus, (14.44) states that this
logarithmic change is equal to the Divisia volume index $\sum_i w_i d(\log_e q_i)$. The
right-hand side of (14.41) is simply a finite-change version of this volume index.
Hence the real-income definition (14.41) used in the demand model (14.40) is
a finite-change version of the Divisia volume index of the consumer's total
expenditure.

REMARKS:

(1) The log-change in real income defined in (14.41) is the sum of the left-
hand variable in (14.40) over all i, so that the latter variable may be viewed
as the contribution of the ith good to the log-change in real income. Equivalently, the model (14.40) describes each such contribution as a linear function

of their sum (the log-change in real income) and the log-changes in the prices, thus emphasizing that it is an allocation model for the change in the demand for each good, given the changes in income and prices.

(2) The real-income definition (14.41) is in terms of quantity changes, not in terms of the change in money income deflated by prices. The latter approach can also be pursued, but it has the disadvantage that if it is applied to (14.40), the disturbances $\epsilon_{1t}, \ldots, \epsilon_{Nt}$ do not add up to zero. The definition (14.41) has the advantage that the ϵ_{it}'s have zero sum, which again emphasizes the fact that (14.40) is an allocation model. The interested reader should consult Problems 3 and 4.

14.3 Statistical Inference in the Rotterdam Model

Estimation Without Slutsky Symmetry

We write (14.35) as $\pi_{iN} = -\pi_{i1} - \cdots - \pi_{i,N-1}$. This shows that the substitution term of (14.40) can be written as

$$\sum_{j=1}^{N-1} \pi_{ij}Dp_{jt} + \pi_{iN}Dp_{Nt} = \sum_{j=1}^{N-1} \pi_{ij}Dp_{jt} - Dp_{Nt}\sum_{j=1}^{N-1} \pi_{ij}$$
$$= \sum_{j=1}^{N-1} \pi_{ij}(Dp_{jt} - Dp_{Nt})$$

so that (14.40) becomes

(14.45) $\bar{w}_{it}Dq_{it} = \mu_i DQ_t + \sum_{j=1}^{N-1} \pi_{ij}(Dp_{jt} - Dp_{Nt}) + \epsilon_{it}$

Suppose that the standard linear model holds for (14.45), with DQ_t and $Dp_{1t} - Dp_{Nt}, \ldots, Dp_{N-1,t} - Dp_{Nt}$ as the tth observations on N explanatory variables and uncorrelated disturbances $\epsilon_{i1}, \epsilon_{i2}, \ldots$ with zero mean and constant variance. We can then apply LS by running a regression of $\bar{w}_{it}Dq_{it}$ on the above-mentioned explanatory variables, which yields estimates $\mu_i, \pi_{i1}, \ldots, \pi_{i,N-1}$, after which the implied estimate of π_{iN} is obtained by means of the constraint (14.35) that was used to eliminate π_{iN}.

The constraint (14.35) is thus incorporated in the formulation (14.45), but the symmetry constraint (14.34) is not incorporated. The issue of Slutsky symmetry will be considered later in this section.

Two Sets of Estimates

The upper part of Table 16 shows the LS estimates for $N = 4$ Dutch and British groups of goods. These groups are food ($i = 1$); beverages, including tobacco ($i = 2$); durables, including textile ($i = 3$); and all other goods and services, labeled remainder ($i = 4$). The table is taken from Theil (1975–1976, Tables 5.6 and 5.7) and is in part based on work done by Goldman (1971). The underlying data are obtained by combining data on smaller groups; see

TABLE 16

Estimates of marginal shares and Slutsky coefficients of Dutch and British commodity groups

Dutch data

Commodity group	μ_i	π_{i1}	π_{i2}	π_{i3}	π_{i4}
Slutsky symmetry not imposed					
Food	153 (33)	−104 (25)	−39 (49)	44 (23)	100 (45)
Beverages	86 (13)	23 (10)	−31 (19)	2 (9)	6 (18)
Durables	490 (34)	53 (26)	15 (52)	−47 (24)	−22 (48)
Remainder	271 (31)	29 (24)	55 (48)	1 (22)	−84 (44)
Symmetry-constrained estimates					
Food	179 (27)	−107 (25)	22 (9)	43 (20)	42 (20)
Beverages	88 (12)		−27 (18)	2 (9)	3 (16)
Durables	482 (28)			−44 (24)	−1 (17)
Remainder	251 (27)				−44 (27)

British data

Commodity group	μ_i	π_{i1}	π_{i2}	π_{i3}	π_{i4}	c_i
Slutsky symmetry not imposed						
Food	182 (46)	−98 (32)	8 (29)	32 (39)	57 (51)	44 (72)
Beverages	184 (23)	35 (16)	−61 (15)	52 (20)	−27 (26)	−207 (36)
Durables	318 (35)	20 (24)	21 (23)	−76 (30)	34 (39)	−11 (56)
Remainder	317 (33)	43 (23)	31 (21)	−9 (29)	−65 (37)	173 (53)
Symmetry-constrained estimates						
Food	188 (44)	−84 (26)	29 (10)	27 (23)	29 (17)	39 (72)
Beverages	174 (22)		−80 (9)	44 (11)	8 (15)	−202 (36)
Durables	330 (34)			−63 (27)	−7 (19)	−17 (55)
Remainder	307 (32)				−30 (27)	180 (52)

Note: All entries, except those in the last column, are to be divided by 1000. The estimates of the c_i's and their standard errors are to be divided by 100,000.

Theil (1975–1976, Sections 5.2 and 6.1) and, for the original sources, Barten (1966) and Stone and Rowe (1966).

The Dutch estimates are based on annual data for the periods 1922–1939 and 1949–1963, and the British estimates on annual data for 1900–1913 and 1921–1938; war years and early postwar years are deleted. Standard errors are shown in parentheses to the right of the corresponding point estimates. All estimates of the μ_i's and π_{ij}'s and their standard errors are multiplied by 1000 in the table; hence, the LS estimate of the marginal share of food obtained from the Dutch data is .153 with a standard error of .033.

Note that the estimates do not satisfy the symmetry constraint (14.34): The LS estimate of the Dutch π_{12} in the first line is $-.039$ and that of π_{21} in the second is .023. The complete array of the Dutch LS Slutsky estimates is given below. The carets above the π's indicate that they are estimates rather than parameters.

$$\hat{\pi}_{11} = -.104 \quad \hat{\pi}_{12} = -.039 \quad \hat{\pi}_{13} = .044 \quad \hat{\pi}_{14} = .100$$
$$\hat{\pi}_{21} = .023 \quad \hat{\pi}_{22} = -.031 \quad \hat{\pi}_{23} = .002 \quad \hat{\pi}_{24} = .006$$
$$\hat{\pi}_{31} = .053 \quad \hat{\pi}_{32} = .015 \quad \hat{\pi}_{33} = -.047 \quad \hat{\pi}_{34} = -.022$$
$$\hat{\pi}_{41} = .029 \quad \hat{\pi}_{42} = .055 \quad \hat{\pi}_{43} = .001 \quad \hat{\pi}_{44} = -.084$$

Note that these estimates do satisfy the negativity condition (14.36), since $\hat{\pi}_{11}, \hat{\pi}_{22}, \hat{\pi}_{33}$, and $\hat{\pi}_{44}$ are all negative. The reader should verify that the British LS estimates of the π_{ii}'s in the upper-right part of Table 16 are also negative. Hence, insofar as the LS estimates are concerned, a price increase reduces the demand for the corresponding commodity group when real income and all other prices remain constant.

The British Constant Terms

Recall from the discussion below (13.18) that the demand equation for textile, when formulated in log-changes, contains no constant term. In (14.40) there is no constant term either. Hence, when real income and all prices do not change from $t-1$ to t, DQ_t and the Dp_{jt}'s being all zero, $\bar{w}_{it}Dq_{it}$ equals ϵ_{it}, so that the change in the ith quantity is then also zero apart from the effect of a random disturbance.

In the British demand equations a constant term c_i is added to the right-hand side of (14.40):

$$(14.46) \qquad \bar{w}_{it}Dq_{it} = c_i + \mu_i DQ_t + \sum_{j=1}^{N} \pi_{ij}Dp_{jt} + \epsilon_{it}$$

This c_i measures the systematic effect of factors other than income and prices on the demand for the ith good. If $c_i > 0$, this means that this demand increases ($\bar{w}_{it}Dq_{it} > 0$ implying $Dq_{it} > 0$) even when real income and all prices remain unchanged (DQ_t and all Dp_{jt}'s equal to zero).

The c_i estimates and their standard errors, multiplied by 100,000, are shown in the last column of Table 16. The largest estimate in absolute value ($-.00207$

with standard error .00036) is that of the beverages group ($i = 2$), which includes tobacco. This is probably related to the substantial change in the share of tobacco in this group, from about 10 percent in the early 1900s to over 35 percent from 1932 onward. Part of this change resulted from the increasing proportion of smokers among women. Further details are provided in Problems 7 and 8.

Testing for Slutsky Symmetry

Slutsky symmetry can be written in the form $\pi_{12} - \pi_{21} = 0$, $\pi_{13} - \pi_{31} = 0$, and so on. Each such constraint is linear in the parameters. We assume that the ϵ_{it}'s are normally distributed and recall the null hypothesis $w_1\beta_1 + w_2\beta_2 = w_0$ considered in Section 12.2, where the w's are given numbers. The test statistic used is (12.11), reproduced here,

$$(14.47) \qquad \frac{w_1 b_1 + w_2 b_2 - w_0}{(s/\sqrt{1 - r^2})\sqrt{(w_1/S_1)^2 + (w_2/S_2)^2 - 2rw_1w_2/S_1S_2}}$$

which is distributed as $t(n')$ if the null hypothesis is true. The numerator of (14.47) is a linear combination of the LS coefficients minus the value w_0, which the null hypothesis assigns to the corresponding parameter combination. The denominator is the square root of the unbiased estimator of the variance of $w_1 b_1 + w_2 b_2$.

Here we are interested in testing the hypothesis $\pi_{12} = \pi_{21}$ for the Dutch data. Hence, the numerator of (14.47) takes the form $\hat{\pi}_{12} - \hat{\pi}_{21}$, where the $\hat{\pi}_{ij}$'s are the LS estimators of the π_{ij}'s, and the denominator becomes the square root of the unbiased estimator of the variance of $\hat{\pi}_{12} - \hat{\pi}_{21}$. This variance is

$$(14.48) \qquad \text{var}\,(\hat{\pi}_{12} - \hat{\pi}_{21}) = \text{var}\,\hat{\pi}_{12} + \text{var}\,\hat{\pi}_{21} - 2\,\text{cov}\,(\hat{\pi}_{12}, \hat{\pi}_{21})$$

Let us assume, temporarily, that $\hat{\pi}_{12}$ and $\hat{\pi}_{21}$ are uncorrelated, so that the right-hand side of (14.48) becomes var $\hat{\pi}_{12}$ + var $\hat{\pi}_{21}$. An estimate of this expression is the sum of the squares of the standard errors of the LS estimates of π_{12} and π_{21}, which equals $(.049)^2 + (.010)^2$ for the Dutch data (see the first two lines of Table 16). Thus, using the corresponding LS estimates also, we obtain

$$\frac{-.039 - .023}{\sqrt{(.049)^2 + (.010)^2}} \approx -1.2$$

which is the value of the Student test statistic. The outcome is far from significant at any reasonable significance level (see the table of the Student distribution at the end of this book), so that the symmetry relation $\pi_{12} = \pi_{21}$ is acceptable in spite of the fact that the LS estimates $\hat{\pi}_{12} = -.039$ and $\hat{\pi}_{21} = .023$ are far apart.

Two Qualifications

The application of the Student test statistic (14.47) to Slutsky symmetry is not a routine application, because π_{12} is a coefficient in the demand equation for the first good and π_{21} occurs in the equation for the second good. Hence, testing for Slutsky symmetry amounts to testing a constraint on two coefficients which occur in two different equations. If these equations have disturbances which are correlated, the covariance in (14.48) does not vanish. In our case, the demand equation for the first good has a disturbance ϵ_{1t} [see (14.40)] and that for the second good has a disturbance ϵ_{2t}; the covariance of ϵ_{1t} and ϵ_{2t} is, in general, not zero, which makes the computations described below (14.48) invalid. The interested reader should consult Problem 12 for some further details.

The second qualification is that if we are interested in Slutsky symmetry, we should not test one single symmetry relation such as $\pi_{12} = \pi_{21}$, but we should test the symmetry relations $\pi_{ij} = \pi_{ji}$ for all pairs (i, j) simultaneously. The Student test is then no longer appropriate; it has to be extended to an F test (see Section 12.3).

In spite of these qualifications it is the case that Slutsky symmetry is an acceptable hypothesis for both the Dutch and the British data at any reasonable significance level; details can be found in Theil (1975–1976, Section 5.3). Given this outcome, an obvious procedure is to accept Slutsky symmetry as valid and to impose it on the estimates. The main objective of this section from here onward is to discuss numerical results.

Imposing Slutsky Symmetry

Imposing linear constraints such as Slutsky symmetry can be performed by means of a generalization of the LS method which is described in Appendix G. Whereas the LS procedure estimates each demand equation separately, the generalization estimates all equations simultaneously. This is necessary in order to incorporate constraints on coefficients of different equations such as $\pi_{12} = \pi_{21}$.

The symmetry-constrained estimates for the Dutch data are shown below. Primes are added to the $\hat{\pi}_{ij}$'s in order to distinguish them from the unconstrained (LS) Slutsky estimates on page 214.

$$
\begin{array}{llll}
\hat{\pi}'_{11} = -.107 & \hat{\pi}'_{12} = .022 & \hat{\pi}'_{13} = .043 & \hat{\pi}'_{14} = .042 \\
\hat{\pi}'_{21} = .022 & \hat{\pi}'_{22} = -.027 & \hat{\pi}'_{23} = .002 & \hat{\pi}'_{24} = .003 \\
\hat{\pi}'_{31} = .043 & \hat{\pi}'_{32} = .002 & \hat{\pi}'_{33} = -.044 & \hat{\pi}'_{34} = -.001 \\
\hat{\pi}'_{41} = .042 & \hat{\pi}'_{42} = .003 & \hat{\pi}'_{43} = -.001 & \hat{\pi}'_{44} = -.044
\end{array}
$$

Note that the estimates are symmetric: $\hat{\pi}'_{12} = \hat{\pi}'_{21}$ ($= .022$), and so on. Also note that the estimates along the main diagonal from upper left to lower right ($\hat{\pi}'_{11}, \hat{\pi}'_{22}, \hat{\pi}'_{33}, \hat{\pi}'_{44}$) are all negative. Since the $\hat{\pi}'_{ij}$'s below this diagonal are equal to the corresponding $\hat{\pi}'_{ji}$'s above the diagonal, there is no need to show them separately. Accordingly, the lower part of Table 16 contains the diagonal and above-diagonal symmetry-constrained estimates, with standard errors in parentheses.

Comparison of the Estimates With and Without Slutsky Symmetry

Imposing symmetry on the π_{ij} estimates affects not only these but also the estimates of the μ_i's. For example, the Dutch marginal share of food has an unconstrained (LS) estimate equal to .153 in the first line of Table 16 and a constrained estimate equal to .179 in the fifth line in spite of the fact that Slutsky symmetry refers to the π_{ij}'s and not to the μ_i's. The cause is the fact that the symmetry-constrained procedure estimates all parameters of all demand equations simultaneously. This includes both the π_{ij}'s and the μ_i's and, in the British case, also the c_i's.

The symmetry-constrained estimate of π_{ij} is usually between the unconstrained estimates of π_{ij} and π_{ji}, but this rule is not without exceptions. For example, the unconstrained estimates of the British π_{14} and π_{41} are .057 and .043, and the symmetry-constrained estimate of $\pi_{14} = \pi_{41}$ is smaller than both, .029. This happens because the constrained estimation procedure is not just a matter of taking a weighted average of the unconstrained estimates of π_{ij} and π_{ji}.

When the unconstrained estimates of π_{ij} and π_{ji} have standard errors of a different order of magnitude, the constrained estimate tends to be closer to the unconstrained estimate with the smaller standard error. For example, the unconstrained estimate of the Dutch π_{12} in the first line is $-.039$ with a standard error of .049, and the π_{21} estimate in the second line is .023 with a much smaller standard error, .010. Accordingly, the symmetry-constrained estimate of $\pi_{12} = \pi_{21}$ in the fifth line, .022, is much closer to the latter estimate than to the former. Also note that the standard error of this constrained estimate, .009, is smaller than those of both unconstrained estimates (.049 and .010). This agrees with intuition; if Slutsky symmetry is a correct hypothesis, we should be able to obtain more precise estimates by imposing this symmetry than by not imposing it. In fact, the reduction of the standard errors is also noticeable for the estimates of the parameters that are not directly involved in this symmetry [μ_i, c_i, and π_{ii} (equal subscripts)], but the effect tends to be much smaller for these estimates.

The Signs of the Symmetry-Constrained Estimates

All estimates of all marginal shares are positive, and their t ratios are substantial. We conclude that when income increases, prices remaining constant, the demand for each of the four groups increases also. This applies to both the Dutch and the British data.

The sign pattern of the symmetry-constrained estimates of the Slutsky coefficients is also the same for the Dutch and the British data: negative signs of the equal-subscript π_{ii}'s and of π_{34} (durables and remainder) and positive signs of all other π_{ij}'s. Thus, when the price of food goes up, real income and all other prices remaining constant, the demand for food decreases ($\pi_{11} < 0$) and that for the three other groups increases ($\pi_{21}, \pi_{31}, \pi_{41} > 0$). Similarly, when the price of beverages goes up (same proviso), the demand for this group decreases and that for the other groups increases. But when the price of durables goes up (same proviso), the demand for both this group and remainder decreases; only for food and for beverages is there an increased demand.

Note, however, that this sign pattern of estimates cannot be guaranteed to hold for the corresponding parameters. For example, the symmetry-constrained estimate of the Dutch π_{34} is $-.001$ with a standard error of .017; hence, a positive value of the true π_{34} can certainly not be excluded.

Implied Estimates of Elasticities

Let us divide (14.40) by $\bar{w}_{it}$:

$$(14.49) \qquad Dq_{it} = \frac{\mu_i}{\bar{w}_{it}} DQ_t + \sum_{j=1}^{N} \frac{\pi_{ij}}{\bar{w}_{it}} Dp_{jt} + \frac{\epsilon_{it}}{\bar{w}_{it}}$$

Since the log-change Dq_{it} is on the left, the coefficient of the log-change in real income (DQ_t) must be the income elasticity of the demand for the ith good. This coefficient is $\mu_i/\bar{w}_{it}$, which is not a constant because $\bar{w}_{it}$ varies over time. Let us take the average budget shares over all observations, which take the following values (in the order food, beverages, durables, and remainder):

$$(14.50) \qquad \begin{array}{cccc} .294 & .096 & .240 & .370 \\ .326 & .113 & .202 & .359 \end{array} \quad \begin{array}{l} \text{(Dutch)} \\ \text{(British)} \end{array}$$

By dividing the symmetry-constrained estimates of $\mu_1, \ldots, \mu_4$ of Table 16 by the corresponding average budget shares shown in (14.50), we obtain estimates of the income elasticities at these average budget shares. These elasticity estimates are given in the first column of Table 17. For both the Dutch and the

TABLE 17

**Estimates of income and Slutsky elasticities
of Dutch and British commodity groups**

Commodity group	Income elasticity	Slutsky elasticity with respect to the price of			
		Food	Beverages	Durables	Remainder
		Dutch			
Food	.61	$-.36$	.07	.15	.14
Beverages	.92	.23	$-.28$	.02	.03
Durables	2.01	.18	.01	$-.18$	$-.00$
Remainder	.68	.11	.01	$-.00$	$-.12$
		British			
Food	.58	$-.26$	.09	.08	.09
Beverages	1.54	.26	$-.71$	.39	.07
Durables	1.63	.13	.22	$-.31$	$-.03$
Remainder	.86	.08	.02	$-.02$	$-.08$

British data, food has the smallest income elasticity of the four (about .6) and durables the largest. Goods with income elasticities exceeding 1 are called *luxuries* and those with income elasticities below 1 *necessities*. Thus, food is a necessity for the Dutch as well as the British.

It follows from (14.49) that the elasticity of the demand for the ith good with respect to the jth price is $\pi_{ij}/\bar{w}_{it}$. This is not equal to $\pi_{ji}/\bar{w}_{jt}$, even when $\pi_{ij} = \pi_{ji}$, so that these elasticities are not symmetric. Their numerical values, obtained from the symmetry-constrained estimates of the π_{ij}'s in Table 16 and the average budget shares given in (14.50), are shown in the last four columns of Table 17. They are labeled Slutsky elasticities in order to distinguish them from the price elasticity $-.83$ in (8.12), which is an elasticity with respect to a relative price (the relative price of textile in this case). Slutsky elasticities are elasticities of demand with respect to absolute (undeflated) prices for a constant real income.

The Slutsky elasticity with the largest estimate in absolute value is that of the British beverages group with respect to its own price $(-.71)$. All other Slutsky elasticity estimates are substantially closer to zero. This modest degree of price sensitivity should be expected when we deal with such broad commodity groups as those which are used here.

*14.4   Groupwise Extensions

Strictly speaking, the theoretical developments leading to the model (14.40) are based on the idea that the N consumer goods are more narrowly defined than the four groups of Tables 16 and 17. To a degree this is unavoidable, because when we distinguish between a large number of goods, the N parameters in (14.45) amount to an unwieldy number of unknowns. However, it is possible to reformulate the approach so that it becomes more manageable when we impose certain separability conditions on the utility function. The implied strategy is then to formulate, first, demand equations for groups of goods and, second, demand equations for individual goods within their respective groups.

Groups of Goods

We divide the N goods into G groups of goods and assume that the consumer's preferences are such that the utility function (14.1) can be written as the sum of G functions, one for each group,

$$(14.51) \qquad u(q_1, \ldots, q_N) = u_1(\quad) + u_2(\quad) + \cdots + u_G(\quad)$$

where the arguments of the G functions on the right are the q_i's of the corresponding group. To verify the implications of this assumption, we consider $\partial u/\partial q_i$, the marginal utility of the ith good. If this good belongs to the first group, then $\partial u/\partial q_i = \partial u_1/\partial q_i$, which depends only on the q_j's of the first group. Thus, the marginal utility of the ith good is under (14.51) independent of the quantities of all goods which belong to groups other than that of the ith.

We consider one particular group, the *g*th, and arrange the goods so that those of this group have subscripts $1, \ldots, N_g$, where N_g is the number of goods of the *g*th group. We define

$$(14.52) \qquad \bar{W}_{gt} = \sum_{i=1}^{N_g} \bar{w}_{it}, \qquad M_g = \sum_{i=1}^{N_g} \mu_i$$

where $\bar{W}_{gt}$ is the budget share of the group (averaged over periods $t-1$ and t) and M_g is its marginal share. The latter share answers the following question: If income increases by one dollar, how much of this increase is allocated to the goods of the *g*th group?

Next we define

$$(14.53) \qquad DQ_{gt} = \sum_{i=1}^{N_g} \frac{\bar{w}_{it}}{\bar{W}_{gt}} Dq_{it}$$

which is the log-change in the volume (quantity) index of the *g*th group. The right-hand side is a weighted mean of the Dq_{it}'s of this group with weights of the form $\bar{w}_{it}/\bar{W}_{gt}$, which should be compared with (14.41) for the log-change in real income.

Demand Equations for Groups of Goods

We multiply (14.53) by $\bar{W}_{gt}$:

$$(14.54) \qquad \bar{W}_{gt} DQ_{gt} = \sum_{i=1}^{N_g} \bar{w}_{it} Dq_{it}$$

The left-hand side is the group version of the left-hand variable $\bar{w}_{it} Dq_{it}$ of the demand equation (14.40) for an individual good. Hence, (14.54) implies that if we want a demand equation for the group with $\bar{W}_{gt} DQ_{gt}$ on the left, we must sum the equations (14.40) for the goods of this group. Using M_g defined in (14.52), the equation for the group thus becomes

$$(14.55) \qquad \bar{W}_{gt} DQ_{gt} = M_g DQ_t + \sum_{i=1}^{N_g} \sum_{j=1}^{N} \pi_{ij} Dp_{jt} + E_{gt}$$

where $E_{gt} = \sum_i \epsilon_{it}$ (sum over $i = 1, \ldots, N_g$) is the sum of the demand disturbances of all goods of the group.

It is possible to simplify the substitution term $\sum_i \sum_j \pi_{ij} Dp_{jt}$ of the group demand equation (14.55) under condition (14.51), but we shall not pursue this here. The objective of the remainder of this section is the formulation of demand equations for goods *within their group*.

Conditional Budget Shares

In (14.28) we obtained the three components of the infinitesimal change in a budget share, one of which was subsequently used as the left-hand variable in the demand equation (14.30). Here we proceed similarly for the infinitesimal change in the ratio of w_i to $W_g = \sum_j w_j$ (sum over $j = 1, \ldots, N_g$). The ratio

w_i/W_g is called the conditional budget share of the ith good within its group. If the consumer spends 20 percent of his income on the group and 3 percent on a good which belongs to this group, then $W_g = .2$ and $w_i = .03$, so that the conditional budget share of this good within the group is $(.03)/(.2) = .15$ or 15 percent. The word "conditional" should in this context be interpreted as "within the group."

We have $d(\log_e x) = dx/x$ and hence $dx = x\,d(\log_e x)$ for any positive variable x. We apply this to $x = w_i/W_g$:

$$d\left(\frac{w_i}{W_g}\right) = \frac{w_i}{W_g}d\left(\log_e \frac{w_i}{W_g}\right) = \frac{w_i}{W_g}d(\log_e w_i) - \frac{w_i}{W_g}d(\log_e W_g)$$

The first term in the third member equals $(w_i/W_g)(dw_i/w_i) = dw_i/W_g$, so that

$$d\left(\frac{w_i}{W_g}\right) = \frac{dw_i}{W_g} - \frac{w_i}{W_g}d(\log_e W_g)$$
$$= \frac{w_id(\log_e p_i) + w_id(\log_e q_i) - w_id(\log_e m)}{W_g} - \frac{w_i}{W_g}d(\log_e W_g)$$

where the second step is based on (14.28). We can write this result in a simpler form,

(14.56) $\quad d\left(\frac{w_i}{W_g}\right) = \frac{w_i}{W_g}d(\log_e p_i) + \frac{w_i}{W_g}d(\log_e q_i) - \frac{w_i}{W_g}d(\log_e W_g m)$

which is a within-group version of (14.28). The first two terms on the right in (14.56) are the price and quantity components of the change in the conditional budget share. The last term results from the change in the total amount spent on the group. This follows from the fact that W_g is the combined budget share of all goods of the group, so that $W_g m$ is the amount spent on this group. By summing (14.56) over $i = 1, \ldots, N_g$, we obtain Divisia indexes of the group, similar to those shown in (14.42); this matter is pursued in Problem 14.

Conditional Demand Equations

Recall that the left-hand variable $\bar{w}_{it}Dq_{it}$ in (14.40) is a finite-change version of the quantity component of dw_i. Thus, when our objective is to formulate a demand equation for the ith good within its group, an obvious choice for its left-hand variable is a finite-change version of $(w_i/W_g)d(\log_e q_i)$, the quantity component of the change in the conditional budget share which is given in (14.56). We choose $(\bar{w}_{it}/\bar{W}_{gt})Dq_{it}$ as this finite-change version, where $\bar{W}_{gt}$ is defined in (14.52). To obtain this variable on the left, we simply divide both sides of (14.40) by $\bar{W}_{gt}$:

(14.57) $\quad \frac{\bar{w}_{it}}{\bar{W}_{gt}}Dq_{it} = \frac{\mu_i}{\bar{W}_{gt}}DQ_t + \sum_{j=1}^{N}\frac{\pi_{ij}}{\bar{W}_{gt}}Dp_{jt} + \frac{\epsilon_{it}}{\bar{W}_{gt}}$

Next we multiply (14.55) by $\mu_i/M_g\bar{W}_{gt}$,

$$\frac{\mu_i}{M_g}DQ_{gt} = \frac{\mu_i}{\bar{W}_{gt}}DQ_t + \sum_{k=1}^{N_g}\sum_{j=1}^{N}\frac{\mu_i\pi_{kj}}{M_g\bar{W}_{gt}}Dp_{jt} + \frac{\mu_iE_{gt}}{M_g\bar{W}_{gt}}$$

and subtract this from (14.57), so that the two terms involving DQ_t cancel each other out. The result may be written as

$$\frac{\bar{w}_{it}}{\bar{W}_{gt}} Dq_{it} - \frac{\mu_i}{M_g} DQ_{gt} = \text{price term} + \frac{\epsilon_{it}}{\bar{W}_{gt}} - \frac{\mu_i E_{gt}}{M_g \bar{W}_{gt}}$$

or, equivalently, as

$$\frac{\bar{w}_{it}}{\bar{W}_{gt}} Dq_{it} = \frac{\mu_i}{M_g} DQ_{gt} + \text{price term} + \epsilon_{it}^*$$

where $\epsilon_{it}^* = \epsilon_{it}/\bar{W}_{gt} - \mu_i E_{gt}/M_g \bar{W}_{gt}$. It is shown in Appendix D that if the utility function satisfies condition (14.51), the price term can be simplified so that the equation takes the form

$$(14.58) \qquad \frac{\bar{w}_{it}}{\bar{W}_{gt}} Dq_{it} = \frac{\mu_i}{M_g} DQ_{gt} + \sum_{j=1}^{N_g} \pi_{ij}^* Dp_{jt} + \epsilon_{it}^*$$

This is a conditional demand equation for each good of the group ($i = 1, \ldots, N_g$) with the coefficients of the Dp_{jt}'s satisfying

$$(14.59) \qquad \pi_{ij}^* = \pi_{ji}^* \qquad\qquad i, j = 1, \ldots, N_g$$

$$(14.60) \qquad \sum_{j=1}^{N_g} \pi_{ij}^* = 0 \qquad\qquad i = 1, \ldots, N_g$$

$$(14.61) \qquad \pi_{ii}^* < 0 \qquad\qquad i = 1, \ldots, N_g$$

Note that these three constraints are similar to (14.34) through (14.36).

Conditional Marginal Shares and Conditional Slutsky Coefficients

A comparison of (14.58) and (14.40) is instructive. In (14.40) we have the quantity component of the change in the ith budget share on the left; in (14.58) it is the quantity component of the change in the ith conditional budget share. In (14.40) the first variable on the right is the log-change in real income; in (14.58) it is the log-change in the volume index of the group. In (14.40) we have the price log-changes of all N goods, but in (14.58) we have only those of the goods of the same group as that of the ith. In fact, all variables of (14.58) refer to the group to which the ith good belongs. This illustrates the role of (14.58) as an allocation model for goods within their group.

The coefficient of DQ_{gt} in (14.58) is μ_i/M_g, which is called the *conditional marginal share* of the ith good within its group. This share answers the following question: If income increases by one dollar, so that an additional amount M_g is spent on the gth group, what proportion of this amount is allocated to the ith good? It can be shown that $M_g > 0$ under condition (14.51), so that μ_i/M_g exists.

The properties (14.59) through (14.61) of the coefficients of the Dp_{jt}'s in (14.58) are similar to (14.34) through (14.36) for the π_{ij}'s in (14.40), but note that these coefficients are not the same. In (14.40), π_{ij} measures the effect of a change in the jth price on the demand for the ith good when real income and the prices of all $N - 1$ other goods remain unchanged. In (14.58), π_{ij}^* measures the effect of this change when the volume index of the group remains constant ($DQ_{gt} = 0$) and the prices of the $N_g - 1$ other goods of this group remain constant. We shall refer to π_{ij}^* as the (i, j)th *conditional Slutsky coefficient* within the group.

Application to the Demand for Meats in the United States

In the application to be described we treat DQ_{gt} and the Dp_{jt}'s of (14.58) as nonstochastic values taken by explanatory variables and ϵ_{it}^* as a random disturbance with zero mean and constant variance which is uncorrelated over time. The application is based on annual U.S. data in 1950–1972 for beef ($i = 1$), pork ($i = 2$), chicken ($i = 3$), and lamb ($i = 4$). Hence, (14.51) implies that the marginal utility of each meat is assumed to be independent of the quantities consumed of all goods consumed outside the meat group. We thus have $N_g = 4$ in (14.58) for the ith meat. The reader should verify, using (14.60), that (14.58) can then be written as

$$(14.62) \qquad \frac{\bar{w}_{it}}{\bar{W}_{gt}} Dq_{it} = \frac{\mu_i}{M_g} DQ_{gt} + \sum_{j=1}^{3} \pi_{ij}^*(Dp_{jt} - Dp_{4t}) + \epsilon_{it}^*$$

which has a form similar to (14.45). Thus, we estimate μ_i/M_g, π_{i1}^*, π_{i2}^*, and π_{i3}^* from an LS regression of $(\bar{w}_{it}/\bar{W}_{gt})Dq_{it}$ on the four right-hand variables in (14.62). The result is shown in the upper half of Table 18. Note that the estimates of π_{12}^* and π_{21}^* in the first and second lines (for beef and pork) are rather close to each other, which is encouraging for the symmetry condition (14.59).

Testing this symmetry and imposing it on the estimates are completely analogous to the corresponding procedures for unconditional demand equations. The meat data pass the symmetry test with flying colors. The constrained estimates are shown in the lower half of Table 18. The reader should verify the

TABLE 18

Estimates of conditional marginal shares and Slutsky coefficients of meats

	μ_i/M_g	π_{i1}^*	π_{i2}^*	π_{i3}^*	π_{i4}^*
		Slutsky symmetry not imposed			
Beef	.712 (.055)	−.197 (.048)	.176 (.020)	.026 (.023)	−.005 (.063)
Pork	.192 (.049)	.157 (.043)	−.219 (.018)	.050 (.020)	.012 (.057)
Chicken	.046 (.022)	.009 (.019)	.030 (.008)	−.087 (.009)	.048 (.025)
Lamb	.050 (.012)	.030 (.010)	.013 (.004)	.012 (.005)	−.055 (.014)
		Symmetry-constrained estimates			
Beef	.692 (.049)	−.227 (.019)	.164 (.014)	.033 (.009)	.029 (.010)
Pork	.199 (.044)		−.214 (.014)	.038 (.007)	.012 (.004)
Chicken	.059 (.021)			−.084 (.009)	.013 (.005)
Lamb	.050 (.012)				−.055 (.014)

reduction of the standard errors caused by the symmetry constraint. He should also verify that these standard errors tend to be smaller relative to the point estimates than those shown in Table 16 for the symmetry-constrained estimates of the unconditional π_{ij}'s. Hence, the estimates of the π_{ij}^*'s in the lower half of Table 18 tend to be more precise than their counterparts in Table 16. This is in large measure due to the fact that the prices of meats are subject to more substantial fluctuations than are the prices on which Table 16 is based.

Conditional Income Elasticities

The conditional marginal share of the ith good equals μ_i/M_g. The conditional budget share is similarly defined as $\bar{w}_{it}/\bar{W}_{gt}$. Their ratio is

$$(14.63) \qquad \frac{\mu_i/M_g}{\bar{w}_{it}/\bar{W}_{gt}} = \frac{\mu_i/\bar{w}_{it}}{M_g/\bar{W}_{gt}}$$

To interpret the right-hand side, we divide (14.55) by $\bar{W}_{gt}$,

$$(14.64) \qquad DQ_{gt} = \frac{M_g}{\bar{W}_{gt}}DQ_t + \frac{1}{\bar{W}_{gt}}\sum_{i=1}^{N_g}\sum_{j=1}^{N}\pi_{ij}Dp_{jt} + \frac{E_{gt}}{\bar{W}_{gt}}$$

which shows that $M_g/\bar{W}_{gt}$ is the income elasticity of the demand for the group [compare the discussion below (14.49)]. Therefore, (14.63) states that the ratio of the conditional marginal share of a good to its conditional budget share is equal to the ratio of its income elasticity to the income elasticity of the group. We refer to the latter ratio as the *conditional income elasticity* of the ith good within its group.

Estimates of these conditional elasticities for meats are shown in the first column of Table 19. Those of beef and lamb exceed 1, indicating that these two meats are luxuries within the meat group, whereas the opposite holds for pork and chicken. These elasticity estimates are computed from the symmetry-constrained estimates of μ_i/M_g in Table 18 and the average budget shares in the period 1950–1972. About 50 percent of the total expenditure on meat is allocated to beef, about 35 percent to pork, 12 percent to chicken, and less than 3 percent to lamb.

TABLE 19
Estimates of conditional income and Slutsky elasticities of meats

	Conditional income elasticity	Conditional Slutsky elasticity with respect to the price of			
		Beef	Pork	Chicken	Lamb
Beef	1.39	−.45	.33	.07	.06
Pork	.57	.47	−.61	.11	.03
Chicken	.49	.27	.31	−.69	.11
Lamb	1.80	1.06	.44	.47	−2.00

Conditional Slutsky Elasticities

Next divide (14.58) by $\bar{w}_{it}/\bar{W}_{gt}$:

(14.65) $$Dq_{it} = \frac{\mu_i/\bar{w}_{it}}{M_g/\bar{W}_{gt}} DQ_{gt} + \sum_{j=1}^{N_g} \frac{\pi_{ij}^* \bar{W}_{gt}}{\bar{w}_{it}} Dp_{jt} + \frac{\epsilon_{it}^* \bar{W}_{gt}}{\bar{w}_{it}}$$

The coefficient $\pi_{ij}^* \bar{W}_{gt}/\bar{w}_{it}$ of Dp_{jt} is the *conditional Slutsky elasticity* of the demand for the ith good with respect to the jth price within the group. This elasticity measures the proportionate effect of a change in p_j on the demand for the ith good when the demand for the group is unchanged ($DQ_{gt} = 0$) and the prices of the other goods of the group are also unchanged.

Estimates of the conditional Slutsky elasticities for meats, based on average budget shares and the symmetry-constrained estimates of the π_{ij}^*'s, are shown in Table 19. The last column indicates that a 1 percent increase in the price of lamb, the three other prices and the volume index of meat consumption remaining constant, reduces the consumption of lamb by 2 percent and raises the consumption of the three other meats by a small fraction of a percent. Notice that the effect of a change in the price of beef on the consumption of the other meats is much larger. A major cause is the fact that beef accounts for a much greater proportion of meat expenditure than does lamb.

Conditional and Unconditional Slutsky Elasticities Compared

The Slutsky elasticities of Table 19 tend to be somewhat larger in absolute value than those of Table 17. However, an unqualified comparison is misleading because we have conditional elasticities in one case and unconditional elasticities in the other. It can be shown that if (14.51) holds with meats being one of the G groups and if the conditional marginal shares are all positive (see Table 18), the unconditional Slutsky elasticities are algebraically smaller than the corresponding conditional elasticities. Thus, the unconditional Slutsky elasticity of beef with respect to its own price takes a larger negative value than the $-.45$ shown in Table 19. In fact, it may be as large as -1 (see Problem 18).

This result can be explained in intuitive terms. For $i = 1$ (beef) in (14.49) the Slutsky elasticity $\pi_{11}/\bar{w}_{1t}$ can be viewed as the proportionate effect of an increase in the price of beef on its demand when the consumer receives an income compensation so that his real income is unchanged. Similarly, the corresponding conditional Slutsky elasticity in (14.65) may be viewed as the proportionate effect of this price increase when it is accompanied by an income compensation so that the volume index of meat is unchanged ($DQ_{gt} = 0$). It stands to reason that the latter compensation has to be larger than the former, because a price increase of beef will have a larger proportionate impact on the volume of meat consumption than on real income. This larger income compensation reduces the decrease in the demand for beef, so that the conditional Slutsky elasticity takes a smaller negative value than the unconditional elasticity.

Problems

Problems 1 and 2 refer to Section 14.1, 3 and 4 to Section 14.2, 5–12 to Section 14.3, and 13–18 to Section 14.4.

1 Prove that (14.9) amounts to $c_{i1} + \cdots + c_{iN} = 0$ and (14.8) to $c_{ii} < 0$ under the demand specification (14.10).

2 Use Figure 25 to verify that an increase in the price of either good, accompanied by an income increase so that the consumer can attain the original indifference curve, always leads to an increase in the quantity consumed of the other good. (*Note*: This result holds only for $N = 2$. When there are three goods or more, it is possible that an increase in the price of some good, accompanied by an income increase so that the consumer attains the original utility level, yields a decrease in the quantity consumed of some other good.)

3 Verify that summation of both sides of (14.40) over $i = 1, \ldots, N$ yields

$$DQ_t = DQ_t + \sum_{i=1}^{N} \epsilon_{it}$$

which implies $\epsilon_{1t} + \cdots + \epsilon_{Nt} = 0$. (*Hint*: Use the constraints on the marginal shares and the Slutsky coefficients.)

4 (*Continuation*) Consider (14.43) and the discussion below that equation to verify that

$$Dm_t - \sum_{i=1}^{N} \bar{w}_{it} Dp_{it}$$

can be viewed as an alternative way of measuring the log-change in real income. Prove that when DQ_t is replaced by this expression in (14.40), the sum of the N disturbances equals

$$\sum_{i=1}^{N} \epsilon_{it} = DQ_t - \left(Dm_t - \sum_{i=1}^{N} \bar{w}_{it} Dp_{it}\right) = \sum_{i=1}^{N} \bar{w}_{it} Dw_{it}$$

[*Hint*: For the second step, derive $Dw_{it} = Dp_{it} + Dq_{it} - Dm_t$ from (14.25), and multiply this by $\bar{w}_{it}$ and sum over i.] Finally, use a numerical example to prove that $\sum_i \bar{w}_{it} Dw_{it}$ can be nonzero.

5 Verify that the price of the Nth good is used as a deflator of the price of the jth good in (14.45) for $j = 1, \ldots, N - 1$. [*Hint*: Compare (13.23).]

6 For $N = 3$, write $\hat{\pi}_{i1}$ and $\hat{\pi}_{i2}$ for the estimators of π_{i1} and π_{i2} obtained from (14.45), and prove

$$\text{var } \hat{\pi}_{i3} = \text{var } \hat{\pi}_{i1} + \text{var } \hat{\pi}_{i2} + 2 \text{ cov } (\hat{\pi}_{i1}, \hat{\pi}_{i2})$$

Then state and prove the corresponding result for general N. [*Note*: This result shows how the sampling variance of $\hat{\pi}_{iN}$ can be derived from the sampling variances and covariances of the estimators of $\pi_{i1}, \ldots, \pi_{i,N-1}$ which occur in (14.45).]

7 When (14.46) is applied to the Dutch data, LS yields the following estimates of c_i (multiplied by 100,000 and with standard errors in parentheses): food,

43 (103); beverages, 14 (45); durables, -310 (100); remainder, 253 (98). Compare the implied t ratios with those of the British c_i's in Table 16, and state your conclusion. [*Note*: In (14.46), c_i serves as a demand trend (upward for $c_i > 0$, downward for $c_i < 0$) which is unrelated to the behavior of the explanatory variables. Usually, such a trend term "explains" little, so that it should preferably be avoided if the data allow it to be avoided.]

8 (*Continuation*) Verify that if the demand model takes the form (14.46), the right-hand side of (14.49) contains an extra term equal to $c_i/\bar{w}_{it}$. Use (14.50) and the relevant symmetry-constrained estimates in Table 16 to verify that this term implies an estimated trend decrease of about 1.8 percent per year of the demand for the British beverages group and estimated trends (increases or decreases) of one-half of 1 percent or less for the three other groups.

9 Use (14.25) and (14.37) to prove that the income elasticity of the demand for a good is equal to the ratio of its marginal share to its budget share:

$$\frac{\partial q_i}{\partial m} \frac{m}{q_i} = \frac{\mu_i}{w_i}$$

Also prove that the weighted mean of the N income elasticities, with weights equal to the corresponding budget shares, is equal to 1.

10 (*Continuation*) The harmonic mean H of $a_1, \ldots, a_N$ is defined as the reciprocal of the arithmetic mean of the reciprocals of the a_i's:

$$\frac{1}{H} = \frac{1}{N} \sum_{i=1}^{N} \frac{1}{a_i}$$

Use (14.39) to prove that $\mu_i/\bar{w}_{it}$ is the harmonic mean of the income elasticities of the ith good in $t - 1$ and t, with μ_i assumed constant.

11 Prove that the income elasticity of a budget share equals the corresponding income elasticity of demand less 1:

$$\frac{\partial w_i}{\partial m} \frac{m}{w_i} = \frac{\partial q_i}{\partial m} \frac{m}{q_i} - 1$$

Use this result and Table 17 to verify Engel's law for the expenditure on food (see the opening paragraph of the chapter).

12 For $i = 1, \ldots, n$, consider

$$y_{1i} = \beta_0 + \beta_1 x_{1i} + \epsilon_{1i}, \qquad y_{2i} = \beta_0' + \beta_2 x_{2i} + \epsilon_{2i}$$

Suppose that the standard linear model applies to both equations and write σ_1 and σ_2 for the standard deviations of ϵ_{1i} and ϵ_{2i}, respectively. Also suppose that ϵ_{1i} and ϵ_{2j} are uncorrelated whenever $i \neq j$ and that the correlation coefficient of ϵ_{1i} and ϵ_{2i} equals ρ for each i. Prove that the LS estimators b_1 of β_1 and b_2 of β_2 have the following sampling covariance:

$$\mathrm{cov}\,(b_1, b_2) = \rho\sigma_1\sigma_2 \frac{\displaystyle\sum_{i=1}^{n} (x_{1i} - \bar{x}_1)(x_{2i} - \bar{x}_2)}{\displaystyle\sum_{i=1}^{n} (x_{1i} - \bar{x}_1)^2 \sum_{i=1}^{n} (x_{2i} - \bar{x}_2)^2}$$

Also prove that the sampling correlation coefficient of b_1 and b_2 equals pr, where r is the correlation coefficient of the observation pairs (x_{1i}, x_{2i}). (*Note*: This result illustrates that LS coefficients of different equations are, in general, correlated when the disturbances of these equations are correlated.)

13 Prove that (14.53) implies $DQ_t = \sum_g \bar{W}_{gt} DQ_{gt}$ (sum over all groups), and verify that this is the extension of (14.41) for groups.

14 Verify that the sum of the left-hand side of (14.56) over $i = 1, \ldots, N_g$ vanishes. Use this to prove that (14.56) implies

$$d(\log_e W_g m) = \sum_{i=1}^{N_g} \frac{w_i}{W_g} d(\log_e p_i) + \sum_{i=1}^{N_g} \frac{w_i}{W_g} d(\log_e q_i)$$

and compare this with (14.42).

15 Verify that the sum of the left-hand variable in (14.58) over $i = 1, \ldots, N_g$ equals DQ_{gt}. Also verify that the sum of the disturbance over $i = 1, \ldots, N_g$ vanishes. Compare these results with remarks (1) and (2) at the end of Section 14.2.

16 Prove that the budget-share-weighted mean of the income elasticities of the goods of a group is equal to the income elasticity of the group:

$$\sum_{i=1}^{N_g} \frac{\bar{w}_{it}}{\bar{W}_{gt}} \frac{\mu_i}{\bar{w}_{it}} = \frac{M_g}{\bar{W}_{gt}}$$

Also prove that the conditional income elasticities of the goods of a group have a budget-share-weighted mean equal to 1.

17 In the discussion preceding (14.62) it is stated that DQ_{gt} in (14.58) is treated as a nonstochastic value taken by one of the explanatory variables. But $\bar{W}_{gt} DQ_{gt}$ has a random component E_{gt} in (14.55). Suppose that E_{gt} and ϵ_{it}^* are correlated random variables. Is it then permissible to treat DQ_{gt} as nonstochastic in (14.58)? [*Note*: Under the theory of rational random behavior, E_{gt} and ϵ_{it}^* are stochastically independent, so that (14.58) may be viewed as a conditional model, given DQ_{gt}; see Theil (1975–1976, Chapters 7 and 8).]

18 Consider the following relation between the unconditional and the conditional Slutsky elasticities:

(14.66) $$\frac{\pi_{ij}}{\bar{w}_{it}} - \frac{\pi_{ij}^* \bar{W}_{gt}}{\bar{w}_{it}} = (-.6) \frac{\mu_i/\bar{w}_{it}}{M_g/\bar{W}_{gt}} \frac{\mu_j}{M_g}$$

Use the relevant entries in Tables 18 and 19 to verify the following estimates (in one decimal place) of the unconditional Slutsky elasticities with respect to the price of beef: -1.0 for the demand for beef, .2 for pork, .1 for chicken, and .3 for lamb. Compare these with the estimates of the corresponding conditional Slutsky elasticities, and state your conclusion. [*Note*: For (14.66), see the following equations in Theil (1975–1976, Chapter 7): (1.15), (3.18), and (6.26) for the estimate $-.6$ of $\phi M_g (1 - M_g)/\bar{W}_{gt}$.]

part three

EXTENSIONS
OF THE
REGRESSION
MODEL

chapter 15

Large-Sample
Distribution Theory

Many estimators discussed in Part Three have a distribution which is not exactly but only approximately known. The approximation becomes better when the sample size increases. This subject is pursued in this chapter. Formal proofs are given for some theorems only; the major objective is to provide an intuitive understanding. For a more extensive treatment, see Theil (1971, Chapter 8).

15.1   Introduction to Large-Sample Theory

Chebyshev's Inequality

A simple lemma, known as Chebyshev's inequality, is a convenient tool in large-sample analysis. Consider a random variable X which has an arbitrary continuous distribution with density function $f(\ )$ and finite mean μ and variance σ^2. We write the variance as

$$(15.1) \qquad \sigma^2 = \int_{-\infty}^{\infty} (x - \mu)^2 f(x)\, dx$$

If the range of the distribution is (a, b) rather than $(-\infty, \infty)$, with a and/or b finite, we can still use the integration limits shown in (15.1), provided $f(x)$ is interpreted as zero for $x < a$ and $x > b$.

Chebyshev's inequality, which is derived in the next subsection, states that

$$(15.2) \qquad P[|X - \mu| \geq k\sigma] \leq \frac{1}{k^2} \qquad \text{for any } k > 0$$

The left-hand side is the probability that the random variable deviates from its expectation by k times the standard deviation or more, where k is any positive number. The inequality states that this probability is at most equal to $1/k^2$.

Chebyshev's inequality is not "sharp" for most distributions (see Problems 1 and 2); its importance results from the fact that it holds for *any* distribution with finite mean μ and variance σ^2, including discrete distributions. The proof for the latter distributions is similar to that which follows in the next subsection, but with integrals replaced by sums.

Proof of Chebyshev's Inequality

The function $(x - \mu)^2 f(x)$ which is integrated in (15.1) is illustrated in Figure 26. This function is nonnegative, and hence the curve in the figure is nowhere below the horizontal axis, because $(x - \mu)^2$ and $f(x)$ are both nonnegative. The function obviously vanishes at $x = \mu$. Also, since σ^2 equals the area below the curve in view of (15.1), the curve must move toward the horizontal axis as $x \longrightarrow \pm\infty$, because otherwise the variance would not take a finite value σ^2.

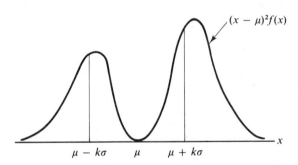

FIGURE 26   The function $(x - \mu)^2 f(x)$

We write the integral in (15.1) as the sum of three integrals,

$$\int_{-\infty}^{\mu-k\sigma} (x - \mu)^2 f(x)\, dx + \int_{\mu-k\sigma}^{\mu+k\sigma} (x - \mu)^2 f(x)\, dx + \int_{\mu+k\sigma}^{\infty} (x - \mu)^2 f(x)\, dx$$

which is indicated in the figure by the vertical lines at $\mu - k\sigma$ and $\mu + k\sigma$. Since the area below the curve and between $\mu \pm k\sigma$ is nonnegative, we have

$$(15.3) \qquad \sigma^2 \geq \int_{-\infty}^{\mu-k\sigma} (x - \mu)^2 f(x)\, dx + \int_{\mu+k\sigma}^{\infty} (x - \mu)^2 f(x)\, dx$$

In the first integral on the right, the integration limits are such that $x \leq \mu - k\sigma$, which implies $x - \mu \leq -k\sigma$ and hence $(x - \mu)^2 \geq k^2\sigma^2$ because both k and σ are positive. Hence,

$$(15.4) \qquad \int_{-\infty}^{\mu-k\sigma} (x - \mu)^2 f(x)\, dx \geq k^2\sigma^2 \int_{-\infty}^{\mu-k\sigma} f(x)\, dx$$

Similarly, in the second integral in the right-hand side of (15.3), the integration limits imply $x \geq \mu + k\sigma$ and hence $(x - \mu)^2 \geq k^2\sigma^2$, so that

$$\int_{\mu+k\sigma}^{\infty} (x - \mu)^2 f(x)\, dx \geq k^2\sigma^2 \int_{\mu+k\sigma}^{\infty} f(x)\, dx$$

On combining this with (15.3) and (15.4), we obtain

$$\sigma^2 \geq k^2\sigma^2 \left[\int_{-\infty}^{\mu-k\sigma} f(x)\, dx + \int_{\mu+k\sigma}^{\infty} f(x)\, dx \right]$$

and hence, after dividing both sides by $k^2\sigma^2$,

(15.5) $$\int_{-\infty}^{\mu-k\sigma} f(x)\, dx + \int_{\mu+k\sigma}^{\infty} f(x)\, dx \leq \frac{1}{k^2}$$

The right-hand side of (15.5) is equal to that of (15.2). The left-hand side is the area below the density curve to the left of $\mu - k\sigma$ plus that to the right of $\mu + k\sigma$. These are the two shaded areas in Figure 27. The area to the right of $\mu + k\sigma$ equals the probability that $X > \mu + k\sigma$ or that $X - \mu > k\sigma$. The area to the left of $\mu - k\sigma$ equals the probability that $X < \mu - k\sigma$, or that $X - \mu < -k\sigma$, or that $-(X - \mu) > k\sigma$. Hence, the sum of the two shaded areas is equal to the probability that either $X - \mu$ or $-(X - \mu)$ exceeds $k\sigma$ and hence to the probability that $X - \mu$ exceeds $k\sigma$ in absolute value, in agreement with (15.2).

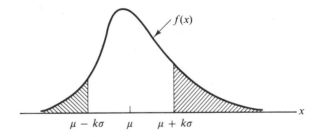

FIGURE 27   The left-hand side of Chebyshev's inequality

Convergence in Probability

Let Y be distributed as $\chi^2(n)$, with mean n and variance $2n$ [see (11.2)]. Hence, Y/n has mean $n/n = 1$ and variance $2n/n^2 = 2/n$. We apply (15.2) to $X = Y/n$, so that μ becomes 1 and σ becomes $\sqrt{2/n}$:

$$P\left[\left| \frac{Y}{n} - 1 \right| \geq \frac{k\sqrt{2}}{\sqrt{n}} \right] \leq \frac{1}{k^2}$$

This holds for any $k > 0$. We specify $k = \delta\sqrt{n/2}$, where δ is an arbitrary small number:

(15.6) $$P\left[\left| \frac{Y}{n} - 1 \right| \geq \delta \right] \leq \frac{2}{n\delta^2}$$

The ratio $2/n\delta^2$ converges to zero as $n \longrightarrow \infty$ no matter how small δ is. Therefore, (15.6) implies that as $n \longrightarrow \infty$ the probability approaches zero that Y/n (a χ^2 variate divided by the number of degrees of freedom) takes a value which differs from 1 by more than *any* given amount:

$$(15.7) \qquad \lim_{n \to \infty} P\left[\left| \frac{Y}{n} - 1 \right| \geq \delta \right] = 0 \qquad \text{for any } \delta > 0$$

This limiting or asymptotic property is expressed by saying that as $n \longrightarrow \infty$, Y/n *converges in probability* to 1.

Consistent Estimators

Let $(X_1, \ldots, X_n)$ be a random sample from some distribution. We write the arithmetic mean of its elements as

$$(15.8) \qquad \bar{X}_n = \frac{1}{n} \sum_{i=1}^{n} X_i$$

where the subscript n of $\bar{X}_n$ serves to indicate explicitly that the underlying sample is of size n. Recall from (4.42) and (4.48) that if the sample is drawn from any distribution with finite mean μ and variance σ^2, $\bar{X}_n$ has mean μ and variance σ^2/n. Thus, when we apply (15.2) to $X = \bar{X}_n$, σ becomes $\sigma/\sqrt{n}$:

$$P\left[|\bar{X}_n - \mu| \geq \frac{k\sigma}{\sqrt{n}} \right] \leq \frac{1}{k^2}$$

Again, this holds for any $k > 0$. We specify $k = (\delta\sqrt{n})/\sigma$:

$$(15.9) \qquad P[|\bar{X}_n - \mu| \geq \delta] \leq \frac{\sigma^2}{n\delta^2}$$

Since $\sigma^2/n\delta^2$ converges to zero as $n \longrightarrow \infty$ for any $\delta > 0$, this proves that $\bar{X}_n$ converges in probability to μ as $n \longrightarrow \infty$. We concluded from (15.7) that Y/n converges in probability to 1 (a known constant). The present convergence in probability is that of the estimator $\bar{X}_n$ to the unknown parameter μ which it serves to estimate. The estimator is then said to be *consistent*.

More generally, let $(X_1, \ldots, X_n)$ be a random sample from some distribution characterized by an unknown parameter θ, which is estimated by $\hat{\theta}_n = \hat{\theta}_n(X_1, \ldots, X_n)$. This $\hat{\theta}_n$ is a consistent estimator of θ if

$$(15.10) \qquad \lim_{n \to \infty} P[|\hat{\theta}_n - \theta| \geq \delta] = 0 \qquad \text{for any } \delta > 0$$

This limiting process is illustrated in Figure 28, which contains the density curve of $\hat{\theta}_n$ for three values of n. The probability whose limit is described in (15.10) is the area below the density curve outside the interval $(\theta \pm \delta)$. Clearly, this area is smaller for $n = 50$ than for $n = 10$ and still smaller for $n = 250$.

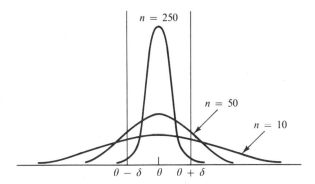

FIGURE 28 Density curves of a consistent estimator

Probability Limits

The notation of (15.7) and (15.10) is cumbersome. A more compact notation is

$$(15.11) \qquad \operatorname*{plim}_{n \to \infty} \frac{Y}{n} = 1, \qquad \operatorname*{plim}_{n \to \infty} \hat{\theta}_n = \theta$$

or, in words, the *probability limit* (abbreviated as plim) of the random sequence $Y_1/1, Y_2/2, \ldots, Y_n/n, \ldots$ is equal to 1 and that of the random sequence $\hat{\theta}_1, \hat{\theta}_2, \ldots, \hat{\theta}_n, \ldots$ is equal to θ. Note that the following statements are all equivalent: (1) $\hat{\theta}_n$ converges in probability to θ as $n \to \infty$; (2) $\hat{\theta}_n$ is a consistent estimator of θ; (3) $\hat{\theta}_n$ has a probability limit equal to θ as $n \to \infty$.

The difference between a probability limit and an ordinary limit should be noted. If $a_1, a_2, \ldots, a_n, \ldots$ is a nonrandom sequence with limit α, we can be *certain* that $|a_n - \alpha|$ is less than any given positive δ when n is sufficiently large. For example, for $a_n = 2 + 1/n$ with limit $\alpha = 2$, we have $|a_n - 2| < \delta$ for any $n > 1/\delta$. But if $a_1, a_2, \ldots, a_n, \ldots$ is a random sequence with probability limit α, we can only say that $|a_n - \alpha| < \delta$ is true *with a probability arbitrarily close to unity* if n is sufficiently large. When the range of a_n is infinite, as is the case, e.g., when a_n is normally distributed, there is always a positive probability that $|a_n - \alpha| > \delta$ no matter how large n is.

Biased Estimators May Be Consistent

We concluded from (15.9) that if $\bar{X}_n$ is the arithmetic mean of a random sample from any distribution with finite mean μ and variance σ^2, then $\bar{X}_n$ is a consistent estimator of μ. This $\bar{X}_n$ is also an unbiased estimator; hence, $\bar{X}_n$ is both unbiased and consistent. But biased estimators can be consistent too. Let $\hat{\theta}_n$ be a biased estimator of θ, $\mathscr{E}\hat{\theta}_n \neq \theta$. If the bias $\mathscr{E}\hat{\theta}_n - \theta$ converges to zero as $n \to \infty$ and if the variance of $\hat{\theta}_n$ also converges to zero as $n \to \infty$, then $\hat{\theta}_n$ is a consistent estimator of θ. The reader should develop an intuitive feeling for this theorem by means of Figure 28, imagining that the mean of the sampling distribution for $n = 10$ differs from θ, that the mean for $n = 50$ is closer to θ, and that the mean for $n = 250$ is still closer to θ. Unbiasedness is a finite-sample property (for finite n); consistency is an asymptotic or large-sample property (for $n \rightarrow \infty$).

The Consistency of LS Coefficient Estimators

The standard linear model takes the values assumed by the explanatory variables as given, which means that the model has nothing to say about these values. But if we want to apply large-sample theory to the standard linear model, we must make some assumption on the behavior of the explanatory variables when we imagine that the number of observations increases. To clarify this, we return to Figure 8 on page 62, where we independently drew at random one household from the group of all households with incomes x_1, x_2, and x_3, so that we obtained three observations: three amounts of consumption, each corresponding to one of the incomes x_1, x_2, and x_3. Suppose we do this again, which gives another batch of three observations; again, each of these corresponds to one of the incomes x_1, x_2, and x_3. By repeating this over and over, we extend the size of the sample indefinitely in multiples of three.

Note that for each group of three observations the explanatory variable (income) takes the same values. This is expressed by saying that this variable is assumed to be *constant in repeated samples*. But the dependent variable y (consumption) is obviously not constant in repeated samples, because its disturbance component differs from one observation to the next. This is illustrated in Table 20 for the case in which the line in the horizontal plane of Figure 8 goes

TABLE 20

The assumption of constancy in repeated samples

Income	First batch	Second batch	Third batch	Fourth batch
	Consumption			
x_1	$y_1 = \beta x_1 + \epsilon_1$	$y_4 = \beta x_1 + \epsilon_4$	$y_7 = \beta x_1 + \epsilon_7$	$y_{10} = \beta x_1 + \epsilon_{10}$
x_2	$y_2 = \beta x_2 + \epsilon_2$	$y_5 = \beta x_2 + \epsilon_5$	$y_8 = \beta x_2 + \epsilon_8$	$y_{11} = \beta x_2 + \epsilon_{11}$
x_3	$y_3 = \beta x_3 + \epsilon_3$	$y_6 = \beta x_3 + \epsilon_6$	$y_9 = \beta x_3 + \epsilon_9$	$y_{12} = \beta x_3 + \epsilon_{12}$

through the origin ($\beta_0 = 0$). In the first row of Table 20, the expectations of all y_i's are equal to βx_1, but the disturbances (ϵ_1, ϵ_4, ϵ_7, ...) are all different.

Suppose that we estimate β of Table 20 by the LS slope coefficient b through the origin. It follows from (5.17) that if we have only the first three observations, the sampling variance of b equals

$$\frac{\sigma^2}{x_1^2 + x_2^2 + x_3^2}$$

and that if we have the first six observations, this variance equals

$$\frac{\sigma^2}{x_1^2 + x_2^2 + x_3^2 + x_1^2 + x_2^2 + x_3^2} = \frac{\sigma^2}{2(x_1^2 + x_2^2 + x_3^2)}$$

Clearly, under the assumption of constancy in repeated samples on the explanatory variable, the sampling variance of b converges to zero as the number of observations increases. Since b is an unbiased estimator of β, we can use Chebyshev's inequality to prove that b is a consistent estimator (see Figure 28 with θ interpreted as β).

This result can be extended straightforwardly to the case of a nonzero constant term and also to multiple regression. In the latter case, the assumption of constancy in repeated samples refers to all explanatory variables jointly. See Problems 4 and 5.

Asymptotic Standard Errors

In addition to convergence in probability, there is a second type of convergence as $n \rightarrow \infty$, which is described in Section 15.2. This second type yields in certain cases asymptotic standard errors of estimates. If the sample is sufficiently large, asymptotic standard errors can be used in the two-sigma rule in the same way as ordinary standard errors (see the end of Section 4.4). A problem is, though, that it is in many cases unclear how large "sufficiently large" is, so that a cautious interpretation is appropriate.

*15.2   Large-Sample Analysis

The Asymptotics of F and t

Consider the ratio (12.16),

(15.12) $$\frac{X/m}{Y/n} = F(m, n)$$

where X and Y are independent χ^2 variates with m and n degrees of freedom, respectively. We know from (15.7) that, as $n \rightarrow \infty$, the left-hand denominator in (15.12) converges in probability to 1. This suggests that, as $n \rightarrow \infty$, (15.12) has the same distribution as X/m (a multiple $1/m$ of a χ^2 variate with m degrees of freedom). Indeed, this is true; in the limit for $n \rightarrow \infty$, the F ratio with m and n degrees of freedom is distributed as a multiple $1/m$ of $\chi^2(m)$.

Next take Student's t with n degrees of freedom, $t(n)$, defined as the ratio of a standardized normal variate to the square root of Y/n, Y being distributed as $\chi^2(n)$ and independent of the normal variate. Since Y/n converges in probability to 1 as $n \rightarrow \infty$, so does its square root. Thus, in the limit for $n \rightarrow \infty$, $t(n)$ is distributed as a standardized normal variate.

Convergence in Probability and in Distribution

When Y/n has a probability limit equal to 1 as $n \longrightarrow \infty$, the implication is that Y/n ceases to be random in the limit. For $n \longrightarrow \infty$, the distribution of Y/n becomes degenerate with all of its density concentrated at 1 (see Figure 28, with θ interpreted as 1). The limiting behavior of $F(m, n)$ and $t(n)$ described in the previous subsection is different. As $n \longrightarrow \infty$, $t(n)$ becomes normal with zero mean and unit variance, which is not a degenerate distribution because it has a positive variance. As $n \longrightarrow \infty$, $F(m, n)$ becomes a multiple $1/m$ of $\chi^2(m)$, which also has a positive variance (equal to $2m/m^2 = 2/m$).

The normal distribution toward which $t(n)$ converges as $n \longrightarrow \infty$ is called the *limiting distribution* of $t(n)$, and $t(n)$ is said to *converge in distribution* to this limiting distribution. Similarly, as $n \longrightarrow \infty$, $F(m, n)$ converges in distribution to $(1/m)\chi^2(m)$, which is the limiting distribution of the F ratio (15.12).

The Central Limit Theorem

Let $(X_1, \ldots, X_n)$ be a random sample from any distribution with finite mean μ and variance σ^2. Since $\bar{X}_n$ defined in (15.8) has mean μ and variance σ^2/n, the ratio

(15.13)
$$\frac{\bar{X}_n - \mu}{\sigma/\sqrt{n}} = \frac{(\bar{X}_n - \mu)\sqrt{n}}{\sigma}$$

has zero mean and unit variance. If the sample is drawn from a normal distribution, the ratio (15.13) is also normally distributed. If the sample is drawn from a nonnormal distribution, the ratio is not normally distributed either. The central limit theorem states that, as $n \longrightarrow \infty$, the ratio (15.13) has a *normal limiting distribution* for random samples from *any* distribution with finite mean μ and variance σ^2. For a proof, see Theil (1971, pp. 368–369).

Asymptotic Distributions

The normal limiting distribution of the ratio (15.13) provides an approximation of the distribution of $\bar{X}_n$ when n is sufficiently large. If we accept the approximation of (15.13) by the normal distribution with zero mean and unit variance, the implied approximation of $\bar{X}_n$ is normal with mean μ and variance σ^2/n. This is expressed by saying that $\bar{X}_n$ is *asymptotically normally distributed with mean μ and variance σ^2/n.* Since $\bar{X}_n$ converges in probability to μ as $n \longrightarrow \infty$, its distribution becomes degenerate with all of its density concentrated at μ; the asymptotic normal distribution of $\bar{X}_n$ provides an approximation of the exact distribution *before* it becomes degenerate, i.e., for values of n smaller than those at which the density is effectively concentrated at μ.

The variance σ^2/n of the asymptotic approximation of the sampling distribution of $\bar{X}_n$ is called the *asymptotic sampling variance* of $\bar{X}_n$. The associated standard deviation is $\sigma/\sqrt{n}$, which is unknown because σ is unknown. When we replace σ by s, the square root of s^2 defined in (4.46), we obtain $s/\sqrt{n}$, which is the *asymptotic standard error* of $\bar{X}_n$. A standard error is an estimate of the standard deviation of the sampling distribution of the estimator; an asymptotic standard error is an estimate of the standard deviation of the *asymptotic approximation* of the sampling distribution of the estimator.

In the particular case of $\bar{X}_n$, the asymptotic standard error $s/\sqrt{n}$ happens to coincide with the ordinary standard error (see the end of Section 4.4). This is by no means always so. The derivation of asymptotic standard errors of other estimators is discussed below. There are many estimators whose exact sampling distributions are either unknown or very complicated, in which case the asymptotic distribution can be useful if the sample is sufficiently large. There are also estimators whose exact distribution has no finite variance, whereas the asymptotic distribution does have a finite variance. If the sample is sufficiently large, asymptotic standard errors can be used in the two-sigma rule in the same way as ordinary standard errors. But, as stated at the end of Section 15.1, a cautious interpretation is appropriate.

The Asymptotic Distribution of Linear and Nonlinear Functions

Given that $\bar{X}_n$ is asymptotically normal with mean μ and variance σ^2/n, any linear function $\alpha + \beta\bar{X}_n$ is also asymptotically normal, with mean $\alpha + \beta\mu$ and variance $\beta^2\sigma^2/n$. A similar result holds for appropriately differentiable nonlinear functions. We write $h(\bar{X}_n)$ for such a function and apply a Taylor expansion,

$$(15.14) \qquad h(\bar{X}_n) - h(\mu) = \frac{dh}{d\bar{X}_n}(\bar{X}_n - \mu) + R$$

where R is a remainder term and the derivative $dh/d\bar{X}_n$ is evaluated at $\bar{X}_n = \mu$. Then square both sides and take the expectation. This yields the expectation of $[h(\bar{X}_n) - h(\mu)]^2$ on the left, which is the variance of $h(\bar{X}_n)$ if it is true (which need not be the case) that $h(\bar{X}_n)$ is an unbiased estimator of $h(\mu)$. On the right we obtain, after squaring and taking the expectation and ignoring the remainder term,

$$(15.15) \qquad \left(\frac{dh}{d\bar{X}_n}\right)^2 \mathcal{E}[(\bar{X}_n - \mu)^2] = \frac{\sigma^2}{n}\left(\frac{dh}{d\bar{X}_n}\right)^2$$

This procedure is of course not rigorous. But it can be proved that, as $n \to \infty$, $h(\bar{X}_n)$ is asymptotically normally distributed with mean $h(\mu)$ and variance (15.15). The proof involves, in addition to the asymptotic normality of $\bar{X}_n$ with mean μ and variance σ^2/n, the condition that $h(\ )$ has a continuous second-order derivative around $\bar{X}_n = \mu$. For details, see Theil (1971, pp. 373–375, 381–382).

As an example we consider μ^3, which we estimate by $h(\bar{X}_n) = \bar{X}_n^3$, with first- and second-order derivatives equal to $3\bar{X}_n^2$ and $6\bar{X}_n$, respectively. The latter derivative is obviously a continuous function of $\bar{X}_n$, at any value of $\bar{X}_n$. The first-order derivative at $\bar{X}_n = \mu$ equals $3\mu^2$, which is $dh/d\bar{X}_n$ in (15.14) and (15.15). We conclude that, as $n \rightarrow \infty$, $\bar{X}_n^3$ is asymptotically normally distributed with mean μ^3 and the following variance obtained from (15.15):

$$\frac{\sigma^2}{n}\left(\frac{dh}{d\bar{X}_n}\right)^2 = \frac{\sigma^2}{n}(3\mu^2)^2 = \frac{9\mu^4\sigma^2}{n}$$

The associated standard deviation is $3\mu^2\sigma/\sqrt{n}$, so that the asymptotic standard error of $\bar{X}_n^3$ is $3\bar{X}_n^2 s/\sqrt{n}$.

The Asymptotic Distribution of LS Coefficient Estimators

Since the LS coefficient estimators are linear functions of the disturbances under the standard linear model, they are normally distributed when the disturbances are normally distributed. If the disturbances are not normally distributed, the LS coefficient estimators are not normally distributed either. But there is the following extension of the central limit theorem: If the disturbances are independently and identically distributed with zero mean and variance σ^2 and if the explanatory variables are constant in repeated samples, the LS coefficient estimators are asymptotically normally distributed with means equal to the corresponding β's. For a proof, which uses a weaker assumption than constancy in repeated samples, see Theil (1971, pp. 378–381).

The asymptotic normality of the LS coefficient estimators can be used to obtain asymptotic distributions of appropriately differentiable functions of these estimators. For example, consider the CES production function in the logarithmic form (13.35):

$$(15.16) \qquad \log_e P_i = \log_e c - \frac{1}{\rho} \log_e [\alpha K_i^{-\rho} + (1 - \alpha)L_i^{-\rho}] + \epsilon_i$$

We use the approximation (13.36),

$$(15.17) \quad \log_e \frac{P_i}{L_i} \approx \log_e c + \alpha \log_e \frac{K_i}{L_i} - \frac{1}{2}\rho\alpha(1 - \alpha)\left(\log_e \frac{K_i}{L_i}\right)^2 + \epsilon_i$$

which we write in the form

$$(15.18) \qquad\qquad y_i = \beta_0 + \beta_1 x_{1i} + \beta_2 x_{2i} + \epsilon_i$$

This implies that y, x_1, and x_2 are interpreted as $\log_e (P/L)$, $\log_e (K/L)$, and $[\log_e (K/L)]^2$ and that the β's are specified as

$$(15.19) \qquad \beta_0 = \log_e c, \qquad \beta_1 = \alpha, \qquad \beta_2 = -\tfrac{1}{2}\rho\alpha(1 - \alpha)$$

We assume that K/L is constant in repeated samples, so that both explanatory variables in (15.17) have this property.

It follows (15.19) that the estimator $\hat{\rho}$ of ρ which is implied by the LS estimators b_1 and b_2 of β_1 and β_2 is

$$(15.20) \qquad\qquad \hat{\rho} = -\frac{2b_2}{b_1(1 - b_1)}$$

In the next subsection we shall show that a Taylor expansion at $b_1 = \beta_1$,

$b_2 = \beta_2$ yields

(15.21) $$\hat{\rho} - \rho = - \frac{\rho(1 - 2\beta_1)(b_1 - \beta_1) + 2(b_2 - \beta_2)}{\beta_1(1 - \beta_1)} + R$$

where R is a remainder term. The asymptotic sampling variance of $\hat{\rho}$ is then obtained by squaring, taking the expectation, and ignoring R, which yields

(15.22) asymptotic variance of $\hat{\rho}$
$$= \frac{\rho^2(1 - 2\beta_1)^2 \operatorname{var} b_1 + 4 \operatorname{var} b_2 + 4\rho(1 - 2\beta_1) \operatorname{cov}(b_1, b_2)}{\beta_1^2(1 - \beta_1)^2}$$

where the variances and covariance of b_1 and b_2 are as shown in (8.33), (8.34), and (8.44). The asymptotic standard error of $\hat{\rho}$ is obtained by substituting estimates for unknown parameters in (15.22) and then taking the square root. The continuity of the second-order derivatives of (15.20) is verified in the next subsection.

Derivations for the CES Function

The first-order derivatives of (15.20) are

(15.23) $$\frac{\partial \hat{\rho}}{\partial b_1} = \hat{\rho}\left(\frac{1}{1 - b_1} - \frac{1}{b_1}\right), \qquad \frac{\partial \hat{\rho}}{\partial b_2} = -\frac{2}{b_1(1 - b_1)}$$

which yield the following Taylor approximation at $b_1 = \beta_1$, $b_2 = \beta_2$:

$$\hat{\rho} - \rho = \rho\left(\frac{1}{1 - \beta_1} - \frac{1}{\beta_1}\right)(b_1 - \beta_1) - \frac{2(b_2 - \beta_2)}{\beta_1(1 - \beta_1)} + \text{remainder}$$

It is readily verified that this is equivalent to (15.21).

It follows from $\partial\hat{\rho}/\partial b_2$ given in (15.23) that the second-order derivative of $\hat{\rho}$ with respect to b_2 vanishes identically. The two other second derivatives are obtained by differentiating $\partial\hat{\rho}/\partial b_1$:

(15.24) $$\frac{\partial^2 \hat{\rho}}{\partial b_1^2} = 2\hat{\rho}\left[\frac{1}{b_1^2} - \frac{1}{b_1(1 - b_1)} + \frac{1}{(1 - b_1)^2}\right]$$

(15.25) $$\frac{\partial^2 \hat{\rho}}{\partial b_1 \partial b_2} = -\frac{2}{b_1(1 - b_1)}\left(\frac{1}{1 - b_1} - \frac{1}{b_1}\right)$$

These second derivatives are continuous around $b_1 = \beta_1$, $b_2 = \beta_2$ if $0 < \beta_1 < 1$, which is equivalent to $0 < \alpha < 1$ [see (15.19)]. If this condition is satisfied, $\hat{\rho}$ is asymptotically normally distributed with mean ρ and variance (15.22).

Note that the variance-covariance formulas mentioned below (15.22) are based on the standard linear model. The interested reader should consult Desai (1976, pp. 113–136) for alternative specifications.

The Normality Assumption on the Disturbances

We assumed in Section 10.3 that the disturbances of the standard linear model are normally distributed. One way of justifying this assumption is by means of a generalization of the central limit theorem which can be described as follows.

Let $X_1, \ldots, X_n$ be independently distributed. The distributions of the X_k's may differ; we write $f_k(\ )$ for the density function of X_k and assume that its mean μ_k and its standard deviation σ_k are finite $(k = 1, \ldots, n)$. Hence, the variance of $X_1 + \cdots + X_n$ equals

$$(15.26) \qquad D_n^2 = \sum_{k=1}^{n} \sigma_k^2$$

Let D_n be the positive square root of this variance. We consider the following ratio:

$$(15.27) \qquad \frac{(X_1 - \mu_1) + \cdots + (X_n - \mu_n)}{D_n} = \frac{1}{D_n}\left(n\bar{X}_n - \sum_{k=1}^{n} \mu_k\right)$$

If $\sigma_1 = \cdots = \sigma_n = \sigma$, D_n equals $\sigma\sqrt{n}$ in view of (15.26). Thus, if we also have $\mu_1 = \cdots = \mu_n = \mu$, the ratio (15.27) is identical to (15.13).

It can be shown that, as $n \to \infty$, the ratio (15.27) converges in distribution to a standardized normal variate if

$$(15.28) \qquad \lim_{n\to\infty} \frac{1}{D_n^2} \sum_{k=1}^{n} \left[\int_{|x-\mu_k|>\delta D_n} (x - \mu_k)^2 f_k(x)\, dx \right] = 0 \qquad \text{for any } \delta > 0$$

The implications of this condition are not obvious, but it can be shown that it requires $D_n \to \infty$ and $\sigma_n/D_n \to 0$ as $n \to \infty$. That is, the variance of $X_1 + \cdots + X_n$ tends to infinity, but the individual X_k's contribute only a small fraction to this variance [see (15.26)].

Suppose now that the disturbance in (15.18) is a linear combination of neglected variables $u_1, u_2, \ldots$. We write u_{ki} for the ith observation on the kth neglected variable and assume that u_{ki} is random with mean μ_k and standard deviation σ_k. Hence, ϵ_i of (15.18) can be written as

$$(15.29) \qquad \epsilon_i = \alpha_1(u_{1i} - \mu_1) + \alpha_2(u_{2i} - \mu_2) + \cdots$$

where each neglected variable is written as a deviation from its expectation. If we interpret $(x_k - \mu_k)/D_n$ in (15.27) as $\alpha_k(u_{ki} - \mu_k)$, the asymptotic normality of the ratio (15.27) is equivalent to the approximate normality of ϵ_i in (15.29) when the number of neglected variables is sufficiently large. Note that the condition $\sigma_n/D_n \to 0$ stated below (15.28) means in the present context that none of the neglected variables should dominate the others. Also note that the asymptotic normality requires these variables to be independently distributed. This is a restrictive condition.

*15.3   More on Maximum Likelihood

The Asymptotics of Maximum Likelihood

Under certain weak conditions, maximum-likelihood estimators and likelihood ratios have certain attractive asymptotic properties, listed below. For proofs and an explanation of the conditions, see Theil (1971, pp. 392–397).

(1) Maximum-likelihood estimators are consistent and have normal asymptotic distributions with expectations equal to the parameters which they serve to estimate.

(2) Maximum-likelihood estimators are efficient for large samples. This means that there is no other estimator of the same parameter whose asymptotic distribution has an expectation equal to this parameter and a variance smaller than that of the asymptotic distribution of the maximum-likelihood estimator.

(3) Let λ be the likelihood ratio for testing the null hypothesis H_0 against some alternative hypothesis. As $n \longrightarrow \infty$, the limiting distribution of $-2 \log_e \lambda$ is $\chi^2(q)$ if H_0 is true, where q is the number of constraints imposed by H_0. For example, the null hypothesis (12.15) imposes two constraints: $\beta_1 = 0$ and $\beta_2 = 0$. Hence, in this case, the limiting distribution of $-2 \log_e \lambda$ is $\chi^2(2)$. This particular case is further analyzed in Problem 11.

The CES Function with Normally Distributed Disturbances

Recall from Section 10.3 that under the standard linear model with normally distributed disturbances the LS and maximum-likelihood coefficient estimators are identical. Below we shall show that the same is true for the CES production function (15.16) in spite of the fact that this function is nonlinear.

Equation (15.17) results from a linearization which is based on the assumption that ρ is not far from zero. We drop this assumption here and use (15.16) rather than (15.17), but we do assume here that $\epsilon_1, \ldots, \epsilon_n$ are independent normal variates with zero mean and variance σ^2. Hence, their joint density function is

$$\frac{1}{(2\pi\sigma^2)^{n/2}} \exp\left\{-\frac{1}{2\sigma^2} \sum_{i=1}^{n} \epsilon_i^2\right\}$$

which implies the following likelihood function for (15.16):

$$L(\log_e P_1, \ldots, \log_e P_n; c, \alpha, \rho, \sigma^2) = \frac{1}{(2\pi\sigma^2)^{n/2}}$$

$$\times \exp\left[-\frac{1}{2\sigma^2} \sum_{i=1}^{n} \left\{\log_e P_i - \log_e c + \frac{1}{\rho} \log_e [\alpha K_i^{-\rho} + (1-\alpha)L_i^{-\rho}]\right\}^2\right]$$

The logarithm of this likelihood function equals

$$(15.30) \quad -\frac{n}{2} \log_e 2\pi - \frac{n}{2} \log_e \sigma^2$$

$$-\frac{1}{2\sigma^2} \sum_{i=1}^{n} \left\{\log_e P_i - \log_e c + \frac{1}{\rho} \log_e [\alpha K_i^{-\rho} + (1-\alpha)L_i^{-\rho}]\right\}^2$$

The parameters c, α, and ρ occur only in the term on the second line, which is a negative multiple $(-1/2\sigma^2)$ of

$$(15.31) \quad \sum_{i=1}^{n} \left\{\log_e P_i - \log_e c + \frac{1}{\rho} \log_e [\alpha K_i^{-\rho} + (1-\alpha)L_i^{-\rho}]\right\}^2$$

We conclude that the maximum-likelihood estimates of c, α, and ρ are the values which minimize the expression (15.31). But note that minimizing (15.31) is equivalent to minimizing the residual sum of squares in (15.16). The reader should verify that the solution for $\log_e c$ is

$$(15.32) \qquad \frac{1}{n} \sum_{j=1}^{n} \log_e P_j + \frac{1}{n\rho} \sum_{j=1}^{n} \log_e [\alpha K_j^{-\rho} + (1 - \alpha)L_j^{-\rho}]$$

When this is substituted for $\log_e c$ in (15.31), an expression in α and ρ emerges which should be minimized with respect to these two coefficients. This expression is not so simple as it is under the standard linear model, but it is nevertheless manageable. For example, we can compute the value of this expression for a number of pairs (α, ρ), plot these values in the α, ρ plane, and search for the minimum. There are computationally more attractive methods, but these are beyond the scope of this book.

The importance of this result is that it enables the analyst to use, for large n, the optimum property (2) stated in the previous subsection. When LS and maximum-likelihood estimators are identical, as is the case here, efficient estimates for large samples are obtained by minimizing the residual sum of squares [see (15.31)]. Asymptotic standard errors of these estimates can be derived from the second-order derivatives of the logarithmic likelihood function; see Theil (1971, pp. 392–396) for details on this matter.

Problems

Problems 1–6 refer to Section 15.1, 7–10 to Section 15.2, and 11–13 to Section 15.3.

1 If X is normally distributed, the probability on the left in (15.2) equals .046 for $k = 2$. Compare this with the upper bound for this probability given by Chebyshev's inequality, and state your conclusion.

2 (*Continuation*) For the distribution (3.4), verify that the probability in (15.2) vanishes for $k = 2$ and that it equals $\frac{1}{3}$ for $k = \sqrt{2}$. Again, compare these results with the Chebyshev upper bound.

3 Let $(X_1, \ldots, X_n)$ be a random sample from a normal distribution with mean μ and variance σ^2. Use (11.2) and the theorem on biased-but-consistent estimators to prove that (4.44) is a consistent estimator of σ^2.

4 Let the explanatory variable x be constant in repeated samples. For a simple regression with constant term, prove that the LS coefficient and constant-term estimators are consistent estimators of β and β_0, respectively. [*Hint*: Use (5.31) and (5.38). Is $\bar{x}$ constant in repeated samples?]

5 (*Continuation*) Extend the assumption of constancy in repeated samples to all explanatory variables of a multiple regression. Prove that all LS slope coefficients are consistent estimators of the corresponding β's. [*Hint*: Use (9.33) and (9.34). Are r and P_h constant in repeated samples?]

6 Verify that the three dummy variables in (13.33) are constant in repeated samples.

7 Use the normal asymptotic distribution of $\bar{X}_n$ with mean μ and variance σ^2/n to prove that $\sqrt{\bar{X}_n}$ is asymptotically normally distributed with mean $\sqrt{\mu}$ and variance $\sigma^2/4n\mu$, provided $\mu > 0$. Also prove that $\frac{1}{2}s/\sqrt{n\bar{X}_n}$ is the asymptotic standard error of $\bar{X}_n$. What goes wrong when $\mu = 0$? What goes wrong when $\mu < 0$?

8 (*Continuation*) Prove that $\log_e \bar{X}_n$ is asymptotically normally distributed with mean $\log_e \mu$ and variance $\sigma^2/n\mu^2$, provided $\mu > 0$. Formulate the asymptotic standard error of $\log_e \bar{X}_n$.

9 Verify the derivatives of (15.20) given in (15.23) to (15.25). Also verify that the derivatives (15.24) and (15.25) are continuous functions of b_1 and b_2 around $b_1 = \beta_1$, $b_2 = \beta_2$ if $0 < \beta_1 < 1$.

10 (*Continuation*) Prove that the asymptotic variance (15.22) equals 64 var b_2 if $\alpha = \frac{1}{2}$.

11 Use (12.26) and (12.28) to prove that $\frac{1}{2}n'(\lambda^{-2/n} - 1)$ is distributed as $F(2, n')$ if (12.15) is true. Then use the convergence property of the F ratio to prove that (for large n') the left-hand side of the following equation is distributed as $\chi^2(2)$, where the second step is based on a Taylor expansion:

$$n'(\lambda^{-2/n} - 1) = n'\left[\exp\left\{-\frac{2}{n}\log_e \lambda\right\} - 1\right]$$
$$\approx n'\left(1 - \frac{2}{n}\log_e \lambda - 1\right)$$
$$= \frac{n'}{n}(-2\log_e \lambda)$$

Combine these results to conclude that, as $n \to \infty$, $-2\log_e \lambda$ converges in distribution to $\chi^2(2)$. (*Note*: The terms that are ignored in the Taylor expansion converge to zero as $n \to \infty$.)

12 Describe the difference in the assumptions made on the CES function in Sections 15.2 and 15.3.

13 Prove that (15.32) is the solution for $\log_e c$ when (15.31) is minimized with respect to $\log_e c$.

chapter 16

Bayesian Inference
and
Rational Random Behavior

In this chapter we shall introduce the last statistical inference method to be discussed, that of Bayesian analysis, as well as the theory of rational random behavior, which provides constraints on the distribution of the disturbances of behavioral equations.

*16.1 Bayesian Inference

Bayesian inference differs from the statistical procedures discussed so far in that it treats parameters as random variables rather than unknown constants. Bayesians require the analyst to have certain prior judgments on the value of the parameter and to express these judgments by means of a prior distribution. When a sample of observations has been drawn, this is used to modify the prior distribution into a posterior distribution, which combines the prior judgments and the evidence supplied by the sample.

The Prior Density Function

Let $(X_1, \ldots, X_n)$ be a random sample from a distribution which is determined by an unknown parameter θ, and let $p(\theta)$ be the prior density function which the analyst uses to express his judgments about θ. For example, if the distribution from which the sample is drawn is normal with mean θ and unit variance, the density function of the sample is

(16.1) $$\frac{1}{(2\pi)^{n/2}} \exp \left\{ -\frac{1}{2} \sum_{i=1}^{n} (x_i - \theta)^2 \right\}$$

Suppose that the analyst knows that θ is in the interval (a, b) and that it is his judgment that, within this interval, all values are equally plausible. These prior judgments can be expressed by the uniform distribution over (a, b):

(16.2)
$$p(\theta) = \begin{cases} \dfrac{1}{b - a} & \text{if } a \leq x < b \\ 0 & \text{if } x < a \text{ or } x \geq b \end{cases}$$

Alternatively, suppose that the analyst considers μ_0 (some numerical value) to be the most plausible value of θ and that he views numerically equal deviations from μ_0 ($\mu_0 + a$ and $\mu_0 - a$) to be equally plausible. This requires a symmetric prior density function centered at μ_0. One possibility is

(16.3)
$$p(\theta) = \frac{1}{\sqrt{2\pi\sigma_0^2}} \exp\left\{ -\frac{1}{2} \frac{(\theta - \mu_0)^2}{\sigma_0^2} \right\}$$

which is the density function of the normal prior distribution with mean μ_0 and standard deviation σ_0. If the analyst has great confidence in his best guess μ_0, σ_0 will be small (the prior distribution is tight around μ_0). If there is less confidence, σ_0 will be larger.

The Posterior Density Function and the Likelihood Function

Recall from Section 4.2 that a conditional density function is obtained by dividing the joint density function by the density function of the condition: $p(y\,|\,z) = p(y, z)/p(z)$ or, equivalently,

(16.4)
$$p(y, z) = p(z)p(y\,|\,z)$$

Note that we use here $p(\ )$ as a general symbol for density functions; we indicate by the arguments within parentheses which particular density function we have in mind.

Interchanging y and z in (16.4) yields $p(y, z) = p(y)p(z\,|\,y)$. We subtract this from (16.4): $p(z)p(y\,|\,z) = p(y)p(z\,|\,y)$. If $p(y) > 0$, this yields

(16.5)
$$p(z\,|\,y) = \frac{p(z)p(y\,|\,z)}{p(y)}$$

which is known as Bayes' theorem. We proceed to interpret z as the parameter θ and y as the random sample $(X_1, \ldots, X_n)$, so that (16.5) becomes

(16.6)
$$p(\theta\,|\,X_1, \ldots, X_n) = \frac{p(\theta)p(X_1, \ldots, X_n\,|\,\theta)}{p(X_1, \ldots, X_n)}$$

Here $p(\theta)$ on the right is the prior density function of θ, and the denominator $p(X_1, \ldots, X_n)$ is the density function of the random sample. On the left is the density function of the conditional distribution of θ, given the sample. This is the *posterior density function*; the derivation of this function is our objective.

Since the posterior density function on the left in (16.6) takes the sample as given, this must also hold for $p(X_1, \ldots, X_n\,|\,\theta)$ on the right, which thus becomes a function of θ, given the sample. Going back to the discussion preceding (10.29), we conclude that this function is simply the likelihood function, so that (16.6) can be written as

$$(16.7) \qquad p(\theta \mid X_1, \ldots, X_n) = \frac{p(\theta)L(X_1, \ldots, X_n; \theta)}{p(X_1, \ldots, X_n)}$$

Note further that $p(X_1, \ldots, X_n)$ is a constant when we take the sample as given. Hence, we can write (16.7) in the form

$$(16.8) \qquad p(\theta \mid X_1, \ldots, X_n) \propto p(\theta)L(X_1, \ldots, X_n; \theta)$$

or, in words, as

$$(16.9) \qquad \text{posterior density} \propto \text{prior density} \times \text{likelihood}$$

where $\propto$ stands for "is proportional to." The value of the proportionality constant (a constant with respect to θ) can be determined from the condition that the total integral of the posterior density function equals 1.

Application to the Mean of the Normal Distribution with Unit Variance

Let $(X_1, \ldots, X_n)$ be a random sample from a normal distribution with mean θ and unit variance. Hence, the likelihood function is as shown in (16.1), with x_i replaced by X_i:

$$(16.10) \qquad L(X_1, \ldots, X_n; \theta) = \frac{1}{(2\pi)^{n/2}} \exp\left\{-\frac{1}{2} \sum_{i=1}^{n} (X_i - \theta)^2\right\}$$

We assume that the analyst uses (16.3) as his prior density function for θ. It thus follows from (16.8) that the posterior density function is obtained by multiplying (16.3) and (16.10):

$$\frac{1}{\sqrt{2\pi\sigma_0^2}} \exp\left\{-\frac{1}{2} \frac{(\theta - \mu_0)^2}{\sigma_0^2}\right\} \frac{1}{(2\pi)^{n/2}} \exp\left\{-\frac{1}{2} \sum_{i=1}^{n} (X_i - \theta)^2\right\}$$

Note that the ratios before the two exponents are constants with respect to θ. Thus, for the posterior density function we obtain

$$(16.11) \quad p(\theta \mid X_1, \ldots, X_n) \propto \exp\left\{-\frac{1}{2} \frac{(\theta - \mu_0)^2}{\sigma_0^2}\right\} \exp\left\{-\frac{1}{2} \sum_{i=1}^{n} (X_i - \theta)^2\right\}$$

Some further algebra is provided in the subsection immediately following the next. The result is

$$(16.12) \quad p(\theta \mid X_1, \ldots, X_n) \propto \exp\left\{-\frac{1}{2}(\sigma_0^{-2} + n)\left(\theta - \frac{\sigma_0^{-2}\mu_0 + n\bar{X}}{\sigma_0^{-2} + n}\right)^2\right\}$$

which is of the normal form $\exp\{-\frac{1}{2}(\theta - \text{mean})^2/\text{variance}\}$ with the mean and variance specified as

$$(16.13) \qquad \text{mean} = \frac{\sigma_0^{-2}\mu_0 + n\bar{X}}{\sigma_0^{-2} + n}, \qquad \text{variance} = \frac{1}{\sigma_0^{-2} + n}$$

where $\bar{X}$ is the arithmetic average of $X_1, \ldots, X_n$.

We conclude from (16.12) that the posterior distribution of θ is normal and that the mean of this distribution [the posterior mean shown in (16.13)] is a weighted average of the prior mean μ_0 and the arithmetic average $\bar{X}$ of the sample values, with weights proportional to σ_0^{-2} and n, respectively. As n increases relative to σ_0^{-2}, the mean and variance in (16.13) become effectively equal to $\bar{X}$ and $1/n$, respectively, which are independent of μ_0 and σ_0 of the prior density function (16.3). This agrees with intuition; as the sample size increases indefinitely, the evidence supplied by it will dominate the prior judgments.

Example

Table 8 on page 53 contains the outcome of a random sample ($n = 50$) of profit margins on Pintos, with average $\bar{X} = 9.845$. The analyst works for a competing automobile maker and is interested in the mean θ of the profit margins on Pintos. Before having seen Table 8, he considers 10 the most plausible value of θ and is willing to bet 20 to 1 that θ is not outside the interval (9, 11). He decides to formalize this by means of a normal prior distribution with mean 10 and standard deviation .5 (which is in approximate agreement with the two-sigma rule). Thus, using (16.12) and (16.13), he concludes that the posterior distribution of θ is normal with mean

(16.14) $$\frac{(.5)^{-2} \times 10 + 50 \times 9.845}{(.5)^{-2} + .50} \approx 9.86$$

and standard deviation $1/\sqrt{(.5)^{-2} + 50} \approx .14$. Hence, the sample has modified the analyst's prior judgments, the mean 10 being reduced to 9.86 and the standard deviation .5 to .14. The latter reduction is substantial; it reflects the decrease in uncertainty on θ which the sample achieves.

Derivations

When we take logarithms in (16.11), the proportionality constant represented by $\propto$ becomes an additive constant (a constant with respect to θ):

(16.15) $$\log_e p(\theta \mid X_1, \ldots, X_n) = -\frac{1}{2}\frac{(\theta - \mu_0)^2}{\sigma_0^2} - \frac{1}{2}\sum_{i=1}^{n}(X_i - \theta)^2$$
$$+ \text{ constant}$$

Next consider the following identity:

$$\sum_{i=1}^{n}(X_i - \theta)^2 = \sum_{i=1}^{n}[X_i - \bar{X} + (\bar{X} - \theta)]^2$$
$$= \sum_{i=1}^{n}(X_i - \bar{X})^2 + n(\bar{X} - \theta)^2 + 2(\bar{X} - \theta)\sum_{i=1}^{n}(X_i - \bar{X})$$

Since the last term on the second line vanishes [because $\sum_i (X_i - \bar{X}) = 0$], we can write the right-hand side of (16.15) as

$$-\frac{1}{2}\frac{(\theta - \mu_0)^2}{\sigma_0^2} - \frac{1}{2}\sum_{i=1}^{n}(X_i - \bar{X})^2 - \frac{n}{2}(\bar{X} - \theta)^2 + \text{ constant}$$

The term $\sum_i (X_i - \bar{X})^2$ is a constant with respect to θ, so that it can be combined with the constant on the far right. Therefore,

$$(16.16) \quad \log_e p(\theta \mid X_1, \ldots, X_n) = -\frac{1}{2} \frac{(\theta - \mu_0)^2}{\sigma_0^2} - \frac{n}{2}(\bar{X} - \theta)^2 + \text{constant}$$

$$= -\frac{1}{2}\left[\frac{(\theta - \mu_0)^2}{\sigma_0^2} + n(\bar{X} - \theta)^2 \right] + \text{constant}$$

Finally, we write the expression in brackets as

(16.17)

$$\frac{(\theta - \mu_0)^2}{\sigma_0^2} + n(\bar{X} - \theta)^2 = \sigma_0^{-2}(\theta^2 - 2\theta\mu_0) + n(\theta^2 - 2\theta\bar{X}) + \text{constant}$$

$$= (\sigma_0^{-2} + n)\left(\theta^2 - 2\theta\frac{\sigma_0^{-2}\mu_0 + n\bar{X}}{\sigma_0^{-2} + n} \right) + \text{constant}$$

$$= (\sigma_0^{-2} + n)\left(\theta - \frac{\sigma_0^{-2}\mu_0 + n\bar{X}}{\sigma_0^{-2} + n} \right)^2 + \text{constant}$$

The reader should verify that the three constants on the far right are indeed constant with respect to θ. The proof is completed by substituting the last line of (16.17) in (16.16) and taking antilogs, which yields (16.12).

Bayesian Estimation

In the Bayesian approach the posterior distribution contains all information provided by the sample and the analyst's prior judgments, so that this distribution may be viewed as the final product of the analysis. In certain cases the analyst will desire to characterize the posterior distribution by measures of central tendency, dispersion, and so on. Such a measure of central tendency of the posterior distribution, which is the Bayesian version of a point estimate of a parameter, may be the mode of the posterior distribution (the parameter value at which the posterior density function takes the largest value, if there is such a maximum) or the mean of this distribution (if it has a finite mean). However, it is more in the spirit of Bayesian thinking to formulate a *loss function* and to minimize expected loss. The approach may be outlined as follows.

Write $\hat{\theta} = \hat{\theta}(X_1, \ldots, X_n)$ for the Bayesian estimator of θ. The analysis is based on the posterior distribution $p(\theta \mid X_1, \ldots, X_n)$ and is thus conditional on the sample, so that $\hat{\theta}$ is treated as a constant. This is in contrast to the non-Bayesian approach, which considers an estimator as a random variable. On the other hand, whereas the latter approach treats the parameter θ as an unknown constant, Bayesians treat θ as a random variable. Thus, *the random/nonrandom distinction of the parameter and its estimator is completely reversed in Bayesian analysis.*

We proceed to formulate a loss function $l(\theta, \hat{\theta})$ which measures the seriousness of a discrepancy between $\hat{\theta}$ and θ and to select the estimator $\hat{\theta}$ which minimizes expected loss. The quadratic loss function is an example:

$$(16.18) \qquad l(\theta, \hat{\theta}) = (\hat{\theta} - \theta)^2$$

We write $\mathcal{E}$ for the expectation operator corresponding to the posterior distribution and evaluate the right-hand side of (16.18) as follows:

$$[\hat{\theta} - \mathcal{E}\theta - (\theta - \mathcal{E}\theta)]^2 = (\hat{\theta} - \mathcal{E}\theta)^2 + (\theta - \mathcal{E}\theta)^2 - 2(\hat{\theta} - \mathcal{E}\theta)(\theta - \mathcal{E}\theta)$$

The expected loss is equal to the sum of the expectations of the three terms on the right. Since $\hat{\theta}$ is a constant, the first term, $(\hat{\theta} - \mathcal{E}\theta)^2$, is nonrandom, and the third has an expectation equal to $-2(\hat{\theta} - \mathcal{E}\theta)$ multiplied by $\mathcal{E}(\theta - \mathcal{E}\theta)$, which is zero. The second term, $(\theta - \mathcal{E}\theta)^2$, is independent of $\hat{\theta}$ and is hence irrelevant from the viewpoint of minimizing expected loss.

We conclude that minimizing the expectation of the loss function (16.18) is equivalent to minimizing the nonrandom expression $(\hat{\theta} - \mathcal{E}\theta)^2$ with respect to $\hat{\theta}$, which yields $\hat{\theta} = \mathcal{E}\theta$. Hence, if the loss function is quadratic, the expectation of the posterior distribution (the posterior mean) is the Bayesian estimator with minimum expected loss. If θ is the mean of the normal distribution with unit variance and if (16.3) is the prior density function, this yields the mean shown in (16.13) as the Bayesian estimator of θ.

Diffuse Prior Distributions

We proceed to consider the more complicated case in which $(X_1, \ldots, X_n)$ is a random sample from a normal distribution with mean μ and variance σ^2, both of which are unknown. To apply Bayesian inference, the analyst must formulate a prior density function $p(\mu, \sigma^2)$ on the two parameters jointly. Suppose that the analyst claims that he knows little or nothing on one or both parameters and that his ignorance is such that he is not in a position to formulate an adequate prior density function $p(\mu, \sigma^2)$. This situation arises frequently, particularly with respect to the variance σ^2.

If the analyst wants to apply Bayesian inference, he *must* specify a prior distribution on *all* parameters of his model. One way of expressing ignorance is by means of "diffuse" or "noninformative" prior distributions. For example, imagine that the mean μ of the normal distribution is considered to be uniformly distributed over the interval $(-A, A)$:

$$(16.19) \qquad p(\mu) = \begin{cases} \dfrac{1}{2A} & \text{if } -A \leq \mu < A \\ 0 & \text{if } \mu < -A \text{ or } \mu \geq A \end{cases}$$

Imagine that A takes larger and larger values, so that we obtain a prior density function of μ which is a constant in the interval $(-\infty, \infty)$. The proponents of this approach would argue that such a density function should not be taken as a literal expression of the analyst's prior judgments on μ but as a device to indicate that in the interval in which the likelihood function takes appreciable values there is little variation in the prior density. This device is designed to ensure that the sample evidence will be given overwhelming weight in the determination of the posterior distribution.

Diffuseness and Independence

A uniform prior density for the variance σ^2 of the normal distribution must obviously be restricted to the interval $(0, \infty)$ rather than $(-\infty, \infty)$. However, a uniform distribution of σ^2 implies a nonuniform distribution of the standard deviation σ. This asymmetry can be avoided by postulating that $\log_e \sigma^2$ has a uniform prior distribution, because $\log_e \sigma = \frac{1}{2} \log_e \sigma^2$ then has the same prior distribution.

Thus, let us assume that both μ and $\log_e \sigma$ have uniform prior distributions; let us also assume that they are independent a priori. By multiplying this joint prior density function by the likelihood function (10.33), reproduced here,

$$L(X_1, \ldots, X_n; \mu, \sigma^2) = \frac{1}{(2\pi\sigma^2)^{n/2}} \exp\left\{-\frac{1}{2\sigma^2} \sum_{i=1}^{n} (X_i - \mu)^2\right\}$$

we obtain $p(\mu, \sigma \mid X_1, \ldots, X_n)$ multiplied by a constant. This $p(\ )$ is the joint posterior density function of μ and σ. If the analyst is interested in μ but not in σ, he computes the marginal posterior density function of μ, which is obtained by integrating the joint posterior density function over σ:

$$(16.20) \qquad p(\mu \mid X_1, \ldots, X_n) = \int_0^\infty p(\mu, \sigma \mid X_1, \ldots, X_n) \, d\sigma$$

It appears that for the diffuse prior distribution discussed above the posterior distribution of μ is such that the ratio of $(\bar{X} - \mu)\sqrt{n}$ to s is distributed as $t(n - 1)$; for a proof, see Theil (1971, pp. 669–670). Note that this ratio is identical to (11.11) for which we proved that it is distributed as $t(n - 1)$. Thus, we obtain the same mathematical result, but again note that in Bayesian analysis μ is random and $\bar{X}$ and s are fixed, whereas the opposite is true in Chapter 11.

Confidence Intervals and Tests of Hypotheses

The result described above illustrates the fact that, given an appropriate mathematical expression of diffuseness, the Bayesian approach yields in many cases the same formulas as those obtained in Chapter 11. This similarity extends to a wide range, but not all, of the best known statistical techniques, including confidence intervals and hypothesis testing. For example, we can obtain a Bayesian interval for μ of the form (11.13) in which $\bar{X}$ and s are fixed and μ is random. What is random in the Bayesian approach is always viewed as a fixed number in the non-Bayesian approach and vice versa. For a Bayesian it makes sense to talk about the probability that a hypothesis is true; for a non-Bayesian (Chapter 12) a hypothesis is either true or false. A summary is given in Table 21.

TABLE 21
Bayes and Non-Bayes compared

	Bayes	*Non-Bayes*
Parameter	Random	Nonrandom
Estimator	Nonrandom	Random
Confidence interval	End points nonrandom	End points random
Hypothesis	True with some probability	Either true or false

*16.2   Bayesian Inference in Econometrics

A number of problems arise when the analyst wants to use the Bayesian approach for inference in econometrics, most of which result from the fact that econometric models contain more than a few parameters.

Prior Distributions for the Parameters of the CES Production Function

The CES production function is a convenient starting point. We write it in the logarithmic form (13.35),

$$(16.21) \qquad \log_e P_i = \log_e c - \frac{1}{\rho} \log_e [\alpha K_i^{-\rho} + (1 - \alpha) L_i^{-\rho}] + \epsilon_i$$

where α is constrained to the interval $(0, 1)$. Thus, if the analyst feels that he is completely ignorant about α, he can use a uniform distribution over this interval to express this feeling.

But it is not sufficient to formulate prior distributions for individual parameters; a joint prior distribution for all parameters is needed. Suppose, then, that the analyst judges α and ρ to be independent a priori, so that the joint prior density of α and ρ is the product of the prior density of α and that of ρ. This is perfectly acceptable, but note that if the CES function is written in the form (13.36),

$$(16.22) \quad \log_e \frac{P_i}{L_i} \approx \log_e c + \alpha \log_e \frac{K_i}{L_i} - \frac{1}{2} \rho \alpha (1 - \alpha) \left(\log_e \frac{K_i}{L_i} \right)^2 + \epsilon_i$$

the parameters α and $-\frac{1}{2} \rho \alpha (1 - \alpha)$ are not independent when α and ρ are independent.

This does not mean that it is impossible to evaluate the joint prior density function of α and $-\frac{1}{2} \rho \alpha (1 - \alpha)$ which is implied by independent prior distributions of α and ρ, but it does show that the formulation of prior distributions is a matter which requires great care. It is also an increasingly complicated matter when there are more parameters. For each additional parameter, the analyst must not only supply a marginal prior distribution, but he must also judge whether this parameter is a priori independent of the others; and if he denies independence, he must specify the nature of the dependence.

Problems of Mathematical Tractability

Once a joint prior distribution of all parameters has been formulated, we obtain the posterior distribution by multiplication by the likelihood function. But note that this is the joint posterior distribution of all parameters and that to obtain the marginal posterior distribution of each parameter separately, we must integrate over all other parameters [see (16.20)]. This leads frequently to considerable complications, because the integration is in many cases analytically intractable. Numerical integration is then necessary, but this is an imperfect substitute.

Under these circumstances it is almost unavoidable that mathematical tractability becomes an important consideration for the formulation of prior distributions. For example, in the case of (16.21) and (16.22), we have four parameters: α, ρ, c, and the variance σ^2 of the ϵ_i's. For the last two parameters, a convenient device is independence of $\log_e c$ and $\log_e \sigma$, each having a diffuse prior marginal distribution of the type discussed below (16.19).

If mathematical tractability is a major consideration for the formulation of prior distributions, there is the risk that the analyst prefers a mathematically convenient prior distribution to the less convenient distribution that would be needed to describe his true prior judgments on the parameters. If this happens, the Bayesian approach defeats its own purpose, which is to incorporate the analyst's prior judgments adequately. Also, the selection of the model which describes the data (and hence determines the likelihood function) may be influenced by considerations of tractability. Few analysts are interested in using a model which promises no results. But it is a serious matter when an otherwise attractive model is rejected because the Bayesian approach cannot handle it.

It is true that the non-Bayesian approach will also use tractability as one of its ingredients. However, Bayesian analysis is much more demanding from a mathematical point of view. The complications described above are a major reason there are few applied Bayesian econometric studies of interest.

Other Problems

The Bayesian approach itself is a matter of considerable controversy. This is not surprising, given that the approach takes such a fundamentally different view of the nature of the parameters by treating them as random variables. For different appreciations of the Bayesian approach to econometrics, see Pratt (1971), Rothenberg (1971a), and Zellner (1971a, b).

Among Bayesians, there is a controversy as to the use of the diffuse prior distributions based on (16.19). If $A \rightarrow \infty$, the density $1/2A$ converges to zero, which yields an *improper* density function in the limit. It can be shown that the use of improper prior distributions may yield internal contradictions [see Stone (1976)]. This should be a matter of concern, since Bayesian econometric theoreticians heavily rely on the use of improper prior distributions to express the analyst's ignorance of a parameter in a tractable way. The Bayesian idea of incorporating the analyst's prior knowledge in statistical inference is attractive, but the complications caused by revealing that no such knowledge exists are not. In Section 19.5 we shall consider a different method of incorporating prior judgments in the estimation of parameters.

Although Bayesian econometrics has considerable problems and has attracted few followers among applied econometricians, the conceptual framework of Bayesian analysis is attractive for applications in decision making. This subject is considered in the next section.

*16.3   Rational Random Behavior

The theory of rational random behavior, which originated with Theil (1974a) and was extended by Barbosa (1975), provides a formal justification of the use of random disturbances in behavioral equations. This theory does not try to explain each particular action of a decision maker but focuses on the stochastic process which generates observed behavior. This process yields a *decision distribution*; it is derived from an optimization procedure, to be described below, which involves the acquisition of information by the decision maker as a fundamental ingredient.

The Theoretically Optimal Decision

Let z be the variable controlled by the decision maker, $\bar{z}$ (a numerical value) the optimal value of this variable, and $l(z, \bar{z})$ the loss function which describes the decision maker's loss when his decision is z rather than $\bar{z}$. To ensure that $\bar{z}$ is unique, we assume

$$(16.23) \qquad \begin{aligned} l(z, \bar{z}) &= 0 \qquad \text{if } z = \bar{z} \\ &> 0 \qquad \text{if } z \neq \bar{z} \end{aligned}$$

For example, we may have a quadratic loss function,

$$(16.24) \qquad l(z, \bar{z}) = (z - \bar{z})^2$$

which obviously satisfies (16.23).

In most cases, the optimal decision $\bar{z}$ depends on numerous factors which are relevant for the decision process. We assume here that the decision maker does not know the values of all these factors, so that he does not know $\bar{z}$ either. To emphasize this aspect, we shall refer to $\bar{z}$ as the *theoretically optimal decision*; it is optimal under perfect knowledge.

The Acquisition of Information

The uncertainty regarding the factors relevant for the decision process will be expressed in probabilistic terms. If no additional information on these factors is acquired, the decision made is described as random with density function

$p_0(z)$. We assume that $p_0(z)$ is differentiable around $\bar{z}$ and that it takes positive values for each $z \in R$, where R is the range of all possible values of z (the feasible region of the decision variable):

(16.25) $$p_0(z) > 0 \quad \text{if } z \in R$$

Our next step is the assumption that the decision maker considers the possibility of acquiring further information on the factors relevant for the decision process so that $p_0(z)$ is transformed into $p(z)$, the density function of the posterior decision distribution. We define

(16.26) $$I = \int_R p(z) \log_e \frac{p(z)}{p_0(z)} \, dz$$

as the amount of information received when the distribution with density function $p_0(\ )$ is transformed into the distribution with density function $p(\ )$. This definition is from information theory; it is the continuous version of a similar discrete definition discussed by Theil (1971, pp. 641–643). We have $I = 0$ if $p(z) = p_0(z)$ for each $z \in R$; hence, no information is received when the two p's are identical, which agrees with intuition. It is shown in the next subsection that $I > 0$ when the two p's are not identical.

For example, let $p_0(z)$ be the density function of the normal distribution with mean μ_0 and standard deviation σ_0, and let $p(z)$ be the density function of the normal distribution with mean μ and standard deviation σ. The reader should verify (see Problem 5) that (16.26) yields

(16.27) $$I = \frac{(\mu - \mu_0)^2}{2\sigma_0^2} + \frac{1}{2}\left[\frac{\sigma^2}{\sigma_0^2} - 1 - \log_e \frac{\sigma^2}{\sigma_0^2}\right]$$

and also (see Problem 6) that the expression in brackets vanishes if $\sigma = \sigma_0$ and is positive if $\sigma \neq \sigma_0$. Note that (16.27) describes the information as the sum of two terms, one involving the difference between the means and the other the difference between the variances. We have $I = 0$ if and only if both $\mu = \mu_0$ and $\sigma = \sigma_0$, in which case the two normal distributions are identical.

The Nonnegativity of Information

We write (16.26) in the form

(16.28) $$-I = \int_R p(z) \log_e \frac{p_0(z)}{p(z)} \, dz$$

and use (13.10), $\log_e x = x - 1$ if $x = 1$ and $< x - 1$ if $x \neq 1$, with x interpreted as $p_0(z)/p(z)$ for $p(z) \neq 0$:

$$\log_e \frac{p_0(z)}{p(z)} = \frac{p_0(z)}{p(z)} - 1 \qquad \text{if } p_0(z) = p(z)$$
$$< \frac{p_0(z)}{p(z)} - 1 \qquad \text{if } p_0(z) \neq p(z)$$

When we multiply this by $p(z)$, we obtain

$$p(z) \log_e \frac{p_0(z)}{p(z)} = p_0(z) - p(z) \qquad \text{if } p_0(z) = p(z)$$
$$< p_0(z) - p(z) \qquad \text{if } p_0(z) \neq p(z)$$

Then by integrating over z and using (16.28), we find that if $p_0(z) \neq p(z)$ for some $z \in R$,

$$-I < \int_R p_0(z)\, dz - \int_R p(z)\, dz = 1 - 1 = 0$$

which implies $I > 0$.

The Cost of Information and the Expected Loss

Information is not costless. We write

(16.29) $$C = C(I)$$

for the cost of acquiring the information (16.26). We assume that $C(\ )$ is a differentiable function with a positive first derivative,

(16.30) $$C' = \frac{dC}{dI} > 0$$

which amounts to a positive *marginal cost of information.*

Since I depends on $p(\ )$ [see (16.26)], so does the cost of information. This cost will be one consideration for the selection of the decision distribution $p(\ )$. The other consideration is the expected loss,

(16.31) $$\bar{l} = \int_R l(z, \bar{z}) p(z)\, dz$$

If the cost (16.29) and the expected loss (16.31) are both measured in dollars, the obvious solution is the decision distribution which minimizes their sum, $C(I) + \bar{l}$.

The Optimal Decision Distribution

The derivation of this optimal decision distribution is described in Appendix E. The result is that a distribution which minimizes $C(I) + \bar{l}$ exists when

(16.32) $$\frac{d^2 C}{dI^2} \geq 0$$

which amounts to nondecreasing marginal cost of information, and that the density function of this distribution is of the form $p(z) = 0$ if $z \notin R$ and

(16.33) $$p(z) \propto p_0(z) \exp\left\{-\frac{l(z, \bar{z})}{C'}\right\} \qquad \text{if } z \in R$$

where $\propto$ is the Bayesian proportionality symbol, the proportionality coefficient being independent of z. Behavior generated by the random process (16.33) is called *rational random behavior.*

For example, take the loss function (16.24) and assume that the density function $p_0(z)$ equals a constant independent of z. Then (16.33) yields

$$(16.34) \qquad p(z) \propto \exp\left\{-\frac{1}{2}\frac{(z-\bar{z})^2}{C'/2}\right\}$$

which amounts to a *truncated* normal decision distribution over the range R. The density curve of this distribution is shown in Figure 29, together with the corresponding normal curve (the broken curve). If the range R is sufficiently large, the density function (16.34) is approximately equivalent to that of the normal distribution with a mean equal to the theoretically optimal decision ($\bar{z}$) and a variance equal to one-half of the marginal cost of information ($\frac{1}{2}C'$).

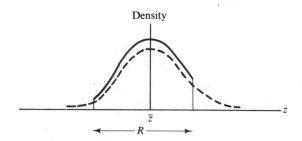

FIGURE 29   A truncated normal decision distribution

Comparison with Bayesian Inference

It is instructive to compare (16.33) with (16.8) for Bayesian inference, reproduced here:

$$(16.35) \qquad p(\theta \mid X_1, \ldots, X_n) \propto p(\theta)L(X_1, \ldots, X_n; \theta)$$

If we identify θ with z, we find that the p's immediately to the right of the proportional signs in (16.33) and (16.35) are prior density functions. The likelihood function in (16.35) represents the information obtained from the sample, which should be compared with the exponent of $-l(z, \bar{z})/C'$ in (16.33), where C' is a function of the information obtained by the decision maker. This comparability is imperfect, since the exponent in (16.33) involves the unknown $\bar{z}$ in addition to z, whereas the likelihood function in (16.35) involves the known sample $(X_1, \ldots, X_n)$ in addition to θ. Nevertheless, it should be clear that (16.33) and (16.35) are similar in that both describe learning processes based on acquiring information.

*16.4   The Asymptotic Theory of Rational Random Behavior

It follows from (16.33) that the optimal decision distribution implied by the theory of rational random behavior depends on the prior density function $p_0(z)$, the loss function $l(z, \bar{z})$, and the marginal cost of information C'. This marginal cost depends on the prices of certain goods and services, which may go up or down. In this section we are interested in the behavior of the optimal decision distribution when C' converges to zero.

The Convergence in Probability to the Theoretically Optimal Decision

We take the logarithm of (16.33),

$$(16.36) \qquad \log_e p(z) = \text{constant} + \log p_0(z) - \frac{l(z, \bar{z})}{C'}$$

where the constant is independent of z. Next we substitute $\bar{z}$ for z and use (16.23):

$$(16.37) \qquad \log_e p(\bar{z}) = \text{constant} + \log_e p_0(\bar{z})$$

Since the constants in (16.36) and (16.37) are equal, subtraction gives

$$(16.38) \qquad \log_e \frac{p(\bar{z})}{p(z)} = \log_e \frac{p_0(\bar{z})}{p_0(z)} + \frac{l(z, \bar{z})}{C'}$$

It follows from (16.23) that as $C' \longrightarrow 0$ the second term on the right increases beyond bounds for any $z \neq \bar{z}$, so that the same must be true for $p(\bar{z})/p(z)$ on the left. Hence, as $C' \longrightarrow 0$, the density function $p(z)$ becomes zero for each $z \neq \bar{z}$, and the optimal decision distribution collapses with all of its mass concentrated at $z = \bar{z}$, irrespective of the prior density function $p_0(\ )$.

It is not difficult to understand intuitively why the random decision generated by (16.33) converges in probability to $\bar{z}$ as $C' \longrightarrow 0$, irrespective of $p_0(\ )$. If the marginal cost of information is zero, information is a free good, and the selection of the optimal decision distribution is exclusively a matter of minimizing the expected loss (16.31). The minimum expected loss is zero, which is attained by selecting a degenerate decision distribution whose mass is concentrated at $\bar{z}$. In the limit for $C' \longrightarrow 0$, $\bar{z}$ is no longer unknown.

The Asymptotic Normality of the Optimal Decision Distribution

We proceed to impose three conditions on the loss function in addition to (16.23). First, the derivatives of $l(z, \bar{z})$ with respect to z exist up to the third order, the third derivative being a continuous function of z for each $z \in R$. Second, the first-order derivative vanishes at $z = \bar{z}$:

$$(16.39) \qquad \frac{d}{dz} l(z, \bar{z}) = 0 \qquad \text{at } z = \bar{z}$$

Third, the second-order derivative is positive at $z = \bar{z}$:

$$(16.40) \qquad \frac{d^2}{dz^2} l(z, \bar{z}) = A > 0 \qquad \text{at } z = \bar{z}$$

The quadratic loss function (16.24) satisfies all three conditions. In fact, these conditions serve to ensure that the loss function behaves approximately as a quadratic function for z close to $\bar{z}$.

Consider a Taylor expansion of $l(z, \bar{z})$ at $z = \bar{z}$:

$$l(z, \bar{z}) = l(\bar{z}, \bar{z}) + (z - \bar{z})\frac{d}{dz}l(z, \bar{z}) + \frac{1}{2}(z - \bar{z})^2 \frac{d^2}{dz^2}l(z, \bar{z}) + \cdots$$

It follows from (16.23), (16.39), and (16.40) that this equation can be simplified to $l(z, \bar{z}) = \frac{1}{2}A(z - \bar{z})^2 + \ldots$, or to

(16.41)
$$\frac{l(z, \bar{z})}{C'} = \frac{A(z - \bar{z})^2}{2C'} + R_1$$

where R_1 is a remainder term. Next recall from the discussion preceding (16.25) that $p_0(\ )$ is assumed to be positive and differentiable around $\bar{z}$, so that a Taylor expansion of its logarithm gives $\log_e p_0(z) = \log_e p_0(\bar{z}) + R_2$, where R_2 is another remainder term. We combine this with (16.36) and (16.41):

(16.42) $$\log_e p(z) = \text{constant} + \log_e p_0(\bar{z}) - \frac{A(z - \bar{z})^2}{2C'} - R_1 + R_2$$

Note that $\log_e p_0(\bar{z})$ does not involve z and is hence a constant. It is shown in Appendix E that R_1 and R_2 converge to zero as $C' \to 0$, so that in the limit $\log_e p(z)$ equals a constant minus $A(z - \bar{z})^2/2C'$. Hence, as $C' \to 0$, the density function of the optimal decision distribution converges to

(16.43) $$\bar{p}(z) \propto \exp\left\{-\frac{1}{2}\frac{(z - \bar{z})^2}{C'/A}\right\}$$

which is the density function of the normal decision distribution with mean $\bar{z}$ and variance C'/A. Note that this asymptotic result is independent of the prior density $p_0(\ )$.

The Variance of the Asymptotic Decision Distribution

The variance C'/A of the asymptotic normal decision distribution is proportional to C' and is thus smaller when information is cheaper in the sense that its marginal cost is smaller. The economic interpretation is that it is advantageous to select a decision distribution which is tight around the theoretically optimal decision $\bar{z}$ when the search for $\bar{z}$ is inexpensive.

Recall from the discussion below (16.34) that a quadratic loss function and a uniform prior density function imply a truncated normal decision distribution when the range R is finite. The word "truncated" can be deleted in the asymptotic analysis. As C' converges to zero, so does the variance C'/A of the asymptotic distribution (16.43). In the limit, the part of the normal decision distribution which is outside the range R ceases to be of significance.

The variance C'/A of the distribution (16.43) is inversely proportional to the second-order derivative A of the loss function at $z = \bar{z}$. Hence, this variance is smaller in the case of Figure 30(a), with large A, than in that of Figure 30(b),

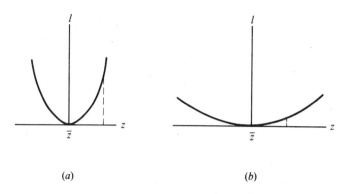

(a) (b)

FIGURE 30   Two loss functions

where A is smaller. This agrees with intuition, because numerically equal deviations of z from the mean $\bar{z}$ of the distribution (16.43) imply a larger loss in Figure 30(a) than in Figure 30(b) (see the broken vertical lines); hence, the decision maker can afford a larger variance in the latter case than in the former.

Extension to Several Decision Variables

The asymptotic results described above can be extended for the case in which the decision maker controls several variables $z_1, z_2, \ldots$. Details are given in Appendix E, the results of which can be summarized as follows:

(1) Let the theoretically optimal decisions be $\bar{z}_1, \bar{z}_2, \ldots$ (one value for each decision variable). We extend (16.23) so that the loss function vanishes when all z_i's are equal to the corresponding $\bar{z}_i$'s and is positive otherwise. Then, as $C' \rightarrow 0$, the multivariate decision distribution collapses with all of its mass concentrated at $\bar{z}_1, \bar{z}_2, \ldots$.

(2) Under regularity conditions on the loss function similar to (16.39) and (16.40), the optimal decision distribution becomes multivariate normal as $C' \rightarrow 0$, with means equal to $\bar{z}_1, \bar{z}_2, \ldots$. The variances and covariances of this multivariate normal distribution converge to zero as $C' \rightarrow 0$. Given C', these variances and covariances are uniquely determined by the second-order derivatives of the loss function. This is a direct extension of the variance C'/A of the asymptotic distribution for one decision variable, because C'/A is determined (given C') by the second-order derivative A of $l(z, \bar{z})$.

Application to Consumer Demand Theory

The application of the theory of rational random behavior to the consumer as decision maker requires that the budget constraint (14.2) be taken into consideration. This can be done by using the constraint to eliminate the quantity of one of the N goods from the utility function (14.1). With the utility function thus modified, the consumer's loss function is then defined as maximum utility minus the utility of the basket selected.

When this approach is applied to the Rotterdam Model described in Section 14.2, the consumer's decision becomes random in agreement with the random disturbance ϵ_{it} of (14.40), reproduced here:

$$(16.44) \qquad \bar{w}_{it}Dq_{it} = \mu_i DQ_t + \sum_{j=1}^{N} \pi_{ij}Dp_{jt} + \epsilon_{it} \qquad i = 1, \ldots, N$$

The variable $\bar{w}_{it}Dq_{it}$ on the left is the quantity component of the change in the ith budget share; this is the consumer's decision variable for the ith good according to the Rotterdam Model. The right-hand side of (16.44) excluding ϵ_{it} is the theoretically optimal decision $(\bar{z}_i)$ for the ith good, which thus involves the changes in real income and all prices. The asymptotic theory of rational random behavior implies that the distribution of the disturbances $\epsilon_{1t}, \epsilon_{2t}, \ldots$ is multivariate normal with zero means.

Recall from property (2) in the previous subsection that the variances and covariances of the asymptotic normal decision distribution are determined (given C') by the second-order derivatives of the loss function. When this is applied to the Rotterdam Model, it appears that the covariance of ϵ_{it} and ϵ_{jt} is proportional to the Slutsky coefficient π_{ij}, as will now be explained for the demand model for meats discussed in Section 14.4.

Application to the Demand for Meats in the United States

The model for meats is a four-equation conditional demand model. Its form is as shown in (14.58) for $N_g = 4$, reproduced here,

$$(16.45) \qquad \frac{\bar{w}_{it}}{\bar{W}_{gt}}Dq_{it} = \frac{\mu_i}{M_g}DQ_{gt} + \sum_{j=1}^{4} \pi_{ij}^* Dp_{jt} + \epsilon_{it}^*$$

where $i = 1$ (beef), 2 (pork), 3 (chicken), and 4 (lamb). The asymptotic theory of rational random behavior implies that the disturbances of this model are normally distributed with zero means and variances and covariances proportional to the corresponding conditional Slutsky coefficients,

$$(16.46) \qquad \text{cov}\,(\epsilon_{it}^*, \epsilon_{jt}^*) = k\pi_{ij}^* \qquad i, j = 1, \ldots, 4$$

where k is a negative proportionality coefficient. Equation (16.46) is the conditional version of the proportionality mentioned at the end of the previous subsection.

It is instructive to compare the normal distribution of the disturbances with the normality result obtained below (15.29), which is based on a large number of stochastically independent neglected variables. The present analysis is based on a low marginal cost of the information needed to approximate the theoretically optimal decision. This decision includes the changes in all prices [see the discussion below (16.44)]; acquiring knowledge of these changes is obviously not a free good.

Note that our present approach is more powerful than that below (15.29). First, we make no assumption that neglected variables are stochastically independent. Second, the present result implies not only asymptotic normality but also strong restrictions on the variances and covariances of the asymptotic distribution. When applied to the conditional model (16.45), these restrictions take the form (16.46), where k is closer to zero when the marginal cost of information is smaller.

Disturbance Covariances Compared with Conditional Slutsky Coefficients

It is obviously of interest to test the validity of (16.46). For this purpose we use the symmetry-constrained estimates of the conditional Slutsky coefficients given in Table 18 on page 223, which are reproduced in the middle part of Table 22. By substituting the symmetry-constrained estimates for the corresponding parameters in (16.45), we obtain the implied residuals, to be written e_{it}^*. The mean squares and products of these residuals are of the form

$$(16.47) \qquad \frac{1}{T} \sum_{t=1}^{T} e_{it}^* e_{jt}^* \qquad\qquad i, j = 1, \ldots, 4$$

where $T = 22$ is the number of annual observations. For $i = j = 1$ this gives 54.1×10^{-6}, which is the mean square of the residuals of the equation for beef; for $i = 1, j = 2$ and $i = 2, j = 1$ it gives -43.3×10^{-6}, which is the mean

TABLE 22

**Estimates of conditional Slutsky coefficients
and residual mean squares and products for meats**

	Beef	Pork	Chicken	Lamb
	*Mean squares and products of residuals**			
Beef	54.1	−43.3	−9.9	−.9
Pork		43.1	1.4	−1.2
Chicken			8.9	−.3
Lamb				2.4
	Symmetry-constrained estimates of conditional Slutsky coefficients			
Beef	−.227	.164	.033	.029
Pork		−.214	.038	.012
Chicken			−.084	.013
Lamb				−.055
	Maximum-likelihood estimates of conditional Slutsky coefficients			
Beef	−.216	.173	.034	.008
Pork		−.216	.035	.007
Chicken			−.079	.009
Lamb				−.024

*All figures shown are to be multiplied by 10^{-6}.

product of the residuals of the beef equation and those of the pork equation. All residual mean squares and products are shown in the first four lines of Table 22.

As an informal preliminary test, let us approximate the conditional Slutsky coefficient in (16.46) by its symmetry-constrained estimate and the covariance by the mean product (16.47). If (16.46) is true, we should expect an approximate proportionality when the parameters are replaced by these estimates. The result is shown in Figure 31 by means of 10 small circles. The Slutsky estimate, multiplied by -1, is measured along the horizontal axis and the mean product (16.47) along the vertical axis. The four circles in the positive quadrant refer to the four disturbance variances and the conditional Slutsky coefficients with equal subscripts; they are indicated by B, P, C, and L for beef, pork, chicken, and lamb, respectively. The six circles to the left of the vertical axis refer to the covariances $(i \neq j)$, with BP indicating that of beef and pork.

Since k in (16.46) is negative and since the Slutsky estimates in Figure 31 are multiplied by -1, the 10 circles should ideally be located on an upward-

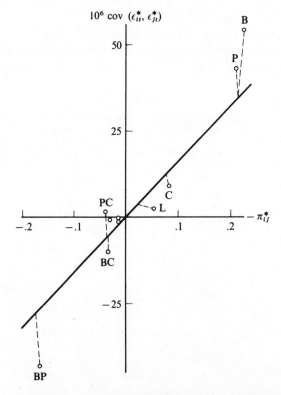

FIGURE 31 The proportionality of the conditional Slutsky coefficients and the disturbance covariances of meats

sloping straight line through the origin. The evidence shows that this is approximately true, which is encouraging.

A Maximum-Likelihood Procedure

A more rigorous test is provided by the maximum-likelihood method. The last four lines of Table 22 contain the Slutsky estimates obtained by means of this method when the proportionality (16.46) is imposed as a constraint. The associated likelihood ratio test shows that (16.46) is an acceptable hypothesis at the 10 percent significance level. For further details, see Theil (1975–1976, Chapter 7).

Most of the maximum-likelihood estimates of Table 22 are close to the corresponding figures in the middle part of the table. The exceptions are the Slutsky estimates involving lamb (π_{ij}^* with $i = 4$ or $j = 4$), which are all pushed in zero direction when (16.46) is imposed. This is caused in part by the small residuals in the equation for lamb, as may be inferred from the small mean square of these residuals (2.4×10^{-6}; see the fourth row of Table 22). If the residuals for lamb are small, this is indicative of small disturbances for lamb and hence also small covariances in (16.46) for $i = 4$ and $j = 4$, which pushes the estimates of the conditional Slutsky coefficients involving lamb in zero direction when (16.46) is imposed. See also Problem 9.

If (16.46) is imposed on the estimates, the 10 points of Figure 31 are forced to be located on a straight line through the origin. The line drawn in the figure is that of the maximum-likelihood estimates, and the broken lines show how the symmetry-constrained estimates (the small circles) are affected when (16.46) is imposed. The three circles immediately to the left of the origin are too close to the line through the origin to permit such a visual display.

Problems

Problems 1 and 2 refer to Section 16.1, 3 and 4 to Section 16.2, 5 and 6 to Section 16.3, and 7–11 to Section 16.4.

1 The analyst decides to use a normal prior distribution with mean 10 and standard deviation .1 for the mean θ of the profit margins on Pintos. Use Table 8 on page 53 to verify that the posterior distribution of θ is normal with mean 9.95 and standard deviation .08 (in two decimal places). Compare this result with that described below (16.14), and state your conclusions.

2 Verify that the first two constants in (16.17) are $(\mu_0/\sigma_0)^2 + n\bar{X}^2$ and that the third equals

$$\sigma_0^{-2}\mu_0^2 + n\bar{X}^2 - \frac{(\sigma_0^{-2}\mu_0 + n\bar{X})^2}{\sigma_0^{-2} + n}$$

3 Suppose that the analyst uses a uniform prior density function over the interval $(0, 1)$ for α in (16.21). Is this an improper density function?

4 Consider Problem 10 on page 169, and suppose that the numbers $-.91$ and $-.75$ are obtained from the posterior distribution of β_2. Would the statement $P[-.91 \leq \beta_2 \leq -.75] = .95$ be acceptable from a Bayesian point of view?

5 Let $p_0(z)$ and $p(z)$ be the density functions of normal distributions, the former with mean μ_0 and standard deviation σ_0 and the latter with mean μ and standard deviation σ. Prove that I defined in (16.26) can be written as the sum of three terms:

$$\frac{1}{\sigma\sqrt{2\pi}} \int_{-\infty}^{\infty} \log_e \frac{\sigma_0}{\sigma} \exp\left\{ -\frac{1}{2} \frac{(z-\mu)^2}{\sigma^2} \right\} dz$$

$$-\frac{1}{2} \frac{1}{\sigma\sqrt{2\pi}} \int_{-\infty}^{\infty} \frac{(z-\mu)^2}{\sigma^2} \exp\left\{ -\frac{1}{2} \frac{(z-\mu)^2}{\sigma^2} \right\} dz$$

$$\frac{1}{2} \frac{1}{\sigma\sqrt{2\pi}} \int_{-\infty}^{\infty} \frac{(z-\mu_0)^2}{\sigma_0^2} \exp\left\{ -\frac{1}{2} \frac{(z-\mu)^2}{\sigma^2} \right\} dz$$

Prove that the first term is equal to $\log_e (\sigma_0/\sigma)$, the second to $-\frac{1}{2}$, and the third to $(\mu - \mu_0)^2 + \sigma^2$ divided by twice the square of σ_0, and use these results to verify (16.27). [*Hint*: Write $z - \mu_0 = (\mu - \mu_0) + (z - \mu)$ in the third term.]

6 (*Continuation*) Use (13.10) to verify that the expression in brackets in (16.27) vanishes if $\sigma = \sigma_0$ and is positive if $\sigma \neq \sigma_0$.

7 Verify that the loss function (16.24) has derivatives of any order, that its first derivative vanishes at $z = \bar{z}$, and that its second derivative equals 2.

8 Is the proportionality (16.46) in agreement with Slutsky symmetry?

9 Consider Table 18 on page 223, and compute t ratios for the symmetry-constrained Slutsky estimates with equal subscripts. Verify that the t ratio for lamb is much smaller than those of the three other meats, and argue that this could be a cause of the relatively substantial change of the estimate for lamb, from $-.055$ to $-.024$ (see Table 22), when (16.46) is imposed.

10 (*Continuation*) Use the relevant figures in Tables 18, 19, and 22 to compute the conditional Slutsky elasticities involving lamb that are implied by the maximum-likelihood estimates of the conditional Slutsky coefficients in Table 22. Compare these elasticities with those shown in Table 19, and state your conclusions.

11 The theory of rational random behavior is formulated for an individual decision maker. Does this agree with the application of this theory to the demand for meats? [*Note*: For an aggregated version of this theory, see Theil (1975–1976, Sections 4.4 and 7.8).]

chapter 17

Specification
and
Observational Errors

Until this point we have assumed that the mathematical form of the relation to be estimated is known. This is frequently not true. The analyst will then consider alternative forms and make a choice, but this may be the wrong choice. Sometimes he knows that a particular form is correct, but he has no data on certain variables. Sometimes he has data, but they are subject to observational error.

17.1 Functional Forms Further Considered

More on the Demand for Textile

The demand equation for textile which we derived from the data of Table 12 on page 96 is linear in the logarithms of three variables: the volume of textile consumption per capita (T), real income per capita (Y), and the relative textile price (p). We write (8.7) in the following form:

(17.1) $\log_{10} T_i = 1.3742 + 1.1430 \log_{10} Y_i - .8289 \log_{10} p_i + \text{residual}$

It is instructive to compare this log-linear specification with that which is linear in T, Y, and p rather than in their logarithms. Thus, we run a regression of column (1) of Table 12 on columns (2) and (3), which gives

(17.2) $T_i = 130.7 + 1.062 Y_i - 1.383 p_i + \text{residual}$

Which specification, (17.1) or (17.2), should be preferred?

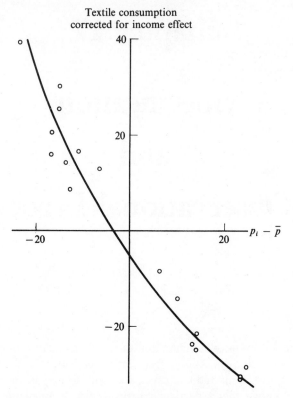

FIGURE 32 **Partial scatter diagram for the relative textile price in the linear specification**

One method of verifying linearity versus log-linearity is by means of partial scatter diagrams. Figure 32 shows the partial scatter diagram for the relative textile price based on (17.2), with $p_i - \bar{p}$ measured horizontally and $T_i - \bar{T} - 1.062(Y_i - \bar{Y})$ vertically, the latter variable being textile consumption per capita corrected for the estimated effect of real income. (The bars indicate the arithmetic means of the three variables.) The 17 points are close to a curve whose slope increases algebraically when p increases. This suggests that the linear specification (17.2) is inappropriate. The reader should compare this figure with the corresponding partial scatter diagram of the log-linear specification in Figure 15 on page 108, which provides no evidence of nonlinearity. The subject of statistical tests against nonlinearity is discussed in Section 19.3.

Does It Matter Which Form Is Selected?

Although the curve of Figure 32 suggests a nonlinear relation, the degree of nonlinearity is actually modest. The reader should verify this by stretching a rubber band over the 17 points, which shows that the linear fit is worse, but not much worse, than that of the curve. If there is so little difference, does it matter whether we use a linear or a log-linear equation?

There are situations in which it matters a great deal, which will be illustrated with an example. A monopolist produces one good, the cost of which varies linearly with output. Hence, the cost function is of the form $c_0 + cq$, where q is output (which will be identified with sales) and c is marginal cost per unit of output. Gross revenue is thus pq, p being the price charged by the monopolist, so that his profit is

$$(17.3) \qquad P = (p - c)q - c_0$$

where q (sales) is a function of p. The monopolist's objective is to set the price p so that profit P is maximized. He is particularly interested in the following question: If marginal cost c increases (because of wage increases or price increases of raw materials), how does this affect the profit-maximizing price?

We shall answer this question for two specifications of the demand function. One is linear,

$$(17.4) \qquad q = \beta_0 + \beta p \qquad\qquad \beta_0 > 0,\ \beta < 0$$

and the other is the constant-elasticity function:

$$(17.5) \qquad q = Ap^\eta \qquad\qquad A > 0,\ \eta < -1$$

For (17.4) we obtain the profit-maximizing price by differentiating (17.3), with $\beta_0 + \beta p$ substituted for q, with respect to p and equating the derivative to zero. This yields

$$(17.6) \qquad p = \frac{\beta_0}{-2\beta} + \frac{1}{2}c$$

which shows that if marginal cost increases by one dollar, the profit-maximizing price increases by one-half dollar.

When we proceed similarly for (17.5), we obtain

$$(17.7) \qquad p = \frac{\eta}{\eta + 1}c$$

We have $\eta/(\eta + 1) > 1$ because $\eta < -1$ [see (17.5)], so that the log-linear demand equation implies that a one-dollar increase in marginal cost raises the profit-maximizing price by more than one dollar, that is, by more than twice the amount which we obtained from (17.6) for the linear demand equation. The inequality $\eta < -1$ ensures that we have a profit maximum; for proofs of the above statements, see Problems 2 and 3.

Two Alternative Explanatory Variables

Suppose that the analyst compares two specifications, one which describes the dependent variable as a linear function of an explanatory variable x,

$$(17.8) \qquad y_i = \beta_0 + \beta x_i + \epsilon_i \qquad\qquad i = 1, \dots, n$$

and a second which expresses y as a linear function of a different variable x':

$$(17.9) \qquad y_i = \beta'_0 + \beta' x'_i + \epsilon'_i \qquad\qquad i = 1, \ldots, n$$

Suppose that one of these two specifications is correct but that the analyst does not know which. How should he choose? Note that we may have $x' = \log_e x$ or $x' = e^x$ or $x' = \sqrt{x}$, in which case the choice between (17.8) and (17.9) is that between alternative functional forms of the relation which describes y in terms of x.

Let us assume that (17.8) is the correct specification and also that $\epsilon_1, \ldots, \epsilon_n$ are uncorrelated random variables with zero mean and variance σ^2 and that the values taken by x and x' are nonstochastic. We consider the LS coefficients of the incorrect specification (17.9),

$$(17.10) \qquad b' = \frac{\sum_{i=1}^{n} (x'_i - \bar{x}')(y_i - \bar{y})}{\sum_{i=1}^{n} (x'_i - \bar{x}')^2}, \qquad b'_0 = \bar{y} - b'\bar{x}'$$

so that $e'_i = y_i - b'_0 - b'x'_i$ is the ith LS residual. We state without proof that the expectation of the sum of their squares is

$$(17.11) \qquad \varepsilon\left(\sum_{i=1}^{n} e'^2_i\right) = (n-2)\sigma^2 + (1-r^2)\beta^2 \sum_{i=1}^{n} (x_i - \bar{x})^2$$

where r is the correlation coefficient of x and x'. This result is a special case of a more general proposition proved by Theil (1971, p. 543).

We conclude from (17.11) that, except for the case $r = \pm 1$, the LS residual sum of squares of the incorrect specification (17.9) has an expectation larger than $(n-2)\sigma^2$. Hence, when we divide this residual sum of squares by the number of degrees of freedom, which is $n-2$ for (17.9), the ratio thus obtained has an expectation exceeding σ^2 except when $r = \pm 1$. But we know from (5.43) and (5.44) that, for the correct specification (17.8), this ratio is s^2 with an expectation equal to σ^2. Therefore, except when the competing variables x and x' are perfectly correlated ($r = \pm 1$), the residual-variance estimator of the incorrect specification has an expectation exceeding that of the correct specification.

The Residual-Variance Criterion

More generally, consider alternative regressions of the same dependent variable on different sets of explanatory variables, one of which represents the correct specification. For each specification a residual-variance estimate is computed by dividing the residual sum of squares by the number of degrees of freedom. The selection of the specification with the smallest residual-variance estimate can be justified by means of the following proposition: If the correct specification has uncorrelated disturbances with zero mean and variance σ^2 and if the values of the explanatory variables of all specifications are nonstochastic, the residual-variance estimator of the correct specification has an expectation which is never larger than that of an incorrect specification. For a proof, see Theil (1971, p. 543); for extensions, see Schmidt (1973, 1974) and Ebbeler (1975).

REMARKS:

(1) The residual-variance criterion for the selection of a specification is widely used but, like any other statistical criterion, it is not a foolproof instrument. For any particular sample we may have a residual-variance estimate of the correct specification which exceeds that of an incorrect specification, so that the criterion makes the wrong choice for that sample.

(2) For each specification we divide the LS residual sum of squares by the number of degrees of freedom. Note that different specifications have different degrees of freedom when they adjust different numbers of coefficients.

(3) The residual-variance criterion presupposes that the competing specifications have the same dependent variable [y in (17.8) and (17.9)]. The case of different dependent variables is considered in the next subsection.

(4) If the analyst considers *many* alternative specifications and if he selects the one with the smallest residual-variance estimate, he should expect that this estimate tends to be well below σ^2. Least squares minimizes the residual sum of squares; we divide this sum by the number of degrees of freedom, rather than the number of observations, in order to estimate σ^2 unbiasedly, but this unbiasedness holds only when we know the correct specification. If the analyst is persistent enough to run 10 or 20 alternative regressions, he is advised to presume that the smallest residual-variance estimate underestimates σ^2. This has implications for the multiple correlation coefficient of the regression selected, as will be argued in the subsection immediately following the next.

The Residual-Variance Criterion for Different Dependent Variables

For the linear specification (17.2) of the demand equation for textile, the residual sum of squares is 433. For the log-linear specification (17.1), it is .00257 in five decimal places [see the discussion preceding (8.39)], which is of a different order of magnitude. In fact, the two numbers are not comparable at all, since 433 refers to residuals of textile consumption and .00257 to residuals of the logarithm of textile consumption.

The following procedure achieves comparability. We compute the LS adjusted values $\hat{T}_1, \ldots, \hat{T}_n$ from the linear specification (17.2), take their logarithms, and compute the sum of the squares of the deviations of these logarithms from the corresponding observed values of the logarithm of textile consumption per capita:

$$(17.12) \qquad \sum_{i=1}^{n} (\log_{10} \hat{T}_i - \log_{10} T_i)^2$$

This yields .00432, which is shown in Table 23 at the top of the second column. This number exceeds .00257, the LS residual sum of squares of the log-linear

TABLE 23

Residual sums of squares with different dependent variables

	Sum of squares of deviations from	
	T_i	$\log_{10} T_i$
Demand for textile		
Linear regression	433	.00432
Log-linear regression	277	.00257
Problem 5		
Linear regression	.00940	.000795
Log-linear regression	.01396	.000555

specification (the second entry in the same column), so that the latter specification is preferable if our criterion is goodness of fit with respect to the logarithm of textile consumption per capita.

However, this criterion may be presumed to be prejudiced in favor of the log-linear specification, because the number .00257 results from direct minimization, whereas .00432 is obtained by minimizing something else and doing some additional computations. To resolve this issue, we replace the above criterion by goodness of fit with respect to the dependent variable of (17.2). Thus, we take antilogs of the LS adjusted values of the log-linear regression (17.1) and compute the sum of squares of the deviations of these antilogs from the corresponding observed values of textile consumption per capita. This yields 277, which is less than the LS residual sum of squares 433 of the linear regression (see the first column of Table 23). Hence, the log-linear regression has a better fit according to both criteria.

REMARKS:

(1) The ratio $433/277 \approx 1.56$ of the entries in the first column is smaller than $.00432/.00257 \approx 1.68$ of those in the second column. This confirms that the linear specification fares a little better relative to the log-linear specification when the criterion used is goodness of fit with respect to its dependent variable (textile consumption per capita) rather than with respect to the logarithm of this variable.

(2) There are cases in which the two ratios are on opposite sides of 1, so that the two comparisons yield opposite conclusions. An example is given in Problem 5.

(3) In the above discussion we paid no attention to degrees of freedom, which may be justified in this case by the fact that both specifications of the demand equation for textile adjust the same number of coefficients. If this is not so, it is good practice always to divide the sums of squares of the deviations for each specification by the excess of the number of observations over the number of coefficients adjusted. However, there is no formal justification for this proce-

dure when the deviations are obtained indirectly, as is the case for (17.12) under the linear specification (17.2).

The Residual-Variance and the Multiple-Correlation Criterion

For $n - 3$ degrees of freedom, consider $\bar{R}^2$ defined in (9.30):

$$(17.13) \qquad 1 - \bar{R}^2 = \frac{[1/(n - 3)] \sum\limits_{i=1}^{n} e_i^2}{[1/(n - 1)] \sum\limits_{i=1}^{n} (y_i - \bar{y})^2}$$

Since the right-hand numerator is the residual-variance estimate, the criterion of the smallest residual-variance estimate is thus equivalent to that of the smallest $1 - \bar{R}^2$, or the largest $\bar{R}^2$, provided that the competing specifications use the same dependent variable. This proviso is important; if one specification uses y and another log y as the dependent variable, this affects the right-hand denominator in (17.13), which makes the two $\bar{R}^2$'s incomparable.

Recall from remark (4) on page 271 that the smallest residual-variance estimate tends to be below σ^2. If the $\bar{R}^2$'s are comparable (see above), this is equivalent to the statement that $\bar{R}^2$ of the selected specification tends to be on the high side. In addition, applied econometric studies that are published tend to be those which are successful, with goodness of fit being among the more important criteria for success. There is no reason for frustration when an $\bar{R}^2$ is obtained that falls short of the $\bar{R}^2$'s of published studies in the same area of application.

Indeed, statistical criteria such as the smallest residual-variance estimate should not be considered as the only tools for selecting the specification. The analyst may be convinced on a priori grounds that one specification is more realistic than another, in which case he should feel justified in using the former even when the latter has a somewhat smaller residual-variance estimate. The real test of the specification selected is provided by prediction based on an independent set of data. It is not self-evident that selections exclusively based on the smallest residual-variance estimate yield the most accurate predictions.

17.2 Regression Strategies

The final remarks in the previous section, on prediction based on an independent set of data, provide an appropriate start for further developments. When the observations are plentiful, a sensible approach is to divide them into three parts. One set of observations should be used for the specification of the mathematical form of the relation. The second set should be used for the estimation of the parameters of this specification, and the third for predictions based on the estimated equation to verify whether the specification selected is acceptable.

Testing and Estimating Based on the Same Sample

A major problem with the approach just mentioned is the fact that the observations are frequently less than plentiful. The analyst will then feel that he would do three poor jobs, each based on very few observations, if he followed this advice. Thus, he decides to use the same set of data for the selection of the specification and for the estimation.

Using the same sample for these two purposes affects the sampling distribution of the estimators. To show this, we consider the quadratic specification

$$(17.14) \qquad y_i = \beta_0 + \beta_1 x_i + \beta_2 x_i^2 + \epsilon_i \qquad\qquad i = 1, \ldots, n$$

where the ϵ_i's are independent normal variates with zero mean and variance σ^2. Suppose that the correct specification is linear ($\beta_2 = 0$). Thus, if the null hypothesis $\beta_2 = 0$ is verified by means of a t test at the 5 percent significance level, the correct specification is rejected with probability .05. If this specification is rejected (which happens 5 percent of the time), we run a multiple regression of y on x and x^2; if it is accepted (which happens 95 percent of the time), we run a simple regression of y on x only. Clearly, the sampling distribution of the estimators is affected when we proceed in this way. The LS coefficient estimators of the correct specification have the familiar normal sampling distribution only if this specification is used 100 percent of the time, not 95 percent of the time. The distribution of these estimators is affected by the fact that a statistical test was performed on the same data prior to the estimation.

Regression Strategies

The following situation is more complicated but, unfortunately, quite common in econometrics. The analyst has a list of K explanatory variables but presumes that several of these may actually be redundant because their coefficients may be zero. However, he is confident that the first $\bar{K}$ variables have nonzero coefficients. His confidence is less for the $(\bar{K} + 1)$st variable, still less for the $(\bar{K} + 2)$nd, and so on. Thus, he should obviously introduce the first $\bar{K}$ variables in his regression, but how should he handle the $K - \bar{K}$ other variables? Note that some of these variables may be squares, products, logarithms, etc., of other variables, so that the situation described here includes that in which there is uncertainty about the mathematical form of the relation.

One approach uses, as a first step, a regression on the first $\bar{K} + 1$ variables and a test of the hypothesis that the $(\bar{K} + 1)$st variable has a zero coefficient. If this hypothesis is accepted, the analyst deletes this variable and also the variables numbered $\bar{K} + 2, \ldots, K$ (because he has even less confidence in nonzero coefficients of these variables). Hence, in this case, the final product consists of a regression on the first $\bar{K}$ variables only.

If the hypothesis of a zero coefficient of the $(\bar{K} + 1)$st variable is rejected, the analyst runs a regression on the first $\bar{K} + 2$ variables and tests whether the coefficient of the $(\bar{K} + 2)$nd variable is zero. If that hypothesis is accepted, the final product is a regression on the first $\bar{K} + 1$ variables; if it is rejected, the analyst runs a regression on the first $\bar{K} + 3$ variables, and so on. Thus, the final result is a regression on the first $\bar{K} + p$ variables, where p $(0 \leq p \leq K - \bar{K})$ is such that the $(\bar{K} + 1)$st, . . . , $(\bar{K} + p)$th variables have significant coefficients in the successive regression attempts, whereas the $(\bar{K} + p + 1)$st variable has a coefficient which is not significantly different from zero.

A *strategy* is any form of decision making in which each successive decision is made dependent on the information available at the time when this decision is taken. The procedure described above may be called a *regression strategy*, since each new computation is made dependent on the outcome of its predecessor.

Comparing Different Regression Strategies

The regression strategy of the previous subsection is by no means the only possible one. The analyst may also start from the set of all K explanatory variables and then reduce the size of this set step by step. If the regression on all K variables yields a significant coefficient of the Kth variable, this regression is the final result. Otherwise the Kth variable is deleted and a regression on $K - 1$ variables is computed. It is accepted as the final result when the $(K - 1)$st variable has a significant coefficient but is rejected in favor of a regression on the first $K - 2$ variables in the opposite case, and so on.

Regression strategies have become very popular because of the availability of computer programs (*stepwise regressions*) which implement such strategies automatically. However, they present considerable theoretical problems. What is the best regression strategy? What is the best significance level in each step of a strategy? Which criterion should be chosen for best? It appears that most properties of regression strategies involve the values of unknown parameters, which means that they provide little guidance for users of this approach.

Given these difficulties, it is wise to proceed conservatively in the interpretation of the standard errors that are obtained from the final regression of a regression strategy. These standard errors may overstate the reliability of the corresponding point estimate, so that a 95 percent confidence coefficient may actually only be, say, an 85 percent confidence coefficient. In the case of hypothesis testing it is similarly wise to presume that errors of the first kind occur more frequently than the significance level indicates.

More Warnings

The example of the monopolist in Section 17.1 has shown [see (17.6) and (17.7)] that different functional forms can have quite different implications, which illustrates the importance of an adequate selection of the functional form. This applies particularly when the number of explanatory variables is large, because the number of possible mishaps increases fast when the number of variables increases.

The applied econometric literature contains numerous estimated equations with close to 10 variables. Such equations deserve the reader's suspicion. They are frequently the product of an unimaginative use of a computer, which (if properly instructed) faithfully produces what the analyst wants it to do. Too many applied econometricians interpret the linearity of the standard linear model in the sense that each explanatory variable should be introduced linearly in its original form, which can lead to numerous misspecifications when there are many variables. When such equations are also the result of experimentation with many alternative explanatory variables, t ratios and similar test statistics have doubtful validity. The problem is particularly serious for cross-sectional data on large numbers of households, because a large number of observations creates the illusion that many coefficients can be estimated with adequate precision. Regressions based on time series data have their own special problems, since their disturbances are frequently correlated (see Section 19.2).

Of course, when we have cross-sectional data on a large number of households, we can estimate many coefficients *if* we know the correct form of the specification (and if there are no multicollinearity problems). But usually we do not know the correct form. It is then much better to proceed as described in the opening paragraph of this section, viz., by dividing the sample into subsamples and using one of these for experimentation with alternative explanatory variables and functional forms. Numerous functional forms can be handled by the standard linear model (see Section 13.1), and relations which are nonlinear in their parameters can frequently be estimated by means of numerical methods (see Section 15.3).

17.3 Specification Analysis

There are situations in which the analyst knows that he commits a specification error, particularly when he needs an explanatory variable on which no data are available. For example, let investment be a function of anticipated profits. If there are no data on anticipated profits, the analyst may decide to replace this variable by observed (realized) profits, which implies the use of a misspecified explanatory variable. Alternatively, he may decide to delete this variable from the list of explanatory variables altogether; this is the case of an omitted variable. The objective of specification analysis is to explore the implications of such specification errors.

A Misspecified Variable

We return to the correct specification (17.8) and the incorrect specification (17.9), with x now interpreted as the variable on which no observations are available and x' as its replacement. We are particularly interested in the LS coefficient b' defined in (17.10), and use the correct specification (17.8) to write its numerator as

$$\sum_{i=1}^{n} (x'_i - \bar{x}')(y_i - \bar{y}) = \sum_{i=1}^{n} (x'_i - \bar{x}')[\beta_0 + \beta x_i + \epsilon_i - (\beta_0 + \beta\bar{x} + \bar{\epsilon})]$$
$$= \beta \sum_{i=1}^{n} (x'_i - \bar{x}')(x_i - \bar{x}) + \sum_{i=1}^{n} (x'_i - \bar{x}')(\epsilon_i - \bar{\epsilon})$$

where $\bar{\epsilon}$ is the arithmetic mean of $\epsilon_1, \ldots, \epsilon_n$. When we divide the expression in the second line by the denominator of b', we obtain

$$(17.15) \qquad b' = \beta \frac{\sum_{i=1}^{n} (x'_i - \bar{x}')(x_i - \bar{x})}{\sum_{i=1}^{n} (x'_i - \bar{x}')^2} + \frac{\sum_{i=1}^{n} (x'_i - \bar{x}')(\epsilon_i - \bar{\epsilon})}{\sum_{i=1}^{n} (x'_i - \bar{x}')^2}$$

If the values taken by x' are constants and if the ϵ_i's have zero expectation, the second term on the right also has zero expectation, so that

$$(17.16) \qquad \mathcal{E}b' = p\beta$$

where

$$(17.17) \qquad p = \frac{\sum_{i=1}^{n} (x'_i - \bar{x}')(x_i - \bar{x})}{\sum_{i=1}^{n} (x'_i - \bar{x}')^2}$$

Note that p may be interpreted as the slope coefficient of the LS regression of the correct explanatory variable x on its replacement x':

$$(17.18) \qquad x_i = \text{constant} + px'_i + \text{residual} \qquad i = 1, \ldots, n$$

We can thus conclude from (17.16) that the expectation of the LS coefficient b' coincides with the slope β of the correct specification (17.8) if and only if the slope p of the regression (17.18) equals 1. This regression is known as the *auxiliary regression* of specification analysis. The usefulness of specification analysis is determined by how much the analyst knows about the coefficients of such an auxiliary regression. Typically, a substitute variable is positively correlated with the variable which it replaces. In that case $p > 0$ in (17.18), so that (17.16) implies that the expectation of b' has the same sign as β.

An Omitted Variable

Next consider the case of two explanatory variables without constant term:

$$(17.19) \qquad y_i = \beta_1 x_{1i} + \beta_2 x_{2i} + \epsilon_i \qquad i = 1, \ldots, n$$

We assume that no data are available on x_2 and that the analyst decides to delete this variable. Thus, he runs a regression of y on x_1, which yields a slope $b = \sum_i x_{1i} y_i / \sum_i x_{1i}^2$. Using the correct specification (17.19), we find that the numerator of this b equals

$$\sum_{i=1}^{n} x_{1i}y_i = \sum_{i=1}^{n} x_{1i}(\beta_1 x_{1i} + \beta_2 x_{2i} + \epsilon_i)$$

$$= \beta_1 \sum_{i=1}^{n} x_{1i}^2 + \beta_2 \sum_{i=1}^{n} x_{1i}x_{2i} + \sum_{i=1}^{n} x_{1i}\epsilon_i$$

Thus, by dividing by $\sum_i x_{1i}^2$, we find that b can be written as

(17.20)
$$b = \beta_1 + \beta_2 \frac{\sum_{i=1}^{n} x_{1i}x_{2i}}{\sum_{i=1}^{n} x_{1i}^2} + \frac{\sum_{i=1}^{n} x_{1i}\epsilon_i}{\sum_{i=1}^{n} x_{1i}^2}$$

We take the expectation,

(17.21)
$$\mathcal{E}b = \beta_1 + p^*\beta_2$$

where $p^* = \sum_i x_{1i}x_{2i}/\sum_i x_{1i}^2$ is the LS coefficient of the auxiliary regression

(17.22)
$$x_{2i} = p^*x_{1i} + \text{residual} \qquad\qquad i = 1, \ldots, n$$

We conclude from (17.21) that if $p^* = 0$, the LS coefficient b of x_1 in the simple regression of y on this variable has an expectation equal to the coefficient β_1 of the same variable in the correct specification (17.19). This special case should cause no surprise, since $p^* = 0$ implies $\sum_i x_{1i}x_{2i} = 0$ and since (7.30) for $K = 2$ (rather than $K = 3$) shows that b is then identical to the LS estimator of β_1 in (17.19). If $p^* \neq 0$, the expectation of b differs from β_1 and the difference $\mathcal{E}b - \beta_1 = p^*\beta_2$ is the *specification bias* of b, which is thus proportional to both p^* and β_2. If it is known that x_2 has a positive effect on y, $\beta_2 > 0$ in (17.19), the specification bias of b is positive when the variables x_1 and x_2 have a positive product sum $\sum_i x_{1i}x_{2i}$ (which is obviously true if x_1 and x_2 are positive variables). Similarly, in the case of the previous subsection, with x' used as replacement of x in (17.8), we can conclude from (17.16) that the specification bias of b' equals $(p - 1)\beta$.

An Omitted Variable with Constant Term

We extend (17.19) so that it contains a constant term:

(17.23)
$$y_i = \beta_0 + \beta_1 x_{1i} + \beta_2 x_{2i} + \epsilon_i \qquad\qquad i = 1, \ldots, n$$

Again we assume that x_2 is deleted. The regression computed is now that of y on x_1 with a constant term, yielding the following slope coefficient:

(17.24)
$$b = \frac{\sum_{i=1}^{n} (x_{1i} - \bar{x}_1)(y_i - \bar{y})}{\sum_{i=1}^{n} (x_{1i} - \bar{x}_1)^2}$$

The reader should verify, by substituting (17.23) in (17.24), that the expectation of this b satisfies (17.21) but with p^* now defined as

$$(17.25) \qquad p^* = \frac{\sum_{i=1}^{n} (x_{1i} - \bar{x}_1)(x_{2i} - \bar{x}_2)}{\sum_{i=1}^{n} (x_{1i} - \bar{x}_1)^2}$$

which is the slope coefficient of the auxiliary regression (17.22) with a constant term added:

$$(17.26) \qquad x_{2i} = \text{constant} + p^* x_{1i} + \text{residual} \qquad i = 1, \ldots, n$$

We conclude from (17.21) and (17.25) that the condition for a zero specification bias is now $\sum_i (x_{1i} - \bar{x}_1)(x_{2i} - \bar{x}_2) = 0$, which means that the observations on the two explanatory variables are uncorrelated. In many cases the analyst knows that these observations are not uncorrelated. He may even know that they are positively correlated in spite of the fact that he has no observations on x_2. For example, let i in (17.23) be the ith household in a sample of n households, and let x_1 be income and x_2 net worth. In most cases income and net worth are positively correlated, which implies $p^* > 0$. Then, if $\beta_2 > 0$, the LS coefficient (17.24) is subject to a positive specification bias [see (17.21)].

The General Procedure of Specification Analysis

The three examples discussed above illustrate the procedure of specification analysis. One specification is assumed correct; given this assumption, we analyze the implications of the use of a different specification for the expectations of the LS coefficients of the latter specification. The tool consists of one or several auxiliary regressions which describe each explanatory variable of the correct specification in terms of those of the specification that is actually used. Note that these auxiliary regressions need not have any particular economic meaning; they are just tools. Also note that, in the examples of the three previous subsections, the approach assumes that the explanatory variables of all specifications take nonstochastic values. The approach can be extended for random values, but this will not be pursued here.

As stated earlier, the usefulness of specification analysis depends on the analyst's knowledge of the coefficients of the auxiliary regressions. An application to observational errors follows in Section 17.4, and a more extensive application to aggregation analysis in Sections 18.1 and 18.2. For other examples and extensions, see Theil (1957a; 1971, pp. 548–556) and Griliches (1957).

More on the Rotterdam Model

There are situations in which we can derive useful results from the approach of specification analysis *without* specifying the true form of the relation. We shall illustrate this for the ith demand equation of the Rotterdam Model given in (14.40) and reproduced here:

$$(17.27) \qquad \bar{w}_{it} Dq_{it} = \mu_i DQ_t + \sum_{j=1}^{N} \pi_{ij} Dp_{jt} + \epsilon_{it}$$

To simplify the discussion, we assume that prices remain unchanged, $Dp_{jt} = 0$ for all pairs (j, t), although a weaker assumption is actually sufficient (see Problem 10). Hence, (17.27) is simplified to

$$(17.28) \qquad \bar{w}_{it} Dq_{it} = \mu_i DQ_t + \epsilon_{it}$$

This equation contains only one unknown parameter, the marginal share μ_i, which we estimate by LS,

$$(17.29) \qquad \hat{\mu}_i = \frac{\sum_t DQ_t(\bar{w}_{it} Dq_{it})}{\sum_t (DQ_t)^2}$$

where the summations over t are over all observations of the sample.

The Rotterdam Model treats the μ_i's and π_{ij}'s of (17.27) as constants. Suppose that this constancy is an incorrect specification and that the marginal share in (17.28) actually varies over time:

$$(17.30) \qquad \bar{w}_{it} Dq_{it} = \mu_{it} DQ_t + \epsilon_{it}$$

The marginal share in this equation may be a function of the levels of income and prices or of any other variables. In fact, (17.30) is not a specification of the true relation at all; it just states that the marginal share may vary over time, as is indicated by the subscript t of μ_{it}.

As in the earlier examples of this section, we are interested in the expectation of the coefficient of the incorrect specification, which in this case is the expectation of the LS estimator (17.29) of the specification (17.28). Thus, we substitute (17.30) in the right-hand numerator of (17.29):

$$\sum_t DQ_t(\bar{w}_{it} Dq_{it}) = \sum_t (DQ_t)^2 \mu_{it} + \sum_t (DQ_t) \epsilon_{it}$$

The second term on the right has zero expectation when the DQ_t's are constants and ϵ_{it} has zero expectation. Hence, taking the expectation of (17.29) gives

$$(17.31) \qquad \mathcal{E}\hat{\mu}_i = \frac{\sum_t (DQ_t)^2 \mu_{it}}{\sum_t (DQ_t)^2}$$

This shows that the expectation of the LS estimator of the ith marginal share is a weighted average of the values taken by this share in the successive periods, with weights proportional to the square of the log-change in real income. This simple result is intuitively easy to understand. If real income does not change from $t - 1$ to t, $DQ_t = 0$, the associated marginal share μ_{it} is ineffective because it is multiplied by zero in (17.30) and, hence, does not affect the left-hand variable of (17.30). If, on the other hand, real income changes substantially from $t - 1$ to t (either upward or downward), the associated μ_{it} is quite effective, which is measured in (17.31) by a weight that increases when DQ_t moves away from zero in either direction.

*17.4   Observational Errors

In the opening paragraph of Section 17.2 we painted a bright picture on how to proceed when the observations are plentiful. This picture is subject to the obvious proviso that the observations should be of "good quality." Data on many economic variables are of modest or even poor quality. This leads to the problem of observational errors, the solution of which is difficult.

An Approach Based on Specification Analysis

We shall start with the simple case in which the dependent variable is proportional to one explanatory variable, apart from a random disturbance:

$$(17.32) \qquad y_i = \beta x_i + \epsilon_i \qquad\qquad i = 1, \ldots, n$$

Let x' be the observed version of x, so that

$$(17.33) \qquad \xi_i = x_i' - x_i \qquad\qquad i = 1, \ldots, n$$

is the ith observational error. We apply specification analysis by running a regression of y on x' and expressing the expectation of the slope coefficient of this regression in terms of that of the auxiliary regression. The reader should verify that this is simply a matter of suppressing constant terms in the first example of Section 17.3 and that the specification bias equals $(p - 1)\beta$, where

$$(17.34) \qquad p = \frac{\sum_{i=1}^{n} x_i x_i'}{\sum_{i=1}^{n} x_i'^2}$$

which is the slope coefficient of the auxiliary regression of x on x' without constant term.

To evaluate (17.34), we write its numerator as

$$\sum_{i=1}^{n} x_i x_i' = \sum_{i=1}^{n} x_i'^2 - \sum_{i=1}^{n} (x_i' - x_i)x_i' = \sum_{i=1}^{n} x_i'^2 - \sum_{i=1}^{n} \xi_i(x_i + \xi_i)$$

where the last step is based on (17.33). Substitution of the third member in (17.34) gives

$$(17.35) \qquad p = 1 - \frac{\sum_{i=1}^{n} \xi_i x_i}{\sum_{i=1}^{n} x_i'^2} - \frac{\sum_{i=1}^{n} \xi_i^2}{\sum_{i=1}^{n} x_i'^2}$$

Suppose that the pairs (ξ_i, x_i) for $i = 1, \ldots, n$ (the observational errors and the true values of x) are uncorrelated. The second right-hand term in (17.35) then vanishes, so that $p - 1$ becomes minus the ratio of two sums of squares (for ξ and for x'). Since this ratio is positive for nonzero ξ's, we conclude that the specification bias $(p - 1)\beta$ is in the zero direction.

Random Observational Errors

Most errors-in-variables models proceed under the assumption that such errors are random. Accordingly, we interpret x_i in (17.32) and (17.33) as non-stochastic but ξ_i and x_i' as random. We shall also assume that the dependent variable is subject to a random observational error η_i,

$$(17.36) \qquad \eta_i = y_i' - y_i \qquad\qquad i = 1, \ldots, n$$

so that the relation between the observed variables is

$$(17.37) \qquad y_i' = \beta x_i' + (\epsilon_i + \eta_i - \beta \xi_i) \qquad\qquad i = 1, \ldots, n$$

To simplify the analysis of the next two subsections, we assume that the disturbances $\epsilon_1, \ldots, \epsilon_n$ and the observational errors $\xi_1, \ldots, \xi_n$ and $\eta_1, \ldots, \eta_n$ are $3n$ independent random variables with zero mean and standard deviations σ_ϵ, σ_ξ, and σ_η, respectively.

Three Special Cases

(1) If $\sigma_\xi = \sigma_\eta = 0$, the observational errors ξ_i and η_i have zero mean and zero variance, so that they vanish with unit probability. The standard linear model can then be applied to (17.32) directly.

(2) If $\sigma_\xi = 0$ but $\sigma_\eta > 0$, the explanatory variable is not subject to measurement error but the dependent variable is. We can then write (17.37) as

$$(17.38) \qquad y_i' = \beta x_i + (\epsilon_i + \eta_i) \qquad\qquad i = 1, \ldots, n$$

and run a regression of y' on x. The reader should verify that this yields an unbiased slope estimator $b' = \sum_i x_i y_i' / \sum_i x_i^2$ with variance

$$(17.39) \qquad \operatorname{var} b' = \frac{\sigma_\epsilon^2 + \sigma_\eta^2}{\sum\limits_{i=1}^{n} x_i^2}$$

This exceeds the variance (5.17) of the corresponding estimator based on data without observational errors, which reflects the fact that there is a penalty on imperfect measurement.

(3) Next consider the case $\sigma_\epsilon = \sigma_\eta = 0$ but $\sigma_\xi > 0$, so that there are zero disturbances [hence, (17.32) is "undisturbed"] and zero measurement errors in the dependent variable but nonzero errors in the explanatory variable. We can now write (17.37) in the form $y_i = \beta x_i' - \beta \xi_i$. If $\beta \neq 0$, this is equivalent to

$$(17.40) \qquad x_i' = \frac{1}{\beta} y_i + \xi_i \qquad\qquad i = 1, \ldots, n$$

Since y_i has no measurement errors ($\sigma_\eta = 0$) and contains no disturbance component ($\sigma_\epsilon = 0$), it can be treated as a constant. Therefore, given the assumption that $\xi_1, \ldots, \xi_n$ are independent random variables with zero mean and variance

σ_ξ^2, the standard linear model is applicable to (17.40) with the role of the two variables reversed. That is, a best linear unbiased estimator of $1/\beta$ is obtained by running a regression of x_i' on y_i for $i = 1, \ldots, n$. Note that this amounts to measuring the deviations in Figure 3 on page 18 horizontally rather than vertically and minimizing the sum of the squares of the deviations thus measured. Also note that "linear" of best linear unbiased means linear in $y_1, \ldots, y_n$, not linear in $x_1', \ldots, x_n'$.

Case (3) can thus be handled straightforwardly, but note that we made the assumption of zero disturbances ($\sigma_\epsilon = 0$). This is quite restrictive, since most behavioral and technical relations are not exact even when their variables are measured without error.

The General Case

The case in which the ϵ's, η's, and ξ's are all nonzero is much more difficult. One problem is that the LS slope estimator obtained from (17.37) is not consistent. This estimator can be written as

$$(17.41) \qquad \frac{\sum_{i=1}^{n} x_i' y_i'}{\sum_{i=1}^{n} x_i'^2} = \beta + \frac{(1/n) \sum_{i=1}^{n} (x_i + \xi_i)(\epsilon_i + \eta_i - \beta \xi_i)}{(1/n) \sum_{i=1}^{n} (x_i + \xi_i)^2}$$

where the equal sign is based on (17.33) and (17.37). The numerator on the right equals the sum of six terms: the arithmetic averages (over $i = 1, \ldots, n$) of $x_i \epsilon_i$, $x_i \eta_i$, $-\beta x_i \xi_i$, $\xi_i \epsilon_i$, $\xi_i \eta_i$, and $-\beta \xi_i^2$. Under appropriate conditions, these terms all converge in probability to zero as $n \to \infty$ except the last, which converges to $-\beta \sigma_\xi^2$ and is the cause of the inconsistency. If $(1/n) \sum_i x_i^2$ converges to a positive limit m as $n \to \infty$, the probability limit of the LS slope estimator (17.41) is

$$(17.42) \qquad \plim_{n \to \infty} \frac{\sum_{i=1}^{n} x_i' y_i'}{\sum_{i=1}^{n} x_i'^2} = \beta \frac{m}{m + \sigma_\xi^2}$$

which has the same sign as β but is closer to zero if $\sigma_\xi \neq 0$. Note that this result is similar to that obtained below (17.35) from specification analysis. For a proof of (17.42), see Theil (1971, pp. 608, 614).

The obvious question is whether a more attractive estimator of β is available. This appears to be a very difficult problem. A major complication is the fact that the true values of the explanatory variable $(x_1, \ldots, x_n)$ act as unknown parameters, the number of which increases when the number of observations (n) increases. The method of maximum likelihood yields attractive estimators for large n in many situations (see Section 15.3), but it yields no useful result for (17.37).

A Reformulation of the Specification

Given these difficulties, the analyst may want to consider whether it is possible to modify the specification in a plausible manner so that the errors-in-variables problem is avoided. We shall illustrate this by means of a simple version of Friedman's (1957) theory of the consumption function.

The consumer's income is assumed to consist of a permanent and a transitory component. The transitory component is that part of his income which the consumer considers as accidental; his consumption decision is determined by the permanent component. We write x_i for the latter component in year i and y_i for consumption and assume that these variables are proportional apart from a random disturbance, $y_i = \beta x_i + \epsilon_i$. Permanent income cannot be measured; observed income (x_i') differs from permanent income (x_i) by the transitory component $\xi_i = x_i' - x_i$, which is assumed to be random. The relationship in terms of observed income is therefore

$$(17.43) \qquad y_i = \beta x_i' + (\epsilon_i - \beta \xi_i)$$

This may be viewed as a relation containing an explanatory variable that is subject to random observational errors. Hence, we have the same problems as those described in the previous subsection.

Two considerations should convince us to reconsider this specification. First, when we combine the proportionality $y_i = \beta x_i + \epsilon_i$ with the assumption that the ϵ_i's have constant variance, the implication is that disturbances play a relatively smaller role in years with a high permanent income than in low-income years, which is probably not realistic. We can meet this objection by specifying the proportionality with a multiplicative disturbance, y_i being equal to βx_i multiplied by the exponent of a disturbance. This is equivalent to

$$(17.44) \qquad \log_e y_i = \log_e \beta + \log_e x_i + \epsilon_i'$$

Second, if the transitory component $\xi_i = x_i' - x_i$ is assumed to have constant variance, it will also play a relatively smaller role in high-income years. This problem can also be resolved by a multiplicative procedure. Write $x_i' = x_i(1 + T_i)$, where T_i is transitory income measured as a fraction of permanent income. Then take logarithms and write $\xi_i' = \log_e (1 + T_i)$,

$$\log_e x_i' = \log_e x_i + \xi_i'$$

On combining this with (17.44), we obtain

$$(17.45) \qquad \log_e \frac{y_i}{x_i'} = \log_e \beta + (\epsilon_i' - \xi_i')$$

Hence, if $\epsilon_i' - \xi_i'$ for $i = 1, \ldots, n$ are uncorrelated random variables with zero mean and constant variance, we can estimate $\log_e \beta$ by simply taking the arithmetic mean of $\log_e (y_i/x_i')$ over i.

Observational Errors and Multicollinearity

So far, we have confined ourselves to one explanatory variable with observational errors. The extension to several such variables is far more troublesome. For example, the simple solution for the case $\sigma_\epsilon = \sigma_\eta = 0$ described below (17.40) does not work when several explanatory variables are subject to error. The reason is that (17.40) uses such a variable as the left-hand variable, which can be done for one variable only.

When errors in one or several explanatory variables are combined with the problem of near-extreme multicollinearity among the observed values of these variables, the situation is even worse. Consider the following case of two explanatory variables and three observations:

$$(17.46) \qquad (x_{1i} - \bar{x}_1, x_{2i} - \bar{x}_2) = \begin{array}{ll} (\ 10, \quad 10) & (i = 1) \\ (-1, \quad\ \ 0) & (i = 2) \\ (-9, -10) & (i = 3) \end{array}$$

Suppose that these are observed values and that the true values of $x_{1i} - \bar{x}_1$ are 0 for $i = 2$ and -10 for $i = 3$, the four other numbers in (17.46) being correct. If we knew the truth, we would realize that there is extreme multicollinearity and refrain from estimating the equation. If we carry out the LS computations based on (17.46), we obtain numerical results which are obviously without any meaning.

Problems

Problems 1–5 refer to Section 17.1, 6 to Section 17.2, 7–11 to Section 17.3, and 12–16 to Section 17.4.

1 The eight points to the right of the vertical axis in Figure 32 all refer to years prior to 1931, and the nine points to the left of the vertical axis all refer to years after 1930. With this knowledge, verify that the evidence shown in the figure is in agreement with the hypothesis that (a) textile consumption per capita is a linear (not log-linear!) function of the relative textile price and (b) the slope of this function is steeper in the 1930s than in the 1920s. (*Note*: This alternative interpretation illustrates that 17 years of observations do not necessarily present conclusive evidence on the functional form of a relation.)

2 Verify that the first two derivatives of (17.3) are

$$\frac{dP}{dp} = q + (p - c)\frac{dq}{dp}, \qquad \frac{d^2P}{dp^2} = 2\frac{dq}{dp} + (p - c)\frac{d^2q}{dp^2}$$

and that the second-order maximum condition for P as a function of p

can be written as

$$2\frac{dq}{dp} + \frac{q}{-dq/dp}\frac{d^2q}{dp^2} < 0$$

where dq/dp and d^2q/dp^2 are evaluated at $dP/dp = 0$.

3 (*Continuation*) For (17.4), verify that $\beta < 0$ is the second-order maximum condition and that (17.6) gives the profit-maximizing price. For (17.5), prove that $\eta < -1$ is the second-order maximum condition and that (17.7) gives the profit-maximizing price.

4 Consider the following three alternative specifications:

$$y_i = \beta_0 + \beta \log_e x_i + \epsilon_i$$
$$y_i = \beta_0' + \beta_1 x_i + \beta_2 x_i^2 + \epsilon_i'$$
$$y_i = \beta_0'' + \frac{\beta''}{x_i} + \epsilon_i''$$

Explain how the residual-variance criterion is applied in this case as well as the underlying conditions.

5 Write T for the volume of textile consumption per capita and x for some explanatory variable. Consider the following $n = 3$ pairs of observations:

$$(x_1, T_1) = (1, 1), \qquad (x_2, T_2) = (4, 1.87), \qquad (x_3, T_3) = (9, 3)$$

Two alternative regressions are compared, linear and log-linear (logs to the base 10), which yields the four sums of squares of deviations shown in the last two lines of Table 23. Verify that one comparison favors the linear specification and the other the log-linear specification. [*Note*: If a definite choice is desired on the basis of these four numbers, the geometric mean of the ratios $940/1396 \approx .673$ and $795/555 \approx 1.432$ can be used. This geometric mean is the square root of $(.673)(1.432)$, which is .98 and hence in favor of the linear specification.]

6 Read the discussion below (17.14) on the problems of testing followed by estimation. Are there such problems in the analysis of Section 14.3?

7 Prove that if (17.23) is the correct specification (with x's that are constants and ϵ's that are random with zero mean), the expectation of the LS slope coefficient (17.24) satisfies (17.21) with p^* defined in (17.25).

8 Verify that all auxiliary regressions discussed in Section 17.3 describe explanatory variables of the correct specification as linear functions of the explanatory variables of the specification that is actually used. Also verify that the auxiliary regressions contain a constant term if and only if the specification used contains such a term.

9 Suppose that x_i' is random and correlated with ϵ_i. Is it then still true that the expectation of (17.15) yields (17.16)?

10 Suppose that all prices change proportionately from $t - 1$ to t. Prove that this implies $Dp_{jt} = k_t$ for $j = 1, \ldots, N$, where k_t is some number independent of j, and prove also that the substitution term in (17.27) then vanishes. [*Hint*: Consider (14.35).]

11 Why are there no auxiliary regressions in the case discussed in the last subsection of Section 17.3?

12 Verify that $b' = \sum_i x_i y_i' / \sum_i x_i^2$ is an unbiased estimator of β in (17.38) under the conditions stated below (17.37) and that its variance is as shown in (17.39). Also verify that the right-hand numerator in (17.39) is estimated unbiasedly by $\sum_i (y_i' - b' x_i)^2$ divided by $n - 1$.

13 Verify that the remark on Figure 3 made below (17.40) provides an answer to one of the questions raised in Section 2.4.

14 (*Continuation*) For (17.40), define

$$\frac{1}{b^*} = \frac{\sum\limits_{i=1}^{n} x_i' y_i}{\sum\limits_{i=1}^{n} y_i^2}, \qquad b = \frac{\sum\limits_{i=1}^{n} x_i' y_i}{\sum\limits_{i=1}^{n} x_i'^2}$$

Prove that b and b^* have the same sign and that b is closer to zero than b^*. (*Hint*: Consider the ratio b/b^*.)

15 (*Continuation*) Under the conditions stated below (17.40), prove that $1/b^*$ is an unbiased estimator of $1/\beta$ and that the variance of $1/b^*$ equals $\sigma_\xi^2 / \sum_i y_i^2$. Also prove the following proposition and state the conditions under which it is true: As $n \longrightarrow \infty$, the asymptotic distribution of b^* is normal with mean β and variance $\beta^4 \sigma_\xi^2 / \sum_i y_i^2$.

16 Prove that under the conditions stated below (17.45) this equation falls under the standard linear model with a constant term (equal to $\log_e \beta$) and without explanatory variables. Also prove that the estimator described below (17.45) is best linear unbiased, and derive the variance of this estimator.

chapter 18

Aggregation

Aggregation theory is concerned with the transition from micro- to macro-models. In Sections 18.1 and 18.2 this subject is approached by means of specification analysis. A different approach is described in Section 18.3.

*18.1 The Specification Approach to the Aggregation Problem

The Micromodel and the Macrovariables

Let y_{ci} be the consumption of sugar (in dollars) by the cth consumer in year i and x_{ci} his income in that year. There are N consumers in the economy, each of whom has a linear demand function of the form

$$(18.1) \qquad y_{ci} = \beta_{0c} + \beta_c x_{ci} + \epsilon_{ci} \qquad\qquad i = 1, \ldots, n$$

where $c = 1, \ldots, N$ and the ϵ_{ci}'s are random disturbances with zero expectation. The model (18.1) is our micromodel.

Our objective is to construct a macromodel for the demand for sugar in macrovariables (or per capita variables). Thus, we introduce y_i, the per capita consumption of sugar in year i, and x_i, per capita income in that year:

$$(18.2) \qquad y_i = \frac{1}{N} \sum_{c=1}^{N} y_{ci}, \qquad x_i = \frac{1}{N} \sum_{c=1}^{N} x_{ci}$$

By combining the equation for y_i with (18.1), we obtain

$$(18.3) \qquad y_i = \frac{1}{N} \sum_{c=1}^{N} (\beta_{0c} + \beta_c x_{ci} + \epsilon_{ci})$$

$$= \frac{1}{N} \sum_{c=1}^{N} \beta_{0c} + \frac{1}{N} \sum_{c=1}^{N} \beta_c x_{ci} + \frac{1}{N} \sum_{c=1}^{N} \epsilon_{ci}$$

The second line of (18.3) describes the per capita consumption of sugar as the sum of three terms. The first is a constant term, equal to the arithmetic mean of the constant terms of the individual demand equations (18.1) over $c = 1, \ldots,$ N, and the third is a random disturbance, which is similarly equal to the arithmetic mean of the disturbances of the microequations. The second term is a weighted sum of the individual incomes with weights $\beta_1/N, \ldots, \beta_N/N$.

It is evident that (18.3) does not, in general, achieve our objective of describing the per capita consumption of sugar in terms of per capita income. But there is a special case in which we do obtain this result, viz., when $\beta_1 = \cdots = \beta_N = \beta$ (say). Using the definition of x_i in (18.2), we can then write (18.3) as

$$(18.4) \qquad y_i = \frac{1}{N} \sum_{c=1}^{N} \beta_{0c} + \beta x_i + \frac{1}{N} \sum_{c=1}^{N} \epsilon_{ci}$$

which is a linear equation in the two per capita variables.

An Approach Based on Specification Analysis

Suppose that the β_c's are not all equal but that the analyst nevertheless uses (18.4) by running a regression of per capita sugar consumption (y_i) on per capita income (x_i). This yields the LS slope coefficient

$$(18.5) \qquad b = \frac{\sum_{i=1}^{n} (x_i - \bar{x})(y_i - \bar{y})}{\sum_{i=1}^{n} (x_i - \bar{x})^2}$$

where $\bar{x}$ and $\bar{y}$ are the arithmetic averages of x_i and y_i over all observations $(i = 1, \ldots, n)$. To evaluate the numerator of (18.5), we average (18.3) over i,

$$(18.6) \qquad \bar{y} = \frac{1}{N} \sum_{c=1}^{N} \beta_{0c} + \frac{1}{N} \sum_{c=1}^{N} \beta_c \bar{x}_c + \frac{1}{N} \sum_{c=1}^{N} \bar{\epsilon}_c$$

where $\bar{x}_c$ and $\bar{\epsilon}_c$ are the arithmetic averages of x_{ci} and ϵ_{ci} over all observations. Next we subtract (18.6) from (18.3),

$$y_i - \bar{y} = \frac{1}{N} \sum_{c=1}^{N} \beta_c (x_{ci} - \bar{x}_c) + \frac{1}{N} \sum_{c=1}^{N} (\epsilon_{ci} - \bar{\epsilon}_c)$$

which we substitute in (18.5):

$$b = \frac{\sum_{i=1}^{n} (x_i - \bar{x}) \sum_{c=1}^{N} \beta_c (x_{ci} - \bar{x}_c)}{N \sum_{i=1}^{n} (x_i - \bar{x})^2} + \frac{\sum_{i=1}^{n} (x_i - \bar{x}) \sum_{c=1}^{N} (\epsilon_{ci} - \bar{\epsilon}_c)}{N \sum_{i=1}^{n} (x_i - \bar{x})^2}$$

If the x_{ci}'s and hence also [see (18.2)] the x_i's are nonstochastic, the second term on the right has zero expectation. Thus, we obtain

(18.7)
$$\mathcal{E}b = \sum_{c=1}^{N} p_c \beta_c$$

where

(18.8)
$$p_c = \frac{\sum_{i=1}^{n} (x_i - \bar{x})(x_{ci} - \bar{x}_c)}{N \sum_{i=1}^{n} (x_i - \bar{x})^2} \qquad c = 1, \dots, N$$

which is the slope of the LS auxiliary regression

(18.9)
$$\frac{1}{N} x_{ci} = \text{constant} + p_c x_i + \text{residual} \qquad i = 1, \dots, n$$

Discussion of the Auxiliary Regressions

We conclude from (18.7) that the slope (18.5) of the LS regression of per capita sugar consumption on per capita income has an expectation equal to a weighted sum of the parameters $\beta_1, \dots, \beta_N$ of the micromodel with weights equal to $p_1, \dots, p_N$. These weights have unit sum:

(18.10)
$$\sum_{c=1}^{N} p_c = 1$$

To prove this we sum the numerator of (18.8) over $c = 1, \dots, N$ and use the x_i definition in (18.2) in the second step:

$$\sum_{c=1}^{N} \left[\sum_{i=1}^{n} (x_i - \bar{x})(x_{ci} - \bar{x}_c) \right] = \sum_{i=1}^{n} (x_i - \bar{x}) \sum_{c=1}^{N} (x_{ci} - \bar{x}_c)$$
$$= N \sum_{i=1}^{n} (x_i - \bar{x})^2$$

Since the expression in the second line is equal to the denominator of (18.8), this completes the proof of (18.10).

The results (18.7) to (18.10) imply that the expectation of the slope b of the macroregression is a weighted sum of $\beta_1, \dots, \beta_N$ with weights (the p_c's) that have unit sum, each weight being the slope of an auxiliary regression (18.9) for some c. In most cases, a majority of the consumers will have incomes that move approximately up and down with the country's per capita income, so that x_{ci} and x_i are positively correlated, and hence $p_c > 0$. In view of (18.7), the slope β_c of the microrelation (18.1) of such a consumer has a positive effect on the expectation of the slope of the macroregression. But we may have a negative correlation of x_{ci} and x_i, and hence $p_c < 0$, in which case the β_c of this consumer has a negative effect on $\mathcal{E}b$. Indeed, when there are negative p_c's, we may have a situation in which $\mathcal{E}b$ is smaller than the smallest among the β_c's or larger than the largest; also, the sign of $\mathcal{E}b$ may then differ from that of each of the β_c's (see Problem 2).

*18.2   An Extension and an Example

The microrelation (18.1) has only one explanatory variable. To extend the analysis to several variables, we shall discuss a study by Boot and de Wit (1960) dealing with investment decisions of $N = 10$ American companies, listed in column (1) of Table 24, in the 20-year period 1935–1954. The firms are listed

TABLE 24

Microparameters and coefficients of auxiliary regressions
for the aggregation of investment equations of ten American companies

Company (1)	LS estimate of		Coefficients of auxiliary regressions			
	β_{1c} (2)	β_{2c} (3)	p_{1c} (4)	p_{2c} (5)	q_{1c} (6)	q_{2c} (7)
General Motors Corporation	.119	.371	.4615	−.0622	.0127	.3698
U.S. Steel Corporation	.175	.390	.1309	−.0729	.0047	.0828
General Electric	.027	.152	.2077	−.0770	−.0108	.1581
Chrysler	.078	.316	.0720	−.0172	.0108	.0580
Atlantic Refining	.162	.003	.0107	.0345	−.0062	.1167
IBM	.131	.085	.0122	.1208	−.0004	.0409
Union Oil	.088	.123	.0121	−.0029	−.0048	.0759
Westinghouse	.053	.093	.0671	.0657	−.0037	.0389
Goodyear Tire and Rubber	.075	.082	.0236	.0146	−.0025	.0572
Diamond Match	.005	.437	.0021	−.0033	.0002	.0016
Sum			1	0	0	1

according to decreasing values of average annual investment in this period. These averages are all between 40 and about 100 million dollars per year (dollars of 1947 purchasing power) with three exceptions: General Motors and U.S. Steel have averages of about 600 and 400 million, respectively, and Diamond Match of about 3 million dollars per year.

Grunfeld's Investment Theory

The aggregation analysis is based on Grunfeld's (1958) investment theory, which implies that the firm's gross investment, including maintenance and repairs, during a year is a linear function of the firm's market value (the total value of the outstanding stock) and its capital stock at the beginning of this year. We write G_{ci} for the cth firm's gross investment in year i and M_{ci} and K_{ci} for its market value and its capital stock, respectively, at the beginning of that year. The micromodel thus takes the form

(18.11) $$G_{ci} = \beta_{0c} + \beta_{1c}M_{ci} + \beta_{2c}K_{ci} + \epsilon_{ci}$$

where ϵ_{ci} is a random disturbance and $c = 1, \ldots, N$ and $i = 1, \ldots, n$, with $N = 10$ and $n = 20$. The LS point estimates of β_{1c} and β_{2c} are shown in columns (2) and (3) of Table 24.

We construct three macrovariables, average investment per firm, average market value, and average capital stock,

$$(18.12) \quad G_i = \frac{1}{N} \sum_{c=1}^{N} G_{ci}, \qquad M_i = \frac{1}{N} \sum_{c=1}^{N} M_{ci}, \qquad K_i = \frac{1}{N} \sum_{c=1}^{N} K_{ci}$$

and obtain the following LS regression for the average investment per firm, with standard errors in parentheses:

$$(18.13) \qquad G_i = \text{constant} + .099 M_i + .260 K_i + \text{residual}$$
$$\phantom{(18.13) \qquad G_i = \text{constant} + } (.025) \qquad (.020)$$

We consider (18.11) as the correct specification, so that the implied model for the average investment per firm is

$$G_i = \frac{1}{N} \sum_{c=1}^{N} \beta_{0c} + \frac{1}{N} \sum_{c=1}^{N} \beta_{1c} M_{ci} + \frac{1}{N} \sum_{c=1}^{N} \beta_{2c} K_{ci} + \frac{1}{N} \sum_{c=1}^{N} \epsilon_{ci}$$

The reader should verify that this is equivalent to a linear equation in G_i, M_i, and K_i if $\beta_{11} = \cdots = \beta_{1N}$ and $\beta_{21} = \cdots = \beta_{2N}$, in which case (18.13) is the estimated version of a correct specification. But what can be said about (18.13) when there are differences among the β_{1c}'s or the β_{2c}'s?

Discussion of the Auxiliary Regressions

Recall from Section 17.3 that the auxiliary regressions of specification analysis describe each explanatory variable of the correct specification in terms of those of the specification which is actually used. Thus, given that M_i and K_i are the explanatory variables used in (18.13), we extend the auxiliary regression (18.9) to

$$(18.14) \qquad \frac{1}{N} M_{ci} = \text{constant} + p_{1c} M_i + p_{2c} K_i + \text{residual}$$

$$(18.15) \qquad \frac{1}{N} K_{ci} = \text{constant} + q_{1c} M_i + q_{2c} K_i + \text{residual}$$

The slope coefficients of these two sets of auxiliary regressions are shown in columns (4) to (7) of Table 24. The p_{1c}'s and the q_{2c}'s are all positive, whereas the p_{2c}'s and the q_{1c}'s are sometimes positive and sometimes negative. This is not surprising, because we have the following extension of (18.10):

$$(18.16) \qquad \sum_{c=1}^{N} p_{1c} = \sum_{c=1}^{N} q_{2c} = 1, \qquad \sum_{c=1}^{N} p_{2c} = \sum_{c=1}^{N} q_{1c} = 0$$

To clarify (18.16) we sum (18.14) over $c = 1, \ldots, N$. It follows from (18.12) that this yields M_i on the left, so that we obtain

$$(18.17) \qquad M_i = \text{constant} + \left(\sum_{c=1}^{N} p_{1c} \right) M_i + \left(\sum_{c=1}^{N} p_{2c} \right) K_i + \text{residual}$$

This shows that the sum of the auxiliary regressions (18.14) is equivalent to a regression of M_i on M_i and K_i. If we want to select the coefficients of (18.17) so that the residual sum of squares is minimized, this can simply be done by making the constant term and the coefficient $\sum_c p_{2c}$ of K_i both zero and the coefficient $\sum_c p_{1c}$ of M_i equal to 1, because (18.17) then becomes $M_i = M_i$ with zero residual. The specifications $\sum_c p_{2c} = 0$ and $\sum_c p_{1c} = 1$ confirm (18.16). A more rigorous proof of (18.16) is given in Appendix F.

Corresponding and Noncorresponding Microparameters

Write b_1 and b_2 for the LS slope estimators corresponding to the estimates .099 and .260, respectively, in (18.13). It is shown in Appendix F that they have the following expectations:

$$(18.18) \qquad \mathcal{E}b_1 = \sum_{c=1}^{N} p_{1c}\beta_{1c} + \sum_{c=1}^{N} q_{1c}\beta_{2c}$$

$$(18.19) \qquad \mathcal{E}b_2 = \sum_{c=1}^{N} p_{2c}\beta_{1c} + \sum_{c=1}^{N} q_{2c}\beta_{2c}$$

It is instructive to view (18.18) and (18.19) as extensions of (18.7). The first right-hand term in (18.18) is a weighted sum of the β_{1c}'s with weights (the p_{1c}'s) that add up to 1 [see (18.16)]. This is directly comparable with (18.7) and (18.10). But note that $\mathcal{E}b_1$ has a second component equal to a weighted sum of the β_{2c}'s. This should be of particular concern, since b_1 is the coefficient of M_i (average market value) in (18.13), whereas the β_{2c}'s are coefficients of a different variable (capital stock) in the micromodel (18.11). We shall refer to the β_{1c}'s as the *corresponding microparameters* with respect to b_1 and to the β_{2c}'s as the *noncorresponding parameters*. Similarly, (18.19) shows that $\mathcal{E}b_2$ also involves corresponding microparameters (the β_{2c}'s for $\mathcal{E}b_2$) as well as noncorresponding microparameters (the β_{1c}'s).

We must conclude that the extension of the aggregation analysis to two explanatory variables yields LS macrocoefficients whose expectations will, in general, involve noncorresponding microparameters, so that such a macro-coefficient represents (at least in part) the influence of explanatory variables which it is not supposed to represent. It is true, there is a difference between the weights of corresponding and noncorresponding microparameters. It follows from (18.16), (18.18), and (18.19) that, both for $\mathcal{E}b_1$ and for $\mathcal{E}b_2$, the weights of the corresponding microparameters have unit sum and those of the noncorresponding microparameters have zero sum. But such a zero sum does not imply that the weights are individually zero. In fact, they are not individually zero in Table 24, as is shown in columns (5) and (6).

The computation of the corresponding and noncorresponding components in (18.18) and (18.19) requires knowledge of the β_{1c}'s and β_{2c}'s in addition to the p's and q's. These β's are unknown, but when they are approximated by their LS estimates [columns (2) and (3) of Table 24], the noncorresponding component of $\mathcal{E}b_1$ is about 7 percent of the corresponding component and that of $\mathcal{E}b_2$ about 1 percent. Needless to say, this is only one particular case; there is no guarantee that other cases will yield similar numerical results. Also, if the β's were known, they could yield results different from those obtained from their LS estimates.

*18.3   The Convergence Approach to the Aggregation Problem

A different approach to aggregation is that which is based on an asymptotic analysis for N increasing indefinitely. Let N be the number of consumers ($c = 1, \ldots, N$), and consider the micromodel

$$(18.20) \qquad y_{ci} = \beta_{0c} + \beta_{1c} x_{1ci} + \beta_{2c} x_{2ci} + \epsilon_{ci} \qquad\qquad i = 1, \ldots, n$$

as well as the per capita variables

$$(18.21) \quad y_i = \frac{1}{N} \sum_{c=1}^{N} y_{ci}, \qquad x_{1i} = \frac{1}{N} \sum_{c=1}^{N} x_{1ci}, \qquad x_{2i} = \frac{1}{N} \sum_{c=1}^{N} x_{2ci}$$

Our objective is to investigate whether the micromodel (18.20) implies a linear equation in per capita variables for large N.

The Random-Selection Assumption

We sum (18.20) over $c = 1, \ldots, N$ and divide the result by N:

$$y_i = \frac{1}{N} \sum_{c=1}^{N} \beta_{0c} + \frac{1}{N} \sum_{c=1}^{N} \beta_{1c} x_{1ci} + \frac{1}{N} \sum_{c=1}^{N} \beta_{2c} x_{2ci} + \frac{1}{N} \sum_{c=1}^{N} \epsilon_{ci}$$

If the x_{1ci}'s and x_{2ci}'s and hence also $\sum_c x_{1ci}$ and $\sum_c x_{2ci}$ are all positive, we can write this as

$$(18.22) \quad y_i = \frac{1}{N} \sum_{c=1}^{N} \beta_{0c} + \frac{\displaystyle\sum_{c=1}^{N} \beta_{1c} x_{1ci}}{\displaystyle\sum_{c=1}^{N} x_{1ci}} x_{1i} + \frac{\displaystyle\sum_{c=1}^{N} \beta_{2c} x_{2ci}}{\displaystyle\sum_{c=1}^{N} x_{2ci}} x_{2i} + \frac{1}{N} \sum_{c=1}^{N} \epsilon_{ci}$$

We can view (18.22) as a linear equation in y_i, x_{1i}, and x_{2i}, but the coefficients of x_{1i} and x_{2i} are, in general, not constant over time. For example, the coefficient of x_{1i} in (18.22) is

$$(18.23) \qquad\qquad \frac{\displaystyle\sum_{c=1}^{N} \beta_{1c} x_{1ci}}{\displaystyle\sum_{c=1}^{N} x_{1ci}}$$

which is a constant when the microvariables $x_{11}, \ldots, x_{1N}$ behave proportionately but not otherwise.

Suppose, then, that we are engaged in a time series analysis of cross-section data on randomly selected consumers. This implies that the microparameters β_{0c}, β_{1c}, and β_{2c} are also random. Specifically, we assume that, for each $c = 1, \ldots, N$, the parameters $(\beta_{0c}, \beta_{1c}, \beta_{2c})$ are a random drawing from a three-dimensional distribution with finite means $\bar{\beta}_0$, $\bar{\beta}_1$, and $\bar{\beta}_2$ and standard deviations σ_0, σ_1, and σ_2. Assuming that the x's in (18.20) to (18.23) are nonstochastic (we shall return to this assumption in the subsection immediately following the next), we conclude that the coefficient (18.23) of x_{1i} is a random variable with the following mean:

$$(18.24) \qquad \frac{\bar{\beta}_1 \sum_{c=1}^{N} x_{1ci}}{\sum_{c=1}^{N} x_{1ci}} = \bar{\beta}_1$$

To find the variance of (18.23), we note that the assumption of random drawings implies stochastic independence, so that we can apply (3.46) or its continuous version (4.38). Hence, the variance of (18.23) becomes

$$(18.25) \qquad \frac{\sigma_1^2 \sum_{c=1}^{N} x_{1ci}^2}{\left(\sum_{c=1}^{N} x_{1ci} \right)^2} = \frac{\sigma_1^2}{N} \frac{(1/N) \sum_{c=1}^{N} x_{1ci}^2}{x_{1i}^2}$$

where the equal sign is based on the x_{1i} definition in (18.21).

The Convergence in Probability

Note that the mean (18.24) of the coefficient (18.23) is independent of i but that the variance (18.25) does involve i. To evaluate this variance, we write the numerator on the right in (18.25) as

$$\frac{1}{N} \sum_{c=1}^{N} x_{1ci}^2 = \frac{1}{N} \sum_{c=1}^{N} [(x_{1ci} - x_{1i}) + x_{1i}]^2$$

$$= \frac{1}{N} \sum_{c=1}^{N} (x_{1ci} - x_{1i})^2 + x_{1i}^2 + \frac{2x_{1i}}{N} \sum_{c=1}^{N} (x_{1ci} - x_{1i})$$

Since the last term in the second line vanishes [see (18.21)], the variance (18.25) can thus be written as

$$(18.26) \qquad \frac{\sigma_1^2}{N} \frac{(1/N) \sum_{c=1}^{N} (x_{1ci} - x_{1i})^2 + x_{1i}^2}{x_{1i}^2} = \frac{\sigma_1^2}{N} (v_{1i}^2 + 1)$$

where

$$(18.27) \qquad v_{1i} = \frac{\sqrt{(1/N) \sum_{c=1}^{N} (x_{1ci} - x_{1i})^2}}{x_{1i}}$$

is the coefficient of variation (i.e., the standard deviation divided by the mean) of the N numbers $x_{11i}, \ldots, x_{1Ni}$.

The coefficient of variation v_{1i} may be different for different observations (i.e., for different values of i), but there is no cogent reason for assuming that it will increase or decrease systematically when the number of consumers (N) increases. Thus, let us assume that v_{1i} converges to a finite limit as $N \to \infty$. Then the right-hand side of (18.26), which is the variance of the coefficient (18.23) of x_{1i} in (18.22), converges to zero as $N \to \infty$. Since the expectation of this coefficient equals $\bar{\beta}_1$ which is independent of N, we can use Chebyshev's inequality to conclude that, as $N \longrightarrow \infty$, the coefficient (18.23) of x_{1i} in (18.22) converges in probability to $\bar{\beta}_1$.

For the coefficient of x_{2i} in (18.22) we can proceed analogously; this is a matter of replacing the subscript 1 by 2 in the two previous paragraphs. For the constant term in (18.22) we have a similar convergence result (see Problem 9). Thus, we find that, for sufficiently large N, we can replace (18.22) by

$$(18.28) \qquad y_i \approx \bar{\beta}_0 + \bar{\beta}_1 x_{1i} + \bar{\beta}_2 x_{2i} + \frac{1}{N} \sum_{c=1}^{N} \epsilon_{ci}$$

which amounts to a linear equation in per capita variables with macroparameters equal to the means of the corresponding microparameters. Note that, in contrast to (18.18) and (18.19), noncorresponding microparameters play no role in the present result.

The Independence Assumption

In the discussion preceding (18.24), we assumed that the x's which occur in (18.20) to (18.23) are nonstochastic. This assumption may seem innocent, but it is not. If we select consumers at random, *all* characteristics of these consumers become random variables. This includes not only the microparameters β_{0c}, β_{1c}, and β_{2c} but also the values x_{1ci} and x_{2ci} (the incomes of the consumers, the prices which they pay for goods and services, etc.). This does not mean that we cannot treat the x's as fixed, as we did in the two previous subsections. It does mean, however, that if we treat them as fixed, we operate conditionally on the x's and we assume implicitly that the conditional distribution of the β's, given the x's, is independent of the x's. Thus, the convergence approach to the aggregation problem assumes that over the set of individuals who are aggregated, there is stochastic independence of the factors determining their behavior (the x's) and the way in which they react to these factors (the β's).

We obtain different results when this condition is violated. Let x_{1ci} in (18.22) be the income of the cth consumer in year i, so that the coefficient (18.23) of x_{1i} in that equation can be written as $\sum_c \theta_{ci} \beta_{1c}$, where

$$(18.29) \qquad \theta_{ci} = \frac{x_{1ci}}{\sum\limits_{d=1}^{N} x_{1di}} = \frac{x_{1ci}}{N x_{1i}}$$

is the share of the cth consumer of the country's total personal income. The coefficient $\sum_c \theta_{ci} \beta_{1c}$ of x_{1i} in (18.22) is thus a weighted average of the income coefficients of the microrelations (the β_{1c}'s) with weights equal to the corresponding income shares. This weighted average can be written as

$$(18.30) \qquad \sum_{c=1}^{N} \theta_{ci} \beta_{1c} = \frac{1}{N} \sum_{c=1}^{N} \beta_{1c} + \sum_{c=1}^{N} \left(\theta_{ci} - \frac{1}{N} \right) \beta_{1c}$$

As $N \longrightarrow \infty$, the first term on the right converges in probability to the expectation $\bar{\beta}_1$. However, the second term will be nonzero when x_{1ci} (and hence also

θ_{ci}) is correlated with β_{1c}. There may also be a nonzero correlation between β_{1c} and a noncorresponding microvariable such as x_{2ci}, which may be compared with the noncorresponding components that occur in (18.18) and (18.19). This comparability is limited, however, because the present analysis is confined to individual observations (one value of i), whereas that of Section 18.2 is based on all observations ($i = 1, \ldots, n$).

The relations considered in this section are all linear. The convergence approach to the aggregation problem can be extended to nonlinear equations under appropriate conditions; see Theil (1971, pp. 573, 580–588).

Problems

Problems 1 and 2 refer to Section 18.1, 3–6 to Section 18.2, and 7–9 to Section 18.3.

1 Prove that p_c in (18.9) vanishes if the cth consumer's income remains constant over the periods $i = 1, \ldots, n$. Verify that $\mathcal{E}b$ in (18.7) is then independent of β_c for this c, and provide an intuitive explanation of this result.

2 For $N = 3$, take $\beta_1 = \beta_2 = .01$, $\beta_2 = .04$, $p_1 = p_2 = p_3 = \frac{1}{3}$. Verify that these p's satisfy (18.10) and that (18.7) yields $\mathcal{E}b = .02$. Next, for the same β's, take $p_1 = p_2 = -p_3 = 1$. Verify that these p's also satisfy (18.10) and that (18.7) yields $\mathcal{E}b = -.02$. Conclude that (a) $\mathcal{E}b$ may be smaller than the smallest β_c and (b) $\mathcal{E}b$ may have a sign opposite to that of each β_c. Also construct an example of p_c's satisfying (18.10) so that $\mathcal{E}b$ exceeds the largest of the above β_c's.

3 Suppose that a regression is desired which describes total investment (rather than the average investment per firm) in terms of total market value and total capital stock. Verify that such a regression is obtained by multiplying both sides of (18.13) by $N = 10$ and that this affects neither the LS slope coefficients nor their standard errors.

4 Prove that if $\beta_{11} = \cdots = \beta_{1N} = \beta_1$ and $\beta_{21} = \cdots = \beta_{2N} = \beta_2$, (18.11) implies a macroequation of the form

$$G_i = \frac{1}{N} \sum_{c=1}^{N} \beta_{0c} + \beta_1 M_i + \beta_2 K_i + \frac{1}{N} \sum_{c=1}^{N} \epsilon_{ci}$$

where G_i, M_i, and K_i are defined in (18.12).

5 Repeat the argument below (18.17) for the sum of the auxiliary regressions (18.15) over $c = 1, \ldots, N$, and compare the result with (18.16).

6 Suppose that for $i = 1, \ldots, n$ the market values of the N firms change proportionately. Prove that this implies $p_{2c} = 0$ for each c in (18.14), and verify what the implication is for the occurrence of noncorresponding parameters in (18.18) and (18.19).

7 Verify that Section 18.3 presents a fourth asymptotic theory in addition to (a) the large-sample theory of Chapter 15, (b) a large number of neglected variables (end of Section 15.2), and (c) a small marginal cost of information (Section 16.4).

8   Prove that if corresponding explanatory microvariables in (18.20) change proportionately over time, $x_{1ci} = k_{1c}x_{1i}$ and $x_{2ci} = k_{2c}x_{2i}$ hold for each pair (c, i) and for some coefficients k_{1c} and k_{2c} that are independent of i. Also prove that (18.22) is then a linear equation in y_i, x_{1i}, and x_{2i} with constant coefficients.

9   Khintchine's theorem states that if $X_1, \ldots, X_n$ are independent random variables, all having the same distribution with finite mean μ, their arithmetic average $(1/n) \sum_i X_i$ has probability limit μ. Use this theorem to prove that the constant term in (18.22) converges in probability to $\bar{\beta}_0$ as $N \rightarrow \infty$. [*Note*: Khintchine's theorem is a powerful result because it does not require the X_i's to have a finite variance; for a proof of this theorem, see Theil (1971, pp. 360, 371).]

chapter 19

Generalized Least Squares and Related Procedures

The standard linear model assumes that the relation to be estimated has uncorrelated disturbances with constant variance, but this assumption is not always realistic. A generalization of the LS procedure is available to handle weaker assumptions.

19.1 Heteroscedasticity and Weighted Least Squares

The Concept of Heteroscedasticity

Figure 8 on page 62 illustrates a consumption-income relation for which the conditional variance of consumption, given income, takes the same value for each income level. It seems more plausible that this variance increases with income: Families with a $10,000 annual income have consumption expenditures between $8,000 and $12,000 with few exceptions, which amounts to a $4,000 range of variation, whereas families with an annual income of $50,000 have expenditures whose range of variation is much larger. This is illustrated in Figure 33, which the reader should compare with Figure 8.

More generally, consider a linear relation of the form

$$(19.1) \qquad y_i = \beta_0 + \beta_1 x_{1i} + \beta_2 x_{2i} + \epsilon_i \qquad i = 1, \ldots, n$$

where $\epsilon_1, \ldots, \epsilon_n$ are uncorrelated disturbances with zero mean and standard deviations $\sigma_1, \ldots, \sigma_n$. If the σ_i's are all equal, as is the case under the standard linear model, the disturbances are said to be *homoscedastic*; if the σ_i's are not all equal, the ϵ_i's are called *heteroscedastic*.

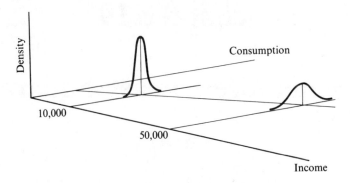

FIGURE 33   Illustration of heteroscedastic disturbances

Weighted Least Squares for Heteroscedastic Disturbances

If ϵ_i has standard deviation σ_i, ϵ_i/σ_i has unit standard deviation for each i, so that we can reduce the heteroscedasticity case to that of homoscedasticity by dividing (19.1) by σ_i:

$$(19.2) \qquad \frac{y_i}{\sigma_i} = \frac{\beta_0}{\sigma_i} + \beta_1 \frac{x_{1i}}{\sigma_i} + \beta_2 \frac{x_{2i}}{\sigma_i} + \frac{\epsilon_i}{\sigma_i} \qquad\qquad i = 1, \ldots, n$$

However, dividing the ith observation by σ_i requires σ_i to be known. If σ_1, $\ldots, \sigma_n$ are unknown, the analyst may want to estimate them; unfortunately, estimating n parameters $\sigma_1, \ldots, \sigma_n$ (along with β_0, β_1, and β_2) from n observations is not a practical idea.

Consider the specific case in which y_i in (19.1) is the expenditure on tea by the ith household, x_{1i} is the household's income, and x_{2i} is the number of persons in the household. Let the standard deviation of ϵ_i be proportional to the household's income:

$$(19.3) \qquad\qquad \sigma_i = k x_{1i} \qquad\qquad i = 1, \ldots, n$$

We divide (19.1) by x_{1i}:

$$(19.4) \qquad \frac{y_i}{x_{1i}} = \frac{\beta_0}{x_{1i}} + \beta_1 + \beta_2 \frac{x_{2i}}{x_{1i}} + \frac{\epsilon_i}{x_{1i}} \qquad\qquad i = 1, \ldots, n$$

It follows from (19.3) that the disturbances $\epsilon_1/x_{11}, \ldots, \epsilon_n/x_{1n}$ all have standard deviations equal to k. Hence, the standard linear model applies to (19.4), and the associated LS procedure amounts to a regression of y_i/x_{1i} (the proportion of income spent on tea) on the reciprocal of income ($1/x_{1i}$) and the reciprocal of income per household member (1 divided by x_{1i}/x_{2i}). Thus, instead of minimizing the residual sum of squares corresponding to the original specification (19.1), we minimize the residual version of $\sum_i (\epsilon_i/x_{1i})^2$. This amounts to *weighted least squares*. In this case each residual is weighted inversely proportionally to the household's income.

Disturbance Variances Involving Unknown Parameters

The case (19.3) is very simple because σ_i is known up to a multiplicative constant k. The following example, from Prais and Houthakker (1955), is not so simple. They had a large sample of household data, which enabled them to divide the households into family size groups and income groups. They found that for each family size-income combination the standard deviation of the amounts spent on tea is approximately proportional to the arithmetic mean of these amounts. If we assume that the grouping approximately eliminates the effect of income and family size on the expenditure on tea, this standard deviation corresponds to the conditional standard deviation σ_i of y_i, given x_{1i} and x_{2i} in (19.1), and the arithmetic mean to the conditional expectation $\mathscr{E}y_i$, given x_{1i} and x_{2i}. Thus, the proportionality takes the form $\sigma_i = c\mathscr{E}y_i$, which can be written as

$$(19.5) \qquad \sigma_i = c(\beta_0 + \beta_1 x_{1i} + \beta_2 x_{2i}) \qquad i = 1, \ldots, n$$

The occurrence of the β's in (19.5) is a problem that we did not have in (19.3). When we repeat the procedure of (19.3) and (19.4) by dividing (19.1) by $\beta_0 + \beta_1 x_{1i} + \beta_2 x_{2i}$, the left-hand side contains the unknown β's, which complicates its use as a regressand. The following two-step procedure provides an approximation. First, we estimate the β's of (19.1) by LS, ignoring the heteroscedasticity, and substitute the LS estimates in (19.5):

$$(19.6) \qquad \hat{\sigma}_i = c(b_0 + b_1 x_{1i} + b_2 x_{2i}) \qquad i = 1, \ldots, n$$

Second, we follow the procedure of (19.3) and (19.4) by dividing both sides of (19.1) by $b_0 + b_1 x_{1i} + b_2 x_{2i}$ and apply LS to the equation thus modified. See Theil (1971, pp. 403–405) for a large-sample justification of this two-step procedure.

A Reformulation of the Specification

It is sometimes possible to change the specification slightly so that the heteroscedasticity problem is avoided. Let us write (19.1) as

$$(19.7) \qquad y_i = (\beta_0 + \beta_1 x_{1i} + \beta_2 x_{2i})(1 + \zeta_i)$$

where $\zeta_i = \epsilon_i/(\beta_0 + \beta_1 x_{1i} + \beta_2 x_{2i})$. If (19.5) is true, the standard deviations of $\zeta_1, \ldots, \zeta_n$ are all equal to c. We assume that the distributions of the ζ_i's are identical (not just their standard deviations) and take logarithms in (19.7):

$$(19.8) \qquad \log y_i = \log (\beta_0 + \beta_1 x_{1i} + \beta_2 x_{2i}) + \log (1 + \zeta_i)$$

This formulation avoids the heteroscedasticity complication, since the logarithms of $1 + \zeta_1, \ldots, 1 + \zeta_n$ cannot have different variances when $\zeta_1, \ldots, \zeta_n$ are identically distributed.

However, note that (19.8) in contrast to (19.1) is nonlinear in the parameters β_0, β_1, and β_2. A possible solution is

$$(19.9) \qquad \log y_i = \beta_0' + \beta_1' \log x_{1i} + \beta_2' \log x_{2i} + \epsilon_i'$$

which is a different specification that avoids both the nonlinearity and the heteroscedasticity problem if $\epsilon_1', \ldots, \epsilon_n'$ have the same variance. Of course, this simple solution fails when $\mathcal{E}(\log y_i)$ is nonlinear in the parameters. [If (19.8) is preferable to (19.9), the LS method for nonlinear functions described in Section 15.3 can be used, provided $\log (1 + \zeta_i)$ is normally distributed.]

19.2   Correlated Disturbances and Autoregressive Transformations

When the data are time series data, successive disturbances are frequently positively correlated. The reason is that most of the neglected variables which are represented by the disturbance tend to change slowly over time, so that the same is true for their combined effect on the dependent variable. If there is such a correlation, this amounts to another violation of the conditions of the standard linear model, which can also be handled by an appropriate generalization of the LS method under suitable conditions.

Disturbances Generated by an Autoregressive Process

Let the observations $i = 1, \ldots, n$ be arranged in the order of successive time periods. We assume that the disturbances are generated by a process which is described by

$$(19.10) \qquad \epsilon_i = \rho\epsilon_{i-1} + \zeta_i$$

where $-1 < \rho < 1$ and the ζ's are uncorrelated random variables with zero mean and standard deviation σ_0. Equation (19.10) describes a first-order autoregressive process; each ϵ_i is expressed linearly in terms of its predecessor and a random variable. The words "first order" indicate that only the most recent predecessor plays a role. There are also second- and higher-order autoregressive processes, but these will not be considered here.

It is shown in the next subsection that (19.10) implies

$$(19.11) \qquad \epsilon_i = \sum_{t=0}^{\infty} \rho^t \zeta_{i-t} \qquad i = 1, \ldots, n$$

The zero-mean condition on the ζ's thus implies that the ϵ's also have zero mean. The following result will also be proved:

$$(19.12) \qquad \operatorname{var} \epsilon_i = \frac{\sigma_0^2}{1 - \rho^2} \qquad i = 1, \ldots, n$$

Since the right-hand side is independent of i, this result shows that the autoregressive process (19.10) yields homoscedastic disturbances.

Furthermore, it can be shown that (19.10) implies the following correlation pattern of the ϵ's. Successive disturbances (ϵ_1 and ϵ_2, ϵ_2 and ϵ_3, etc.) have a correlation coefficient equal to ρ. Disturbances which are two periods apart (ϵ_1 and ϵ_3, ϵ_2 and ϵ_4, etc.) have a correlation coefficient equal to ρ^2; for ϵ's which are three periods apart the correlation coefficient is ρ^3, and so on. Thus, when $0 < \rho < 1$, all such correlation coefficients are positive, but they converge to zero when the distance in time increases. The reader who is interested in the derivation of this correlation pattern should consult Problem 3.

Derivations

By lagging (19.10) by one time period, we obtain $\epsilon_{i-1} = \rho\epsilon_{i-2} + \zeta_{i-1}$, which we substitute in (19.10) to obtain $\epsilon_i = \rho^2\epsilon_{i-2} + \zeta_i + \rho\zeta_{i-1}$. We repeat this once more:

$$\epsilon_i = \rho^2(\rho\epsilon_{i-3} + \zeta_{i-2}) + \zeta_i + \rho\zeta_{i-1}$$
$$= \rho^3\epsilon_{i-3} + \zeta_i + \rho\zeta_{i-1} + \rho^2\zeta_{i-2}$$

When we repeat this t times, we obtain

$$\epsilon_i = \rho^{t+1}\epsilon_{i-t-1} + \zeta_i + \rho\zeta_{i-1} + \rho^2\zeta_{i-2} + \cdots + \rho^t\zeta_{i-t}$$

The result (19.11) then follows from $\lim_{t\to\infty} \rho^{t+1} = 0$, which is implied by the condition $-1 < \rho < 1$.

The variance of ϵ_i is obtained by squaring (19.11),

$$(\zeta_i + \rho\zeta_{i-1} + \rho^2\zeta_{i-2} + \cdots)^2 = \zeta_i^2 + (\rho\zeta_{i-1})^2 + (\rho^2\zeta_{i-2})^2 + \cdots$$
$$+ 2\rho\zeta_i\zeta_{i-1} + 2\rho^2\zeta_i\zeta_{i-2} + \cdots$$

and then taking the expectation. Since the ζ's are uncorrelated random variables with zero mean, the product terms in the second line also have zero mean [e.g., $\mathcal{E}(\zeta_i\zeta_{i-1}) = \mathcal{E}\zeta_i\mathcal{E}\zeta_{i-1} = 0$]. Moreover, the ζ's all have variance σ_0^2, so that the expectation of the sum of the other terms is

$$\mathcal{E}[\zeta_i^2 + (\rho\zeta_{i-1})^2 + (\rho^2\zeta_{i-2})^2 + \cdots] = \sigma_0^2(1 + \rho^2 + \rho^4 + \cdots)$$

which yields (19.12).

An Autoregressive Transformation

Consider again (19.1), where $i = 1, \ldots, n$ now refers to successive time periods. We assume that the disturbances of (19.1) are generated by the autoregressive process (19.10). We lag (19.1) by one time period and multiply by ρ,

$$\rho y_{i-1} = \beta_0\rho + \beta_1\rho x_{1,i-1} + \beta_2\rho x_{2,i-1} + \rho\epsilon_{i-1}$$

which we subtract from (19.1), using $\epsilon_i - \rho\epsilon_{i-1} = \zeta_i$ [see (19.10)]:

$$(19.13) \qquad y_i - \rho y_{i-1} = \beta_0(1 - \rho) + \beta_1(x_{1i} - \rho x_{1,i-1})$$
$$+ \beta_2(x_{2i} - \rho x_{2,i-1}) + \zeta_i$$

This lagging-and-subtracting procedure is known as an autoregressive transformation. It changes (19.1) with correlated ϵ's into (19.13) with uncorrelated ζ's that have zero mean and constant variance. Hence, the standard linear model is applicable to (19.13), so that we can apply LS by running a regression of $y_i - \rho y_{i-1}$ on $x_{1i} - \rho x_{1,i-1}$ and $x_{2i} - \rho x_{2,i-1}$. This requires ρ to be known; the case of an unknown ρ is considered in the next subsection.

REMARKS:

(1) When the observations are $i = 1, \ldots, n$, we must confine (19.13) to $i = 2, \ldots, n$ because of the occurrence of the subscript $i - 1$ in this equation. Thus, the autoregressive transformation loses the first observation. Problem 4 shows how this loss can be eliminated.

(2) When we apply LS to (19.13) for $i = 2, \ldots, n$, this amounts to minimizing the residual version of

$$\sum_{i=2}^{n} \zeta_i^2 = \sum_{i=2}^{n} (\epsilon_i - \rho\epsilon_{i-1})^2 = \sum_{i=2}^{n} \epsilon_i^2 + \rho^2 \sum_{i=2}^{n} \epsilon_{i-1}^2 - 2\rho \sum_{i=2}^{n} \epsilon_{i-1}\epsilon_i$$

The second term in the last member equals ρ^2 multiplied by the sum of the squares of $\epsilon_1, \ldots, \epsilon_{n-1}$. Hence, the above expression is equal to

$$(19.14) \quad \rho^2\epsilon_1^2 + \epsilon_n^2 + (1 + \rho^2)(\epsilon_2^2 + \cdots + \epsilon_{n-1}^2) - 2\rho(\epsilon_1\epsilon_2 + \cdots + \epsilon_{n-1}\epsilon_n)$$

which shows that LS applied to (19.13) gives different weights to the first and last ϵ's (ρ^2 and 1, to be compared with $1 + \rho^2$ for the $n - 2$ other ϵ's) and that it also involves products of successive ϵ's.

The Case of an Unknown Autoregressive Parameter

When ρ is unknown, it can be replaced by an estimate or by an assumed value. For example, if the correlation coefficient of successive disturbances is assumed not to be far below 1, we can use the approximation $\rho = 1$ in (19.13), which gives

$$(19.15) \quad y_i - y_{i-1} = \beta_1(x_{1i} - x_{1,i-1}) + \beta_2(x_{2i} - x_{2,i-1}) + \zeta_i$$

This is a *first-difference transformation*. (A first difference is a change, $\Delta y_i = y_i - y_{i-1}$; a second difference is a change in a change, $\Delta^2 y_i = \Delta y_i - \Delta y_{i-1}$, etc.) An example (first differences in logarithms) is provided by (13.18). Another example is the Rotterdam Model (14.40), the variables of which are all changes over time (quantity components of changes in budget shares and log-changes in real income and prices).

Alternatively, a two-step procedure can be used similar to that described below (19.5) for heteroscedasticity. First, we compute the LS residuals $e_1, \ldots, e_n$, ignoring the correlation of the corresponding ϵ's, and we compute an estimate $\hat{\rho}$ of ρ from these residuals. Second, we run a regression based on (19.13) with ρ replaced by $\hat{\rho}$. One way of defining $\hat{\rho}$ is as the correlation coefficient of the

$n - 1$ pairs of successive LS residuals $(e_1, e_2), \ldots, (e_{n-1}, e_n)$,

$$(19.16) \qquad \hat{\rho} = \frac{\sum_{i=2}^{n} (e_i - \bar{e}')(e_{i-1} - \bar{e}'')}{\sqrt{\sum_{i=2}^{n} (e_i - \bar{e}')^2 \sum_{i=2}^{n} (e_{i-1} - \bar{e}'')^2}}$$

where

$$(19.17) \qquad \bar{e}' = \frac{1}{n-1} \sum_{i=2}^{n} e_i, \qquad \bar{e}'' = \frac{1}{n-1} \sum_{i=2}^{n} e_{i-1}$$

There are several possible definitions other than (19.16), including some versions which are based on iterative procedures; the interested reader should consult Johnston (1972, pp. 259–266). An asymptotic justification of the use of $\hat{\rho}$ can be derived from Theil (1971, Sections 8.6 and 8.7). See also Problem 6.

19.3 Some Statistical Testing Procedures

In addition to the statistical tests described in Chapter 12, there are several others which perform a useful role in regression analysis. The most common among these test the null hypothesis that successive disturbances are uncorrelated against the alternative hypothesis that they are correlated; this alternative hypothesis is frequently expressed by saying that the disturbances are *autocorrelated*. A convenient start is provided by the Von Neumann ratio, which has applications beyond regression also.

The Von Neumann Ratio

Let $X_1, X_2, \ldots, X_n$ be a series of successive random variables with zero mean and unit variance. We want to test their independence against the alternative hypothesis that they are autocorrelated. For this purpose we consider the following identity:

$$(19.18) \qquad \mathcal{E}[(X_i - X_{i-1})^2] = \mathcal{E}(X_i^2) + \mathcal{E}(X_{i-1}^2) - 2\mathcal{E}(X_i X_{i-1})$$

When successive X_i's are positively correlated, the left-hand side will be smaller than when they are uncorrelated because $-2\mathcal{E}(X_i X_{i-1})$ is then negative. The minimum of this left-hand side is obviously zero, which is reached when the autocorrelation coefficient is 1, $\mathcal{E}(X_i X_{i-1}) = \mathcal{E}(X_i^2)$; the maximum is 4, which is reached when this coefficient is -1. The sample counterpart of the left-hand side of (19.18) is the numerator of the following ratio:

$$(19.19) \qquad Q = \frac{[1/(n-1)] \sum_{i=2}^{n} (X_i - X_{i-1})^2}{(1/n) \sum_{i=1}^{n} (X_i - \bar{X})^2}, \qquad \text{where } \bar{X} = \frac{1}{n} \sum_{i=1}^{n} X_i$$

This Q is the Von Neumann ratio. Significance limits for Q are available under the condition that $X_1, \ldots, X_n$ are independent normal variates with mean

μ and variance σ^2. A table of these limits for $n \leq 60$ is given at the end of this book; for $n > 60$ the distribution of Q can be approximated by the normal distribution with mean $2n/(n-1)$ and variance $4/n$. If the null hypothesis of zero autocorrelation is true, Q has an expectation close to 2 and a variance which converges to zero as $n \longrightarrow \infty$. Values of Q sufficiently below (above) 2 are indicative of positive (negative) autocorrelation of the X_i's; this follows from the statement made below (19.18).

The Durbin-Watson Statistic

We return to the LS residuals $e_1, \ldots, e_n$ and define

(19.20)
$$d = \frac{\sum_{i=2}^{n} (e_i - e_{i-1})^2}{\sum_{i=1}^{n} e_i^2}$$

which is the Durbin-Watson statistic for testing the disturbances $\epsilon_1, \ldots, \epsilon_n$ against autocorrelation. A comparison with (19.19) shows that d equals $(n-1)Q/n$ with X_i interpreted as e_i, provided $\bar{X} = 0$. This proviso is satisfied when the equation contains a constant term, because the LS residuals have a zero arithmetic mean in that case. See Problem 7 for the relation between d and ρ of (19.10).

Durbin and Watson (1950, 1951) considered the distribution of d under the standard linear model (including a constant term) when the disturbances are independent normal variates with zero mean and variance σ^2. It appears that this distribution depends on the values taken by the explanatory variables, which leads to complicated calculations in applications. To avoid these problems, Durbin and Watson provided lower and upper bounds (d_L and d_U) for the significance limits of d at which the null hypothesis of zero autocorrelation must be rejected in favor of positive autocorrelation. These bounds hold for any values taken by the explanatory variables. The procedure is as follows:

(1) If $d < d_L$, reject the hypothesis of zero autocorrelation in favor of positive autocorrelation.

(2) If $d > d_U$, accept the hypothesis of zero autocorrelation.

(3) If $d_L < d < d_U$, do not draw any conclusion; the test is inconclusive.

An example is instructive. Table 13 on page 105 contains the LS residuals of the demand equation for textile: .0142, .0030, $\ldots$, $-.0241$, .0216. Thus, we obtain

(19.21)
$$d = \frac{(.0030 - .0142)^2 + \cdots + (.0216 + .0241)^2}{(.0142)^2 + \cdots + (.0216)^2} = 1.93$$

We select the 5 percent significance level, so that the probability is .05 that the zero-autocorrelation hypothesis of the ϵ's will be rejected when in fact it is true. For this significance level and for $n = 17$ observations on two explanatory variables (plus constant term) we have $d_L = 1.02$ and $d_U = 1.54$. The observed $d = 1.93$ exceeds $d_U = 1.54$, so that the hypothesis of zero autocorrelation is acceptable [case (2) above]. If the observed d had been between 1.02 and 1.54, no conclusion could have been drawn [case (3)]. If the observed d had been below 1.02, we would have concluded that the ϵ's are positively autocorrelated [case (1)]. Tables of d_L and d_U are given at the end of this book.

Remarks on the Durbin-Watson Test

A major difficulty in the application of the Durbin-Watson test is the fact that the interval (d_L, d_U) of inconclusive tests is large for modest numbers of observations, yielding a substantial proportion of inconclusive d's in applied econometric studies. There is the risk that such cases are viewed as "no evidence against zero autocorrelation," whereas in fact the disturbances are auto-correlated. Attempts have been made by Henshaw (1966) and Durbin (1970) to eliminate the region of inconclusive tests, but the procedures proposed by these authors are much more complicated and not widely used. It was shown by Theil and Nagar (1961) that if the explanatory variables change slowly over time, the significance limit of d is close to the upper bound d_U. If we approximate this limit by d_U, cases (1) and (3) above are combined so that the hypothesis of zero autocorrelation is rejected when $d < d_U$ and accepted when $d > d_U$ [case (2)]. However, note that the condition of slowly changing explanatory variables is usually not satisfied when the model is formulated in first-difference form [see (19.15)] and certainly not when there are dummy variables among the explanatory variables (see Section 13.3).

Why does the distribution of d depend on the values taken by the explanatory variables? The answer is that (19.20) is formulated in terms of LS residuals, not in terms of disturbances. If we had ϵ's rather than e's in the right-hand side of (19.20), the distribution of d could be obtained directly from that of the Von Neumann ratio (19.19). But we use e's rather than ϵ's in (19.20) because the ϵ's are not observable. The problem is that the e's are not uncorrelated even when the ϵ's are uncorrelated, nor do the e's all have the same variance (see Problem 9). It is possible to replace the LS residuals by other residuals which are uncorrelated random variables with variance σ^2 when $\epsilon_1, \ldots, \epsilon_n$ are uncorrelated and have variance σ^2. This leads to the subject of BLUS residuals, which can be used for a variety of tests; we refer to Theil (1971, Chapter 5).

We conclude by noting that the Durbin-Watson test is unsatisfactory when there are lagged values of the dependent variable among the explanatory variables. Such lagged values have not yet been introduced; we refer to Section 21.1.

Other Tests

The Durbin-Watson procedure can be easily modified so as to yield a test against nonlinearity. In Figure 34 we measure the LS residuals vertically and the values taken by the hth explanatory variable horizontally. If the dependent variable is linear in this explanatory variable, we should expect that the residuals are scattered more or less randomly around the horizontal axis, as is the

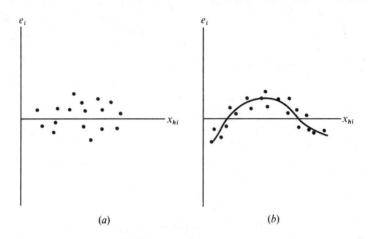

(a) (b)

FIGURE 34   A test against nonlinearity

case in Figure 34(a). If, on the other hand, the relation is nonlinear, the residuals tend to be positive for some range of x_h and negative elsewhere. This is illustrated in Figure 34(b) by a smooth curve that goes through the observed points. Residuals that correspond to nearly equal values of x_h will then, on the average, be rather close to each other in numerical value. Thus, if we rearrange the observations according to increasing values of x_h,

$$(19.22) \qquad\qquad x_{h1} \leq x_{h2} \leq \cdots \leq x_{hn}$$

the numerator of (19.20) will take a relatively small value. This means that, after the rearrangement (19.22) has been made, the Durbin-Watson procedure can be used for a test against nonlinearity.

Goldfeld and Quandt (1965) proposed a test against heteroscedasticity. Suppose that the analyst is interested in the question of whether n_1 of the n observations have disturbances with either larger or smaller variance than another group of n_2 observations ($n_1 + n_2 \leq n$). The procedure is to compute LS regressions for both groups of observations separately and then to take the ratio of the two residual sums of squares. If the null hypothesis of equal variances is true, this ratio can be tested with an F distribution (see Section 12.3). A different test against heteroscedasticity was proposed by Glejser (1969).

*19.4   The Use of Extraneous Estimators

An Extraneous Estimate of an Income Elasticity

Let (19.1) be the demand equation for textile considered in Chapter 8, with y_i, x_{1i}, and x_{2i} the logarithms of, respectively, the volume of textile consumption per capita, real income per capita, and the relative textile price, and with β_1

and β_2 the income and price elasticities. We assume that the ϵ's are uncorrelated and have zero mean and variance σ^2.

Imagine that a cross-section analysis of households yields an estimate of the income elasticity of the demand for textile. We want to use this estimate in conjunction with the time series data (Table 12 on page 96) to obtain better estimates of β_1 and β_2. Before plunging into algebra, it is appropriate to stress that a time series income elasticity is not necessarily identical to a cross-section income elasticity. The former measures the effect on textile consumption of a change in per capita income from level A to level B over time, whereas the latter deals with the transition from a household with income A to another household with income B. It is conceivable that a change in income has a lagged effect on textile consumption. This would be relevant for the time series regression but not for the cross-section analysis if we assume that the two households have earned incomes equal to A and B, respectively, over a sufficiently long period of time. In such a case the cross-section income elasticity may be expected to differ from the time series income elasticity. However, for the argument which follows we assume that no such difference exists.

The Incorporation of an Extraneous Estimator

We write p_1 for the extraneous (cross-section) estimator of the income elasticity β_1 in (19.1). We assume that p_1 is an unbiased estimator with variance σ_1^2 and that it is independent of the time series data. We write this as

$$(19.23) \qquad p_1 = \beta_1 + v_1$$

where v_1 is the sampling error of p_1. This error has zero mean and variance σ_1^2 and is independent of the disturbances $\epsilon_1, \ldots, \epsilon_n$ of (19.1).

Next multiply (19.23) by σ/σ_1:

$$(19.24) \qquad \frac{p_1 \sigma}{\sigma_1} = \beta_1 \frac{\sigma}{\sigma_1} + \frac{v_1 \sigma}{\sigma_1}$$

Since $v_1 \sigma/\sigma_1$ has variance $\sigma_1^2 (\sigma/\sigma_1)^2 = \sigma^2$, the $n+1$ random variables $\epsilon_1, \ldots,$ $\epsilon_n, v_1 \sigma/\sigma_1$ are all uncorrelated with zero mean and variance σ^2. Thus, we can combine the time series data and the extraneous information by means of an LS regression for $n+1$ observations. Out of these, n refer to the time series data (the 17 annual observations of Table 12) and one refers to (19.24). An example follows in the next subsection.

Extraneous Estimators and Multicollinearity

The use of extraneous information is particularly important in a multicollinear situation. As an example, we consider the $n = 13$ fictitious observations of Table 25 for a regression of y on x_1 and x_2 (with constant term). The sums

TABLE 25

Multicollinearity and an extraneous estimate

i	y_i	x_{1i}	x_{2i}
1	30	15	12
2	15	10	7
3	10	4	3
4	5	0	0
5	0	−4	−3
6	−20	−10	−7
7	−30	−15	−12
8	−25	−15	−12
9	−10	−10	−7
10	−5	−4	−3
11	0	4	3
12	10	10	7
13	20	15	12
Extraneous	$p_1\sigma/\sigma_1$	σ/σ_1	0

of squares and products are

$$(19.25) \qquad \sum_{i=1}^{13} x_{1i}^2 = 1364, \qquad \sum_{i=1}^{13} x_{2i}^2 = 808, \qquad \sum_{i=1}^{13} x_{1i}x_{2i} = 1048$$

$$(19.26) \qquad \sum_{i=1}^{13} x_{1i}y_i = 2185, \qquad \sum_{i=1}^{13} x_{2i}y_i = 1690, \qquad \sum_{i=1}^{13} y_i^2 = 3800$$

All three variables have a zero average over the 13 observations. Hence, the normal equations (7.8) and (7.9) take the form

$$(19.27) \qquad \begin{aligned} 1364b_1 + 1048b_2 &= 2185 \\ 1048b_1 + 808b_2 &= 1690 \end{aligned}$$

with the following solution:

$$(19.28) \qquad b_1 = -1.5 \ (2.3), \qquad b_2 = 4.0 \ (3.0)$$

The standard errors in parentheses show that the estimates are worthless. This is the result of a high degree of multicollinearity; Table 25 shows that the values taken by x_2 are all almost exactly equal to three-quarters of the corresponding x_1 values.

But suppose that there is an extraneous unbiased estimator p_1 of β_1 with variance σ_1^2. Since $v_1\sigma/\sigma_1$ in (19.24) has the same variance as the 13 disturbances associated with the data of Table 25, we can identify the left-hand variable $p_1\sigma/\sigma_1$ in (19.24) with y_{14} and the coefficient σ/σ_1 of β_1 in (19.24) with $x_{1,14}$. These two expressions are shown in the last row of Table 25; the zero value of $x_{2,14}$ results from the fact that β_2 does not occur in (19.24). For example, let the extraneous estimate of β_1 be .8 with variance .04. We substitute .8 for p_1 and $\sqrt{.04} = .2$ for σ_1 and approximate σ by the square root of

$$(19.29) \qquad s^2 = 25.49$$

which is the unbiased σ^2 estimate obtained from the 13 observations. It is shown in the next subsection that incorporating this extraneous estimate yields a β_1 estimate of .78 and a β_2 estimate of 1.08; their standard errors are .20 and .31, respectively. The β_1 estimate and its standard error are almost identical to the extraneous values, so that the sample provides virtually no additional information on β_1. But the β_2 estimate 1.08 and its standard error .31 are a considerable improvement over the values shown in (19.28); hence, the sample is valuable for β_2 when it is used in conjunction with the extraneous β_1 estimate.

Derivations

Writing $i = 14$ for the extraneous estimate, we have the following results from Table 25 and (19.25):

$$\sum_{i=1}^{14} x_{1i} = \frac{\sigma}{\sigma_1}, \qquad \sum_{i=1}^{14} x_{1i}^2 = 1364 + \frac{\sigma^2}{\sigma_1^2}$$

Thus, we conclude from (2.18) that

(19.30) $$\sum_{i=1}^{14} (x_{1i} - \bar{x}_1)^2 = 1364 + \frac{13\sigma^2}{14\sigma_1^2}$$

where $\bar{x}_1 = (x_{11} + \cdots + x_{1,14})/14$. Similarly,

(19.31) $$\sum_{i=1}^{14} (x_{1i} - \bar{x}_1)(y_i - \bar{y}) = 2185 + \frac{13p_1\sigma^2}{14\sigma_1^2}$$

Since $x_{2,14} = 0$, the sums (over $i = 1, \ldots, 14$) of squares and products involving x_2 are equal to the corresponding expressions in (19.25) and (19.26). Therefore, incorporating the extraneous estimate changes the normal equations (19.27) into

(19.32) $$\left(1364 + \frac{13\sigma^2}{14\sigma_1^2}\right)\hat{\beta}_1 + 1048\hat{\beta}_2 = 2185 + \frac{13p_1\sigma^2}{14\sigma_1^2}$$

(19.33) $$1048\hat{\beta}_1 + 808\hat{\beta}_2 = 1690$$

The solution of this equation system is $\hat{\beta}_1 = .78$, $\hat{\beta}_2 = 1.08$ for $p_1 = .8$, $\sigma_1 = .2$, and σ^2 approximated by 25.49. The standard errors of $\hat{\beta}_1$ and $\hat{\beta}_2$ (.20 and .31) are derived in Appendix G.

*19.5   Mixed Estimation

We extend the approach of the previous section by interpreting the extraneous information as the analyst's prior judgments on the values of certain parameters. Thus, returning to the demand for textile, we assume that the analyst argues as follows: "I consider unity the most plausible value of the income elasticity β_1, and I am willing to bet 20 to 1 that this elasticity is not outside the interval (.7, 1.3)." Applying the two-sigma rule, we can argue that these prior judgments are approximately equivalent to an unbiased point estimate of β_1 equal to 1 with a standard deviation of .15. Let us also assume that the analyst's prior judgments on the price elasticity β_2 can be similarly translated into an unbiased point estimate equal to $-.7$ with standard deviation $.15$ (a two-sigma range from -1 to $-.4$). The latter judgments refer to (19.23) with the subscript 1 replaced by 2,

$$(19.34) \qquad p_2 = \beta_2 + v_2$$

with $-.7$ the numerical value of p_2.

The Mixed Estimation Procedure

In our present problem we thus have two extraneous estimates in addition to the n time series observations (the 17 annual observations of Table 12 on page 96). To make the standard linear model applicable to these $n + 2$ sources of information, we must transform them so that their $n + 2$ random components are uncorrelated and have the same variance. This is pursued in the next subsection. The result is the following estimated demand equation for textile, which includes the prior judgments described above:

$$(19.35) \qquad y = 1.467 + 1.089x_1 - .821x_2 + \text{residual}$$
$$ (.203) \quad (.103) \qquad (.035)$$

We compare this with the original regression (8.12), adding an extra decimal place:

$$(19.36) \qquad y = 1.374 + 1.143x_1 - .829x_2 + \text{residual}$$
$$ (.306) \quad (.156) \qquad (.036)$$

Equation (19.35) is the result of the *mixed estimation* procedure, from Theil and Goldberger (1961) and Theil (1963). This terminology reflects the fact that (19.35) is based on both the data and the prior judgments. This is in contrast to (19.36), which is exclusively based on the data, given the log-linear specification of the demand equation for textile.

Note that the standard errors are smaller in (19.35) than in (19.36). This difference reflects the gain in precision which results from the use of prior judgments. Note also that the reduction of the standard error of the income elasticity (from .156 to .103) is much larger than that of the price elasticity (from .036 to .035). This is not surprising, given the standard deviations of the two prior estimates (both .15) mentioned in the opening paragraph of this section. The income elasticity estimate in (19.36), based on data only, has a standard error of .156, but that of the price elasticity is much smaller, .036; hence, the prior judgments on the latter elasticity provide little additional precision.

Derivation of the Mixed Estimates

If v_1 and v_2 in (19.23) and (19.34) are uncorrelated, a simple procedure for obtaining $n + 2$ uncorrelated random components with the same variance [see the discussion preceding (19.35)] consists of writing (19.23) in the form (19.24) and proceeding similarly for (19.34). But v_1 and v_2 may be correlated. For example, the analyst may argue that if his best guess overstates the true income sensitivity of the demand for textile, this is probably also the case for the price sensitivity. This implies a nonzero correlation of v_1 and v_2, and the numerical value of this correlation must be specified before the mixed estimates can be obtained.

The prior judgments stated in the opening paragraph of this section imply that the standard deviations of v_1 and v_2 are $\sigma_1 = \sigma_2 = .15$. We use a covariance of v_1 and v_2 equal to $-.01$, so that their correlation coefficient equals

$$(19.37) \qquad \rho = \frac{-.01}{\sqrt{(.15)^2(.15)^2}} = -\frac{4}{9}$$

Given that the income and price elasticities β_1 and β_2 have opposite signs, this negative correlation implies that if p_1 overstates β_1, $|p_2|$ will probably also overestimate $|\beta_2|$, in agreement with the analyst's argument in the previous paragraph. See Theil (1971, pp. 351–352) for the consequences of selecting correlation values other than (19.37).

One way of obtaining uncorrelated random components for $\rho \neq 0$ is by means of suitable linear combinations of (19.23) and (19.34). The interested reader should consult Problem 12; a computationally more efficient procedure, which requires matrix algebra, is given in Appendix G.

Comparison with Bayesian Inference

The mixed estimation procedure is similar to Bayesian inference (Sections 16.1 and 16.2) in that both methods combine the analyst's prior judgments with the evidence supplied by the sample. There are two important differences. First, Bayesians treat parameters as random variables, whereas in the mixed estimation technique parameters are unknown constants, and prior estimators are random. These estimators vary in successive applications of the technique. Second, Bayesian inference requires a prior distribution of all parameters of the demand equation for textile, including the constant term (β_0) and the disturbance variance (σ^2), whereas the mixed estimation technique permits the analyst to confine his prior judgments to those parameters about which he feels that he knows something. The implementation of this technique is therefore much simpler, and the problems of improper prior density functions are completely avoided (see the end of Section 16.2).

The mixed estimation procedure can be extended in various ways. If v_1 and v_2 in (19.23) and (19.34) as well as the ϵ_i's are normally distributed, a χ^2 test can be designed for the hypothesis that the prior information and sample information are compatible with each other. Other extensions allow the prior estimates to be biased and correlated with the ϵ_i's. For details, see Theil (1971, pp. 350–352; 1974b).

Mixed Estimation of Numerous Parameters

The use of prior judgments on parameters is particularly important for models with many parameters. An example is the Rotterdam Model for a large number of goods. Paulus (1972) estimated this model for a 14-commodity classification. The parameters are the coefficients of the log-change in real income and those of log-changes in prices. Prior judgments are formulated for the former coefficients only; these are the marginal shares [see (14.37) and (14.40)]. Since it is somewhat easier to speculate on income elasticities than on marginal shares, we shall start with prior estimates of these elasticities, after which a translation into prior estimates of marginal shares will follow.

Column (1) of Table 26 lists the 14 commodity groups. Column (2) contains prior estimates of the income elasticities with standard deviations in parentheses. For bread the prior estimate is .2 with standard deviation .1, which means that this good is judged to have a low income elasticity (a two-sigma range from 0 to .4). For groceries the prior estimate is twice as large, but the standard deviation is also larger. The latter feature reflects the fact that groceries are a more heterogeneous commodity group than bread, which implies greater uncertainty as to the value of its income elasticity.

Recall from the discussion below (14.49) that the marginal share of each good equals the product of the income elasticity and the budget share of this good. By multiplying the prior estimate of the income elasticity by the average budget share of the same good (averaged over all observations), we obtain the implied prior estimate of the marginal share. These estimates are shown in column (3) of Table 26, with standard deviations in parentheses (see Problem 13). Columns (4) and (5) contain the sample and mixed estimates of the marginal shares. The figures for bread indicate that the sample estimate is weak, with a large standard error, so that it is not surprising to find that the mixed estimate is dominated by the prior judgments. The opposite is true for several other groups such as the group labeled other durables. Also notice that it is not true that the mixed estimate is always between the corresponding prior and sample estimates (see, for example, clothing and other textiles); this is so because mixed estimation is more complicated than just taking a weighted or unweighted average.

The most instructive way of inspecting the results is by analyzing the extent to which the sample evidence changes the prior judgments on the income elasticities. Column (6) contains the estimates (and standard errors) of the income elasticities that are implied by the mixed estimates of the marginal shares, obtained by dividing the latter by average budget shares. A comparison of columns (2) and (6) shows that the sample does not change the prior estimates to a great extent but that it reduces their uncertainty as measured by the figures in parentheses. Thus, the sample confirms the prior judgments on the whole and makes them more precise.

The above discussion does not include the covariances of the prior estimates.

TABLE 26

Prior, sample, and mixed estimates of income elasticities and marginal shares

Commodity group (1)	Income elasticity: prior (2)	Marginal share Prior (3)	Marginal share Sample (4)	Marginal share Mixed (5)	Implied income elasticity (6)
1. Bread	.2 (.10)	.0070 (.0035)	.0005 (.0068)	.0056 (.0027)	.16 (.08)
2. Groceries	.4 (.15)	.0227 (.0085)	.0567 (.0121)	.0280 (.0060)	.50 (.11)
3. Dairy products	.6 (.15)	.0434 (.0108)	.0327 (.0084)	.0351 (.0056)	.49 (.08)
4. Vegetables and fruit	.6 (.20)	.0265 (.0088)	.0333 (.0103)	.0276 (.0058)	.62 (.13)
5. Meat	1.0 (.20)	.0760 (.0152)	.0517 (.0144)	.0676 (.0094)	.89 (.12)
6. Fish	.8 (.25)	.0057 (.0018)	.0049 (.0045)	.0050 (.0012)	.71 (.16)
7. Beverages	1.5 (.30)	.0406 (.0081)	.0316 (.0063)	.0382 (.0044)	1.41 (.16)
8. Tobacco products	.6 (.25)	.0225 (.0094)	.0301 (.0085)	.0234 (.0055)	.62 (.15)
9. Pastry, chocolate, etc.	.8 (.25)	.0249 (.0078)	.0227 (.0068)	.0243 (.0041)	.78 (.13)
10. Clothing and other textiles	2.0 (.40)	.2656 (.0531)	.2353 (.0203)	.2263 (.0159)	1.70 (.12)
11. Footwear	1.5 (.30)	.0215 (.0043)	.0297 (.0040)	.0238 (.0023)	1.66 (.18)
12. Other durables	2.0 (.50)	.1882 (.0471)	.2233 (.0150)	.2125 (.0106)	2.26 (.11)
13. Water, light, and heat	.8 (.30)	.0439 (.0165)	.0592 (.0111)	.0462 (.0076)	.84 (.14)
14. Other goods and services	.7 (.35)	.2115 (.1100)	.1883 (.0277)	.2364 (.0200)	.75 (.06)

315

There is a temptation to postulate zero covariances, but this should be resisted when it is not realistic. In the analysis described here, prior estimates of income elasticities for several goods are obtained by making a comparison with the prior estimate for another good. Hence, if the latter estimate exceeds the true value, this is probably also the case for the former. Accordingly, positive covariances are postulated for the prior estimates of the income elasticities of several pairs of goods. For details, see Paulus (1972) and Theil (1975–1976, Chapter 6).

Problems

Problems 1 and 2 refer to Section 19.1, 3–6 to Section 19.2, 7–9 to Section 19.3, 10 and 11 to Section 19.4, and 12 and 13 to Section 19.5.

1 Verify that LS applied to (19.2) amounts to running a regression on three variables without constant term.

2 It is stated below (19.2) that estimating n parameters $\sigma_1, \ldots, \sigma_n$ from n observations is not a practical idea. Verify that the proposals to solve this problem in Section 19.1 amount to either (a) formulating a model for the σ_i's which involves only one (rather than n) additional unknown parameter or (b) reformulating the specification so that the heteroscedasticity problem is avoided.

3 To obtain the covariance of ϵ_i and ϵ_{i+1} under (19.10), use (19.11) to prove that this covariance is equal to the expectation of

$$(\zeta_i + \rho\zeta_{i-1} + \rho^2\zeta_{i-2} + \cdots)(\zeta_{i+1} + \rho\zeta_i + \rho^2\zeta_{i-1} + \cdots)$$

Verify that this yields cov $(\epsilon_i, \epsilon_{i+1}) = \rho\sigma_0^2/(1 - \rho^2)$, and combine this with (19.12) to prove that the correlation coefficient of ϵ_i and ϵ_{i+1} equals ρ. Then extend this result to obtain the covariance and correlation coefficient of ϵ_i and ϵ_{i+2}.

4 Multiply (19.1) for $i = 1$ by $\sqrt{1 - \rho^2}$:

$$y_1\sqrt{1 - \rho^2} = \beta_0\sqrt{1 - \rho^2} + \beta_1 x_{11}\sqrt{1 - \rho^2} + \beta_2 x_{21}\sqrt{1 - \rho^2} + \epsilon_1\sqrt{1 - \rho^2}$$

Prove that the disturbance of this equation has zero mean, that it is uncorrelated with $\zeta_2, \ldots, \zeta_n$ of (19.13), and that its variance is equal to that of these ζ's. [*Hint*: For the variance, use (19.12); for the correlations, use (19.11) to prove that $\epsilon_1\sqrt{1 - \rho^2}$ involves only ζ's with subscripts $i \leq 1$.] Conclude that the standard linear model applies to the above equation as the first observation and to (19.13) for $i = 2, \ldots, n$ as the $n - 1$ other observations and that the dependent variable of the associated regression takes the n values $y_1\sqrt{1 - \rho^2}, y_2 - \rho y_1, \ldots, y_n - \rho y_{n-1}$.

5 (*Continuation*) Verify that this n-observation approach modifies (19.14) so that the coefficient of ϵ_1^2 is 1 rather than ρ^2. Also verify that the first-difference transformation (19.15) deletes the additional observation of Problem 4.

6 Verify that (19.17) yields $\bar{e}' = -e_1/(n-1)$ and $\bar{e}'' = -e_n/(n-1)$ if the LS regression contains a constant term. This shows that, unless n is small, $\bar{e}'$ and $\bar{e}''$ will typically be close to zero. Prove that if $\bar{e}'$ and $\bar{e}''$ are approximated by zero, the numerator of (19.16) becomes $e_1 e_2 + \cdots + e_{n-1} e_n$ and the denominator becomes

$$(19.38) \qquad \sqrt{\sum_{i=2}^{n} e_i^2 \sum_{i=2}^{n} e_{i-1}^2} \approx \frac{n-1}{n} \sum_{i=1}^{n} e_i^2$$

yielding

$$\hat{\rho}' = \frac{n}{n-1} \frac{\sum\limits_{i=2}^{n} e_i e_{i-1}}{\sum\limits_{i=1}^{n} e_i^2}$$

as an alternative estimator of ρ. Discuss the approximation implied by the $\approx$ sign in (19.38).

7 (Continuation) With d defined in (19.20), consider $\hat{\rho}'' = 1 - \frac{1}{2}d$. Verify that $\hat{\rho}''$ can be viewed as another estimator of ρ in (19.10). [Hint: Approximate e_i's by ϵ_i's in (19.20), and take the expectations of the numerator and the denominator.]

8 (Continuation) A test against negative autocorrelation of disturbances is obtained by replacing d by $4 - d$. Verify whether the numerical result (19.21) provides evidence in favor of negatively autocorrelated disturbances.

9 For the two-variable standard linear model without constant term (Section 5.2), prove that the LS residual $e_i = y_i - bx_i$ satisfies

$$\text{var } e_i = \sigma^2 \left(1 - \frac{x_i^2}{\sum\limits_{k=1}^{n} x_k^2} \right)$$

$$\text{cov } (e_i, e_j) = -\frac{\sigma^2 x_i x_j}{\sum\limits_{k=1}^{n} x_k^2} \qquad i \neq j$$

Conclude that, in general, different LS residuals are not uncorrelated and have different variances. [Hint: Prove $e_i = \epsilon_i - (b - \beta)x_i$. For the variance of e_i, square both sides and take the expectation. Proceed analogously for the covariance.]

10 Verify that $b_1 = -1.4811$, $b_2 = 4.0126$ satisfy the normal equations (19.27). Next use (9.18) and (19.26) to verify that $R^2 = 3545.1/3800 = .93292$, and use this to verify the unbiased σ^2 estimate given in (19.29). Finally, verify the two standard errors shown in (19.28).

11 Prove (19.30) and (19.31). Also verify the solution $\hat{\beta}_1 = .782$, $\hat{\beta}_2 = 1.077$ of (19.32) and (19.33).

12 With ρ defined as the correlation coefficient of v_1 and v_2, verify that the following equation results from a linear combination of (19.23) and (19.34):

$$\sigma \frac{p_2/\sigma_2 - \rho p_1/\sigma_1}{\sqrt{1-\rho^2}} = \sigma \frac{\beta_2/\sigma_2 - \rho \beta_1/\sigma_1}{\sqrt{1-\rho^2}} + \sigma \frac{v_2/\sigma_2 - \rho v_1/\sigma_1}{\sqrt{1-\rho^2}}$$

Prove that the second term on the right is uncorrelated with the random component $v_1\sigma/\sigma_1$ of (19.24) and that its variance equals σ^2, and conclude that the mixed estimation technique amounts to LS applied to the 17 time series observations (Table 12 on page 96) as well as the above equation and (19.24). [*Note*: The result (19.35) is based on the estimate (8.39) as an approximation of σ^2.]

13 Write $\bar{w}_i$ for the average budget share of the ith good, $\hat{E}_i$ for the prior estimate of its income elasticity, and σ_i for the standard deviation of this estimate. Prove that if $\bar{w}_i$ is treated as a constant, the implied estimate $\bar{w}_i\hat{E}_i$ of the ith marginal share has a standard deviation equal to $\bar{w}_i\sigma_i$. Also prove that for each good the ratio of the prior estimate to its standard deviation is the same for the income elasticity and the marginal share, and check this rule for columns (2) and (3) of Table 26.

chapter 20

Introduction to Simultaneous-Equation Problems: Static Equation Systems

The standard linear model assumes that the values taken by the explanatory variables are constants. However, this assumption may be contradicted by the general interdependence of economic phenomena. For example, the demand analysis for textile in Chapter 8 treats the textile price level in any year as fixed; given this assumption, we ask what can be said about the associated random value of textile consumption. But if textile prices depend on textile consumption, either directly or indirectly, it becomes difficult to argue that the textile price level is fixed and given with respect to textile consumption. To handle such problems, we must consider several equations simultaneously.

20.1 Endogenous and Exogenous Variables

Supply and Demand

Consider an agricultural good with a supply and a demand equation. The former describes the producers' response to changes in the price of the good; the latter describes the consumers' response to changes in this price and the consumers' income. We assume that the market is cleared in every year, so that we can use one symbol, q_i, for the quantity bought and sold in year i. We write p_i for the price and Y_i for the consumers' income in that year. Hence, if the equations are linear, they take the form

$$
\text{(20.1)} \qquad q_i = \alpha_0 + \alpha_1 p_i + \epsilon_i \qquad \text{(supply)}
$$
$$
\text{(20.2)} \qquad q_i = \beta_0 + \beta_1 p_i + \beta_2 Y_i + \epsilon_i' \qquad \text{(demand)}
$$

where ϵ_i and ϵ'_i are the random supply and demand disturbances, respectively, in year i and the α's and β's are unknown parameters.

A Keynesian Model

For the developments which follow it is convenient to consider a Keynesian model which is even simpler than (20.1) and (20.2). This model consists of the following two equations:

$$(20.3) \qquad C_i = \beta Y_i + \epsilon_i$$
$$(20.4) \qquad C_i + I_i = Y_i$$

Equation (20.3) is a macroeconomic consumption function which describes total consumption in year i (C_i) as proportional to the consumers' income (Y_i), apart from a random disturbance (ϵ_i). Equation (20.4) is a definitional relation which states that consumption plus investment (I_i) equals income in each year.

Note that (20.3) and (20.4) contain only one unknown parameter: the proportionality constant β of the consumption function. Our objective is to estimate β from observations on the variables (for $i = 1, \ldots, n$) under the condition that $\epsilon_1, \ldots, \epsilon_n$ are uncorrelated disturbances with zero mean and variance σ^2. Thus, to check the validity of the standard linear model for (20.3), we must verify whether the values $Y_1, \ldots, Y_n$ of the explanatory variable can be regarded as constants. For this purpose we subtract (20.3) from (20.4):

$$(20.5) \qquad I_i + \epsilon_i = (1 - \beta)Y_i$$

If Y_i is a constant, so is the right-hand side of (20.5), and hence the left-hand side also. But if $I_i + \epsilon_i$ is a constant for each i, the implication is that investment has a random component which is always exactly equal to minus the disturbance of the consumption function. This is highly implausible. However, if we abandon the assumption of a nonrandom $I_i + \epsilon_i$, Y_i in (20.5) and hence also in (20.3) becomes random, so that the standard linear model does not apply to (20.3).

Complete Equation Systems

The above discussion of the Keynesian model involves a disturbance of one equation and a variable (investment) which does not occur in that equation but in another. This indicates that our further discussion should not be confined to one equation but extended to a system of equations. Such a system usually contains more variables than equations: three variables (C, Y, I) and two equations, (20.3) and (20.4). The objective of an equation system is to describe some of its variables, the *endogenous variables*, in terms of the other variables, the *exogenous variables*. The latter variables are determined "from the outside," i.e., independently of the process described by the equation system. The former (endogenous) variables are simultaneously determined by the exogenous variables and the disturbances in the way prescribed by the equations of the system. The word "simultaneously" should clarify why these equations are known as *simultaneous equations*.

In (20.3) and (20.4) we designate I as exogenous and C and Y as endogenous variables. Similarly, Y will be considered as exogenous and p and q as endogenous in (20.1) and (20.2). [This illustrates that a variable (Y) may be endogenous in one model and exogenous in another.] Hence, both models are two-equation systems with two endogenous variables. When the numbers of equations and endogenous variables are equal, the equation system is said to be *complete*. Therefore, (20.1) and (20.2) form a complete system that describes price and quantity (p and q) in terms of the consumers' income (the exogenous Y) and the supply and demand disturbances. In the same way, (20.3) and (20.4) form a complete system which describes consumption and income in terms of investment and the disturbance of the consumption function.

The Statistical Interpretation of "Exogenous"

For estimation purposes it is necessary to specify what exogenous ("determined from the outside") means in statistical terms. This specification amounts to the assumption that the values taken by the exogenous variables are stochastically independent of the disturbances of the system. Thus, we assume that income in (20.2) is independent of the supply and demand disturbances in (20.1) and (20.2) and that investment in (20.4) is independent of the disturbance in (20.3).

If the n investment values $I_1, \ldots, I_n$ are stochastically independent of the disturbances $\epsilon_1, \ldots, \epsilon_n$ of the consumption function (20.3), we can (and shall) operate conditionally on the I_i's by regarding them as constants. This is similar to what we did with the values of the explanatory variables in the standard linear model. However, in the present analysis we may have explanatory variables which are not exogenous and whose values are not independent of the disturbances. An example is (20.2), where p_i on the right is an endogenous explanatory variable which takes random values.

20.2   Structural Equations and the Reduced Form

The Reduced Form of a Complete Equation System

Assume $\beta \neq 1$ and divide both sides of (20.5) by $1 - \beta$:

$$(20.6) \qquad Y_i = \frac{1}{1-\beta} I_i + \frac{1}{1-\beta} \epsilon_i$$

Next subtract I_i from both sides and use (20.4):

$$(20.7) \qquad C_i = \frac{\beta}{1-\beta} I_i + \frac{1}{1-\beta} \epsilon_i$$

These two equations describe an endogenous variable in terms of the exogenous I_i and the disturbance ϵ_i. The reader should verify that if $\alpha_1 > 0$ and $\beta_1 < 0$, (20.1) and (20.2) yield the following solution for p_i and q_i:

$$(20.8) \qquad p_i = -\frac{\alpha_0 - \beta_0}{\alpha_1 - \beta_1} + \frac{\beta_2}{\alpha_1 - \beta_1} Y_i + \frac{\epsilon'_i - \epsilon_i}{\alpha_1 - \beta_1}$$

$$(20.9) \qquad q_i = \frac{\alpha_1 \beta_0 - \alpha_0 \beta_1}{\alpha_1 - \beta_1} + \frac{\alpha_1 \beta_2}{\alpha_1 - \beta_1} Y_i + \frac{\alpha_1 \epsilon'_i - \beta_1 \epsilon_i}{\alpha_1 - \beta_1}$$

The solution (20.6) and (20.7) of the Keynesian model is called the *reduced form* of this model. Each reduced-form equation describes one endogenous variable [Y in (20.6) and C in (20.7)] in terms of the exogenous variables and the disturbances. Similarly, (20.8) and (20.9) constitute the reduced form of the model consisting of the supply equation (20.1) and the demand equation (20.2).

Structural Equations

To distinguish the original equations from those of the reduced form, we call the former *structural equations*. This reflects the fact that each such equation serves to describe some component of the structure of the economy. For example, the consumption function (20.3) describes the behavior of consumers with respect to all goods and services jointly; the demand equation (20.2) describes their behavior with respect to one agricultural good; and the supply equation (20.1) describes the behavior of the producers of this good.

The Use of the Reduced Form

The economic interpretation of structural equations is much simpler than that of the reduced form, but this form is more convenient for computing the effect of a change in an exogenous variable on an endogenous variable. For example, (20.6) and (20.7) show that a one-million-dollar increase in investment raises income and consumption by $1/(1 - \beta)$ and $\beta/(1 - \beta)$ million dollars, respectively. Similarly, (20.9) implies that the change in q caused by a change in Y equals a multiple $\alpha_1 \beta_2/(\alpha_1 - \beta_1)$ of the latter change. In (20.2) this multiple is β_2, but note that (20.2) describes the demand response only. When demand changes due to a change in the consumers' income, supply changes also because demand and supply are equal (we assume that the market is cleared in every year). When supply and hence the left-hand variable in (20.1) change, the price on the right will also change, and this price change affects demand in (20.2), and so on. The reduced-form equation (20.9) gives the effect of a change in Y on the quantity bought and sold which results from this supply-and-demand interaction.

Another important feature of the reduced form is the fact that its right-hand variables are all exogenous, so that their values can be assumed to be constants. This is in contrast to the structural equation (20.2), which has the endogenous price on the right. Therefore, in a statistical sense the reduced form is closer to the standard linear model than are the structural equations.

20.3   Least Squares, Indirect Least Squares, and Instrumental Variables

The Inconsistency of LS Applied to a Structural Equation

Let us estimate β of (20.3) by LS:

$$(20.10) \qquad b = \frac{\sum\limits_{i=1}^{n} Y_i C_i}{\sum\limits_{i=1}^{n} Y_i^2}$$

To evaluate this estimator we substitute (20.3) in the numerator,

$$\sum_{i=1}^{n} Y_i C_i = \sum_{i=1}^{n} Y_i(\beta Y_i + \epsilon_i) = \beta \sum_{i=1}^{n} Y_i^2 + \sum_{i=1}^{n} Y_i \epsilon_i$$

which we substitute in (20.10):

$$b = \frac{\beta \sum\limits_{i=1}^{n} Y_i^2 + \sum\limits_{i=1}^{n} Y_i \epsilon_i}{\sum\limits_{i=1}^{n} Y_i^2} = \beta + \frac{\sum\limits_{i=1}^{n} Y_i \epsilon_i}{\sum\limits_{i=1}^{n} Y_i^2}$$

This is equivalent to

$$(20.11) \qquad b - \beta = \frac{\sum\limits_{i=1}^{n} Y_i \epsilon_i}{\sum\limits_{i=1}^{n} Y_i^2}$$

This result is identical to the equation for $b - \beta$ in (5.12), reproduced here,

$$(20.12) \qquad b - \beta = \frac{\sum\limits_{i=1}^{n} x_i \epsilon_i}{\sum\limits_{i=1}^{n} x_i^2}$$

except that x_i in (20.12) becomes Y_i in (20.11). But this exception has important consequences. Since the x_i's in (20.12) are constants, the numerator $\sum_i x_i \epsilon_i$ in that equation has zero expectation. The numerator in (20.11) is, in view of (20.6), equal to

$$\sum_{i=1}^{n} Y_i \epsilon_i = \sum_{i=1}^{n} \left(\frac{1}{1-\beta} I_i + \frac{1}{1-\beta} \epsilon_i \right) \epsilon_i$$

$$= \frac{1}{1-\beta} \sum_{i=1}^{n} I_i \epsilon_i + \frac{1}{1-\beta} \sum_{i=1}^{n} \epsilon_i^2$$

which has expectation $n\sigma^2/(1 - \beta)$ because $\sum_i I_i \epsilon_i$ has zero expectation (the I_i's are constants) and ϵ_i^2 has expectation σ^2.

The cause of the problem is the fact that the explanatory variable Y_i in (20.3) is a random variable which is correlated with the disturbance ϵ_i of that equation. Such a correlation implies that the LS coefficient estimator is neither unbiased nor consistent. No matter how large n is, the LS estimator (20.10) fails to converge in probability to the parameter β of (20.3).

Indirect Least Squares

It is obviously of interest to know whether a consistent estimator of β can be obtained. The reduced-form equation (20.6) provides a clue. This equation contains the exogenous I_i on the right, which we treat as a constant. If $\epsilon_1, \ldots, \epsilon_n$ are uncorrelated random variables with zero mean and variance σ^2, the disturbances $\epsilon_1/(1 - \beta), \ldots, \epsilon_n/(1 - \beta)$ of (20.6) are uncorrelated random variables with zero mean and variance $\sigma^2/(1 - \beta)^2$. Therefore, (20.6) satisfies the conditions of the standard linear model, so that an LS regression of Y_i on I_i (without constant term) yields a best linear unbiased estimator of the coefficient $1/(1 - \beta)$ of I_i. We indicate the slope of this regression by

$$(20.13) \qquad \frac{1}{1 - \hat\beta} = \frac{\sum_{i=1}^{n} I_i Y_i}{\sum_{i=1}^{n} I_i^2}$$

and take reciprocals of both sides,

$$1 - \hat\beta = \frac{\sum_{i=1}^{n} I_i^2}{\sum_{i=1}^{n} I_i Y_i} = \frac{\sum_{i=1}^{n} I_i(Y_i - C_i)}{\sum_{i=1}^{n} I_i Y_i} = \frac{\sum_{i=1}^{n} I_i Y_i - \sum_{i=1}^{n} I_i C_i}{\sum_{i=1}^{n} I_i Y_i} = 1 - \frac{\sum_{i=1}^{n} I_i C_i}{\sum_{i=1}^{n} I_i Y_i}$$

where the second step is based on (20.4). By equating the first and last members, we obtain

$$(20.14) \qquad \hat\beta = \frac{\sum_{i=1}^{n} I_i C_i}{\sum_{i=1}^{n} I_i Y_i}$$

which is the estimator of β that is implied by the estimator (20.13) of the parameter $1/(1 - \beta)$ of the reduced-form equation (20.6). This procedure illustrates how a parameter of a structural equation [β of (20.3)] can be estimated *indirectly by applying LS to the reduced form.*

The estimator (20.14) is, in contrast to (20.10), consistent with respect to β when the exogenous variable (investment) is constant in repeated samples. We know from Section 15.1 that, under this constancy, the LS estimator (20.13) is consistent with respect to $1/(1 - \beta)$. The consistency of (20.14) then follows from the general proposition that if $\hat\theta_n$ is a consistent estimator of θ, any function $f(\hat\theta_n)$ is a consistent estimator of $f(\theta)$, provided only that $f(\ )$ is continuous at θ. In this case $\hat\beta$ equals 1 minus the reciprocal of (20.13), which satisfies the continuity condition if $\beta \neq 1$.

The Instrumental-Variable Technique

An alternative interpretation of (20.14) is very useful, because it will enable us to obtain an important generalization. We multiply both sides of (20.3) by I_i and sum over i:

(20.15)
$$\sum_{i=1}^{n} I_i C_i = \beta \sum_{i=1}^{n} I_i Y_i + \sum_{i=1}^{n} I_i \epsilon_i$$

Since $I_1, \ldots, I_n$ are constants, $\sum_i I_i \epsilon_i$ is a random variable with zero expectation. For the purpose of estimating β, let us replace this variable by its expectation. This yields

(20.16)
$$\sum_{i=1}^{n} I_i C_i = \hat{\beta} \sum_{i=1}^{n} I_i Y_i$$

where $\hat{\beta}$ is the estimator of β implied by this procedure. It is readily verified that this $\hat{\beta}$ is identical to the estimator (20.14).

The previous paragraph illustrates the instrumental-variable technique, with investment used as the instrumental variable. Such a variable, the values of which are written $x_1, \ldots, x_n$, has the property that $\sum_i x_i \epsilon_i$ has zero expectation. As (20.15) shows, the technique amounts to multiplying the equation by x_i and summing over i, after which a replacement of the disturbance term $\sum_i x_i \epsilon_i$ by its zero expectation yields an estimation equation of a form similar to (20.16).

The instrumental-variable approach includes LS under the standard linear model as a special case. For example, consider the reduced-form equation (20.6), which satisfies the conditions of the standard linear model. We use investment (the right-hand variable) as the instrumental variable. Thus, we multiply (20.6) by I_i and sum over i:

$$\sum_{i=1}^{n} I_i Y_i = \frac{1}{1-\beta} \sum_{i=1}^{n} I_i^2 + \frac{1}{1-\beta} \sum_{i=1}^{n} I_i \epsilon_i$$

The disturbance term on the right has zero expectation. If we replace this term by its expectation, we obtain an equation that yields the LS estimator (20.13) of $1/(1-\beta)$.

Instrumental-Variable Estimation of the Supply Equation

Recall that the consumers' income (Y) is the exogenous variable in the supply-and-demand system (20.1) and (20.2). Thus, to estimate the supply equation, we multiply (20.1) by Y_i and sum over i:

(20.17)
$$\sum_{i=1}^{n} Y_i q_i = \alpha_0 \sum_{i=1}^{n} Y_i + \alpha_1 \sum_{i=1}^{n} Y_i p_i + \sum_{i=1}^{n} Y_i \epsilon_i$$

By replacing $\sum_i Y_i \epsilon_i$ by its expectation (zero), we obtain an estimation equation for α_0 and α_1.

But since we have two unknown parameters, we need a second estimation equation. For this purpose, note that the constant term α_0 in (20.1) may be viewed as the coefficient of a variable which equals 1 for each i: $\alpha_0 = \alpha_0 \times 1$. Since the value 1 is obviously nonstochastic, this variable is exogenous. The reader should verify that its use as an instrumental variable amounts to

(20.18)
$$\sum_{i=1}^{n} q_i = n\alpha_0 + \alpha_1 \sum_{i=1}^{n} p_i + \sum_{i=1}^{n} \epsilon_i$$

with $\sum_i \epsilon_i$ replaced by its expectation (zero). He should also verify that when the disturbance terms of (20.17) and (20.18) are replaced by zero, estimators a_1 of α_1 and a_0 of α_0 result of the form

$$(20.19) \qquad a_1 = \frac{\sum\limits_{i=1}^{n}(Y_i - \bar{Y})(q_i - \bar{q})}{\sum\limits_{i=1}^{n}(Y_i - \bar{Y})(p_i - \bar{p})}, \qquad a_0 = \bar{q} - a_1\bar{p}$$

where

$$(20.20) \qquad \bar{Y} = \frac{1}{n}\sum_{i=1}^{n}Y_i, \qquad \bar{q} = \frac{1}{n}\sum_{i=1}^{n}q_i, \qquad \bar{p} = \frac{1}{n}\sum_{i=1}^{n}p_i$$

20.4   The Identification Problem

Instrumental-Variable Estimation of the Demand Equation

When we proceed similarly for (20.2), we obtain the following demand versions of (20.17) and (20.18):

$$\sum_{i=1}^{n}Y_i q_i = \beta_0 \sum_{i=1}^{n}Y_i + \beta_1 \sum_{i=1}^{n}Y_i p_i + \beta_2 \sum_{i=1}^{n}Y_i^2 + \sum_{i=1}^{n}Y_i\epsilon_i'$$

$$\sum_{i=1}^{n}q_i = n\beta_0 + \beta_1 \sum_{i=1}^{n}p_i + \beta_2 \sum_{i=1}^{n}Y_i + \sum_{i=1}^{n}\epsilon_i'$$

This yields two estimation equations when we replace the disturbance terms by their expectations (zero in both cases). But we need three such equations, since there are three unknown parameters: β_0, β_1, and β_2. Is there a third estimation equation?

The answer is no. To illustrate the nature of the problem, we first assume that Y_i in (20.2) takes a particular numerical value, so that $\beta_0 + \beta_2 Y_i$ becomes the constant term in (20.2). This implies that both the supply and the demand equation describe q as a linear function of p, apart from a random disturbance. The two equations are represented by straight lines in Figure 35(a) for $\alpha_1 > 0$ and $\beta_1 < 0$. The model specifies that the data satisfy both equations, apart from random disturbances. Hence, the observation points must be randomly scattered around the intersection point of the two lines, as is illustrated in Figure 35(a).

When the consumers' income (Y_i) takes different values in (20.2), the intercept of the demand line also takes different values. This is illustrated in Figure 35(b) by means of three demand lines, all with slope β_1. As in the case of Figure 35(a), the observation points must be scattered around the intersection point of the demand and supply lines. But since the demand line shifts when Y changes, we obtain a series of points around the supply line, which enables us to estimate the parameters of the supply equation (20.1) but not those of the demand equation (20.2). The latter parameters are said to be *unidentifiable* or *underidentified*.

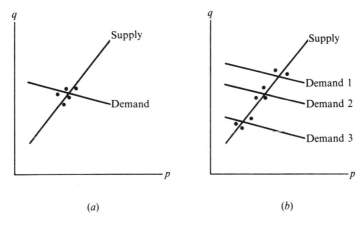

FIGURE 35   **Illustration of the identification problem**

A Condition for Identification

The discussion of Figure 35 is the geometric counterpart of the algebraic discussion which started at (20.17). The estimators a_0 and a_1 in (20.19) are obtained from two instrumental variables [see (20.17) and (20.18)]. When we tried the same approach for the demand equation, it failed because two instrumental variables are insufficient to estimate the three parameters of (20.2).

The instrumental variables used in (20.15) and (20.17) are the variables that are exogenous in the equation system [I in (20.15), Y in (20.17)]. If the system contains one or several equations with a constant term, it is convenient to count the associated variable also as an exogenous variable. [This variable takes the unit value for each observation; see the discussion preceding (20.18).] A necessary condition for the identifiability of the parameters of a structural equation is that *the number of exogenous variables in the equation system be at least equal to the number of parameters of the equation.* In (20.1) and (20.2) we have two exogenous variables: Y and the constant-term variable. The supply equation has two parameters, and the demand equation three. Hence, the identification condition is satisfied by the former equation and violated by the latter, in agreement with the conclusions drawn from Figure 35(*b*).

If the term $\beta_2 Y_i$ is deleted from (20.2), the supply-and-demand system has only one exogenous variable, viz., the constant-term variable. The number of parameters in both (20.1) and (20.2) is then two [β_2 being deleted from (20.2)], so that the identification condition is violated by both. This agrees with the fact that deleting β_2 yields Figure 35(*a*) in which the observation points are scattered around the intersection point of the supply and demand lines. Such a single intersection point is obviously insufficient to enable us to infer on the slope of either line.

Underidentified, Just-Identified, and Overidentified Equations

When an equation contains more parameters than there are exogenous variables in the system, these parameters are underidentified and cannot be estimated. When the numbers of parameters and exogenous variables are equal, as is the case for (20.1), the parameters are *just-identified*; we can then estimate them by using the exogenous variables as instrumental variables [see (20.17) to (20.20)]. When the number of parameters is below the number of exogenous variables, the parameters are called *overidentified*. The instrumental-variable approach of Section 20.3 will then yield more equations from which the estimates are to be solved than there are parameters to be estimated. An estimation procedure for the overidentified case is described in Section 20.5.

Note that the identification condition stated in the previous subsection is a necessary, not a sufficient, condition. Counting numbers of parameters in each equation and of exogenous variables in the system is usually enough, but sometimes the parameters of an equation are not identifiable in spite of the fact that their number does not exceed that of the exogenous variables. An example is given in Theil (1971, p. 449).

20.5 Two-Stage Least Squares

A Second Supply-and-Demand System

We return to (20.1) and (20.2), but assume now that supply depends on the wage rate (w_i in year i) and the cost of raw materials (C_i). Hence, the supply-and-demand system takes the following form:

$$(20.21) \qquad q_i = \alpha_0 + \alpha_1 p_i + \alpha_2 w_i + \alpha_3 C_i + \epsilon_i \qquad \text{(supply)}$$

$$(20.22) \qquad q_i = \beta_0 + \beta_1 p_i + \beta_2 Y_i + \epsilon_i' \qquad \text{(demand)}$$

We assume that w and C are exogenous, so that the total number of exogenous variables in the two-equation system is now four: Y, w, C, and the constant-term variable. Since the demand equation still contains three parameters (β_0, β_1, and β_2), it is now over- rather that underidentified. Our objective is to estimate these parameters from n observations under the condition that the random pairs $(\epsilon_1, \epsilon_1'), \ldots, (\epsilon_n, \epsilon_n')$ are independently and identically distributed with zero means and finite variances.

2SLS Estimation of the Demand Equation

If (20.22) contained only exogenous variables (whose values are constants) on the right, we could estimate its parameters by LS. The problem is the endogenous p_i. With the two additional exogenous variables (w and C), the reduced-form equation for p_i is changed from (20.8) into

$$(20.23) \quad p_i = -\frac{\alpha_0 - \beta_0}{\alpha_1 - \beta_1} - \frac{\alpha_2}{\alpha_1 - \beta_1} w_i - \frac{\alpha_3}{\alpha_1 - \beta_1} C_i + \frac{\beta_2}{\alpha_1 - \beta_1} Y_i + \zeta_i$$

where

(20.24) $$\zeta_i = \frac{\epsilon_i' - \epsilon_i}{\alpha_1 - \beta_1}$$

Let us write (20.22) in the following form:

(20.25) $$q_i = \beta_0 + \beta_1(p_i - \zeta_i) + \beta_2 Y_i + (\epsilon_i' + \beta_1 \zeta_i)$$

The subtraction of ζ_i from p_i should be viewed as an attempt to "purify" this endogenous variable. As (20.23) shows, this subtraction yields a linear combination of exogenous variables. Since the values taken by the latter variables are constants, the same holds for this linear combination.

Thus, (20.25) suggests an LS regression of q_i on $p_i - \zeta_i$ and Y_i for $i = 1, \ldots, n$. The problem is that subtracting ζ_i from p_i requires the supply and demand disturbances to be known [see (20.24)]. The following is a simple, although approximate, solution for this problem. We estimate the reduced-form equation (20.23) by LS,

(20.26) $$p_i = c_0 + c_1 w_i + c_2 C_i + c_3 Y_i + \hat{\zeta}_i$$

where $c_0, \ldots, c_3$ are LS coefficients and $\hat{\zeta}_i$ is the ith LS residual, which is used to approximate the corresponding disturbance ζ_i in (20.25):

(20.27) $$q_i = \beta_0 + \beta_1(p_i - \hat{\zeta}_i) + \beta_2 Y_i + (\epsilon_i' + \beta_1 \hat{\zeta}_i)$$

The two variables on the right take known values ($p_i - \hat{\zeta}_i$ and Y_i). The procedure is completed by an LS regression of q_i on $p_i - \hat{\zeta}_i$ and Y_i with constant term for $i = 1, \ldots, n$.

The previous paragraph summarizes the *two-stage least-squares* (2SLS) estimation of the demand equation (20.22). The first stage consists of LS applied to the reduced-form equation for the right-hand endogenous variable p_i, followed by subtraction of the reduced-form residual $\hat{\zeta}_i$ from p_i, which changes (20.22) into (20.27). The second stage consists of applying LS to (20.27).

Remarks on 2SLS Estimation

(1) Since $\hat{\zeta}_i$ is an LS residual, $\hat{p}_i = p_i - \hat{\zeta}_i$ is an LS adjusted value, so that (20.27) can be written as

(20.28) $$q_i = \beta_0 + \beta_1 \hat{p}_i + \beta_2 Y_i + (\epsilon_i' + \beta_1 \hat{\zeta}_i)$$

Hence, the second step of 2SLS amounts to an LS regression on the explanatory variables of the original equation (20.22) but with the right-hand endogenous variable (p) replaced by its LS adjusted value. We emphasize that this adjusted value results from LS applied to the reduced form, not to any structural equation.

(2) If 2SLS is applied to a just-identified equation, the estimates obtained are identical to those of the instrumental-variable approach of Section 20.3. For example, the consumption function (20.3) is just-identified in the Keynesian

model. When we faithfully carry out the two steps of 2SLS (see Problem 13), we obtain the β estimator (20.14).

(3) Sometimes we have several endogenous variables in the right-hand side of a structural equation. The first step of 2SLS involves the subtraction of reduced-form residuals from each of these variables. However, the actual computation of 2SLS estimates does not require the individual reduced-form residuals. The most convenient procedure is in terms of matrix algebra, as explained in Appendix H. Further details are provided in Section 21.3, which contains an example with 2SLS point estimates and asymptotic standard errors.

Problems

Problems 1 and 2 refer to Section 20.1, 3 and 4 to Section 20.2, 5–7 to Section 20.3, 8 and 9 to Section 20.4, and 10–13 to Section 20.5.

1 Verify that p_t and Y_t in (20.2) can be both nonstochastic only if the supply and demand disturbances of (20.1) and (20.2) are identically equal. [*Hint*: Subtract (20.2) from (20.1), and assume $\alpha_1 \neq \beta_1$.]

2 Consider the Rotterdam Model (14.40) as an N-equation demand system, with DQ_t and the Dp_{jt}'s as the tth observations on $N + 1$ exogenous variables. Is this system an N-equation system in the sense of Section 20.1, or does it simply consist of N one-equation systems? (*Hint*: Read the last paragraph of Section 20.1.)

3 Substitute the right-hand sides of (20.6) and (20.7) for Y_t and C_t in (20.3) to check the reduced form of the Keynesian model.

4 Verify (20.8) by subtracting (20.2) from (20.1). Then derive (20.9) by substituting (20.8) in (20.1). Do you consider the assumptions $\alpha_1 > 0$ and $\beta_1 < 0$ plausible? Explain your answer.

5 Multiply (20.5) by ϵ_t, and take the expectation to verify that the covariance of Y_t and ϵ_t equals $\sigma^2/(1 - \beta)$. Next, for $i \neq j$, multiply (20.5) by ϵ_j; prove that Y_i and ϵ_j have a zero covariance and are hence uncorrelated. [*Note*: These results show that in the system (20.3) and (20.4) income and the consumption disturbance are correlated when they refer to the same observation and uncorrelated when they refer to different observations.]

6 Read the proposition on the consistency of $f(\hat{\theta}_n)$ in the paragraph below (20.14). Give an intuitive proof-in-words of this proposition; include the continuity condition in your discussion.

7 In (20.17) and (20.18), replace α_0 by a_0, α_1 by a_1, and the disturbance terms by zero:

$$\sum_{i=1}^{n} Y_i q_i = a_0 \sum_{i=1}^{n} Y_i + a_1 \sum_{i=1}^{n} Y_i p_i \quad \text{and} \quad \sum_{i=1}^{n} q_i = n a_0 + a_1 \sum_{i=1}^{n} p_i$$

Verify that these equations yield the solution (20.19).

8 Verify that the consumption function (20.3) satisfies the identification condition in the Keynesian model (with investment exogenous). Also verify
that (20.3) is just-identified.

9 Let C_i be the cost of producing an agricultural good in year i, and consider
the following supply-and-demand system for this good:

$$q_i = \alpha_0 + \alpha_1 p_i + \alpha_2 C_i + \epsilon_i \qquad \text{(supply)}$$
$$q_i = \beta_0 + \beta_1 p_i + \epsilon_i' \qquad \text{(demand)}$$

Verify that if C is exogenous, the demand equation does but the supply
equation does not satisfy the identification condition. Illustrate this result
geometrically, similarly to Figure 35(b).

10 Apply the instrumental-variable approach of Section 20.3 to the demand
equation (20.22) in the supply-and-demand system (20.21) and (20.22).
Verify that this approach yields four equations from which the estimates of
only three parameters (β_0, β_1, and β_2) are to be solved.

11 (Continuation) Apply the same approach to the supply equation (20.21).
Does it work here? Is the supply equation underidentified, just-identified,
or overidentified?

12 Verify the reduced-form equation (20.23).

13 Write $c = \sum_i I_i Y_i / \sum_i I_i^2$ for the LS reduced-form coefficient (20.13). Verify
that the first step of 2SLS estimation of (20.3) amounts to writing this
equation as $C_i = \beta(cI_i) + \epsilon_i + \beta(Y_i - cI_i)$. Next verify that the second
step yields an estimator of β equal to the ratio of $\sum_i (cI_i)C_i$ to $\sum_i (cI_i)^2$,
and prove that this ratio equals $\hat{\beta}$ defined in (20.14).

chapter 21

Dynamic
Equation Systems

The two models discussed in Section 20.1 are both static. Most systems of simultaneous equations are dynamic in the sense that they contain variables which refer to different points or periods of time. The implied extensions involve complications that occur even when the system contains only one equation. Accordingly, Section 21.1 is devoted to dynamic one-equation systems. To emphasize the time series nature of the models discussed in this chapter, we replace the observation subscript i by t.

21.1 Distributed Lags

The Distributed-Lag Concept

A person receives a $1000 salary increase and reacts by raising his consumption expenditures by $600 in the curent year, by another $200 next year, and by another $100 in the third year. Hence, the ultimate effect is a $900 increase in consumption, and the implied consumption function is of the form

$$(21.1) \qquad y_t = \text{constant} + .6x_t + .2x_{t-1} + .1x_{t-2} + \text{disturbance}$$

where y_t and x_t are consumption and income, respectively, in year t. If the equation were of the form $y_t = .9x_{t-1} + \text{constant} + \text{disturbance}$, we would have the same ultimate effect, but it would take place with a fixed lag of one year. But in (21.1) we have a *distributed lag*; the lag is distributed over three years.

When there are several explanatory variables, each occurring with several lags, the equation takes the form

(21.2) $y_t = \beta_0 + \beta_1 x_{1t} + \beta_2 x_{2t} + \cdots + \beta_1' x_{1,t-1} + \beta_2' x_{2,t-1} + \cdots + \epsilon_t$

If the values taken by the x's are constants and if the ϵ's are uncorrelated random variables with zero mean and constant variance, LS yields best linear unbiased estimates of the β's in (21.2). But "best" is not necessarily very good. One problem is that the number of unknown parameters in (21.2) can easily be quite large when we have several x's with several lags. Another is that successive values taken by the same explanatory variable, such as x_t and x_{t-1} for $t = 1, 2,$ $\ldots$ in (21.1) and x_{1t} and $x_{1,t-1}$ in (21.2), will in many cases be rather highly correlated, leading to a multicollinearity problem in the LS estimation of the β's.

Koyck's Method

To solve this problem, we impose constraints on the coefficients of successive values taken by the same explanatory variable. Let us consider the case of one explanatory variable:

(21.3) $y_t = \beta_0 + \beta_1 x_t + \beta_2 x_{t-1} + \beta_3 x_{t-2} + \cdots + \epsilon_t$

In many cases it is plausible that the coefficient series $\beta_1, \beta_2, \ldots$ converges to zero in a rather regular manner. Let this decline be geometric, starting at the first lag: $\beta_2 = \rho\beta_1$, $\beta_3 = \rho^2\beta_1, \ldots$, where $0 < \rho < 1$, so that (21.3) becomes

(21.4) $y_t = \beta_0 + \beta_1 x_t + \rho\beta_1 x_{t-1} + \rho^2\beta_1 x_{t-2} + \cdots + \epsilon_t$

We lag this equation by one period and multiply by ρ,

$$\rho y_{t-1} = \rho\beta_0 + \rho\beta_1 x_{t-1} + \rho^2\beta_1 x_{t-2} + \cdots + \rho\epsilon_{t-1}$$

and subtract this equation from (21.4). The result can be written as

(21.5) $y_t = (1 - \rho)\beta_0 + \beta_1 x_t + \rho y_{t-1} + (\epsilon_t - \rho\epsilon_{t-1})$

This equation has the same dependent variable as (21.3) but different variables on the right. The original explanatory variable now occurs only in current form (x_t), and we also have the lagged dependent variable (y_{t-1}) about which we shall have more to say in the next subsection.

When we use (21.5) by running an LS regression of y_t on x_t and y_{t-1}, we avoid the multicollinearity problem of successive x's, because the only x in (21.5) is x_t. This regression is the simplest version of Koyck's (1954) method of estimating distributed lags.

The Problem of Lagged Dependent Variables

The explanatory variables in (21.5) are x_t and y_{t-1}. The standard linear model assumes that the values of the explanatory variables can be treated as constants, but this cannot apply to y_{t-1}. For $t = 1$, the dependent variable of (21.5) takes the random value y_1, but this is also the second value ($t = 2$) of y_{t-1}. Since it is impossible to maintain that y_1 is both random and nonstochastic, we must face the fact that one of the explanatory variables in (21.5) takes random values.

Also, y_{t-1} may be correlated with the disturbance $\epsilon_t - \rho\epsilon_{t-1}$ in (21.5). Since ϵ_t is the random component of y_t in (21.4), ϵ_{t-1} must be the random component of y_{t-1}, so that it would not be surprising if y_{t-1} and $\epsilon_t - \rho\epsilon_{t-1}$ were correlated. Indeed, this can be shown to be true if $\epsilon_1, \epsilon_2, \ldots$ are uncorrelated random variables.

Suppose, however, that the ϵ's are generated by the autoregressive process (19.10), written here as

$$(21.6) \qquad \epsilon_t = \rho\epsilon_{t-1} + \zeta_t$$

where the ζ's are independently and identically distributed with zero mean and constant variance. We can then write (21.5) as

$$(21.7) \qquad y_t = (1 - \rho)\beta_0 + \beta_1 x_t + \rho y_{t-1} + \zeta_t$$

We still face the problem that y_{t-1} is random, but it can be shown that y_{t-1} is stochastically independent of the disturbance ζ_t in (21.7). This saves the situation for large samples: The LS point estimators obtained from (21.7) are consistent, and the conventional expressions for the LS standard errors remain valid in the sense that they can be interpreted as asymptotic standard errors. For proofs, see Theil (1971, pp. 260–261, 417).

Qualifications and Extensions

The results obtained above are pleasing because of their simplicity. However, note the restrictive assumption that the same parameter ρ applies to the geometric decline of the coefficients in (21.4) and also to the autoregressive process (21.6). If we have different ρ's in these two equations, ρ_1 in (21.4) and ρ_2 in (21.6) and $\rho_1 \neq \rho_2$, the regression of y_t on x_t and y_{t-1} [see (21.5)] does not yield consistent estimators. Restrictive assumptions are needed to handle the presence of a lagged dependent variable among the explanatory variables. Also, this presence causes the Durbin-Watson statistic (19.20) to be biased toward the acceptance of the hypothesis of uncorrelated ζ_t's in (21.7); see Theil (1971, pp. 408–425) for details on this matter.

Koyck's method can be extended in various directions (see Problems 1 and 2). A different approach is that of the Almon or polynomial distributed lags (see Problem 3). The latter approach does not involve a regression on a lagged dependent variable and thus avoids one of the problems of Koyck's method, but it requires that the degree of the polynomial be specified.

21.2   An Example of a Dynamic Equation System

When we extend a single equation to a system of several simultaneous equations, we have several endogenous variables rather than a single dependent variable. If the system is dynamic, we have one or several lagged endogenous and exogenous variables. This is illustrated below by means of one of the models constructed by Klein (1950) for the U.S. economy, the so-called Klein Model I.

The Behavioral Equations of Klein's Model I

One of the equations of the model is a consumption function which describes total consumption (C_t in year t) in terms of current and lagged profit income (P_t and P_{t-1}) and current wage income:

$$(21.8) \qquad C_t = \beta_0 + \beta_1 P_t + \beta_2 P_{t-1} + \beta_3(W_t + W_t') + \epsilon_t$$

Here W_t is the total wage bill paid by private industry, W_t' is the government wage bill, and ϵ_t is the disturbance of the consumption function (all in year t). The model refers to the years 1920–1941; its variables are all measured in billions of dollars of 1934 purchasing power per year, except when stated otherwise.

Let I_t be net investment in year t. The investment function is

$$(21.9) \qquad I_t = \beta_0' + \beta_1' P_t + \beta_2' P_{t-1} + \beta_3' K_{t-1} + \epsilon_t'$$

where K_t is the stock of capital goods at the end of year t (measured in billions of 1934 dollars, not per year, because K is a stock rather than a flow variable). The presumption is $\beta_3' < 0$, implying that if the capital stock at the beginning of the year (K_{t-1}) is larger, the addition to capital stock in the form of net investment is reduced. The investment function (21.9) is similar to the consumption function (21.8) in that both contain current profits (P_t) and profits lagged one year (P_{t-1}).

The third behavioral equation of the model is a demand-for-labor function. This demand is measured by the wage bill of private industry in billions of 1934 dollars per year, which is W_t of (21.8). The demand for labor is assumed to depend on the total production of private industry, both current and with a one-year lag (X_t and X_{t-1}). The equation takes the form

$$(21.10) \qquad W_t = \beta_0'' + \beta_1'' X_t + \beta_2'' X_{t-1} + \beta_3''(t - 1931) + \epsilon_t''$$

where t is time measured in calendar years. Thus, the wage bill of private industry contains a linear trend, which the author of the model ascribes to the increasing strength of labor unions in the period between the wars.

The Definitional Equations of Klein's Model I

The model contains three identities in addition to the above behavioral relations. One states that the change in capital stock equals net investment. This may be written as

$$(21.11) \qquad K_t = K_{t-1} + I_t$$

The second identity states that the production of the private sector (X_t) is for either consumption (C_t) or investment (I_t) or the government. We write this as

$$(21.12) \qquad X_t = C_t + I_t + G_t$$

where G_t is government nonwage expenditure.

Finally, there is a profit identity for the private sector as a whole: Subtract from total output (X_t) the amounts paid as wages (W_t) and taxes, and what remains is total profits (P_t). This gives

(21.13) $$P_t = X_t - W_t - T_t$$

where T_t stands for business taxes in year t.

Which Variables Are Exogenous?

The model (21.8) to (21.13) is a six-equation system in 10 variables. These variables and their symbols are listed in columns (1) and (2) of Table 27 in the order in which they appear in the successive equations. Column (3) indicates by L whether the variable occurs with a one-year lag. For example, consumption appears in current form in (21.8) and (21.12) and is nowhere lagged, but profits appear in current form in (21.8), (21.9), and (21.13) and also in lagged form in (21.8) and (21.9).

TABLE 27

The variables of Klein's Model I

Symbol (1)	Description (2)	Lagged (3)	Endogenous (4)	Exogenous (5)
C	Consumption		x	
P	Profits	L	x	
W	Wage bill paid by private industry		x	
W'	Government wage bill			x
I	Net investment		x	
K	Capital stock at year-end	L	x	
X	Total output of private industry	L	x	
t	Time (in calendar years)			x
G	Government nonwage expenditure			x
T	Business taxes			x

Calendar time (t) is obviously an exogenous variable. The time passes independently of anything and hence certainly independently of the economy of the United States which the model serves to describe. Next consider the three government variables W', G, and T. If we imagine that the government controls these variables, their values are fixed and given from the viewpoint of the behavioral equations (21.8) to (21.10). Thus, we have four exogenous and six endogenous variables, as indicated by crosses in the last two columns of Table 27, and the model (21.8) to (21.13) has become a complete six-equation system.

We should add that it is not quite satisfactory to say that the government controls a variable such as T (business tax revenue in billions of 1934 dollars). It is preferable to say that the government controls *tax rates*. This can be handled by the introduction of a seventh equation which describes tax revenue in terms of a tax rate (and possibly other determining factors); tax revenue then becomes the seventh endogenous variable. The designation of W', G, and T as exogenous variables should be viewed as a convenient simplification. Although Klein's Model I is larger than the two models discussed in Section 20.1, it is still a very small and oversimplified model.

The Reduced Form with Lagged Endogenous Variables

The reduced-form equations (20.6) to (20.9) describe endogenous variables in terms of exogenous variables and disturbances of structural equations. When the system is dynamic, we may have lagged endogenous variables. This holds for P, K, and X in Klein's Model I (see Table 27). In such a case we extend the reduced-form concept; each reduced-form equation describes a current endogenous variable in terms of (1) current exogenous variables, (2) lagged variables, and (3) disturbances of structural equations. In a complete six-equation system we have six current endogenous variables; the reduced form of this system will then consist of six equations. For example, in the case of Klein's Model I we obtain for the total output of private industry in year t (X_t), after some tedious algebra,

$$(21.14) \quad X_t = \text{constant} + \frac{\beta_3 W'_t - (\beta_1 + \beta'_1)T_t + G_t - \beta''_3 \gamma(t - 1931)}{D}$$
$$+ \frac{(\beta_2 + \beta'_2)P_{t-1} + \beta'_3 K_{t-1} - \beta''_2 \gamma X_{t-1}}{D} + \frac{\epsilon_t + \epsilon'_t - \gamma \epsilon''_t}{D}$$

where

$$(21.15) \qquad\qquad \gamma = \beta_1 - \beta_3 + \beta'_1$$

$$(21.16) \qquad\qquad D = 1 - (\beta_1 + \beta'_1)(1 - \beta''_1) - \beta_3 \beta''_1$$

The condition for the existence of the solution (21.14) is $D \neq 0$. This condition is further considered in Problem 4.

Equation (21.14) illustrates the reduced form of a dynamic equation system. The first ratio on the right contains the current exogenous variables (W'_t, G_t, T_t, and t), the second contains lagged variables (P_{t-1}, K_{t-1}, and X_{t-1}), and the third contains the disturbances ϵ_t, ϵ'_t, and ϵ''_t of the structural equations (21.8) to (21.10).

Jointly Dependent and Predetermined Variables

The statistical justification for including lagged endogenous variables among the right-hand variables of the reduced form is based on the assumption that the disturbance triples (ϵ_t, ϵ'_t, ϵ''_t) for $t = 1, 2, \ldots$ are independently distributed. This assumption implies that the lagged endogenous variables are independent of the *current operation* of the equation system; this will be clarified at the end of Section 21.4.

Consider then the following 2×2 classification:

	Endogenous variables	Exogenous variables
Current variables	Current endogenous	Current exogenous
Lagged variables	Lagged endogenous	Lagged exogenous

Current endogenous variables (C_t, P_t, W_t, I_t, K_t, X_t in Klein's Model I) are called *jointly dependent variables*. They are the left-hand variables of the reduced-form equations. (We shall usually delete "jointly" when we consider only one such variable.) All other variables are called *predetermined*; they are either lagged or exogenous or both. For a lagged endogenous variable such as P_{t-1} we should interpret predetermined in a temporal sense. For a current exogenous variable such as T_t we interpret it in a causal sense, the variable being determined "from the outside." Both interpretations apply to a lagged exogenous variable, but such variables do not occur in Klein's Model I.

Arrow Schemes

The function of the reduced form under the new interpretation is thus to describe the behavior of the jointly dependent variables in terms of the predetermined variables and the disturbances. The structural equations provide an equivalent description, but they do so in terms of more elementary (structural) concepts. It is instructive to display the latter description in graphical form, as shown in Figure 36 for the consumption function (21.8), reproduced below with the subscript t deleted and $t - 1$ abbreviated as -1:

$$(21.17) \qquad C = \beta_0 + \beta_1 P + \beta_2 P_{-1} + \beta_3(W + W') + \epsilon$$

In the shaded bar we have the current exogenous variables: W' in (21.17). Above the bar we have the lagged variable P_{-1}. Below the bar we have the current

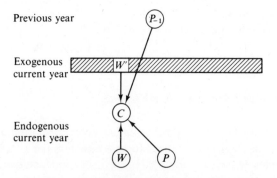

FIGURE 36   **Arrow scheme for the consumption function of Klein's Model I**

endogenous variables of (21.17): C, W, and P. These variables are connected with arrows pointing to C, the left-hand variable of (21.17).

Arrow schemes can be drawn for each equation of the system. The investment equation (21.9) contains only endogenous variables. Arrows in this case come in at I (a current endogenous variable and hence below the bar) from P, P_{-1}, and K_{-1}; the last two are above the bar since they are lagged. The two equations, (21.8) and (21.9), make up the scheme shown in Figure 37. When we continue in this way for the other four equations of the system, we obtain the rather intricate arrow scheme drawn in Figure 38.

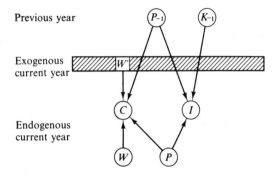

FIGURE 37   Arrow scheme for the consumption and investment functions of Klein's Model I

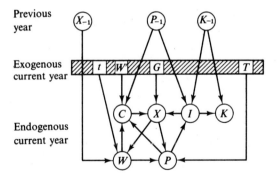

FIGURE 38   Arrow scheme for all equations of Klein's Model I

Such an arrow scheme clearly shows the interdependencies of the jointly dependent variables that are implied by the structural equations. For example, W influences C [the upward-pointing arrow, resulting from (21.8)], C influences X [the arrow pointing to the right, from (21.12)], and X influences W [the arrow pointing southwest, from (21.10)]. Even more importantly, the arrow scheme shows that there are two kinds of variables. On the one hand, there are the variables where arrows arrive and depart; these are the current endogenous variables (the jointly dependent variables) that are drawn below the bar. On the other hand, there are the variables from which arrows only depart. These are the exogenous variables in the bar and the lagged variables above the bar, which are the predetermined variables in the dynamic equation system.

21.3   Identification and Estimation in Dynamic Equation Systems

Identifying the Parameters of Klein's Model I

We assume that the disturbances of the structural equations are independent over time. In the case of Klein's Model I this means that the triples $(\epsilon_t, \epsilon_t', \epsilon_t'')$ of (21.8) to (21.10) for $t = 1, 2, \ldots$ are independently distributed.

Under this assumption, the identification and 2SLS estimation procedures of Sections 20.4 and 20.5 apply directly to dynamic equation systems, the only change being that exogenous variables are replaced by predetermined variables. Thus, a necessary condition for the identification of the parameters of a structural equation in a dynamic equation system is that *the number of predetermined variables in the system be at least equal to the number of parameters in the equation.* In Klein's Model I we have four current exogenous variables, no lagged exogenous variables, and three endogenous variables with a one-year lag (see Table 27). This yields seven predetermined variables, which is raised to eight when we take the constant-term variable into account [see β_0, β_0', and β_0'' in (21.8) to (21.10)]. The number of parameters is four in each of the behavioral equations (21.8) to (21.10). Therefore, these parameters are all overidentified.

2SLS Estimation of the Parameters of Klein's Model I

Consider the demand-for-labor function (21.10), reproduced here:

$$W_t = \beta_0'' + \beta_1'' X_t + \beta_2'' X_{t-1} + \beta_3''(t - 1931) + \epsilon_t''$$

All variables on the right are predetermined except X_t. Thus, we write the equation in the form

$$(21.18) \quad W_t = \beta_0'' + \beta_1''\left(X_t - \frac{\epsilon_t + \epsilon_t' - \gamma\epsilon_t''}{D}\right) + \beta_2'' X_{t-1} + \beta_3''(t - 1931)$$
$$+ \left(\epsilon_t'' + \beta_1''\frac{\epsilon_t + \epsilon_t' - \gamma\epsilon_t''}{D}\right)$$

where $(\epsilon_t + \epsilon_t' - \gamma\epsilon_t'')/D$ is the disturbance of the reduced-form equation (21.14) for X_t. Following the example of (20.25) to (20.27), we approximate this disturbance by the corresponding LS residual. Thus, we estimate (21.14) by LS,

$$(21.19) \quad X_t = c_0 + c_1 W_t' + c_2 T_t + c_3 G_t + c_4(t - 1931)$$
$$+ c_5 P_{t-1} + c_6 K_{t-1} + c_7 X_{t-1} + v_t$$

where $c_0, \ldots, c_7$ are LS coefficients and v_t is the tth LS residual. We replace (21.18) by

$$(21.20) \quad W_t = \beta_0'' + \beta_1''(X_t - v_t) + \beta_2'' X_{t-1} + \beta_3''(t - 1931) + (\epsilon_t'' + \beta_1'' v_t)$$

after which we run a regression of W_t on $X_t - v_t$, X_{t-1}, and $t - 1931$.

When this procedure is applied to the consumption and investment equations also, we obtain the following 2SLS estimated versions of the behavioral equations of Klein's Model I, with asymptotic standard errors in parentheses:

$$(21.21) \quad C_t = 16.6 + .02P_t + .22P_{t-1} + .81(W_t + W_t') + \text{residual}$$
$$ (1.3) \ (.12) \quad (.11) \quad\quad (.04)$$

$$(21.22) \quad I_t = 20.3 + .15P_t + .62P_{t-1} - .16K_{t-1} + \text{residual}$$
$$ (7.5) \ (.17) \quad (.16) \quad\quad (.04)$$

$$(21.23) \quad W_t = 1.5 + .44X_t + .15X_{t-1} + .13(t - 1931) + \text{residual}$$
$$ (1.1) \ (.04) \quad (.04) \quad\quad (.03)$$

Remarks on the 2SLS Procedure

(1) The investment function (21.9) is similar to the demand-for-labor function (21.10) in that it contains only one dependent variable on the right, P_t, but the consumption function (21.8) contains two such variables: P_t and the sum $W_t + W_t'$. This sum involves a dependent variable (W_t) and a predetermined variable (W_t'). Since W_t is random and stochastically dependent on the disturbances in t, the same holds for $W_t + W_t'$. Accordingly, the 2SLS procedure for (21.8), yielding (21.21), amounts to an LS regression after the reduced-form residual of P_t is subtracted from P_t and that of W_t from $W_t + W_t'$.

(2) The statistical justification of the 2SLS approach is of the large-sample type. When there are no lagged endogenous variables (as in the case discussed in Chapter 20), the 2SLS coefficient estimators are consistent if the exogenous variables are constant in repeated samples and if the disturbance triples (ϵ_t, ϵ_t', ϵ_t'') for $t = 1, 2, \ldots$ are independently and identically distributed with zero means and finite variances. If these two conditions are satisfied, the sampling distribution of the 2SLS coefficient estimators becomes approximately normal for large samples, and the asymptotic standard errors shown in parentheses in (21.21) to (21.23) can be used to assess the sampling variability of the 2SLS estimates. The derivation of the asymptotic standard errors is described in Appendix H.

(3) When the equation system contains lagged endogenous variables, the consistency and large-sample normality of the 2SLS coefficient estimators require an additional condition. This third condition ensures that as the sample size increases the mean square of the values taken by each lagged endogenous variable converges in probability to a positive limit; see Theil (1971, Sections 10.1 and 10.3) for details on this matter.

(4) If the triples (ϵ_t, ϵ_t', ϵ_t'') for $t = 1, 2, \ldots$ are *not* independently distributed, lagged endogenous variables are not independent of the current operation of

the equation system (see the end of Section 21.4 below), which means that these variables are not really predetermined. If these variables are nevertheless treated as predetermined in the 2SLS procedure, the resulting estimators are not consistent.

21.4   The Final Form of a Dynamic Equation System

We showed in Section 20.2 how the reduced form can be used to assess the effect of a change in an exogenous variable on an endogenous variable. Further analysis is needed to obtain a complete picture of such effects when the system contains lagged endogenous variables.

The Final Form

Consider again the reduced-form equation (21.14), reproduced here:

$$(21.24) \quad X_t = \text{constant} + \frac{\beta_3 W'_t - (\beta_1 + \beta'_1)T_t + G_t - \beta''_3\gamma(t - 1931)}{D}$$
$$+ \frac{(\beta_2 + \beta'_2)P_{t-1} + \beta'_3 K_{t-1} - \beta''_2\gamma X_{t-1}}{D} + \frac{\epsilon_t + \epsilon'_t - \gamma\epsilon''_t}{D}$$

The first ratio on the right shows that a unit increase in the exogenous W' (government wage bill) raises the endogenous X (the volume of total private production) by β_3/D units in the same year. The effects of a unit increase in T and G are similarly equal to $-(\beta_1 + \beta'_1)/D$ and $1/D$ units, respectively, in the same year. We have no lagged exogenous variable in (21.24), but it would be wrong to conclude that a change in an exogenous variable has a zero effect on X one year later.

The reason is that the second ratio in the right-hand side of (21.24) contains lagged endogenous variables, including X_{t-1}. By lagging (21.24) by one year, we obtain

$$X_{t-1} = \text{constant} + \frac{\beta_3 W'_{t-1} - (\beta_1 + \beta'_1)T_{t-1} + G_{t-1} - \beta''_3\gamma(t - 1932)}{D}$$
$$+ \frac{(\beta_2 + \beta'_2)P_{t-2} + \beta'_3 K_{t-2} - \beta''_2\gamma X_{t-2}}{D} + \frac{\epsilon_{t-1} + \epsilon'_{t-1} - \gamma\epsilon''_{t-1}}{D}$$

When we substitute this in (21.24) and proceed similarly for the other lagged endogenous variables (P_{t-1} and K_{t-1}), we find that X_t becomes a linear function of (1) exogenous variables and disturbances in t and $t - 1$ and (2) endogenous variables in $t - 2$, including X_{t-2}. Next, by lagging (21.24) by two years, we obtain an equation for X_{t-2} in terms of exogenous variables and disturbances in $t - 2$ and endogenous variables in $t - 3$, and so on.

When we continue in this way, we obtain the *final form* of the equation system, which describes current endogenous variables (such as X_t) in terms of current and lagged exogenous variables and disturbances. All lagged endogenous variables are eliminated by successive lagged application of the reduced form.

Impact, Interim, and Total Multipliers

Table 28 contains estimates of the successive final-form coefficients for all six endogenous variables of Klein's Model I and for three exogenous variables: W', G, and T. The exogenous time trend $(t - 1931)$ is not considered because it is less interesting.

The first row of the table displays the current effect of an exogenous change on the endogenous variables. Thus, a one-million-dollar increase in the government wage bill (W') raises consumption (C) by 1.34 million dollars and profits (P) by .89 million dollars in the same year. These numbers (1.34, .89, etc.), which measure the immediate impact of exogenous changes, are known as the *impact multipliers* of the equation system. Note that the impact multipliers of business taxes (T) are all negative.

The final-form coefficients in the next rows, corresponding to positive lags, are called the *interim multipliers* of the system. Thus, whereas a one-million-dollar increase in T has a modest negative effect on C in the same year, it reduces C by about one million dollars in each of the next two years. This suggests that Klein's Model I is characterized by substantial lagged effects. Figure 39 illustrates the impact and interim multipliers in the form of vertical distances from a horizontal time axis; successive points are connected by straight lines to yield a clearer picture. These lines indicate a damped oscillatory behavior. *Oscillatory* means that the successive final-form coefficients tend to be positive first, then negative, then positive again, and so on, or vice versa. *Damped* means that the coefficients ultimately converge to zero when the lag becomes sufficiently large.

The last row of Table 28 contains the sum of all impact and interim multipliers of each column, which is known as the *total multiplier*. For example, the ultimate effect of a one-million-dollar increase in W' on C is an increase of

$$1.34 + .94 + .69 + .32 - .03 - .27 - \ldots = 1.86 \text{ million dollars}$$

Hence, the total multiplier of C with respect to W' is 1.86. Note that the increase in W' must be interpreted as a nonsustained increase, for one year only. The effects of sustained increases are obtained by adding final-form coefficients (see Problem 8).

Lagged Endogenous Variables and the Current Operation of the System

We concluded at the end of the first subsection that the final form describes a current endogenous variable such as X_t in terms of exogenous variables and disturbances in $t, t - 1, t - 2, \ldots$. When we lag this equation by one year, we obtain X_{t-1} expressed in terms of exogenous variables and disturbances in $t - 1, t - 2, t - 3, \ldots$. The random component of X_{t-1} is thus a function of $(\epsilon_{t-1}, \epsilon'_{t-1}, \epsilon''_{t-1}), (\epsilon_{t-2}, \epsilon'_{t-2}, \epsilon''_{t-2}), \ldots$ but *not* of $(\epsilon_t, \epsilon'_t, \epsilon''_t)$. Hence, if the disturbance triples are independently distributed over time, lagged endogenous vari-

TABLE 28

Impact, interim, and total multipliers of Klein's Model I

Lag in years	Unit increase in W'						Unit increase in T						Unit increase in G					
	C	P	W	I	K	X	C	P	W	I	K	X	C	P	W	I	K	X
0	1.34	.89	.65	.21	.21	1.54	-.19	-1.28	-.20	-.30	-.30	-.48	.67	1.12	.81	.26	.26	1.93
1	.94	.64	.90	.61	.81	1.54	-1.01	-1.03	-.88	-.89	-1.19	-1.91	1.17	.80	1.13	.76	1.02	1.93
2	.69	.32	.67	.31	1.12	.99	-1.01	-.57	-.95	-.52	-1.71	-1.52	.86	.40	.84	.38	1.40	1.24
3	.32	.03	.30	.02	1.14	.34	-.54	-.12	-.52	-.09	-1.80	-.63	.40	.04	.38	.02	1.42	.42
4	-.03	-.18	-.04	-.19	.95	-.22	-.03	.24	-.01	.25	-1.54	.23	-.03	-.23	-.04	-.24	1.18	-.27
5	-.27	-.30	-.28	-.31	.64	-.57	.37	.44	.38	.46	-1.09	.82	-.34	-.37	-.35	-.38	.80	-.72
6	-.39	-.33	-.40	-.33	.31	-.72	.59	.51	.60	.52	-.57	1.11	-.49	-.41	-.50	-.41	.39	-.90
7	-.41	-.29	-.41	-.29	.02	-.70	.64	.46	.65	.47	-.10	1.11	-.51	-.36	-.52	-.36	.03	-.87
8	-.35	-.21	-.35	-.21	-.19	-.55	.56	.34	.56	.35	.24	.91	-.43	-.26	-.43	-.26	-.23	-.69
9	-.24	-.11	-.24	-.11	-.30	-.35	.40	.20	.40	.20	.44	.60	-.30	-.14	-.30	-.14	-.37	-.44
10	-.12	-.03	-.12	-.02	-.32	-.14	.22	.06	.21	.06	.50	.28	-.15	-.03	-.15	-.03	-.40	-.18
11	-.01	.04	-.01	.04	-.28	.03	.05	-.05	.04	-.05	.45	-.00	-.02	.05	-.02	.05	-.35	.03
12	.06	.08	.06	.08	-.20	.14	-.08	-.11	-.08	-.12	.33	-.20	.08	.10	.08	.10	-.25	.18
13	.10	.09	.11	.09	-.11	.20	-.15	-.14	-.16	-.14	.19	-.30	.13	.11	.13	.12	-.13	.25
14	.12	.08	.12	.08	-.02	.20	-.18	-.13	-.18	-.14	.05	-.31	.14	.10	.14	.11	-.03	.25
15	.10	.06	.10	.06	.04	.16	-.16	-.10	-.16	-.10	-.05	-.27	.13	.08	.13	.08	.05	.21
16	.07	.04	.07	.04	.08	.11	-.12	-.06	-.12	-.06	-.11	-.19	.09	.05	.09	.05	.10	.14
17	.04	.01	.04	.01	.09	.05	-.07	-.02	-.07	-.02	-.14	-.10	.05	.01	.05	.01	.11	.06
18	.01	-.01	.01	-.01	.08	.00	-.02	.01	-.02	.01	-.13	-.01	.01	-.01	.05	-.01	.10	.00
19	-.01	-.02	-.01	-.02	.06	-.03	.02	.03	.02	.03	-.10	.05	-.02	-.03	-.02	-.03	.08	-.04
20	-.03	-.03	-.03	-.03	.04	-.05	.04	.04	.04	.04	-.06	.08	-.03	-.03	-.03	-.03	.04	-.07
Total multiplier	1.86	.77	1.09	0	4.10	1.86	-.57	-1.24	-.33	0	-6.56	-.57	1.32	.96	1.36	0	5.12	2.32

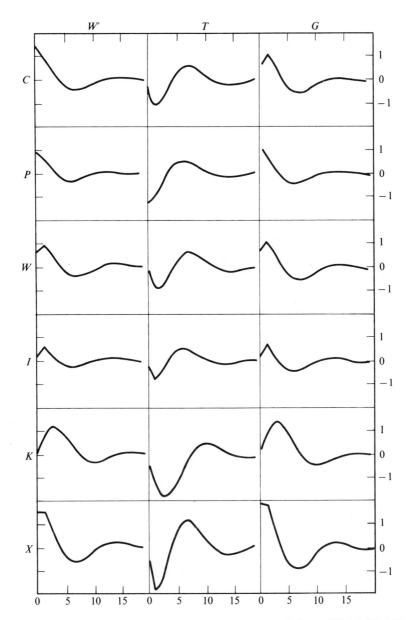

FIGURE 39   The behavior of the successive final-form coefficients of Klein's Model I

ables such as X_{t-1} are stochastically independent of the current operation of the equation system as described by the current disturbances ϵ_t, ϵ_t', and ϵ_t''.

On the other hand, if the disturbances are not independent over time, X_{t-1} will not be stochastically independent of ϵ_t, ϵ_t', and ϵ_t'' in spite of the fact that the final form does not describe X_{t-1} as a function of these three ϵ's. The stochastic dependence of X_{t-1} on these ϵ's is then caused by the dependence of the ϵ's in t on the ϵ's in $t-1$. As stated in remark (4) on page 341, X_{t-1} is not really predetermined in this case, and 2SLS estimates which treat X_{t-1} as predetermined are not consistent.

*21.5   Recursive Systems

Equation Systems of a Special Form

Consider the following three-equation system, where the y's are jointly dependent variables, the x's predetermined variables, and the ϵ's random disturbances:

$$
\begin{align}
(21.25) \qquad & \gamma_1 y_{1t} && + \beta_1 x_{1t} + \beta_2 x_{2t} = \epsilon_{1t} \\
(21.26) \qquad & \gamma_2 y_{1t} + \gamma_3 y_{2t} && + \beta_3 x_{1t} + \beta_4 x_{2t} = \epsilon_{2t} \\
(21.27) \qquad & \gamma_4 y_{1t} + \gamma_5 y_{2t} + \gamma_6 y_{3t} + \beta_5 x_{1t} + \beta_6 x_{2t} = \epsilon_{3t}
\end{align}
$$

Equation (21.25) contains only one dependent variable. If we divide both sides by γ_1, we obtain an equation that describes this variable in terms of the two predetermined variables and a disturbance:

$$
y_{1t} = -\frac{\beta_1}{\gamma_1} x_{1t} - \frac{\beta_2}{\gamma_1} x_{2t} + \frac{\epsilon_{1t}}{\gamma_1}
$$

This is a reduced-form equation, which can be estimated directly by LS. Thus, we can solve the estimation problem for (21.25) by means of an LS regression of y_1 on x_1 and x_2.

In (21.26) we have two jointly dependent variables, one in addition to that which occurs in (21.25), and in (21.27) we have three such variables, one in addition to the two of (21.26). Suppose that, for each t, the three disturbances ϵ_{1t}, ϵ_{2t}, and ϵ_{3t} are independently distributed. Since ϵ_{1t} may be viewed as the random component of $\gamma_1 y_{1t}$ in (21.25), this independence suggests that we can regard (21.25) as a one-equation system which determines y_1, so that y_1 becomes predetermined in the two other equations. Continuing this line of thought, we conclude that (21.26) is a one-equation system with three predetermined variables (x_1, x_2, y_1) which determines y_2 and that (21.27) is a one-equation system with four predetermined variables (x_1, x_2, y_1, y_2) which determines y_3. Thus, the three-equation system is interpreted as a hierarchy of one-equation systems, each containing only one dependent variable. Can we estimate such one-equation systems by LS?

Recursive Systems

Consider the following conditions:
(1) The structural equations can be arranged so that the first contains one dependent variable, the second, two—one in addition to the dependent variable of the first equation—and so on. This is satisfied by the model (21.25) to (21.27).

(2) The disturbances of the structural equations are independent across equations and across observations. Recall from remark (2) on page 341 that, in the case of Klein's Model I, the disturbance triples $(\epsilon_t, \epsilon'_t, \epsilon''_t)$ for $t = 1, 2, \ldots$ are assumed to be independently distributed. This is independence across observations, which is also assumed for the triples $(\epsilon_{1t}, \epsilon_{2t}, \epsilon_{3t})$ of the model (21.25) to (21.27). We now also assume that, for each t, the three disturbances $\epsilon_{1t}, \epsilon_{2t}$, and ϵ_{3t} are independently distributed; this is *contemporaneous* independence across equations. The implication is that the joint density function of *all* ϵ_{it}'s is equal to the product of the univariate density functions of the ϵ_{it}'s separately.

If conditions (1) and (2) are satisfied, the equation system is called *recursive*; successive dependent variables are determined recursively by the successive structural equations. If the disturbances are normally distributed with zero mean and constant variances (the variances of $\epsilon_{1t}, \epsilon_{2t}$, and ϵ_{3t} being independent of t), the maximum-likelihood approach yields estimators identical to those obtained from LS applied to each structural equation separately. In (21.25) to (21.27) there are two x's and no constant terms, but this result holds for any number of x's with and without constant terms. For a proof, see Theil (1971, p. 525).

We conclude that there is no real simultanity in recursive systems. However, when we run LS regressions to estimate the equations of such a system, we should be careful in the selection of the regressors and the regressands, as the following example will show.

A Dynamic Model of Supply and Demand

Consider the following supply-and-demand system:

(21.28)
$$q_t = \alpha_0 + \alpha p_{t-1} + \epsilon_t \qquad \text{(supply)}$$

(21.29)
$$q_t = \beta_0 + \beta p_t + \epsilon'_t \qquad \text{(demand)}$$

Our observations are $t = 1, 2, \ldots$; we assume that the disturbances $\epsilon_1, \epsilon'_1, \epsilon_2, \epsilon'_2, \ldots$ are independently distributed. Hence, p_{t-1} is a predetermined variable, so that the supply equation is in reduced form and can be estimated by means of an LS regression of q_t on p_{t-1}.

Given that (21.28) is a one-equation system determining q_t, this variable is predetermined in the demand equation (21.29). Hence, p_t is the only dependent variable in (21.29); the role of this variable is to ensure that demand equals supply. Therefore, when we solve (21.29) for p_t,

(21.30)
$$p_t = -\frac{\beta_0}{\beta} + \frac{1}{\beta} q_t - \frac{\epsilon'_t}{\beta}$$

we have the dependent variable on the left and the predetermined variable on the right. Thus, we can estimate $-\beta_0/\beta$ and $1/\beta$ by means of an LS regression of p on q. Note that (21.29) contains these variables in reverse order, suggesting a regression of q on p. The two regressions are illustrated in Figure 40. The regression which we need, based on (21.30), is that of p on q. Since p is measured horizontally, this regression minimizes the sum of the squared discrepancies in

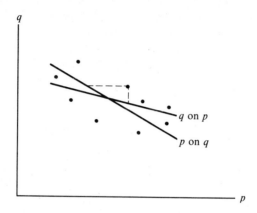

FIGURE 40 Regressions of price on quantity
and of quantity on price

the horizontal direction. This is in contrast to the regression of q on p, for which the discrepancies are measured vertically (see the horizontal and vertical broken lines, both corresponding to the same observation point). The "horizontal" minimization yields a steeper demand line than its vertical counterpart unless the observation points are all exactly on a straight line. This is illustrated in Figure 40 and pursued algebraically in Problem 10. The slope of the estimated demand line is the estimate of β, which measures the price sensitivity of demand in (21.29). Therefore, a predetermined q yields a higher degree of price sensitivity of demand in this model than does a predetermined p.

Block-Recursive Systems

Let there be several goods, each with a supply and a demand equation, and let the prices in the supply equations all be lagged. For three goods we thus have the following supply equations:

$$q_{1t} = \alpha_0 + \alpha_1 p_{1,t-1} + \alpha_2 p_{2,t-1} + \alpha_3 p_{3,t-1} + \text{disturbance}$$
$$q_{2t} = \beta_0 + \beta_1 p_{1,t-1} + \beta_2 p_{2,t-1} + \beta_3 p_{3,t-1} + \text{disturbance}$$
$$q_{3t} = \gamma_0 + \gamma_1 p_{1,t-1} + \gamma_2 p_{2,t-1} + \gamma_3 p_{3,t-1} + \text{disturbance}$$

When these equations are combined with the three demand equations, we obtain a six-equation system. If the six supply and demand disturbances are stochastically independent across observations, the supply equations are in reduced form. If the supply disturbances are stochastically independent of the demand disturbances for each t, the six-equation supply and demand system is *block-recursive* in the sense that the three demand equations form a three-equation block in which the three quantities can be treated as predetermined variables. These quantities are predetermined by the three supply equations in the same way that q_t in (21.29) is predetermined by the supply equation (21.28).

Application to the Rotterdam Model

Consider the conditional demand model (14.58) for meats,

(21.31) $$\frac{\bar{w}_{it}}{\bar{W}_{gt}} Dq_{it} = \frac{\mu_i}{M_g} DQ_{gt} + \sum_{j=1}^{4} \pi_{ij}^* Dp_{jt} + \epsilon_{it}^*$$

where $i = 1$ refers to beef, 2 to pork, 3 to chicken, and 4 to lamb. This is a demand model in log-changes. Imagine that the supply equations are also in log-changes, with prices occurring in lagged form $(Dp_{1,t-1}, \ldots, Dp_{4,t-1})$, that the market is cleared in the sense that the log-change in supply equals the log-change in demand for each meat and each t, that the demand disturbances $(\epsilon_{1t}^*, \ldots, \epsilon_{4t}^*)$ are stochastically independent of the supply disturbances for each t, and that the supply and the demand disturbances are stochastically independent across observations. The implication is that (21.31) for $i = 1, \ldots, 4$ is a four-equation block in which the four quantity log-changes are predetermined.

Note that (21.31) cannot be estimated by LS because it has several jointly dependent variables $(Dp_{1t}, \ldots, Dp_{4t})$ on the right. However, we can use the predetermined quantity log-changes as instrumental variables (see Problem 13 for details). The result is shown in Table 29 to the right of the corresponding estimates of Table 18 on page 223, which are reproduced to facilitate the comparison. The latter estimates are LS estimates which treat the Dp_{jt}'s as predetermined, whereas the instrumental-variable estimates assign this role to the Dq_{jt}'s.

When Slutsky symmetry $(\pi_{ij}^* = \pi_{ji}^*)$ is imposed, we obtain the estimates shown in the lower-right part of the table. Note that the Slutsky estimates in this part of the table all have the same sign as, but are larger in absolute value than, the corresponding estimates for predetermined price changes in the lower-left part. Hence, the estimated price sensitivity of demand under predetermined quantity changes exceeds that under predetermined price changes, in agreement with the conclusion drawn from Figure 40 for the case of a single good.

The derivation of the asymptotic standard errors of the instrumental-variable estimates and of the symmetry-constrained point estimates is beyond the scope of this book. For details on these matters, see Theil (1975–1976, Sections 9.1 to 9.4).

*21.6   Extensions

Limited Information, Full Information, and Nonlinear Systems

The 2SLS estimator uses the predetermined variables of the equation system to estimate the parameters of each structural equation separately. The estimator uses the fact that certain variables are excluded from the equation. For example, the right-hand side of the investment equation (21.9) contains P_t, P_{t-1}, and K_{t-1}

TABLE 29

Instrumental-variable estimates of conditional marginal shares and Slutsky coefficients of meats

	μ_i/M_g	π^*_{i1}	π^*_{i2}	π^*_{i3}	π^*_{i4}	μ_i/M_g	π^*_{i1}	π^*_{i2}	π^*_{i3}	π^*_{i4}
	Unconstrained (LS) estimates of Table 18					*Unconstrained instrumental-variable estimates*				
Beef	712 (55)	−197 (48)	176 (20)	26 (23)	−5 (63)	669 (73)	−307 (90)	171 (30)	46 (29)	90 (116)
Pork	192 (49)	157 (43)	−219 (18)	50 (20)	12 (57)	191 (60)	186 (74)	−236 (25)	43 (24)	7 (96)
Chicken	46 (22)	9 (19)	30 (8)	−87 (9)	48 (25)	60 (28)	33 (35)	37 (12)	−106 (11)	36 (45)
Lamb	50 (12)	30 (10)	13 (4)	12 (5)	−55 (14)	81 (22)	88 (27)	28 (9)	17 (9)	−133 (35)
	Symmetry-constrained estimates of Table 18					*Symmetry-constrained instrumental-variable estimates*				
Beef	692 (49)	−227 (19)	164 (14)	33 (9)	29 (10)	669 (57)	−306 (31)	171 (18)	47 (13)	89 (27)
Pork	199 (44)		−214 (14)	38 (7)	12 (4)	183 (47)		−239 (15)	40 (8)	28 (9)
Chicken	59 (21)			−84 (9)	13 (5)	67 (24)			−105 (11)	18 (9)
Lamb	50 (12)				−55 (14)	81 (22)				−135 (35)

Note: All entries are to be divided by 1000.

but no other variables and that of the demand-for-labor equation (21.10) similarly contains only three variables (X_t, X_{t-1}, and $t - 1931$) and no others. Note that the 2SLS estimator of (21.9) does *not* use the knowledge that certain variables are excluded from *other* structural equations [such as those which are excluded from (21.10)]. This is expressed by saying that 2SLS is a *limited-information* estimation method.

Full-information methods estimate the parameters of all equations of the system simultaneously and use the knowledge of the exclusion of variables from all structural equations. There is, for example, a full-information maximum-likelihood method for the estimation of the parameters of all structural equations jointly. The estimated final-form coefficients shown in Table 28 are derived from the structural coefficient estimates obtained by this method. There is also a three-stage least-squares (3SLS) method, which uses the two steps of 2SLS to estimate the parameters of each structural equation separately, followed by a third step in which the parameters of all equations are estimated simultaneously. Details can be found in Theil (1971, Sections 10.5 to 10.7).

The equations of Klein's Model I are all linear. Estimation methods for nonlinear equation systems exist, but they are obviously more complicated. If a system is nonlinear, its final-form coefficients are not constants but functions of the values taken by the exogenous variables.

More on Identification and Related Matters

The identification condition stated in Section 21.3 is in terms of the number of unknown parameters in a structural equation relative to the number of predetermined variables in the system. There are other ways of identifying equations under appropriate assumptions. For example, the knowledge that supply and demand disturbances are uncorrelated may identify an equation which would otherwise not be identifiable. An example is given in Problem 15. For this and other extensions, see Fisher (1966) and Rothenberg (1971b).

For large- and medium-sized equation systems, the identification condition in terms of numbers of parameters in the equation and of predetermined variables in the system is almost always satisfied. The reason is that when we consider a larger system, the number of predetermined variables is usually also larger, but the number of unknown parameters in each equation remains within fairly narrow limits. In fact, the presence of a large number of predetermined variables may present another problem. When this number exceeds that of the observations, the first step of 2SLS cannot be implemented because the reduced-form equations will then have too many unknown parameters. [Imagine that there are so many predetermined variables that (21.19) has more c's than there are observations.] See Theil and Laitinen (1977) and the references quoted in that article for attempts to solve this problem.

Historical Note

The first economy-wide econometric model was the equation system of the Dutch economy constructed by J. Tinbergen in 1936. His article has been translated into English; see Tinbergen (1959, pp. 37–84). Among the well-known later models are Tinbergen's League of Nations study (1939) and the models of Klein (1950) and Klein and Goldberger (1955). Today there are numerous economy-wide econometric models both for the United States and for other countries; see Fromm and Klein (1976) and Waelbroeck (1975).

Tinbergen's estimation method was LS for each structural equation separately. In 1943 Haavelmo considered the implications of simultaneity, which inspired considerable research activity in this area by the Cowles Commission for Research in Economics at The University of Chicago. This led to two monographs, Koopmans (1950) and Hood and Koopmans (1953), which stress maximum-likelihood methods in particular. There are precursors to Haavelmo, in particular Sewall Wright, but their work has been less influential; the interested reader should consult Goldberger (1972).

The 2SLS method was proposed by Theil (1953a, 1953b, 1961) and by Basmann (1957). The multiplier terminology for the final-form coefficients originated with Goldberger (1959). The importance of recursive systems was stressed particularly by Wold (1954).

Problems

Problems 1–3 refer to Section 21.1, 4 and 5 to Section 21.2, 6 and 7 to Section 21.3, 8 and 9 to Section 21.4, 10–14 to Section 21.5, and 15 and 16 to Section 21.6.

1 Extend (21.4) to the case of two explanatory variables:

$$y_t = \beta_0 + \beta_1 x_{1t} + \rho\beta_1 x_{1,t-1} + \rho^2\beta_1 x_{1,t-2} + \cdots \\ + \beta_2 x_{2t} + \rho\beta_2 x_{2,t-1} + \rho^2\beta_2 x_{2,t-2} + \cdots + \epsilon_t$$

Apply the procedure described below (21.4). Prove that if (21.6) is true, the result is

$$y_t = (1 - \rho)\beta_0 + \beta_1 x_{1t} + \beta_2 x_{2t} + \rho y_{t-1} + \zeta_t$$

Compare this with (21.7), and give your comments.

2 When the time period is short (a quarter or a month), β_2 may exceed β_1 in (21.3), so that (21.4) is not applicable. To solve this problem, we let the geometric decline of the β's start at the second lag:

$$y_t = \beta_0 + \beta_1 x_t + \beta_2 x_{t-1} + \rho\beta_2 x_{t-2} + \rho^2\beta_2 x_{t-3} + \cdots + \epsilon_t$$

Prove that if (21.6) is true, this specification implies

$$y_t = (1 - \rho)\beta_0 + \beta_1 x_t + (\beta_2 - \rho\beta_1)x_{t-1} + \rho y_{t-1} + \zeta_t$$

Compare this result with (21.7), and give your comments.

3 Write the relation which expresses y in terms of current and lagged x's as

(21.32) $y_t = \text{constant} + \beta_0 x_t + \beta_1 x_{t-1} + \cdots + \beta_k x_{t-k} + \epsilon_t$

Koyck's method imposes the constraint $\beta_i = \rho^i \beta_0$ and does not impose a finite maximum lag. Here we postulate a maximum lag of k periods and impose the quadratic constraint $\beta_i = \alpha_0 + \alpha_1 i + \alpha_2 i^2$:

$$
\begin{aligned}
\beta_0 &= \alpha_0 && (\text{set } i = 0) \\
\beta_1 &= \alpha_0 + \alpha_1 + \alpha_2 && (\text{set } i = 1) \\
\beta_2 &= \alpha_0 + 2\alpha_1 + 4\alpha_2 && (\text{set } i = 2)
\end{aligned}
$$

.

.

.

$$\beta_k = \alpha_0 + k\alpha_1 + k^2\alpha_2 \qquad (\text{set } i = k)$$

Substitute this in (21.32) to verify that this equation becomes

(21.33) $$y_t = \text{constant} + \sum_{r=0}^{2} \alpha_r z_{rt} + \epsilon_t$$

where

(21.34) $$z_{0t} = \sum_{i=0}^{k} x_{t-i}, \qquad z_{1t} = \sum_{i=0}^{k} i x_{t-i}, \qquad z_{2t} = \sum_{i=0}^{k} i^2 x_{t-i}$$

[*Note*: The result (21.33) shows that when we have a lagged relation (21.32) involving k lags, a quadratic specification of the β's can be handled by a regression on only three variables (z_0, z_1, and z_2) in the same way that the Koyck specification yields (21.5) with only two variables on the right. Note that the z's defined in (21.34) do not involve lagged values of the dependent variable. The quadratic specification of the β's can be extended to a polynomial of higher order.]

4 The condition for the existence of the reduced-form solution (21.14) is $D \neq 0$ or, equivalently [see (21.16)],

$$\beta_1'' \beta_3 + (1 - \beta_1'')(\beta_1 + \beta_1') \neq 1$$

Use (21.8) to (21.10) to verify that the left-hand side of this inequality is a weighted average of the marginal propensities to spend out of current wage income and out of current profit income, the weights being determined by β_1'' (i.e., by the short-run change in the private wage bill induced by a unit increase in total private production).

5 Consider the arrow scheme in Figure 38; imagine that an arrow goes from one of the variables below the bar to one of the variables inside the bar. What would you conclude?

6 In remark (1) on page 341 it is stated that for the 2SLS estimation of (21.8) we subtract the reduced-form residual of W_t from $W_t + W'_t$. Why don't we subtract the reduced-form residual of W'_t?

7 Suppose that the disturbances of the demand-for-labor function (21.10) are stochastically independent over time but that those of (21.8) and (21.9) are not independent over time. Are the 2SLS estimators of the parameters of (21.10) then consistent? Explain your answer.

8 Let W' increase by one million dollars in year 0; let this increase be maintained in years 1 and 2, after which W' returns to the original level at the beginning of year 3. Use Table 28 to verify that the implied increases in C (in millions of dollars) are 1.34 in year 0, 2.28 in year 1, 2.97 in year 2, 1.95 in year 3, .98 in year 4, .02 in year 5, and then negative in the next several years. Also verify that the total (accumulated) net change in C is an increase of 5.58 million dollars.

9 Let δ be the total multiplier of K_t (end-of-year capital stock) with respect to some exogenous variable. Use (21.11) to verify that the corresponding total multiplier of net investment equals $\delta - \delta = 0$, and compare this with the last row of Table 28. (*Hint*: As $t \to \infty$, the total effect of a given change in any exogenous variable on K_t and K_{t-1} must be the same.)

10 Let ϵ'_t for $t = 1, 2, \ldots$ in (21.29) be a sequence of uncorrelated random variables with zero mean and constant variance; prove that the disturbance of (21.30) then has the same properties. Next verify that the LS estimator of $1/\beta$ obtained from (21.30) equals

$$\frac{\sum_t (p_t - \bar{p})(q_t - \bar{q})}{\sum_t (q_t - \bar{q})^2}$$

where $\bar{p}$ and $\bar{q}$ are the arithmetic means of p_t and q_t, respectively, over t. Then prove that the implied estimator of β has the same sign as, and is never smaller in absolute value than, the LS estimator of β obtained from a regression of q on p. [*Hint*: Prove that the product of the latter estimator and the LS estimator of $1/\beta$ based on (21.30) equals the square of the correlation coefficient of $(p_1, q_1), (p_2, q_2), \ldots$.]

11 (*Continuation*) Compare the discussion of Figure 40 with Problem 13 on page 287, and make your comments.

12 Verify that LS estimation of (21.30) is equivalent to instrumental-variable estimation of (21.29) with q_t and a constant-term variable as instrumental variables.

13 Write (21.31) in the form (14.62):

$$\frac{\bar{w}_{it}}{\bar{W}_{gt}} Dq_{it} = \frac{\mu_i}{M_g} DQ_{gt} + \sum_{j=1}^{3} \pi^*_{ij}(Dp_{jt} - Dp_{4t}) + \epsilon^*_{it}$$

To apply the instrumental-variable technique with the quantity log-changes of the four meats as instrumental variables, multiply both sides by Dq_{kt} and sum over t:

$$\sum_t Dq_{kt}\left(\frac{\bar{w}_{it}}{\bar{W}_{gt}}Dq_{it}\right) = \frac{\mu_i}{M_g}\sum_t Dq_{kt}DQ_{gt}$$
$$+ \sum_{j=1}^{3} \pi_{ij}^* \sum_t Dq_{kt}(Dp_{jt} - Dp_{4t}) + \sum_t Dq_{kt}\epsilon_{it}^*$$

Verify that when the disturbance term is replaced by zero, this approach yields four linear estimation equations for four unknown parameters of each demand equation. [*Note*: The instrumental-variable estimates of Table 29 are actually based on quantity components of changes in conditional budget shares ($\bar{w}_{kt}Dq_{kt}/\bar{W}_{gt}$), rather than quantity log-changes, as predetermined instrumental variables. This ensures that the log-change in the volume index of meat as a group is also predetermined; see (14.53).]

14 The average budget shares of beef, pork, chicken, and lamb in the period 1950–1972 are .02763, .01940, .00675, and .00152, respectively. Use these shares and the symmetry-constrained estimates in the lower-right part of Table 29 to obtain the implied estimates of the conditional income and Slutsky elasticities. Compare these elasticity estimates with those shown in Table 19 on page 224, and state your conclusions.

15 Multiply (20.1) by a constant $k \neq -1$ and add this to (20.2). Verify that the result can be written as

$$(21.35) \qquad q_i = \frac{\beta_0 + k\alpha_0}{1 + k} + \frac{\beta_1 + k\alpha_1}{1 + k}p_i + \frac{\beta_2}{1 + k}Y_i + \frac{\epsilon_i' + k\epsilon_i}{1 + k}$$

This is an equation in the same variables as those of the demand equation (20.2), which is another way of saying that the parameters of the latter equation are not identifiable. But suppose that ϵ_i and ϵ_i' of (20.1) and (20.2) are uncorrelated random variables with zero means and standard deviations σ_1 and σ_2. Prove that the supply disturbance ϵ_i is then uncorrelated with the disturbance of (21.35) only if $k = 0$, i.e., only if (21.35) is identical to the demand equation (20.2). Verify that this is equivalent to saying that the zero-correlation condition on the supply and demand disturbances ϵ_i and ϵ_i' identifies the demand equation.

16 (*Continuation*) Verify that (21.26) and (21.27) are identified by the zero correlations of ϵ_{1t}, ϵ_{2t}, and ϵ_{3t}, not by the excess of the number of predetermined variables in the three-equation system over the number of parameters in each equation.

part four

PREDICTION AND CONTROL

chapter 22

The Evaluation
of
Economic Predictions

The opening paragraph of Chapter 14 emphasized that the combined use of economic theory and statistical data is important for successful econometric modeling. This should not be interpreted in the sense that looking at data without much modeling is an illegitimate activity. Quite to the contrary—there is considerable merit in statistically analyzing what data have to say. The objective of this chapter is to illustrate this proposition by means of an evaluation of economic predictions. In particular, we shall be interested in the degree to which predictions become less accurate when they are made for a more distant future.

22.1 Predictions and Prediction Errors

We showed in Section 13.2 that if a variable takes positive values only, the use of natural logarithms is very convenient for the analysis of its changes over time. These logarithms are also convenient for the analysis of predictions, as the account which follows will show.

Logarithmic Prediction Errors

Let x_t be the value of some variable x at time t. Let this x_t be predicted by some numerical value $\hat{x}_t$, so that $\hat{x}_t - x_t$ is the prediction error. The analyst is frequently interested in predicted and observed changes over time. The observed change is $x_t - x_{t-1}$, and the predicted change is $\hat{x}_t - x_{t-1}$; hence, the error of the predicted change is

$$\hat{x}_t - x_{t-1} - (x_t - x_{t-1}) = \hat{x}_t - x_t$$

which is thus identical to the error of the predicted level. But suppose that the analyst is more interested in $(\hat{x}_t - x_{t-1})/x_{t-1}$ and $(x_t - x_{t-1})/x_{t-1}$, which are the predicted and observed relative changes. The error of the predicted relative change is

$$(22.1) \qquad \frac{\hat{x}_t - x_{t-1}}{x_{t-1}} - \frac{x_t - x_{t-1}}{x_{t-1}} = \frac{\hat{x}_t - x_t}{x_{t-1}}$$

which is thus equal to the error of the predicted level divided by the observed level in $t - 1$.

An even simpler picture emerges when we work with natural logarithms. The logarithmic error of the predicted level is

$$(22.2) \qquad \log_e \hat{x}_t - \log_e x_t = \log_e \frac{\hat{x}_t}{x_t}$$

The predicted change is now $\log_e \hat{x}_t - \log_e x_{t-1} = \log_e (\hat{x}_t/x_{t-1})$, and the observed change is similarly $\log_e (x_t/x_{t-1})$. Hence, the logarithmic error of the predicted change is

$$(22.3) \qquad \log_e \frac{\hat{x}_t}{x_{t-1}} - \log_e \frac{x_t}{x_{t-1}} = \log_e \frac{\hat{x}_t}{x_t}$$

which is identical to the logarithmic error of the predicted level given in (22.2). Therefore, if we work with logarithms, the error analysis of predicted levels includes that of predicted changes and vice versa. This is not true when we work with relative prediction errors, although the left-hand side of (22.1) is close to the right-hand sides of (22.2) and (22.3) when $\hat{x}_t - x_{t-1}$ and $x_t - x_{t-1}$ are both small in absolute value compared with x_{t-1} (see Problem 1).

Application to Predictions of the U.S. Gross National Product

Since 1968, quarterly forecasts of several macroeconomic variables have been made by members of the Business and Economic Statistics Section of the American Statistical Association. Among these variables is gross national product at current prices ("money-GNP"). Thus, if x_t is money-GNP in quarter t and $\hat{x}_t$ is its prediction, (22.2) provides the logarithmic error of the predicted level, and (22.3) similarly provides the logarithmic error of the predicted change from the level of the previous quarter ($t - 1$).

The GNP price deflator is also among the variables predicted. Let this deflator be y_t in quarter t, and let $\hat{y}_t$ be its prediction, so that the logarithmic error of the predicted level of this deflator is

$$(22.4) \qquad \log_e \hat{y}_t - \log_e y_t = \log_e \frac{\hat{y}_t}{y_t}$$

Real GNP (GNP in constant dollars) is defined as money-GNP divided by the GNP price deflator. Hence, it equals x_t/y_t in quarter t, and its prediction is $\hat{x}_t/\hat{y}_t$; this is the prediction implied by the prediction $\hat{x}_t$ of money-GNP and the prediction $\hat{y}_t$ of the deflator. The logarithmic error of this implied prediction is

$$(22.5) \qquad \log_e \frac{\hat{x}_t}{\hat{y}_t} - \log_e \frac{x_t}{y_t} = \log_e \frac{\hat{x}_t}{x_t} - \log_e \frac{\hat{y}_t}{y_t}$$

and hence, in view of (22.2) and (22.4), simply equal to the difference between the logarithmic errors of the predictions $\hat{x}_t$ and $\hat{y}_t$. Note that the left-hand side of (22.5) is identical to

$$\log_e \frac{\hat{x}_t/\hat{y}_t}{x_{t-1}/y_{t-1}} - \log_e \frac{x_t/y_t}{x_{t-1}/y_{t-1}}$$

which is the logarithmic error of the predicted change in real GNP that is implied by $\hat{x}_t$ and $\hat{y}_t$. For nonlogarithmic prediction errors of real GNP, see Problem 2.

The use of logarithms has another advantage besides the identity of the prediction errors of level and change. Money-GNP can be written as the product of the population, real GNP per capita, and the GNP price deflator. The American population increases over time and so does real GNP per capita in most years (economic growth) and also the price deflator (inflation). Therefore, money-GNP is subject to an increasing trend; it was around 900 billion dollars per year in the late 1960s and around 1500 billion in the mid-1970s. Thus, it is obvious that an extra 1-billion-dollar prediction error for money-GNP in the 1960s is much more serious than in the 1970s. The logarithmic error (22.2) avoids this problem because the ratio $\hat{x}_t/x_t$ eliminates the upward trend.

Mean-Square-Error Analysis of the GNP Predictions

Suppose that we have predictions and realizations for T quarters, $t = 1, \ldots, T$. The mean square prediction error is a frequently used measure for the seriousness of the prediction errors. When applied to the error (22.2) of the prediction of money-GNP, we thus have the following mean square error:

$$(22.6) \qquad \frac{1}{T} \sum_{t=1}^{T} (\log_e \hat{x}_t - \log_e x_t)^2 = \frac{1}{T} \sum_{t=1}^{T} \left(\log_e \frac{\hat{x}_t}{x_t} \right)^2$$

We can proceed similarly for the GNP deflator by squaring (22.4) and averaging over t. When we apply this to (22.5) also, we obtain

$$(22.7) \quad \frac{1}{T} \sum_{t=1}^{T} \left(\log_e \frac{\hat{x}_t}{\hat{y}_t} - \log_e \frac{x_t}{y_t} \right)^2 = \frac{1}{T} \sum_{t=1}^{T} \left(\log_e \frac{\hat{x}_t}{x_t} \right)^2 + \frac{1}{T} \sum_{t=1}^{T} \left(\log_e \frac{\hat{y}_t}{y_t} \right)^2$$

$$- \frac{2}{T} \sum_{t=1}^{T} \left(\log_e \frac{\hat{x}_t}{x_t} \right) \left(\log_e \frac{\hat{y}_t}{y_t} \right)$$

The left-hand side is the mean square logarithmic prediction error of real GNP. The first two terms on the right are the analogous mean square errors of money-GNP and the deflator, and the last term is minus twice the mean product of the prediction errors of the latter two variables.

Su and Su (1975) used the forecast survey mentioned above to analyze the decomposition (22.7) for $T = 19$ quarterly forecasts from the last quarter of 1968 to the second quarter of 1973, with the following result:

$$(22.8) \quad .4319 \times 10^{-4} = .7563 \times 10^{-4} + .5063 \times 10^{-4} - .8307 \times 10^{-4}$$

A term-by-term comparison with (22.7) shows that the mean square logarithmic prediction errors of real GNP, money-GNP, and the deflator are .4319, .7563, and .5063, respectively (all to be multiplied by 10^{-4}). Taking square roots, we obtain root-mean-square prediction errors, which are $10^{-2}\sqrt{.4319} \approx .0066$ or .66 percent for real GNP, .87 percent for money-GNP, and .71 percent for the deflator.

The last term in (22.8) is negative, which amounts to a positive mean product of the prediction errors for money-GNP and the deflator [see the corresponding term in (22.7)]. Hence, for the predictions considered here, the errors of these two variables tend to have the same sign. If the mean product were zero rather than positive, the mean square errors for money-GNP and the deflator being as they are in (22.8), the mean square prediction error for real GNP would be $.7563 + .5063 = 1.2626$ ($\times 10^{-4}$), which is almost three times as large as the actual value $.4319 \times 10^{-4}$ shown in (22.8). Therefore, the positive mean product of the prediction errors for money-GNP and the deflator is advantageous from the viewpoint of accurate prediction of real GNP. This is caused by the fact that the tendency toward equal sign of the errors of $\hat{x}_t$ and $\hat{y}_t$ cancels such errors when we take the ratio $\hat{x}_t/\hat{y}_t$.

22.2   Predicting the Future and Estimating the Past

When we discussed predicted and observed changes from the level at time $t - 1$, we assumed that this level is known. But it often happens that when x_t is predicted, x_{t-1} is not known with certainty. Economic data on previous periods are frequently revised, which means that the past is unknown, as is the future.

Prediction Errors and Estimation Errors of Past Values

Let $\hat{x}_t$ be the prediction of x_t. Let x'_{t-1} be the estimate of x_{t-1} which is available when this prediction is made. Hence, $(\hat{x}_t - x'_{t-1})/x'_{t-1}$ is the implied prediction of the relative change (from the estimated level in $t - 1$). The error of this prediction is

$$(22.9) \quad \frac{\hat{x}_t - x'_{t-1}}{x'_{t-1}} - \frac{x_t - x_{t-1}}{x_{t-1}} = \frac{\hat{x}_t}{x'_{t-1}} - \frac{x_t}{x_{t-1}}$$

which obviously differs from the prediction error (22.1) that is based on perfect knowledge of the past.

Next consider the logarithmic predicted change from the estimated level in $t - 1$, $\log_e \hat{x}_t - \log_e x'_{t-1} = \log_e (\hat{x}_t/x'_{t-1})$. The corresponding actual logarithmic change is $\log_e (x_t/x_{t-1})$ as before, so that the logarithmic error of the predicted change is now

(22.10)
$$\log_e \frac{\hat{x}_t}{x'_{t-1}} - \log_e \frac{x_t}{x_{t-1}} = \log_e \frac{\hat{x}_t}{x_t} - \log_e \frac{x'_{t-1}}{x_{t-1}}$$

The right-hand side is the difference between the logarithmic prediction error of the level of x in t and the logarithmic estimation error of the level of x in $t-1$. This result provides a simple decomposition of the logarithmic error of the predicted change in terms of two elementary errors. The decomposition (22.9) for relative changes is less attractive, since neither $\hat{x}_t/x'_{t-1}$ nor x_t/x_{t-1} can be interpreted as an error.

Also note that, in view of (22.3), the first right-hand term in (22.10) is identical to the logarithmic error of the predicted change based on the true x_{t-1}. Hence, (22.10) implies that the error of the predicted change based on the estimate x'_{t-1} is equal to the corresponding error based on the true x_{t-1} minus the estimation error of x'_{t-1}, with all three errors measured logarithmically. See also Problem 3 for applications to money-GNP, real GNP, and the GNP price deflator.

Revisions of Predictions and Estimates

When time proceeds, new data become available, so that the estimate x'_{t-1} is replaced by a new (revised) estimate x''_{t-1}. Suppose that the prediction of x_t is also revised, from $\hat{x}_t$ to $\hat{x}'_t$. Hence, the new logarithmic predicted change is $\log_e (\hat{x}'_t/x''_{t-1})$, and its error is

(22.11)
$$\log_e \frac{\hat{x}'_t}{x''_{t-1}} - \log_e \frac{x_t}{x_{t-1}} = \log_e \frac{\hat{x}'_t}{x_t} - \log_e \frac{x''_{t-1}}{x_{t-1}}$$

which is identical to (22.10) except that $\hat{x}_t$ and x'_{t-1} are replaced by the corresponding revised values.

Next subtract (22.10) from (22.11), so that the left-hand side becomes

$$\log_e \frac{\hat{x}'_t}{x''_{t-1}} - \log_e \frac{\hat{x}_t}{x'_{t-1}}$$

which is the revision of the logarithmic predicted change (i.e., the revised prediction minus the original prediction of this change). On the right we obtain

$$\log_e \frac{\hat{x}'_t}{x_t} - \log_e \frac{x''_{t-1}}{x_{t-1}} - \left(\log_e \frac{\hat{x}_t}{x_t} - \log_e \frac{x'_{t-1}}{x_{t-1}}\right) = \log_e \frac{\hat{x}'_t}{\hat{x}_t} - \log_e \frac{x''_{t-1}}{x'_{t-1}}$$

so that the result is

(22.12)
$$\log_e \frac{\hat{x}'_t}{x''_{t-1}} - \log_e \frac{\hat{x}_t}{x'_{t-1}} = \log_e \frac{\hat{x}'_t}{\hat{x}_t} - \log_e \frac{x''_{t-1}}{x'_{t-1}}$$

or, in words, the revision of the predicted change from $t-1$ to t is equal to the revision of the predicted level in t minus the revision of the estimated level in $t-1$. This convenient result is another advantage of the use of logarithms.

Seven Sets of Successive Forecasts and Estimates

We proceed to consider predictions and estimates of annual changes for a number of Dutch macroeconomic variables. Consider year t, which is marked by a shaded bar above the horizontal time axis of Figure 41. The predictions and estimates are made at seven points in time, indicated by $1, \ldots, 7$ below the time axis, with S indicating September and D December.

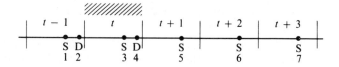

FIGURE 41   Seven successive forecasts and estimates

(1) In September of year $t - 1$, budget proposals for year t are presented to Parliament. These proposals include forecasts for year t, to be called the stage-1 forecasts of that year.

(2) Two months later, in December of year $t - 1$, revised forecasts for year t are made. These are the stage-2 forecasts.

(3) The documents presented to Parliament in September of year t contain estimates of the values taken by the various variables in that year. Two-thirds of the year has passed, but the uncertainty with respect to this year is greater than this fraction suggests, since statistical data lag behind the events which they describe. Therefore, these stage-3 figures are still forecasts to a considerable extent.

(4) In December of year t the stage-4 figures are released simultaneously with the stage-2 forecasts for $t + 1$.

(5) Preliminary estimates of the values taken by the variables in year t are released in September of $t + 1$. These estimates are the stage-5 figures.

(6) The stage-6 figures are the revised estimates that are released one year later, in September of $t + 2$.

(7) The stage-7 figures are made available in September of $t + 3$. They will be considered as the definite (true) values, even though it occurs from time to time that such values are again revised at a later date, for example, when new census data become available.

The stage-1 through -7 forecasts and estimates will be expressed as predicted or estimated log-changes from the estimated level of $t - 1$ which was available when the prediction or estimate was made. For example, these log-changes for the volume of total private consumption in 1955 are as shown below, with $s = 1, \ldots, 7$ indicating the successive stages:

$s = 1$	$s = 2$	$s = 3$	$s = 4$	$s = 5$	$s = 6$	$s = 7$
.0119	.0225	.0459	.0589	.0695	.0695	.0650

The last figure (.0650) amounts to an increase of almost 7 percent. The first (.0119) is the prediction made in September 1954; it is evidently much too low. The successive revisions are improvements up to $s = 5$ (the preliminary estimate released in September 1956) when the mark is overshot.

22.3 Mean-Square-Error Analysis of Predictions and Estimates

In (22.8) we considered mean square prediction errors of three variables for 19 observations. We can compute such mean square errors for the Dutch variables of Section 22.2 also, but this is less attractive because there are only 10 observations (the available data refer to 1953–1962). In addition, there are as many as 19 variables, and there are seven stages to be analyzed. These considerations should convince us to describe the mean square errors in terms of a simple statistical model.

A Model for Expected Square Errors

For the ith variable ($i = 1, \ldots, 19$), let x_{its} be the predicted or estimated log-change in year t according to stage s, where t refers to the years 1953, $\ldots$, 1962 and s to the successive stages $1, \ldots, 7$. Since the stage-7 figure is interpreted as the true value, the error of x_{its} equals $x_{its} - x_{it7}$. We interpret this error as random and consider the following model for the expectation of its square:

$$(22.13) \qquad \mathcal{E}[(x_{its} - x_{it7})^2] = \alpha_i^2 \beta_t^2 \gamma_s^2$$

The right-hand side of this equation describes the expected square error as the product of three factors: one for the variable (α_i^2), one for the year which is predicted or estimated (β_t^2), and one for the stage of prediction or estimation (γ_s^2). A large α_i implies that the ith variable is subject to large prediction and estimation errors, a large β_t that year t is predicted and estimated relatively unsuccessfully, and a large γ_s that stage s has considerable errors.

When we multiply α_i for each i by some number $k > 0$ and divide γ_s for each s by the same k, the right-hand side of (22.13) becomes

$$(22.14) \qquad (k\alpha_i)^2 \beta_t^2 \left(\frac{\gamma_s}{k}\right)^2 = \alpha_i^2 \beta_t^2 \gamma_s^2$$

This shows that the model (22.13) is not affected when we multiply all α_i's by k and all γ_s's by $1/k$. When we select $k = \gamma_1$, γ_s becomes γ_s/γ_1, and hence γ_1 becomes $\gamma_1/\gamma_1 = 1$. This selection means that we *normalize* the coefficients of (22.13) so that $\gamma_1 = 1$, which can be done without loss of generality.

Implementation of the Model

The numerical values of the α_i's of the 19 variables, the β_t's of the 10 years, and the γ_s's of the 7 stages are shown in Table 30; see Theil (1967, pp. 399–401) for the derivation of these values. The α_i's differ substantially among each other,

TABLE 30

Decomposition of mean square errors by variables, years, and stages of prediction or estimation

Coefficients of variables (square of α_i)		Coefficients of years (square of β_t)	
Volume of total private consumption	.0011	1953	2.28
Price index of private consumption	.0002	1954	3.06
Value of nonwage income	.0082	1955	1.38
Total production volume (private sector)	.0008	1956	1.06
Total employment (private sector)	.0001	1957	.83
Gross investment volume (excl. housing)	.0109	1958	1.20
Volume of residential construction	.0108	1959	.63
Wage rate (private sector)	.0017	1960	.58
Price index of investment goods	.0008	1961	.56
Value of indirect taxes less subsidies	.0025	1962	.48
Value of government wage bill	.0022		
Value of government nonwage consumption	.0112	Coefficients of stages (square of γ_s)	
Value of gross government investment	.0220		
Volume of imported commodities	.0013		
Volume of exported commodities	.0020	Stage 1	1
Volume of world trade	.0033	Stage 2	.676
Price index of imported commodities	.0006	Stage 3	.261
Price index of exported commodities	.0007	Stage 4	.137
Price index of foreign commodities	.0007	Stage 5	.123
		Stage 6	.092

and so do the β_t's, but the discussion of this phenomenon is postponed until later in this section. Here we are interested in the γ_s's, which measure the gradual decline of the mean square error when we move from one stage to the next. Given the normalization $\gamma_1 = 1$, (22.13) implies

$$(22.15) \qquad \frac{\mathcal{E}[(x_{its} - x_{it7})^2]}{\mathcal{E}[(x_{it1} - x_{it7})^2]} = \gamma_s^2$$

Since $\gamma_2^2 = .676$ in Table 30, this means that for each variable and each year (each i and each t) the mean square error of the stage-2 forecast is $1 - .676 = .324$ or almost one-third below that of the stage-1 forecast. The mean-square-error reduction achieved by stage 3 is $.676 - .261 = .415$, which is more than 60 percent of the figure .676 of the previous stage. Similarly, stage 4 achieves an almost 50 percent mean-square-error reduction below the level of its predecessor. The relatively small reduction of stage 5 (September of year $t + 1$) indicates that it is not necessarily true that the uncertainty regarding year t is substantially reduced when this year has become past.

REMARKS:

(1) The assumption that the stage-7 estimate is the true value implies $\gamma_7 = 0$ in the model (22.13). This assumption is obviously a simplifying approximation. It can be relaxed under certain conditions; see Theil (1967, pp. 408–409).

(2) We concluded from (22.14) that we can equate γ_1 to 1 without loss of

generality. Problem 5 shows that there is even more freedom, but this will not affect the analysis which follows.

The GNP Forecasts Further Considered

We return to the GNP forecasts discussed in Section 22.1. These forecasts refer to quarter t and are made at the end of quarter $t - 1$ or a little later. At the same point of time, forecasts are also made for quarters $t + 1$, $t + 2$, and $t + 3$. Equivalently, money-GNP x_t is predicted at the end of quarter $t - 1$, in which case next quarter is predicted, but x_t is also predicted one, two, and three quarters earlier.

Table 31, from Su and Su, presents an extension of eq. (22.8). In the first

TABLE 31

Mean-square-error analysis of GNP predictions*

Quarter predicted (1)	Mean square errors			Minus twice mean product† (5)	RMS errors		
	Real GNP (2)	Money- GNP (3)	GNP deflator (4)		Real GNP (6)	Money- GNP (7)	GNP deflator (8)
Third after next	3.16	2.09	3.00	−1.94	1.78	1.45	1.73
Second after next	1.79	1.79	1.73	−1.73	1.34	1.34	1.31
First after next	.93	1.37	1.13	−1.56	.97	1.17	1.06
Next	.43	.76	.51	−.83	.66	.87	.71

*All entries in columns (2) to (5) are to be multiplied by 10^{-4}. The entries in columns (6) to (8) are RMS errors in percentage form.
†Minus twice the mean product of the logarithmic prediction errors of money-GNP and the GNP deflator.

line we interpret $\hat{x}_t$ and $\hat{y}_t$ in (22.7) as the money-GNP and GNP deflator predictions for t that are made at the end of quarter $t - 4$; those in the second line are made at the end of $t - 3$; and so on. The figures in the last line correspond to those shown in (22.8).

Columns (2) to (4) show that the mean square prediction errors for all three variables decline when the quarter predicted becomes nearer future. This should be compared with the decline of the successive γ_s's in Table 30. Column (5) of Table 31, corresponding to the last right-hand term in (22.7), indicates that in all four cases the mean product of the prediction errors of money-GNP and the deflator is positive, which contributes to the accuracy of the real-GNP predictions in the sense that the mean square errors of these predictions are reduced [see the paragraph below (22.8)]. Columns (6) to (8) contain root-mean-square (RMS) prediction errors, obtained by taking the square roots of the corresponding entries in columns (2) to (4). They show that the RMS errors of real GNP and the GNP deflator decrease rapidly for predictions made in successive quarters, from about $1\frac{3}{4}$ to less than $\frac{3}{4}$ percent, and that the decline for money-GNP is much slower.

The Inequality Coefficient

If a prediction has an RMS error of $1\frac{3}{4}$ percent, is it worthwhile to engage in predictive activity at all? We should obviously take a skeptical view when a simple (and cheaper!) extrapolation method exists which yields the same or a smaller RMS error. To pursue this matter, we write $P_1, \ldots, P_n$ for the predicted changes in a variable in n successive periods and $A_1, \ldots, A_n$ for the corresponding actual changes. The simplest extrapolation method is that of no-change, each A_i being predicted by zero, yielding errors equal to $-A_1, \ldots, -A_n$ and a mean square error equal to $(1/n) \sum_i A_i^2$. The ratio of the RMS prediction error to the RMS no-change extrapolation error is thus

$$(22.16) \qquad U = \sqrt{\frac{(1/n) \sum_{i=1}^{n} (P_i - A_i)^2}{(1/n) \sum_{i=1}^{n} A_i^2}}$$

which is known as the *inequality coefficient* of the predictions $P_1, \ldots, P_n$ with respect to the corresponding realizations $A_1, \ldots, A_n$. This coefficient vanishes when all forecasts are perfect ($P_i = A_i$ for each i), and it is positive otherwise. It takes the unit value when the mean square prediction error equals the mean square no-change extrapolation error. Therefore, if we use mean square errors as our criterion, the inequality coefficient of $P_1, \ldots, P_n$ should be less than 1 before we can consider these predictions worthwhile in the sense of being more accurate than no-change extrapolations.

The division by $\sum_i A_i^2$ under the square-root sign in (22.16) may be viewed as an attempt to take into consideration that variables with small changes are usually easier to predict than variables with larger changes. For example, we find in the last line of Table 31 that the RMS prediction error of next quarter's real GNP is smaller than that of next quarter's money-GNP. But money-GNP is subject to larger quarter-to-quarter log-changes than is real GNP. Therefore, when we compute inequality coefficients for these two variables by dividing the RMS prediction error by the RMS no-change extrapolation error, it may well be that the larger RMS prediction error of money-GNP is overcompensated by a larger RMS no-change extrapolation error, yielding a smaller inequality coefficient for money-GNP than for real GNP. We refer to McNees (1975), who analyzed numerous forecasts of American macrovariables using inequality coefficients.

The Seven Successive Stages Further Considered

We return to Table 30, which shows that the coefficients of different variables take quite different values and that there are also rather substantial differences between the coefficients of different years. Following the arguments of the previous paragraph, we recognize that different variables are subject to annual changes of a different order of magnitude. We also recognize that different years are characterized by changes of a different order. With x_{it7} interpreted as the true log-change of the ith variable in year t, we formalize these two features by assuming that this log-change is the outcome of a stochastic process with the following expected square:

$$(22.17) \qquad \mathcal{E}(x_{it7}^2) = a_i^2 b_t^2$$

A large a_i implies that the ith variable is normally subject to large changes over time and a large b_t that year t is characterized by larger changes than a year t' with a smaller coefficient $b_{t'}$.

When we divide (22.13) by (22.17), we obtain

$$(22.18) \qquad \frac{\mathcal{E}[(x_{its} - x_{it7})^2]}{\mathcal{E}(x_{it7}^2)} = \left(\frac{\alpha_i}{a_i}\right)^2 \left(\frac{\beta_t}{b_t}\right)^2 \gamma_s^2$$

and, in particular, for $s = 1$ under the normalization $\gamma_1 = 1$,

$$(22.19) \qquad \frac{\mathcal{E}[(x_{it1} - x_{it7})^2]}{\mathcal{E}(x_{it7}^2)} = \left(\frac{\alpha_i}{a_i}\right)^2 \left(\frac{\beta_t}{b_t}\right)^2$$

Consider the special case in which all years are characterized by the same degree of change and are predicted and estimated equally accurately: $b_t = \beta_t = 1$ for each t. The right-hand side of (22.19) is then equal to the square of α_i/a_i. Since $-x_{it7}$ is the error of no-change extrapolation [see the discussion preceding (22.16)], the left-hand side of (22.19) equals the expected mean square error of the stage-1 forecasts divided by the expected mean square no-change extrapolation error. Thus, if $b_t = \beta_t = 1$ for each t, we can identify α_i/a_i with the inequality coefficient (22.16) of the stage-1 forecasts of the ith variable. The only difference is that we have expectations in the left-hand sides of (22.18) and (22.19) and arithmetic means in (22.16).

We know from Table 30 that the β_t's are not all equal to 1. Instead, they are subject to a declining trend, from a value exceeding 2 in the first two years to about $\frac{1}{2}$ at the end of the ten-year period, which suggests that the forecasts and estimates have become substantially more accurate during this period. The criterion (22.18) enables us to evaluate this trend by means of the ratio β_t/b_t. This ratio takes the following values:

1953	1954	1955	1956	1957	1958	1959	1960	1961	1962
.97	1.43	1.10	.94	.90	1.29	.92	.67	1.07	.92

These ratios fluctuate around 1 and are not subject to any noticeable trend. Hence, on the basis of the models (22.13) and (22.17), the accuracy of the forecasts and estimates has remained approximately constant during the ten-year period.

Different Variables Are Predicted with Different Accuracy

The ratios α_i/a_i of the 19 variables are shown in Table 32. They range between .32 (volume of imported commodities) and 1.23 (volume of residential construction). Note that these ratios provide a picture of the accuracy of the forecasts

TABLE 32

The ratios α_i/a_i of 19 variables

Volume of total private consumption	.59
Price index of private consumption	.54
Value of nonwage income	1.13
Total production volume (private sector)	.52
Total employment (private sector)	.67
Gross investment volume (excl. housing)	.78
Volume of residential construction	1.23
Wage rate (private sector)	.58
Price index of investment goods	.82
Value of indirect taxes less subsidies	.56
Value of government wage bill	.44
Value of government nonwage consumption	1.02
Value of gross government investment	.99
Volume of imported commodities	.32
Volume of exported commodities	.50
Volume of world trade	.72
Price index of imported commodities	.63
Price index of exported commodities	.96
Price index of foreign commodities	.99

that differs from that of Table 30. The smallest α_i in Table 30 is that of total employment in the private sector; the ratio α_i/a_i of this variable is .67, which happens to be the median of the 19 ratios (nine ratios being larger and nine others being smaller than .67).

Recall from (22.19) that if $\beta_t/b_t = 1$, the ratio α_i/a_i equals the inequality coefficient of the stage-1 forecasts of the ith variable. Table 32 shows that this ratio exceeds 1 for three variables, so that the stage-1 forecasts of these variables are worse than no-change extrapolations if $\beta_t/b_t = 1$. We know from the previous subsection that the ratios β_t/b_t fluctuate around 1; hence, an α_i/a_i smaller than but close to 1 will yield an inequality coefficient exceeding 1 for several years. There are three variables (value of gross government investment and the price indexes of exported and foreign commodities) for which α_i/a_i is between .95 and 1. Therefore, there are six variables for which the stage-1 forecasts are about as bad as or worse than no-change extrapolations.

We conclude from (22.18) that the inequality coefficients of the stage-2 forecasts are obtained from the corresponding coefficients of the stage-1 forecasts by multiplication by $\gamma_2 = \sqrt{.676} \approx .82$ (see Table 30), and those of the stage-3 forecasts by multiplication by $\gamma_3 \approx .51$, and so on. When such multiplications are performed, it appears that only one variable has stage-2 forecasts whose accuracy is equal to or below that of no-change extrapolations and none for which this holds in the subsequent stages.

22.4   Some Useful Diagrams

We know from Section 7.3 that some simple diagrams can be of great value for our understanding of regression results. The same is true for our understanding of the relation between forecasts and the corresponding observed values.

An Investment Survey

Since World War II the Dutch Central Bureau of Statistics has organized an investment survey by sending a questionnaire to a large number of firms, asking about the realized investment in the past year and the planned investment in the coming year. Each participating firm belongs to one of 13 industries. Figures for the predicted and actual investment of each industry and each year are derived under the assumption that within the same industry the investment per employee is the same for the participating and the nonparticipating firms.

The upper part of Figure 42, from Mouchart and others (1963), illustrates the industry predictions and realizations for the four-year period 1953–1956. Each industry is represented by a point in each year, so there are $13 \times 4 = 52$ points. The variable measured horizontally is the predicted log-change in the

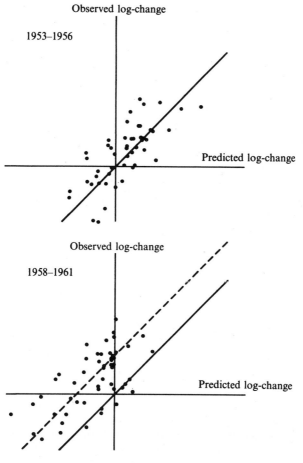

FIGURE 42   Prediction-realization diagrams for an investment survey

industry's investment from the level of the previous year, and the vertical variable is the corresponding observed log-change. Hence, if no change is predicted and observed, the point is at the origin; if the predicted log-change equals the observed log-change, the point is located on the straight line drawn through the origin with a 45-degree angle with respect to the positive direction of the two axes. This is the *line of perfect forecasts*. The 52 points in the upper half of Figure 42 are not all on this line, but they are at least scattered around it, which is encouraging.

The lower part of the figure, dealing with the four-year period 1958–1961, presents an entirely different picture. About 90 percent of the points are to the left of and above the line of perfect forecasts. In fact, these points are scattered more nicely around the broken line parallel to the line of perfect forecasts than they are around the perfect-forecast line itself. Evidently, the predictions for 1958–1961 are systematically too low, whereas no such effect existed in 1953–1956.

The cause of all this is a change in the definition of "investments." Prior to 1957 the question concerned the cost of the buildings and machines *installed* during the past year and the expenditures on fixed assets *to be installed* in the coming year. Since 1957 the question is how much has been *ordered* during the past year and how much the firm *will order* in the coming year. What will be installed in the coming year is frequently ordered a long time in advance; the amount involved is largely known, which leads to relatively small discrepancies from the corresponding amount observed one year later, in agreement with the evidence shown in the upper part of Figure 42. But the prediction of investments that remain to be ordered is far more difficult, as shown in the lower part of the figure. These investment predictions are systematically too low. The Central Bureau of Statistics made this change in definition to look farther into the future, but the price to be paid is a much lower accuracy of the predictions.

The Prediction-Realization Diagram

The two diagrams of Figure 42 are examples of a prediction-realization diagram, which is further considered in Figure 43. In the upper-right quadrant, both the prediction and the actual development amount to an increase. If the point representing the prediction and realization is in this quadrant but below and to the right of the line of perfect forecasts, the predicted increase exceeds the actual increase; hence, the prediction overestimates the actual change. If the point is above and to the left of the perfect-forecast line in this quadrant, the prediction underestimates the actual change. Similarly, the line of perfect forecasts divides the lower-left quadrant into an area in which the actual change is underestimated and an area in which this change is overestimated. The predicted and actual changes both amount to decreases in this quadrant.

The two other quadrants contain the cases in which the predicted and observed changes have opposite sign, an increase being predicted by a decrease or vice versa. These cases represent turning point errors, which are illustrated in

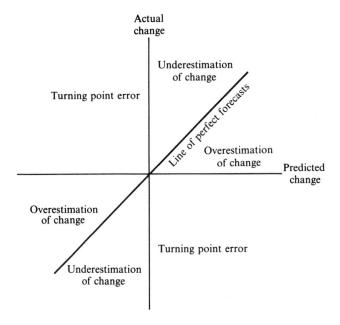

FIGURE 43   The areas of a prediction-realization diagram

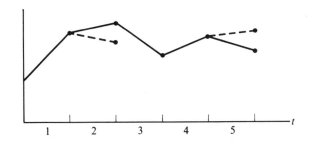

FIGURE 44   Turning point errors

Figure 44. The solid line is the actual behavior of a variable; the broken lines at $t = 2$ and $t = 5$ are predictions. In $t = 1$ there is an increase; the prediction for $t = 2$ is a decrease, which amounts to a predicted turning point. The actual behavior is a further increase in $t = 2$; hence, the predicted turning point did not materialize. In $t = 5$ there is a turning point, the increase in $t = 4$ being followed by a decrease in $t = 5$. But the prediction for $t = 5$ is a continued increase; hence, the forecaster missed a turning point that actually took place.

Evidence on the Three Types of Errors

It follows from Figure 43 that unless points are located exactly on one or both axes or on the line of perfect forecasts all predictions are either turning point errors or they under- or overestimate the actual change. For the stage-1 forecasts described in Section 22.2, the relative frequency of turning point errors is about 20 percent. This frequency decreases rapidly in the later stages until it becomes less than 5 percent after stage 3. The cases of underestimation of change exceed those of overestimation by about 3 to 1 in stages 1 and 2 and by about 2 to 1 in stage 3 [see Theil (1966, pp. 146–148)]. This *preponderance of underestimation of changes* appears to be a general feature of economic forecasts, although the evidence is more overwhelming for changes which are increases than for those which are decreases (partly because there have been many more increases than decreases since World War II).

A triangular illustration is convenient for three nonnegative numbers which add up to 1, as in the case of the relative frequencies of turning point errors and under- and overestimation of change. Figure 45(*a*) shows a point *P* within an equilateral triangle and the projections (*A'*, *B'*, and *C'*) of *P* on the three sides.

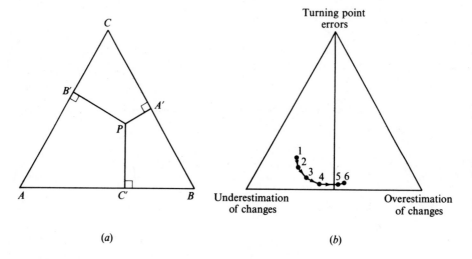

FIGURE 45   **Turning point errors and under- and overestimation of changes in six successive stages**

For any point within the triangle, the sum of the distances from the three sides equals a constant *c*:

$$PA' + PB' + PC' = c$$

When we put $c = 1$, identify PA' with the relative frequency of A, and proceed similarly for PB' and PC', we can represent each triple of fractions by a point in the triangle. This is applied in Figure 45(*b*) with A and B interpreted as under- and overestimation of changes, respectively, and C as turning point errors. The six successive points illustrate that in the six successive stages both the occurrence of turning point errors and the preponderance of change underestimation are largely eliminated. Note that the last two stages (5 and 6) represent estimates of past changes rather than predictions of future changes.

Problems

Problems 1 and 2 refer to Section 22.1, 3 and 4 to Section 22.2, 5 and 6 to Section 22.3, and 7–11 to Section 22.4.

1 Expand $\hat{x}_t/x_{t-1} = \exp\{\log_e(\hat{x}_t/x_{t-1})\}$ to obtain

$$\frac{\hat{x}_t}{x_{t-1}} = 1 + \log_e\frac{\hat{x}_t}{x_{t-1}} + \frac{1}{2}\left(\log_e\frac{\hat{x}_t}{x_{t-1}}\right)^2 + \cdots$$

where third- and higher-order terms are ignored. Proceed in the same way for x_t/x_{t-1} to verify that

$$\frac{\hat{x}_t - x_t}{x_{t-1}} = \left(1 + \frac{1}{2}\log_e\frac{\hat{x}_t x_t}{x_{t-1}^2}\right)\log_e\frac{\hat{x}_t}{x_t} + \cdots$$

State your conclusions for the case in which $\hat{x}_t$ and x_t are both close to x_{t-1}.

2 Prove that $\hat{x}_t/\hat{y}_t - x_t/y_t$ is the error of the predicted level of real GNP implied by the predictions $\hat{x}_t$ (money-GNP) and $\hat{y}_t$ (GNP deflator) and that the ratio of $\hat{x}_t/\hat{y}_t - x_t/y_t$ to x_{t-1}/y_{t-1} is the error of the predicted relative change. Can either of these errors be written as the sum or the difference of money-GNP and the deflator errors?

3 Let y'_{t-1} be the estimate of the GNP deflator which is available when the predictions $\hat{x}_t$ (for money-GNP) and $\hat{y}_t$ are made. Verify that the logarithmic error of the implied predicted change of real GNP is

$$\log_e\frac{\hat{x}_t/\hat{y}_t}{x'_{t-1}/y'_{t-1}} - \log_e\frac{x_t/y_t}{x_{t-1}/y_{t-1}}$$
$$= \left(\log_e\frac{\hat{x}_t}{x_t} - \log_e\frac{\hat{y}_t}{y_t}\right) - \left(\log_e\frac{x'_{t-1}}{x_{t-1}} - \log_e\frac{y'_{t-1}}{y_{t-1}}\right)$$

Interpret this result, and compare it with (22.5).

4 (*Continuation*) Let $\hat{y}'_t$ be a revised prediction and y''_{t-1} a revised estimate of the deflator in t and $t-1$, respectively. Extend (22.12) to

$$\log_e\frac{\hat{x}'_t/\hat{y}'_t}{x''_{t-1}/y''_{t-1}} - \log_e\frac{\hat{x}_t/\hat{y}_t}{x'_{t-1}/y'_{t-1}}$$
$$= \left(\log_e\frac{\hat{x}'_t}{\hat{x}_t} - \log_e\frac{\hat{y}'_t}{\hat{y}_t}\right) - \left(\log_e\frac{x''_{t-1}}{x'_{t-1}} - \log_e\frac{y''_{t-1}}{y'_{t-1}}\right)$$

Interpret the left-hand side as a revision for real GNP and each expression in parentheses on the right as the difference between two revisions.

5 Consider (22.13) for $i = 1, \ldots, 19$; $t = 1953, \ldots, 1962$; and $s = 1, \ldots, 7$. Multiply α_i by $k > 0$ for each i, β_t by $k' > 0$ for each t, and γ_s by $1/kk'$ for each s. Prove that these multiplications do not affect the model (22.13). [*Note*: This result shows that the coefficients of (22.13) are subject to two multiplicative degrees of freedom, which have been used in Table 30 to equate both γ_1 and the geometric mean of the β_t's to 1. (The geometric mean of n positive numbers is defined as the nth root of the product of these numbers.) The b_i's of (22.17) are also normalized so that their geometric mean equals 1.]

6 For the successive GNP predictions of Table 31, draw a time axis similar to Figure 41.

7 It is stated in the first subsection of Section 22.4 that industry-wide predictions and realizations are obtained under the assumption that investment per employee is the same for the participating and the nonparticipating firms. Provide a numerical example to show that if this assumption is not satisfied, the industry-wide prediction may differ from the realization even when the predictions of the individual firms are all exact. (*Note*: This aspect is ignored in the text.)

8 Why is the year 1957 deleted from Figure 42?

9 The equation of the broken line in Figure 42 is

$$\log_e y = -\log_e .7 + \log_e x$$

where x and y are the predicted and actual log-changes in investment. Verify that saying that the points are scattered around this broken line is equivalent to saying that, on average, the predictions are about 70 percent of the corresponding realizations.

10 Make a comparison of the two kinds of turning point errors in Figure 44 with the two kinds of errors in hypothesis testing.

11 Suppose that all predictions are turning point errors. Indicate the point which represents this situation in Figure 45(*b*).

chapter 23

Prediction
and
Control

Why are predictions made? The answer is that most decision makers dislike uncertainty. They hope that the degree of uncertainty of future events given the predictions of these events is less than would be the case without such predictions. Decision makers hope that if this uncertainty is reduced by these predictions, they are in a better position to take actions which are optimal from their point of view.

*23.1 Typology of Predictions

In Section 11.4 we discussed regression predictions. The analysis of Chapter 22 includes GNP predictions by business economists and economic statisticians, investment plans of firms, and several stages of successive predictions made for the Dutch Parliament; several other examples are given by Zarnowitz (1972, pp. 183–239). A typology of predictions is in order.

The Time Span of Prediction

A forecast or prediction is a statement about an unknown event. Such events are usually future events. If a prediction refers to a period of a year or less, it is called a short-term prediction. All predictions considered in Chapter 22 are short-term.

Medium-term predictions are those whose time span is between one and five years, and long-term predictions are those which have a longer time span. The latter are used when a decision is made on building a new plant, acquiring control over an existing firm, adding or abandoning units in a state university system, and so on.

Conditional and Unconditional Predictions

In Section 11.4 our objective was to predict y_*, defined in (11.30) and reproduced here,

$$(23.1) \qquad y_* = \beta_0 + \beta_1 x_{1*} + \beta_2 x_{2*} + \epsilon_*$$

where x_{1*} and x_{2*} are values assumed by two explanatory variables. These two values are taken as given. Accordingly, the prediction $\hat{y}_*$ defined in (11.32),

$$(23.2) \qquad \hat{y}_* = b_0 + b_1 x_{1*} + b_2 x_{2*}$$

is a conditional prediction of y_*, given $x_1 = x_{1*}$ and $x_2 = x_{2*}$.

Predictions are called unconditional when they are not made dependent on the validity of other future statements (such as the statements $x_1 = x_{1*}$ and $x_2 = x_{2*}$). All predictions considered in Chapter 22 are unconditional.

Point Predictions and Interval Predictions

The prediction (23.2) is a point prediction, but the double inequality shown in (11.44),

$$(23.3) \qquad bx_* - t_\alpha s\sqrt{1 + x_*^2/S^2} \le y_* \le bx_* + t_\alpha s\sqrt{1 + x_*^2/S^2}$$

provides an interval prediction. The interval whose end points are the first and third members of (23.3) is constructed in such a way that it will contain the predictand y_* with probability $1 - 2\alpha$.

Most economic predictions, including those considered in Chapter 22, concern variables that are continuous or approximately continuous (approximately when we ignore the fact that a dollar amount must be a multiple of .01). When a future value of such a variable is predicted by one single numerical value, as is the case in Chapter 22, this is a point prediction.

Verifiability of Predictions

Predictions should be verifiable. This means that (1) it must be possible to conclude unambiguously, after a certain time, whether the prediction has turned out to be correct or not, and (2) the two possibilities (correct and incorrect) must both exist.

Condition (1) requires that there be no ambiguity as to the concepts used in the prediction. It also requires that there be no ambiguity with respect to the time or time interval to which the prediction refers and that the distance between this time and the moment of prediction be finite. If this distance is left unspecified, the forecaster can always assert that his audience should be more patient, which is unacceptable.

Condition (2) excludes trivial predictions which are true with unit probability, such as "The value of Iowa's agricultural output in 1985 will be nonnegative." There is no possibility that this statement will not be true. Also excluded are conditional predictions whose conditions have zero probability, such as "Iowa's agricultural output (properly defined) will increase by 150 percent in 1985 if its agricultural area is doubled by that time." Since the condition has zero probability, it will not be possible to verify whether the prediction is correct or not.

The General Nature of Prediction Procedures

To obtain a prediction, the forecaster uses two inputs: *theory* and *observations*. The theory, which may range from naive to sophisticated, always states that *something remains constant*. This something is the variable itself in the case of no-change extrapolation; it is the set of coefficients of an econometric model if such a model is the theoretical prediction tool. No-change extrapolation requires only one observation—that of the variable to be predicted in the most recent period. Constructing an econometric model is more demanding and requires a number of observations on each of several variables in order that the coefficients of the model can be estimated.

In general, the more sophisticated the theory is, the more extensive the data requirements will be. To explain this, let us consider predictive activity as a production process. Given that the objective of prediction is to reduce uncertainty and given that the prediction procedure uses two inputs (theory and observations), the marginal revenues of the two inputs with respect to the uncertainty reduction must be equal in order that this reduction be maximized for a given dollar amount spent on the two inputs. In most production processes, the demand for individual inputs increases as output increases. Predictive activity, with output interpreted as reduction of uncertainty, is no exception to this general rule. Therefore, it is usually the case that an increased forecasting budget will both raise the sophistication of the theories used and also enlarge the data bases for implementing these theories.

Implications of the Constancy Assumption

The constancy assumption which is used by the prediction theory has two important implications. First, since reality is less impressed by this constancy than the forecaster is, we typically find that predictions are characterized by more regularity than the corresponding observed development justifies. For example, projection curves are usually smooth curves, whereas the actual curves have numerous irregularities.

A second implication is the tendency toward underestimation of changes which was noted at the end of Section 22.4. Consider two extremes, one being the naive forecaster who systematically predicts a zero change. He cannot be surpassed in terms of change underestimation. The other extreme is the perfect forecaster who always hits the bull's-eye. In terms of Figure 43 on page 373, the points of the first extreme are all located on the vertical axis. Imagine that a forecaster tries to improve his performance, starting as a no-change extrapolator, so that he attempts to move his points horizontally from the vertical axis to the line of perfect forecasts. In some cases he will move a point in the wrong direction, which leads to a turning point error; in other cases he will move his point in the right direction but too far, which yields an overestimate of the actual change. But given that the point of departure is the vertical axis and that the objective is the line of perfect forecasts, we should expect that in a substantial proportion of all cases a moderately successful forecaster will arrive at a point between these two lines. Each such point represents a situation in which the change is underestimated, both above and below the horizontal axis.

*23.2   Predictions Based on Econometric Models

The prediction $\hat{y}_*$ in (23.2) is conditional on known values (x_{1*} and x_{2*}) of two explanatory variables. If it is unknown which values these variables will take, the forecaster can try to predict them. Let these predictions be $\hat{x}_{1*}$ and $\hat{x}_{2*}$; substitution of these predictions in (23.2) yields the implied prediction $b_0 + b_1\hat{x}_{1*} + b_2\hat{x}_{2*}$ of y_*. This is an unconditional prediction of y_* because it does not involve given values taken by the explanatory variables.

Reduced-Form Predictions

The extension of this approach to the equation systems of Chapter 20 is straightforward. Consider the reduced-form equation (20.7) for consumption of the Keynesian model:

$$(23.4) \qquad C_i = \frac{\beta}{1-\beta}I_i + \frac{1}{1-\beta}\epsilon_i$$

Let investment (exogenous) take a given value I_* in some future year, and let our objective be to predict consumption C_* in that year. Such a prediction can be obtained by substituting I_* for I_i, the 2SLS estimate for β, and zero for the disturbance. The resulting prediction of C_* is conditional, given $I = I_*$. If I_* is unknown, the forecaster can try to predict it and substitute the prediction in (23.4), which yields an unconditional prediction of C_*.

Thus, when the standard linear model is generalized to the static equation systems of Chapter 20, we predict endogenous variables by means of the reduced form; the exogenous variables of the system take on the role of the x's in (23.1) and (23.2). For the dynamic equation systems of Chapter 21, we use predetermined rather than exogenous variables. Consider the reduced-form equation (21.14) of Klein's Model I:

$$(23.5) \quad X_t = \text{constant} + \frac{\beta_3 W_t' - (\beta_1 + \beta_1')T_t + G_t - \beta_3''\gamma(t - 1931)}{D}$$

$$+ \frac{(\beta_2 + \beta_2')P_{t-1} + \beta_3' K_{t-1} - \beta_2''\gamma X_{t-1}}{D} + \frac{\epsilon_t + \epsilon_t' - \gamma\epsilon_t''}{D}$$

Given the predetermined variables in the first two ratios on the right, we obtain a conditional prediction of X_t by substituting estimates for the parameters and zero for the three disturbances.

Predictions Several Periods Ahead

The prediction based on (23.5) can be made at the beginning of year t when P_{t-1}, K_{t-1}, and X_{t-1} are known. This amounts to a prediction one year ahead. The procedure is not applicable when we want to predict two years ahead: If X_t is to be predicted at the beginning of $t - 1$, the endogenous values P_{t-1}, K_{t-1}, and X_{t-1} are still future.

However, we can lag the reduced-form equations of P_t, K_t, and X_t in order to express P_{t-1}, K_{t-1}, and X_{t-1} in terms of (1) exogenous variables and disturbances in $t - 1$ and (2) endogenous variables in $t - 2$. These lagged reduced-form equations are then substituted in (23.5). Thus, at the beginning of $t - 1$, given the values of the exogenous variables in $t - 1$ and t, we can obtain a conditional prediction of X_t by substituting estimates for the parameters and zero for the disturbances in $t - 1$ and t. The reader will notice that this lagging procedure is similar to that which we applied in Section 21.4 for the derivation of the final form. For a prediction three periods ahead, we must apply the lagging procedure once more.

A Comparison of Mean Square Prediction Errors

When postsample observations become available, it is possible to check the accuracy of an estimated simultaneous-equation model. Conditional or *ex post* forecasts of C_t and X_t are obtained by substituting the observed values for the predetermined variables in the right-hand sides of (23.4) and (23.5) as well as estimates for the parameters and zero for the disturbances. Ex post means that these observed values are inserted "after the fact." This should be contrasted with the *ex ante* forecasts, which are the unconditional predictions of the endogenous variables. These are the actual predictions released by the forecaster, based on predictions of the future behavior of the exogenous variables.

A comparison of the two sets of forecasts is obviously of interest. Table 33 contains RMS errors of the predicted log-changes in 14 variables which are endogenous in the model used for the successive stages of prediction (see Figure

TABLE 33

Root-mean-square errors of two sets of predictions

Variable	Conditional (ex post)	Unconditional (ex ante)
Volume of total private consumption	2.25	1.87
Price index of private consumption	1.54	1.22
Value of nonwage income	5.11	7.07
Total production volume (private sector)	2.51	2.54
Total employment (private sector)	1.25	.58
Gross investment volume (excl. housing)	9.80	10.45
Wage rate (private sector)	2.87	1.83
Price index of investment goods	2.43	3.12
Value of indirect taxes less subsidies	6.92	3.63
Taxes on wage income	6.65	6.19
Taxes on nonwage income	11.16	10.24
Volume of imported commodities	6.25	5.01
Volume of exported commodities	6.66	5.32
Price index of exported commodities	2.24	1.82

Note: RMS errors are all in percentage form.

41 on page 364). There are only four variables out of 14 whose conditional predictions have an RMS error smaller than that of the unconditional predictions. Hence, on average, the conditional predictions are less accurate than the unconditional ones. This may seem surprising, since the conditional predictions are based on the observed values of the exogenous variables, whereas the unconditional predictions use predictions for these values which are usually imperfect. Nevertheless, the superiority of the unconditional predictions which Table 33 displays is not at all an isolated case; see, for example, Haitovsky and others (1974) for an analysis of American model predictions.

Two considerations serve to explain this result. First, the construction of economy-wide econometric models is an imperfect art. Second, the unconditional predictions released by econometric model builders usually involve certain information which is not contained in the original model. Details on these matters follow in the remainder of this section.

Problems in Specifying Economy-Wide Models

A convenient starting point is the system of consumer demand equations discussed in Sections 14.2 to 14.4, 16.4, and 21.5. When the mathematical form of these equations is specified as discussed in these sections, the statistical implementation (testing and estimation) is in principle straightforward. The construction of a large economy-wide model is a different matter. Its components are much more heterogeneous and include, in addition to consumer demand equations, structural equations explaining prices, output, employment, imports, and numerous other variables.

The model builder's task is to specify the mathematical form of each of these equations, using the underlying economic theory such as the utility theory of

Section 14.1 in the case of consumer demand. But there may be conflicting economic theories, or there may be no data on a variable which is needed to apply a theory, or these data may be of low quality. In such cases, the specification of the form of a relation, including the variables to be introduced in the relation, becomes a matter of choice. The model builder frequently feels that this choice is rather arbitrary and that his best decision is bound to be imperfect. This leads to misspecifications (see Chapter 17). If the model contains several dozen structural equations, which is not an exaggerated number by present-day standards, the number of possible misspecifications is obviously very substantial.

In practice, the specification of a structural equation is a matter of large-scale experimentation with alternative functional forms and alternative sets of variables. This experimentation is almost always performed by applying LS as if the right-hand variables would satisfy the assumptions of the standard linear model. In most cases, goodness of fit is an important criterion for the specification selected.

The Published Form of the Model

The use of LS in the experimentation is perfectly understandable, because it is impossible to apply a simultaneous-equation approach to one equation as long as the other equations of the model are not specified. For example, the use of 2SLS requires all predetermined variables of the system, and the list of these variables is not available when we know only one equation. However, if the model builder decides on a particular specification of his structural equations on the basis of such experiments and if he uses the same set of data to reestimate these equations by 2SLS, the distribution of these 2SLS estimators may differ substantially from their theoretical distribution. The published form of most economy-wide models is such a reestimate obtained from the same data as those which were used for experimentation. It is wise to presume that the statistical quality of this reestimate is below the level which is suggested by its standard errors.

Big models have big problems. Each additional equation presents a heavy burden on the specification problem of the model as a whole. This is comparable to the implementation problem of Bayesian inference, where each additional parameter presents a heavy burden for the analyst who wants to specify a prior distribution for all parameters [see the paragraph below (16.22)]. Be that as it may, it should be clear that if the statistical quality of published models is as indicated at the end of the previous paragraph, their ability to predict becomes a matter of major importance.

The Use of Previous Prediction Errors and Extraneous Information

Typically, the postsample predictions of economy-wide models are poorer than the fit of the reduced form indicates. That is, the RMS errors of ex post predictions are usually larger than the corresponding RMS values of the reduced-form residuals of the sample. An important cause is *overfitting*, the selection of the specification being too exclusively based on goodness of fit during the sample period. The size of the random component of the model is then underestimated.

Also, the level of ex post predictions is in many cases systematically either too low or too high. If a quarterly model overpredicts GNP by 4 to 6 percent for the fifth consecutive quarter, the model builder may decide to lower the next GNP prediction by 5 percent. This amounts to subtracting the average of the five previous prediction errors from the next prediction. Model builders are acutely aware of such discrepancies and frequently adjust their models by raising or lowering the constant terms of their structural equations. In fact, they are revising their equations almost continuously, so that the selection of one particular model for the verification of ex post forecasts is not always a simple matter. The reader may want to consult Theil (1966, Chapter 4) for further details relating to Table 33.

The above-mentioned correction by means of previous prediction errors is frequently an improvement. This is one reason ex ante forecasts are sometimes better than ex post forecasts based on one fixed model. Ex ante forecasts are less mechanical and can be improved not only by the use of evidence from the recent past but also by means of the results of an investment survey and a consumer buying intention survey. If the latter survey indicates that consumers plan to buy more cars next quarter than they are doing this quarter, the model builder may decide to adjust the constant term of his demand equation for automobiles.

Some model builders encourage a dialogue between the model and its users. The first ex ante forecasts, based on the model builder's best judgments of the future behavior of the exogenous variables, are sent to experts of various economic sectors who express their opinions. The model builder will then change some of the exogenous predictions and perhaps some coefficients of the model, after which a new set of ex ante forecasts results. The interaction with the experts may go on for a few more rounds. The final ex ante forecasts are considered to be consistent both with the experts' opinion on future developments and also with the observed behavior of the variables during the sample period. In this dialogue the econometric model is used to process all available information. There is no other tool which performs this service as efficiently. This explains why the construction and updating of economy-wide econometric models have become a flourishing industry in many Western countries. However, commercial success should not conceal the fact that the product delivered by this industry is imperfect.

*23.3   Some Problems of Optimal Control

In this section we shall consider a macroeconomic decision maker whose objective is to minimize a loss function subject to the constraints under which the economy operates. This approach may be viewed as an extension of the consumer's problem of maximizing a utility function subject to a budget constraint (see Section 14.1). In the case of the macroeconomic decision maker, the constraints on the economy will be expressed by means of an econometric model, so that appropriate attention must be paid to the random components of its equations. To keep the discussion within reasonable limits, we shall discuss a simple pilot study from Van den Bogaard and Theil (1959) and Theil (1964).

The Objective: Restoring Prosperity in the 1930s

The period considered is the first Administration of President Franklin D. Roosevelt from January 1933 through December 1936. We assume that the decision maker's objective is ending the depression, using Klein's Model I as a description of the operation of the U.S. economy. Accordingly, we designate W' (government wage bill), T (business taxes), and G (government nonwage expenditure) as the government's policy variables. The decision maker's task is to select appropriate values for these three variables at the beginning of each of the years 1933–1936 so that his objective is reached.

To specify this objective, we consider three variables that are not government-controlled. One is total consumption (C), which had declined considerably below the 1929 level of 57.8 billions of dollars per year (dollars of 1934 purchasing power). We formulate a *desired value* of total consumption in 1936, written $\bar{C}_{36}$, by requiring that the per capita consumption level of 1929 be restored in 1936 under the assumption of a 1 percent annual population increase. This yields

$$(23.6) \qquad \bar{C}_{36} = 57.8 \times 1.01^7 = 61.97$$

The second noncontrolled variable is net investment (I), which was of the order of 10 percent of consumption during the 1920s but had declined to negative values in the early 1930s. We wish to restore the original ratio and put the desired value of investment in 1936 equal to 10 percent of the desired consumption value shown in (23.6). The third variable to be considered is the ratio of profits to the wage bill of the private sector, P/W, which had fluctuated around $\frac{1}{2}$ in the 1920s but declined to less than $\frac{1}{4}$ in 1932. Our desire is to have the original ratio $\frac{1}{2}$ by 1936. Since it is more convenient to work with differences than with ratios, we introduce a *distribution variable*,

$$(23.7) \qquad D = W - 2P$$

and put its desired 1936 value equal to zero: $\bar{D}_{36} = 0$. This is equivalent to the desire $P/W = \frac{1}{2}$ in 1936.

The two previous paragraphs specify the desired values of the noncontrolled variables in 1936. We also need desired values for the earlier years 1933 to 1935. This is done by linear interpolation between the observed values of 1932 and the corresponding desires for 1936. The results are shown in the first three columns of Table 34.

TABLE 34

Desired values, 1933–1936

	$\bar{C}$	$\bar{I}$	$\bar{D}$	$\bar{W}'$	$\bar{T}$	$\bar{G}$
1933	49.69	−3.10	11.25	5.04	7.40	5.40
1934	53.78	.00	7.50	5.25	7.64	5.61
1935	57.88	3.10	3.75	5.47	7.87	5.83
1936	61.97	6.20	.00	5.68	8.11	6.04

Note: All entries are in billions of 1934 dollars per year.

A Quadratic Loss Function

The three policy variables (W', T, and G) will be used to affect the noncontrolled variables (C, I, and D) in the desired direction. But policy variables have their own desired values. For example, when the U.S. economy expands, certain federal services must expand too, which raises the government wage bill (W') and government nonwage expenditure (G). The simple solution chosen consists of LS regressions of the three policy variables on time during the period 1920–1932, followed by the use of extrapolated values in 1933–1936 as desired values. These values are shown in the last three columns of Table 34.

It is, in general, not possible to realize all desires of Table 34, so that the decision maker must formulate a loss function which expresses his misgivings when the actual values deviate from the corresponding desired values. Our loss function is the sum of squares of all these deviations. Hence, the loss can be written as the sum of four components,

$$(23.8) \qquad l = \sum_{t=1}^{4} l_t$$

where l_t is the loss caused by the deviations in the tth year after 1932:

$$(23.9) \quad l_t = (C_{32+t} - \bar{C}_{32+t})^2 + (I_{32+t} - \bar{I}_{32+t})^2 + (D_{32+t} - \bar{D}_{32+t})^2$$
$$+ (W'_{32+t} - \bar{W}'_{32+t})^2 + (T_{32+t} - \bar{T}_{32+t})^2$$
$$+ [G_{32+t} + W'_{32+t} - (\bar{G}_{32+t} + \bar{W}'_{32+t})]^2$$

REMARKS:

(1) In the case discussed here, there are as many policy variables as noncontrolled variables (both three). This equality should be regarded as accidental.

(2) The desired values of Table 34 have been obtained in an oversimplified way, particularly those of the policy variables. The specification used here is that of a pilot study. In (23.8) and (23.9), all squared deviations are given the same weight. It is possible to generalize this so that deviations of different variables in different years all have different weights. It is also possible to add product terms (see Problem 6). Another extension is the addition of the square of the difference between two successive values of a policy variable. Such a term serves to reduce large changes in a policy variable from one year to the next.

(3) The expression in the last line of (23.9) involves the variable $G + W'$, government expenditure including the government wage bill. It would be more in line with the other terms in (23.9) to replace this term by $(G_{32+t} - \bar{G}_{32+t})^2$. The combination of G and W' dates back to Klein's (1950) original formulation of his model.

The Expected Loss

Let us consider the goal of selecting those values of the three policy variables in the four years 1933–1936 which minimize, subject to the constraints on the U.S. economy described by Klein's Model I, the loss function given in (23.8) and (23.9). As will be explained later in this section, this is a matter of replacing the endogenous values which occur in (23.9) by the right-hand sides of the corresponding reduced-form equations, lagged appropriately, after which the loss function is minimized by varying the policy variables. However, the goal stated above cannot really be attained, since the reduced-form equations contain random disturbances. To handle this problem, we change the criterion into a minimum *expected loss*.

For the developments which follow it is important to note that the decisions for the years 1933–1936 can be made consecutively (not all at once), so that later decisions can be made dependent on future information that will be available when they must be made. This situation calls for a strategy similar to the regression strategies discussed in Section 17.2. To further clarify this concept, we consider a simple example from Boot (1964).

A Digression on Strategies

A manager must choose between two investment projects. He can invest $100,000 in a machine in year 1, which will yield savings of $35,000 in years 2 to 4 and $20,000 in year 5. Alternatively, he can spend $13,500 on research in year 1 and $100,000 in year 2. Then there will be four years to reap the harvest, which is considerable if the research is successful. As of today, the probability of success is .4. *After one year* (after $13,500 has been spent) *it will be known for certain whether or not the research will pay off*. The financial data are summarized in Table 35.

The bottom row of the table gives the (internal) rate of return, i.e., the discount rate which makes the present value of the expenditures and returns equal to zero. For example, the rate of return of the machine is 10 percent because the present value (in thousands of dollars) at the 10 percent discount rate is

$$-100 + \frac{35}{1.1} + \frac{35}{1.1^2} + \frac{35}{1.1^3} + \frac{20}{1.1^4} \approx 0$$

The higher the rate of return, the more profitable the investment. Thus, we assume that the manager uses a maximum expected rate of return as his cri-

TABLE 35
Financial data on two investment projects

Year	Machine	Research	
		If successful	If not
1	−100,000	−13,500	−13,500
2	35,000	−100,000	−100,000
3	35,000	50,000	30,000
4	35,000	50,000	30,000
5	20,000	50,000	30,000
6	0	20,000	27,000
Rate of return	10%	20%	1%

terion. Looking at Table 35, he may then decide to buy the machine with its 10 percent rate of return, arguing that the expected rate of return of research is $.4 \times 20 + .6 \times 1 = 8.6$ percent. But this decision would be wrong.

The manager should use the information that after spending $13,500 on research in year 1 he will know whether the research is successful or not. At that time, if it proved unsuccessful, *he could switch to the machine*. This would imply $13,500 spent on research in year 1, $100,000 spent on the machine in year 2, and savings of $35,000 in years 3 to 5 and of $20,000 in year 6. The corresponding rate of return is 4 percent (larger than the 1 percent of continued unsuccessful research). Therefore, the manager should consider the following strategy: For year 1, decide on research; for year 2, continue the research if it is successful (probability .4) but switch to the machine if it is not. The expected rate of return of this strategy is $.4 \times 20 + .6 \times 4 = 10.4$ percent. This exceeds the 10 percent rate of the machine, so that the optimal decision for year 1 is to go into research.

When Is the Use of Strategies Appropriate?

Suppose that decisions must be made at successive moments, that there is uncertainty regarding the outcome but that information on the outcome will be forthcoming, and, finally, that it will be possible to react to this information when it becomes available. Under these conditions it is advantageous to consider a strategy, i.e., a series of successive decisions each of which is a function of the information available when that decision must be made. In the above example, the decision for year 2 of the best strategy is made dependent on whether the research is successful or not. This information is available at the beginning of year 2. If the manager confines himself to those chains of successive decisions which do not use information that will be available in the future, he obtains a lower expected rate of return.

As a second example, consider the macroeconomic decision maker whose objective is to minimize, subject to Klein's Model I, the expectation of the loss function given in (23.8) and (23.9). The policy variables (W', T, and G) are three of the four exogenous variables of the model; the fourth, t (calendar time), presents no problem because its behavior is perfectly predictable in 1933–1936. The other variables in which the decision maker is interested are either endogenous (C and I) or a linear function of endogenous variables ($D = W - 2P$). Hence, these variables involve disturbances: ϵ_t, ϵ_t', and ϵ_t'' of (21.8) to (21.10) during 1933–1936. We assume that the decision maker knows the 1933 disturbances at the beginning of 1934, the 1934 disturbances at the beginning of 1935, and so on. Therefore, a strategy for 1933–1936 requires that the 1934 decision be made dependent on the 1933 disturbances, that the 1935 decision be made dependent on the 1933 *and* 1934 disturbances, and so on. Of course, disturbances are not observable (see Table 9 on page 64) and are hence never known, but we ignore this issue here and will come back to it at the end of this section.

First-Period Certainty Equivalence

Note that the macroeconomic decision maker's problem has a particular mathematical form: (1) The loss function whose expectation is minimized is *quadratic*, and (2) this minimization is subject to constraints (Klein's Model I) which are *linear* equations. If, moreover, (3) the disturbances of these equations have a distribution with finite variances which is independent of the values taken by the policy variables, then a simple result can be proved for the optimal strategy (i.e., the strategy which minimizes the expectation of the quadratic loss function subject to the linear constraints): This strategy has a first-period component identical to that of the decision that would be made if the uncertainty were disregarded by equating all disturbances to their expectations (zero).

This result, known as *first-period certainty equivalence*, is very convenient for the computation of the optimal strategy for the first period: Our decision maker will take the correct decision for 1933 by acting as if the disturbances of 1933–1936 are all zero. The certainty equivalence theorem is from Simon (1956) and Theil (1957b); its proof is beyond the scope of this book.

Application of the Certainty Equivalence

To implement this result, we consider (23.9) for $t = 1$, which contains C_{33}, I_{33}, and D_{33}. We use the reduced form to express these 1933 variables as linear functions of predetermined variables and disturbances of 1933. The predetermined variables include W_{33}', T_{33}, G_{33}, and calendar time as well as lagged (1932) endogenous variables whose values are known at the beginning of 1933. Thus, when we replace the 1933 disturbances by zero, as the certainty equivalence theorem permits us to do, C_{33}, I_{33}, and D_{33} become linear functions of W_{33}', T_{33}, and G_{33}, and the first three right-hand terms in (23.9) for $t = 1$ become quadratic functions of W_{33}', T_{33}, and G_{33}.

Next consider (23.9) for $t = 2$, containing C_{34}, I_{34}, and D_{34}. The reduced form expresses these three variables as linear functions of the 1934 disturbances (to be replaced by zero), of W'_{34}, T_{34}, G_{34}, calendar time, and of endogenous variables of 1933. Lagged application of the reduced form expresses these 1933 variables linearly in terms of W'_{33}, T_{33}, G_{33}, calendar time, disturbances of 1933 (to be replaced by zero), and known values of 1932. Hence, C_{34}, I_{34}, and D_{34} become linear functions of the six variables W'_{33}, T_{33}, G_{33}, W'_{34}, T_{34}, G_{34}, and the first three right-hand terms in (23.9) for $t = 2$ become quadratic functions of these six variables.

So we continue with (23.9) for $t = 3$, writing C_{35}, I_{35}, and D_{35} as linear functions of W', T, and G with subscripts 33 to 35, and for $t = 4$, so that C_{36}, I_{36}, and D_{36} become linear in W', T, and G with subscripts 33 to 36. When these linear functions are substituted in (23.9), the loss function (23.8) becomes quadratic in 12 variables: W'_{32+t}, T_{32+t}, and G_{32+t} for $t = 1, \ldots, 4$. Minimizing this function is a matter of computing 12 derivatives, which are all linear, and solving the associated 12-equation system.

The results are shown in the first row of Table 36. The entries relevant for the decision maker are those in the three 1933 columns, marked by an asterisk, because the certainty equivalence theorem states only that the first-year decision (for 1933) of the optimal strategy is identical to the corresponding decision obtained by replacing the disturbances by zero. One year later, the decision maker faces a three-year horizon with 1934 as the first year, so that he can then use the certainty equivalence theorem to obtain W'_{34}, T_{34}, and G_{34}. Note that the 1933 disturbances are known at this moment and that W'_{33}, T_{33}, and G_{33} are now fixed. Therefore, he adjusts the algebra of the three previous paragraphs by putting W'_{33}, T_{33}, G_{33}, and the 1933 disturbances at their known values, after which he minimizes the loss function with respect to nine variables: W'_{32+t}, T_{32+t}, and G_{32+t} for $t = 2$, 3, and 4. The results are shown in the second row of Table 36. Again, only the first-year components, now of 1934, are used by the decision maker (see the three asterisks in the second row).

He then continues for 1935 in the same way, using the observed disturbances of 1933 and 1934 as well as the given values of W', T, and G in these two years, and similarly for 1936. The results are shown in the third and fourth rows of Table 36. The lower part of the table is discussed later in this section.

Discussion of the Results

Table 37 contains the numerical values of the six variables which result from the optimal strategy, together with the desired values of Table 34 and the values which were actually observed from 1932 to 1936. The strategy values of the policy variables W', T, and G are the entries marked by asterisks in the first four rows of Table 36. The implied values of C, I, and D are obtained by substituting these strategy values and the observed disturbance values in the relevant reduced-form equations.

TABLE 36

The results of the optimal strategy: realizations and predictions

Computations made at the beginning of	W' 1933	W' 1934	W' 1935	W' 1936	T 1933	T 1934	T 1935	T 1936	G 1933	G 1934	G 1935	G 1936
1933	6.13*	6.26	6.20	6.36	8.62*	8.45	7.64	6.99	8.13*	7.66	7.51	6.94
1934		5.64*	5.96	6.30		8.34*	7.43	6.87		7.56*	7.70	7.06
1935			6.05*	6.34			7.37*	6.92			7.78*	7.02
1936				6.28*				6.91*				7.03*

Computations made at the beginning of	C 1933	C 1934	C 1935	C 1936	I 1933	I 1934	I 1935	I 1936	D 1933	D 1934	D 1935	D 1936
1933	47.36	51.77	56.37	60.73	−6.23	−2.38	.90	3.59	8.25	5.02	1.91	.05
1934	49.57*	52.72	56.68	60.79	−4.80*	−1.54	.89	3.38	6.76*	5.34	1.95	.08
1935		52.74*	56.52	60.75		−1.81*	.67	3.40		6.41*	1.94	.06
1936			56.69*	60.83			.81*	3.47			1.83*	.08
1937				64.43*				6.03*				−6.76*

Note: Asterisks indicate realizations; all other entries are predictions. All entries are in billions of 1934 dollars per year.

TABLE 37

Strategy values compared with desired and actual values

	Strategy	Desire	Actual	Strategy	Desire	Actual
	C			W'		
1932			45.6			5.3
1933	49.57	49.69	46.5	6.13	5.04	5.6
1934	52.74	53.78	48.7	5.64	5.25	6.0
1935	56.69	57.88	51.3	6.05	5.47	6.1
1936	64.43	61.97	57.7	6.28	5.68	7.4
	I			T		
1932			−6.2			8.3
1933	−4.80	−3.10	−5.1	8.62	7.40	5.4
1934	−1.81	.00	−3.0	8.34	7.64	6.8
1935	.81	3.10	−1.3	7.37	7.87	7.2
1936	6.03	6.20	2.1	6.91	8.11	8.3
	D			G		
1932			15.0			4.9
1933	6.76	11.25	6.1	8.13	5.40	3.7
1934	6.41	7.50	6.0	7.56	5.61	4.0
1935	1.83	3.75	5.2	7.78	5.83	4.4
1936	−6.76	.00	1.6	7.03	6.04	2.9

Note: All entries are in billions of 1934 dollars per year.

The results for consumption and investment show that the 1936 desires are adequately satisfied by the optimal strategy. Also in 1936, consumption and investment are at considerably higher levels under this strategy than under the regime that was actually followed. This indicates that the strategy was successful in its effort to bring the depression to an end. However, for the distribution variable $D = W - 2P$ the mark is overshot in 1936. The strategy value is negative, which implies a ratio P/W larger than $\frac{1}{2}$.

The behavior of the policy variables shows that the optimal strategy emphasizes government spending. Nonwage expenditure (G) is about twice as high under the strategy as it is under the actual regime followed. It was only in 1940 that the observed G reached a level of the same order of magnitude as that of the strategy values of this variable in 1933–1936.

Linear Decision Rules

The 12 entries in the first row of Table 36 are obtained by assuming that the disturbances of 1933–1936 are all zero. The next three rows use successively the observed disturbance values of these years. If it happened to be true that these observed values are all zero, the 1934 to 1936 entries in the first row would be equal to the corresponding strategy values obtained later. That is, the 1934 strategy value of W' would then be 6.26 rather than 5.64, the 1935 value would be 6.20 rather than 6.05, and so on. But, of course, these disturbances are not all zero and the 1934–1936 strategy values are functions of these disturbances. More precisely, the strategy which minimizes the expectation of a quadratic loss function subject to linear constraints consists of successive decisions (successive values taken by policy variables) which are linear functions of disturbances. Accordingly, such a strategy is known as a *linear decision rule*.

The values of C, I, and D implied by the strategy values of the policy variables are obtained by substituting these and the disturbances in the relevant reduced-form equations. For example, $C_{33} = 49.57$ (upper left in Table 37) is a linear function of $W'_{33} = 6.13$, $T_{33} = 8.62$, $G_{33} = 8.13$, and the 1933 disturbances. Hence, $C_{33} = 49.57$ can be computed at the beginning of 1934 when the 1933 disturbances are known. This explains why 49.57 appears in the 1934 row of the lower part of Table 36.

Predicting Future Decisions and Their Consequences

Since the strategy values of the policy variables in 1934 depend on the 1933 disturbances, they cannot be determined at the beginning of 1933. But we can predict them at that moment by replacing the 1933 disturbances by their zero expectations; in fact, this is what the 1933 computations shown in the first row of Table 36 do. Since the 1934 strategy value is a linear function of the 1933 disturbances, this predicted value minus the strategy value (the prediction error) has zero expectation. Hence, the prediction is unbiased.

Similarly, the 1933 computations yield unbiased predictions of the 1935 and 1936 strategy values, which are revised when later disturbances are observed. For example, the last column of Table 36 shows that at the beginning of 1933 G_{36} is predicted to be 6.94, that this was revised to 7.06 one year later and to 7.02 two years later, and that the actual strategy decision made is 7.03. All three successive predictions are unbiased conditionally on the information available when they are made. Note that on the whole, as early as the beginning of 1933, the decision maker has a fairly accurate idea of what is to be done during the four-year period: He should reduce G gradually from 8.1 billion dollars per year to about 7, reduce T from 8.6 billion dollars per year to about 7, and keep W' approximately constant just above 6 billion dollars per year. This is in agreement with the actual strategy values except for the 1934 value (5.64 billion) of W'.

Since the C, I, and D values implied by the strategy values of the policy variables are linear functions of the latter values and the disturbances, we can predict these C, I, and D values unbiasedly by substituting the predictions for the values of the policy variables and zero for the disturbances. Thus, at the beginning of 1933, we obtain a prediction of C_{33} equal to 47.36 by substituting $W'_{33} = 6.13$, $T_{33} = 8.62$, $G_{33} = 8.13$, and zero for the 1933 disturbances, and we obtain a prediction of C_{34} equal to 51.77 by also using the 1933 predictions of W'_{34}, T_{34}, and G_{34} as well as zero for the 1934 disturbances. The predictions of C_{33} and C_{34} (47.36 and 51.77) are shown in the first and second columns of

Table 36. One year later, at the beginning of 1934, we compute the realization of C_{33} (49.57 billion) and a revised prediction (52.72 billion) of C_{34}.

As a whole, there are 30 predictions of the 1933–1936 values of C, I, and D. Most of them are rather accurate, but the predictions of the three 1936 values (C_{36}, I_{36}, D_{36}) are all much worse. This is due to the large absolute values of the 1936 disturbances, which are predicted to be zero prior to 1936. All predictions of D_{36} are close to zero, suggesting that D_{36} will be close to the desired value $\bar{D}_{36} = 0$, but the realization is a large negative value. This result illustrates that when we have a series of successive predictions of the same predictand which are all virtually the same (predictions of D_{36} ranging between .05 and .08), there is nevertheless no guarantee that the predictand will be close to any of these predictions.

Concluding Remarks

The above results show that the framework of a quadratic loss function and a linear model yields important results. However, there are several qualifications that should be kept in mind:

(1) The certainty equivalence theorem requires a quadratic loss function and a linear model. It is not true, however, that the preferences of each decision maker can be adequately represented by a quadratic loss function. Also, many econometric models—particularly the larger ones—have several nonlinearities. One approach, pursued particularly by Friedman (1975), consists of approximating a nonlinear model by different linear models in different regions and proceeding similarly for nonquadratic loss functions. The certainty equivalence result will then also be only approximately true; see also Malinvaud (1969).

(2) The certainty equivalence theorem requires the coefficients of the linear model to be known. When estimates of coefficients are used, as has been done for Table 36, we have another approximation. The estimates used here are full-information maximum-likelihood estimates; see Theil (1964, pp. 77–78) for details. Therefore, the feedback to observed previous disturbances is actually a feedback to maximum-likelihood residuals.

(3) We assumed that the 1933 disturbances (residuals) are known at the beginning of 1934. This is another simplifying approximation, because what has just become past is not always immediately known with full accuracy (see Section 22.2). It is obvious that the 1934 strategy decision based on imperfect estimates of 1933 will in general not be optimal. For further details on this important matter, see Johansen (1972), who referred to earlier work by Friedman (1953). Also, the 1933–1936 period considered here is part of the sample period used for fitting Klein's Model I. Any actual application would refer to a postsample period during which the fit may well be worse than it is during the sample period.

(4) We know from Section 23.2 that the specification of an economy-wide econometric model, whether linear or nonlinear, is not an easy matter. It is

equally true that the specification of a macroeconomic loss function, whether quadratic or nonquadratic, is a matter involving uncertainties. The best procedure is to present alternative specifications, both for the model and for the loss function, and to verify the extent to which the optimal strategy decisions are sensitive to such changes in the specifications. If they are insensitive, the associated policy advice has a relatively firm basis. If they are sensitive, the implication is that further analysis is appropriate.

Problems

Problems 1–3 refer to Section 23.1, 4 and 5 to Section 23.2, and 6–8 to Section 23.3.

1 Does the interval shown in (23.3) provide a conditional or an unconditional interval prediction for y_*? Explain your answer.

2 Read the discussion of predictive activity as a production process on page 379. Does the use of a more complicated theory guarantee a greater reduction of uncertainty? Explain your answer.

3 Read the discussion in the last paragraph of Section 23.1. Illustrate graphically the horizontal movements of points in Figure 43, both above and below the horizontal axis, and give your comments.

4 It is stated in the second subsection of Section 23.2 that prediction based on (23.5) is possible at the beginning of t when P_{t-1}, K_{t-1}, and X_{t-1} are known. How should this be amended when the past is not known with full accuracy? (*Hint*: See Section 22.2.)

5 (*Continuation*) Assuming that the past is completely known, describe how X_t can be predicted at the beginning of $t - 2$.

6 Interpret the loss function (23.8) as a disutility function and each of its derivatives as a marginal disutility. Then add the following term to the right-hand side of (23.9):

$$(C_{32+t} - \bar{C}_{32+t})(I_{32+t} \quad \bar{I}_{32+t})$$

Verify that this implies that the marginal disutility of the discrepancy of C_{32+t} from its desired value is an increasing function of the discrepancy of I_{32+t} from its desired value and vice versa.

7 Verify that Table 36 contains nine revisions of predictions of values taken by policy variables and that eight of these are successful in the sense that the revised prediction is closer to the actual strategy value. Also verify that there are 18 revisions of predictions of values taken by noncontrolled variables; indicate the successful and unsuccessful predictions, and do so separately for the 1936 values and the earlier values.

8 (*Continuation*) Why is it that the predictions for W', T, and G in 1936 are so much better than those for C, I, and D in that year?

Appendix

The material which follows will be useful for mathematically more advanced readers. Matrices are indicated by boldface uppercase letters (such as **A**), column vectors by boldface lowercase letters (**a**), and row vectors by boldface lowercase letters with a prime added (**a′**) to indicate that they are the transposes of the corresponding column vectors.

A   Least-Squares Adjustment in Matrix Notation
(Chapter 7)

Matrix Notation

We introduce the $n \times 1$ observation vector **y** and the $n \times K$ observation matrix **X**:

$$(A.1) \qquad \mathbf{y} = \begin{bmatrix} y_1 \\ y_2 \\ \cdot \\ \cdot \\ \cdot \\ y_n \end{bmatrix}, \qquad \mathbf{X} = \begin{bmatrix} x_{11} & x_{21} & \cdots & x_{K1} \\ x_{12} & x_{22} & \cdots & x_{K2} \\ \cdot & \cdot & & \cdot \\ \cdot & \cdot & & \cdot \\ \cdot & \cdot & & \cdot \\ x_{1n} & x_{2n} & \cdots & x_{Kn} \end{bmatrix}$$

The n rows of **y** and **X** refer to the n observations. The K columns of **X** refer to the different x variables.

If there were an exact linear relation for all n observations, we would have

(A.2)
$$
\begin{bmatrix} y_1 \\ y_2 \\ \cdot \\ \cdot \\ \cdot \\ y_n \end{bmatrix}
=
\begin{bmatrix} x_{11} & x_{21} & \cdots & x_{K1} \\ x_{12} & x_{22} & \cdots & x_{K2} \\ \cdot & \cdot & & \cdot \\ \cdot & \cdot & & \cdot \\ \cdot & \cdot & & \cdot \\ x_{1n} & x_{2n} & \cdots & x_{Kn} \end{bmatrix}
\begin{bmatrix} b_1 \\ b_2 \\ \cdot \\ \cdot \\ \cdot \\ b_K \end{bmatrix}
$$

which can be simplified to

(A.3) $\qquad\qquad \mathbf{y} = \mathbf{Xb}, \qquad$ where $\mathbf{b} = [b_1 \quad b_2 \quad \cdots \quad b_K]'$

The matrix $\mathbf{X}$ and the vector $\mathbf{b}$ defined in (A.1) and (A.3) refer to LS adjustment through the origin. A minor modification is sufficient to handle the presence of a constant term b_0. We replace (A.2) by

$$
\begin{bmatrix} y_1 \\ y_2 \\ \cdot \\ \cdot \\ \cdot \\ y_n \end{bmatrix}
=
\begin{bmatrix} 1 & x_{11} & \cdots & x_{K1} \\ 1 & x_{12} & \cdots & x_{K2} \\ \cdot & \cdot & & \cdot \\ \cdot & \cdot & & \cdot \\ \cdot & \cdot & & \cdot \\ 1 & x_{1n} & \cdots & x_{Kn} \end{bmatrix}
\begin{bmatrix} b_0 \\ b_1 \\ \cdot \\ \cdot \\ \cdot \\ b_K \end{bmatrix}
$$

This shows that the observation matrix $\mathbf{X}$ has an additional column consisting of units and that the coefficient vector $\mathbf{b}$ has an additional element equal to the constant term b_0. It will be convenient in our matrix developments to work with the notation (A.1) to (A.3). It should simply be understood that if there is a constant term, this is one of the elements of the vector $\mathbf{b}$ and that the corresponding column of $\mathbf{X}$ consists of n unit elements.

The LS Normal Equations

If there is no exact linear relation, we must replace (A.3) by

(A.4) $\qquad\qquad\qquad \mathbf{y} = \mathbf{Xb} + \mathbf{e}$

where $\mathbf{e} - [e_1 \ \ldots \ e_n]'$ is the residual vector. The sum of the squares of the residuals is $\mathbf{e'e}$, the squared length of the residual vector. It follows from (A.4) that $\mathbf{e'e}$ can be written as

(A.5) $\qquad G(\mathbf{b}) = (\mathbf{y} - \mathbf{Xb})'(\mathbf{y} - \mathbf{Xb}) = \mathbf{y'y} - 2\mathbf{y'Xb} + \mathbf{b'X'Xb}$

This expression is minimized by LS by varying $\mathbf{b}$. Thus, we compute its gradient (the vector of first-order derivatives),

(A.6) $\qquad\qquad\qquad \dfrac{\partial G}{\partial \mathbf{b}} = -2\mathbf{X'y} + 2\mathbf{X'Xb}$

which we equate to zero. The result may be written as

(A.7) $\qquad\qquad\qquad\qquad \mathbf{X'Xb} = \mathbf{X'y}$

The vector $\mathbf{X'y}$ consists of K elements equal to those shown in the right-hand side of (7.30) for the special case $K = 3$, and the matrix $\mathbf{X'X}$ equals

$$(A.8) \qquad \mathbf{X'X} = \begin{bmatrix} \sum x_{1i}^2 & \sum x_{1i} x_{2i} & \cdots & \sum x_{1i} x_{Ki} \\ \sum x_{2i} x_{1i} & \sum x_{2i}^2 & \cdots & \sum x_{2i} x_{Ki} \\ \cdot & \cdot & & \cdot \\ \cdot & \cdot & & \cdot \\ \cdot & \cdot & & \cdot \\ \sum x_{Ki} x_{1i} & \sum x_{Ki} x_{2i} & \cdots & \sum x_{Ki}^2 \end{bmatrix}$$

where all summations are over $i = 1, \ldots, n$. We conclude that (A.7) is a concise form of the normal equations (7.30). See Problem 1 at the end of the Appendix for the normal equations (7.35).

The Hessian matrix of $G(\ )$, which contains all second-order derivatives, is obtained by differentiating the gradient (A.6) with respect to $\mathbf{b'}$:

$$(A.9) \qquad \frac{\partial^2 G}{\partial \mathbf{b}\, \partial \mathbf{b'}} = 2\mathbf{X'X}$$

This Hessian matrix is constant with respect to $\mathbf{b}$ because $G(\ )$ is a quadratic function of $\mathbf{b}$. For $G(\ )$ to have a minimum it is sufficient that this Hessian matrix is positive definite, which amounts to full column rank of $\mathbf{X}$ in view of (A.9). If $\mathbf{X}$ has less than full column rank, a vector $\mathbf{c} \neq \mathbf{0}$ exists so that $\mathbf{Xc} = \mathbf{0}$, which amounts to extreme multicollinearity (see Sections 8.3 and 9.3). The matrix $\mathbf{X'X}$ is then singular, and the normal equations (A.7) do not have a unique solution.

The LS Coefficient Vector and Residual Vector

If $\mathbf{X}$ has full column rank, so that $\mathbf{X'X}$ is nonsingular, the LS coefficient vector $\mathbf{b}$ is obtained by premultiplying the normal equations (A.7) by $(\mathbf{X'X})^{-1}$:

$$(A.10) \qquad \mathbf{b} = (\mathbf{X'X})^{-1} \mathbf{X'y}$$

This may be written as

$$(A.11) \qquad \mathbf{b} = \mathbf{X}^+ \mathbf{y}$$

where

$$(A.12) \qquad \mathbf{X}^+ = (\mathbf{X'X})^{-1} \mathbf{X'}$$

is the Moore-Penrose inverse of $\mathbf{X}$. Such an inverse of an $m \times n$ matrix $\mathbf{A}$ is defined as the $n \times m$ matrix $\mathbf{A}^+$ which satisfies the following four conditions:

$$(A.13) \qquad \mathbf{AA^+A} = \mathbf{A}$$
$$(A.14) \qquad \mathbf{A^+AA^+} = \mathbf{A^+}$$
$$(A.15) \qquad (\mathbf{AA^+})' = \mathbf{AA^+}$$
$$(A.16) \qquad (\mathbf{A^+A})' = \mathbf{A^+A}$$

The checks for X^+ defined in (A.12) are

$$XX^+X = X(X'X)^{-1}X'X = X$$
$$X^+XX^+ = (X'X)^{-1}X'X(X'X)^{-1}X' = (X'X)^{-1}X' = X^+$$

which agrees with (A.13) and (A.14). Similarly, $XX^+ = X(X'X)^{-1}X'$ and $X^+X = (X'X)^{-1}X'X = I$ are symmetric matrices, in agreement with (A.15) and (A.16). It can be shown that each matrix has a unique Moore-Penrose inverse; see, for example, Theil (1971, pp. 269–270). The reader should verify that if A is square and nonsingular, its Moore-Penrose inverse A^+ equals the ordinary inverse A^{-1}.

The LS residual vector e is obtained from (A.4) and (A.10),

(A.17) $$e = y - Xb = [I - X(X'X)^{-1}X']y$$

where I is the $n \times n$ unit matrix. Using (A.12), we can simplify this to

(A.18) $$e = (I - XX^+)y$$

Hence, the LS residual vector is a linear transformation of y, with a transformation matrix equal to $I - XX^+$. If X is square and nonsingular, then $X^+ = X^{-1}$ and $I - XX^+ = I - I = 0$, so that $e = 0$. This is the trivial case in which the LS fit is exact due to the equality of the number of observations and the number of coefficients adjusted.

Premultiplication of the first and third members of (A.17) by X' gives

$$X'e = [X' - X'X(X'X)^{-1}X']y$$

Since the matrix in brackets is zero, this proves

(A.19) $$X'e = 0$$

so that each column of X is orthogonal to the LS residual vector. If X contains a column of units corresponding to the constant term, the orthogonality of this column to the residual vector implies that the n residuals have zero sum.

B   Least-Squares Estimation in Matrix Notation
(Chapter 8)

The Standard Linear Model

We use the notation of (A.1) to (A.3) and assume, as before, that if there is a constant term, this is one of the elements of the vector b and that the corresponding column of X consists of n unit elements. We write (8.3) for $i = 1, \ldots, n$ and an arbitrary number of explanatory variables as

(B.1) $$y = X\beta + \epsilon$$

where ϵ is an n-element disturbance vector and β is the parameter vector (with a number of elements equal to that of b).

The standard linear model treats all elements of $\mathbf{X}$ as known constants. Condition (8.4) for $i = 1, \ldots, n$ is written as

(B.2) $$\mathcal{E}\boldsymbol{\epsilon} = \mathbf{0}$$

where $\mathcal{E}\boldsymbol{\epsilon}$ stands for the expectation of the vector $\boldsymbol{\epsilon}$, which is defined as the vector whose elements are the expectations of the elements of $\boldsymbol{\epsilon}$:

$$\mathcal{E}\boldsymbol{\epsilon} = \mathcal{E}\begin{bmatrix} \epsilon_1 \\ \cdot \\ \cdot \\ \cdot \\ \epsilon_n \end{bmatrix} = \begin{bmatrix} \mathcal{E}\epsilon_1 \\ \cdot \\ \cdot \\ \cdot \\ \mathcal{E}\epsilon_n \end{bmatrix} = \begin{bmatrix} 0 \\ \cdot \\ \cdot \\ \cdot \\ 0 \end{bmatrix}$$

Similarly, $\mathcal{E}(\boldsymbol{\epsilon}\boldsymbol{\epsilon}')$ stands for the expectation of the matrix $\boldsymbol{\epsilon}\boldsymbol{\epsilon}'$, which is defined as the matrix whose elements are the expectations of the elements of $\boldsymbol{\epsilon}\boldsymbol{\epsilon}'$:

$$\mathcal{E}(\boldsymbol{\epsilon}\boldsymbol{\epsilon}') = \mathcal{E}\begin{bmatrix} \epsilon_1^2 & \epsilon_1\epsilon_2 & \cdots & \epsilon_1\epsilon_n \\ \epsilon_2\epsilon_1 & \epsilon_2^2 & \cdots & \epsilon_2\epsilon_n \\ \cdot & \cdot & & \cdot \\ \cdot & \cdot & & \cdot \\ \cdot & \cdot & & \cdot \\ \epsilon_n\epsilon_1 & \epsilon_n\epsilon_2 & \cdots & \epsilon_n^2 \end{bmatrix} = \begin{bmatrix} \mathcal{E}(\epsilon_1^2) & \mathcal{E}(\epsilon_1\epsilon_2) & \cdots & \mathcal{E}(\epsilon_1\epsilon_n) \\ \mathcal{E}(\epsilon_2\epsilon_1) & \mathcal{E}(\epsilon_2^2) & \cdots & \mathcal{E}(\epsilon_2\epsilon_n) \\ \cdot & \cdot & & \cdot \\ \cdot & \cdot & & \cdot \\ \cdot & \cdot & & \cdot \\ \mathcal{E}(\epsilon_n\epsilon_1) & \mathcal{E}(\epsilon_n\epsilon_2) & \cdots & \mathcal{E}(\epsilon_n^2) \end{bmatrix}$$

It follows from (8.5) that the matrix in the third member has zero off-diagonal elements and that its diagonal elements are all equal to σ^2. Therefore, the matrix version of (8.5) is

(B.3) $$\mathcal{E}(\boldsymbol{\epsilon}\boldsymbol{\epsilon}') = \sigma^2\mathbf{I}$$

where $\mathbf{I}$ is the $n \times n$ unit matrix. The matrix $\mathcal{E}(\boldsymbol{\epsilon}\boldsymbol{\epsilon}')$ is the variance-covariance matrix or, for short, the covariance matrix of the disturbance vector.

The Mean and Covariance Matrix of the LS Coefficient Vector

Substitution of (B.1) in (A.10) yields

$$\mathbf{b} = (\mathbf{X}'\mathbf{X})^{-1}\mathbf{X}'(\mathbf{X}\boldsymbol{\beta} + \boldsymbol{\epsilon}) = \boldsymbol{\beta} + (\mathbf{X}'\mathbf{X})^{-1}\mathbf{X}'\boldsymbol{\epsilon}$$

which may be written as

(B.4) $$\mathbf{b} - \boldsymbol{\beta} = (\mathbf{X}'\mathbf{X})^{-1}\mathbf{X}'\boldsymbol{\epsilon}$$

Since $\mathbf{X}$ consists of constant elements and $\mathcal{E}\boldsymbol{\epsilon} = \mathbf{0}$, this proves $\mathcal{E}(\mathbf{b} - \boldsymbol{\beta}) = \mathbf{0}$, so that $\mathbf{b}$ is an unbiased estimator of $\boldsymbol{\beta}$. Note that this result is independent of the validity of condition (B.3).

The covariance matrix of $\mathbf{b}$, to be written $\mathcal{V}(\mathbf{b})$, is the matrix whose typical element is

$$\mathcal{E}[(b_h - \mathcal{E}b_h)(b_k - \mathcal{E}b_k)] = \mathcal{E}[(b_h - \beta_h)(b_k - \beta_k)]$$

where the equal sign is based on the unbiasedness ($\mathcal{E}b_h = \beta_h$). We conclude that the covariance matrix of $\mathbf{b}$ takes the form

(B.5) $$\mathcal{V}(\mathbf{b}) = \mathcal{E}[(\mathbf{b} - \boldsymbol{\beta})(\mathbf{b} - \boldsymbol{\beta})']$$

To evaluate the right-hand side we use (B.4),

$$\mathcal{E}[(\mathbf{b} - \boldsymbol{\beta})(\mathbf{b} - \boldsymbol{\beta})'] = \mathcal{E}[(\mathbf{X'X})^{-1}\mathbf{X'\epsilon\epsilon'X(X'X)}^{-1}]$$
$$= (\mathbf{X'X})^{-1}\mathbf{X'}\mathcal{E}(\mathbf{\epsilon\epsilon'})\mathbf{X(X'X)}^{-1}$$
$$= \sigma^2(\mathbf{X'X})^{-1}\mathbf{X'X(X'X)}^{-1}$$

where the second step is based on the constancy of the elements of $\mathbf{X}$ and the third on (B.3). We can write the result in the simple form

(B.6) $$\mathcal{V}(\mathbf{b}) = \sigma^2(\mathbf{X'X})^{-1}$$

Note that (B.3) can also be written as $\mathcal{V}(\boldsymbol{\epsilon}) = \sigma^2\mathbf{I}$ because $\mathcal{E}\boldsymbol{\epsilon} = \mathbf{0}$ [compare (B.5)].

The Gauss-Markov Theorem

The LS vector $\mathbf{b} = (\mathbf{X'X})^{-1}\mathbf{X'y}$ is linear in the vector $\mathbf{y}$ because the elements of $\mathbf{X}$ are constants. Any other linear estimator of $\boldsymbol{\beta}$ can be written as

(B.7) $$\mathbf{b^*} = [(\mathbf{X'X})^{-1}\mathbf{X'} + \mathbf{A}]\mathbf{y}$$

for some suitably selected matrix $\mathbf{A}$ consisting of constant elements. Using (B.1), we can write this estimator as

(B.8) $$\mathbf{b^*} = [(\mathbf{X'X})^{-1}\mathbf{X'} + \mathbf{A}](\mathbf{X}\boldsymbol{\beta} + \boldsymbol{\epsilon})$$
$$= (\mathbf{I} + \mathbf{AX})\boldsymbol{\beta} + [(\mathbf{X'X})^{-1}\mathbf{X'} + \mathbf{A}]\boldsymbol{\epsilon}$$

Hence $\mathcal{E}\mathbf{b^*} = (\mathbf{I} + \mathbf{AX})\boldsymbol{\beta}$, which should be identically equal to $\boldsymbol{\beta}$ in order that $\mathbf{b^*}$ be unbiased. This requires

(B.9) $$\mathbf{AX} = \mathbf{0}$$

in which case (B.8) can be written as

$$\mathbf{b^*} - \boldsymbol{\beta} = [(\mathbf{X'X})^{-1}\mathbf{X'} + \mathbf{A}]\boldsymbol{\epsilon}$$

To obtain $\mathcal{V}(\mathbf{b^*})$ we postmultiply both sides of this equation by their transposes and then take the expectation. Using the constancy of the elements of $\mathbf{X}$ and $\mathbf{A}$, we obtain

$$\mathcal{V}(\mathbf{b^*}) = [(\mathbf{X'X})^{-1}\mathbf{X'} + \mathbf{A}]\mathcal{E}(\mathbf{\epsilon\epsilon'})[\mathbf{X(X'X)}^{-1} + \mathbf{A'}]$$
$$= \sigma^2[(\mathbf{X'X})^{-1}\mathbf{X'} + \mathbf{A}][\mathbf{X(X'X)}^{-1} + \mathbf{A'}]$$
$$= \sigma^2[(\mathbf{X'X})^{-1} + (\mathbf{X'X})^{-1}\mathbf{X'A'} + \mathbf{AX(X'X)}^{-1} + \mathbf{AA'}]$$

where the second step is based on (B.3). It follows from (B.9) that the last line can be simplified to

(B.10) $$\mathcal{V}(\mathbf{b^*}) = \sigma^2(\mathbf{X'X})^{-1} + \sigma^2\mathbf{AA'}$$
$$= \mathcal{V}(\mathbf{b}) + \sigma^2\mathbf{AA'}$$

where use is made of (B.6) in the second step.

Next we consider the linear parameter combination $\mathbf{w'}\boldsymbol{\beta}$, with LS estimator $\mathbf{w'b}$ and with $\mathbf{w'b^*}$ as the estimator based on (B.7). If the weight vector $\mathbf{w}$ consists of constant elements, both $\mathbf{w'b}$ and $\mathbf{w'b^*}$ are unbiased estimators of $\mathbf{w'}\boldsymbol{\beta}$. The variance of $\mathbf{w'b}$ is then equal to the expectation of

$$(\mathbf{w'b} - \mathbf{w'\beta})^2 = [\mathbf{w'(b - \beta)}]^2 = \mathbf{w'(b - \beta)(b - \beta)'w}$$

The expectation of the third member is equal to $\mathbf{w'\mho(b)w}$. Similarly, the variance of $\mathbf{w'b^*}$ equals $\mathbf{w'\mho(b^*)w}$. Using (B.10), we obtain

(B.11)
$$\begin{aligned} \text{var } \mathbf{w'b^*} &= \mathbf{w'\mho(b)w} + \sigma^2 \mathbf{w'AA'w} \\ &= \text{var } \mathbf{w'b} + \sigma^2 (\mathbf{A'w})'\mathbf{A'w} \end{aligned}$$

Since $\sigma^2 (\mathbf{A'w})'\mathbf{A'w}$ is the sum of the squares of the elements of the vector $\sigma \mathbf{A'w}$ and therefore nonnegative, this proves the Gauss-Markov theorem, which states that the LS estimator $\mathbf{w'b}$ of $\mathbf{w'\beta}$ has the smallest possible sampling variance in the class of all unbiased linear estimators of $\mathbf{w'\beta}$ for any vector $\mathbf{w}$ consisting of constant elements. This theorem can also be formulated in terms of generalized variances and positive semidefinite quadratic forms in sampling errors; see Theil (1971, pp. 121, 124–125).

The LS Estimator of the Disturbance Variance

We substitute (B.1) in (A.18),

(B.12)
$$\mathbf{e} = (\mathbf{I} - \mathbf{XX^+})(\mathbf{X\beta} + \boldsymbol{\epsilon}) = (\mathbf{I} - \mathbf{XX^+})\boldsymbol{\epsilon}$$

where the second step is based on $(\mathbf{I} - \mathbf{XX^+})\mathbf{X} = \mathbf{0}$, which follows from property (A.13) of the Moore-Penrose inverse. We conclude from (B.12) that the sum of the squares of the LS residuals equals

$$\mathbf{e'e} = \boldsymbol{\epsilon}'(\mathbf{I} - \mathbf{XX^+})'(\mathbf{I} - \mathbf{XX^+})\boldsymbol{\epsilon}$$

It follows from the symmetry property (A.15) that this can be written as

(B.13)
$$\mathbf{e'e} = \boldsymbol{\epsilon}'(\mathbf{I} - \mathbf{XX^+})^2 \boldsymbol{\epsilon}$$

Hence, the LS residual sum of squares is equal to a quadratic form in the disturbances with a matrix equal to the square of $\mathbf{I} - \mathbf{XX^+}$. This matrix is idempotent, i.e., it is equal to its own square:

(B.14)
$$(\mathbf{I} - \mathbf{XX^+})^2 = \mathbf{I} - \mathbf{XX^+}$$

To prove this we write the left-hand side as

$$\begin{aligned} (\mathbf{I} - \mathbf{XX^+})(\mathbf{I} - \mathbf{XX^+}) &= \mathbf{I} - \mathbf{XX^+} - \mathbf{XX^+} + \mathbf{XX^+XX^+} \\ &= \mathbf{I} - \mathbf{XX^+} - \mathbf{XX^+} + \mathbf{XX^+} \\ &= \mathbf{I} - \mathbf{XX^+} \end{aligned}$$

where the second step is based on (A.13).

Thus, using (B.14), we simplify (B.13) to

(B.15)
$$\mathbf{e'e} = \boldsymbol{\epsilon}'(\mathbf{I} - \mathbf{XX^+})\boldsymbol{\epsilon}$$

To evaluate this further we introduce the trace (tr) of a square matrix, which is defined as the sum of the diagonal elements of this matrix, and we use the property $\text{tr } \mathbf{AB} = \text{tr } \mathbf{BA}$ (for $\mathbf{A}$ of order $p \times q$ and $\mathbf{B}$ of order $q \times p$, so that the product matrices $\mathbf{AB}$ and $\mathbf{BA}$ are both square). The right-hand side of (B.15) is a

1×1 matrix and hence equal to its own trace. Thus, we can write it as

(B.16) $$\text{tr } \mathbf{\epsilon}'(\mathbf{I} - \mathbf{X}\mathbf{X}^+)\mathbf{\epsilon} = \text{tr } (\mathbf{I} - \mathbf{X}\mathbf{X}^+)\mathbf{\epsilon}\mathbf{\epsilon}'$$

where the equal sign is based on $\text{tr } \mathbf{AB} = \text{tr } \mathbf{BA}$ with $\mathbf{A}$ interpreted as $\mathbf{\epsilon}'$ and $\mathbf{B}$ as $(\mathbf{I} - \mathbf{X}\mathbf{X}^+)\mathbf{\epsilon}$. By combining (B.15) and (B.16), we obtain

(B.17) $$\mathbf{e}'\mathbf{e} = \text{tr } (\mathbf{I} - \mathbf{X}\mathbf{X}^+)\mathbf{\epsilon}\mathbf{\epsilon}'$$

The expectation of the LS residual sum of squares is obtained by taking the expectation of both sides of (B.17). Using the constancy of the elements of $\mathbf{X}$ as well as the fact that the trace is a linear operator, we find

(B.18) $$\mathcal{E}(\mathbf{e}'\mathbf{e}) = \text{tr } (\mathbf{I} - \mathbf{X}\mathbf{X}^+)\mathcal{E}(\mathbf{\epsilon}\mathbf{\epsilon}') = \sigma^2 \text{ tr } (\mathbf{I} - \mathbf{X}\mathbf{X}^+)$$

where the second step is based on (B.3) and on $\text{tr } (k\mathbf{A}) = k \text{ tr } \mathbf{A}$ for a scalar k. Next we use $\text{tr } (\mathbf{A} - \mathbf{B}) = \text{tr } \mathbf{A} - \text{tr } \mathbf{B}$ to write (B.18) as

(B.19) $$\begin{aligned} \mathcal{E}(\mathbf{e}'\mathbf{e}) &= \sigma^2(\text{tr } \mathbf{I} - \text{tr } \mathbf{X}\mathbf{X}^+) \\ &= \sigma^2[n - \text{tr } \mathbf{X}(\mathbf{X}'\mathbf{X})^{-1}\mathbf{X}'] \\ &= \sigma^2[n - \text{tr } (\mathbf{X}'\mathbf{X})^{-1}\mathbf{X}'\mathbf{X}] \end{aligned}$$

where the second step is based on the order $(n \times n)$ of $\mathbf{I}$ and on (A.12) and the third on $\text{tr } \mathbf{AB} = \text{tr } \mathbf{BA}$ with $\mathbf{A} = \mathbf{X}$, $\mathbf{B} = (\mathbf{X}'\mathbf{X})^{-1}\mathbf{X}'$. The trace in the last line is equal to that of the unit matrix whose order is equal to the number of columns of $\mathbf{X}$. Hence, this trace is equal to this number. Since the number of columns of $\mathbf{X}$ equals the number of coefficients adjusted (i.e., the number of elements of $\mathbf{b}$), this proves that $\mathcal{E}(\mathbf{e}'\mathbf{e})$, the expectation of the LS residual sum of squares, equals σ^2 multiplied by the number of degrees of freedom of the regression.

For the textile example we have $17 - 3 = 14$ degrees of freedom. Using the unbiased estimate (8.39) of σ^2, we have the following unbiased estimate of the covariance matrix (B.6):

(B.20) $$s^2(\mathbf{X}'\mathbf{X})^{-1} = \begin{bmatrix} .093617 & -.046604 & .000077 \\ -.046604 & .024324 & -.001251 \\ .000077 & -.001251 & .001304 \end{bmatrix}$$

The successive rows and columns refer to b_0, b_1, and b_2.

C   The Normal and Associated Distributions
(Chapters 10 and 11)

The Multivariate Normal Distribution

A vector of n random variables is said to follow the multivariate normal distribution with mean $\mathbf{\mu}$ and nonsingular covariance matrix $\mathbf{\Sigma}$ if its density function takes the form

(C.1) $$f(\mathbf{x}) = \frac{1}{(2\pi)^{n/2}|\mathbf{\Sigma}|} \exp\left\{-\frac{1}{2}(\mathbf{x} - \mathbf{\mu})'\mathbf{\Sigma}^{-1}(\mathbf{x} - \mathbf{\mu})\right\}$$

where $|\mathbf{\Sigma}|$ is the determinant value of the covariance matrix. The exponent in (C.1) agrees with (10.20) when we identify a_{ij} with the (i, j)th element of $\mathbf{\Sigma}^{-1}$. If the n random variables are all uncorrelated, Σ and Σ^{-1} are diagonal matrices, in which case the expression in curled brackets in (C.1) can be written as a weighted sum of n squares, in agreement with (10.23).

For proofs of the propositions that any linear function of a multinormal vector is normally distributed and that the conditional distributions associated with (C.1) are normal, see Theil (1971, pp. 78–79, 188–190).

The Chi-Square Distribution of Idempotent Quadratic Forms

Let $\mathbf{A}$ be an idempotent matrix, $\mathbf{A}^2 = \mathbf{A}$ [see the discussion below (B.13)]. All idempotent matrices in the Appendix are symmetric, so that it is convenient to make the implicit assumption that $\mathbf{A}$ is symmetric when it is idempotent: $\mathbf{A} = \mathbf{A}^2 = \mathbf{A'A}$.

Since the latent roots of the square of any square matrix are squares of the latent roots of the matrix that is squared, an idempotent matrix $\mathbf{A}$ of order $n \times n$ and rank r must have r unit latent roots and $n - r$ zero roots. Hence, there exists an $n \times n$ orthogonal matrix $\mathbf{C}$ so that $\mathbf{C'AC} = \boldsymbol{\Lambda}$, where $\boldsymbol{\Lambda}$ is a diagonal matrix whose first r diagonal elements are 1 and whose last $n - r$ diagonal elements are 0. Let $\mathbf{x}$ be a vector consisting of n independent standardized normal variates $[\mathcal{E}\mathbf{x} = \mathbf{0}, \mathcal{E}(\mathbf{xx'}) = \mathbf{I}]$. We define $\mathbf{y} = \mathbf{C'x}$ and consider the quadratic form

(C.2)
$$\mathbf{x'Ax} = \mathbf{x'(CC')A(CC')x} = \mathbf{y'(C'AC)y} = \mathbf{y'\Lambda y}$$
$$= [\mathbf{y'_1} \ \ \mathbf{y'_2}] \begin{bmatrix} \mathbf{I}_r & \mathbf{0} \\ \mathbf{0} & \mathbf{0} \end{bmatrix} \begin{bmatrix} \mathbf{y}_1 \\ \mathbf{y}_2 \end{bmatrix} = \mathbf{y'_1 y_1}$$

where $\mathbf{y}_1$ is the subvector of $\mathbf{y}$ consisting of the first r elements and $\mathbf{I}_r$ is the $r \times r$ unit matrix. The vector $\mathbf{y} = \mathbf{C'x}$ is multivariate normal because it is a linear function of the normal vector $\mathbf{x}$. It has zero expectation: $\mathcal{E}\mathbf{y} = \mathbf{C'}\mathcal{E}\mathbf{x} = \mathbf{0}$. Its covariance matrix is

$$\mathcal{E}(\mathbf{C'xx'C}) = \mathbf{C'}\mathcal{E}(\mathbf{xx'})\mathbf{C} = \mathbf{C'C} = \mathbf{I}$$

Hence, $\mathbf{y}_1$ in (C.2) is an r-element vector of independent standardized normal variates, so that the sum of the squares of these elements, $\mathbf{y'_1 y_1}$ in the last member of (C.2), is distributed as $\chi^2(r)$. Therefore, (C.2) implies that if $\mathbf{x}$ consists of independent standardized normal variates, any idempotent quadratic form $\mathbf{x'Ax}$ of rank r is distributed as $\chi^2(r)$.

Applications

It may be verified that the right-hand side of (11.7) is a special case for $\mathbf{x} = [(X_1 - \mu)/\sigma \ \ \cdots \ \ (X_n - \mu)/\sigma]'$ and

(C.3)
$$\mathbf{A} = \mathbf{I} - \frac{1}{n}\boldsymbol{\imath}\boldsymbol{\imath}'$$

where $\boldsymbol{\imath} = [1 \ \ \cdots \ \ 1]'$ is a column vector consisting of n unit elements. The trace of the matrix (C.3) is $n - 1$, so that its rank is also $n - 1$ (because the trace of a square matrix equals the sum of its latent roots, and the nonzero roots of A are all 1). Hence, the right-hand side of (11.7) is distributed as $\chi^2(n - 1)$, as stated in proposition (I) below (11.7).

It follows from (B.15) that

(C.4) $$\frac{e'e}{\sigma^2} = \frac{\epsilon'(I - XX^+)\epsilon}{\sigma^2}$$

which is an idempotent quadratic form with rank n' (the number of degrees of freedom of the regression) in the vector $(1/\sigma)\epsilon$. Hence, if ϵ consists of independent normal variates with zero mean and variance σ^2, (C.4) is distributed as $\chi^2(n')$. Since the left-hand side of (C.4) equals the right-hand side of (11.19), this proves proposition (I) below (11.19).

Independence Properties of Idempotent Quadratic Forms

Let $x'Ax$ be an idempotent quadratic form in a vector x which consists of independent standardized normal variates. Since A satisfies $A = A^2 = A'A$, the quadratic form can be written as $x'A'Ax$, which equals the sum of squares of the elements of the vector Ax. Let Lx be a vector whose elements are linear in x. If the condition

(C.5) $$LA = 0$$

is satisfied, each element of Lx is uncorrelated with each element of Ax, because the covariances of all pairs of such elements are elements of the matrix

$$\mathcal{E}(Lxx'A') = L\mathcal{E}(xx')A' = LA' = LA = 0$$

Since x and hence also Lx and Ax are normally distributed, uncorrelated means are independent. Therefore, (C.5) is a sufficient condition for the independence of Lx and Ax and, given that $x'Ax$ equals the sum of the squares of the elements of Ax, also for the independence of Lx and the idempotent quadratic form $x'Ax$.

For the arithmetic mean $\bar{X}$ we specify $L = (1/n)\iota'$, which satisfies (C.5) for A defined in (C.3); this proves proposition (II) below (11.7). For the corresponding proposition below (11.19) we use (B.4), which states that $b - \beta$ equals $(X'X)^{-1}X'\epsilon$ $= X^+\epsilon$. Hence, the sampling error of the LS coefficient vector is a linear function of ϵ with transformation matrix X^+. This matrix satisfies $X^+(I - XX^+) = 0$ in view of property (A.14) of the Moore-Penrose inverse. The independence of b and s^2 then follows from (C.4) and (C.5).

D   The Slutsky Matrix
(Chapter 14)

The Conditions for a Utility Maximum

We write the utility function (14.1) and the budget constraint (14.2) as $u = u(q)$ and $p'q = m$, respectively, where p and q are N-element column vectors. We assume that $u(\ )$ has continuous second-order derivatives, so that its

Hessian matrix,

(D.1)
$$\mathbf{U} = \frac{\partial^2 u}{\partial \mathbf{q} \, \partial \mathbf{q}'}$$

exists and is symmetric.

To maximize $u(\mathbf{q})$ subject to $\mathbf{p}'\mathbf{q} = m$ we form the Lagrangean function,

(D.2)
$$u(\mathbf{q}) - \lambda(\mathbf{p}'\mathbf{q} - m)$$

where λ is an undetermined (Lagrangean) multiplier. We differentiate (D.2) with respect to $\mathbf{q}$,

(D.3)
$$\frac{\partial u}{\partial \mathbf{q}} - \lambda \mathbf{p}$$

and equate (D.3) to zero. This yields, in scalar form,

(D.4)
$$\frac{\partial u}{\partial q_i} = \lambda p_i \qquad\qquad i = 1, \ldots, N$$

which is the familiar proportionality of the marginal utilities and the corresponding prices. These N equations plus the budget constraint are equal in number to the N unknown optimal quantities plus the associated value of λ, which is known as the marginal utility of income.

The zero value of the vector (D.3) implies a stationary utility value subject to the budget constraint. To ensure that this stationary value is a maximum, we assume that the matrix of second-order derivatives of the Lagrangean function (D.2) with respect to $q_1, \ldots, q_N$ is negative definite at the stationary point. This matrix is obtained by differentiating (D.3) with respect to $\mathbf{q}'$ and is thus equal to the Hessian matrix $\mathbf{U}$ defined in (D.1). Hence, we assume that $\mathbf{U}$ is symmetric negative definite. Note that, from now on, $\mathbf{U}$ will be interpreted as the Hessian matrix of $u(\ )$ at the point of the budget-constrained utility maximum.

The Fundamental Matrix Equation

We write the demand systems (14.3) and (14.6) in vector form as

(D.5) $$\mathbf{q} = \mathbf{f}(m, \mathbf{p})$$
(D.6) $$\mathbf{q} = \mathbf{q}(\bar{m}, \mathbf{p})$$

where $\mathbf{f}(\ )$ and $\mathbf{q}(\ )$ are both column vectors consisting of N functions.

We are interested in the derivatives of these functions. For this purpose, note that the budget constraint and the proportionality (D.4) hold for any values of income and prices; hence, we can differentiate both with respect to income and prices. Thus, we differentiate $\mathbf{p}'\mathbf{q} = m$ with respect to m to obtain

(D.7)
$$\mathbf{p}' \frac{\partial \mathbf{f}}{\partial m} = 1$$

where $\partial \mathbf{f}/\partial m$ stands for the column vector of derivatives of (D.5) with respect to m. Similarly, differentiation of $\mathbf{p}'\mathbf{q} = m$ with respect to p_k gives $\sum_i p_i(\partial f_i/\partial p_k)$

$+ q_k = 0$ or, in vector form, $\mathbf{p}'(\partial \mathbf{f}/\partial p_k) + q_k = 0$. When we repeat this for all prices, we obtain

(D.8) $$\mathbf{p}' \frac{\partial \mathbf{f}}{\partial \mathbf{p}'} + \mathbf{q}' = \mathbf{0}$$

where $\partial \mathbf{f}/\partial \mathbf{p}'$ is the $N \times N$ matrix with $\partial f_i/\partial p_j$ as (i, j)th element.

Next we differentiate (D.4) with respect to m,

$$\sum_{j=1}^{N} \frac{\partial^2 u}{\partial q_i\, \partial q_j} \frac{\partial f_j}{\partial m} = p_i \frac{\partial \lambda}{\partial m} \qquad\qquad i = 1, \ldots, N$$

which can be written in matrix form as

(D.9) $$\mathbf{U} \frac{\partial \mathbf{f}}{\partial m} = \frac{\partial \lambda}{\partial m} \mathbf{p}$$

Finally, we differentiate (D.4) with respect to p_k, which gives

$$\sum_{j=1}^{N} \frac{\partial^2 u}{\partial q_i\, \partial q_j} \frac{\partial f_j}{\partial p_k} = \begin{cases} p_i \dfrac{\partial \lambda}{\partial p_k} & \text{if } k \neq i \\[2ex] p_i \dfrac{\partial \lambda}{\partial p_i} + \lambda & \text{if } k = i \end{cases}$$

or, in matrix form,

(D.10) $$\mathbf{U} \frac{\partial \mathbf{f}}{\partial \mathbf{p}'} = \mathbf{p} \frac{\partial \lambda}{\partial \mathbf{p}'} + \lambda \mathbf{I}$$

where $\partial \lambda/\partial \mathbf{p}'$ is the row vector of the derivatives of λ with respect to all prices and $\mathbf{I}$ is the $N \times N$ unit matrix.

The results (D.7) to (D.10) can be combined in partitioned form:

(D.11) $$\begin{bmatrix} \mathbf{U} & \mathbf{p} \\ \mathbf{p}' & 0 \end{bmatrix} \begin{bmatrix} \partial \mathbf{f}/\partial m & \partial \mathbf{f}/\partial \mathbf{p}' \\ -\partial \lambda/\partial m & -\partial \lambda/\partial \mathbf{p}' \end{bmatrix} = \begin{bmatrix} \mathbf{0} & \lambda \mathbf{I} \\ 1 & -\mathbf{q}' \end{bmatrix}$$

This result, from Barten (1964), is known as the fundamental matrix equation of consumer demand theory.

Solving the Fundamental Matrix Equation

The inverse of the bordered Hessian on the far left in (D.11) is

(D.12) $$\frac{1}{\mathbf{p}'\mathbf{U}^{-1}\mathbf{p}} \begin{bmatrix} (\mathbf{p}'\mathbf{U}^{-1}\mathbf{p})\mathbf{U}^{-1} - \mathbf{U}^{-1}\mathbf{p}(\mathbf{U}^{-1}\mathbf{p})' & \mathbf{U}^{-1}\mathbf{p} \\ (\mathbf{U}^{-1}\mathbf{p})' & -1 \end{bmatrix}$$

Premultiplication of both sides of (D.11) by (D.12) yields

(D.13) $$\frac{\partial \lambda}{\partial m} = \frac{1}{\mathbf{p}'\mathbf{U}^{-1}\mathbf{p}}$$

(D.14) $$\frac{\partial \mathbf{f}}{\partial m} = \frac{1}{\mathbf{p}'\mathbf{U}^{-1}\mathbf{p}} \mathbf{U}^{-1}\mathbf{p}$$

(D.15) $$\frac{\partial \mathbf{f}}{\partial \mathbf{p}'} = \lambda \mathbf{U}^{-1} - \frac{\lambda}{\mathbf{p}'\mathbf{U}^{-1}\mathbf{p}} \mathbf{U}^{-1}\mathbf{p}(\mathbf{U}^{-1}\mathbf{p})' - \frac{1}{\mathbf{p}'\mathbf{U}^{-1}\mathbf{p}} \mathbf{U}^{-1}\mathbf{p}\mathbf{q}'$$

We use (D.13) to write (D.14) as

(D.16)
$$\frac{\partial \mathbf{f}}{\partial m} = \frac{\partial \lambda}{\partial m} \mathbf{U}^{-1} \mathbf{p}$$

We also use (D.13) and (D.14) to write (D.15) as

(D.17)
$$\frac{\partial \mathbf{f}}{\partial \mathbf{p}'} = \lambda \mathbf{U}^{-1} - \frac{\lambda}{\partial \lambda / \partial m} \frac{\partial \mathbf{f}}{\partial m} \frac{\partial \mathbf{f}'}{\partial m} - \frac{\partial \mathbf{f}}{\partial m} \mathbf{q}'$$

or, in scalar form,

(D.18)
$$\frac{\partial f_i}{\partial p_j} = \lambda u^{ij} - \frac{\lambda}{\partial \lambda / \partial m} \frac{\partial f_i}{\partial m} \frac{\partial f_j}{\partial m} - \frac{\partial f_i}{\partial m} q_j$$

where u^{ij} is the (i, j)th element of $\mathbf{U}^{-1}$.

Real Income and the Income Effect of Price Changes

Suppose that p_j increases by dp_j. One implication is that the basket $(q_1, \ldots, q_N)$ which was optimal prior to this price increase becomes more expensive. The consumer needs an income compensation equal to $q_j dp_j$ to be able to buy this basket in the new price situation. If he receives this compensation, he faces two changes: a price increase dp_j and an income increase $dm = q_j dp_j$. Their combined effect on the demand for the ith good is

(D.19)
$$\left(\frac{\partial f_i}{\partial p_j} + \frac{\partial f_i}{\partial m} q_j \right) dp_j = \left(\lambda u^{ij} - \frac{\lambda}{\partial \lambda / \partial m} \frac{\partial f_i}{\partial m} \frac{\partial f_j}{\partial m} \right) dp_j$$

where the equal sign is based on (D.18). Note that the last term in (D.18) occurs on the left in (D.19). This term reflects the fact that an increase in p_j makes the consumer poorer, so that an income compensation is needed to offset this effect. Accordingly, the last term in (D.18) is called the *income effect* of dp_j on q_i. The two other terms in that equation are considered in the next subsection.

The left-hand side of (D.19) is the effect of dp_j on q_i when there is an appropriate income compensation or, equivalently, when real income is held constant. Suppose now that all prices change infinitesimally, so that their combined effect on real income equals $- \sum_k q_k \, dp_k$. If the actual change in money income is dm, the change in real income is

(D.20)
$$d\bar{m} = dm - \sum_{k=1}^{N} q_k \, dp_k$$
$$= dm - m \sum_{k=1}^{N} w_k d(\log_e p_k)$$

where $w_k = p_k q_k / m$ is the budget share of the kth good. Note that (D.20) specifies only the change in real income and thus leaves its level undefined. If we define this level equal to that of money income (m), we obtain the following result after dividing (D.20) by m:

(D.21)
$$d(\log_e \bar{m}) = d(\log_e m) - \sum_{k=1}^{N} w_k d(\log_e p_k)$$

The second term on the right equals minus the logarithmic change in the Divisia price index which is given in (14.43). Therefore, (D.21) implies that this index is the deflator used to transform money income into real income.

The Substitution Matrix

Since the left-hand side of (D.19) measures the effect of dp_j on the demand for the ith good when real income ($\bar{m}$) remains constant, the expression by which dp_j is multiplied in (D.19) must be a price derivative of the demand equations (D.6). Thus, using the right-hand side of (D.19), we have

$$(D.22) \qquad \frac{\partial q_i}{\partial p_j} = \lambda u^{ij} - \frac{\lambda}{\partial \lambda/\partial m} \frac{\partial f_i}{\partial m} \frac{\partial f_j}{\partial m}$$

which is equivalent to (D.18) except that the term on the far right (the income effect of dp_j) is missing. Note that we have

$$(D.23) \qquad \frac{\partial f_i}{\partial m} = \frac{\partial q_i}{\partial m} \qquad\qquad i = 1, \ldots, N$$

because the partial-derivative procedure implies that prices are kept constant. Therefore, we can write (D.22) in the equivalent form

$$\frac{\partial q_i}{\partial p_j} = \lambda u^{ij} - \frac{\lambda}{\partial \lambda/\partial m} \frac{\partial q_i}{\partial m} \frac{\partial q_j}{\partial m}$$

which is the (i, j)th element of the matrix equation

$$(D.24) \qquad \frac{\partial \mathbf{q}}{\partial \mathbf{p}'} = \lambda \mathbf{U}^{-1} - \frac{\lambda}{\partial \lambda/\partial m} \frac{\partial \mathbf{q}}{\partial m} \frac{\partial \mathbf{q}'}{\partial m}$$

The left-hand side of (D.24) is the *substitution matrix*; each of its N^2 elements describes the substitution effect of the change in the price of some good on the demand for some good. The right-hand side of (D.24) is a symmetric matrix, which proves (14.7). Next we premultiply (D.24) by $\mathbf{p}'$:

$$(D.25) \qquad \mathbf{p}' \frac{\partial \mathbf{q}}{\partial \mathbf{p}'} = \lambda \mathbf{p}' \mathbf{U}^{-1} - \frac{\lambda}{\partial \lambda/\partial m} \left(\mathbf{p}' \frac{\partial \mathbf{q}}{\partial m} \right) \frac{\partial \mathbf{q}'}{\partial m}$$

The first term on the right is, in view of (D.16), equal to

$$\frac{\lambda}{\partial \lambda/\partial m} \frac{\partial \mathbf{f}'}{\partial m} = \frac{\lambda}{\partial \lambda/\partial m} \frac{\partial \mathbf{q}'}{\partial m}$$

where the equal sign is based on (D.23). The second right-hand term in (D.25) takes the same value apart from sign [see (D.7) and (D.23)], so that $\mathbf{p}'(\partial \mathbf{q}/\partial \mathbf{p}')$ = $\mathbf{0}$. This confirms (14.9) and establishes that $\partial \mathbf{q}/\partial \mathbf{p}'$ is a singular matrix. In the next subsection we shall prove that this matrix is negative semidefinite of rank $N - 1$, so that its diagonal elements are all negative in accordance with (14.8).

The Negative Semidefiniteness of the Substitution Matrix

The substitution matrix (D.24) equals a (positive) multiple λ of the matrix

$$\mathbf{A} = \mathbf{U}^{-1} - \frac{1}{\mathbf{p}'\mathbf{U}^{-1}\mathbf{p}}\mathbf{U}^{-1}\mathbf{p}(\mathbf{U}^{-1}\mathbf{p})'$$

which follows from (D.13), (D.16), and (D.23). Thus, for any column vector $\mathbf{x}$ consisting of N elements,

(D.26) $\qquad \mathbf{x}'\mathbf{A}\mathbf{x} = \frac{1}{\mathbf{p}'\mathbf{U}^{-1}\mathbf{p}}[(\mathbf{x}'\mathbf{U}^{-1}\mathbf{x})(\mathbf{p}'\mathbf{U}^{-1}\mathbf{p}) - (\mathbf{x}'\mathbf{U}^{-1}\mathbf{p})^2]$

Since $\mathbf{U}$ and hence $\mathbf{U}^{-1}$ are symmetric negative definite, a nonsingular matrix $\mathbf{B}$ exists so that $\mathbf{U}^{-1} = -\mathbf{B}'\mathbf{B}$. Hence, we can write (D.26) as

$$\mathbf{x}'\mathbf{A}\mathbf{x} = \frac{1}{\mathbf{p}'\mathbf{U}^{-1}\mathbf{p}}[(\mathbf{x}'\mathbf{B}'\mathbf{B}\mathbf{x})(\mathbf{p}'\mathbf{B}'\mathbf{B}\mathbf{p}) - (\mathbf{x}'\mathbf{B}'\mathbf{B}\mathbf{p})^2]$$

$$= \frac{1}{\mathbf{p}'\mathbf{U}^{-1}\mathbf{p}}[(\mathbf{a}'\mathbf{a})(\mathbf{b}'\mathbf{b}) - (\mathbf{a}'\mathbf{b})^2]$$

where $\mathbf{a} = \mathbf{B}\mathbf{x}$ and $\mathbf{b} = \mathbf{B}\mathbf{p}$. Schwartz' inequality states that the last expression in brackets vanishes if a scalar k exists so that $\mathbf{a} = k\mathbf{b}$ and that it is positive otherwise. Therefore, given that $\mathbf{p}'\mathbf{U}^{-1}\mathbf{p}$ before the brackets is negative, $\mathbf{A}$ and hence also $\partial\mathbf{q}/\partial\mathbf{p}'$ are negative semidefinite of rank $N - 1$.

The Slutsky Matrix

It follows from (14.33) that the $N \times N$ matrix $[\pi_{ij}]$ of Slutsky coefficients is obtained by premultiplying (D.24) by $(1/m)\mathbf{P}$ and postmultiplying by $\mathbf{P}$, where $\mathbf{P}$ is the $N \times N$ diagonal matrix which contains the prices $p_1, \ldots, p_N$ in the diagonal:

$$[\pi_{ij}] = \frac{\lambda}{m}\mathbf{P}\mathbf{U}^{-1}\mathbf{P} - \frac{\lambda/m}{\partial\lambda/\partial m}\mathbf{P}\frac{\partial\mathbf{q}}{\partial m}\left(\mathbf{P}\frac{\partial\mathbf{q}}{\partial m}\right)'$$

Since $\mathbf{P}(\partial\mathbf{q}/\partial m)$ is the vector $[\mu_1 \ \cdots \ \mu_N]'$ of marginal shares, we can write this result as

(D.27) $\qquad [\pi_{ij}] = \frac{\lambda}{m}\mathbf{P}\mathbf{U}^{-1}\mathbf{P} - \phi \begin{bmatrix} \mu_1 \\ \cdot \\ \cdot \\ \cdot \\ \mu_N \end{bmatrix} [\mu_1 \ \cdots \ \mu_N]$

where ϕ is the reciprocal of the income elasticity of λ (i.e., the reciprocal of the income elasticity of the marginal utility of income):

(D.28) $\qquad \frac{1}{\phi} = \frac{\partial\lambda}{\partial m}\frac{m}{\lambda}$

It should be evident from the way in which (D.27) is derived from (D.24) that $[\pi_{ij}]$ is a symmetric negative semidefinite matrix with rank $N - 1$. Also, $\phi < 0$

because $\partial\lambda/\partial m$ in (D.28) is the reciprocal of a negative definite quadratic form [see (D.13)].

Block-Independence

Let the N goods consist of two groups of goods, S_1 and S_2, so that the utility function can be written as

(D.29) $$u(\mathbf{q}) = u_1(\mathbf{q}_1) + u_2(\mathbf{q}_2)$$

where $\mathbf{q}_1$ and $\mathbf{q}_2$ are the vectors of q_i's that fall under S_1 and S_2, respectively. The utility specification (D.29) is identical to (14.51) for $G = 2$ groups.

It follows from (D.29) that the second-order cross-derivative of $u(\ )$ with respect to q_i and q_j vanishes whenever i and j belong to different groups. Therefore,

(D.30) $$\mathbf{P}\mathbf{U}^{-1}\mathbf{P} = \begin{bmatrix} \mathbf{P}_1\mathbf{U}_1^{-1}\mathbf{P}_1 & \mathbf{0} \\ \mathbf{0} & \mathbf{P}_2\mathbf{U}_2^{-1}\mathbf{P}_2 \end{bmatrix}$$

where $\mathbf{U}_1$ and $\mathbf{U}_2$ are the Hessian matrices of $u_1(\ )$ and $u_2(\ )$ in (D.29) and $\mathbf{P}_1$ and $\mathbf{P}_2$ are submatrices of $\mathbf{P}$. A comparison of (D.27) and (D.30) shows that

(D.31) $$\pi_{ij} = -\phi\mu_i\mu_j \qquad \begin{array}{l} \text{if } i \in S_1 \text{ and } j \in S_2 \\ \text{or } i \in S_2 \text{ and } j \in S_1 \end{array}$$

so that if i belongs to S_1, the demand equation (14.40) can be written as

(D.32) $$\bar{w}_{it}Dq_{it} = \mu_i DQ_t + \sum_{j \in S_1} \pi_{ij}Dp_{jt} - \phi\mu_i \sum_{j \in S_2} \mu_j Dp_{jt} + \epsilon_{it}$$

Conditional Demand Equations Under Block-Independence

We sum (D.32) over $i \in S_1$. Using (14.54) for $g = 1$, we obtain

(D.33) $$\bar{W}_{1t}DQ_{1t} = M_1 DQ_t + \sum_{j \in S_1}\left(\sum_{i \in S_1}\pi_{ij}\right)Dp_{jt} - \phi M_1 \sum_{j \in S_2}\mu_j Dp_{jt} + E_{1t}$$

where M_1 and E_{1t} are the sums of μ_i and ϵ_{it}, respectively, over $i \in S_1$. In the next subsection we shall prove that

(D.34) $$\sum_{i \in S_1}\pi_{ij} = \phi M_2 \mu_j \qquad \text{if } j \in S_1$$

where M_2 is the sum of μ_k over $k \in S_2$. Thus, we can write (D.33), after multiplication by μ_i/M_1, as

$$\frac{\mu_i}{M_1}\bar{W}_{1t}DQ_{1t} = \mu_i DQ_t + \frac{\phi M_2 \mu_i}{M_1}\sum_{j \in S_1}\mu_j Dp_{jt} - \phi\mu_i \sum_{j \in S_2}\mu_j Dp_{jt} + \frac{\mu_i}{M_1}E_{1t}$$

which we subtract from (D.32):

$$\bar{w}_{it}Dq_{it} - \frac{\mu_i}{M_1}\bar{W}_{1t}DQ_{1t} = \sum_{j \in S_1}\left(\pi_{ij} - \frac{\phi M_2 \mu_i \mu_j}{M_1}\right)Dp_{jt} + \epsilon_{it} - \frac{\mu_i}{M_1}E_{1t}$$

Finally, we divide by $\bar{W}_{1t}$ to obtain

(D.35)
$$\frac{\bar{w}_{it}}{\bar{W}_{1t}} Dq_{it} = \frac{\mu_i}{M_1} DQ_{1t} + \sum_{j \in S_1} \pi_{ij}^* Dp_{jt} + \epsilon_{it}^*$$

where

(D.36)
$$\pi_{ij}^* = \frac{\pi_{ij}}{\bar{W}_{1t}} - \frac{\phi M_2 \mu_i \mu_j}{M_1 \bar{W}_{1t}} \qquad\qquad i, j \in S_1$$

(D.37)
$$\epsilon_{it}^* = \frac{\epsilon_{it}}{\bar{W}_{1t}} - \frac{\mu_i E_{1t}}{M_1 \bar{W}_{1t}} \qquad\qquad i \in S_1$$

The result (D.35) is the conditional demand equation (14.58) for $g = 1$. It is shown in the next subsection that the conditional Slutsky coefficients defined in (D.36) satisfy the properties (14.59) to (14.61).

Derivations for Conditional Demand Equations

Let ι_1 be the column vector which consists of as many unit elements as there are goods in S_1. The left-hand side of (D.34) is then the jth element of the row vector

(D.38)
$$[\iota_1' \quad 0][\pi_{ij}] = \frac{\lambda}{m}[\iota_1' \quad 0]PU^{-1}P - \phi M_1[\mu_1 \quad \cdots \quad \mu_N]$$

where the equal sign is based on (D.27). It follows from (D.30) that the first term on the right in (D.38) equals

(D.39)
$$\frac{\lambda}{m}[\iota_1'P_1U_1^{-1}P_1 \quad 0] = \frac{\lambda}{m}[p_1'U_1^{-1}P_1 \quad 0]$$

where p_1 is the column vector of the prices of the goods of S_1. The reader should verify, using (D.16) and (D.28), that the jth element of the right-hand side of (D.39) equals $\phi\mu_j$ if $j \in S_1$ and 0 if $j \in S_2$, after which he obtains (D.34) by taking the second right-hand term of (D.38) into account and using $1 - M_1 = M_2$. He should also note that (D.34) implies $\sum_i \sum_j \pi_{ij} = \phi M_1 M_2$ (sums over $i, j \in S_1$). This double sum must be negative because $[\pi_{ij}]$ is negative semi-definite with rank $N - 1$. Hence, given $\phi < 0$, M_1 and M_2 must be either both positive or both negative under (D.29). They cannot both be negative (because $M_1 + M_2 = 1$), and therefore both must be positive.

The symmetry property (14.59) of the conditional Slutsky coefficients follows directly from (D.36). Summation of (D.36) over $i \in S_1$ gives zero in view of (D.34); the result (14.60) then follows from (14.59). The negativity of the equal-subscript coefficients stated in (14.61) is implied by the fact that the conditional Slutsky matrix is negative semidefinite with a rank one less than its order (see Problem 4).

E   Rational Random Behavior
(Chapter 16)

The General Form of the Optimal Decision Distribution

We write $\mathbf{z} = [z_1 \quad \ldots \quad z_k]'$ for the vector of decision variables, so that (16.26) and (16.31) become

(E.1)
$$I = \int_R p(\mathbf{z}) \log_e \frac{p(\mathbf{z})}{p_0(\mathbf{z})} \, dz_1 \ldots dz_k$$

(E.2)
$$\bar{l} = \int_R l(\mathbf{z}, \bar{\mathbf{z}}) p(\mathbf{z}) \, dz_1 \ldots dz_k$$

where in both cases the integration is over the k-dimensional feasible region R of the decision vector $\mathbf{z}$.

It is shown in the next subsection that the decision distribution $p(\;)$ which minimizes $C(I) + \bar{l}$ takes the form $p(\mathbf{z}) = 0$ if $\mathbf{z} \notin R$ and

(E.3)
$$p(\mathbf{z}) \propto p_0(\mathbf{z}) \exp \left\{ -\frac{l(\mathbf{z}, \bar{\mathbf{z}})}{C'} \right\} \qquad \text{if } \mathbf{z} \in R$$

This is the extension of (16.33) for k decision variables.

Derivations

The calculus-of-variations approach implies that if a function

(E.4)
$$\int_R F_0(\mathbf{z}, p) \, dz_1 \ldots dz_k$$

is to be minimized for variations in $p(\;)$ subject to r constraints,

(E.5)
$$\int_R F_i(\mathbf{z}, p) \, dz_1 \ldots dz_k = c_i \qquad\qquad i = 1, \ldots, r$$

where the c_i's are constants, the solution $p(\;)$ is obtained from

(E.6)
$$\frac{\partial F_0}{\partial p} + \lambda_1 \frac{\partial F_1}{\partial p} + \cdots + \lambda_r \frac{\partial F_r}{\partial p} = 0$$

with the λ's interpreted as undetermined multipliers. Note the similarity to the Lagrangean approach of (D.2) to (D.4); the second-order condition is also similar (see the paragraph immediately following the next). Details on the technique of the calculus of variations can be found in Elsgolc (1962, pp. 139–147) and Gelfand and Fomin (1963, pp. 42–46 and Chapter 7).

In our case the function (E.4) takes the form $C(I) + \bar{l}$, where I and $\bar{l}$ are given in (E.1) and (E.2). Applying the chain rule to $C(I)$, we obtain

(E.7)
$$\frac{\partial F_0}{\partial p} = C'[1 + \log_e p(\mathbf{z}) - \log_e p_0(\mathbf{z})] + l(\mathbf{z}, \bar{\mathbf{z}})$$

The minimization of $C(I) + \bar{l}$ is subject to one constraint,

$$\int_R p(\mathbf{z})\, dz_1 \dots dz_k = 1$$

so that we have $r = 1$ and $F_1(\mathbf{z}, p) \equiv p$ in (E.5). On combining this with (E.7), we find that the left-hand side of (E.6) becomes

(E.8) $$C'[1 + \log_e p(\mathbf{z}) - \log_e p_0(\mathbf{z})] + l(\mathbf{z}, \bar{\mathbf{z}}) + \lambda_1$$

We obtain the solution (E.3) by equating this to zero and taking antilogs, noting that λ_1 is a constant with respect to $\mathbf{z}$.

To ensure that the solution corresponds to a minimum of $C(I) + \bar{l}$, we consider the derivative of the left-hand side of (E.6) with respect to p. Using (E.8), we obtain

(E.9) $$C''[1 + \log_e p(\mathbf{z}) - \log_e p_0(\mathbf{z})]^2 + \frac{C'}{p(\mathbf{z})} \qquad \mathbf{z} \in R$$

where $C'' = d^2C/dI^2$. For $C(I) + \bar{l}$ to be minimal it is sufficient that the derivative (E.9) is positive. This is the case when $C'' = d^2C/dI^2$ is nonnegative, as is assumed in (16.32).

The Asymptotics of the Multivariate Decision Distribution

When we extend (16.23) to the case in which z and $\bar{z}$ are vectors, the convergence in probability based on (16.38) can be proved straightforwardly for the multivariate case. To prove the asymptotic normality of the multivariate decision distribution, we assume that the loss function has a zero gradient at $\mathbf{z} = \bar{\mathbf{z}}$,

(E.10) $$\frac{\partial}{\partial \mathbf{z}} l(\mathbf{z}, \bar{\mathbf{z}}) = 0 \qquad \text{at } \mathbf{z} = \bar{\mathbf{z}}$$

and that its Hessian matrix is a symmetric positive definite matrix $\mathbf{A}$ at $\mathbf{z} = \bar{\mathbf{z}}$:

(E.11) $$\frac{\partial^2}{\partial \mathbf{z}\, \partial \mathbf{z}'} l(\mathbf{z}, \bar{\mathbf{z}}) = \mathbf{A} \qquad \text{at } \mathbf{z} = \bar{\mathbf{z}}$$

We also assume that all third-order derivatives of $l(\ )$ exist and are continuous functions of $\mathbf{z}$ for each $\mathbf{z} \in R$. These conditions are extensions of those made in Section 16.4.

We define the vector

(E.12) $$\mathbf{x} = \frac{1}{\sqrt{C'}} (\mathbf{z} - \bar{\mathbf{z}})$$

so that $l(\mathbf{z}, \bar{\mathbf{z}})$ equals $l(\bar{\mathbf{z}} + \sqrt{C'}\mathbf{x}, \bar{\mathbf{z}})$. We apply a Taylor expansion to $l(\mathbf{z}, \bar{\mathbf{z}})/C'$, using the conditions listed in the previous paragraph:

(E.13) $$\frac{l(\mathbf{z}, \bar{\mathbf{z}})}{C'} = \frac{1}{C'}\left[\frac{1}{2}(\sqrt{C'}\mathbf{x})'\mathbf{A}(\sqrt{C'}\mathbf{x}) + O(C'^{3/2})\right]$$

$$= \frac{1}{2}\mathbf{x}'\mathbf{A}\mathbf{x} + O(\sqrt{C'})$$

As in the discussion preceding (16.25), we assume that $p_0(\mathbf{z})$ is positive and differentiable around $\bar{\mathbf{z}}$. Using (E.12), we thus have

(E.14) $\log_e p_0(\mathbf{z}) = \log_e p_0(\bar{\mathbf{z}}) + O(\sqrt{C'})$

On combining this with (E.13) and the logarithm of (E.3), we find that $\log_e p(\mathbf{z})$ equals a constant minus $\frac{1}{2}\mathbf{x}'\mathbf{A}\mathbf{x}$ plus the sum of two remainder terms which both converge to zero as $C' \to 0$. Hence, in view of (E.12), $p(\mathbf{z})$ is asymptotically equivalent to

(E.15) $$\bar{p}(\mathbf{z}) \propto \exp\left\{-\frac{1}{2}(\mathbf{z} - \bar{\mathbf{z}})'\left(\frac{1}{C'}\mathbf{A}\right)(\mathbf{z} - \bar{\mathbf{z}})\right\}$$

which is the density function of the multivariate normal decision distribution with mean vector $\bar{\mathbf{z}}$ and covariance matrix $C'\mathbf{A}^{-1}$. Given C', this covariance matrix is determined by the Hessian matrix of the loss function given in (E.11).

Application to the Rotterdam Model

In consumer demand theory we can interpret the loss function as the excess of the maximum value of the utility function over the actual value attained when some quantity vector is selected. The subtraction of the latter value implies that the Hessian matrix $\mathbf{A}$ of the loss function becomes $-\mathbf{U}$, where $\mathbf{U}$ is the Hessian matrix of the utility function. In addition, we must take into consideration that the utility function is not maximized unconditionally but subject to the budget constraint. This can be handled by eliminating one of the N quantities. The result is that the covariances of the disturbances of the model (14.40) are proportional to the corresponding Slutsky coefficients,

(E.16) $\text{cov}(\epsilon_{it}, \epsilon_{jt}) = c\pi_{ij}$ $i, j = 1, \ldots, N$

where c is a negative proportionality coefficient. The derivation of this result is rather lengthy and not given here; we refer to Theil (1975–1976, Sections 2.6 and 2.7). However, some understanding of (E.16) can be obtained from a comparison with (D.27). The first term on the right in (D.27) contains $\mathbf{U}^{-1}$, in agreement with (E.15) and the discussion preceding (E.16). The second term in (D.27), containing marginal shares, results from the budget constraint.

The covariance model (16.46) can be derived from (E.16). The following result follows from (D.37) for $i, j \in S_1$:

(E.17) $\text{cov}(\epsilon_{it}^*, \epsilon_{jt}^*) = \frac{1}{\bar{W}_{1t}^2}\left[\text{cov}(\epsilon_{it}, \epsilon_{jt}) + \frac{\mu_i\mu_j}{M_1^2}\text{var}\,E_{1t}\right.$

$\left. - \frac{\mu_i}{M_1}\text{cov}(E_{1t}, \epsilon_{jt}) - \frac{\mu_j}{M_1}\text{cov}(E_{1t}, \epsilon_{it})\right]$

The disturbance E_{1t} of the demand equation for the group S_1 equals the sum of ϵ_{it} over $i \in S_1$. Thus, using (E.16) and (D.34), we have

$$\text{var}\,E_{1t} = \sum_{i \in S_1}\sum_{j \in S_1}\text{cov}(\epsilon_{it}, \epsilon_{jt}) = c\sum_{i \in S_1}\sum_{j \in S_1}\pi_{ij} = c\phi M_1 M_2$$
$$\text{cov}(E_{1t}, \epsilon_{jt}) = \sum_{i \in S_1}\text{cov}(\epsilon_{it}, \epsilon_{jt}) = c\sum_{i \in S_1}\pi_{ij} = c\phi M_2\mu_j$$

Substitution of these results in (E.17) yields (16.46), with π_{ij}^{*} as specified in (D.36) and k as $c/\bar{W}_{1t}$.

F   Aggregation
(Chapter 18)

The Micromodel and the Macrovariables

Let there be N economic agents, each having a behavioral equation of the form

(F.1) $$\mathbf{y}_c = \mathbf{X}_c\boldsymbol{\beta}_c + \boldsymbol{\epsilon}_c \qquad c = 1, \ldots, N$$

where $\mathbf{y}_c$ and $\boldsymbol{\epsilon}_c$ are n-element column vectors and $\mathbf{X}_c$ is a matrix of order $n \times K$, K being independent of c. We assume that, for each pair (c, d) of economic agents, any column of $[\mathbf{y}_c \quad \mathbf{X}_c]$ has the same interpretation as the corresponding column of $[\mathbf{y}_d \quad \mathbf{X}_d]$ except that it refers to a different agent. The parameter vectors $\boldsymbol{\beta}_1, \ldots, \boldsymbol{\beta}_N$ can then be arranged in a $K \times N$ matrix,

(F.2) $$[\boldsymbol{\beta}_1 \quad \boldsymbol{\beta}_2 \quad \ldots \quad \boldsymbol{\beta}_N] = \begin{bmatrix} \beta_{11} & \beta_{12} & \cdots & \beta_{1N} \\ \beta_{21} & \beta_{22} & \cdots & \beta_{2N} \\ \cdot & \cdot & & \cdot \\ \cdot & \cdot & & \cdot \\ \cdot & \cdot & & \cdot \\ \beta_{K1} & \beta_{K2} & \cdots & \beta_{KN} \end{bmatrix}$$

Each row of this matrix consists of corresponding parameters belonging to N different economic agents.

Macrovariables are defined as averages of corresponding microvariables. The observations on the macrovariables are elements of $[\bar{\mathbf{y}} \quad \bar{\mathbf{X}}]$, where

(F.3) $$\bar{\mathbf{y}} = \frac{1}{N} \sum_{c=1}^{N} \mathbf{y}_c, \qquad \bar{\mathbf{X}} = \frac{1}{N} \sum_{c=1}^{N} \mathbf{X}_c$$

Substitution of (F.1) in the equation of $\bar{\mathbf{y}}$ gives

(F.4) $$\bar{\mathbf{y}} = \frac{1}{N} \sum_{c=1}^{N} \mathbf{X}_c\boldsymbol{\beta}_c + \frac{1}{N} \sum_{c=1}^{N} \boldsymbol{\epsilon}_c$$

$$= \begin{bmatrix} \frac{1}{N}\mathbf{X}_1 & \cdots & \frac{1}{N}\mathbf{X}_N \end{bmatrix} \begin{bmatrix} \boldsymbol{\beta}_1 \\ \cdot \\ \cdot \\ \cdot \\ \boldsymbol{\beta}_N \end{bmatrix} + \frac{1}{N} \sum_{c=1}^{N} \boldsymbol{\epsilon}_c$$

This result expresses the dependent macrovariable in terms of all explanatory microvariables. If all columns of the matrix (F.2) are equal (to $\boldsymbol{\beta}$, say), (F.4) becomes $\bar{\mathbf{y}} = \bar{\mathbf{X}}\boldsymbol{\beta} + (1/N) \sum_c \boldsymbol{\epsilon}_c$. Here we are interested in the more general case in which the $\boldsymbol{\beta}_c$'s are not necessarily equal.

The Specification Approach to the Aggregation Problem

We assume that the analyst runs a regression of $\bar{\mathbf{y}}$ on $\bar{\mathbf{X}}$, so that he obtains the LS coefficient vector

(F.5) $$\mathbf{b} = (\bar{\mathbf{X}}'\bar{\mathbf{X}})^{-1}\bar{\mathbf{X}}'\bar{\mathbf{y}}$$

To analyze the relationship between this vector and the $\boldsymbol{\beta}_c$'s we substitute the second line of (F.4) for $\bar{\mathbf{y}}$ and then take the expectation under the assumption that $\boldsymbol{\epsilon}_c$ has zero expectation and $\mathbf{X}_c$ is nonstochastic for each c:

(F.6) $$\mathcal{E}\mathbf{b} = (\bar{\mathbf{X}}'\bar{\mathbf{X}})^{-1}\bar{\mathbf{X}}'\left[\frac{1}{N}\mathbf{X}_1 \cdots \frac{1}{N}\mathbf{X}_N\right]\begin{bmatrix}\boldsymbol{\beta}_1 \\ \vdots \\ \vdots \\ \boldsymbol{\beta}_N\end{bmatrix} = \sum_{c=1}^{N}\mathbf{B}_c\boldsymbol{\beta}_c$$

Here $\mathbf{B}_c$ is defined as

(F.7) $$\mathbf{B}_c = (\bar{\mathbf{X}}'\bar{\mathbf{X}})^{-1}\bar{\mathbf{X}}'\left(\frac{1}{N}\mathbf{X}_c\right) \qquad\qquad c = 1, \ldots, N$$

which is thus the coefficient matrix of the auxiliary regressions whose left-hand variables are $1/N$ times the explanatory variables of the micromodel (F.1) and whose right-hand variables are those represented in the matrix $\bar{\mathbf{X}}$. These auxiliary regressions can therefore be written as

(F.8) $$\frac{1}{N}\mathbf{X}_c = \bar{\mathbf{X}}\mathbf{B}_c + \mathbf{U}_c \qquad\qquad c = 1, \ldots, N$$

where $\mathbf{U}_c$ is the associated residual matrix:

(F.9) $$\mathbf{U}_c = [\mathbf{I} - \bar{\mathbf{X}}(\bar{\mathbf{X}}'\bar{\mathbf{X}})^{-1}\bar{\mathbf{X}}']\frac{1}{N}\mathbf{X}_c \qquad\qquad c = 1, \ldots, N$$

The matrices (F.7) and (F.9) satisfy

(F.10) $$\sum_{c=1}^{N}\mathbf{B}_c = \mathbf{I}, \qquad \sum_{c=1}^{N}\mathbf{U}_c = \mathbf{0}$$

which is verified as follows:

$$(\bar{\mathbf{X}}'\bar{\mathbf{X}})^{-1}\bar{\mathbf{X}}'\left(\frac{1}{N}\sum_{c=1}^{N}\mathbf{X}_c\right) = (\bar{\mathbf{X}}'\bar{\mathbf{X}})^{-1}\bar{\mathbf{X}}'\bar{\mathbf{X}} = \mathbf{I}$$

$$[\mathbf{I} - \bar{\mathbf{X}}(\bar{\mathbf{X}}'\bar{\mathbf{X}})^{-1}\bar{\mathbf{X}}']\frac{1}{N}\sum_{c=1}^{N}\mathbf{X}_c = [\mathbf{I} - \bar{\mathbf{X}}(\bar{\mathbf{X}}'\bar{\mathbf{X}})^{-1}\bar{\mathbf{X}}']\bar{\mathbf{X}} = \mathbf{0}$$

The result (F.10) proves (18.16). The right-hand sides of (18.18) and (18.19) are the two elements of the vector

(F.11) $$\sum_{c=1}^{N}\begin{bmatrix}p_{1c} & q_{1c} \\ p_{2c} & q_{2c}\end{bmatrix}\begin{bmatrix}\beta_{1c} \\ \beta_{2c}\end{bmatrix}$$

which agrees with (F.6) except that (F.11) does not contain the constant terms

β_{0c} of the micromodel (18.11). But this is correct, because it can be shown (see Problem 6) that the expectations of the multiplicative LS macrocoefficients are independent of the constant terms of the micromodel.

G   Generalized Least Squares
(Chapter 19)

The discussion starts with generalized least squares (GLS) and Aitken's theorem, followed by constrained GLS and its application to the Rotterdam Model. In the last two subsections we shall be concerned with mixed estimation and two standard errors of Section 19.4.

GLS and Aitken's Theorem

We return to eqs. (B.1) to (B.3) and generalize (B.3) to

$$(G.1) \qquad\qquad \mathcal{E}(\epsilon\epsilon') = \sigma^2 V$$

where V is a symmetric positive definite $n \times n$ matrix. Hence, V^{-1} is also symmetric positive definite, so that a nonsingular $n \times n$ matrix P exists which satisfies $P'P = V^{-1}$. We premultiply (B.1) by P:

$$(G.2) \qquad\qquad Py = PX\beta + P\epsilon$$

The disturbance vector $P\epsilon$ has zero expectation, and its covariance matrix is

$$\mathcal{V}(P\epsilon) = P\mathcal{E}(\epsilon\epsilon')P' = \sigma^2 PVP' = \sigma^2 P(P'P)^{-1}P' = \sigma^2 PP^{-1}(P')^{-1}P' = \sigma^2 I$$

where the third step is based on $P'P = V^{-1}$ and the fourth on the nonsingularity of P.

We conclude that the disturbance vector $P\epsilon$ satisfies the assumptions of the standard linear model. Hence, the Gauss-Markov theorem implies that LS applied to (G.2) yields a best linear unbiased estimator:

$$\hat{\beta} = [(PX)'PX]^{-1}(PX)'Py = (X'P'PX)^{-1}X'P'Py$$

It follows from $P'P = V^{-1}$ that this can be simplified to

$$(G.3) \qquad\qquad \hat{\beta} = (X'V^{-1}X)^{-1}X'V^{-1}y$$

which is the GLS estimator of β. Its covariance matrix is

$$(G.4) \qquad\qquad \mathcal{V}(\hat{\beta}) = \sigma^2(X'V^{-1}X)^{-1}$$

Aitken's theorem, which is a generalization of the Gauss-Markov theorem, states that the GLS estimator (G.3) is a best linear unbiased estimator of β under (G.1) in the same way that the LS estimator b is best linear unbiased under (B.3).

In the case discussed below (19.1), V can be viewed as a diagonal matrix whose diagonal elements are the squares of $\sigma_1, \ldots, \sigma_n$, so that P can be specified as a diagonal matrix with $1/\sigma_1, \ldots, 1/\sigma_n$ as diagonal elements. The estimator (G.3) is then equivalent to LS applied to (19.2). The autoregressive process

(19.10) implies that $\mathbf{V}^{-1}$ takes the form of a band matrix, with nonzero elements in the diagonal and immediately above and below the diagonal and zero elements elsewhere; see Theil (1971, pp. 252–253).

Constrained GLS

Let $\boldsymbol{\beta}$ be subject to q linear constraints,

$$(G.5) \qquad\qquad \mathbf{R}\boldsymbol{\beta} = \mathbf{r}$$

where $\mathbf{r}$ is a known q-element vector and $\mathbf{R}$ is a known $q \times K$ matrix with rank q. The constrained GLS estimator of $\boldsymbol{\beta}$ is obtained by minimizing, subject to the constraint (G.5), a quadratic form in the residuals with $\mathbf{V}^{-1}$ as matrix (see Problem 8). The result is

$$(G.6) \qquad \hat{\boldsymbol{\beta}}^* = \hat{\boldsymbol{\beta}} + (\mathbf{X}'\mathbf{V}^{-1}\mathbf{X})^{-1}\mathbf{R}'[\mathbf{R}(\mathbf{X}'\mathbf{V}^{-1}\mathbf{X})^{-1}\mathbf{R}']^{-1}(\mathbf{r} - \mathbf{R}\hat{\boldsymbol{\beta}})$$

which satisfies the constraint: $\mathbf{R}\hat{\boldsymbol{\beta}}^* = \mathbf{r}$. If we want to test the hypothesis that (G.5) is true, we can use the following test statistic:

$$(G.7) \qquad \frac{n-K}{q} \times \frac{(\mathbf{r} - \mathbf{R}\hat{\boldsymbol{\beta}})'[\mathbf{R}(\mathbf{X}'\mathbf{V}^{-1}\mathbf{X})^{-1}\mathbf{R}']^{-1}(\mathbf{r} - \mathbf{R}\hat{\boldsymbol{\beta}})}{(\mathbf{y} - \mathbf{X}\hat{\boldsymbol{\beta}})'\mathbf{V}^{-1}(\mathbf{y} - \mathbf{X}\hat{\boldsymbol{\beta}})}$$

If $\boldsymbol{\epsilon}$ is normally distributed, the test statistic (G.7) is distributed as $F(q, n - K)$ under the null hypothesis (G.5).

For example, consider the Rotterdam Model (14.45) for $N = 4$:

$$(G.8) \qquad \bar{w}_{it}Dq_{it} = \mu_i DQ_t + \sum_{j=1}^{3} \pi_{ij}(Dp_{jt} - Dp_{4t}) + \epsilon_{it}$$

Since it can be shown that the fourth equation ($i = 4$) is equivalent to the sum of the first three, we may confine our attention to (G.8) for $i = 1, 2$, and 3, so that Slutsky symmetry amounts to three equations:

$$(G.9) \qquad \pi_{12} = \pi_{21}, \qquad \pi_{13} = \pi_{31}, \qquad \pi_{23} = \pi_{32}$$

We write the parameters of (G.8) for $i = 1, 2$, and 3 in the following vector form:

$$(G.10) \quad \boldsymbol{\beta} = [\mu_1 \ \ \pi_{11} \ \ \pi_{12} \ \ \pi_{13} \ \ \mu_2 \ \ \pi_{21} \ \ \pi_{22} \ \ \pi_{23} \ \ \mu_3 \ \ \pi_{31} \ \ \pi_{32} \ \ \pi_{33}]'$$

We can then write the constraints (G.9) in the form (G.5) when we specify $\mathbf{r} = \mathbf{0}$ and

$$(G.11) \quad \mathbf{R} = \begin{bmatrix} 0 & 0 & 1 & 0 & 0 & -1 & 0 & 0 & 0 & 0 & 0 & 0 \\ 0 & 0 & 0 & 1 & 0 & 0 & 0 & 0 & 0 & -1 & 0 & 0 \\ 0 & 0 & 0 & 0 & 0 & 0 & 0 & 1 & 0 & 0 & -1 & 0 \end{bmatrix}$$

For further details on the estimator (G.6), its asymptotic covariance matrix, and the statistic (G.7), see Theil (1975–1976, Section 5.3).

Mixed Estimation

We assume that the analyst has unbiased prior estimates of q linear combinations of the parameter vector $\boldsymbol{\beta}$. We write this as

(G.12) $$\mathbf{r} = \mathbf{R}\boldsymbol{\beta} + \mathbf{v}$$

where $\mathbf{R}$ is a known $q \times K$ matrix of rank q and $\mathbf{v}$ is the error component of the prior estimate $\mathbf{r}$. Note that (G.12) is similar to (G.5) but that $\mathbf{r}$ is now subject to error.

The vector $\mathbf{v}$ has zero mean and covariance matrix $\mathbf{V}_0$. We combine this with (B.1), (B.2), and (G.1) in the form

(G.13) $$\begin{bmatrix} \mathbf{y} \\ \mathbf{r} \end{bmatrix} = \begin{bmatrix} \mathbf{X} \\ \mathbf{R} \end{bmatrix} \boldsymbol{\beta} + \begin{bmatrix} \boldsymbol{\epsilon} \\ \mathbf{v} \end{bmatrix}, \qquad \mathcal{E}\begin{bmatrix} \boldsymbol{\epsilon} \\ \mathbf{v} \end{bmatrix} = \mathbf{0}, \qquad \mathcal{V}\begin{bmatrix} \boldsymbol{\epsilon} \\ \mathbf{v} \end{bmatrix} = \begin{bmatrix} \sigma^2 \mathbf{V} & \mathbf{0} \\ \mathbf{0} & \mathbf{V}_0 \end{bmatrix}$$

Application of (G.3) and (G.4) yields the mixed estimator,

(G.14) $$\left(\frac{1}{\sigma^2} \mathbf{X}' \mathbf{V}^{-1} \mathbf{X} + \mathbf{R}' \mathbf{V}_0^{-1} \mathbf{R} \right)^{-1} \left(\frac{1}{\sigma^2} \mathbf{X}' \mathbf{V}^{-1} \mathbf{y} + \mathbf{R}' \mathbf{V}_0^{-1} \mathbf{r} \right)$$

and the following covariance matrix of this estimator:

(G.15) $$\left(\frac{1}{\sigma^2} \mathbf{X}' \mathbf{V}^{-1} \mathbf{X} + \mathbf{R}' \mathbf{V}_0^{-1} \mathbf{R} \right)^{-1}$$

The parameter vector of (19.1) is $\boldsymbol{\beta} = [\beta_0 \quad \beta_1 \quad \beta_2]'$. Thus, when (19.1) is interpreted as the demand equation for textile, with β_1 and β_2 the income and price elasticities, the prior estimates 1 (of β_1) and $-.7$ (of β_2) and their standard deviations (both .15) and covariance ($-.01$) are all contained in

(G.16) $$\mathbf{r} = \begin{bmatrix} 1 \\ -.7 \end{bmatrix}, \qquad \mathbf{R} = \begin{bmatrix} 0 & 1 & 0 \\ 0 & 0 & 1 \end{bmatrix}, \qquad \mathbf{V}_0 = \begin{bmatrix} .0225 & -.01 \\ -.01 & .0225 \end{bmatrix}$$

Application of (G.14) and (G.15) requires knowledge of σ^2. Since $\mathbf{V}$ for the demand equation for textile is $\mathbf{I}$, we approximate σ^2 by the unbiased estimate s^2 given in (8.39), which yields (19.35). The standard errors shown in (19.35) are the square roots of the diagonal elements of

(G.17) $$\left(\frac{1}{s^2} \mathbf{X}' \mathbf{X} + \mathbf{R}' \mathbf{V}_0^{-1} \mathbf{R} \right)^{-1} = \begin{bmatrix} .04139 & -.01997 & -.00064 \\ -.01997 & .01069 & -.00082 \\ -.00064 & -.00082 & .00122 \end{bmatrix}$$

This matrix should be compared with the estimated covariance matrix (B.20) of the LS estimates that are based on the sample only. The sampling correlation coefficient of b_0 and b_1 in (B.20) is quite high, and the reduction of the standard error which the mixed estimation method achieves for the constant term estimate is primarily due to the prior information on the income elasticity.

Two Standard Errors

The data shown in Table 25 on page 310 refer to a regression with constant term. We introduce a constant-term variable x_0, so that the table takes the following form:

	y_i	x_{0i}	x_{1i}	x_{2i}
$i = 1$	30	1	15	12
.	.	.	.	.
.	.	.	.	.
.	.	.	.	.
$i = 13$	20	1	15	12
Extraneous	$p_1\sigma/\sigma_1$	0	σ/σ_1	0

The two zeros in the last row indicate that (19.24) contains neither the constant term nor the parameter β_2.

We write **X** for the 14×3 observation matrix of the explanatory variables (including the extraneous observation and the constant-term variable). Using (19.25), we find that

$$
(G.18) \qquad \mathbf{X'X} = \begin{bmatrix} 13 & 0 & 0 \\ 0 & 1364 + \sigma^2/\sigma_1^2 & 1048 \\ 0 & 1048 & 808 \end{bmatrix}
$$

which has the following determinant value:

$$
(G.19) \qquad |\mathbf{X'X}| = 13\left[808\left(1364 + \frac{\sigma^2}{\sigma_1^2}\right) - 1048^2 \right]
$$

The variance of $\hat{\beta}_1$ is equal to the cofactor of the second diagonal element of $\mathbf{X'X}$ multiplied by $\sigma^2/|\mathbf{X'X}|$. Hence, the reciprocal of this variance is

$$
\frac{13\{808[1364 + (\sigma^2/\sigma_1^2)] - 1048^2\}}{13 \times 808\sigma^2} \approx \frac{4.713}{\sigma^2} + \frac{1}{\sigma_1^2}
$$

which becomes 25.2 for $\sigma_1 = .2$ and σ approximated by $\sqrt{25.49}$ [see (19.29)]. The implied standard error of $\hat{\beta}_1$ is $1/\sqrt{25.2} \approx .20$. The reciprocal of the variance of $\hat{\beta}_2$ is similarly equal to the ratio of (G.19) to $13\sigma^2(1364 + \sigma^2/\sigma_1^2)$. This yields a standard error of $\hat{\beta}_2$ equal to .31 under the same numerical specification of σ and σ_1.

H   Two-Stage Least Squares
(Chapters 20 and 21)

Notation

We consider a complete linear L-equation system and write the jth structural equation ($j = 1, \ldots, L$) for all n observations in matrix form as

$$
(H.1) \qquad \mathbf{y}_j = \mathbf{Y}_j\boldsymbol{\gamma}_j + \mathbf{X}_j\boldsymbol{\beta}_j + \boldsymbol{\epsilon}_j
$$

where y_j is the n-element column vector of values taken by the left-hand variable, $[Y_j \quad X_j]$ is the matrix of values taken by the explanatory variables, γ_j and β_j are parameter vectors to be estimated, and ϵ_j is the n-element column vector of disturbances.

The $n \times L_j$ matrix Y_j in (H.1) contains the values of the explanatory variables in the jth equation which are jointly dependent in the equation system. Accordingly, the associated parameter vector γ_j consists of L_j elements. The $n \times K_j$ matrix X_j contains values of predetermined variables, and β_j consists of K_j elements. The matrix X_j is a submatrix of the $n \times K_S$ matrix X_S, which consists of the values of all K_S predetermined variables in the equation system. A necessary condition for the identification of the jth structural equation is $K_S \geq K_j + L_j$.

In what follows we shall confine ourselves to one equation of the system, so that no confusion arises when we drop the subscript j. Thus, we write (H.1) in the form

(H.2) $$y = Y\gamma + X\beta + \epsilon$$

which contains $K + L$ parameters.

The Two Steps of 2SLS

We know from (A.18) that the residual vector in the LS regression of z on X_S equals $(I - X_S X_S^+)z$. For two regressands, z_1 and z_2, the residuals in the LS regressions on X_S can thus be written as

$$[(I - X_S X_S^+)z_1 \quad (I - X_S X_S^+)z_2] = (I - X_S X_S^+)[z_1 \quad z_2]$$

Therefore, the LS residuals in the regressions of the L columns of Y on X_S can be written in the form of an $n \times L$ matrix,

(H.3) $$V = (I - X_S X_S^+)Y$$

and the orthogonality result (A.19) implies

(H.4) $$X_S' V = 0$$

The first step of 2SLS consists of writing (H.2) in the form

(H.5) $$y = (Y - V)\gamma + X\beta + \epsilon + V\gamma$$
$$= [Y - V \quad X]\begin{bmatrix} \gamma \\ \beta \end{bmatrix} + \epsilon + V\gamma$$

which includes (21.20) as a special case for $L = 1$, X_t being the only dependent variable in the right-hand side of (21.10). The second step consists of LS applied to (H.5), with $[Y - V \quad X]$ used as the matrix of values of the regressors. This yields 2SLS normal equations of the form

(H.6) $$\begin{bmatrix} (Y - V)'y \\ X'y \end{bmatrix} = \begin{bmatrix} (Y - V)'(Y - V) & (Y - V)'X \\ X'(Y - V) & X'X \end{bmatrix}\begin{bmatrix} c \\ b \end{bmatrix}$$

where $\mathbf{c}$, $\mathbf{b}$ is the 2SLS estimator of $\boldsymbol{\gamma}$, $\boldsymbol{\beta}$. It is shown in Problem 9 that (H.6) can be simplified to

(H.7)
$$\begin{bmatrix} (\mathbf{Y} - \mathbf{V})'\mathbf{y} \\ \mathbf{X}'\mathbf{y} \end{bmatrix} = \begin{bmatrix} \mathbf{Y}'\mathbf{Y} - \mathbf{V}'\mathbf{V} & \mathbf{Y}'\mathbf{X} \\ \mathbf{X}'\mathbf{Y} & \mathbf{X}'\mathbf{X} \end{bmatrix} \begin{bmatrix} \mathbf{c} \\ \mathbf{b} \end{bmatrix}$$

and in Problem 10 that the expressions involving $\mathbf{V}$ can be computed from the mean squares and products of the observed variables.

The estimated asymptotic covariance matrix of $\mathbf{c}$, $\mathbf{b}$ is

(H.8)
$$\hat{\sigma}^2 \begin{bmatrix} \mathbf{Y}'\mathbf{Y} - \mathbf{V}'\mathbf{V} & \mathbf{Y}'\mathbf{X} \\ \mathbf{X}'\mathbf{Y} & \mathbf{X}'\mathbf{X} \end{bmatrix}^{-1}$$

where $\hat{\sigma}^2$ is the mean square of the 2SLS residuals of (H.2). This $\hat{\sigma}^2$ is an estimator of the variance σ^2 of the elements of $\boldsymbol{\epsilon}$. The asymptotic standard errors shown in parentheses in (21.21) to (21.23) are computed as the square roots of the diagonal elements of the matrix (H.8). See Theil (1971, Section 10.3) for the properties of this matrix and the underlying conditions.

Alternative Derivation of 2SLS

We define

(H.9)
$$\mathbf{Z} = [\mathbf{Y} \quad \mathbf{X}], \qquad \boldsymbol{\delta} = \begin{bmatrix} \boldsymbol{\gamma} \\ \boldsymbol{\beta} \end{bmatrix}$$

so that (H.2) can be simplified to

(H.10)
$$\mathbf{y} = \mathbf{Z}\boldsymbol{\delta} + \boldsymbol{\epsilon}$$

where $\boldsymbol{\delta}$ is a column vector of $K + L = N$ parameters. Next we premultiply (H.10) by the transpose of $\mathbf{X}_S$:

(H.11)
$$\mathbf{X}_S'\mathbf{y} = \mathbf{X}_S'\mathbf{Z}\boldsymbol{\delta} + \mathbf{X}_S'\boldsymbol{\epsilon}$$

This is a vector equation which consists of K_S scalar equations and contains N unknown parameters. If the equation is just-identified, $K_S = N$, we can use the K_S predetermined variables as instrumental variables by replacing $\mathbf{X}_S'\boldsymbol{\epsilon}$ by zero in (H.11), which yields $(\mathbf{X}_S'\mathbf{Z})^{-1}\mathbf{X}_S'\mathbf{y}$ as the instrumental-variable estimator of $\boldsymbol{\delta}$.

If the equation is overidentified, (H.11) consists of more scalar equations than there are parameters to be estimated ($K_S > N$). Let us assume that all predetermined variables are exogenous, so that $\mathbf{X}_S$ can be viewed as a matrix with non-stochastic elements. Then, if $\boldsymbol{\epsilon}$ has zero mean vector and covariance matrix $\sigma^2\mathbf{I}$, the disturbance vector of (H.11) has zero mean and a covariance matrix equal to

(H.12)
$$\mathcal{E}(\mathbf{X}_S'\boldsymbol{\epsilon}\boldsymbol{\epsilon}'\mathbf{X}_S) = \mathbf{X}_S'\mathcal{E}(\boldsymbol{\epsilon}\boldsymbol{\epsilon}')\mathbf{X}_S = \sigma^2\mathbf{X}_S'\mathbf{X}_S$$

We apply GLS to (H.11), using the covariance matrix (H.12), which yields the following estimator of $\boldsymbol{\delta}$:

(H.13)
$$\mathbf{d} = [\mathbf{Z}'\mathbf{X}_S(\mathbf{X}_S'\mathbf{X}_S)^{-1}\mathbf{X}_S'\mathbf{Z}]^{-1}\mathbf{Z}'\mathbf{X}_S(\mathbf{X}_S'\mathbf{X}_S)^{-1}\mathbf{X}_S'\mathbf{y}$$
$$= (\mathbf{Z}'\mathbf{X}_S\mathbf{X}_S^{+}\mathbf{Z})^{-1}\mathbf{Z}'\mathbf{X}_S\mathbf{X}_S^{+}\mathbf{y}$$

It can be shown (see Problem 11) that this estimator is identical to the 2SLS estimator $\mathbf{c}, \mathbf{b}$ obtained from (H.7) and that it reduces to the simple expression $(\mathbf{X}_s'\mathbf{Z})^{-1}\mathbf{X}_s'\mathbf{y}$ when $\mathbf{X}_s'\mathbf{Z}$ is square and nonsingular (see the end of the previous paragraph).

Problems

Problems 1 and 2 refer to Appendix A, 3 to Appendix B, 4 to Appendix D, 5 to Appendix E, 6 to Appendix F, 7 and 8 to Appendix G, and 9–11 to Appendix H.

1 For LS with constant term, partition $\mathbf{X} = [\mathbf{\iota} \quad \mathbf{Z}]$, where $\mathbf{\iota}$ is a column vector consisting of n unit elements, and prove

$$\mathbf{X}'\mathbf{y} = \begin{bmatrix} \mathbf{\iota}'\mathbf{y} \\ \mathbf{Z}'\mathbf{y} \end{bmatrix}, \qquad \mathbf{X}'\mathbf{X} = \begin{bmatrix} n & \mathbf{\iota}'\mathbf{Z} \\ \mathbf{Z}'\mathbf{\iota} & \mathbf{Z}'\mathbf{Z} \end{bmatrix}$$

$$(\mathbf{X}'\mathbf{X})^{-1} = \begin{bmatrix} \dfrac{1}{n} + \dfrac{1}{n^2}\mathbf{\iota}'\mathbf{Z}(\mathbf{Z}'\mathbf{AZ})^{-1}\mathbf{Z}'\mathbf{\iota} & -\dfrac{1}{n}\mathbf{\iota}'\mathbf{Z}(\mathbf{Z}'\mathbf{AZ})^{-1} \\ -\dfrac{1}{n}(\mathbf{Z}'\mathbf{AZ})^{-1}\mathbf{Z}'\mathbf{\iota} & (\mathbf{Z}'\mathbf{AZ})^{-1} \end{bmatrix}$$

where $\mathbf{A} = \mathbf{I} - (1/n)\mathbf{\iota}\mathbf{\iota}'$. Next use (A.10) to obtain

$$\mathbf{b} = \begin{bmatrix} \dfrac{1}{n}\mathbf{\iota}'\mathbf{y} - \dfrac{1}{n}\mathbf{\iota}'\mathbf{Z}(\mathbf{Z}'\mathbf{AZ})^{-1}\mathbf{Z}'\mathbf{Ay} \\ (\mathbf{Z}'\mathbf{AZ})^{-1}\mathbf{Z}'\mathbf{Ay} \end{bmatrix}$$

Prove finally that $(\mathbf{Z}'\mathbf{AZ})^{-1}\mathbf{Z}'\mathbf{Ay}$ equals the solution obtained from normal equations of the form (7.38) and that the top element of $\mathbf{b}$ equals b_0 defined in (7.36). [*Hint*: See Theil (1971, pp. 38–40).]

2 Use eqs. (A.13) through (A.16) to verify that if $\mathbf{A}$ is square and nonsingular, $\mathbf{A}^+ = \mathbf{A}^{-1}$. Also prove that if $\mathbf{A}$ is the $m \times n$ zero matrix, $\mathbf{A}^+$ is the $n \times m$ zero matrix.

3 Consider the LS point estimates in the first four lines of Table 16 on page 213. Verify that, for both the Dutch and the British data, the standard errors of corresponding point estimates in the first two demand equations are proportional apart from rounding errors:

$$\tfrac{33}{13} \approx \tfrac{25}{10} \approx \tfrac{49}{19} \approx \tfrac{23}{9} \approx \tfrac{45}{18}, \qquad \tfrac{46}{23} \approx \tfrac{32}{16} \approx \cdots \approx \tfrac{72}{36}$$

Extend this to the other demand equations, and use (B.6) and (14.45) to prove that this result must necessarily hold. Repeat this for Table 18 on page 223.

4 Use (16.46) with $k < 0$ to prove that the matrix of conditional Slutsky coefficients must be negative semidefinite. [*Note*: The singularity of this matrix follows from (14.60); its rank is one less than its order.]

5 Let the loss function satisfy $l(\mathbf{z}, \bar{\mathbf{z}}) = 0$ if $\mathbf{z} = \bar{\mathbf{z}}$, $l(\mathbf{z}, \bar{\mathbf{z}}) > 0$ if $\mathbf{z} \neq \bar{\mathbf{z}}$. Prove that if $p_0(\mathbf{z})$ equals a constant independent of $\mathbf{z}$ for each $\mathbf{z} \in R$, the density function (E.3) of the optimal decision distribution has a mode at $\mathbf{z} = \bar{\mathbf{z}}$. Also prove that if this distribution has several modes, the mode at $\bar{\mathbf{z}}$ is the highest.

6 Suppose that the micromodel (F.1) contains constant terms, represented by a first column of $\mathbf{X}_c$ consisting of unit elements ($c = 1, \ldots, N$). Verify that the first column of $\mathbf{B}_c$ in (F.8) then consists of zero elements except for the top element. Use this result and (F.6) to prove that the expectations of the multiplicative LS macrocoefficients are independent of the constant terms of the micromodel.

7 Prove that minimizing $(\mathbf{y} - \mathbf{X}\boldsymbol{\beta})'\mathbf{V}^{-1}(\mathbf{y} - \mathbf{X}\boldsymbol{\beta})$ with respect to $\boldsymbol{\beta}$ yields the solution $\boldsymbol{\beta} = \hat{\boldsymbol{\beta}}$ as specified in (G.3).

8 (*Continuation*) Prove that minimizing the same expression with respect to $\boldsymbol{\beta}$ subject to the constraint (G.5) yields $\boldsymbol{\beta} = \hat{\boldsymbol{\beta}}^*$ as specified in (G.6).

9 Use (H.4) and the fact that $\mathbf{X}$ is a submatrix of $\mathbf{X}_S$ to prove that $\mathbf{X}'\mathbf{V} = \mathbf{0}$. Next verify that $\mathbf{Y} - \mathbf{V}$ equals $\mathbf{X}_S\mathbf{P}$, where $\mathbf{P} = \mathbf{X}_S^+\mathbf{Y}$, and use this to prove that

$$(\mathbf{Y} - \mathbf{V})'(\mathbf{Y} - \mathbf{V}) = \mathbf{Y}'\mathbf{X}_S\mathbf{P} = \mathbf{Y}'\mathbf{Y} - \mathbf{Y}'\mathbf{V}$$

Prove finally that $\mathbf{Y}'\mathbf{V} = \mathbf{V}'\mathbf{V}$, and verify that this completes the proof of the equivalence of (H.6) and (H.7).

10 (*Continuation*) Verify that

$$\mathbf{Y}'\mathbf{Y} - \mathbf{V}'\mathbf{V} = \mathbf{Y}'\mathbf{X}_S(\mathbf{X}_S'\mathbf{X}_S)^{-1}\mathbf{X}_S'\mathbf{Y}$$
$$(\mathbf{Y} - \mathbf{V})'\mathbf{y} = \mathbf{Y}'\mathbf{X}_S(\mathbf{X}_S'\mathbf{X}_S)^{-1}\mathbf{X}_S'\mathbf{y}$$

and combine this with (H.7) to conclude that the computation of the 2SLS estimates requires only the matrices $\mathbf{X}_S'\mathbf{X}_S$, $\mathbf{X}_S'\mathbf{Y}$, and $\mathbf{X}_S'\mathbf{y}$.

11 (*Continuation*) With $\mathbf{Z}$ defined in (H.9), prove that

$$\mathbf{Z}'\mathbf{X}_S(\mathbf{X}_S'\mathbf{X}_S)^{-1}\mathbf{X}_S' = \begin{bmatrix} \mathbf{P}'\mathbf{X}_S' \\ \mathbf{X}'\mathbf{X}_S(\mathbf{X}_S'\mathbf{X}_S)^{-1}\mathbf{X}_S' \end{bmatrix} = \begin{bmatrix} \mathbf{Y}' - \mathbf{V}' \\ \mathbf{X}' \end{bmatrix}$$

[*Hint*: $\mathbf{X}'\mathbf{X}_S(\mathbf{X}_S'\mathbf{X}_S)^{-1}$ is a submatrix of $\mathbf{X}_S'\mathbf{X}_S(\mathbf{X}_S'\mathbf{X}_S)^{-1} = \mathbf{I}$.] Then post-multiply the above equation by $\mathbf{y}$ and $\mathbf{Y}$ to prove that $\mathbf{d}$ defined in (H.13) is identical to $\mathbf{c}$, $\mathbf{b}$ obtained from (H.7). Also prove that this $\mathbf{d}$ equals $(\mathbf{X}_S'\mathbf{Z})^{-1}\mathbf{X}_S'\mathbf{y}$ when $\mathbf{X}_S'\mathbf{Z}$ is square and nonsingular.

References

I have experienced that it is quite useful to discuss some published scatter diagrams at the end of Chapter 2. Interesting examples are the cost function of a British busline derived by Johnston (1960, p. 79), which is also quoted by Fox (1968, pp. 80–81); the distribution of interarrival times of planes at the airport of Amsterdam discussed by Theil, Boot and Kloek (1965, pp. 157–159); and Malinvaud's (1970, pp. 1–7) analysis of the depreciation of Citroën cars and his scatter diagram for the expenditure on clothing by families of French civil servants. The last example is particularly useful because Malinvaud considers both the regression of clothing expenditure on total expenditure and that of total expenditure on clothing expenditure; these alternative procedures are related to one of the questions raised in Section 2.4. Another useful feature is that Malinvaud's depreciation curve is similar to that of the distribution of interarrival times of planes. This similarity illustrates that the same mathematical relationship can be used for the description of entirely different phenomena. Houthakker's (1957) article on income and other elasticities (obtained from budget data of various countries) is an appropriate source when Engel's law is discussed in the opening paragraph of Chapter 14.

Barbosa, F. de H. (1975). *Rational Random Behavior: Extensions and Applications*. Doctoral dissertation, The University of Chicago.

Barten, A. P. (1964). "Consumer Demand Functions Under Conditions of Almost Additive Preferences." *Econometrica*, 32, pp. 1–38.

Barten, A. P. (1966). "Het verbruik door gezinshuishoudingen in Nederland,

1921–1939 en 1948–1962." Report 6604 of the Econometric Institute of the Netherlands School of Economics.

Basman, R. L. (1957). "A Generalized Classical Method of Linear Estimation of Coefficients in a Structural Equation." *Econometrica*, 25, pp. 77–83.

Bogaard, P. J. M. van den, and H. Theil (1959). "Macrodynamic Policy-Making: An Application of Strategy and Certainty Equivalence Concepts to the Economy of the United States, 1933–1936." *Metroeconomica*, 11, pp. 149–167.

Boot, J. C. G. (1964). "Strategy: The Concept." *De Economist*, 112, pp. 190–205.

Boot, J. C. G., and G. M. de Wit (1960). "Investment Demand: An Empirical Contribution to the Aggregation Problem." *International Economic Review*, 1, pp. 3–30.

Desai, M. (1976). *Applied Econometrics*. New York: McGraw-Hill Book Company.

Durbin, J. (1970). "An Alternative to the Bounds Test for Testing for Serial Correlation in Least-squares Regression." *Econometrica*, 38, pp. 422–429.

Durbin, J., and G. S. Watson (1950, 1951). "Testing for Serial Correlation in Least Squares Regression." *Biometrika*, 37, pp. 409–428; 38, pp. 159–178.

Ebbeler, D. H. (1975). "On the Probability of Correct Model Selection Using the Maximum $\bar{R}^2$ Choice Criterion." *International Economic Review*, 16, pp. 516–520.

Elsgolc, L. E. (1962). *Calculus of Variations*. London: Pergamon Press, Ltd.

Fisher, F. M. (1966). *The Identification Problem in Econometrics*. New York: McGraw-Hill Book Company.

Fox, K. A. (1968). *Intermediate Economic Statistics*. New York: John Wiley and Sons, Inc.

Friedman, B. (1975). *Economic Stabilization Policy: Methods in Optimization*. Amsterdam and New York: North-Holland Publishing Company and Elsevier/North-Holland, Inc.

Friedman, M. (1953). "The Effects of a Full-Employment Policy on Economic Stability: A Formal Analysis." Pages 117–132 of *Essays in Positive Economics* (The University of Chicago Press).

Friedman, M. (1957). *A Theory of the Consumption Function*. Princeton University Press.

Fromm, G., and L. R. Klein (1976). "The NBER/NSF Model Comparison Seminar: An Analysis of Results." *Annals of Economic and Social Measurement*, 5, pp. 1–28.

Gelfand, I. M., and S. V. Fomin (1963). *Calculus of Variations*. Englewood Cliffs, New Jersey: Prentice-Hall, Inc.

Glejser, H. (1969). "A New Test for Heteroskedasticity." *Journal of the American Statistical Association*, 64, pp. 316–323.

Goldberger, A. S. (1959). *Impact Multipliers and Dynamic Properties of the Klein-Goldberger Model*. Amsterdam: North-Holland Publishing Company.

Goldberger, A. S. (1972). "Structural Equation Methods in the Social Sciences." *Econometrica*, 40, pp. 979–1001.

Goldfeld, S. M., and R. E. Quandt (1965). "Some Tests for Homoscedasticity." *Journal of the American Statistical Association*, 60, pp. 539–547.

Goldman, S. (1971). *An Empirical Comparison of Alternative Functional Forms of Demand Systems*. Doctoral dissertation, The University of Chicago.

Griliches, Z. (1957). "Specification Bias in Estimates of Production Functions." *Journal of Farm Economics*, 39, pp. 8–20.

Grunfeld, Y. (1958). *The Determinants of Corporate Investment*. Doctoral dissertation, The University of Chicago.

Haavelmo, T. (1943). "The Statistical Implications of a System of Simultaneous Equations." *Econometrica*, 11, pp. 1–12.

Haitovsky, Y., G. Treyz, and V. Su (1974). *Forecasts with Quarterly Macroeconometric Models*. New York: National Bureau of Economic Research.

Hart, B. I. (1942). "Significance Levels for the Ratio of the Mean Square Successive Difference to the Variance." *Annals of Mathematical Statistics*, 13, pp. 445–447.

Henshaw, R. C., Jr. (1966). "Testing Single-Equation Least Squares Regression Models for Autocorrelated Disturbances." *Econometrica*, 34, pp. 646–660.

Hood, W. C., and T. C. Koopmans (editors) (1953). *Studies in Econometric Method*. New York: John Wiley and Sons, Inc.

Houthakker, H. S. (1957). "An International Comparison of Household Expenditure Patterns, Commemorating the Centenary of Engel's Law." *Econometrica*, 25, pp. 532–551.

Johansen, L. (1972). "On the Optimal Use of Forecasts in Economic Policy Decisions." *Journal of Public Economics*, 1, pp. 1–24.

Johnston J. (1960). *Statistical Cost Analysis*. New York: McGraw-Hill Book Company.

Johnston, J. (1972). *Econometric Methods*. Second edition (first edition, 1963). New York: McGraw-Hill Book Company.

Klein, L. R. (1950). *Economic Fluctuations in the United States, 1921-1941*. New York: John Wiley and Sons, Inc.

Klein, L. R., and A. S. Goldberger (1955). *An Econometric Model of the United States, 1929-1952*. Amsterdam: North-Holland Publishing Company.

Kmenta, J. (1967). "On Estimation of the CES Production Function." *International Economic Review*, 8, pp. 180–189.

Koopmans, T. C. (editor) (1950). *Statistical Inference in Dynamic Economic Models*. New York: John Wiley and Sons, Inc.

Koyck, L. M. (1954). *Distributed Lags and Investment Analysis*. Amsterdam: North-Holland Publishing Company.

Malinvaud, E. (1969). "First Order Certainty Equivalence." *Econometrica*, 37, pp. 706–718.

Malinvaud, E. (1970). *Statistical Methods of Econometrics*. Second edition (first edition, 1966). Amsterdam and New York: North-Holland Publishing Company and Elsevier/North-Holland, Inc.

McNees, S. K. (1975). "An Evaluation of Economic Forecasts." *The New England Economic Review*, November/December, 1975.

Mouchart, M., H. Theil, and J. I. Vorst (1963). "On the Predictive Value of Investment Surveys." *Statistica Neerlandica*, 17, pp. 287–297.

Paulus, J. D. (1972). *The Estimation of Large Systems of Consumer Demand Equations Using Stochastic Prior Information*. Doctoral dissertation, The University of Chicago.

Prais, S. J., and H. S. Houthakker (1955). *The Analysis of Family Budgets*. Cambridge University Press.

Pratt, J. W. (1971). "Comments on the Above Two Papers." Pages 207–209 of *Frontiers of Quantitative Economics*, edited by M. D. Intriligator (Amsterdam: North-Holland Publishing Company).

Rothenberg, T. J. (1971a). "The Bayesian Approach and Alternatives in Econometrics." Pages 194–204 of *Frontiers of Quantitative Economics*, edited by M. D. Intriligator (Amsterdam: North-Holland Publishing Company).

Rothenberg, T. J. (1971b). "Identification in Parametric Models." *Econometrica*, 39, pp. 577–591.

Schmidt, P. (1973). "Calculating the Power of the Minimum Standard Error Choice Criterion." *International Economic Review*, 14, pp. 253–255.

Schmidt, P. (1974). "A Note on Theil's Minimum Standard Error Criterion When the Disturbances Are Autocorrelated." *Review of Economics and Statistics*, 66, pp. 122–123.

Simon, H. A., (1956). "Dynamic Programming Under Uncertainty with a Quadratic Criterion Function." *Econometrica*, 24, pp. 74–81.

Slutsky, E. (1915). "Sulla teoria del bilancio del consumatore." *Giornale degli Economisti*, 51, pp. 1–26. An English translation appeared under the title "On the Theory of the Budget of the Consumer" as Chapter 2 of *Readings in Price Theory*, edited by G. J. Stigler and K. E. Boulding (Chicago, Illinois: Richard D. Irwin, Inc., 1952).

Stone, M. (1976). "Strong Inconsistency for Uniform Priors." *Journal of the American Statistical Association*, 71, pp. 114–116.

Stone, R., and D. A. Rowe (1966). *The Measurement of Consumers' Expenditure and Behaviour in the United Kingdom, 1920–1938*. Volume II. Cambridge University Press.

Su, V., and J. Su (1975). "An Evaluation of the ASA/NBER Business Outlook Survey Forecasts." *Explorations in Economic Research*, 2, pp. 588–618.

Theil, H. (1953a). "Repeated Least-Squares Applied to Complete Equation Systems." The Hague: Central Planning Bureau (mimeographed).

Theil, H. (1953b). "Estimation and Simultaneous Correlation in Complete Equation Systems." The Hague: Central Planning Bureau (mimeographed).

Theil, H. (1954). *Linear Aggregation of Economic Relations*. Amsterdam: North-Holland Publishing Company.

Theil, H. (1957a). "Specification Errors and the Estimation of Economic Relationships." *Review of the International Statistical Institute*, 25, pp. 41–51.

Theil, H. (1957b). "A Note on Certainty Equivalence in Dynamic Planning." *Econometrica*, 25, pp. 346–349.

Theil, H. (1961). *Economic Forecasts and Policy*. Second edition (first edition, 1958). Amsterdam: North-Holland Publishing Company.

Theil, H. (1963). "On the Use of Incomplete Prior Information in Regression Analysis." *Journal of the American Statistical Association*, 58, pp. 401–414.

Theil, H. (1964). *Optimal Decision Rules for Government and Industry*. Amsterdam and New York: North-Holland Publishing Company and Elsevier/North-Holland, Inc.

Theil, H. (1966). *Applied Economic Forecasting*. Amsterdam and New York: North-Holland Publishing Company and Elsevier/North-Holland, Inc.

Theil, H. (1967). *Economics and Information Theory*. Amsterdam and New York: North-Holland Publishing Company and Elsevier/North-Holland, Inc.

Theil, H. (1971). *Principles of Econometrics*. New York and Amsterdam: John Wiley and Sons, Inc., and North-Holland Publishing Company.

Theil, H. (1974a). "A Theory of Rational Random Behavior." *Journal of the American Statistical Association*, 69, pp. 310–314.

Theil, H. (1974b). "Mixed Estimation Based on Quasi-Prior Judgments." *European Economic Review*, 5, pp. 33–40.

Theil, H. (1975–1976). *Theory and Measurement of Consumer Demand*. Two volumes. Amsterdam and New York: North-Holland Publishing Company and Elsevier/North-Holland, Inc.

Theil, H., J. C. G. Boot, and T. Kloek (1965). *Operations Research and Quantitative Economics: An Elementary Introduction*. New York: McGraw-Hill Book Company.

Theil, H., and A. S. Goldberger (1961). "On Pure and Mixed Statistical Estimation in Economics." *International Economic Review*, 2, pp. 65–78.

Theil, H., and K. Laitinen (1977). "A Maximum Entropy Approach to the Problem of Undersized Samples in Simultaneous Equation Estimation." Report 7713 of the Center for Mathematical Studies in Business and Economics, The University of Chicago.

Theil, H., and A. L. Nagar (1961). "Testing the Independence of Regression Disturbances." *Journal of the American Statistical Association*, 56, pp. 793–806.

Tinbergen, J. (1939). *Statistical Testing of Business Cycle Theories*. Volume 1, *A Method and Its Application to Investment Activity*. Volume 2, *Business Cycles in the United States of America, 1919–1932*. Geneva: League of Nations.

Tinbergen, J. (1959). *Selected Papers*, edited by L. H. Klaassen, L. M. Koyck, and J. H. Witteveen. Amsterdam: North-Holland Publishing Company.

Van den Bogaard, P. J. M., *see* Bogaard, P. J. M. van den.

Waelbroeck, J. (1975). "A Survey of Short-Run Model Research Outside the United States." Chapter 10 of *The Brookings Model: Perspective and Recent Developments*, edited by G. Fromm and L. R. Klein (Amsterdam: North-Holland Publishing Company).

Wald, A. (1940). "The Fitting of Straight Lines If Both Variables Are Subject to Error." *Annals of Mathematical Statistics*, 11, pp. 284–300.

Wold, H. (1954). "Causality and Econometrics." *Econometrica*, 22, pp. 162–177.

Zarnowitz, V. (editor) (1972). *The Business Cycle Today*. New York: National Bureau of Economic Research.

Zellner, A. (1971a). *An Introduction to Bayesian Inference in Econometrics*. New York: John Wiley and Sons, Inc.

Zellner, A. (1971b). "The Bayesian Approach and Alternatives in Econometrics." Pages 178–193 of *Frontiers of Quantitative Economics*, edited by M. D. Intriligator (Amsterdam: North-Holland Publishing Company).

Statistical Tables

The tables of the t, normal, χ^2, and F distributions have been reproduced from the third edition (1966) of *Biometrika Tables for Statisticians*, Vol. 1. The table of the Von Neumann ratio is reproduced from Hart (1942). The tables of the Durbin-Watson statistic are reproduced from Durbin and Watson (1951).

The t distribution and the normal distribution[a]

Degrees of freedom	Pb	.25 / .5	.1 / .2	.05 / .1	.025 / .05	.01 / .02	.005 / .01
	1	1.000	3.078	6.314	12.706	31.821	63.657
	2	.816	1.886	2.920	4.303	6.965	9.925
	3	.765	1.638	2.353	3.182	4.541	5.841
	4	.741	1.533	2.132	2.776	3.747	4.604
	5	.727	1.476	2.015	2.571	3.365	4.032
	6	.718	1.440	1.943	2.447	3.143	3.707
	7	.711	1.415	1.895	2.365	2.998	3.499
	8	.706	1.397	1.860	2.306	2.896	3.355
	9	.703	1.383	1.833	2.262	2.821	3.250
	10	.700	1.372	1.812	2.228	2.764	3.169
	11	.697	1.363	1.796	2.201	2.718	3.106
	12	.695	1.356	1.782	2.179	2.681	3.055
	13	.694	1.350	1.771	2.160	2.650	3.012
	14	.692	1.345	1.761	2.145	2.624	2.977
	15	.691	1.341	1.753	2.131	2.602	2.947
	16	.690	1.337	1.746	2.120	2.583	2.921
	17	.689	1.333	1.740	2.110	2.567	2.898
	18	.688	1.330	1.734	2.101	2.552	2.878
	19	.688	1.328	1.729	2.093	2.539	2.861
	20	.687	1.325	1.725	2.086	2.528	2.845
	21	.686	1.323	1.721	2.080	2.518	2.831
	22	.686	1.321	1.717	2.074	2.508	2.819
	23	.685	1.319	1.714	2.069	2.500	2.807
	24	.685	1.318	1.711	2.064	2.492	2.797
	25	.684	1.316	1.708	2.060	2.485	2.787
	26	.684	1.315	1.706	2.056	2.479	2.779
	27	.684	1.314	1.703	2.052	2.473	2.771
	28	.683	1.313	1.701	2.048	2.467	2.763
	29	.683	1.311	1.699	2.045	2.462	2.756
	30	.683	1.310	1.697	2.042	2.457	2.750
	40	.681	1.303	1.684	2.021	2.423	2.704
	60	.679	1.296	1.671	2.000	2.390	2.660
	120	.677	1.289	1.658	1.980	2.358	2.617
(Normal)	∞	.674	1.282	1.645	1.960	2.326	2.576

[a]The smaller probability shown at the head of each column is the area in one tail; the larger probability is the area in both tails. Example: With 20 degrees of freedom, a t value larger than 1.725 has a .05 probability and a t value exceeding 1.725 in absolute value has a .1 probability.

The χ^2 distribution[a]

Degrees of freedom	0.995	0.990	0.575	0.950	0.900	0.750	0.500	0.250	0.100	0.050	0.025	0.010	0.005	0.001
1	392704.10^{-10}	157088.10^{-9}	982069.10^{-9}	393214.10^{-8}	0.0157908	0.1015308	0.454936	1.32330	2.70554	3.84146	5.02389	6.63490	7.87944	10.828
2	0.0100251	0.0201007	0.0506356	0.102587	0.210721	0.575364	1.38629	2.77259	4.60517	5.99146	7.37776	9.21034	10.5966	13.816
3	0.0717218	0.114832	0.215795	0.351846	0.584374	1.212534	2.36597	4.10834	6.25139	7.81473	9.34840	11.3449	12.8382	16.266
4	0.206989	0.297109	0.484419	0.710723	1.063623	1.92256	3.35669	5.38527	7.77944	9.48773	11.1433	13.2767	14.8603	18.467
5	0.411742	0.554298	0.831212	1.145476	1.61031	2.67460	4.35146	6.62568	9.23636	11.0705	12.8325	15.0863	16.7496	20.515
6	0.675727	0.872090	1.23734	1.63538	2.20413	3.45460	5.34812	7.84080	10.6446	12.5916	14.4494	16.8119	18.5476	22.458
7	0.989256	1.239043	1.68987	2.16735	2.83311	4.25485	6.34581	9.03715	12.0170	14.0671	16.0128	18.4753	20.2777	24.322
8	1.34441	1.64650	2.17973	2.73264	3.48954	5.07064	7.34412	10.2189	13.3616	15.5073	17.5345	20.0902	21.9550	26.125
9	1.73493	2.08790	2.70039	3.32511	4.16816	5.89883	8.34283	11.3888	14.6837	16.9190	19.0228	21.6660	23.5894	27.877
10	2.15586	2.55821	3.24697	3.94030	4.86518	6.73720	9.34182	12.5489	15.9872	18.3070	20.4832	23.2093	25.1882	29.588
11	2.60322	3.05348	3.81575	4.57481	5.57778	7.58414	10.3410	13.7007	17.2750	19.6751	21.9200	24.7250	26.7568	31.264
12	3.07382	3.57057	4.40379	5.22603	6.30380	8.43842	11.3403	14.8454	18.5493	21.0261	23.3367	26.2170	28.2995	32.909
13	3.56503	4.10692	5.00875	5.89186	7.04150	9.29907	12.3398	15.9839	19.8119	22.3620	24.7356	27.6882	29.8195	34.528
14	4.07467	4.66043	5.62873	6.57063	7.78953	10.1653	13.3393	17.1169	21.0641	23.6848	26.1189	29.1412	31.3194	36.123
15	4.60092	5.22935	6.25214	7.26094	8.54676	11.0365	14.3389	18.2451	22.3071	24.9958	27.4884	30.5779	32.8013	37.697
16	5.14221	5.81221	6.90766	7.96165	9.31224	11.9122	15.3385	19.3689	23.5418	26.2962	28.8454	31.9999	34.2672	39.252
17	5.69722	6.40776	7.55419	8.67176	10.0852	12.7919	16.3382	20.4887	24.7690	27.5871	30.1910	33.4087	35.7185	40.790
18	6.26480	7.01491	8.23075	9.39046	10.8649	13.6753	17.3379	21.6049	25.9894	28.8693	31.5264	34.8053	37.1565	42.312
19	6.84397	7.63273	8.90652	10.1170	11.6509	14.5620	18.3377	22.7178	27.2036	30.1435	32.8523	36.1909	38.5823	43.820
20	7.43384	8.26040	9.53078	10.8508	12.4426	15.4518	19.3374	23.8277	28.4120	31.4104	34.1696	37.5662	39.9968	45.315
21	8.03365	8.89720	10.28293	11.5913	13.2396	16.3444	20.3372	24.9348	29.6151	32.6706	35.4789	38.9322	41.4011	46.797
22	8.64272	9.54249	10.9823	12.3380	14.0415	17.2396	21.3370	26.0393	30.8133	33.9244	36.7807	40.2894	42.7957	48.268
23	9.26043	10.19567	11.6886	13.0905	14.8480	18.1373	22.3369	27.1413	32.0069	35.1725	38.0756	41.6384	44.1813	49.728
24	9.88623	10.8564	12.4012	13.8484	15.6587	19.0373	23.3367	28.2412	33.1962	36.4150	39.3641	42.9798	44.5585	51.179
25	10.5197	11.5240	13.1197	14.6114	16.4734	19.9393	24.3366	29.3389	34.3816	37.6525	40.6465	44.3141	46.9279	52.618
26	11.1602	12.1981	13.8439	15.3792	17.2919	20.8434	25.3365	30.4346	35.5632	38.8851	41.9232	45.6417	48.2899	54.052
27	11.8076	12.8785	14.5734	16.1514	18.1139	21.7494	26.3363	31.5284	36.7412	40.1133	43.1945	46.9629	49.6449	55.476
28	12.4613	13.5647	15.3079	16.9279	18.9392	22.6572	27.3362	32.6205	37.9159	41.3371	44.4608	48.2782	50.9934	56.892
29	13.1211	14.2565	16.0471	17.7084	19.7677	23.5666	28.3361	33.7109	39.0875	42.5570	45.7223	49.5879	52.3356	58.301
30	13.7867	14.9535	16.7908	18.4927	20.5992	24.4776	29.3360	34.7997	40.2560	43.7730	46.9792	50.8922	53.6720	59.703
40	20.7065	22.1643	24.4330	26.5093	29.0505	33.6603	39.3353	45.6160	51.8051	55.7585	59.3417	63.6907	66.7660	73.402
50	27.9907	29.7067	32.3574	34.7643	37.6886	42.9421	49.3349	56.3336	63.1671	67.5048	71.4202	76.1539	79.4900	86.661
60	35.5345	37.4849	40.4817	43.1880	46.4589	52.2938	59.3347	66.9815	74.3970	79.0819	83.2977	88.3794	91.9517	99.607
70	43.2752	45.4417	48.7576	51.7393	55.3289	61.6983	69.3345	77.5767	85.5270	90.5312	95.0232	100.425	104.215	112.317
80	51.1719	53.5401	57.1532	60.3915	64.2778	71.1445	79.3343	88.1303	96.5782	101.879	106.629	112.329	116.321	124.839
90	59.1963	61.7541	65.6466	69.1260	73.2911	80.6247	89.3342	98.6499	107.565	113.145	118.136	124.116	128.299	137.208
100	67.3276	70.0649	74.2219	77.9295	82.3581	90.1332	99.3341	109.141	118.498	124.342	129.561	135.807	140.169	149.449

[a]The probability shown at the head of the column is the area in the right-hand tail. Example: With 4 degrees of freedom, a χ^2 value larger than 7.78 has a .1 probability.

5 percent points of the F distribution[a]

Degrees of freedom for numerator

	1	2	3	4	5	6	7	8	9	10	12	15	20	24	30	40	60	120	∞
1	161.4	199.5	215.7	224.6	230.2	234.0	236.8	238.9	240.5	241.9	243.9	245.9	248.0	249.1	250.1	251.1	252.2	253.3	254.3
2	18.51	19.00	19.16	19.25	19.30	19.33	19.35	19.37	19.38	19.40	19.41	19.43	19.45	19.45	19.46	19.47	19.48	19.49	19.50
3	10.13	9.55	9.28	9.12	9.01	8.94	8.89	8.85	8.81	8.79	8.74	8.70	8.66	8.64	8.62	8.59	8.57	8.55	8.53
4	7.71	6.94	6.59	6.39	6.26	6.16	6.09	6.04	6.00	5.96	5.91	5.86	5.80	5.77	5.75	5.72	5.69	5.66	5.63
5	6.61	5.79	5.41	5.19	5.05	4.95	4.88	4.82	4.77	4.74	4.68	4.62	4.56	4.53	4.50	4.46	4.43	4.40	4.36
6	5.99	5.14	4.76	4.53	4.39	4.28	4.21	4.15	4.10	4.06	4.00	3.94	3.87	3.84	3.81	3.77	3.74	3.70	3.67
7	5.59	4.74	4.35	4.12	3.97	3.87	3.79	3.73	3.68	3.64	3.57	3.51	3.44	3.41	3.38	3.34	3.30	3.27	3.23
8	5.32	4.46	4.07	3.84	3.69	3.58	3.50	3.44	3.39	3.35	3.28	3.22	3.15	3.12	3.08	3.04	3.01	2.97	2.93
9	5.12	4.26	3.86	3.63	3.48	3.37	3.29	3.23	3.18	3.14	3.07	3.01	2.94	2.90	2.86	2.83	2.79	2.75	2.71
10	4.96	4.10	3.71	3.48	3.33	3.22	3.14	3.07	3.02	2.98	2.91	2.85	2.77	2.74	2.70	2.66	2.62	2.58	2.54
11	4.84	3.98	3.59	3.36	3.20	3.09	3.01	2.95	2.90	2.85	2.79	2.72	2.65	2.61	2.57	2.53	2.49	2.45	2.40
12	4.75	3.89	3.49	3.26	3.11	3.00	2.91	2.85	2.80	2.75	2.69	2.62	2.54	2.51	2.47	2.43	2.38	2.34	2.30
13	4.67	3.81	3.41	3.18	3.03	2.92	2.83	2.77	2.71	2.67	2.60	2.53	2.46	2.42	2.38	2.34	2.30	2.25	2.21
14	4.60	3.74	3.34	3.11	2.96	2.85	2.76	2.70	2.65	2.60	2.53	2.46	2.39	2.35	2.31	2.27	2.22	2.18	2.13
15	4.54	3.68	3.29	3.06	2.90	2.79	2.71	2.64	2.59	2.54	2.48	2.40	2.33	2.29	2.25	2.20	2.16	2.11	2.07
16	4.49	3.63	3.24	3.01	2.85	2.74	2.66	2.59	2.54	2.49	2.42	2.35	2.28	2.24	2.19	2.15	2.11	2.06	2.01
17	4.45	3.59	3.20	2.96	2.81	2.70	2.61	2.55	2.49	2.45	2.38	2.31	2.23	2.19	2.15	2.10	2.06	2.01	1.96
18	4.41	3.55	3.16	2.93	2.77	2.66	2.58	2.51	2.46	2.41	2.34	2.27	2.19	2.15	2.11	2.06	2.02	1.97	1.92
19	4.38	3.52	3.13	2.90	2.74	2.63	2.54	2.48	2.42	2.38	2.31	2.23	2.16	2.11	2.07	2.03	1.98	1.93	1.88
20	4.35	3.49	3.10	2.87	2.71	2.60	2.51	2.45	2.39	2.35	2.28	2.20	2.12	2.08	2.04	1.99	1.95	1.90	1.84
21	4.32	3.47	3.07	2.84	2.68	2.57	2.49	2.42	2.37	2.32	2.25	2.18	2.10	2.05	2.01	1.96	1.92	1.87	1.81
22	4.30	3.44	3.05	2.82	2.66	2.55	2.46	2.40	2.34	2.30	2.23	2.15	2.07	2.03	1.98	1.94	1.89	1.84	1.78
23	4.28	3.42	3.03	2.80	2.64	2.53	2.44	2.37	2.32	2.27	2.20	2.13	2.05	2.01	1.96	1.91	1.86	1.81	1.76
24	4.26	3.40	3.01	2.78	2.62	2.51	2.42	2.36	2.30	2.25	2.18	2.11	2.03	1.98	1.94	1.89	1.84	1.79	1.73
25	4.24	3.39	2.99	2.76	2.60	2.49	2.40	2.34	2.28	2.24	2.16	2.09	2.01	1.96	1.92	1.87	1.82	1.77	1.71
26	4.23	3.37	2.98	2.74	2.59	2.47	2.39	2.32	2.27	2.22	2.15	2.07	1.99	1.95	1.90	1.85	1.80	1.75	1.69
27	4.21	3.35	2.96	2.73	2.57	2.46	2.37	2.31	2.25	2.20	2.13	2.06	1.97	1.93	1.88	1.84	1.79	1.73	1.67
28	4.20	3.34	2.95	2.71	2.56	2.45	2.36	2.29	2.24	2.19	2.12	2.04	1.96	1.91	1.87	1.82	1.77	1.71	1.65
29	4.18	3.33	2.93	2.70	2.55	2.43	2.35	2.28	2.22	2.18	2.10	2.03	1.94	1.90	1.85	1.81	1.75	1.70	1.64
30	4.17	3.32	2.92	2.69	2.53	2.42	2.33	2.27	2.21	2.16	2.09	2.01	1.93	1.89	1.84	1.79	1.74	1.68	1.62
40	4.08	3.23	2.84	2.61	2.45	2.34	2.25	2.18	2.12	2.08	2.00	1.92	1.84	1.79	1.74	1.69	1.64	1.58	1.51
60	4.00	3.15	2.76	2.53	2.37	2.25	2.17	2.10	2.04	1.99	1.92	1.84	1.75	1.70	1.65	1.59	1.53	1.47	1.39
120	3.92	3.07	2.68	2.45	2.29	2.17	2.09	2.02	1.96	1.91	1.83	1.75	1.66	1.61	1.55	1.50	1.43	1.35	1.25
∞	3.84	3.00	2.60	2.37	2.21	2.10	2.01	1.94	1.88	1.83	1.75	1.67	1.57	1.52	1.46	1.39	1.32	1.22	1.00

Degrees of freedom for denominator

[a]Example: With $m = 5$ degrees of freedom for the numerator and $n = 20$ for the denominator, an F value larger than 2.71 has .05 probability.

1 percent points of the F distribution[a]

Degrees of freedom for numerator

	1	2	3	4	5	6	7	8	9	10	12	15	20	24	30	40	60	120	∞
1	4052	4999.5	5403	5625	5764	5859	5928	5981	6022	6056	6106	6157	6209	6235	6261	6287	6313	6339	6366
2	98.50	99.00	99.17	99.25	99.30	99.33	99.36	99.37	99.39	99.40	99.42	99.43	99.45	99.46	99.47	99.47	99.48	99.49	99.50
3	34.12	30.82	29.46	28.71	28.24	27.91	27.67	27.49	27.35	27.23	27.05	26.87	26.69	26.60	26.50	26.41	26.32	26.22	26.13
4	21.20	18.00	16.69	15.98	15.52	15.21	14.98	14.80	14.66	14.55	14.37	14.20	14.02	13.93	13.84	13.75	13.65	13.56	13.46
5	16.26	13.27	12.06	11.39	10.97	10.67	10.46	10.29	10.16	10.05	9.89	9.72	9.55	9.47	9.38	9.29	9.20	9.11	9.02
6	13.75	10.92	9.78	9.15	8.75	8.47	8.26	8.10	7.98	7.87	7.72	7.56	7.40	7.31	7.23	7.14	7.06	6.97	6.88
7	12.25	9.55	8.45	7.85	7.46	7.19	6.99	6.84	6.72	6.62	6.47	6.31	6.16	6.07	5.99	5.91	5.82	5.74	5.65
8	11.26	8.65	7.59	7.01	6.63	6.37	6.18	6.03	5.91	5.81	5.67	5.52	5.36	5.28	5.20	5.12	5.03	4.95	4.86
9	10.56	8.02	6.99	6.42	6.06	5.80	5.61	5.47	5.35	5.26	5.11	4.96	4.81	4.73	4.65	4.57	4.48	4.40	4.31
10	10.04	7.56	6.55	5.99	5.64	5.39	5.20	5.06	4.94	4.85	4.71	4.56	4.41	4.33	4.25	4.17	4.08	4.00	3.91
11	9.65	7.21	6.22	5.67	5.32	5.07	4.89	4.74	4.63	4.54	4.40	4.25	4.10	4.02	3.94	3.86	3.78	3.69	3.60
12	9.33	6.93	5.95	5.41	5.06	4.82	4.64	4.50	4.39	4.30	4.16	4.01	3.86	3.78	3.70	3.62	3.54	3.45	3.36
13	9.07	6.70	5.74	5.21	4.86	4.62	4.44	4.30	4.19	4.10	3.96	3.82	3.66	3.59	3.51	3.43	3.34	3.25	3.17
14	8.86	6.51	5.56	5.04	4.69	4.46	4.28	4.14	4.03	3.94	3.80	3.66	3.51	3.43	3.35	3.27	3.18	3.09	3.00
15	8.68	6.36	5.42	4.89	4.56	4.32	4.14	4.00	3.89	3.80	3.67	3.52	3.37	3.29	3.21	3.13	3.05	2.96	2.87
16	8.53	6.23	5.29	4.77	4.44	4.20	4.03	3.89	3.78	3.69	3.55	3.41	3.26	3.18	3.10	3.02	2.93	2.84	2.75
17	8.40	6.11	5.18	4.67	4.34	4.10	3.93	3.79	3.68	3.59	3.46	3.31	3.16	3.08	3.00	2.92	2.83	2.75	2.65
18	8.29	6.01	5.09	4.58	4.25	4.01	3.84	3.71	3.60	3.51	3.37	3.23	3.08	3.00	2.92	2.84	2.75	2.66	2.57
19	8.18	5.93	5.01	4.50	4.17	3.94	3.77	3.63	3.52	3.43	3.30	3.15	3.00	2.92	2.84	2.76	2.67	2.58	2.49
20	8.10	5.85	4.94	4.43	4.10	3.87	3.70	3.56	3.46	3.37	3.23	3.09	2.94	2.86	2.78	2.69	2.61	2.52	2.42
21	8.02	5.78	4.87	4.37	4.04	3.81	3.64	3.51	3.40	3.31	3.17	3.03	2.88	2.80	2.72	2.64	2.55	2.46	2.36
22	7.95	5.72	4.82	4.31	3.99	3.76	3.59	3.45	3.35	3.26	3.12	2.98	2.83	2.75	2.67	2.58	2.50	2.40	2.31
23	7.88	5.66	4.76	4.26	3.94	3.71	3.54	3.41	3.30	3.21	3.07	2.93	2.78	2.70	2.62	2.54	2.45	2.35	2.26
24	7.82	5.61	4.72	4.22	3.90	3.67	3.50	3.36	3.26	3.17	3.03	2.89	2.74	2.66	2.58	2.49	2.40	2.31	2.21
25	7.77	5.57	4.68	4.18	3.85	3.63	3.46	3.32	3.22	3.13	2.99	2.85	2.70	2.62	2.54	2.45	2.36	2.27	2.17
26	7.72	5.53	4.64	4.14	3.82	3.59	3.42	3.29	3.18	3.09	2.96	2.81	2.66	2.58	2.50	2.42	2.33	2.23	2.13
27	7.68	5.49	4.60	4.11	3.78	3.56	3.39	3.26	3.15	3.06	2.93	2.78	2.63	2.55	2.47	2.38	2.29	2.20	2.10
28	7.64	5.45	4.57	4.07	3.75	3.53	3.36	3.23	3.12	3.03	2.90	2.75	2.60	2.52	2.44	2.35	2.26	2.17	2.06
29	7.60	5.42	4.54	4.04	3.73	3.50	3.33	3.20	3.09	3.00	2.87	2.73	2.57	2.49	2.41	2.33	2.23	2.14	2.03
30	7.56	5.39	4.51	4.02	3.70	3.47	3.30	3.17	3.07	2.98	2.84	2.70	2.55	2.47	2.39	2.30	2.21	2.11	2.01
40	7.31	5.18	4.31	3.83	3.51	3.29	3.12	2.99	2.89	2.80	2.66	2.52	2.37	2.29	2.20	2.11	2.02	1.92	1.80
60	7.08	4.98	4.13	3.65	3.34	3.12	2.95	2.82	2.72	2.63	2.50	2.35	2.20	2.12	2.03	1.94	1.84	1.73	1.60
120	6.85	4.79	3.95	3.48	3.17	2.96	2.79	2.66	2.56	2.47	2.34	2.19	2.03	1.95	1.86	1.76	1.66	1.53	1.38
∞	6.63	4.61	3.78	3.32	3.02	2.80	2.64	2.51	2.41	2.32	2.18	2.04	1.88	1.79	1.70	1.59	1.47	1.32	1.00

Degrees of freedom for denominator

[a]Example: With $m = 5$ degrees of freedom for the numerator and $n = 20$ for the denominator, an F value larger than 4.10 has .01 probability.

5, 1, and .1 percent points of the Von Neumann ratio

Number of observations	5%	1%	.1%	5%	1%	.1%
	One-tailed test against positive correlation			One-tailed test against negative correlation		
4	1.0406	.8341	.7864	4.2927	4.4992	4.5469
5	1.0255	6724	.5201	3.9745	4.3276	4.4799
6	1.0682	.6738	.4361	3.7318	4.1262	4.3639
7	1.0919	.7163	.4311	3.5748	3.9504	4.2356
8	1.1228	.7575	.4612	3.4486	3.8139	4.1102
9	1.1524	.7974	.4973	3.3476	3.7025	4.0027
10	1.1803	.8353	.5351	3.2642	3.6091	3.9093
11	1.2962	.8706	.5717	3.1938	3.5294	3.8283
12	1.2301	.9033	.6062	3.1335	3.4603	3.7574
13	1.2521	.9336	.6390	3.0812	3.3996	3.6944
14	1.2725	.9618	.6702	3.0352	3.3458	3.6375
15	1.2914	.9880	.6999	2.9943	3.2977	3.5858
16	1.3090	1.0124	.7281	2.9577	3.2543	3.5386
17	1.3253	1.0352	.7548	2.9247	3.2148	3.4952
18	1.3405	1.0566	.7801	2.8948	3.1787	3.4552
19	1.3547	1.0766	.8040	2.8675	3.1456	3.4182
20	1.3680	1.0954	.8265	2.8425	3.1151	3.3840
21	1.3805	1.1131	.8477	2.8195	3.0869	3.3523
22	1.3923	1.1298	.8677	2.7982	3.0607	3.3228
23	1.4035	1.1456	.8866	2.7784	3.0362	3.2953
24	1.4141	1.1606	.9045	2.7599	3.0133	3.2695
25	1.4241	1.1748	.9215	2.7426	2.9919	3.2452
26	1.4336	1.1883	.9378	2.7264	2.9718	3.2222
27	1.4426	1.2012	.9535	2.7112	2.9528	3.2003
28	1.4512	1.2135	.9687	2.6969	2.9348	3.1794
29	1.4594	1.2252	.9835	2.6834	2.9177	3.1594
30	1.4672	1.2363	.9978	2.6707	2.9016	3.1402

5, 1, and .1 percent points of the Von Neumann ratio

Number of observations	5%	1%	.1%	5%	1%	.1%
	One-tailed test against positive correlation			One-tailed test against negative correlation		
31	1.4746	1.2469	1.0115	2.6587	2.8864	3.1219
32	1.4817	1.2570	1.0245	2.6473	2.8720	3.1046
33	1.4885	1.2667	1.0369	2.6365	2.8583	3.0882
34	1.4951	1.2761	1.0488	2.6262	2.8451	3.0725
35	1.5014	1.2852	1.0603	2.6163	2.8324	3.0574
36	1.5075	1.2940	1.0714	2.6068	2.8202	3.0429
37	1.5135	1.3025	1.0822	2.5977	2.8085	3.0289
38	1.5193	1.3108	1.0927	2.5889	2.7973	3.0154
39	1.5249	1.3188	1.1029	2.5804	2.7865	3.0024
40	1.5304	1.3266	1.1128	2.5722	2.7760	2.9898
41	1.5357	1.3342	1.1224	2.5643	2.7658	2.9776
42	1.5408	1.3415	1.1317	2.5567	2.7560	2.9658
43	1.5458	1.3486	1.1407	2.5494	2.7466	2.9545
44	1.5506	1.3554	1.1494	2.5424	2.7376	2.9436
45	1.5552	1.3620	1.1577	2.5357	2.7289	2.9332
46	1.5596	1.3684	1.1657	2.5293	2.7205	2.9232
47	1.5638	1.3745	1.1734	2.5232	2.7125	2.9136
48	1.5678	1.3802	1.1807	2.5173	2.7049	2.9044
49	1.5716	1.3856	1.1877	2.5117	2.6977	2.8956
50	1.5752	1.3907	1.1944	2.5064	2.6908	2.8872
51	1.5787	1.3957	1.2010	2.5013	2.6842	2.8790
52	1.5822	1.4007	1.2075	2.4963	2.6777	2.8709
53	1.5856	1.4057	1.2139	2.4914	2.6712	2.8630
54	1.5890	1.4107	1.2202	2.4866	2.6648	2.8553
55	1.5923	1.4156	1.2264	2.4819	2.6585	2.8477
56	1.5955	1.4203	1.2324	2.4773	2.6524	2.8403
57	1.5987	1.4249	1.2383	2.4728	2.6465	2.8331
58	1.6019	1.4294	1.2442	2.4684	2.6407	2.8260
59	1.6051	1.4339	1.2500	2.4640	2.6350	2.8190
60	1.6082	1.4384	1.2558	2.4596	2.6294	2.8120

Lower and upper bounds of the 5 percent points of the Durbin-Watson test statistic[a]

n	Number of explanatory variables									
	1		2		3		4		5	
	d_L	d_U	d_L	d_U	d_L	d_U	d_L	d_U	d_L	d_U
15	1.08	1.36	.95	1.54	.82	1.75	.69	1.97	.56	2.21
16	1.10	1.37	.98	1.54	.86	1.73	.74	1.93	.62	2.15
17	1.13	1.38	1.02	1.54	.90	1.71	.78	1.90	.67	2.10
18	1.16	1.39	1.05	1.53	.93	1.69	.82	1.87	.71	2.06
19	1.18	1.40	1.08	1.53	.97	1.68	.86	1.85	.75	2.02
20	1.20	1.41	1.10	1.54	1.00	1.68	.90	1.83	.79	1.99
21	1.22	1.42	1.13	1.54	1.03	1.67	.93	1.81	.83	1.96
22	1.24	1.43	1.15	1.54	1.05	1.66	.96	1.80	.86	1.94
23	1.26	1.44	1.17	1.54	1.08	1.66	.99	1.79	.90	1.92
24	1.27	1.45	1.19	1.55	1.10	1.66	1.01	1.78	.93	1.90
25	1.29	1.45	1.21	1.55	1.12	1.66	1.04	1.77	.95	1.89
26	1.30	1.46	1.22	1.55	1.14	1.65	1.06	1.76	.98	1.88
27	1.32	1.47	1.24	1.56	1.16	1.65	1.08	1.76	1.01	1.86
28	1.33	1.48	1.26	1.56	1.18	1.65	1.10	1.75	1.03	1.85
29	1.34	1.48	1.27	1.56	1.20	1.65	1.12	1.74	1.05	1.84
30	1.35	1.49	1.28	1.57	1.21	1.65	1.14	1.74	1.07	1.83
31	1.36	1.50	1.30	1.57	1.23	1.65	1.16	1.74	1.09	1.83
32	1.37	1.50	1.31	1.57	1.24	1.65	1.18	1.73	1.11	1.82
33	1.38	1.51	1.32	1.58	1.26	1.65	1.19	1.73	1.13	1.81
34	1.39	1.51	1.33	1.58	1.27	1.65	1.21	1.73	1.15	1.81
35	1.40	1.52	1.34	1.58	1.28	1.65	1.22	1.73	1.16	1.80
36	1.41	1.52	1.35	1.59	1.29	1.65	1.24	1.73	1.18	1.80
37	1.42	1.53	1.36	1.59	1.31	1.66	1.25	1.72	1.19	1.80
38	1.43	1.54	1.37	1.59	1.32	1.66	1.26	1.72	1.21	1.79
39	1.43	1.54	1.38	1.60	1.33	1.66	1.27	1.72	1.22	1.79
40	1.44	1.54	1.39	1.60	1.34	1.66	1.29	1.72	1.23	1.79
45	1.48	1.57	1.43	1.62	1.38	1.67	1.34	1.72	1.29	1.78
50	1.50	1.59	1.46	1.63	1.42	1.67	1.38	1.72	1.34	1.77
55	1.53	1.60	1.49	1.64	1.45	1.68	1.41	1.72	1.38	1.77
60	1.55	1.62	1.51	1.65	1.48	1.69	1.44	1.73	1.41	1.77
65	1.57	1.63	1.54	1.66	1.50	1.70	1.47	1.73	1.44	1.77
70	1.58	1.64	1.55	1.67	1.52	1.70	1.49	1.74	1.46	1.77
75	1.60	1.65	1.57	1.68	1.54	1.71	1.51	1.74	1.49	1.77
80	1.61	1.66	1.59	1.69	1.56	1.72	1.53	1.74	1.51	1.77
85	1.62	1.67	1.60	1.70	1.57	1.72	1.55	1.75	1.52	1.77
90	1.63	1.68	1.61	1.70	1.59	1.73	1.57	1.75	1.54	1.78
95	1.64	1.69	1.62	1.71	1.60	1.73	1.58	1.75	1.56	1.78
100	1.65	1.69	1.63	1.72	1.61	1.74	1.59	1.76	1.57	1.78

[a]The bounds shown, which assume that the regression contains a constant term, refer to a one-tailed test against positive autocorrelation of the disturbances.

Lower and upper bounds of the 1 percent points of the Durbin-Watson test statistic[a]

					Number of explanatory variables				
	1		2		3		4		5
n	d_L	d_U	d_L	d_U	d_L	d_U	d_L	d_U	d_L	d_U
15	.81	1.07	.70	1.25	.59	1.46	.49	1.70	.39	1.96
16	.84	1.09	.74	1.25	.63	1.44	.53	1.66	.44	1.90
17	.87	1.10	.77	1.25	.67	1.43	.57	1.63	.48	1.85
18	.90	1.12	.80	1.26	.71	1.42	.61	1.60	.52	1.80
19	.93	1.13	.83	1.26	.74	1.41	.65	1.58	.56	1.77
20	.95	1.15	.86	1.27	.77	1.41	.68	1.57	.60	1.74
21	.97	1.16	.89	1.27	.80	1.41	.72	1.55	.63	1.71
22	1.00	1.17	.91	1.28	.83	1.40	.75	1.54	.66	1.69
23	1.02	1.19	.94	1.29	.86	1.40	.77	1.53	.70	1.67
24	1.04	1.20	.96	1.30	.88	1.41	.80	1.53	.72	1.66
25	1.05	1.21	.98	1.30	.90	1.41	.83	1.52	.75	1.65
26	1.07	1.22	1.00	1.31	.93	1.41	.85	1.52	.78	1.64
27	1.09	1.23	1.02	·1.32	.95	1.41	.88	1.51	.81	1.63
28	1.10	1.24	1.04	1.32	.97	1.41	.90	1.51	.83	1.62
29	1.12	1.25	1.05	1.33	.99	1.42	.92	1.51	.85	1.61
30	1.13	1.26	1.07	1.34	1.01	1.42	.94	1.51	.88	1.61
31	1.15	1.27	1.08	1.34	1.02	1.42	.96	1.51	.90	1.60
32	1.16	1.28	1.10	1.35	1.04	1.43	.98	1.51	.92	1.60
33	1.17	1.29	1.11	1.36	1.05	1.43	1.00	1.51	.94	1.59
34	1.18	1.30	1.13	1.36	1.07	1.43	1.01	1.51	.95	1.59
35	1.19	1.31	1.14	1.37	1.08	1.44	1.03	1.51	.97	1.59
36	1.21	1.32	1.15	1.38	1.10	1.44	1.04	1.51	.99	1.59
37	1.22	1.32	1.16	1.38	1.11	1.45	1.06	1.51	1.00	1.59
38	1.23	1.33	1.18	1.39	1.12	1.45	1.07	1.52	1.02	1.58
39	1.24	1.34	1.19	1.39	1.14	1.45	1.09	1.52	1.03	1.58
40	1.25	1.34	1.20	1.40	1.15	1.46	1.10	1.52	1.05	1.58
45	1.29	1.38	1.24	1.42	1.20	1.48	1.16	1.53	1.11	1.58
50	1.32	1.40	1.28	1.45	1.24	1.49	1.20	1.54	1.16	1.59
55	1.36	1.43	1.32	1.47	1.28	1.51	1.25	1.55	1.21	1.59
60	1.38	1.45	1.35	1.48	1.32	1.52	1.28	1.56	1.25	1.60
65	1.41	1.47	1.38	1.50	1.35	1.53	1.31	1.57	1.28	1.61
70	1.43	1.49	1.40	1.52	1.37	1.55	1.34	1.58	1.31	1.61
75	1.45	1.50	1.42	1.53	1.39	1.56	1.37	1.59	1.34	1.62
80	1.47	1.52	1.44	1.54	1.42	1.57	1.39	1.60	1.36	1.62
85	1.48	1.53	1.46	1.55	1.43	1.58	1.41	1.60	1.39	1.63
90	1.50	1.54	1.47	1.56	1.45	1.59	1.43	1.61	1.41	1.64
95	1.51	1.55	1.49	1.57	1.47	1.60	1.45	1.62	1.42	1.64
100	1.52	1.56	1.50	1.58	1.48	1.60	1.46	1.63	1.44	1.65

[a]The bounds shown, which assume that the regression contains a constant term, refer to a one-tailed test against positive autocorrelation of the disturbances.

Index